11/15 Donation

M
L
C
D0682054
Accession _____
Location _____L_____

INTRODUCING
PSYCHOLOGY

Approaches, Topics & Methods

Edited by **DONALD PENNINGTON**

MIDDLESBROUGH COLLEGE
LEARNING RESOURCES CENTRE
WITHDRAWN

Middlesbrough College

00098616

INTRODUCING
PSYCHOLOGY

Approaches, Topics & Methods

Middlesbrough College

Learning Resources Centre

Class No .... 150 Pen ....

Accession .... 098816 ....

Location .... L ....

Learning Resources Centre
Middlesbrough College
Dock Street
Middlesbrough
TS2 1AD

Edited by **DONALD PENNINGTON**

Hodder & Stoughton

A MEMBER OF THE HODDER HEADLINE GROUP

Orders: please contact Bookpoint Ltd, 130 Milton Park, Abingdon, Oxon
OX14 4SB. Telephone: (44) 01235 827720. Fax: (44) 01235 400454. Lines are
open from 9.00–6.00, Monday to Saturday, with a 24-hour message answering
service. You can also order through our website: www.hodderheadline.co.uk

British Library Cataloguing in Publication Data
A catalogue record for this title is available from the British Library

ISBN 0 340 84778 6

First Published 2002
Impression number   10 9 8 7 6 5 4 3 2
Year   2008 2007 2006 2005 2004 2003 2002

Copyright © 2002 Donald Pennington, Karen Boswell, Liz Dancer, Julie
McLoughlin, Dave Robinson and Richard Smithson

All rights reserved. No part of this publication may be reproduced or
transmitted in any form or by any means, electronic or mechanical, including
photocopy, recording, or any information storage and retrieval system, without
permission in writing from the publisher or under licence from the Copyright
Licensing Agency Limited. Further details of such licences (for reprographic
reproduction) may be obtained from the Copyright Licensing Agency Limited,
of 90 Tottenham Court Road, London W1P 9HE.

Typeset by GreenGate Publishing Services, Tonbridge, Kent.
Printed in Great Britain for Hodder & Stoughton Educational, a division of
Hodder Headline Plc, 338 Euston Road, London NW1 3BH by
Martins the Printers, Berwick upon Tweed.

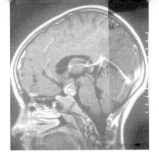

Contents

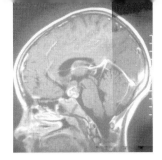

How to use this book

This book has been designed to meet the needs of students and teachers following the GCE AS level Psychology Specification B offered by the Assessment and Qualifications Alliance (AQA). Each of the twelve chapters covers the topic areas in *Unit 1 Introducing Psychology* and *Unit 2 Social and Cognitive Psychology*. Each chapter covers all the syllabus content of these two units and provides short descriptions of empirical studies and experiments directly relating to the topic areas.

Each chapter also provides two types of activities that individuals and small groups can engage in, both inside and outside the classroom. It is recommended that you carry out as many of these activities as possible, since they will help you to both remember the material and think in a deeper and more evaluative way about psychology.

The chapters offer numerous comments which will help you to analyse, discuss and apply theory, concepts and research in psychology. The intellectual skills fostered by these comments will help you gain the extra marks required to achieve high grades in the examinations.

Questions

Towards the end of each chapter, you will find a number of questions. These have been set in the style that appears in the AQA Specification B AS examinations. Each question shows the number of marks available for each sub-section and the marks for each of the two main assessment objectives. These are Assessment Objective 1 (AO1), concerned with knowledge and understanding of theory, concepts and research in psychology. The other is Assessment Objective 2 (AO2), which is concerned with the intellectual skills of critical evaluation, analysis and application of psychology. Please read Appendix 1 for more detail on assessment objectives. It is important that you understand what assessment objectives are and how they are examined, since all examination questions are based on them.

Further reading

At the end of each chapter, you will find suggestions for further reading. This is given in two parts: introductory books and more specialist sources. The introductory texts should be accessible for all students. The specialist books are more demanding and may be of value to students who wish to achieve higher grades or are just interested to find out more about psychology and teachers.

Appendices

There are three appendices at the back of the book.

Appendix 1 provides information about the principles used to guide how questions are set and structured for the AQA GCE Psychology Specification B at AS level. It also provides information on Assessment Objectives; these are important to understand, since they determine how marks are allocated to each question and how question answers that you give are marked.

Appendix 2 provides guidance on study skills, including advice on note-taking, revision techniques, how to prepare for the examinations and how to approach answering questions under examination conditions.

Appendix 3 provides detailed information concerning the Practical Investigation which you are required to conduct and write up for Unit 3 of the AS level. Guidelines are given on the kind of study that you might conduct and the skills that are assessed in the written report.

We hope you enjoy reading this book, both from the point of view of studying psychology and by engaging in the suggested activities.

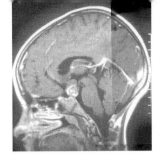

Using the Internet and websites

Access to websites via the Internet offers a valuable resource for teaching and learning; a resource which can be used effectively to supplement material found in the twelve chapters in this book. However, just using a search engine such as Google or Ask Jeeves will throw up numerous suggestions for websites to visit but will not give any indication in advance whether a site is of any use. You won't know if the material is relevant to the area of psychology that you are trying to find out more about or even if what is given there is correct. This is a major obstacle and clearly a problem if you assume that the material is accurate but later on find out there are errors or serious omissions. This may cause you to write material in a examination which is wrong, with the consequence that you will not get the marks that you think you should.

What is needed is some kind of system that suggests websites to visit but which has been checked in advance by qualified psychologists so that you can be confidence that the material is correct, up to date and relevant to the area of psychology that you are interested in.

The *Resource Discovery Network* or *RDN* for short, is a search engine that has been developed as a resource for students, lecturers and researchers and a wide range of professions, such as psychology, nursing, law, engineering and economics. The RDN is a collaboration of over 60 educational and research institutions and the British Library. The RDN checks material on websites and connects you to sites which are relevant to your learning, teaching and research needs.

To use the RDN, you need to type in the following website address: www.rdn.ac.uk. This takes you to the home page on which you will see major headings for the following:

Business
Computing
Engineering
Geography & environment
Health and medicine
Humanities
Law
Life sciences
Mathematics
Physical sciences
Reference
Social sciences
Sport, tourism & leisure

Psychology is under the *Social Sciences* main heading. Click on *Psychology* and you will then bring up a page with *Psychology Gateway* at the top. You will then see the following topic areas of psychology given in bold print and underlined:

General Psychology
Animal Psychology
Communication Systems

Intelligent Systems
Mental Health
Methodology

Consumer Psychology

Developmental Psychology

Educational Psychology

Environmental Psychology

Forensic and Legal Psychology

Human Experimental Psychology

Organizational Psychology

Personality Psychology

Psychological Disorders

Social Processes and Issues

Social Psychology

Sport Psychology

Many of these headings directly relate to chapters in this book and are of obvious relevance. You can click on any one of these headings to go to a page full of material relevant to that topic. Alternatively, you can use the box at the top of the Psychology gateway page to search by word. So, suppose we wanted to find out more about Sigmund Freud. Type in *Sigmund Freud* and press *go*. You can then click on one of the suggestions to be taken to that website. The RDN is a very useful resource that you should aim to make maximum use of in your studies of psychology, or just to broaden your general knowledge about psychology without having to go out and buy lots of books in the first instance.

Whilst most of the topic areas for psychology are under the Social Science heading on the homepage of the RDN, some areas appear under Life Sciences. Topic areas related to physiological psychology, the nervous system and the brain fall under life sciences. For more health-related areas, you may wish to explore Health and Medicine.

Other websites that you may find valuable are www.bps.org.uk and www.apa.org which are the addresses for the British Psychological Society and the American Psychological Association respectively. These sites are particularly useful for find out more about careers in psychology and, especially, ethical issues to do with research and the use of humans and animals in experiments in psychology.

Happy surfing and browsing on the Internet!

Donald Pennington

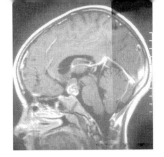

Acknowledgements

The authors wish to acknowledge and thank the Assessment and Qualifications Alliance (AQA) for their support and help in producing teacher support material for the AS Psychology, Specification B. In particular, earlier versions of the chapters on Gender, Attitudes, Social Psychology and Sport, and Cognition and Law were all developed with help from AQA. The earlier versions have all been substantially modified for chapters in this book.

The authors would like to thank Tim Gregson-Williams and Emma Woolf, at Hodder & Stoughton, for guidance, advice and support in developing, designing and producing this book. Thanks also to two readers of selected chapters; their comments and advice have helped greatly to improve the overall quality.

As Editor of this book I would like to thank all the authors for their patience and persistence in making what must have seemed like endless revisions to their chapters. Finally, thanks to Joginder Lully and Kathleen Williams for their skills in typing chapters of this book.

Donald Pennington, Editor

The authors and publisher would like to thank the following for permission to use photographs:

© Copyright British Photographers' Liaison Committee/Finers Stephens Innocent As agreed by BAPLA, AOP, NUJ, MPA and the BFP: page 1; © Steve Bloom/stevebloom.com: top two photos page 245, page 293; Action Plus: pages 205, 209, 217, 269, 273, 281; Alvis Upitis/Getty Images: page 236; Chabruken/Getty Images: page 321; Copyright 1965 by Stanley Milgram from the film Obedience, distributed by the Pennsylvania State University, Audio Visual Services (from Milgram 1974): page 170; Corbis: page 6; Corbis-Bettman: bottom right page 9, pages 12, 15, 139; Daniel Allan/Getty Images: page 151; Erin Hogan/Getty Images: page 306; Eyewire collection: page 300; GDT/Getty Images: page 152; General Photographic Agency/Getty Images: page 2; Hulton Archive/Getty Images: page 265; Illustrated London News: top left page 9; News International plc (News International plc is the holding company for the News International group of companies and is registered in England No 81701, with its address at 1 Virginia St, London E98 1XY): page 91; The Press Association Ltd: pages 168, 323; The Press Association/Neil Munns: page 89; The Ronald Grant Archive: page 165; V.C.L./Getty Images: page 246; World Wide Photo, Inc: page 7.

While every effort has been made to trace copyright holders, this has not been possible in all cases; any omissions brought to our attention will be remedied in future printings.

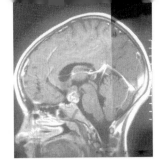

1

Key Approaches and the Study of Psychology

Introduction

Consider the following activities:

* a researcher looking at how a mother and baby communicate with each other;
* a specialist advising the police on the personality profile of a criminal;
* a therapist dealing with somebody suffering depression;
* a researcher observing rats in a maze seeking food;
* a specialist working for a large company advising on morale of the workers.

These diverse activities are all linked by a common factor: each person is a psychologist. Psychology as a discipline is concerned with a very wide range of areas, topics and applications. Those listed above represent only a very few, and you will come across many more as you read through this book.

The word **psychology** is derived from two Greek words: *psyche*, which literally means 'the mind or soul', and *logos* which means 'the study of'. Hence, as a word, psychology means 'the study of mind or soul'. However, few definitions of psychology as a discipline would restrict it just to the study of mind. A more useful definition, and one which reflects what psychologists actually do, is as follows:

> 'Psychology is the scientific study of human and animal behaviour and mental processes.'

This definition reflects the fact that psychology is concerned with both mind (mental processes) and behaviour. It also emphasises that both humans and animals are legitimate objects of study, although with animals this tends to be limited to the study of behaviour. This is because we do not have the same insight into the mental processes of animals as we do with people – humans can reflect and report on what they think and feel, whereas animals can't. We could add to this definition that psychologists are interested in how behaviour and mind are affected by the organism's (person or animal) physical and mental state, and external environment.

The word psychology derives from two Greek words: psyche meaning 'mind' and logos meaning 'the study of'

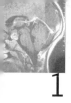

1   Reflective Activity

Consider your own behaviour and state of mind over the past couple of weeks.

- *Identify one specific example of how your physical state (e.g. a cold) affected you.*

- *Identify a time when you were in a bad mood (mental state) – how did this affect your behaviour towards other people?*

- *Finally, identify one occasion when an external environmental factor (this may be another person or a physical factor) affected both your behaviour and how you thought.*

These all highlight the areas of interest of psychology.

What is psychology?

The definition we considered earlier states that psychology is the scientific study of humans and other animals. This is a very important feature of psychology, one that has allowed it to become a separate and respected area of **science** in its own right. We shall now consider psychology in relation to other disciplines, look in more detail at what it means for psychology to be a science, and distinguish between science and **common sense**.

Psychology and other disciplines

The terms **social sciences** or 'behavioural sciences' refer to a family or cluster of disciplines of which psychology is a member. The other disciplines that are commonly put in this cluster are sociology, anthropology and biology. They are all united by an interest in studying humans and animals – why they behave as they do, how they interact and how, where appropriate, their social organisation or society works.

Sociology is the study of **groups** and institutions within society. As such, sociology is concerned with groups such as the family, ethnic groups, sub-cultures (such as Hell's Angels or punks), religious institutions, the workplace and differences between societies. Sociologists are less interested in personality, interaction between two or more people, and social perception (how people think about other people). These areas are more the province of social psychology. Sociology is concerned with larger groups and operates at a macro-level, whilst social psychology operates more at the micro-level of understanding human behaviour.

Anthropology is concerned with the different cultures that exist across the world and their historical origins and development. Anthropologists tend to work at a macro-level, concentrating on whole communities, tribes or the whole society. Anthropologists are interested in how people lead their daily lives in different cultures, and usually go to live amongst a culture for a period of time in order to observe and study behaviour and traditions. The customs, practices and religions of a culture are all of interest. Anthropology is related to an area of psychology called **cross-cultural psychology**. Cross-cultural psychology is concerned with psychological differences (for example, personality, child development, social interaction) between different cultures.

Anthropologists study other cultures as communities; cross-cultural psychologists study differences between cultures

Finally, **biology** is concerned with understanding how organisms (including human beings) are structured and how they function. Structures include muscles, the skeleton, organs, such as the heart and liver, and the nervous system. It is the study of the nervous system, particularly of humans, that relates biology to the biological approach in psychology (see Chapter 2). Figure 1.1 depicts the relationships between psychology and these three other disciplines.

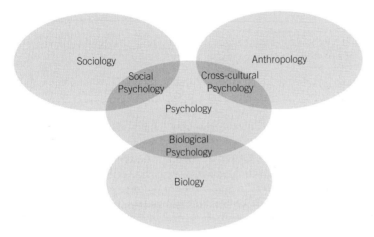

Figure 1.1: Relationship and overlap between psychology and the disciplines of sociology, anthropology and biology

---

Practical Activity

Consider the example of two people in love with each other and the development of a long-term relationship.

Discuss with two or three other people how you think a psychologist, sociologist, anthropologist and biologist would approach this situation.

Make a list of the main interests of each approach, and identify where there may be overlaps.

Psychology as science

The definition we considered earlier emphasised that psychology is a scientific discipline. But precisely what does it mean to call something a science? Karl Popper (1963), a famous philosopher of science, characterised science as the application of a scientific method to gather data or evidence. This evidence is then used to test a *hypothesis*, which is a prediction derived from a *theory*. If the evidence supports the hypothesis, then support is also provided for the theory. If the evidence does not support the hypothesis, the hypothesis is refuted. This may result in the theory being rejected. Popper (1963) also claimed that it was logically impossible to prove a theory to be true, since a scientist cannot rightly or logically claim that refuting evidence will not be found in the future. However, Popper did state that a theory could be rejected if the evidence failed to support it. An example might help clarify all this.

Suppose a psychologist puts forward a theory that all people with blue eyes have an extrovert personality (an extrovert is someone who is outgoing, likes to be with people, and is the life and soul of a party). From this theory, a hypothesis could be made that people with blue eyes will score as extroverts on a personality questionnaire. The psychologist gives this questionnaire to 1,000 people with blue eyes and finds that only 550 score as extroverts. This finding refutes the hypothesis and in consequence casts doubt on (or refutes) the theory. This is shown in Figure 1.2.

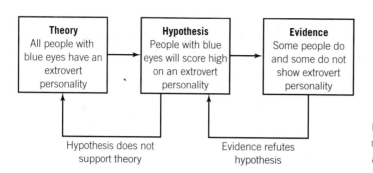

| **Theory** All people with blue eyes have an extrovert personality | → | **Hypothesis** People with blue eyes will score high on an extrovert personality | → | **Evidence** Some people do and some do not show extrovert personality |

Hypothesis does not support theory

Evidence refutes hypothesis

Figure 1.2: The scientific method of theory, hypothesis and evidence

The next matter to consider, if we are to regard psychology as a science, is the way in which evidence is collected. Evidence must be collected in an objective way which other scientists or psychologists can replicate. Science uses an *empirical* method to collect evidence; this means that data is collected through observation and experiment. Observations must be objective, which means that more than one person would record them in the same way. Behaviour is observable and hence objective; how you think is not directly observable and can only be inferred. Hence psychologists, especially behaviourists (see page 12), have placed great emphasis on the need to focus on behaviour for psychology to be a science.

The use of the **experimental** method is also important in psychology. Experiments allow the psychologist to control conditions and then observe how people behave; they also allow cause-and-effect relationships to be established. Knowing what causes us to behave in certain ways allows hypotheses and theories to be tested.

Evaluative Comment

The laboratory method is widely used in psychology. This allows the psychologist to control conditions into which people are put. However, the laboratory is often regarded as an artificial environment, and critics argue that findings from a laboratory cannot easily be generalised or made to apply to people's everyday lives. Also, the very fact of being observed by a psychologist may make people behave differently than they would when not being observed. Therefore, the use of the experimental method to test psychological hypotheses and theory is scientific, but has shortcomings when applied to people.

Thomas Kuhn (1970) characterises psychology as a pre-science rather than a fully fledged science like physics or chemistry. Kuhn says that a true science is characterised by a *paradigm*. A paradigm is where there is agreement about the subject matter and methods of study of a discipline. Psychologists, as we shall see later in this chapter, do not agree about the subject matter and even less about the methods that should be used in research. The various approaches to psychology – psychodynamic, behaviourist, humanistic and cognitive – all differ in what they consider the subject matter of psychology to be. Each approach also uses different methods to study people, hence Kuhn's description of psychology as a pre-science.

Science and common sense

In your study of psychology, you will probably come across many findings from, for example, the use of **laboratory experiments** which you might say were 'obvious' and a matter of 'common sense'. Psychology does at times confirm what many people know, but it also produces findings opposite to those people think to be true. Much of what people know is based on common sense, which includes a person's own subjective experience of the world in which they live, the so-called 'university of life'. The problem here is that different people have different experiences and may, as a result, come up with different common sense views. For example, you may think your psychology teacher is wonderful because you are interested in psychology. Your friend may think the teacher is awful because he or she finds psychology boring. Each of you will have different subjective experiences and views about the teacher.

As we have seen, science uses rigorous methods, including laboratory experiments, and precise measurement of behaviour and attitudes to collect evidence or data. The scientific approach is **objective**, whilst using common sense is **subjective**. Objective methods are much more likely to produce evidence you can trust than subjective methods.

Reflective Activity

Consider the following proverbs which represent common sense views held by people:

- *Birds of a feather flock together*

- *Actions speak louder than words*

- *Too many cooks spoil the broth*

- *You cannot teach an old dog new tricks*

- *More haste, less speed.*

For each of these proverbs, try to think of another saying that contradicts it. For example, for the first saying you might give 'opposites attract' or for the fourth 'you are never too old to learn'. This shows that different people hold different common sense views which may contradict each other.

In many ways, all of us are psychologists, since we all try to predict and explain what other people do and why they do it. Heider (1944) characterised people as **naïve scientists**; by this, he meant the lay person acts informally like a scientist because of the desire to predict and explain behaviour, but is 'naïve' because scientific methods are not used. Legge (1975) distinguished between formal and informal psychology, where the latter is characterised by common sense and the former by science.

Evaluative Comment

Common sense views are not based on sound scientific procedures and evidence. However, psychology as a science may confirm or refute a common sense view. When this happens, we can have a great deal of confidence in the findings.

Historical context of psychology

Historically, psychology has its historical roots in two disciplines – philosophy and physiology. Ever since the times of the ancient Greeks, between 600 and 300 BC, philosophers have been interested in human thinking, emotions and behaviour. Similarly, over the past 500 years, physiologists have been interested in how the brain and nervous system work. However, ideas have changed in both disciplines – before 1700, it was thought that a muscle would respond the instant the brain told it to; but careful experiments showed that a nerve impulse from the brain takes time to reach the muscle – even though it seems to happen instantly, it does take a few milliseconds (thousandths of a second)!

1

Philosophical roots

Philosophy uses reason, argument and experience to try to understand the world in which we live. As such, philosophy has many branches including logic, theory of knowledge and truth, morals and ethics, and human identity. Of special relevance to psychology is what is known as the **mind–body problem**. This is to do with how the physical body interacts or relates to the mind or 'mental life'. Mental life does not *seem* to be physical, but the mind and body do work together to produce behaviour. The mind–body debate was first raised by the French philosopher René Descartes (1596–1650). However, the distinction between mind and body can be traced back to the Greek philosopher Plato (c. 428–348 BC). Plato argued that the mind resides within the brain, whilst Aristotle (384–322 BC) said that the mind was in the heart. Aristotle put forward the view that knowledge about the world (physical and mental) can only be achieved through observation. Plato, by contrast, said that knowledge results from philosophical argument and discussion, and what our inner thoughts tell us. Both views have been influential in the development of psychology, especially since Aristotle talks about empirical methods of objective observation. Plato talks about the value of inner knowledge, awareness of our own thoughts and the meaning of dreams, which is reflected in the psychodynamic and humanistic approaches which we will look at later in this chapter.

Descartes was concerned with how the mind and body interact

The Greek physician Hippocrates (c. 460–377 BC) changed the way the Greeks thought about disease and mental illness. The accepted view before this was that illness (physical or mental) was a punishment of the gods. Hippocrates taught people to believe that illness was a biological disorder and that the body or mind should be treated rather than sacrifices made to the gods.

These early Greek ideas influenced philosophers such as Descartes and John Locke (1632–1704). John Locke put forward the idea of a **tabula rasa** (literally a 'blank slate') as the state in which humans enter the world. Thus Locke first promoted the view that human knowledge and behaviour come only from experience. This relates to the nature–nurture debate – genetics/biology versus environment – which is central in psychology.

Evaluative Comment

Philosophers discussed and produced arguments for many issues that are important to modern psychology; but they used reason and logic rather than empirical or scientific methods when attempting to support their claims and refute the ideas of other philosophers. Historically, psychology was a part of philosophy and not a separate discipline.

Wundt and psychology as a science

Wilhelm Wundt (1832–1920), who trained in medicine and philosophy, was the first scientist to set up a psychological laboratory, established in 1879 in Leipzig in Germany. Wundt was widely read in philosophy and stated in 1873 that he wanted to take psychology out of philosophy and establish it as a science in its own right.

Wundt was interested in the areas of sensation, mental images, reaction times, perception and attention; he did not attempt to research into personality and abnormal behaviour. For example, Wundt attempted to measure the speed of thought, and devised a device called a 'thought metre'.

One of Wundt's most commonly used research methods was that of **introspection**. Wundt would train his researchers to carefully analyse their own mental experiences – sensations, images and emotional reactions. Introspection would take place under controlled laboratory conditions, and before he would allow someone to take part in an experiment a person had to make 10,000 practice introspections first. Once trained to introspect, Wundt's researchers took as long as twenty minutes to report on their inner experiences from a one-second experiment! Wundt claimed that trained introspectionists would produce reliable results which could be replicated by other introspectionists in different laboratories. However, it soon became apparent that reporting on inner experiences in this way was too subjective. Disagreement cannot be resolved since one person can never experience exactly what another person experiences.

Wilhelm Wundt established the first psychology laboratory in an attempt to make psychology a science

---

Practical Activity

One of Wundt's experiments used a metronome and asked trained introspectionists to report sensations, images and feelings when listening to different speeds of 'click'.

Get together with three or four others and set a metronome to 'click' at different speeds (a loud clock will do if you cannot get a metronome).

Each person should listen to the sound for two minutes then report back on sensations, images and feelings.

List what each person reports. Where there are differences between people, can you say one is right and one wrong? Or is it that subjective experience is different from person to person?

Key influences on psychology

Wundt wanted to establish psychology as a separate scientific discipline. The creation of the first psychology laboratory influenced the development of the subject, and soon resulted in similar laboratories being set up elsewhere in Europe, America and Great Britain. Whilst Wundt's methods, particularly introspection, became regarded as not sufficiently objective, the idea that people need to be studied under controlled conditions was and still is highly influential.

Wundt influenced the next generation of psychologists through the development of what was called *structuralism*. Edward Titchener, a researcher trained by Wundt, influenced the development of psychology in the USA. Titchener used introspection in an attempt to analyse consciousness, in the hope that sensations, images and feelings could be broken down into basic elements, as a chemist might reduce water to hydrogen and oxygen. Titchener regarded the experimental method as the only one to be used by psychology. However, whilst this idea has remained in modern psychology, introspection and hence structuralism have not because of their subjective natures. Wilhem Wundt, for these reasons, is regarded as the 'founding father of psychology'.

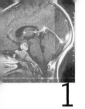

1

Darwin and biological psychology

Charles Darwin published *On the Origin of Species* in 1859 and *The Descent of Man* in 1971, both of which detail his **theory of evolution** and the mechanism to explain how evolution works, ie the concept of **natural selection**. Darwin argued that behavioural and physical changes to a species happen randomly. Some changes help the organism adapt better to its environment, whilst others are maladaptive and are not beneficial to the organism. The principle of natural selection ensures that adaptive characteristics are passed onto future generations whilst maladaptive ones die out.

Darwin also stated that human beings are a product of evolution and are closely related to other primates such as monkeys, chimpanzees and apes. Human beings have evolved over millions of years from the same primitive ancestors as other mammals, such as dogs and cats. Figure 1.3 provides a simplified sketch of the evolutionary tree and shows how all animals have primitive ancestors in common.

The publication of these books and the theory of evolution caused great controversy and were rejected by many at the time. Darwin challenged the accepted religious view that human beings were created by God, as laid down in the Bible. For Darwin, it was natural forces and not higher forces that were responsible for human beings. Eventually Darwin's view was accepted, and most people now regard this as part of the explanation of how we come to be as we are.

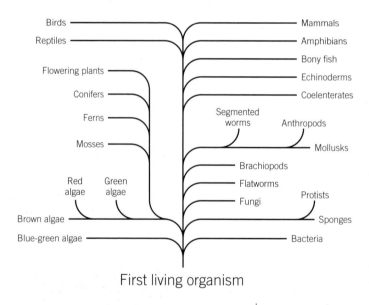

First living organism

Figure 1.3: This simplified 'tree of evolution' shows that humans have the same evolutionary background as other animals

Darwin also emphasised the importance of reproduction in a species. Adaptive changes to an organism can only be passed on to another generation through sexual reproduction in mammals. Hence, the sexual instinct has evolved from primitive to more complex organisms. Without a sexual instinct many species, especially mammals, would fail to reproduce and eventually die out.

Darwin published another book in 1872 called *The Expression of the Emotions in Man and Animals*. In this book, Darwin produced evidence from his travels around the world that a limited number of emotions are expressed by the face in the same way in different cultures: happiness (smiling), hatred (glaring), displeasure (frowning) and surprise (raised eyebrows/eyes wide open). Furthermore, these expressions of emotion resulted from evolution and are genetically 'wired in'.

Key influences on psychology

Darwin's influences on psychology are numerous. His theory of evolution, showing humans had evolved in the same way as other mammals, resulted in many psychologists, especially behaviourists, studying the behaviour of rats, pigeons, cats and monkeys. Behaviourists argued that because humans share the same evolutionary background as other animals, then the principles explaining their behaviour should also apply to human beings.

Darwin also influenced the development of **evolutionary psychology**. Evolutionary psychologists (Buss, 1995) try to explain behaviour in terms of how people adapt to a constantly changing environment. They claim that genes account for not only physical characteristics such as height but also psychological characteristics such as personality traits and **intelligence**. They also claim that aggressiveness and musical ability result from genes passed down by parents (Plomin & DeFries, 1998).

A third influence of Darwin was on Freud's theories, in particular the importance of the sexual instinct. Freud developed his theories to account for how the sexual instinct affects a person at a psychological level. The sexual instinct is central to Darwin's theory of evolution and is also of central importance in Freud's theories (see below).

Darwin's theory of evolution allowed psychologists to study animal behaviour to help understand how humans behave

A fourth influence of Darwin was on the development of cross-cultural psychology. His claim that facial expressions are universal for some emotions can be regarded as the first cross-cultural study. Psychologists have been interested in the study of emotional expression in different cultures ever since (Ekman, 1992).

Practical Activity

Ask a male and female friend to express the emotions of happiness, surprise, fear and hatred. Take pictures of each of their facial expressions.

Show these pictures to other people you know and ask them to identify the emotion. How many gave the correct answer and how many the wrong answer? Were there any differences between males and females?

Freud and psychodynamics

Sigmund Freud (1856–1939), a qualified medical doctor, developed a theory of mental life called **psychoanalysis**. Psychologists and others who adopt this approach emphasise the **psychodynamics** of the mind. This means that different forces operate in the mind, and at times cause inner mental conflict which may be painful to the person. Psychoanalysis as a therapy was developed by Freud to help people come to terms with their inner conflicts, many of which are said to have their origin in early childhood.

Sigmund Freud claimed that the mind was largely unconscious and that human motives are largely determined by the sex instinct

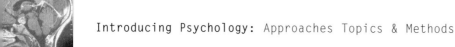

1

Assumptions of the psychodynamic approach

Freud (1933) assumed that a large part of our mental life operates at an **unconscious** level. By this, he meant that we have thoughts and ideas that we are not directly aware of. For example, Freud believed that slips of the tongue and accidents have an unconscious explanation. For example, if you knocked a vase off the mantelpiece claiming it happened accidentally, Freud would not accept this. Freud might have wanted to know about the vase: who bought it, whether it had sentimental value, etc. For Freud, the destruction of the vase might represent a symbolic act of harming the person who bought the vase. Freud assumed that these thoughts were held in the unconscious by a defence mechanism called **repression**. Repression is a type of forgetting where a painful or disturbing memory is unconsciously forgotten. The memory still exists in the mind, but at an unconscious level.

Freud (1900) also assumed that dreams that take place during sleep are meaningful and require interpretation. To interpret dreams, he used the technique of **free association**. This technique requires a person to think of part of the dream and say the first thing that comes to mind, no matter how odd or silly it may seem. The free associations are like pieces of a jigsaw puzzle that Freud would help the person put together to build the whole picture.

Reflective Activity

Write down a dream you had last night or recently. Select a part of it which seems not to make sense to you. Think about this part of the dream and write down whatever comes to mind. If nothing comes to mind at all, you may be repressing the meaning. Keep trying, and some free associations will come to you. When they do, see if any pattern or meaning can be given to this part of the dream. Often a dream is triggered by events of the previous day or childhood memories.

Another assumption that Freud (1909) made in his psychodynamic approach was that early childhood was very important for the development of the adult personality. Freud claimed that development took place through three stages of psychosexual development: the oral, anal and phallic stages. The phallic stage is by far the most important because it contains the **Oedipus complex**. This is an unconscious conflict in the four- to six-year-old child whereby the child wants to possess the opposite-sex parent and remove the same-sex parent. The conflict is resolved by identifying with the same-sex parent (see Chapter 4 on Gender). Memories of the conflict are repressed in childhood, but may return to trouble the person in adulthood.

Freud's main and most important assumption was that the primary driving force in a person's mental life, which also affects behaviour, is the sexual instinct. This operates at an unconscious level in a part of the personality Freud called the **id**. The sexual instinct operates according to the pleasure principle, and it is the task of another part of the personality, the **ego**, to satisfy the demands of the id. At the same time, a third part of the personality, the **superego**, represents the person's conscience and ideal self. The id and the superego represent opposing forces, and it is the task of the ego to try to reduce conflict. Figure 1.4 depicts this.

Evaluative Comment

*Many of Freud's ideas and assumptions about people have been regarded as unscientific. This is because it is not easy to see how, for example, the unconscious can be scientifically studied. The contents of the unconscious can only be inferred, never directly seen or even experienced. Over the past decade, a major controversy has raged over what are called **recovered memories** (British Psychological Society, 1995). These are memories which a person is supposed to have repressed in childhood and the adult 'recovers' in therapy. The problem is that you can never be sure if the recovered memory is really a memory of an actual experience in childhood, or whether it has been made up in psychotherapy.*

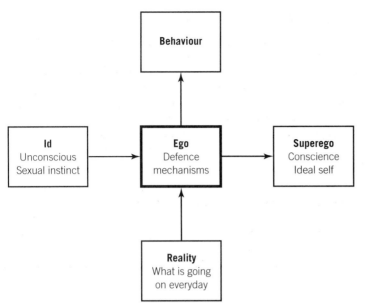

Figure 1.4: The tripartite structure of the personality proposed by Sigmund Freud. The ego attempts to deal with the demands of the id, superego and reality to find an appropriate behavioural response

Key influences on psychology

Freud's psychodynamic approach has had four key influences on the development of psychology. First, the assumption that much of our mental life happens at an unconscious level greatly changed the way in which people viewed themselves. By saying some parts of our mind are beyond our awareness means that we cannot fully know ourselves. This influenced many other psychologists who worked in a psychodynamic approach, such as Carl Jung (1964), Erik Erikson (1968) and Anna Freud (Sigmund Freud's daughter) (1966). Whilst their theories differed in some ways from Freud's (for example, Jung and Erikson did not consider the sexual instinct to be of central importance), they all assumed the unconscious existed.

Freud's second influence on psychology was the acceptance that early childhood experiences are important in determining adult personality. These days this is taken for granted, but this was not so in Freud's time. He put forward the idea of stages of development in childhood which were a result of the sexual instinct. The idea that a young child, from birth onwards, goes through stages of development has influenced other developmental psychologists such as Piaget (1963) and Kohlberg (1984).

The third influence follows on from the previous one. It is that painful or traumatic childhood experiences may have effects later in adult life. One very important experience is if the child is separated from his or her mother for significant periods of time. Maternal deprivation was investigated by Bowlby (1969, 1973) who was trained as a psychoanalyst. To understand maternal separation, Bowlby used Freudian ideas.

The fourth key influence of the psychodynamic approach has been on psychiatry and the development of different therapies to treat people who suffer mental problems. Freud pioneered the use of a psychological approach to treating mental disorders which has had a profound and lasting impact on psychology and psychiatry, although many of the therapies available these days are not based on Freudian concepts and theory.

Overall, whilst many of Freud's ideas and assumptions have been questioned (and in some cases rejected) by modern psychology, his influence on psychology has been profound and widespread.

1

Skinner and behaviourism

At the same time that Freud was developing psychoanalysis, a Russian physiologist called Ivan Pavlov was developing a form of behaviourism called 'classical conditioning'. Meanwhile, in the USA, John Watson, a psychologist, published an article in 1913 called 'Psychology as the behaviourist views it'. Both Pavlov and Watson were responsible for establishing the behaviourist approach in psychology. One of the reasons why behaviourism developed was as a reaction to the introspective method developed by Wundt (see page 6). The behaviourists wanted psychology to adopt an objective approach based on observable behaviour. They criticised introspection because it was subjective and not observable, and hence could not be scientific.

Skinner claimed that scientific study must be based on observable and measurable behaviour

Assumptions of the behaviourist approach

The basic assumption of the behaviourist approach in psychology is that all behaviour is learned from the experiences a person has in their environment. This means that behaviourists are strongly on the side of nurture in the nature–nurture debate and regard genetic influences on behaviour as minimal. The behaviourists further argue that all behaviour is learned through the *reinforcement* or *punishment* of behavioural responses. They claimed that reinforcement, a reward, strengthens the link between a stimulus (something in the environment) and a behavioural response.

Reflective Activity

Think of two or three specific things you have done today. For each, try to identify the stimulus, i.e. what triggered or caused you to behave in that way. Then think about what the reinforcement or reward was for the behaviour. Then think of another behaviour for which you received some sort of punishment – will the punishment stop you behaving that way again?

The behaviourist approach also assumed that laws of human and animal behaviour could be developed. The general law, proposed by Thorndike (1911), was called the **law of effect**. This states:

> 'the tendency of an organism to produce a behaviour depends on the effect the behaviour has on the environment'. (Westen, 1999)

If the effect is rewarding for the organism, then the behaviour will tend to be reproduced again in the future. If the effect is punishing, the behaviour is not likely to be reproduced in the future. The more occasions the behaviour has been rewarded, the more strongly it is 'stamped' into the organism and the more likely it is to be repeated. The law of effect also relates to another assumption of behaviourism: that behaviour is *determined* by the environment and as a consequence people do not have **free will**. That is, behaviour is controlled by forces in the environment rather than by the will of the person.

Evaluative Comment

Behaviourism has received strong criticism because of its denial of free will. People like to believe that they are free to choose. This idea is a basic assumption of the humanistic approach (see page 15). At the same time, many psychologists agree with the behaviourists that animal behaviour is determined by the environment.

Burrhus Frederic Skinner (1904–1990) developed the behaviourist approach which he called **radical behaviourism** (Skinner, 1953, 1996). Radical behaviourism states that psychologists should use scientific methods and focus only on observable behaviour and its consequences. Skinner claimed that all behaviour is learned from environmental consequences or **operant conditioning**. Operant conditioning is where a behaviour becomes more or less likely as a result of its consequences (reward or punishment). Skinner conducted most of his experiments on animals such as rats and pigeons in a device he invented called a Skinner box. In this box, a hungry rat has to learn to press a lever to get the reward of food. Since pressing the lever is not a normal part of a rat's behaviour, it has to be taught to do so. Only if the rat presses the lever does it get food. Hence it has to operate on its environment to gain reinforcement. If the rat is reinforced every time it presses the bar, the behaviour becomes 'stamped in' and it has learned to press the bar to get food. The process of operant conditioning is shown in Figure 1.5.

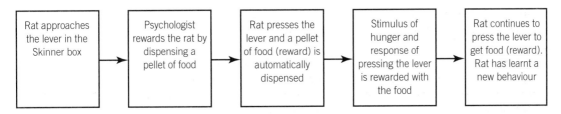

Figure 1.5: The process of operant conditioning. Note that the rat is first rewarded for approaching the lever; this is because the normal behaviour of a rat does not involve pressing levers. Pressing the lever has to be learned as a new behaviour

Pavlov's form of behaviourism is called **classical conditioning**. The key difference between this and operant conditioning is that classical conditioning relies on a behaviour the animal already possesses. For example, Pavlov conditioned a hungry dog who would salivate at the sight of food to salivate at the sound of a bell. This is shown in Figure 1.6.

Behaviourism also produces laws of behaviour and regards all behaviour as a product of the environment.

Figure 1.6: Classical conditioning. In (1), the food causes the hungry dog to salivate. Every time food is given to the dog, a bell is rung. After a while, only the bell is rung and the dog salivates. The dog has learned to associate food with the sound of the bell. So when the dog hears the bell, it expects food and salivates in anticipation

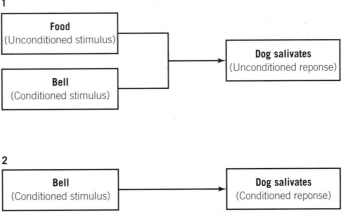

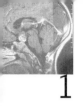

1

Evaluative Comment

The basic assumption that all learning is a result of the environmental consequences of a person's behaviour was challenged in the 1960s. Social-learning theorists such as Albert Bandura (1986) showed that people also learn from observing others and through insight. Observational learning takes mental processes or cognitions within the individual into account. Radical behaviourists did not think that mental processes were a proper area for scientific study.

Key influences on psychology

The behaviourist approach has had three main influences on the development of psychology. First, the highly scientific nature of the approach, exemplified by the use of experiments, has influenced all areas of psychology. For example, cognitive psychology (see page 16), social psychology and developmental psychology all use the experimental method in their areas of study. However, unlike behaviourism, most of the experiments in these areas use humans as participants rather than animals. The scientific approach of behaviourism also influenced psychology to focus firmly on observable, objective measures of behaviour.

The second main influence has been in the practical applications of behaviourism. For example, behaviourist principles have been effectively used to treat people who suffer from **phobias**, such as fear of spiders, fear of flying or fear of going in a lift. These phobias are treated with a therapy called *systematic desensitisation* (Wolpe, 1958). With this technique, the person is progressively exposed to more threatening situations. A person with a fear of spiders would first be shown a picture of spiders and be rewarded for looking at the picture. They would then be rewarded for holding the picture. Next, a film of spiders might be shown. This might be followed by a real spider in a jar on the table, and so on. The therapy has been shown to be effective with anxiety disorders and obsessive–compulsive disorders. However, some psychologists, especially psychodynamic psychologists, have claimed that systematic desensitisation only treats the symptoms and not the cause of the disorder.

The third main influence has been as a result of the emphasis on learning from the environment, or nurture. The behaviourist approach dominated psychology from about 1920 until the 1950s. As a consequence, educational policy was also influenced. If all learning comes from nurture, then achievement at school and college, according to behaviourists, is a matter of creating the right environment. Poor achievement is due to the negative or poor educational environment which the child experiences.

The behaviourist approach has been one of the most dominant and influential in modern psychology. The insistence on precision and objectivity in the application of the scientific method has provided psychology with respect as a discipline and many beneficial, practical applications.

Rogers and humanistic psychology

The humanistic approach emerged in the USA in the 1960s and was called the 'third force' in psychology. The other two forces were behaviourism and psychoanalysis, or the psychodynamic approach. Humanistic psychologists such as Abraham Maslow (1970) and Carl Rogers (1961) thought that the deterministic assumptions of the other two approaches neglected essential aspects of what it is to be a human being. Humanistic psychologists also thought that relying only on observable behaviour and the use of scientific methods to understand people ignored the richness of human experience. They criticised psychoanalysis because it dwelt too much on unconscious mental forces and early childhood, ignoring conscious experience of the here and now. The humanistic approach is called a *phenomenological* approach because of its focus on human experience.

Assumptions of the humanistic approach

The humanistic approach assumes that each person is unique and, because of this, psychology should focus on the subjective experiences, feelings and thoughts of a person. This is called an **ideographic approach** in psychology, since the emphasis is on understanding the uniqueness of a person rather than laws or common aspects of personality that may exist within all people. The humanistic approach also assumes that people have free will, i.e. they are free to choose what they do and what kind of person they can be. A further assumption is that people must be looked at from a holistic perspective rather than trying to reduce behaviour to smaller elements. The humanists argued that trying to break down behaviour and thought into smaller parts results in the whole person being lost in such a reductionist process.

Carl Rogers (1902–1987) was a leading humanistic psychologist who believed that every person has an innate tendency to *self-actualise*. Self-actualisation is where people attempt to achieve their full potential; this can be applied to all aspects of human behaviour – from cooking food to writing poetry. Each individual may self-actualise in a different way or through different achievements.

Carl Rogers was a leading humanistic psychologist who played a important role in the development of the third force in psychology

Practical Activity

Get together in a group of four or five other people. Get each person to list three things which give them great satisfaction and enjoyment.

For each of these, get each person to indicate how much more could be achieved and how great their achievement is.

Finally, ask each person to pick the one thing that would give them the greatest sense of self-actualisation. Compare findings for each of the people in the group. Are there any gender differences?

Rogers (1980) also assumed that we all need a kind of love from other people which he called *unconditional positive regard*. Rogers believed that the unconditional love of the mother for her child is essential to the development of a well-adjusted adult. Many of the problems and mental distress that people face as adults are, according to Rogers, a result of lack of this regard as children. Rogers would treat a client in therapy with unconditional positive regard in order to restore the lack in infancy and help the individual to gain positive self-worth. For this reason, Rogers' form of humanistic therapy is called *client-centred*. Client-centred therapy assumes that people come to therapy not for cures but for help in solving the everyday problems of life.

Rogers thought that people experienced problems in life when their concept of themselves was incongruent with their actual experience. For example, other people may think a person who gets a B grade for their psychology essay has done well. However, the person who wrote the essay may be disappointed because he or she expected to get an A grade. Rogers attempted to help people achieve congruence between their self-concept and how other people think of them. Balance or congruence leads to satisfaction with life and achievements; incongruence leads to conflict.

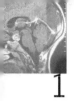

1

Evaluative Comment

Humanistic psychology rejected the scientific approach and the use of experiments to understand and predict human behaviour. Because of this, there is little objective evidence to support the claims and assumptions made. However, humanistic psychologists do not worry much about this. They claim that if people benefit from the approach, and lead more satisfying and problem-free lives as a result, then the approach is valuable.

Key influences on psychology

Humanistic psychologists put forward a picture of the person as an active agent, able to change and determine their own development. In contrast, the behaviourist approach largely characterises humans as passively responding to stimuli in the environment, for which rewards or punishments follow. Viewing people as active means that they can control and change the environment in which they live. This means that each individual is responsible for his or her actions, and for their own personal growth. Humanistic psychology has had a great influence on psychology by promoting the idea of personal responsibility.

Another influence of humanistic psychology is to recognise everybody as unique and individual, with each person having their own needs. To understand someone an in-depth knowledge is required which looks not only at life experiences, but also how he or she feels here and now. This leads to another important influence of humanistic psychology – recognition that the subjective experience of a person is of value and importance. We saw earlier that Wundt, in a way, tried to analyse people's experience using what he thought to be a scientific method. This failed because subjective experience cannot be measured or assessed objectively. In a sense, Wundt's mistake was to apply the scientific method to experiences rather than to actual behaviour. By contrast, humanistic psychologists do not claim to operate in a scientific framework; because of this, the experience of a person can be valued, since the approach is not trying to be objective. As we saw at the end of the last section, this brings other problems, such as the lack of scientific evidence to support the theories and claims of the humanistic approach.

The cognitive approach

The cognitive approach in psychology, which is to do with the study of thought, dates back over 100 years to the work of Ebbinghaus (1885). Ebbinghaus wanted to measure pure memory loss – by 'pure', he meant the investigation of memory in the absence of personal experience or associations to events or meanings that a person may have. To do this, he used nonsense words such as *bok, waf* or *ged*. He then memorised long lists of these nonsense words and tested his memory, or retention, for these words regularly over a period of weeks. What he found, shown in Figure 1.7, is that most forgetting occurred soon after learning and then levelled off. This basic method of giving people lists of words, pictures, sounds, etc. and then subsequently testing their recall has been used by cognitive psychologists ever since.

The point of citing this 100-year-old study by Ebbinghaus is that cognitive psychologists study mental processes by measuring some kind of behaviour (often verbal responses). The objective measurement of behaviour allows cognitive psychologists to create theories concerning what might be going on inside a person's head. You obviously cannot see a person's memory, but you can take measures of it.

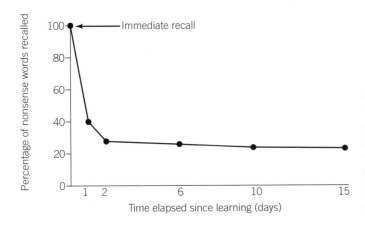

Figure 1.7: The curve of forgetting nonsense syllables found by Ebbinghaus. Notice that most forgetting takes place within the first day, and after six days remains steady

---

Practical Activity

Create twenty nonsense words of your own and memorise them all so that you can recall each one perfectly. Then test your memory for these nonsense words two hours later, six hours later, the next day and a week later.

Draw a graph of the number of words correctly recalled on each occasion and compare to the graph in Figure 1.7. Look at the words you have recalled after a day and a week. Are there some which you can give some kind of sense to? For example, if you created the word mcd, *you might have associated it with McDonalds. This is one the shortcomings of Ebbinghaus's research in that some nonsense words are more memorable than others. This is because people try to impose meaning on something that at first sight appears meaningless. He was therefore not studying pure memory as he intended.*

Areas of study of cognitive psychology

The main areas of interest of the cognitive approach are memory, perception, attention, cognitive development (including language development) and social cognition. The cognitive approach has also enjoyed a range of practical applications, including therapy, criminological psychology (improving eye-witness testimony, for example) and education.

Theory and research into memory looks at short-term and long-term memory techniques that aid memory, why we forget, autobiographical memory, and emotional memory. Perception is concerned with how we view the world using all our different senses, although visual perception is probably the most researched. Research into visual perception uses illusions to investigate how we come to interpret the world in which we live.

Cognitive developmental psychologists, such as Piaget (1963) and Kohlberg (1984), were interested in how development from a baby to an adult takes place in relation to how we come to know and understand the world in which we live. Kohlberg (1984) was also interested in how we develop our sense of morals and distinguish between good and bad behaviour, and between what is right and what is wrong.

An important application of the cognitive approach has been a cognitive therapy developed by Albert Ellis (1962, 1989) called **rational–emotive therapy**. The basic idea is that people who are, for example, depressed or anxious need to change the way they think. To quote Ellis (1962) the client:

'can rid himself of most of his emotional or mental unhappiness, ineffectuality and disturbance if he learns to maximise his rational and minimise his irrational thinking.'

1

A rational–emotive therapist will explore how a person thinks about a specific matter and identify illogical or self-defeating thoughts. The task then is to get the person to see how these thoughts feed the depression and to think more logically and positively. Cognitive therapy has proved highly successful with depressive and anxiety disorders.

Evaluative Comment

Cognitive psychologists are criticised for tending to ignore the physical and social environment in which people live. The focus on cognitions may be regarded as remote from people's lives, and not take account of family situations, employment, social conditions and the experience of a person. On the positive side, the cognitive approach has been highly successful in establishing how various mental processes, such as memory and attention, work, and that the findings apply to people generally. Hence the approach is nomothetic *rather than* ideographic.

The information-processing approach

The development of the computer in the 1950s and 1960s had an important influence on psychology and was, in part, responsible for the cognitive approach becoming the dominant approach in present-day psychology. The computer gave cognitive psychologists a metaphor, or example, to which they could compare human mental processes. Essentially, a computer codes information, stores information, uses information and produces an output. This idea of *information-processing* was adopted by cognitive psychologists as a model of how human thought works. For example, the eye receives visual information and codes that information into neural activity which is fed to the back of the brain in an area called the visual cortex. This information can be used by other parts of the brain and relates to memory, perception and attention. The output might be, for example, to read what you can see on a printed page.

Hence, the information-processing approach characterises thinking as the environment providing input of data, which is then transformed by our senses. The information can be stored, retrieved and transformed using 'mental programs', with the result being behavioural responses. This is depicted in Figure 1.8.

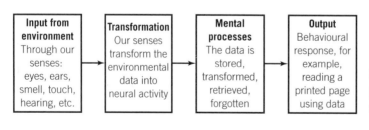

Figure 1.8: The information-processing approach to mental processes

Reflective Activity

Get access to a computer and open up a specific software program which you know how to use, for example, Microsoft Word.

Input some data (words), then use 'tools' to change the data you have inputted, for example, put the text in bold or italics. Then print out the changes.

Now think about your sense of sight or hearing (or any other sense). Compare what you know about this sense as an information-processing system to the software programme. Identify differences and similarities. How good an analogy do you think it is?

Evaluative Comment

The cognitive approach is a highly scientific approach because the vast majority of the research uses laboratory experiments to study mental processes. Whilst this method produces reliable and replicable evidence, it can be criticised for giving people artificial tasks to carry out that do not relate to their every-day lives, for example learning lists of words or nonsense syllables. More recently, cognitive psychology has attempted to be more 'realistic' by, for example, studying autobiographic memory and the interaction between memory and emotions (Lazarus, 1991; Teasdale & Barnard, 1993).

Distinguishing features of each approach

Figure 1.9 provides a summary of the main distinguishing features of each approach using seven areas of comparison. Each of these areas has been covered in our consideration of the five main approaches to psychology. Whilst the biological approach has not been covered in any depth (see Chapter 2 for a fuller discussion), sufficient detail has been provided in this chapter to allow the main distinguishing features of this approach to be identified. Notice that a question mark has been placed against the cognitive approach for nature/nurture and free-will/deterministic categories. This is because it is not clear exactly how the cognitive approach relates to each of these issues.

Approach	Nature/ nurture	Free-will v Deterministic	Ideographic/ Nomothetic	Method of study	Areas of study	Key influence	Therapeutic application
Psycho-dynamic	Both, but emphasis on nature	Deterministic	Ideographic	Case studies	Unconscious conflict	Sexual instinct, childhood important	Psycho-analytic therapy – unconscious repressions
Behaviourism	Nurture, environ-mental experience	Deterministic	Nomothetic	Experiments, mainly with animals (rats)	Observable behaviour – learning	Psychology as science, objective	Systematic desensitis-ation
Humanistic	Nurture, with other people	Free-will	Ideographic	Case studies, studies of different cultures	Human experience	Subjective experience important to psychology	Person-centred therapy of Carl Rogers
Cognitive	?	?	Nomethetic	Laboratory experiment	Human mental processes	Humans as information processors	Rational–emotive therapy
Biological	Nature	Deterministic	Nomothetic	Experiments on humans and animals	Brain processes	Importance of genetics in human psychology	Drug therapies

Figure 1.9: Summary of the main distinguishing features of the five approaches to psychology

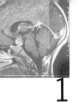

1 Practical Activity

In groups of four, select two approaches and two distinguishing features (the same two for each approach). For example, look at the 'Nature/nurture' and 'Methods of study' features of the Behaviourist and Humanistic approaches.

Each person in the group takes a feature and reads the relevant section of this chapter, making notes in relation to the approach/distinguishing feature.

Then come together as a group and tell each other what you have found. Summarise the key points from each of the four sets of findings.

Evaluative Comment

You may wonder why there are so many different approaches to psychology and whether one approach is correct and others wrong! Psychologists would probably agree that no one approach is correct, although in the past, in the early days of psychology, behaviourists would have said that their approach was the only truly scientific one. The fact that there are different approaches represents the complexity and richness of human (and animal) life. A scientific approach, such as behaviourism or cognition, tends to ignore the subjective experiences that people have. The humanistic approach does recognise human experience, but largely at the expense of being non-scientific in its methods and ability to provide evidence. The psychodynamic approach concentrates too much on the unconscious and our early experiences and repressions made before the age of six. As such, it tends to lose sight of everyday problems facing adults today and the social circumstances in which a person lives. The biological approach reduces humans to a set of mechanisms and physical structures which are clearly essential and important. However, it fails to account for consciousness and how we interact and are influenced by other people.

As a result, each approach brings something different to our understanding of people. For this reason, it is important that psychology does have different approaches to the understanding and study of humans and other animals.

See Appendix 1 for information concerning questions that appear in the examination paper. The assessment of knowledge and understanding (AO1) and analysis and evaluation (AO2) assessment objectives is also given in Appendix 1.

Sample questions

Sample question 1

(a) Outline one way in which psychology scientifically studies human behaviour.

(AO1 = 2) *(2 marks)*

(b) Explain the difference between scientific and common sense explanations of human behaviour.

(AO1 = 1, AO2 = 2) *(3 marks)*

(c) Identify and discuss one key influence of Darwin on the development of psychology.

(AO1 = 2, AO2 = 3) *(5 marks)*

(d) Describe and discuss two assumptions of the cognitive approach in psychology.

(AO1 = 5, AO2 = 5) *(10 marks)*

Total AO1 marks = 10   Total AO2 marks = 10   Total = 20 marks

Questions, answers and comments

(a) Sally has just completed a course in psychology and is telling her friend Irene how interesting she has found the scientific study of behaviour. Describe one reason Sally could give Irene to show that psychology is scientific.

(AO1 = 3) *(3 marks)*

(b) Identify and outline one contribution of Wundt to the development of psychology.

(AO1 = 3) *(3 marks)*

(c) Explain what psychologists mean when they describe human beings as information processors. Use an example to illustrate your answer.

(AO1 = 1, AO2 = 3) *(4 marks)*

(d) Identify and discuss two assumptions of the behaviourist approach.

(AO1 = 3, AO2 = 7) *(10 marks)*

Total AO1 marks = 10   Total AO2 marks = 10   Total = 20 marks

Answer to (a)

Sally could tell Irene that psychology is scientific because experiments are used and empirical results are obtained. The experiments are often carried out in laboratories, which are thought to be linked to a scientific approach. Also experiments are conducted in laboratories where variables are controlled.

Comment

This answer gained the full three marks available. The candidate identified science as the use of experiments and empirical data, then went on to write about the use of laboratories and the control of variables that can be achieved.

1

Sample questions, answers and comments

Answer to (b)

Wundt was the founding father of psychology and introduced the use of introspection. Introspection is concerned with analysing and interpreting an individual's mind, thought and memories. Introspection is a very subjective method because the participant can select what they report.

Comment

This answer achieved two out of the three marks available. The candidate correctly identified Wundt as the founding father of psychology – an important influence in the development of psychology – then went on to write about introspection. However, although what is written is correct, it is not really relevant to the question. The answer needed to be swung round to state the contribution of Wundt. For example, if the answer had said that Wundt thought introspection was scientific and that he wanted to make psychology a science, then the full three marks would have been achieved.

Answer to (c)

This means that psychologists believe humans to be like a computer. Information goes in the computer/brain, it gets processed, which results in a response. For example, when we are hungry, our stomach tells us we are hungry. Our brain registers (it processes information) that we are hungry, and we respond by eating. Some psychologists believe our behaviour is instinctive, but this is not always true. For example, if we are hungry but on a diet, we might process this information but not eat. We are not like a machine, we think about actions before we act.

Comment

Three out of four marks awarded. The answer relates the idea of information-processing to a computer, and the example is acceptable, but one from cognitive psychology, such as memory or attention may have been more appropriate. There is good use of the example comparing instinct of hunger to dieting and how thought may overrule instinct. However, it is not expressed as clearly as it might be; the answer is a little confused in the middle.

Answer to (d)

One assumption of the behaviourist approach is that we learn as a result of reinforcement. Operant conditioning is one example of where we learn a certain behaviour as a result of reinforcement. It is what happens after an event has occurred that determines whether or not a behaviour is learned. The reinforcement may be positive or negative. For example, when a young child is learning to talk and it says the word 'mama'. The parent would positively reinforce this behaviour by smiling at the child. The child will repeat this behaviour again to get a positive reaction from parents.

Another assumption of the behaviourist approach is that we learn our behaviour from the environment. It is what goes on around us that determines what we learn. For example, if we are in a classroom where all the pupils are loud and disruptive, we may learn to be loud and disruptive. Our behaviour is influenced by our environment, however, it may also be influenced by our genetic inheritance.

Comment

This answer scored seven out of the ten marks available. Two assumptions were clearly identified with some discussion given to each. With the first assumption about reinforcement, the example works quite well, but some application of punishment and negative reinforcement would have provided a better answer. The example became too descriptive and needed to discuss more. With the second assumption of learning from the environment, the example is not a good one. The candidate would have done better to develop the nature/nurture side of the debate, which is mentioned at the end of the essay. The seven marks would be made up of AO1 = 3 and AO2 = 4, so more analysis and evaluation was needed to score higher.

Further reading

Introductory texts

Gross, R. (2001), *Psychology: The Science of Mind and Behaviour,* 4th edition (Chapters 1, 2 and 3), London, Hodder & Stoughton

Pennington, D.C. (2003), *Essential Personality* (Chapters 2, 4 and 5), London, Hodder Arnold

Sternberg, R.J. (2001), *Psychology: In Search of the Human Mind* (Chapters 1 and 15), Fort Worth, Harcourt College Publishers

Westen, D. (1999), *Psychology: Mind, Brain and Culture,* 2nd edition (Chapter 1), New York, John Wiley

Specialist sources

Eysenck, M.W. (1994), *Perspectives on Psychology,* Hove, Lawrence Erlbaum

Fancher, R.E. (1996), *Pioneers of Psychology,* 3rd edition, New York, Norton

Gross, R. (1995), *Themes, Issues and Debates in Psychology* (Chapter 11), London, Hodder & Stoughton

Nye, R.E. (2000), *Three Psychologies Perspectives from Freud, Skinner and Rogers,* 6th edition, Belmont, LA, Wadsworth

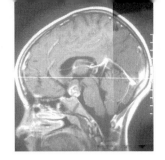

2

The Biological Approach to Psychology

Introduction

Imagine that you have been involved in a car accident and that whilst you only sustained minor cuts and bruises, you were knocked unconscious for a couple of hours. You wake up in a hospital bed, look around you and try to explain what you are doing in hospital! You cannot remember how you came to be there, nor can you remember the events of the previous day. A nurse comes up to talk to you and asks your name – you think and think but cannot remember it. Over the next few days, your memory comes back and you can remember your name and the car accident. What this example demonstrates, perhaps alarmingly, is that physical damage to your head (being knocked out) affects your brain, which in turn has caused memory loss.

The **biological approach** in psychology is interested in how our physical structures, especially the central nervous system, including the brain, and our genes influence how we think and behave. Biological psychology investigates behaviour both in humans and other animals and seeks to explain the causes of behaviour based upon our anatomy and physiology. Biological psychology also includes the study of **behaviour genetics** which sees our behaviour and human characteristics, such as intelligence and personality, as being a result of our genetic make-up.

The biological approach also assumes that the mind and the brain are the same, whereas philosophers and many psychologists think of the brain as physical and the mind as mental. One of the great philosophical questions in psychology is how the mental and physical come together in a person. Biological psychologists basically assume that the mind is the brain.

Reflective Activity

Look at the picture of the human brain in Figure 2.1. Think about the fact that inside your head is your brain. Think about your brain. What evidence from your mental processes do you have that thought, vision, hearing, etc. all occur because you do have a brain? Probably very little. Only when you have a headache are you more aware of your brain.

Genetic basis of behaviour

A distinction needs to be made between genetics and heredity as follows:

* **Genetics** is the study of the genetic make-up of organisms and how this influences physical and behavioural characteristics.

* **Heredity** is the traits, tendencies and characteristics inherited from a person's parents and their ancestors.

(Carlson & Buskist, 1997)

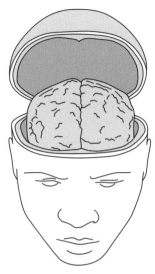

Figure 2.1: Representation of the human brain in the skull. The only visible parts are the two hemispheres of the cerebral cortex

We can see from these definitions that genetics and heredity are similar, except that heredity concentrates on what we inherit from our parents. Genetics, by contrast, is less interested in inheritance but more on how genes determine the physical and psychological characteristics of a person.

In relation to the nature/nurture debate in psychology (whether behaviour is a result of genetics and heredity or a result of the environment), the biological approach comes down firmly on the nature side.

It is important to realise that there are no genes for behaviour as such. This is because one of the main functions of genes is to make proteins. Genes are part of a chromosome (of which there are 46, or 23 pairs, in the normal human). Chromosomes are made up of DNA (deoxyribonucleic acid), which has a structure that looks like a twisted ladder. Genes are bits of DNA which make up a chromosome and direct the synthesis of proteins. It is the protein which then sets off certain physiological responses which result in behaviour. This is shown in Figure 2.2.

Figure 2.2: Representation of the action of genes in causing behaviour

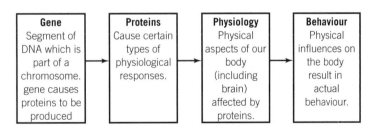

Gene	**Proteins**	**Physiology**	**Behaviour**
Segment of DNA which is part of a chromosome. gene causes proteins to be produced	Cause certain types of physiological responses.	Physical aspects of our body (including brain) affected by proteins.	Physical influences on the body result in actual behaviour.

Evolution and human behaviour

Charles Darwin, as we saw in Chapter 1, had a dramatic and fundamental influence on science and, more generally, on how people think about themselves. Basically, Darwin's theory of evolution states that humans have developed biologically and share common ancestors with all other living creatures, especially mammals. It may help to re-read the section on Darwin (page 8) again now. Darwin's theory of evolution has had a lasting and important influence on psychology for three main reasons:

• All animals, including humans, are related, hence brains and central nervous systems must also be related.

- Since human beings share common ancestors or descendants, behaviour between animals must be related, especially where the genetic relatedness is greatest (for example, humans and chimpanzees).

- Brain and behaviour have been gradually built up through evolution, from more simple to more complex.

For these reasons, biological psychology regards it as legitimate to attempt to understand human behaviour, brain function and other aspects of physiology through the study of other animals.

Reflective Activity

Consider a fish, mouse, chimpanzee and human being. Can you think of behaviours or responses to environmental events which they all have in common? To get you started, think about how each might react to something unexpected happening – depending on other circumstances, you might get either a flight (runs/swims away) or fight (attacks) response. Think of other examples and list them.

One of the key concepts in the theory of evolution is that of **natural selection**. Natural selection is an evolutionary process in which genetically influenced characteristics (physical or psychological) either help an individual survive better in its environment or do not aid survival. Those that aid survival are said to help the individual adapt better to the environment. Such characteristics will survive and be passed on to more individuals in the species and ultimately be common in the population, hence the term 'survival of the fittest'. For example, a polar bear has white fur, which makes the bear difficult to see in snow, which helps it to catch other animals for food.

Study

Aim *Bishop & Cook (1975) conducted a naturalistic study looking at how a particular type of peppered moth had changed its colour over the past 150 years.*

Method *Colours of the same type of moth were compared from records and contemporary pictures. The moths were compared from industrial and rural areas of England.*

Results *As the environment changed, so did the colour of the moth. In industrial cities, since the industrial revolution, the moth had changed from light to dark to light again in colour.*

Conclusions *With pollution in the early 1900s, the change to a dark colour helped the moth survive from predators. As the air became clearer in the latter part of the twentieth century, a lighter colour was a better adaptation to the changed environment. This demonstrates natural selection.*

Human beings have a common ancestry and evolutionary history. This means that we should expect some behaviours and characteristics to be common to all humans. These may be present at birth or develop as the child matures. So what human psychological characteristics might we regard as innate and a product of human evolution?

Evolutionary psychologists (Barkow *et al.*, 1992) argue that characteristics such as exploring the environment, personality or temperament, play and gregariousness (wanting to be with other people) are innate. For example, all primates (humans, monkeys, etc.) explore their environment and engage in play as infants. Human babies in particular grasp whatever is put into their hands. A general personality characteristic called temperament has also been suggested to be a product of evolution (Kagan, 1994). Shortly after birth, babies can be classified as having an 'easy' or 'difficult' temperament, and these temperaments have been shown to follow through to childhood and adolescence. Sutton & Davidson (1997) have linked a personality trait, whereby people feel inhibited from action when threatened, to greater activity in the left hemisphere of the brain. Geary (1995), an evolutionary psychologist, has argued that certain arithmetic skills are innate and result from evolutionary demands. For example, at the age of one week, babies can distinguish between a set of three items and a set of two items (Geary, 1995). Biological aspects of gender are considered in Chapter 4.

Evaluative Comment

One danger of taking an evolutionary perspective in psychology and applying it to humans is that very quickly all behaviours and aspects of the mind become explained in this way. The trouble is that it is not easy to refute or find evidence against such explanations. What is needed is scientific evidence supporting an evolutionary or heredity explanation of specific behaviours. We will look at this general issue again when we come to consider schizophrenia and intelligence in this chapter (pages 44 and 46). Evolutionary psychologists have also used comparisons between different cultures in an attempt to establish evidence for an evolutionary explanation of human behaviour. However, this does not provide the strong evidence produced from experiments in psychology.

Genotype and phenotype

The **genotype** of a person is their actual genetic make-up as represented in the 23 pairs of chromosomes. Each person, apart from identical twins, has a unique genotype. Identical twins have exactly the same genetic make-up. The genotype of brother and sister shares more genetic similarity than between you and your best friend (assuming your best friend is not your brother or sister!). The **phenotype** is the actual expression of a person's genetic make-up – their physical appearance, behavioural characteristics and psychological characteristics that result from heredity. Identical twins, for example, have exactly the same genotype. However, if for some reason they were separated at birth and one twin was fed a better diet than the other, the twin fed a better diet is likely to be taller and physically stronger. Thus each twin would exhibit a different phenotype.

Each of the 23 chromosome pairs in humans contains many pairs of genes; one gene in each pair comes from each of the parents. Each of the pair of genes may be a *dominant gene* or a *recessive gene*. A dominant gene controls the expression of a physical or behavioural characteristic when either both gene pairs are dominant, or one is dominant and one is recessive. A recessive gene does not influence the expression of a physical characteristic or behaviour unless both genes of the pair are recessive. Figure 2.3 shows some physical characteristics that are the result (phenotype) of dominant and recessive genes.

The example of eye colour (brown eyes or blue eyes) shows how this works. The gene for brown eyes is dominant and the gene for blue eyes is recessive. Suppose one parent has brown eyes and

Dominant gene characteristics	Recessive gene characteristic
Brown eyes	Blue eyes
Dark eyes	Blond/red hair
Curly hair	Straight hair
Normal colour vision	Colour blindness
Normal sight	Night blindness
Normal blood	Haemophilia
Normal hearing	Congenital deafness

Figure 2.3: Some examples of human physical characteristics resulting from dominant or recessive genes

2

the other has blue eyes. What colour will the eyes of their child be? It depends on how the gene pairs in each parent are configured. If the father has two dominant brown eye genes and the mother two recessive blue eye genes, their child will have brown eyes. This is shown in Figure 2.4.

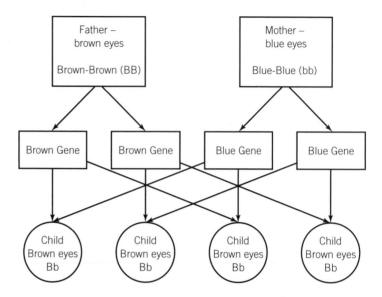

Figure 2.4: Dominant and recessive genes for eye colour, showing the effect of a dominant gene (brown eyes) on a phenotype

Reflective Activity

Imagine a father has brown eyes and the genotype for the gene pair is one brown-eye and one blue-eye gene. The mother has blue eyes and two recessive blue-eye genes. Work out the four different combinations of the two eye-colour genes and the colour of eyes for the four different combinations. You should end up with two brown- and two blue-eyed combinations.

The genetic make-up, or genotype, of an individual can interact with environmental factors to result in the genotype. An example of this is a rare genetic disorder called **phenylketonuria** (PKU). This results from a double recessive gene pair (like blue eyes) which can cause severe learning difficulties for the individual. Children born with PKU are unable to metabolise an amine called phenylanaline. If not diagnosed at birth, the build-up of this amine in the bloodstream causes brain damage and intellectual impairment. However, if the baby is put on a special diet, free of this amine, it will grow and develop normally, with no adverse effect on its intellectual development.

Evaluative Comment

We have seen with PKU that our genotype can be influenced by environmental factors, and thus influence that phenotype. This example highlights the nature/nurture debate in psychology, and suggests that neither one on its own is sufficient to explain human behaviour. What is important is the interaction of genetic and environmental factors, especially for psychological characteristics such as schizophrenia and intelligence (see pages 44 and 46).

Physiological psychology

Physiology is the scientific study of living organisms and is concerned with functions and processes which sustain life. In contrast, anatomy is the study of the structure of living organisms.

Psychologists are interested in the physiology of animals, especially human beings. This is because of the importance of our nervous system, especially the brain, in influencing how we behave and think. Physiological psychologists are also interested in the interaction of the physical body and mind. For example, the body can affect the mind, as shown by the effects of alcohol, and the mind can affect the body – extreme stress may cause tiredness and lethargy.

Practical Activity

Get together with two or three friends or classmates. Discuss ways in which the body affects the mind (for example, feeling sick and the ability to concentrate) and vice versa (for example, feeling anxious and coming out in a rash). List what you come up with. How certain are you that one causes the other?

In what follows, we shall first look at the basic building blocks of the nervous system, the **neuron**, then consider the nervous system as a whole, especially the brain.

Structure and function of neurons

It is estimated that there are 100 billion neurons or nerve cells in the average human nervous system. Neurons vary in size and shape; some are extremely small and others over a metre long! The neuron is specialised for communication, whether between other neurons, or to and from muscles, or with other organs in the body, such as the heart or stomach.

Figure 2.5 depicts a neuron, and although no two neurons are exactly alike, their cellular structure is basically the same. Each neuron has a cell body, axon terminal buttons and dendrites. The cell body, or soma, includes a nucleus which contains the genetic material (chromosomes) of the cell.

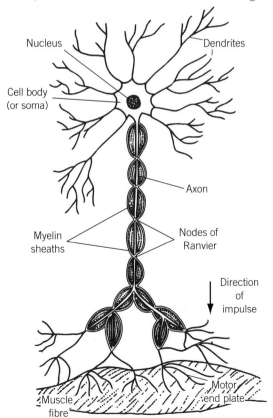

Figure 2.5: The structure of a neuron, showing dendrites cell body, axon, collat~ branches and termin~ buttons

2

Surrounding the nucleus are other components which are essential for the functioning of the whole neuron. The axon is a long extension from the cell body, which may be nearly a metre in length in some neurons. The axon usually has two or more branches called *collateral branches*. Nearly all axons in the human nervous system are covered with a myelin sheath. The myelin sheath insulates or protects the axon from external influences which might affect the transmission of the nerve impulse down the axon. The myelin sheath is what gives the brain its white appearance (the 'white matter'), whilst cell bodies give a grey colour (the 'grey matter') to the brain. The myelin sheath also helps to increase the speed of transmission of the nerve impulse down the axon.

At the end of the axon are what are called terminal buttons. Terminal buttons of one axon send signals to an adjacent cell (another neuron, muscle cell, etc.). If the adjacent cell is another neuron, it is the dendrites (and cell bodies) that receive the nerve impulse or signal from the adjacent neuron. In this way, information is passed between neurons through electrical signals.

The connection between neurons is at the **synapse**. Neurons do not actually touch at the synapse; the electrical impulse 'jumps' between cells at what is called the *synaptic cleft*.

Figure 2.6 depicts a typical synapse. The terminal buttons, or synaptic knobs, at the end of the axon contain small structures called *synaptic vesicles*. These contain certain chemicals called **neurotransmitters**. Neurotransmitters can either increase or decrease the firing of the neuron and the transmission of the electrical impulse from one cell to another. Where a neurotransmitter increases the firing of a cell it is called an *excitatory synapse*, and where it decreases the firing of the cell it is called an *inhibitory synapse*.

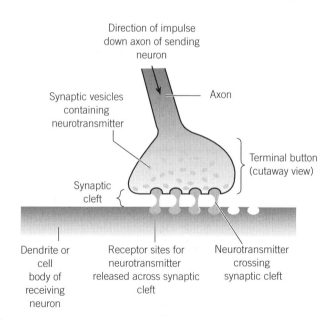

Figure 2.6: A typical synapse between two neurons. The nerve impulse travels from the pre-synaptic neuron, across the synaptic cleft, to the post-synaptic neuron

The function of the neuron is to pass and receive electrical information, or nerve impulses, either from other neurons or other cells, such as muscle cells, heart cells, etc. There are basically three types of neurons: *sensory neurons* receive messages from the outside world through our different senses (eyes, ears, smell, touch, etc.). These messages are then sent to the central nervous system. *Motor neurons* receive messages or nerve impulses from the central nervous system, which are ˙imately passed to other cells. For example, if you touch something very hot, a withdrawal action happens automatically (called a *reflex*). Here, the motor neuron receives a message from the muscle; this goes to the central nervous system which then sends a message back to the muscle, and you withdraw your hand from the hot object. Finally, *interneurons*, or connecting neurons, in the central nervous system connect to other neurons, including sensory and motor neurons. Interneurons represent over 95 per cent of all neurons in the nervous system, with most being in the brain.

The neurotransmitters found in the synaptic vesicles are known to have effects on behaviour and mental processes. For example, acetylcholine (ACH) is a neurotransmitter present at all synapses where a motor neuron is adjacent to a muscle cell. Drugs that block the release of ACH, such as curare, can cause fatal muscle paralysis. Nerve gas, used in warfare, works in the opposite way and aids release of ACH. This results in death through prolonged contraction of all the muscles in the body. The hallucinogenic drug LSD is similar to a neurotransmitter called *serotonin*. LSD causes neurons to fire in the absence of nerve impulses from sense organs. Hence the person taking LSD hears and sees things which are not in the outside world – hallucinations.

The nervous system

The purpose of the nervous system is to collect, process and respond to information, and co-ordinate the workings of different cells in the body. Simple organisms, such as earthworms and jellyfish, have simple, rudimentary nervous systems, but mammals, and especially humans, have extremely complex and highly developed nervous systems. The nervous system in humans is divided into the central nervous system and the peripheral nervous system. Each of these is sub-divided into sub-systems, as shown in Figure 2.7.

The **central nervous system** is made up of the brain and spinal cord, as shown in Figure 2.8. The human brain has three major parts: the brain stem, the cerebellum and the cerebral hemispheres. The brain stem is the oldest (in evolutionary terms) and one of the most primitive parts of the

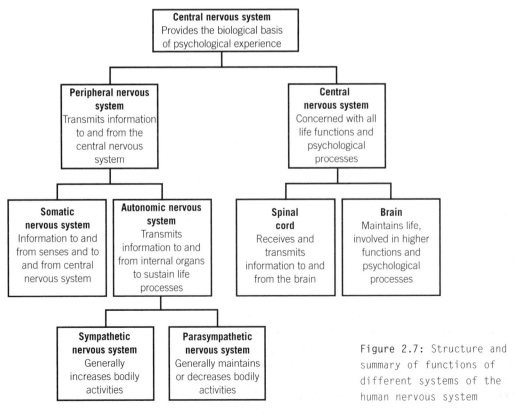

Figure 2.7: Structure and summary of functions of different systems of the human nervous system

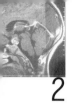

human brain. It controls basic functions such as sleeping and waking, and bodily functions such as breathing and heart rate. The cerebellum is involved in regulating movement and sense of balance. The cerebellum co-ordinates the muscles so that movement and delicate hand co-ordination is smooth and precise. Damage to the cerebellum would result in a person being clumsy, awkward and poorly co-ordinated. Skills such as riding a bicycle, writing with a pen and threading a needle would all be severely affected. Fiez (1996) also claims that the cerebellum is involved in mental tasks such as problem-solving and word generation.

Study

AIM *Krupa* et al. *(1993) conducted a series of experiments on rabbits to investigate the role of the cerebellum in memory.*

METHOD *Rabbits were conditioned to blink their eyes in response to a certain sound. Once the rabbit had been conditioned to make this response, a drug was administered which temporarily stopped the action of the cerebellum.*

RESULTS *The rabbit failed to blink to the sound that had been conditioned whilst the drug was active; however, as the drug wore off, the conditional response returned.*

CONCLUSIONS *The results show that the cerebellum is involved in simple memory tasks.*

The cerebral hemispheres or cerebrum perform higher functions such as vision and memory. We will look at the brain in more detail in the next section.

The *spinal cord* is really an extension of the brain and runs from the base of the brain down the centre of the back. The spinal cord is responsible for certain reflex or automatic behaviours such as pulling your hand away from a very hot object. The spinal cord receives and passes messages from and to the brain, and connects to nerves in the peripheral nervous system. Hence a person who has an accident and has their spinal cord severed at the neck will be both paralysed and without any feeling below the neck.

The *peripheral nervous system* is made up of neurons that transmit messages or information from and to the central nervous system. The peripheral nervous system has two sub-systems, the somatic and autonomic nervous systems, as shown in Figure 2.7. The *somatic nervous system* transmits information from our senses (eyes, ears, skin, nose, tongue, etc.), through receptors, to the central nervous system. It also receives information from the central nervous system which instructs muscles to act, resulting in walking or running. Reading this sentence is a result of the action of the somatic nervous system.

The *autonomic nervous system* consists of two sub-systems, the sympathetic and parasympathetic nervous systems. The autonomic nervous system transmits

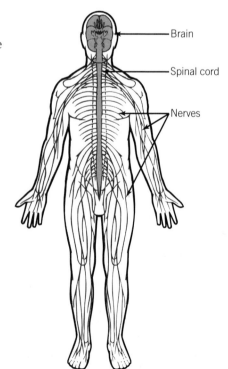

Figure 2.8: The central and peripheral nervous systems, including the brain and spinal cord

information to and from internal bodily organs to carry out life processes such as breathing, digestion and sexual arousal. We will look in more detail at the system on page 37.

Localisation of cortical function

The human brain, and the brains of closely related primates such as the chimpanzee or gorilla, have two cerebral hemispheres that make up the largest part of the brain. These hemispheres are the most recently evolved sections of the brain and are involved in higher cognitive functions such as vision and memory. The left and right hemispheres are symmetrical in shape and are divided into two separate halves which are joined by a bundle of fibres called the *corpus callosum*. The corpus callosum allows the two hemispheres to communicate with or transfer information between each other. As a general rule, the right hemisphere is concerned with the left-hand side of the body, and the left hemisphere with the right-hand side of the body. If you stub your right toe and cause pain, this information will go to the left hemisphere of your cerebral cortex. The two hemispheres also perform different functions, as we shall see a little later.

The cerebral cortex is divided up into what are called frontal, parietal, temporal and occipal lobes, as shown in Figure 2.9.

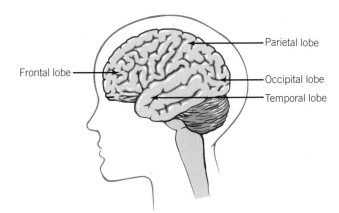

Figure 2.9: The location of the frontal, parietal, temporal and occipital lobes of the brain

The occipital lobe is at the back of the brain, the parietal lobe at the top side and the temporal lobe at the lower side of the brain. Each lobe has different functions, as shown below, but also communicates with the others to perform more complex psychological processes.

- Frontal lobe: motor processing, higher thought processes such as abstract reasoning.

- Parietal lobe: processing of sensations from the skin and muscles of the bodies.

- Temporal lobe: mainly involved in processing auditory information. Sometimes called the auditory cortex.

- Occipital lobe: mainly responsible for processing visual information. Sometimes called the visual cortex.

The idea that different parts of the brain perform different tasks and are involved with different parts of the body is known as **localisation of function**. The idea that the brain has specialised areas of function dates back to Joseph Gall (1758–1828). Gall was an anatomist and he thought that different areas of the brain related to different aspects of personality. Gall created the pseudo-science of phrenology, which claimed that the 'bumps' or contours of the skull revealed different psychological characteristics.

2

Whilst Gall was wrong about the ideas of phrenology, the underlying concept of localisation of function was correct. Whilst the four lobes have the general functions as listed above, certain areas of the brain have more specific localisation of function, as shown in Figure 2.10.

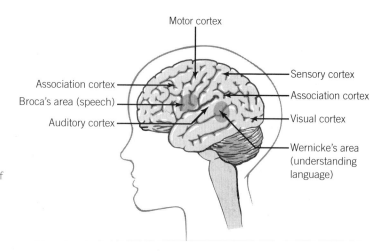

Figure 2.10: Localisation of cortical function. Areas of the brain with specific functions including Broca's and Wernicke's areas

An area of the left frontal lobe is called **Broca's area** and is responsible for the function of speech. To produce meaningful speech, the brain needs to convert memories and thoughts into speech, operated through the vocal cords. Damage to Broca's area causes a particular type of language disorder or aphasia. Here, speech is typically slow, laborious and lacking in fluency. However, recent research has shown that damage only to Broca's area will not cause this type of aphasia. The damage has to be to the immediately surrounding area also (Naesar et al., 1989).

An area of the left-handed temporal lobe is responsible for speech comprehension or recognition of spoken words. This is called **Wernicke's area.** Damage to this area causes a different type of aphasia, where a person has difficulty understanding what another person says and produces speech which is meaningless. In contrast to Broca's aphasia, the speech is fluent and without hesitations; however, it is ungrammatical and does not make a lot of sense. Notice that Wernicke's area is part of the auditory cortex, so it is not surprising that the hearing of what another person says is affected. Also notice that both Broca's area and Wernicke's area are located in the left hemisphere. Generally, the left hemisphere is responsible for most aspects of language.

Study

Aim Petersen et al. (1988) conducted a study to demonstrate different levels of activity in the brain resulting from different types of language tasks.

Method A specialised scanner was used to measure different levels of brain activity in the left hemisphere of the cerebral cortex. People were asked at one time to listen passively to a list of nouns on a tape recorder; at another time to think of verbs to attach to a noun (for example, 'to eat a cake'); and at another time to silently read the list of nouns.

Results As can be seen from Figure 2.11, the scans showed that different parts of the left hemisphere were active according to the task the people were engaged with. In (a) Wernicke's area is activated from listening passively to nouns. In (b) Broca's area is activated by silently repeating the nouns, and in (c) thinking of verbs to attach to a noun activated Broca's area and other parts of the brain.

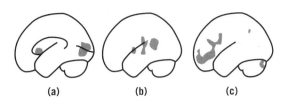

CONCLUSIONS *The scan demonstrated that certain areas of the brain are involved with different aspects of language. The brain scans also showed that other areas of the brain were involved, especially with getting people to link nouns and verbs together.*

Figure 2.12 shows that two areas of the cortex are also specialised for sensory and motor functions. These are symmetrical for both hemispheres, unlike language functions. The motor cortex of the frontal lobe is responsible for stimulating activities in your muscles to cause movement. If the motor cortex is artificially stimulated with electricity, different parts of the body would move, depending on the area stimulated. Figure 2.12 shows a map of the different parts of the body associated with different parts of your body. This is also relevant to the sensory cortex of the parietal lobe. The sensory cortex receives information from your various senses. Notice in Figure 2.12 that the relative size of different parts of the body relate to the density or number of neurons associated with each part. The face, tongue and hands have many more neurons than the trunk and legs.

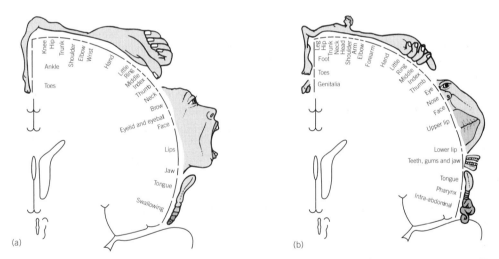

Figure 2.12: Representation of different parts of the body on the sensory cortex. Notice that the face and hands take up more than half of the cortex

Practical Activity

Find a friend or classmate to work with. Take a pair of dividers and get your partner to close his or her eyes. Ask them to report whether they can feel one or two points on their skin.

Very carefully, put the dividers close together and gently touch your partner's legs. One point should be reported.

Widen the dividers a little and repeat. Keep widening until your partner reports feeling two points. Measure the distance between the two points of the dividers and make a note of it.

2

Now repeat this on different parts of the body (lips, cheeks, upper arms, hands, forehead). For each part of the body, note down the distance of the two points of the dividers at which the person reports feeling two points. You should find that the dividers are close together for areas like lips and hands and further apart for legs and upper arms, thus reflecting the density of neurons on the skin which are represented on the sensory cortex, as shown in Figure 2.12.

We have seen with localisation of function of different aspects of language – Broca's and Wernicke's areas – that these are located in the left hemisphere. The two hemispheres also have some different functions, and this is called **lateralisation of function** or hemispheric specialisation. Whilst no one hemisphere has sole responsibility for a function, it is generally accepted that the left hemisphere is dominant for language. It is also regarded as dominant for logical thought, complex motor behaviour and analytic thought. The right hemisphere is dominant for non-linguistic functions, such as the recognition of faces, music and non-logical thought such as intuition. This is the case for right-handed people, and reversed for left-handed people. Gannon *et al.* (1998) showed lateralisation of function to hold for macaque monkeys with respect to vocalisations. Cerebral lateralisation has typically been studied using what are called 'split-brain' patients. These are people who, for some reason, have had the corpus callosum surgically cut, hence stopping communication between the two hemispheres. In a sense, 'split-brain' people have two minds, where each hemisphere operates independently of the other. Sperry (1984) and Gazzaniga (1967) conducted a series of experiments using participants with split-brains and showed that for visual tasks, each hemisphere does see different things.

Evaluative Comment

Where are thoughts and memories stored in the brain? Those who support the idea of localisation of function try to identify specific areas of the brain for memory. However, others claim that information is stored across the brain as well. Lashley (1950) conducted research on rats' brains to try to find specific areas for memory. After 25 years of research, he was not able to find any one area of the rat's brain which specifically remembered how to run around a maze. He thus concluded that learned information is stored in every part of the cortex. This is called a holistic theory *of brain function. One advantage of a holistic theory is that it is able to explain what is called* brain plasticity. *People with damage to certain parts of the brain, as a result of a stroke or accident, may recover some or a lot of the function that has been lost after months or a few years. A head injury may damage a part of the motor cortex so that the person is unable to walk, yet after a period of physiotherapy they may regain that ability. It seems that, whilst a specific area of the normal brain may have a specific function, another part of the brain may take this over a period of time if the original area is damaged. However, some people do recover certain functions, but others do not.*

Methods of investigating cortical function

Broadly speaking, two methods are available to physiological psychologists to find out how the brain works and functions. One set of methods measures the activity of a normal brain, whether in humans or other animals. Another set of methods attempts to relate brain damage (either accidental or deliberate) to deficits in behavioural or psychological processes.

There are three main measurement techniques, which can be used on both normal and damaged brains.

One technique is recording activity at the level of the neuron. Here, microelectrodes are actually inserted into a single neuron, and the electrical activity of the neuron is recorded. This technique was used by Hubel & Wiesel (1989) to investigate the role of different neurons in the visual cortex with respect to vision. This is a very accurate technique, but one that requires high levels of training and use of expensive equipment. The technique is invasive in that an area of the skull has to be removed to expose the brain so that electrodes can be inserted. For this reason, it is used on animals and not humans, but raises ethical issues about whether we should be doing this to animals.

Another technique, which is not invasive, is to record the activity of the brain from electrodes placed on the outside of the skull. This measures global, or more general, activity in the brain and produces an electrocephalogram (ECG). The advantage of this technique is that it is not invasive and can be used on humans and other animals alike. The downside is that the activity of the brain overall is measured rather than the activity of a specific area.

The third measurement technique is the use of scanners. One common type is what is called the **positron emission tomography** or PET for short. Here, substances such as mildly radioactive glucose are injected into the bloodstream. Those areas of the brain that are the most active use up the glucose by converting it into energy. These scans are commonly used in research, but the scanners are expensive and to conduct a PET scan requires an injection into the bloodstream.

Techniques that relate behaviour to damaged brains make use of naturally occurring events, such as brain damage resulting from a car accident, or damage resulting from strokes or tumours of the brain. The disadvantage of exploring naturally or accidentally occurring events is that the damaged area cannot be controlled. Also, it is rarely possible to compare how a person behaved before brain damage and afterwards. A technique that gets over this latter problem, but raises ethical issues, is where the brain of an animal is deliberately damaged. Here, an area of the brain is deliberately removed or destroyed, and psychological functions such as memory and aggression are investigated. Such methods allow the experimenter a high degree of precision over what area of the brain is removed. However, the damage is irreversible, and there are problems when generalising findings from animal studies to humans. Of course, ethical issues also arise concerning whether or not we should subject animals to such irreversible brain damage.

Evaluative Comment

No one method is best for investigating the function of the brain; each has advantages and disadvantages as indicated above. However, the use of computer modelling and 3D pictures on a computer has greatly complemented these methods.

Reflective Activity

Consider any two of the techniques outlined above. List the ethical issues you consider that each technique raises (you may wish to refer to Chapter 3 on ethical issues in psychology).

From an ethical point of view, is any one of the techniques less of a problem than the others? Also, think about whether the knowledge which is gained justifies the ethical problems caused by the technique.

Repeat this exercise for another two of the techniques given above.

The autonomic nervous system

The autonomic nervous system controls the functions of blood vessels, glands and the internal organs of the body (bladder, stomach, heart, etc.). As shown in Figure 2.7, the autonomic nervous system is part of the peripheral nervous system, and transmits information to and from the central nervous system (spinal cord and the brain). It is given the name 'autonomic' because most of the system works automatically and without conscious control. For example, if you have just been to see a scary movie, you may have felt your heart pound and your hands get sweaty. This is the effect of the action of the autonomic nervous system.

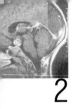

2 Evaluative Comment

Whilst the autonomic nervous system operates largely beyond the conscious control of a person, use of biofeedback can result in someone gaining a degree of control. Biofeedback is where monitoring devices are attached to a person's body to provide information such as body temperature, blood pressure and heart rate. Using biofeedback, some people are able to exert voluntary, conscious control over these bodily functions. In India, yogis are trained to control their bodily systems, and some can make their body temperature stay warm when in a cold environment. However, this requires a lot of training, and most people have little conscious control over their autonomic nervous system.

The autonomic nervous system is sub-divided into the sympathetic and parasympathetic nervous systems. These two systems work together but in opposition to each other. The **sympathetic nervous system** basically prepares the body for action in situations where you are threatened. For example, if you are walking home alone at night and it is very dark, an unusual noise may scare you. The autonomic nervous system prepares you for flight (run away) or fight (stay and confront what is there). It does this by diverting blood from the stomach to the muscles, increasing heart rate, dilating the pupils of the eyes and making the hairs on your body stand on end. However, the sympathetic nervous system may also affect performance in an adverse way. For example, when giving a speech to an audience or a presentation to your class, you may feel anxious and uptight. The sympathetic nervous system causes a dry mouth, sweating and shaking – all this may make your speech hesitant and unclear to those listening. At the extreme, panic attacks, which are extremely debilitating, are the result of the action of the sympathetic nervous system.

The **parasympathetic nervous system** supports normal body activity, conserving and storing bodily energy. It also acts as a brake and reduces the activities of the body that have been increased by the sympathetic nervous system. Figure 2.13 summarises the key functions of each of these systems.

Sympathetic nervous system	Parasympathetic nervous system
Dilates pupils	Contracts pupils
Inhibits saliva production	Stimulates saliva production
Increases rate of breathing	Decreases rate of breathing
Inhibits digestion	Stimulates digestion
Releases the bladder (decreases urination)	Contracts the bladder (increases urination)
Increases heart rate	Decreases heart rate
Stimulates ejaculation in males (orgasm in females)	Stimulates sexual arousal (males and females)
Increases actions of adrenal glands	Decreases actions of adrenal glands
Generally, prepares the body to expend energy for fight or flight	Generally, maintains and conserves body energy and functions

Figure 2.13: The opposing actions of the sympathetic and parasympathetic systems of the autonomic nervous system

Evaluative Comment

The interaction and interdependence of these two systems is highlighted by considering physical effects of the body during sexual activity. In males, the parasympathetic nervous system controls the flow of blood to the penis and is therefore responsible for causing an erection. However, ejaculation is an effect of the sympathetic nervous system. In females, the parasympathetic system causes the emission of lubricating liquid in the vagina, whilst an orgasm is the effect of the action of the sympathetic system. If a person is anxious about sex, the parasympathetic nervous system will be inhibited and sexual performance will be adversely affected.

The endocrine system: the adrenal glands

The **endocrine system** is made up of a number of glands that secrete chemicals, called *hormones,* into the bloodstream. The hormones travel through the bloodstream and affect different body organs. Thus the endocrine system provides another means of communication to the nervous system. The chemical structure of hormones is very similar to that of the neurotransmitters found in the synaptic vesicles of neurons (see page 30). For example, the hormone adrenalin is chemically the same as the neurotransmitter epinephrine. Much of the time, the endocrine system and the autonomic nervous system send the same messages to the body. For example, in a threatening situation, the sympathetic nervous system acts as in Figure 2.13. At the same time, the endocrine system sends hormones through the bloodstream as a parallel action. People feel anxious or jittery for some time after the threat has gone away because the hormones take time to disappear from the bloodstream.

The main glands of the endocrine system are shown in Figure 2.14.

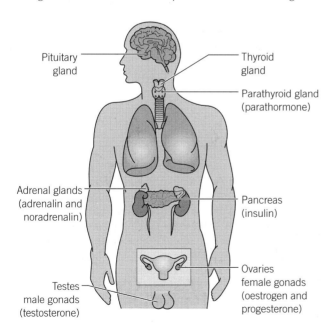

Figure 2.14: The endocrine system showing the major glands in males and females

The pituitary gland is located deep in the brain and is often called the 'master gland' because some of the hormones it releases also regulate and stimulate other glands to secrete hormones. The interaction between the endocrine system and the central nervous system occurs in a small structure in the brain called the **hypothalamus**. The hypothalamus controls the pituitary gland and hence the whole of the endocrine system.

2

The thyroid gland releases hormones that affect general metabolism, energy levels of the organism and mood.

The testes in the male release the male hormone testosterone, and the ovaries in the female release the female hormones oestrogen and progesterone.

The **adrenal glands** are located immediately above the kidneys and secrete a number of hormones, the most important psychologically being *adrenalin*. As we have seen, adrenalin is very similar to epinephrine; both chemicals prepare the body in an emergency for flight or fight.

Evaluative Comment

Adrenalin has been linked to stress reactions shown by people and has sometimes been called the 'stress hormone'. Events are said to be stressful if they have an arousing effect on both our bodily and central nervous system functions (Sapolsky, 1992). A wide variety of quite different events can cause us to become stressed (taking examinations, break-up of an intimate relationship, death of someone we love, moving house, losing a job). When the brain perceives a stressful event, two separate chemical actions take place – one fast and one slow. The fast chemical response is where the brain stimulates the sympathetic nervous system, which in turn instructs the adrenal gland to release the hormone adrenalin. This is the so-called 'adrenalin rush' that is experienced in moments of stress or high anxiety. The slow chemical response is where the hypothalamus in the brain stimulates the pituitary gland in the brain. This then instructs the adrenal gland to release a hormone called cortisol *into the brain. Cortisol inhibits reproductive functions and allows glucose to be released into the bloodstream, thus creating energy.*

Under normal circumstances, stressors are short-lived (a presentation to a class is soon over and you can relax). However, stress prolonged over days or weeks causes hormones to remain in the bloodstream and the stress response to be maintained. This is both physically damaging and mentally exhausting for the person.

Inheritance and behaviour: investigating the genetic basis of behaviour

The nature/nurture debate in psychology is often seen as trying to determine and provide evidence for the extent to which behaviours, or a characteristic such as intelligence, are the product of inheritance or genes, or environmental influences. However, most psychologists and behaviour geneticists nowadays believe that differences between people such as intelligence, mental illness (specifically schizophrenia) and personality are due to the interaction of both genetic inheritance and the environment. The extent to which a behaviour or psychological characteristic is heredity is often expressed in terms of a **heritability coefficient**. A heritability coefficient can vary between 0 and 1.0. A coefficient of 1.0 means that the behaviour or characteristic is determined solely by heredity, and a coefficient of 0.50 would mean a 50 per cent contribution by heredity and 50 per cent from the environment. For example, studies of personality characteristics such as neuroticism, aggressiveness and assertiveness have produced estimated coefficients of between 0.15 and 0.50 heritability (Plomin *et al.*, 1997).

It is important to be aware that heritability refers to genetic influences on variability among individuals. It does not tell you specifically that a behavioural or personality trait is genetically determined. For example, having two ears is genetically determined in humans. However, practically speaking, humans show no variability in the number of ears that they have. That is, you do not see some people with one ear, some with two ears, some with three ears, etc. The heritability of two ears has a coefficient of 0 because there is no variability. Contrast this with eye colour, where there is a high degree of variability and it is also high in heritability – a coefficient of 1.0 exists. The same applies to the search for heritability in psychological characteristics – people do show high degrees of variability. Hence it is legitimate to try to establish the extent to which such characteristics are hereditary.

Evaluative Comment

Psychologists and behaviour geneticists are not able to provide a direct estimate of the heritability of a trait. For obvious ethical reasons, it is not feasible to attempt to manipulate the genes of people through artificial breeding programmes. Manipulating people's environments to look at the nurture contribution is also unethical and would be in breach of human rights. To get round these problems, researchers look to naturally occurring phenomena such as twins and child adoption or manipulate the genetics of animals through **selective breeding***. We will now look at these methods of investigation in attempts to determine heritability.*

Twin studies

The use of twins to estimate heritability of behaviour or psychological characteristics is a commonly used method. There are two types of twins. First, **monozygotic twins** who share exactly the same genetic make-up because they develop from one fertilised egg which divides into two separate embryos. Second, **dizygotic twins**, or fraternal, twins that develop from two separate eggs that are fertilised by different sperm. Dizygotic twins are no more alike genetically than any two siblings (brothers or sisters). Obviously, identical twins are the same sex, whilst dizygotic twins may be the same or different sexes.

Research using twin studies looks for the degree of concordance (or similarity) between identical and fraternal twins. Twins are concordant for a trait if both or neither of the twins exhibits the trait. Twins are said to be disconcordant for a trait if one shows it and the other does not. Identical twins have the same genetic make-up, and fraternal twins have just 50 per cent of genes in common. Because of this, psychologists argue that if identical twins show a higher heritability coefficient than fraternal twins for a particular trait, then this is evidence for heritability of the trait. Figure 2.15 shows concordance rates between identical and fraternal twins for a number of characteristics. (We will look specifically at schizophrenia and intelligence on pages 44 and 46.)

It could be argued that you might expect higher levels of concordance between identical twins than fraternal twins for psychological characteristics because identical twins are treated the same. That is, the environmental experiences are more alike for identical twins than for fraternal twins. To get

Trait	Concordance	
	Identical twins	**Fraternal twins**
Blood types	100%	66%
Eye colour	99%	28%
Learning difficulties	97%	37%
Epilepsy	72%	15%
Diabetes	65%	18%
Allergies	59%	5%
Tuberculosis	57%	23%

Figure 2.15: Concordance rates of identical and fraternal twins for a number of traits (Adapted from Klug & Cummings, 1986)

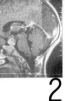

round this criticism, psychologists have studied identical twins that were separated at birth or very early in life and brought up separately and in different environments. The argument here is that if identical twins show high levels of concordance for a trait such as intelligence or personality, having been brought up in different environments, then heritability plays a major role in that trait.

Evaluative Comment

Caution is necessary when looking at research findings from identical twins said to have been reared apart. This is because it is highly unusual to separate identical twins, and where it happens, the environments of each twin are often very similar. Sometimes each twin lives in the same street or neighbourhood with a different member of the extended family. These days, the authorities responsible for placing children in homes will go to great lengths to ensure that twins are not separated. Rarely do identical twins get reared in separate, different environments.

Adoption studies

Adoption studies are another method used to investigate heritability. This involves comparing a trait or characteristic between adopted children and the children of their biological parents. Biological parents pass on their genes to their children, adoptive parents provide their adopted children with the same environment but none of their genes. Normally, adoption studies compare adopted children in one family with biological children in another family. However, sometimes it is possible to look at families with both adopted and biological children. This has the added advantage of all children sharing a similar environment. If a trait or psychological characteristic is heritable, then the biological children should show greater similarity for that characteristic with their biological parents compared to children of adopted parents. For example, an adoption study conducted in Sweden by Cloniger (1987) reported that sons of alcoholic biological parents were more likely to become alcoholic themselves compared to children reared by adopted parents. Often, it is found that the heritability coefficient for adopted children is higher with their natural parents than their adoptive parents.

Evaluative Comment

Ideally adoption studies need to compare children in adopted families to children reared by their biological parents who both share identical environments. This is not really achievable, since no two environments are identical, not even for identical twins. Hence, criteria have to be developed to clarify to what extent the two environments are the same. Only when the two environments can be shown to be highly similar can differences between adopted children and children living with their biological parents be attributed to heritability.

Practical Activity

Get together with two or three people. Decide on up to ten different aspects of the environment in which you live (one might be type of house you live in – terraced, semi-detached, detached, etc.). Each person then writes down what their environment is like in relation to each of the ten aspects.

Come together and compare notes, identifying which aspects of the environment are the same for all of you and which aspects are different.

Now think about trying to set up an adoption study. How easy do you think it would be to get twenty families where the children are adopted and twenty where the children live with the biological parents, where all these environmental aspects are the same?

Selective breeding

Selective breeding of animals to produce a desired characteristic has a history dating back over many thousands of years. Racehorse owners, for example, select which horses to mate; farmers use artificial insemination techniques to fertilise cows; and surrogacy is also used in the animal world of breeding. Selective breeding needs to be distinguished from natural breeding. In selective breeding, there is artificial selection of the male and female animals that are put together to breed and produce offspring. With natural breeding, animals, especially humans, are free to choose who they mate with; there is no artificial interference. Breeding animals with selected traits and observing these traits in their offspring is an important method for the hereditary influences on behaviour. The classic study of Robert Tyron (1940), conducted with the selective breeding of rats who were fast to learn how to run a maze or slow to learn how to run a maze, demonstrates the value of selective-breeding experiments.

Study

Aim *Tyron (1940) conducted a selective breeding study with rats with the aim of identifying whether genetics influenced learning.*

Method *A large number of rats were trained to learn to run a maze, and the number of errors each rat made in running the maze was recorded. From this, Tyron selected those rats which learned to run the maze the quickest and those which learned the slowest. The former were called 'maze bright' and the latter 'maze dull' rats. Tyron mated 'bright' rats with other 'bright' rats, and 'dull' rats with other 'dull' rats. Tyron continued this selective breeding programme over a number of generations. For each generation, the speed with which the rats learned the maze was recorded.*

Results *'Maze bright' rats which were selectively bred learned to run a maze faster at each generation and made fewer errors. By contrast, 'maze dull' rats took longer to learn and made more errors over the generations. This is shown in Figure 2.16.*

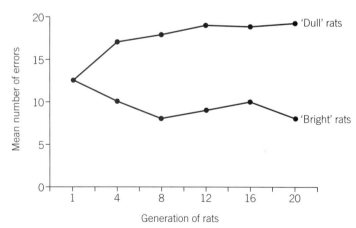

Figure 2.16: Mean number of errors made by 'bright' and 'dull' selectively bred rats when learning to run a maze (Adapted from Tyron, 1940)

Conclusions *Tyron demonstrated that maze learning in rats could be manipulated through selective breeding. This indicates that learning is a heritable characteristic in rats.*

Evaluative Comment

Whilst this may demonstrate a genetic basis to learning in rats, the findings may not generalise very well to human beings, since they are much more complicated in their interaction with the environment.

2

Cooper & Zubek (1958) showed that differences in maze learning in rats were virtually eliminated when 'maze bright' and 'maze dull' rats were reared either in an enriched environment or an impoverished environment. An enriched environment consisted of tunnels, ramps and blocks designed to aid learning. An impoverished environment was a cage with only food and water in it. This shows that the environment in which an animal is reared can more than override or compensate for genetic predispositions.

Genetic basis of schizophrenia

Schizophrenia is a serious mental disorder characterised by hallucinations (visual and auditory), delusions, thought disturbance and emotional and social withdrawal. The most common hallucination consists of hearing voices and the belief that one's thoughts are being controlled by other people or an external force. It is a psychotic disorder with typical onset in the late teens and twenties. It affects just under one per cent of the adult population. For people diagnosed as schizophrenic, about one third recover, one third improve significantly and one third do not get well. There are many theories as to the cause of schizophrenia, and a biological or genetic explanation has received considerable empirical support. The heritability, or genetic, view has been studied through research on relatives of people with schizophrenia, twin studies, adoption studies and what is called 'chromosomal mapping'.

Gottesman (1991) and Kendler *et al.* (1993) have produced clear evidence that schizophrenia is more common in relatives of people with the disorder. The greater the genetic similarity between people, then the greater the incidence of schizophrenia. This is shown in Figure 2.17, where it can be seen that the concordance for schizophrenia with identical twins is 48 per cent. In contrast, with fraternal twins it is only 17 per cent, and ordinary siblings nine per cent. If both parents are schizophrenic, the chances are nearly 50:50 (46 per cent) that their child will also develop schizophrenia.

Relationship to person with schizophrenia	Percentage concordance
Identical twin	48%
Offspring of two schizophrenic parents	46%
Fraternal twins	17%
Offspring of one schizophrenic parent	13%
Sibling (brother or sister)	9%
Parent	6%
Grandchild	5%
Nephew/niece	4%
Uncle/aunt	2%
General population	1%

Figure 2.17: Percentage of people with schizophrenia in relation to biological relatedness (Adapted from Gottesman, 1991)

Evaluative Comment

The finding that concordance between identical twins is 48 per cent shows that schizophrenia is not solely determined by inheritance or genetic factors. Environmental influences also play an important role. The most widely accepted theory of schizophrenia is called the diathesis–stress theory. This states that certain people have a genetic predisposition to develop schizophrenia, but that this is only triggered by stressful environmental experiences. This model implies that some people have a 'schizophrenic gene' but do not become schizophrenic.

Study

AIM *Gottesman & Bertelsen (1989) conducted a study to test the diathesis–stress theory of schizophrenia by looking at the children of twins who were discordant for schizophrenia (that is, one twin had schizophrenia and the other did not).*

METHOD *The children of discordant monozygotic and dizygotic twins were looked at to see which children, if any, were schizophrenic.*

RESULTS *The researchers found that in children of discordant monozygotic twins, the percentage diagnosed as schizophrenic was almost identical at 17 per cent. For children of dizygotic twins, 17 per cent were schizophrenic where the parent twin was schizophrenic. However, where the parent twin was not schizophrenic this dropped to two per cent.*

CONCLUSIONS *These results provide good evidence that schizophrenia is heritable but that this does not mean that someone will go on to become schizophrenic.*

Adoption studies also provide support for the heritability of schizophrenia. Such studies look at adults diagnosed as schizophrenic who were adopted when young and compare them with both their biological and adoptive parents. If the evidence of schizophrenia is higher in comparison with biological parents this is evidence for a genetic influence.

Study

AIM *Kety (1988) conducted an adoption study in Denmark over a twenty-year period to investigate the incidence of schizophrenia in children of adoptive and biological parents.*

METHOD *Over 5,000 adults who were adopted in early life were contacted and the incidence of schizophrenia noted. The biological and adoptive parents of these adults were also found and levels of schizophrenia noted.*

RESULTS *Thirty-three of the 5,000 adults were found to have schizophrenia. Fourteen per cent of the biological parents were found to have schizophrenia, compared to 2.7 per cent of adoptive parents.*

CONCLUSIONS *The findings provide strong evidence for a genetic factor in schizophrenia, since biological parents showed a much higher incidence of schizophrenia than adoptive parents, or the level of incidence in the general population.*

Evaluative Comment

Researchers have sought to explain how the genetic factor may be important in determining schizophrenia. One explanation is that the genes involved produce chemical abnormalities in the brain – specifically a chemical called dopamine. *Dopamine is a neurotransmitter (see page 30), and high levels of dopamine are thought to cause neurons to fire and transmit messages to other neurons much more than is normal. This high level of neural activity may be the cause of hallucinations and thought disorders commonly found in schizophrenics.*

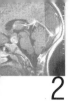

2 Genetic basis of intelligence

Intelligence is a very broad concept and may be defined as follows:

> 'A person's ability to learn and remember information, to recognise concepts and their relations, and to apply the information to their own behaviour in an adaptive way.' (Carlsen & Buskist, 1997)

Practical Activity

Discuss the above definition of intelligence with two or three other people. Before doing so, each write down what you think intelligence is.

Share what each of you has written and identify common themes. You should discover that intelligence can be seen to be many things and defined in a number of different ways.

The idea that intelligence is a product of the influences of both nature (inheritance) and nurture (experience) is widely accepted in psychology (Sternberg, 1997). However, proponents of the heritability of intelligence date back to the 1860s with the publication of a book by Sir Francis Galton (a relative of Darwin) called *Hereditary Genius*.

Galton (1869) studied eminent people in society and looked at how successful their children were. Finding a high correlation, Galton argued that this was genetic; what he omitted to take into account was that such people were also often born into privileged positions in society – inheritance of status, not intelligence.

Most research investigating the heritability of intelligence has used twin and adoption studies and measured intelligence through the use of standardised tests of intelligence. The measures of intelligence of, for example, twins, are then compared to see how alike they are. The comparison is made using a correlation statistic (see Chapter 3), where a figure of 1.0 indicates total similarity, and a figure of 0 indicates no similarity. Henderson (1982) summarised findings from a number of studies which looked at varying degrees of relatedness and correlations in intelligence. This is summarised in Figure 2.16. You can see that the correlation for identical twins reared together is high (0.86), indicating a strong genetic role in intelligence. For fraternal twins, the correlation is lower, and for parent/child even lower still. Notice the correlation for the same individual at 0.87. This is determined from giving the same intelligence test to the same person at different times. The correlation is not perfect (1.0) because the individual performs slightly differently on each occasion. However, this correlation is nearly the same as for identical twins.

Adoption studies examining the importance of genetics in determining intelligence correlate the intelligence of adopted children with both their biological and their adoptive parents.

Relationship	Reared	% genetic similarity	Correlation
Same individual	–	100	0.87
Identical twins	Together	100	0.86
Fraternal twins	Together	50	0.62
Siblings (brother or sister)	Together	50	0.41
Parent–child	Together	50	0.35
Adoptive parent–child	Together	0(?)	0.16

Figure 2.18: Correlations in intelligence between people of different genetic relatedness (Adapted from Henderson, 1982)

Study

AIM *Scarr & Weinberg (1978) compared specific intellectual abilities, such as arithmetic, vocabulary and picture arrangement, of parents and their adopted and biological children.*

METHOD *A standardised intelligence test measuring different aspects of intelligence called the Wechster Adult Intelligence Scale (WAIS) was given to parents and their adopted and biological children.*

RESULTS *Correlations for the different aspects on intelligence were higher between parents and their biological children than between parents and adopted children.*

CONCLUSIONS *This shows that genetic factors play a more significant role in determining intelligence than environmental influences.*

Evaluative Comment

Plomin (1988) argues that much of the above type of research underestimates the importance of environmental influences on intelligence. This is because the environment for siblings in one family is different for each one. No two children are treated exactly the same – for example, differences in appearance may affect how each is treated. Also, birth order has been identified as a factor in intelligence (Zajonc & Markus, 1975; Zajonc, 1983). Children may go to different schools and study different subjects as teenagers. Once children leave home, the environment of each is often quite different. Hence it may be wrong to assume that because siblings or twins are brought up in the same family they are exposed to the same environmental influences.

Limitations of the biological approach

We will now consider four limitations of the biological approach: reductionism; neglect of environmental factors; the mind–body problem; and genetics and ethical issues.

The biological approach is a reductionist approach in that it attempts to reduce human (and animal) psychological processes to physical processes. The physical processes, such as the nervous system, are then reduced to smaller component parts. Some psychologists claim that this loses sight of the person as a whole, and fails to reflect experience and everyday interaction with other people.

The biological approach tends to come down on the nature side of the nature/nurture debate. As such, the importance of environmental factors is often ignored. For example, one of the defining features of being human is that we are social creatures – we seek and enjoy the company of other people. How we relate to and interact with others strongly influences our behaviour. The biological approach tends to take the person out of this social context and only study physical processes within the body.

The biological approach focuses on the body; that is, on physical processes and in particular the structure and function of the central nervous system. Consciousness and conscious thought is a mental process which seems qualitatively different from physical processes. The mind–body debate in philosophy and psychology is about how the physical and mental interact and come together in one person. Since the biological approach focuses on the physical, it does not have an answer to the mind–body problem. In many respects, it does not concern itself with the issue.

The final limitation is to do with ethical issues that the biological approach raises. The Human Genome Project is mapping the entire genetic make-up of people. This involves determining the location of genes on specific chromosomes and then looking to discover the function of each gene. In time, this may allow genetic manipulation and selective breeding in future generations of people.

2

This raises the question, should scientists tamper with human genetic make-up? Whilst there may be many benefits, for example, discovering the genes that give an individual a predisposition to develop schizophrenia, there are many dangers as well. Some scientists may be unethical in their use of these scientific advances.

To end on a positive note, the biological approach does have great strengths and advantages. It does provide an understanding of how psychological processes occur in the brain. It also enjoys applications in respect of the use of drugs to treat disorders such as schizophrenia, depression and anxiety. The drugs act on the nervous system, many at the synapse affecting neurotransmitters. Whilst drugs for depression such as Prozac can have unfortunate side effects, they have also given millions of people relief from depression.

The strengths and weaknesses of the biological approach in psychology can only be fully appreciated by comparison to other approaches, such as humanistic, psychodynamic and behaviourist (see Chapter 1).

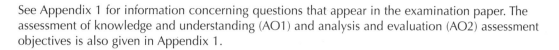

See Appendix 1 for information concerning questions that appear in the examination paper. The assessment of knowledge and understanding (AO1) and analysis and evaluation (AO2) assessment objectives is also given in Appendix 1.

Sample questions

Sample question 1

(a) Describe what is meant by the term evolution.

  (AO1 = 3) *(3 marks)*

(b) Describe one method used to identify cortical specialisation.

  (AO1 = 3) *(3 marks)*

(c) Explain, using an example, what is meant by the term localisation of cortical function.

  (AO1 = 1, AO2 = 3) *(4 marks)*

(d) Discuss two limitations of the biological approach in psychology.

  (AO1 = 3, AO2 = 7) *(10 marks)*

Total AO1 marks = 10 Total AO2 marks = 10 Total = 20 marks

Questions, answers and comments

(a) Name any three parts of the neuron.

  (AO1 = 3) *(3 marks)*

(b) Phenylketonuria (PKU) is a disorder caused by a defective gene resulting in severe learning difficulties for individuals who inherit the condition. With reference to PKU, distinguish between phenotype and genotype.

  (AO1 = 1, AO2 = 2) *(3 marks)*

(c) Outline two examples of cortical localisation of function.

  (AO1 = 4) *(4 marks)*

(d) With reference to at least one study, discuss how localisation of function has contributed to our understanding of human behaviour.

  (AO1 = 3, AO2 = 7) *(10 marks)*

Total AO1 marks = 11 Total AO2 marks = 9 Total = 20 marks

Answer to (a)

Cell body, axon and dendrites.

Comment

Three parts of the neuron correctly identified so scores the full three marks. Could also have given terminal buttons, synapse, synaptic vesicles.

Answer to (b)

Genotype is the genes inherited from your parents found in your chromosomes. Phenotype is how the genes are expressed, so if your inherited genes have the defective gene which causes PKU, your phenotype will suffer from the severe learning difficulty.

2

Comment

Clear answer, although the expression is a little awkward. Candidate clearly understands the difference between genotype and phenotype and relates this to PKU quite well. Just about scores the full three marks available.

Answer to (c)

One example is Broca's area which is involved in the production of speech – Broca's aphasia causes a person to have a problem with this, and they are said to be 'lost for words'. Wernicke's area is also involved with speech and is close to the auditory areas of the brain. A person with Wernicke's aphasia can talk but not make a lot of sense.

Comment

Candidate understands the idea of localisation of function. Correctly described the function of Broca's area in the brain and what happens when damaged to cause Broca's aphasia. Two marks for this. Wernicke's area is a correct example of localisation of function but not clearly enough stated to get two marks. So three marks for this answer overall.

Answer to (d)

Localisation of function has enabled us to understand a great deal about articulation of speech, speech comprehension and written communication. Through studies where the brain has been damaged, we have been able to localise functions of Wernicke's and Broca's areas in speech. Also, the angular gyrus is responsible for visual communication and damage results in dyslexia.

Broca's area is near to the motor strip of the cortex so it is conceivable that a problem there would affect articulation of speech, as the motor strip is in charge of movement.

However, although these functions have been localised, others have not. Lashley conducted an experiment with rats and got them to learn to run a maze. Lashley destroyed parts of the brain to try to find out which part was responsible for learning. However, he could not find a specific part. This suggests learning is not localised.

By understanding which functions are localised in the brain, we can predict what problems result from damage of those areas and know what problems a person will have.

Comment

The answer addresses the question directly and gives other examples of localisation of function. The second paragraph makes a good point about Broca's area being near the motor cortex. The third paragraph provides good analysis and evaluation, since a study is cited which argues against localisation of function for certain things like learning.

The final paragraph gives good analysis to the value of knowing about which functions are localised in the brain. The answer would gain three AO1 marks and five AO2 marks, giving eight out of ten altogether.

Overall, for (a), (b), (c) and (d), this answer would gain seventeen marks out of twenty. A very good answer.

Further reading

Introductory texts

Carlson, R. & Buskist, W. (1997), *Psychology: The Science of Behaviour* (Chapters 3 and 4), Boston, Allyn & Bacon

Gross, R. (2001), *Psychology: The Science of Mind and Behaviour*, 4th edition (Chapters 4, 41 and 45), London, Hodder & Stoughton

Western, D. (1999), *Psychology: Mind, Brain and Culture*, 2nd edition (Chapters 3, 8 and 15), New York, John Wiley & Sons

Specialist sources

Carlson, R. (1994), *Physiology of Behaviour*, 5th edition, Boston, Allyn & Bacon

Kolb, B. & Whishaw, I.Q. (2000), *An Introduction to Brain and Behaviour*, New York, Worth Publishers

Loria, A.R. (1973), *The Working Brain*, Harmondsworth, Penguin

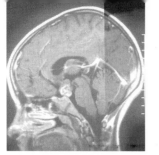

3

Methods of Research in Psychology

Introduction

Psychology is generally defined as *the scientific study of human behaviour* (see Chapter 1). This definition helps to explain why psychologists often adopt methods of investigation which follow those used by more traditional sciences, such as experiments conducted in chemistry or physics laboratories. However, there is no 'rule' which says that all psychologists must conduct their research in a particular way. As you will see from this chapter, there are many methods of investigation used by psychologists to discover and understand behaviour and thought. The purpose of psychological research is to gain an accurate understanding of human behaviour. This is not the same as 'common sense' explanations of behaviour. The research method chosen by a psychologist must aim to challenge common sense ideas by checking the facts. For example, a researcher is likely to design an experiment to find out exactly what happens to memory for information under conditions of noise and silence. If the researcher wants to know how people respond to traumatic events in their lives, then the method used to find this out is likely to involve interviews with people who have had such experiences. The experiment is not 'better' than the interview; each has its place in providing accurate information about human behaviour.

Planning research

Formulating research questions

Psychologists study groups of people to find out what they have in common, and they study individuals in order to identify what makes each person unique. When groups are studied, behaviours or experiences common to many people are investigated. The explanation for the behaviour produced from those studied is then generalised and said to be applicable to all members of the group. Studying groups is called *nomothetic research*. When an individual is studied, then the explanations for the behaviour of that individual cannot be applied to all people; this approach is called *ideographic research*. The different approaches can be seen in the method chosen by the researcher to find out about behaviour. For example, an experiment is a method which compares the behaviour of a group of people in one condition with a group of people in a different condition. In contrast, a **case study** is often used to investigate the in-depth reasons for the behaviour of a person.

A key aspect of choosing a research method is the ability to formulate an appropriate *aim* for an investigation and then to develop research *hypotheses* from this aim. It is important to distinguish between the aim of an investigation and the hypotheses under test in a piece of research.

An example here may help to clarify the difference between the aims of research and research hypotheses. Consider a psychologist who wishes to find out whether or not television influences gender-role stereotypes held by teenagers. The aim of the research is the general interest that the psychologist has concerning television and its possible influence on gender-role stereotypes. By contrast, hypotheses make specific predictions concerning how television may influence gender-role stereotypes. For example, one hypothesis might be 'teenagers who regularly watch *EastEnders* will see males as more aggressive than females, compared to teenagers who rarely, if ever, watch *EastEnders*'. The aim of the research is general, therefore, whereas hypotheses are specific and make precise predictions (see below for more about different types of hypotheses).

Reflective Activity

Using common sense and your knowledge of psychology, state two hypotheses appropriate to each of the research aims given below:

- *Aim 1: to investigate the effect of alcohol on a person's ability to drive a car.*

- *Aim 2: to investigate the stereotype that overweight people are seen to be happy and carefree.*

On the basis of the two related hypotheses given below, state an appropriate aim of the research:

- *Hypothesis 1: people with blue eyes are perceived as more intelligent than people with green eyes.*

- *Hypothesis 2: people with brown eyes are perceived as more logical than people with green eyes.*

Stating the aims of research

In any piece of research, the aim is a straightforward expression of what the researcher is trying to find out from conducting the investigation. For example, if you are given a description of an investigation, the aim may be identified by phrases such as 'the researcher wanted to find out/to see if/to see whether/to investigate ...' These expressions indicate that the aim of the study is being described.

Reflective Activity

Identify the aim of the following investigations:

- *A student wanted to see whether more words would be remembered if they were learned and recalled in the same room or if learning took place in one room and recall took place in a different room.*

- *A researcher wanted to find out if men are more likely to obey traffic-light signals than women.*

Formulating hypotheses

Every investigation begins with an hypothesis which is a *testable statement*, usually proposing a possible relationship between two *variables*. A variable is anything which can change or be changed, i.e. anything which can vary. Examples of variables are intelligence, gender, memory ability, time taken to sort cards, age or eye colour.

In research, there is a convention that the hypothesis is written in two forms: the **null hypothesis**, or H_0, and the **alternative hypothesis** (called the *experimental hypothesis* when the method of investigation is an experiment), or H_a or H_1 (either of these shorthand versions of the alternative hypotheses are acceptable). Briefly, the hypothesis can be expressed in the following ways:

- the H_0 states that there is no relationship between the two variables being studied (or one variable does not affect the other);

- the H_1 states that there is a relationship between the two variables being studied (or one variable has an effect on the other).

3

In order to write the H_1 and H_0 for an investigation, you need to identify the key variables in the study. In the activity above, you were asked to state the aim of two studies briefly described. For the first study, the variables under investigation are:

- The location of learning and recall. In one condition of the study the participants would learn and recall the words in the same room (called Room A). In the other condition, learning would take place in Room A but recall would be in a different room (called Room B). Therefore the variable is whether or not the location of learning and recall is the same or different. This is what psychologists mean by the term 'operationalisation of a variable' – how the variable is actually and specifically realised in an experiment.

- The number of words recalled accurately.

This means that the hypotheses for the study could be expressed in the following way:

H_0: There will be no difference in the number of words recalled when the learning and recall locations are the same and when the learning and recall locations are different.

H_1: There will be a difference in the number of words recalled when the learning and recall locations are the same and when the learning and recall locations are different.

Note that the term *significant difference* has not been used in both the H_0 and H_1. This reflects the fact that some kind of inferential statistic will not be used to determine whether any difference found is statistically significant. It is beyond the scope and need of this chapter to go further into inferential statistics.

Practical Activity

Write the H_0 and H_1 for the second example given in the second activity on page 53. Remember, you will need to identify the key variables in the study before you can write the hypotheses.

Populations, samples and sampling techniques

As already stated, research in psychology is concerned with establishing theories about human behaviour so that we can understand and predict the behaviour of people. Obviously, we cannot expect every person in the world to take part in an investigation, so we have to consider carefully how **sampling** is carried out to find people to act as participants in psychological research.

Target population

The target population is the large group of people whose behaviour we are interested in measuring. A target population could be all sixteen- to nineteen-year-old students, or all four-year-old children, or all dentists and so on. Once the target population has been identified, then a method for gathering a group of people who are *representative* of that target population has to be devised. If the small group gathered to take part in the investigation is representative of the specific population, then when the results of the investigation are analysed, it is possible to *generalise* from the small group and say that these results apply to the target population.

Samples

The sample is the small group of people gathered together to take part in the investigation. It is important that these people are referred to as *participants* and not *subjects*, since the term 'subject' implies that the people have been 'subjected to' an unwelcome experience or are passive subjects of the demands of the researcher.

Sampling bias can be said to have occurred if the sample gathered contains an over-representation of a section of the target population. This might occur if, for example, from a target population of teachers, a sample of twenty teachers consisted of sixteen males and four females. Females would appear to be under-represented in the sample.

Sampling methods

There are six main ways of collecting people to take part in research.

● **Quota sampling** occurs when the sample selected contains specified groups in numbers which are proportional to their size in the target population.

● **Systematic sampling** means that every nth member of the target population is selected, for example, every fifth person on a register.

● **Random sampling** means that every member of the identified target population has an equal chance of being selected for the sample. Random sampling requires a way of naming or numbering all the population members and then using some kind of raffle method, such as names in a hat or a computer program or random number tables, to identify those who should make up the sample.

Evaluative Comment

In practice, random sampling is extremely difficult to achieve unless the target population is a very restricted group and its members are easily identified. Obviously this is time-consuming, and even when the sample is selected, there may still be difficulties for the researcher. People who are selected may refuse to take part or a particular member of the target population may not be suitable as a participant in research. Finally, the composition of the randomly selected sample may not actually be representative of the original target population. So, a random sample of twenty participants may by chance be nineteen males and one female, even though the target population has a 50:50 male–female composition. However, this method means the researcher has no control over who will be selected for the sample, so the method is unbiased.

● **Stratified sampling** is a combination of quota sampling and random sampling. It means that the researcher identifies the different strata, or types, of people who make up the population and works out the proportions needed for the sample to be representative. So, if the population consisted of ten per cent teachers and five per cent hairdressers, then ten per cent of the sample should be teachers and five per cent hairdressers and so on. The actual sample should be selected randomly from each stratum – the teachers and hairdressers and other groups in the target population.

● **Opportunity sampling** means that the sample selected consists of people who are willing, available, and suitable to take part, and are members of the target population. They are not a random sample, because the researcher chooses them, but they may still be representative because the researcher can attempt to balance who is chosen. This is an efficient way of gathering people to be in the sample, but may not yield a very representative sample.

● **Cluster sampling**. If the target population is spread out across the country (which is highly likely), then random sampling would be expensive and time-consuming. Cluster sampling means selecting certain areas at random, for example, Manchester and London, and then randomly selecting a sample from these areas. As the prospective participants are located in clusters round a geographical area, it will be easier to collect the data.

3

Sampling technique	Description of behaviour	Example
Quota sampling	A representative sample of the target population is obtained by specifying quotas of people that need to be included in the study	Suppose dentists are made up of 70% male and 30% female. The quota sample should reflect this
Systematic sampling	Sample obtained by selecting every nth person from the target population	List all students at a college and select every 10th one for the study
Random sampling	Every member of the target population is identified and a random sample taken by, for example, taking names from a hat	All names are put into a hat and a sample of 50 taken by selecting from the hat
Stratified sampling	The sample is divided into strata or separate subgroups, then a random sample is taken from each of the strata or subgroups	Population made up of 50% blue-eyed people, 30% green-eyed people and 20% brown-eyed people. Sample randomly from each strata
Opportunity sampling	Take a sample from the population depending on availability and who happens to come along	Select a sample of students from those coming out of the library
Cluster sampling	When the population is widely spread geographically, select clusters and then take random sample from each cluster	To sample Irish people living in England select clusters in three large cities and take random sample from each cluster

Figure 3.1: Different sampling techniques used in psychological research

Practical Activity

Imagine you want to study the memory ability of students studying AS psychology. Explain how you would gather a sample of this target population using the following sampling methods (see Figure 3.1):

* *random sampling*
* *stratified sampling*
* *opportunity sampling.*

Which of the above sampling methods would you be most likely to implement in your own research? Discuss this with a small group of classmates.

Methods of investigation 1

Experiments

In this section we will examine the most often-used method of investigation in psychology, the *experiment*. As shown in Figure 3.2, there are two main types of experiment, the laboratory and field experiment, and it is important to be able to distinguish between these and identify which one is most appropriate for the aim of the research. Before looking at each of these, we will consider the general characteristics of the experiment in psychology.

The experiment

As already stated, a variable is anything that can vary, i.e. change or be changed, such as memory ability or time taken to sort cards. The hypothesis is a testable statement in which we are concerned with the possible relationship between two variables. In an experiment, all of these

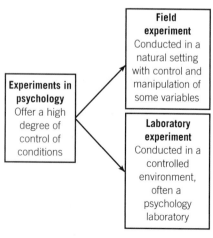

Experiments in psychology
Offer a high degree of control of conditions

Field experiment
Conducted in a natural setting with control and manipulation of some variables

Laboratory experiment
Conducted in a controlled environment, often a psychology laboratory

Figure 3.2: Types of experiment in psychology

concepts come together. The variables are given special names which only apply to an investigation which is an experiment. One is called the **independent variable** (IV) and the other is the **dependent variable** (DV). In an experiment, the researcher is specifically looking for the possible effect on the dependent variable which might be caused by changing the independent variable. Put another way, the psychologist is looking to see if the independent variable causes the effects measured by the dependent variable. This means that the definition of an experiment is:

'An investigation in which the independent variable is manipulated (or altered) in order to cause a change in the dependent variable.'

This means that the independent variable is that which is manipulated by the researcher. The dependent variable is the measure taken or the behaviour recorded.

Of course, the researcher wants to be sure that it is the manipulation of the independent variable which has caused the change in the dependent variable. Hence, all other variables which could cause the DV to change are controlled. These other variables are called *extraneous* or *confounding variables*. Figure 3.3 shows the different types of variables.

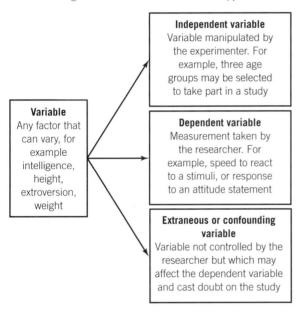

Figure 3.3: Types of variable in psychology experiments

Laboratory experiment

This type of experiment is conducted in a well-controlled environment – not necessarily a laboratory – and therefore accurate measurements are possible. Often students use this method by conducting their experiment in one particular place, like a classroom, so that the noise levels, lighting, and other factors are as similar as possible for all participants in the study.

Evaluative Comment

A major problem with the laboratory experiment is that once people are given precise instructions about what they have to do and very strict limits on their time to do it, the behaviour they produce is often very different from the behaviour they would normally exhibit. Experiments conducted in laboratory settings have a major disadvantage in that the results collected often lack ecological validity. This means that the results may have been produced in such an artificial environment that they do not reflect human behaviour in everyday life. For example, a memory experiment which involves people learning a list of words in 90 seconds is not the way people normally use their memories in everyday life.

3

Field experiment

This is an experiment carried out in a more natural environment. The participants usually have some aspect of their environment manipulated by the researcher, and changes in behaviour can be recorded. An example would be studying obedience in the way Bickman (1974) did when people walking in the street were asked to pick up litter they had not dropped by researchers dressed casually or in 'uniforms'. The participants were unaware that they were in an experiment, and their environment was real; they were just walking along the street. However, their environment was changed because the researcher spoke to them. Therefore, the behaviour produced was their natural, spontaneous response to the instruction given by the researcher.

Natural experiment

When a natural or planned event is about to take place in some aspect of everyday life (for example, a school may be about to introduce a new teaching method into its classrooms), psychologists can exploit these events to conduct research. The key thing about natural experiments is that the researcher does not have control over the independent variable(s). However, the psychologist may be able to determine what measures of the dependent variable to make.

Evaluative Comment

Ecological validity is higher in field experiments than in laboratory experiments. If people are unaware that they are in a study, then their responses tend to be truer to the situation. When a study has ecological validity, it means the data are true or valid for that natural setting, or ecology. However, there may be ethical problems because participants have not been informed in advance that they are taking part in a psychology experiment.

One way to understand all these terms is to consider the following practical example. Imagine you want to find out if organised word lists are easier to recall than randomised word lists. An organised word list would have the words grouped into categories such as:

● *Horse, cat, camel, frog, tiger* ('creatures' word list)

● *Pencil, book, desk, teacher, uniform* ('education' word list)

● *Hospital, nurse, bed, pill, theatre* ('ill-health' word list)

The randomised version of the word list could have the same words on it but they could be jumbled as follows: *Hospital, desk, theatre, cat, pencil, book, camel, hospital* and so on.

The first thing to do is to identify the independent variable (IV) and the dependent variable (DV) for the experiment.

Ask yourself: What is being investigated in this experiment? Answer: The experiment is looking at the effect of [*the independent variable*] on [*the dependent variable*]. The key to identifying the independent and dependent variables is to fill in the blank spaces with the two experimental variables and complete the statement. One way of doing this would be:

> The experiment is looking at the effect of whether a word list is organised or not organised (IV) on the number of words recalled correctly (DV).

If 'whether the word list is organised or not' is the independent variable, then how will you manipulate or change this variable? It is likely that you would set up two trials, or *conditions*, so that a comparison between the performances of people or *participants* in each condition can be made. One solution would be to have a condition in which participants in the experiment learn an organised list of words, and a second condition in which a randomised or jumbled list can be learned. Designing the experiment so that people take part in these two conditions is 'manipulating the IV'. Whenever you are asked to identify the independent variable in an experiment, you must make sure that your description includes both or more conditions in the experiment. In this case, there will be two types of word list: organised and not organised. The independent variable is not 'the organised list', but the format of the two lists. Similarly, the dependent variable should be a description of how the behaviour of the participants is measured in the experiment. In the above example, the measurement is the number of words correctly recalled from the list.

Extraneous or confounding variables

An extraneous variable is one which is not the independent variable, but which has an effect on the dependent variable if it is not controlled. The results of a study will be confounded if they were caused by something other than the independent variable. When designing an experiment, you have to find ways of controlling these extraneous variables so that they do not affect the dependent variable. Any effect on the dependent variable will introduce experimental error.

In the above experiment, having identified the independent variable and the dependent variable, it is now necessary to identify possible extraneous or confounding variables which might be present in the study. To do this, you might ask yourself, 'What else might affect the recall of the words in addition to the way the word lists have been constructed (organised or randomised)?' A possible answer is, 'The amount of time participants in each condition are given to learn the list'. A solution to this would be to allocate a set period of time for learning and ensure that all participants are given this set amount.

There are three main types of confounding variables: *participant variables*, *situational variables* and *experimenter bias*.

* **Participant variables** are to do with how well sampling guidelines have been followed. Suppose, for example, that in an experiment to investigate the speed with which people respond to a green light, all participants were male and over 60 years of age. The results could not be generalised beyond this limited group of people. Experimental error may also arise, for example, if participants are required to do three similar tasks, and learning from one task may influence how they perform on the other two tasks. A special type of experimental design is used to overcome this problem (see page 60).

* **Situational variables**, if not controlled, may also affect behaviour of participants in an experiment. For example, if one group of participants is given an intelligence test in a very cold room and another group is given the same test but in a very hot room, it will not be possible to compare results. The confounding variable of room temperature may cause one group to do well and the other group to do poorly for no other reason than external conditions. To avoid this, the researcher should ensure that participants in each group undertake the task in the same situational conditions.

* **Experimenter bias** may be a confounding variable where the experimenter treats, perhaps inadvertently, participants in one group differently from those in another group. For example, non-verbal cues, such as head nods, may reinforce or encourage certain types of behaviour, and shaking of the head discourage other types of behaviour. If the experimenter nods with one group and shakes his head with another group, even inadvertently, the measures of the dependent variable will show error, not due to the independent variable but due to experimenter bias.

Evaluative Comment

The results of the investigation will be confounded if they were produced by a variable which was not the independent variable, but was extraneous. At the end of an experiment, it is essential that the researcher is confident that it was the manipulation of the IV which caused the DV to change, and not anything else. Therefore, control of extraneous variables is a key feature of a good design.

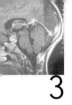

Here is a summary of the variables in the memory experiment:

Independent variable	Dependent variable	Possible confounding variables
Organised and not-organised word lists	Number of words recalled	Time for learning Time for recall Background noise Difficulty of words

Evaluative Comment

The main strengths of the use of the experiment in psychological research are as follows:

● *High degree of control over the independent and dependent variables.*

● *Cause–effect relationships between the independent and dependent variables can be established.*

● *Specific variables can be isolated to manipulate or measure in ways not possible in everyday life.*

● *The null or alternative hypothesis related to the aim of the research can be tested resulting in acceptance or rejection.*

● *Precise and careful measurement of the dependent variable can be made.*

● *Objective and reliable observation and recording of behaviour can be achieved.*

The main weaknesses of the use of the experiment in psychological research are as follows:

● *Research conducted in a psychology laboratory may lack ecological validity, resulting in the research findings not being generalisable to everyday life.*

● *Uncontrolled influences on the dependent variable caused by confounding variables, experimenter bias or participants behaving in ways they think the experimenter wants them to behave may render the findings invalid or meaningless.*

● *Some experiments may suffer ethical problems (see later in this chapter).*

● *The artificial nature of the laboratory may cause people to behave in unusual ways, or ways in which they do not normally behave.*

Experimental designs

This term refers to how participants are allocated to or distributed between the different conditions in an experiment. Once a sample of people has been selected, the researcher needs to make a decision about how their behaviour or performance will be measured or recorded. There are three main experimental designs used in psychological research: repeated measures, matched pairs and independent groups, as shown in Figure 3.4.

Repeated measures

This means that the same people are used in both or all of the conditions of the experiment. In the organisation of word lists and memory experiment described on page 58, there would be one group of people in the study. Each participant would learn the organised list as well as the randomised list of words.

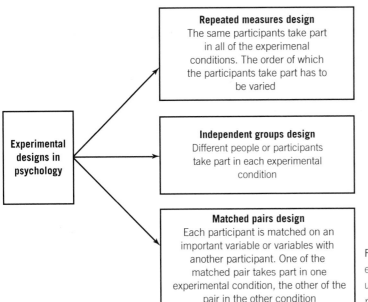

Figure 3.4: Three types of experimental design commonly used in psychological research

---

Evaluative Comment

There are advantages and disadvantages of the repeated measures design.

Advantages

- *As the people are the same in both conditions, we can be sure that there are no differences in performance due to differences in the people, so participant variables are eliminated.*

- *Because each participant performs twice, once in each condition, this experimental design provides two pieces of data for each participant, i.e. ten participants provide twenty 'scores'.*

Disadvantages

- *There may be order effects. Performance in the second condition might be better because the participants now know what to do, i.e. they have a practice effect. Or they may do worse in the second condition because they are tired – they have a fatigue effect. It is not possible to eliminate order effects because in repeated measures, each participant must do both conditions and normally one will be first and the other second. However,* counterbalancing, *in which half the participants do Task A then Task B and the other half do Task B then Task A, will mean that order effects are shared by both conditions.*

- *In this design, you will need extra stimulus material, a set for each condition, because once people have completed the first task, they cannot be given exactly the same material in the second condition.*

Independent groups

This involves using different people in each of the conditions in the experiment. The sample of participants is divided to provide two separate groups. Sometimes the IV under test requires that there are quite different people in each condition. For example, if the experiment is comparing males and females, or young and older people, then each group must have the correct type of person for the comparison to be made. If the experiment is like the 'organisation in memory' one

3

described earlier, then the sample will be divided into the two groups needed. There is a bias which might occur in this process; for example, all the people with good memories could by chance end up in one group. The difference between the groups could be caused by this fact, and so a procedure called *random allocation* should be used. This means each person has an equal chance of being in either condition; in practical terms, it can be achieved like this:

- for a sample of twenty people, put ten As and ten Bs in a bag;
- each person picks out a letter;
- the letter chosen determines which condition the person experiences.

Evaluative Comment

Advantages

- *There are no order effects, such as practice or fatigue, as people participate in one condition only.*
- *The same/very similar task can be used in both conditions, as in the organisation in memory experiment where the same words written in an organised and randomised version could be used in the two conditions. This is because people only take part in one condition of the experiment.*

Disadvantages

- *There may be participant variables present which could confound the results because the people in one condition are not the same as those in the other condition.*
- *You need twenty participants to collect twenty pieces of data, so it can be more time-consuming.*

Matched pairs

In this design, the experimenter uses two different groups of participants, one for each condition. A matching process is used to ensure that the two groups are as similar as possible in any variable that might be relevant to the study, such as age, sex, background, intelligence, etc. In effect, each participant in Condition A has a matched partner in Condition B. One member of the pair experiences the task under Condition A, the other under Condition B. Once people have been matched up, they should be randomly allocated to the different experimental conditions to eliminate any possible bias on the part of the researcher. When the results are collected, they are treated as if they have been provided by *one person*.

A great deal of research in psychology relies on using twins, who may be considered to be naturally occurring matched pairs.

Evaluative Comment

Advantages

- *This eliminates most participant variables because the researcher has tried to pair up the participants so that each condition has people with very similar qualities or abilities.*
- *There are no order effects because each participant only produces a performance or score in one condition.*
- *The same or a very similar task can be used, as each person only experiences it once.*

Disadvantages

- *Some participant variables still exist – the pairs of people are still different people.*

- *Matching is very difficult. (Should we really assume that even twins are the 'same' person?)*

- *The matching process can be expensive and time-consuming.*

Pilot studies

A **pilot study** is an initial run-through of the procedures to be used in an investigation; it involves selecting a few people to be participants and trying out the study on them. It is possible to save time and, in some cases, money, by identifying any flaws in the procedures designed by the researcher. A pilot study can help the researcher spot any ambiguities or confusion in the information given to participants or problems with the task devised. Sometimes the task is too hard, and the researcher may get a *floor effect*, because none of the participants can score at all or can complete the task – all performances are low. The opposite effect is a *ceiling effect*, when the task is so easy that all achieve virtually full marks or top performances and are 'hitting the ceiling'. Therefore, piloting means checking the design of a study before conducting it in full so that if there are differences between conditions, they will show up in the results.

Questionnaires or surveys are often subject to a pilot study. This enables the researcher to establish how easily questions are understood, how long the questionnaire takes to complete, etc. Modifications can then be made to produce a final questionnaire for the main study. A little time invested early on in the design of a study or questionnaire pays off in terms of the main study being well thought through.

Questionnaires

A survey is a technique for collecting information from a large number of people by asking them questions. There are two major methods used in surveys: questionnaires and interviews, as shown in Figure 3.5 on page 64. Questionnaires are often used for survey work in order to obtain current views of people on a particular issue. For example, a researcher might be interested in finding out about attitudes to child rearing and the issues of day care and working mothers. Also, questionnaires can help a researcher to collect information (especially with a yes/no answer) about usual behaviour, for example, the ways parents and carers discipline children, sexual habits, typical leisure activities, moral principles, voting behaviour and so on.

The following items could appear on questionnaires designed to investigate people's thoughts and feelings about happiness.

Example 1: Can you tell me about how happy you feel right now?

Example 2: Do you feel happy right now? YES or NO

Example 3: On a scale of 1–100, where 50 represents your normal level of happiness and 100 is the most happy you could feel, estimate how happy you feel right now.

Example 1 is an *open question*. The value here is in the richness of the information given when the individual answers the question. People are allowed to present all they wish to say – there is no restriction on their responses. There is also less chance of ambiguity because the respondent can say what she or he thinks, rather than being forced to choose from a set of fixed possible answers. There may be less frustration experienced by the participant when answering open questions, and the whole approach is more realistic. We rarely want to just agree or disagree to a statement or question without comment. The data produced from open questions are **qualitative**, which means they will be expressed in description rather than a numerical-type score.

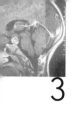

3 Evaluative Comment

A problem with the use of open-ended questions is that it is difficult to combine the individual responses from all the participants, as each person will have produced unique answers. Collating all the responses and summarising the data concisely might mean the researcher has first to combine responses into broad categories, with the result that differences between people's responses might be lost.

Example 2 is a *closed question*. These provide answers that are 'yes' or 'no' – just two categories of response, permitting the researcher to divide people into just two major groups. On some questionnaires, there may be a third choice where people can choose 'don't know'. The data from closed questionnaires are very easy to collate and summarise – for example, the categories of responses can be turned into percentages. This means that the data from closed questionnaires are often **quantitative** or in numerical form. Only very broad responses are collected, and there is little depth or richness to the data, as people cannot explain their answers.

Example 3 above has potential for allowing the researcher to make finer comparisons between people. Once the responses are spread using a rating scale, there is some indication of the depth of feeling of respondents. However, we cannot be sure that two people both choosing to say '60' on the scale are actually expressing the same level of happiness as each other.

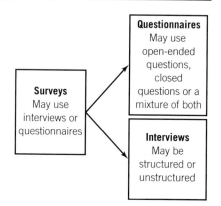

Figure 3.5: Types of surveys, questionnaires and interviews used in psychological research

---

Practical Activity

Imagine you have decided to write a questionnaire to find out about the leisure activities of sixteen- to nineteen-year-old students. Write three open questions and three closed questions with an appropriate rating scale that might be suitable for your questionnaire.

Questionnaire items must be phrased very clearly in order to avoid ambiguity in answering. Ideally, everyone should interpret each item in the questionnaire in the same way. Consider the following items that may be found on a questionnaire investigating television viewing habits.

1 I enjoy watching television. YES/NO

2 I would describe myself as a person who watches television:

    (a) every day.　**(b)** evenings only.　**(c)** weekends only.

3 Which is the happiest soap on TV? Choose from: Neighbours or EastEnders.

What should normally be avoided is any overlap, such as in Question 2 above, where both (a) and (b) could be ticked.

Similarly, the researcher must be careful when drawing conclusions based on closed questions. It could be misleading to draw the conclusion from answers to Question 3 that *Neighbours* is the happiest soap on TV. Fixing the possible choice in the question means that other soaps, which people might have thought were happier than *Neighbours*, were not offered. The conclusion which should be drawn is, 'in a sample of X people asked which of two soaps was the happier, the respondents thought *Neighbours* was a happier soap than *EastEnders*'.

Evaluative Comment

Strengths of the questionnaire method

● *It enables the collection of large amounts of standardised data very quickly and conveniently, especially when the items are closed questions.*

● *Questionnaires can be highly replicable and easy to score (unless open questions are used).*

● *The data can be rich in detail if the items are open questions.*

Weaknesses of the questionnaire method

● *Questionnaires are based on self-report data and may be biased by motivation levels of the respondents.*

● *The data can be biased by socially desirable responses, acquiescence (agreeing with items) and response set (replying in the same way by failing to read the questions properly and ticking all 'yes' answers).*

Interviews

Face-to-face interviews can range from being *unstructured* to completely *structured*. The data from an unstructured interview will be qualitative and rich in personal detail. The data from structured interviews is usually quantitative. The data can be combined because if all respondents were given the same closed questions, their responses can be collated and summarised, using for example, percentages. In essence, an interview is two people talking, but as a research method it is very different from an ordinary conversation.

Structured interview

Here there is a fixed set of questions and often a fixed set of possible responses for the interviewee (the person being asked the questions) to choose from. The advantage is that the method is standardised (the same procedure is used with all interviewees), and therefore the data can be summarised easily and presented as percentages found for particular responses. The disadvantage is that any interesting responses which occur spontaneously cannot be pursued, as the interviewer is restricted to asking all respondents exactly the same questions in the same order. This is the type of interview mostly used in surveys.

Unstructured (informal) interview

Here the interviewee is prompted to talk about a designated topic. The interviewer listens carefully and sympathetically, and offers intelligent comments, but gives no advice or argument. The interviewer may prompt further expansion on a point and offer a direction for the interviewee to move towards and must adjust to the respondent's answers as they occur. The main advantage is the data gathered can be rich in detail, and the interviewer might find an explanation for the behaviour of the particular person being interviewed. It might also allow a professional to reach a diagnosis for a particular client's disorder (the interview is the method of the clinical psychologist who uses it as part of the evidence needed when compiling a case study (see page 72)). Again, there is the problem of collation of the data, since it is difficult to collate the data from different and non-standardised interviews.

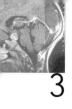

3 Evaluative Comment

Strengths of the interview method

* Generally, interviews produce large amounts of detailed data, especially about internal mental states/beliefs.

* Structured interviews are easy to quantify and analyse. They are reliable, replicable and generalisable.

* Unstructured interviews yield highly detailed and valid data. They are extremely flexible, natural and unconstrained.

Weaknesses of the interview method

* Generally interviews rely on self-report data which may be untrue. Cause and effect cannot be inferred.

* Structured interviews are less valid and distort or ignore data due to restricted answers or insensitivity.

* Unstructured interviews are very unstandardised, therefore not very replicable, reliable or generalisable. They are difficult to quantify and analyse.

Correlation

Correlation is not a method of study or research technique, but a statistical technique that is widely used to assess the extent to which two variables are related to each other. For example, are people who are musical also likely to be good at maths? Are those who are intelligent also creative? Psychologists often want to find the relationship between two variables. A researcher might want to find out whether there is a relationship between the amount of television that people watch and their intelligence. To do this, the researcher could ask people to record the amount of television they watched over a period of a week and also give them an test of intelligence.

Practical Activity

Suppose the results shown below were obtained from measuring the intelligence and the hours spent watching television for eight people. With the intelligence score, the higher the number, the higher the level of intelligence.

Participant	Hours spent watching TV	Intelligence score
1	30	100
2	15	125
3	25	110
4	28	105
5	30	105
6	14	140
7	20	115
8	10	150

Can you see any pattern in the raw data presented in the data shown above? If so, what pattern do you think there is?

The relationship between two variables can be displayed in a **scattergram**. This is a type of graph on which pairs of measurement, for example, number of hours of television watched and intelligence score, are plotted. When producing a scattergram, the vertical axis represents one variable (hours watching TV) and the horizontal axis represents the other variable (intelligence score). One point on the scattergram represents the score for two variables. The pattern that results indicates the relationship between the measurements.

The relationship between two variables can reflect a positive, a negative or a zero relationship. Figure 3.6 shows three scattergrams representing the three types of correlation.

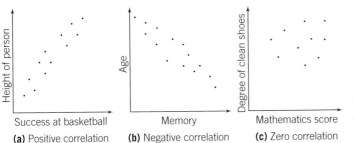

Success at basketball	Memory	Mathematics score
(a) Positive correlation	**(b)** Negative correlation	**(c)** Zero correlation

Figure 3.6: Scattergrams showing positive, negative and zero correlations

Positive correlation

This means that as the values/scores on one variable increase, the values/scores on the other variable increase. That is, high values are paired with high values and low values paired with low values. In Figure 3.6a, the taller the person, the more successful they are at basketball.

Negative correlation

This means that as the values/scores on one variable increase, so the values/scores on the other variable decrease. Thus, high values are paired with low values, and low values paired with high values. In Figure 3.6b, the older the person, the worse their memory.

Both positive and negative correlations show there is a degree of association between the two variables. If we know what the direction of the relationship is, we can measure an individual on one variable and attempt to predict their likely performance on the other variable. For example, if we know that the more television a child watches, the more aggressive their behaviour (positive correlation), then we can predict that a child who watches a great deal of television is likely to have a high score for aggression. Similarly, if the correlation between numerical ability and artistic ability is a negative one, then we can predict that someone who is good at mathematics is likely to be poor at drawing, or somebody who is good at drawing is likely to be poor at mathematics.

Zero correlation

This means that there is no linear relationship between the two variables, either positive or negative. Hence, we are unable to predict a person's likely performance on one variable even when we know their score or value on the other variable. In Figure 3.6c, some people with clean shoes have high mathematics scores, but others with high mathematics scores have dirty shoes. There is no correlation or relationship between ability at mathematics and how clean a person's shoes are – as you would expect!

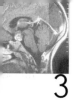

3   Evaluative Comment

Correlation is a valuable technique, since it allows a researcher to establish that two variables are related in some way. This often gives the researcher an idea about which variables might need further investigation. However, there is one major difference between correlation and experimentation. Identifying two variables that are either positively or negatively correlated with each other does not tell the researcher that one variable has caused the other. For example, being tall does not cause a person to be good at basketball (although it helps). There may be several variables that are interrelated, and it is difficult to know whether or not the two that have been correlated by a scattergram are related by cause and effect. Remember, only an experiment can establish cause-and-effect relationships. This means that an alternative hypothesis for an investigation using correlational analysis should not contain a statement that one variable will have an effect on the other. In a correlational analysis, the two variables under test are simply measured; there is often no requirement to control extraneous variables.

Practical Activity

Draw a scattergram to display the data given in the activity on page 66. To plot the pairs of data correctly, you must put one of the variables on the vertical axis and the other on the horizontal axis. You need to choose an appropriate scale for each variable. Plot each point by moving up the scale on the x-axis and across the scale on the y-axis, putting a dot or cross where the two values intersect.

Interpret the scattergram you have drawn by writing a couple of sentences to explain the relationship shown in the graph. Remember to write an appropriate heading for the scattergram.

Methods of investigation 2

Observational studies

Observation in *natural settings* means that the researcher has chosen to observe naturally occurring behaviour, and participants are studied in their own real-life environments. The observation takes place in the setting where such behaviours might normally be expected to occur. For example, playground aggression could be studied by watching children in school playgrounds, and crowd behaviour by watching people at a football match. Observations in natural settings lack control over extraneous variables, but do have high *ecological validity*.

Sylva *et al.* (1980) studied children's play in playgroups. Decisions were taken as to what categories of behaviour to observe, at what time intervals, what the important features of the setting were and how to minimise the effects of the children's awareness of being observed. For the children who were observed, the experience did not seem to affect their natural play behaviour. This is because they had become accustomed to the observers being in the playground area.

Sometimes the researcher will manipulate the natural environment by causing a particular event to occur. This might happen, for example, in a study of obedience in which a researcher approaches a member of the public and gives him or her an unusual instruction. The aim of the research would be to find out how pedestrians in the street respond to such orders. As far as the member of the public is concerned, the setting is natural, but the researcher has controlled the event so that people's behaviour can be observed and recorded.

Direct observation may also be carried out in a laboratory setting in carefully controlled conditions. This type of observation has many of the advantages, as well as some of the disadvantages, of experimentation. In sleep laboratories, for example, participants are allowed to sleep naturally, but with electrodes attached to points on their scalps to measure the electrical activity in the brain. The conditions are very carefully controlled, which means measurement of responses is easy, but the artificial environment means the study can lack ecological validity. It is likely that sleeping in a laboratory environment is not exactly the same as sleeping in your own bed. Hence, the electrical activity of the brain may be different in the laboratory compared to sleeping in your own bed at home.

Participant and non-participant observation

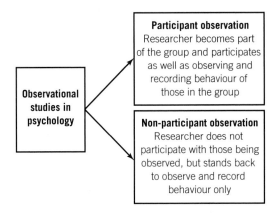

Figure 3.7: Types of observational studies used in psychological research

Figure 3.7 shows the two main types of observational studies. When the researcher actually becomes part of the group being observed, the type of observation being conducted is called **participant observation**. This has the effect of allowing detailed observation and description of behaviours, and also allows the researcher to note the precise context in which the behaviour is taking place. For example, Hargreaves (1967) studied social relationships in a secondary school and became a member of the teaching staff for a period of one year. He was able to observe the attitudes and behaviour of both pupils and teachers at the school. There is, however, the possibility that the observer might become so fully a member of the group that she or he loses objectivity. This means the observations made could be affected by the fact that the observer may have become committed to the group.

In **non-participant observation**, the observer dissociates him or herself from the group and from what is taking place when the group interacts. This means the observer remains more objective and avoids involvement with the people in the group. However, the presence of an observer may well affect the behaviour of the participants, creating what is known as an *observer effect*. Here, the behaviour of the genuine participants is changed in some way because they are aware of being observed. To avoid this, the observer could either allow the participants to become familiar with his or her presence beforehand or remain unobtrusive and watch from a place where he or she cannot be seen, such as behind a one-way mirror.

Evaluative Comment

There are ethical issues surrounding participant and non-participant observation. One issue is to do with research being conducted where the people being observed are not aware of this or have not been informed about being part of the research. The ethical guidelines of the British Psychological Society state that participants in a study must be informed that they are in a study and have the right to withdraw at any time. In observational studies where the participants are unaware that they are being observed, they cannot exercise this right to withdraw if they wish to.

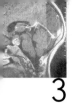

3

Data collection in observational studies

Social behaviour is complex. Consider the behaviour involved in being sociable. Each of us might be able to make a personal decision about whether a friend is sociable or not, but such subjective analysis is not very scientific. Some data collection methods used by psychologists are taken from the field of ethology, which is the study of living creatures in their natural environments. As a first step, researchers often devise a set of *behavioural categories* that reflect the behaviour they wish to quantify. For example, if the target behaviour is aggression in children, the following behavioural categories might be used: hitting, kicking, shouting, pushing and face-pulling.

For a **category** system to be useful, the observer should be able to place in the categories all or most forms of the behaviour that are likely to occur. The first step is to carry out a short preliminary observation or pilot study (see page 63). This is done to create a pilot category system that is tried out, checked and amended if necessary. Having constructed a final behaviour category system, the observers can then simply record on a tally chart or record sheet the instances of each of the behaviours occurring during the period of observation.

There are different ways of recording the behaviours which might occur during an observation. These include *continuous recording* and *time, point* and *event sampling.*

- Continuous recording is where all behaviours observed during the period are recorded.

- Time sampling is where the time is split up into intervals, for example every 30 seconds, and at each time interval (at 30 then 60 then 90 seconds), a recording of the behaviour actually taking place is made.

- Point sampling is where an individual is observed until enough detail about his or her behaviour is collected. Then the observer moves on to the next person to be watched.

- Event sampling is where observations are made of a specific event whenever it occurs, for example, if the target behaviour is fighting, then each fight will be observed, but nothing else, thus avoiding collection of irrelevant data.

Evaluative Comment

You will have noted that whichever method is used for data collection, it is quite a time-consuming and detailed form of research. Due to the technical and practical difficulties involved, it is usually not possible to observe large numbers of people at one time. Also, it is not practical to observe every aspect of an individual's actions. In both cases, some behaviours will be missed during the observation. The researcher has to decide which sampling method best suits his or her needs or purposes.

All observations should be checked for reliability or consistency in recording of the data. This means the researcher wants to be sure that every time a target behaviour occurs, there will be an accurate recording made. If the observation study involves a single person collecting the data, there is the possibility that the record made will be inaccurate. Also, since the behaviour is likely to have passed, there would be no way to go back to the event and check what did happen. If the behaviour had been video-recorded, then a check could be more easily made.

Researchers try to deal with this problem by establishing *inter-observer reliability.* Two or more observers, each using the same category system and watching the same participants at the same time, carry out the observation. The individual record sheets are then compared. The more similar the records, the more reliable the data is considered to be. If they are quite different, we must assume that either the category system is ambiguous, or at least one of the researchers is interpreting it incorrectly. Either way, the data cannot be interpreted if there is no inter-observer reliability. The observation would need to be carried out again, with an improved design, and when the records are consistent, the data can be analysed. Establishing inter-observer reliability is made easier if the behaviour is video-recorded. The recording can then be replayed many times so that different observers can independently categorise the behaviours.

Reflective Activity

Imagine that you and a friend have decided to observe the road-crossing behaviour of people at a pedestrian crossing. You choose to record (a) whether the person crossing was male or female, and (b) whether they obeyed the pedestrian signal or not.

Construct a record sheet that could be used by you and your friend to collect the data. Consider the following questions:

- *How many times will you carry out the observation?*
- *Will you observe people at different times of the day or not? Explain your answer.*
- *How will you try to establish that your records are an accurate account of what happened?*
- *Can you think of any practical difficulties you might encounter when conducting the observation?*

Strengths and weaknesses of observational studies

Observational studies can be natural or laboratory based, and participant or non-participant. The strengths and weaknesses of the study will depend on the actual combination of setting and involvement of the researcher. Some points are summarised below.

Strengths

- Many observational studies are carried out in natural environments, so the participants respond naturally and the data has high ecological validity.

- Observational studies are likely to be more holistic and less reductionist than is often the case with experimental studies. This is because observations are recorded looking at total behaviour, a whole sequence of actions, rather than with small actions, such as learning 30 words in 90 seconds, in a laboratory setting.

- Observations can provide hypotheses for more searching examination and experimentation; that is, they can tell the researcher what to concentrate on in the future.

Weaknesses

- Participants may be affected by the fact that they are aware of being watched. There may be expectancy and *demand characteristics* (features of the study which help the participants to work out what is being investigated), which affect the accuracy of the data. For example, this may result in those being observed changing their behaviour to what they think the observer wants to see or is looking for.

- It is harder to determine causes of behaviour in observational studies. For example, Hargreaves (1967) observed that boys in lower class sets had poorer attitudes towards school and lower attainment than boys in the higher stream. However, this may have been due to the streaming in the school or socio-economic conditions or any number of other variables.

- Observer bias can be a problem – when the researcher is looking for a particular behaviour, it is more likely that actions will be interpreted in ways which fit these expectations.

3

Case studies

Case studies are often conducted in clinical medicine and involve collecting and reporting descriptive information about a particular person or specific environment, such as a school. In psychology, case studies are often confined to the study of a particular individual. The information is mainly biographical and relates to events in the individual's past, as well as to significant events which are currently occurring in his or her everyday life. In order to produce a fairly detailed and comprehensive profile of the person, the psychologist may use various types of accessible data, such as medical records, employer's reports, school reports or psychological test results. The interview is also an extremely effective procedure for obtaining information about an individual, and it may be used to collect comments from the person's friends, parents, employer, workmates and others who have a good knowledge of the person, as well as to obtain facts from the person him or herself.

The case study consists of:

- a description of the person's personal history;
- a description of symptoms;
- a formal diagnosis;
- a record of treatment;
- a record of the eventual outcome of the process.

This makes it clear that the case study is a method that should only be used by a psychologist, therapist or psychiatrist, i.e. someone with a professional qualification. There is an ethical issue of *competence* (see page 80). Only someone qualified to diagnose and treat a person can conduct a formal case study relating to atypical behaviour or atypical development.

The procedure used in a case study means that the researcher provides a description of the behaviour. This comes from interviews and other sources, such as observation. The client also reports detail of events from his or her point of view. The researcher then writes up the information from both sources above as the case study, and interprets the information.

Interpreting the information means the researcher decides what to include or leave out. A good case study should always make clear which information is factual description and which is **inference** or the opinion of the researcher. Some famous psychologists, such as Sigmund Freud (see Chapter 1), have been criticised for producing case studies in which the information was sometimes distorted to fit their particular theories about behaviour.

A case study is not an exercise in creative writing. If it is to be of scientific value, it must be linked to a clear theoretical background. It is possible that case studies may enhance a theory or cause a theory to be altered if the evidence in the case study refutes, or goes against, the original theory.

Evaluative Comment

Strengths of the case study method

- *Case studies capture and describe changes which happen over time rather than the 'snapshot' of an experiment.*
- *Data gathered are qualitative rather than the quantitative information from experiments, which tends to reduce behaviour to very small actions.*
- *Case studies remind us that the study of human behaviour is the study of unique individuals, and the methods used must not ignore or deny this.*

- *A single case study which contradicts a theory is enough to cause that theory to be altered to accommodate the new evidence.*

Weaknesses of the case study method

- *The method is often non-standardised, which can prevent replication.*

- *The data are retrospective, involving the recall of events and experiences which might be prone to confabulation (replacing fact with fantasy), and therefore reliability might be reduced.*

- *There is the possibility that information and inference are blurred in the report and that the researcher's beliefs might affect the analysis of the behaviour studied.*

- *As the approach is idiographic, i.e. focused on the individual, it is unlikely that the findings can be applied to explanations of the behaviour of people in general.*

When thinking about how a case study might be conducted by a psychologist, you would need to consider the person the psychologist is interested in studying and then refer to the following points:

- Obtain the permission of the person (or people) to be studied – remember there are special issues if the person is a child. Consider *informed consent* (see page 80) and how this might be affected by age.

- Decide on the method – the psychologist will be able to choose from a variety of methods, including interview, observation of child/person, reports from parents or teachers or significant others.

- Gather the data.

- Present and interpret the findings.

Qualitative and quantitative methods

There is much debate in psychology about the strengths and weaknesses of different research methods. The arguments often centre on discussion of the 'best way' to measure behaviour. A researcher who adopts a qualitative approach in a study will collect data which focuses on the feelings and thoughts participants have about a particular experience. The data are therefore likely to be expressed in words rather than numbers. If a researcher is interested in measuring 'how much' there is of something, then the approach is quantitative. A method of research does not have to be entirely qualitative or quantitative in emphasis on every occasion, but it is clear that some methods have a tendency to produce either qualitative or quantitative data. For example, unstructured interviews, case studies, open questionnaires and many observational studies usually collect qualitative data; experiments and correlational studies usually generate quantitative data. Some strengths and weaknesses of qualitative and quantitative approaches are given in Figure 3.8 (see page 74).

It is important to be aware that no single method is 'better' than any other. The choice of methodology depends on the aim and hypotheses of the researcher and the practical constraints of conducting the research.

Representing data and descriptive statistics

This section introduces the **descriptive statistics** and graphical displays which can be used to summarise and present the results of an investigation. Research often collects a great deal of information in the form of scores or answers to questions. However, the reader of a report will not want to see the *raw data,* that is, every response of every participant. Instead, a summary of the results is needed so that the reader can quickly see the overall pattern of the results and any differences that may be present.

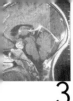

Type of method	Evaluation	
	Strengths	Weaknesses
Qualitative methods	Data are detailed and rich, providing explanation of behaviours under investigation	Lack of standardisation and control of variables means studies may be difficult to replicate
	Settings are natural and therefore data have ecological validity	Data may be difficult to summarise statistically
	Participants are not dehumanised by the process of participating	Data may be less reliable due to subjectivity or use of retrospective information
Quantitative methods	Standardised procedures and control of variables increase the opportunity to replicate studies	Behaviour may be reduced to very narrow, almost meaningless actions
	Data collected are easy to collate and analyse statistically	Laboratory-based studies lack ecological validity
	Objectivity may be increased	Participants may feel dehumanised by the procedures of the study

Figure 3.8: Strengths and weaknesses of qualitative and quantitative methods of data collection in psychological research

Descriptive statistics

When the observations and measurements of the behaviour of the people in an investigation have been collected, the researcher must make decisions about how to summarise the results. When the data are in numerical form, such as scores on a test or time taken to complete a task, then the raw data must be converted into a statistic which will provide a summary of the results. This helps the reader to understand quickly which of the hypotheses set out at the start of the investigation (the null, alternative or experimental) has been supported by the data. The summary statistics or descriptive statistics commonly used are called measures of central tendency and measures of dispersion.

Measures of central tendency

Measures of central tendency provide a single number or value to describe a set of raw scores or data values. A large amount of data may look confusing, with little overall pattern obvious. Using summary statistics, such as measures of central tendency, provides a representative score for the researcher to see what is going on with the data.

There are three commonly used descriptive statistics which are known collectively as measures of central tendency: these are the **mean**, the **median** and the **mode**. Each is easy to calculate, and the following example should help you to understand what each one tells you about the data collected in a study.

A researcher wanted to find out if the level of organisation of a word list would affect the number of words that could be recalled. An independent groups design was used with an opportunity sample of seventeen people, who were randomly allocated to either the organised or the non-organised condition. In each condition, the word lists contained the same words but the order in which they were written was changed from organised to not organised (see page 58). All procedures in the study, such as instructions to participants and time allowed to complete the task, were standardised. The raw data shown in Figure 3.9 were obtained.

Condition A	Condition B
Words recalled by participants given an organised list of words	Words recalled by participants given a non-organised list of words
15	11
16	10
14	10
12	7
17	10
16	8
14	11
16	5
15	
n = 9	n = 8

Figure 3.9: Number of words correctly recalled by participants given either an organised or non-organised list of words

The mean

The mean is the most widely used measure of central tendency, and is often referred to as the *average*. Technically, the mean is the arithmetic average of all the scores in a data set. The mean has the advantage of taking into account all the scores in a data set because each raw score contributes to the *mean value*.

The mean is easy to calculate. Simply add the values in a set of data together and divide that total by the number of values in the set. In this case, for the first set of values (from Condition A), the mean is found by:

15 + 16 + 14 + 12 + 17 + 16 + 14 + 16 + 15 = 135 (total in the set)

$\frac{135}{9}$ (total in set divided by number of values in set)

= 15 (the mean for the set)

Formula

$$\bar{x} = \frac{\Sigma x}{N}$$

where:
$\bar{x}$ stands for 'the mean' x stands for 'individual values'
Σ stands for 'the sum of' N stands for 'the number of values in the set'

Evaluative Comment

The advantage of using the mean to summarise all the values in a set of values is that it is a very sensitive statistic. Its calculation uses each individual value in the set. However, if one of the values is extremely high or low (such a value is usually referred to as anomalous*), then the overall mean can be very distorted. An example of this can be seen in the following set of values:*

4, 8, 5, 9, 7, 7, 32

These values produce a mean of 12, but without the anomalous sixth value of 32 the mean would have been 8, a number which summarises the first five values better.

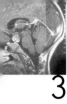

The median

This statistic is the central value in the set of values. It is found by putting all the values in rank order, from lowest to highest, and identifying the value in the middle of the ordered list. If the set has an odd number of values, the middle one is easy to find. When the set has an even number of values, two values will be in the middle. The procedure is then to add these two values together and divide the total by two. Using the data for Condition A in Figure 3.9:

> 15, 16, 14, 11, 17, 16, 13, 16, 14

when rank-ordered becomes

> 11, 13, 14, 14, **15**, 16, 16, 16, 17

and the middle value is the fifth value, 15.

The median is not distorted by any very high or low values, but is usually less precise than the mean.

The mode

This refers to the value which occurs most often in the set. It is very easy to find if the values have been arranged so that the median can be identified, as all the similar values line up next to each other. Look again at the data for Condition A in Figure 3.9:

> 11, 13, 14, 14, 15, **16, 16, 16**, 17

The mode is 16, as this is the value which occurs most often.

The mode is rarely useful when the set of data contains a small number of values, and often there is no mode value in a set. On the other hand, sometimes there are so many modes that the data cannot be described using this statistic.

Practical Activity

Calculate the measures of central tendency for the scores obtained by the participants in Condition B in Figure 3.9.

Measures of dispersion

The measures of central tendency are statistics which summarise a set of values, but they are not necessarily the only way of describing the data. Consider the following set of values:

> 58, 59, 60, 60, 61, 62

The mean, median and mode are all 60. If you calculate the three measures of central tendency for this next set of values, you will see that they are also all 60:

> 27, 36, 60, 60, 84, 93

The fact that the mean, median and mode are the same for each set of data would seem to indicate that there is no difference between the two sets of data. Clearly, looking at the raw data, it is apparent that they are different in one particular aspect: the first set of data consists of values which are very similar to each other, and the second set has values which are spread out. In order to summarise these sets of data, we need a statistic which displays this difference in spread or dispersion.

There are two commonly used **measures of dispersion**; these are the **range** and the **standard deviation**.

The range

The range is the difference between the lowest and highest value in a set. It is very simple to calculate: you simply subtract the lowest value from the highest value. However, it can be distorted by an extremely high or low value which is very different from the rest of the values in the set. For the Condition A data in Figure 3.9, the range would be:

17 – 11 = 6

For Condition B in Figure 3.9, it would be:

12 – 6 = 6

And for the second list of data on page 76, it would be:

93 – 27 = 66

The standard deviation

This statistic is a measure of dispersion which takes into account the difference between each value in the set and the mean value for the set. It is therefore a very sensitive measure of dispersion, although it is time-consuming to calculate without the aid of a scientific calculator. There are two versions of the formula for calculating standard deviation; in psychology the following formula is most commonly used:

$$s = \sqrt{\frac{\Sigma d^2}{N-1}}$$

where:
s is the standard deviation   N is the sample size
Σ is sum of d^2 is each difference between the mean and each new score, then squared

This formula gives the standard deviation for a group of values from a sample that is being used to estimate the dispersion of a larger population. Research in psychology normally investigates samples of people rather than studying every member of the population.

Using the raw data in Condition A in Figure 3.9, the standard deviation is 1.87 (see page 83 for calculation).

The smaller the standard deviation, the closer together the values in the set are; a larger standard deviation indicates that the values are more spread out from the mean.

Practical Activity

Calculate the standard deviation for the data given for Condition B in Figure 3.9.

Representing data

Once the data for a study have been collected, decisions have to be made about how the data will be represented or displayed visually. It is important to distinguish between tabular and graphical displays. A tabular display refers to a table of results, and it is essential that the table presents a summary of the behaviour of the people who took part in the study. All tables must be fully labelled with a clear title and column headings. For the organisation in memory study, all the statistics calculated for Condition A and Condition B in Figure 3.9 would be presented as shown in Figure 3.10.

A second way of presenting a summary of the data is using a *graphical display*. There are four types of graphical display you need to be able to recognise. These are *bar charts, histograms, line graphs* and *scattergrams*.

	Condition A organised word list	Condition B non-organised word list
Mean (x̄)	14.67	9.13
Median	15	9.5
Mode	16	10
Range	11 – 17 = 6	6 – 12 = 6
Standard deviation	1.87	2.03

Figure 3.10: Measures of central tendency and measures of dispersion for data shown in Figure 3.9

Bar charts

A bar chart displays frequencies of discrete variables. *Frequency* refers to how often something has occurred and *discrete* means that the variables are separate categories. The discrete variables are usually displayed on the x-axis and the frequencies on the y-axis. For the organisation in memory study, a bar chart displaying the mean values for Conditions A and B could be drawn, as shown in Figure 3.11.

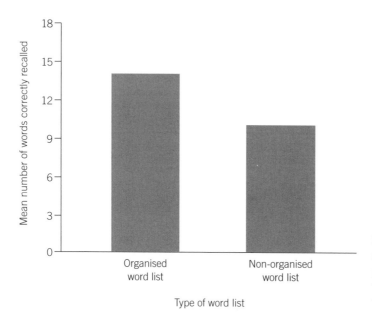

Figure 3.11: Bar chart showing mean number of words recalled from an organised list and a non-organised list of words

Histograms

A histogram displays frequencies of continuous data. *Continuous data* means that the variable being investigated has been divided into intervals that are all the same numerical size. The continuous variable, or class intervals, are usually displayed on the x-axis and the frequency of occurrence on the y-axis. If a particular class interval has no frequency, then the interval is left on the x-axis as an empty space. The midpoint of each column drawn on a histogram can be plotted and the points joined to produce a *frequency polygon,* as shown in Figure 3.12.

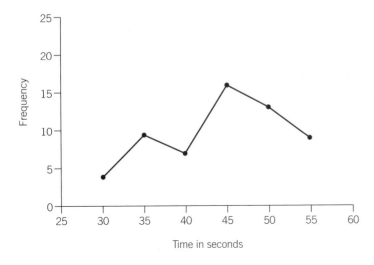

Figure 3.12: Frequency polygon showing frequency of time intervals people take to eat a standard bar of chocolate

Line graphs

A line graph is often used to show the relationship between independent and dependent variables. The IV is usually displayed on the x-axis, and the DV on the y-axis. For instance, in memory research, it has been shown that the position of a word on a word list affects the likelihood of that word being recalled. The resulting graph would look something like that shown in Figure 3.13.

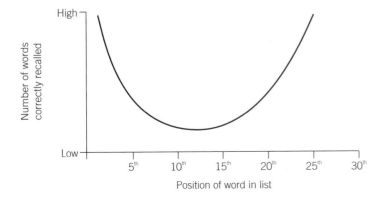

Figure 3.13: Line graph showing that words appearing first and last on a word list are recalled more often than those words appearing in the middle of the list

Joining the frequencies together is appropriate because there is a connection between the scale points on the x-axis; the order of the words on the list is a continuous variable.

Scattergrams

A scattergram is a graphical display of the data obtained using a correlation technique. The data is in pairs: the y-axis displays the scale for one of the paired values, and the x-axis displays the scale for the other. In Figure 3.14, you can see the scattergram produced from data for a study in which the relationship between the self-esteem of mothers and daughters was measured.

As you can see, the scattergram shows a positive correlation, in which mothers who have high self-esteem scores are paired with daughters who also have high self-esteem scores and vice versa. Remember, this relationship does not mean that having a mother with high self-esteem will cause the daughter also to have high self-esteem. It could just mean that the daughter causes the mother to have high self-esteem, or that another factor, such as being rich, cause both to have high self-esteem. An experiment would have to be conducted to try to establish if that were true or not.

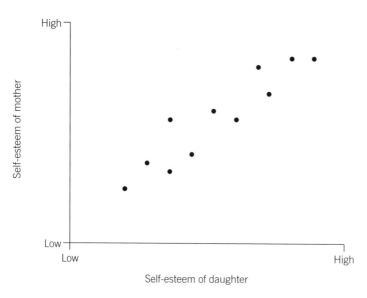

Figure 3.14: Scattergram showing a positive correlation between the level of self-esteem of mother and daughter. High self-esteem in the mother is generally related to high self-esteem in the daughter and vice versa

Ethics

The British Psychological Society (1998) has issued a code of ethics in psychology which provides guidelines for the conduct of research. This is called *Ethical Principles for Conducting Research with Human Participation*. You must be able to understand ethical issues, as well as be able to identify them in psychological research and implement them appropriately in your own investigations. The main ethical principles are given below.

Consent

All people who participate in a psychological investigation must be informed of the nature of the study and agree to participate. The BPS Ethical Principles state that 'participants should be informed of the objectives of the investigation and all other aspects of the research which might reasonably affect their willingness to participate'. A distinction is drawn between *consent* and *informed consent*. The extract given above relates to informed consent, in that prospective participants are informed about the objectives and other aspects of the research. Simple consent would give the prospective participant little if any information about the research. The experimenter seeking to gain simple consent may just ask someone to take part in an experiment without offering any more information. This would be unacceptable, since it would be counter to the BPS guidelines. There is an issue concerning how 'informed' consent can be. Some argue (Gale, 1995) that a person can only truly be informed once he or she has taken part in the experiment. Of course, this way of looking at informed consent is not really possible, since a dummy run through the experiment for the participant would render the findings from the 'real' experiment of little use. In addition, if the participants are under sixteen years of age then parents or people *in loco parentis* (which means acting for the parents) must also consent to the participation for legal reasons. This is because the law regards people under sixteen years as juvenile and not able to make such decisions for themselves.

Deception

Deception is where participants in a study are misled or wrongly informed about the aims of the research. For example, in the famous study on **obedience to authority** by Milgram (1963) (see Chapter 6), participants were led to believe that they were giving real electric shocks to learners when they got a question wrong. In reality, no electric shocks were given and the 'learners' were confederates of Milgram. Some psychologists (Baumrind, 1985) have argued that the use of intentional deception is unethical, imprudent and unwarranted scientifically. The Ethical Principles state that 'intentional deception of the participants over the general nature of the investigation should be avoided whenever possible'. Note that this does say 'wherever possible', and some psychologists argue that, for certain types of research, deception cannot be avoided. In the case of the Milgram study referred to above (see Chapter 6 for a full description of this study), if participants were told in advance that they were not really giving electric shocks but asked to pretend that they were, the experiment would be largely pointless. The whole point of the study was to see whether or not people obey an order even when they think that they are harming another person. Few experiments in psychology do employ deception. The American Psychological Association (APA) set out the following four conditions which have to be met before deception may be used in an experiment:

- The research is of great importance and cannot be conducted without the use of deception.

- Participants can expect the procedures to be reasonable once they are informed after the experiment has finished.

- Participants can withdraw from the experiment at any time.

- Experimenters debrief the participants at the end of the experiment, explain the purpose of the study, and remove any stressful after-effects that the participants may feel.

Some psychologists overcome the problem of deception by asking prospective participants if they would mind be deceived temporarily in an experiment. By doing this, participants have given a type of informed consent to be deceived without knowing the true purpose of the study.

Ideally, when people consent to participate in an investigation, they should not be misled about the nature of the study, but should have enough information to give informed consent to take part. However, it is possible to give a general outline of the study such as, 'You will be required to learn a list of words and then you will have to recall the list', without having to explain the full hypothesis under test. The general rule is to avoid deception in a study.

Debriefing

After participation in a study, there must be a full explanation of its aims and purpose and the procedures used to collect all the data. The psychologist must ensure that the participant fully understands the purpose of the investigation and does not go away anxious about any part they may have played in the research. After being debriefed, the participant should feel comfortable, at ease and, as far as possible, in the same frame of mind that they were at the start of the study. If a participant has been upset through taking part, then it is the duty of the psychologist to reassure the participant and do everything possible to make the person feel better. Where deception has taken place (see above), the researcher must explain the nature of the deception and why it was necessary to deceive the participant. The debriefing helps to avoid the participant suffering any physical or mental harm through taking part in the research. Remember that participants should be told before taking part that they can withdraw at any time; if someone does get upset halfway through, they must feel able to say that they do not want to continue and pull out of the study.

Withdrawal from the investigation

From the very start of the investigation, people must be aware of their right to stop participating in the study. When first approached to participate, they can refuse to go further. During the procedure, they can stop at any point. At the end of participation, after debriefing, the participant has a final opportunity to withdraw the data he or she provided for the research. The right of a participant to withdraw at any time during the study is important because it can avoid further upset, especially

3

where deception is used, or the participant is confused or unhappy about continuing with the experiment. The right to withdraw protects the participant from potential physical, mental or emotional harm.

Confidentiality

People must be aware that the information they provide in an investigation is confidential; they must be assured that all data is anonymous and no names will be used in the report. It should not be possible to identify an individual from the data collected, unless prior consent has been given to be identified. This is especially important with case studies, where in-depth information about a person has been gathered and identification is more of a risk because of the uniqueness of information about a person. For example, Freud (see Chapter 1) published a number of detailed case studies for which he did not gain consent of the individuals concerned. The individuals in the case studies were later identified and interviewed by other psychologists, although they had not given consent originally to have quite intimate details about themselves published and hence made available to the public. Information about a person can be kept anonymous by making sure that any unique identifying information is removed. The psychologist could also go to the lengths of showing the information to the person before publishing the material. Although this approach is not common, it may be necessary with particularly sensitive material to do with, for example, sexual abuse. In general, confidentiality ensures that the rights of the individual are protected.

Protection of participants

When people agree to participate, they have the right to expect that participation will not cause them any mental or physical harm. They should feel no worse about themselves following their involvement in the study than they did before.

Observational research issues

This type of research must respect the privacy and psychological well-being of the people studied. If consent has not been obtained, then observation is only acceptable in those circumstances where people could expect to be watched by strangers, i.e. in public places. However, any observations that do take place should not infringe people's rights to privacy, so for example the content of conversations should not be recorded. As a general rule, do not do anything to others which you yourself would find offensive. Remember, different ethnic groups or people of different ages may vary as to what they find acceptable.

Giving advice

Only professionally qualified psychologists can advise participants. Professionally qualified psychologists include: Chartered Psychologists, Chartered Occupational Psychologists, Chartered Clinical Psychologists, Chartered Criminological Psychologists and Chartered Health Psychologists.

Reflective Activity

1   Jacob et al. (1991) conducted research to investigate the interaction of alcoholic fathers with their adolescent children. One condition in the study made alcoholic drinks available to the fathers, which they drank. The fathers and their children were paid to take part in the research.

*   ●   *Do you think it ethical to pay alcoholics to drink alcohol? Justify your answer.*

*   ●   *Can you think of ways round this ethical problem?*

2 *Kassin & Kiechal (1996) investigated false confessions. To do this, they told participants that they were taking part in a typing test with another participant, who was really a confederate to the experimenters. The participants were told not to touch the 'Alt' key on the keyboard, since to do so would 'crash' the computer. After the participants had been typing for a minute, their computer broke down. The experimenter rushed into the room, accusing the participant of touching the 'Alt' button. In one condition, the confederate working alongside the participant admitted to having touched the 'Alt' button when they had not done so. The researchers were interested in how many participants would make false confessions about having touched the 'Alt' button when they had not done so.*

* *Identify the ethical issues raised by this study.*

* *Try to devise an experiment investigating false confessions, but which does not use deception.*

Calculation of standard deviation (see page 77)

Condition A	d(x–x̄)	d²
15	–1	1
16	1	1
14	–1	1
12	–3	9
17	2	4
16	1	1
14	–1	1
16	1	1
15	0	

Mean (x̄) = 15   **Total = 19 = Σd^2**

$$s = \sqrt{\frac{\Sigma d^2}{N-1}} = \sqrt{\frac{19}{8}} = \sqrt{2.375} = 1.541$$

standard deviation = 1.541

Note:

(a) Answer to practical activity on page 76: mean (x̄) = 9, median = 10, mode = 10
(b) Answer to practical activity on page 77: standard deviation = 2

3

See Appendix 1 for information concerning questions that appear in the examination paper. The assessment of knowledge and understanding (AO1) and analysis and evaluation (AO2) assessment objectives is also given in Appendix 1.

Sample questions

Sample question 1

A psychologist wanted to find out whether or not pairing pictures with words would aid recall for words. The psychologist conducted an experiment in which twenty participants were randomly assigned to one of two conditions. In Condition A, participants were given 30 nouns where each word was paired with an appropriate picture. For example, the word 'car' was presented with a picture of a car. In Condition B, the same 30 nouns were presented without pictures to the other ten participants. The results are shown in Figure 3.15.

Condition A (words and pictures)		Condition B (words only)	
Participant	Number of words recalled	Participant	Number of words recalled
P1	17	P11	13
P2	15	P12	14
P3	14	P13	8
P4	22	P14	10
P5	19	P15	15
P6	21	P16	9
P7	17	P17	11
P8	23	P18	12
P9	20	P19	11
P10	16	P20	16

Figure 3.15: Number of words correctly recalled by participants either shown words paired with pictures (Condition A) or words only (Condition B)

(a) Calculate the mean and median for the data in Condition A and Condition B.
(AO1 = 2, AO2 =1) *(3 marks)*

(b) Calculate the range for the data in Condition A.
(AO1 = 1) *(2 marks)*

(c) Represent the means you have calculated in (a) on a bar chart. Correctly label your chart.
(AO2 = 4) *(4 marks)*

(d) State the aim of the study.
(AO1 = 2) *(2 marks)*

(e) Write a suitable experimental hypothesis for the study.
(AO1 = 2) *(2 marks)*

(f) Identify the independent and dependent variables in the study.
(AO1 = 2) *(2 marks)*

(g) What is meant by the term random allocation? Describe one way the psychologist could have assigned participants to each of the two conditions.
(AO1 = 1, AO2 = 2) *(3 marks)*

(h)   What is meant by the term extraneous variable? Explain why psychologists attempt to control extraneous variables.

(AO1 = 1, AO2 = 2)   (3 marks)

Total AO1 marks = 10   Total AO2 marks = 10   Total = 20 marks

Questions, answers and comments

A group of five people were given a new treatment for their high levels of anxiety. The treatment involved talking to each other about their difficulties in controlling their anxiety. The group was led by a psychologist who wished to discover how people talked to each other during treatment. A non-participant observer recorded how many times each person spoke and the length of time each person spent speaking. The findings are shown in Figure 3.16.

Person	Number of times each person spoke	Mean length of time (in seconds) spent speaking
1	4	50
2	10	15
3	18	23
4	20	11
5	14	27

Figure 3.16: Number of times and mean length of time (in seconds) spent speaking by each person in the group

(a)   (i)   Describe the findings shown in Figure 3.16.

      (AO1 = 2)   (2 marks)

      (ii)   Sketch a graph of the mean length of time spent speaking by each person in the group. Correctly label your graph.

      (AO2 = 4)   (4 marks)

(b)   (i)   Distinguish between participant and non-participant observation.

      (AO1 = 2, AO2 = 1)   (3 marks)

      (ii)   Outline one strength and one weakness of participant observation in psychological research.

      (AO1 = 2, AO2 = 2)   (4 marks)

(c)   (i)   State an appropriate null hypothesis for this study.

      (AO1 = 2)   (2 marks)

      (ii)   State an appropriate alternative hypothesis for this study.

      (AO1 = 2)   (2 marks)

(d)   Discuss one ethical issue the psychologist should have addressed before conducting the study.

      (AO1 = 1, AO2 = 2)   (3 marks)

Total AO1 marks = 9   Total AO2 marks = 11   Total = 20 marks

Answer to (a) (i)

The findings show that the person who speaks least often (Person 1, who only speaks four times) speaks on average for the longest each time (50 seconds). The person who speaks most often (Person 4) speaks for the shortest time.

Sample questions, answers and comments

3

Comment

> Full answer given using data and reference to two people in the study. General relationship between the number of times spoken and length of time each person spoken indicated, but perhaps could have been more clearly stated. This answer would score the full two marks.

Answer to (a) (ii)

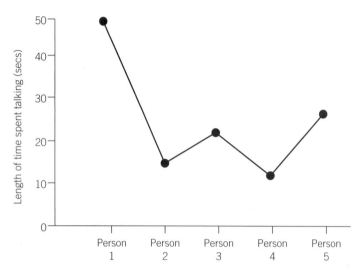

Figure 3.17: Graph showing length of time (in seconds) spent speaking by each of the five persons in the group

Comment

> The graph or bar chart provided would score three out of the four marks available. The graph is correctly labelled, and bars for each of the five people in the study correctly drawn. The axis for the mean length of time spent speaking is inappropriate; however, the axis for representing each person is fine. One mark lost because of the axis being too short.

Answer to (b) (i)

> A participant observer is one that actually takes part in the group activities, a non-participant observer does not take part but simply observes.

Comment

> Two out of the three marks would be awarded for this answer. The difference between participant and non-participant observation is stated through briefly defining each. Some comment on the actual difference is needed for the third mark.

Answer to (b) (ii)

> One strength of participant observation is that the observer will not miss anything going on in the group because he is part of the group all the time. One weakness is that the observer may influence the results.

Comment

> Answer identifies the strength and goes on to state why it is a strength, so two marks for this part of the answer. A weakness is correctly identified, but not expanded upon, so just one mark for this. Overall three marks for this answer.

Answer to (c) (i)

> The treatment of getting people to talk to each other about their difficulties will not have any effect on their level of anxiety.

Answer to (c) (ii)

The talking treatment will change anxiety.

Comment

The null hypothesis is clear and well stated; however the alternative hypothesis, whilst basically correct, is too vague. Two marks for the null hypothesis and just one mark for the alternative hypothesis.

Answer to (d)

One ethical issue the psychologist should have dealt with is that participants already have a high level of anxiety before the start of the study. Talking about their difficulties to another person may make their anxiety even worse. It is not ethical for a treatment to make someone worse. This could have been addressed by the psychologist first asking each person if they felt able to talk about their anxiety.

Comment

Good, full answer with the ethical issue clearly stated. Answer then goes on to say why this is wrong and what the psychologist could have done before conducting the study. Full three marks awarded.

The answer to this whole question would score fifteen out of twenty, so a good answer overall.

Further reading

Introductory texts

Coolican, H. (2000), *Research Methods and Statistics in Psychology*, 2nd edition, London, Hodder & Stoughton

Gross, R. (2001), *Psychology: The Science of Mind and Behaviour,* 4th edition (Chapter 48), London, Hodder & Stoughton

Searle, A. (2000), *Introducing Research and Data in Psychology: A Guide to Methods and Analysis*, Routledge Modular Series, London, Routledge

Specialist sources

Code of Conduct, Ethical Principles and Guidelines, published by the British Psychological Society (1998), www.bps.org.uk

Breakwell, G.M., Hammond, S. & Fife-Shaw, C. (2000), *Research Methods in Psychology*, 2nd edition, London, Sage Publications

Everitt, B.S. & Wykes, S. (1999), *A Dictionary of Statistics for Psychologists*, London, Arnold

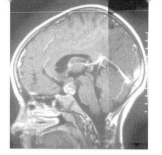

4
Psychology of Gender

Introduction

If you meet someone only once and forget everything about that person, the one fact you will remember is whether they were male or female. Gender is so important to us that we often make judgements about whether someone is male or female on such limited information as handwriting – neater handwriting often being judged as by a female.

Differences in biological sex lead us to expect differences in gender roles. Psychologists have been interested in the cause of these differences almost since the beginning of psychology itself. Early psychological theorists suggested that differences were inborn and therefore unchangeable. Differences were often judged to be in degree as well as kind. Later, theorists took the view that environment was more important than nature. The last 30 years have seen many changes in our attitudes towards gender role and expectations.

Psychology is a science and should be *objective* and *value free*, but in the study of the psychology of gender this is not always the case. Many early studies were conducted with male participants, and the results were then generalised (unfavourably) to females. There have also been studies by female researchers trying to redress the balance which have been equally biased in their methodology and conclusions.

This chapter begins by considering different ways in which gender has been studied and the issues involved in research, including specific ethical issues. It then considers competing explanations of how gender identity develops, together with evidence which supports and disputes these ideas.

Studying gender: concepts

Sex and gender

Sex is a biological term. Across time and culture, sex is defined in terms of reproduction, and all societies make the same distinction. It is customary to define two distinct biological groups and associate specific gender characteristics with these groups. There are some societies which accept the notion of a third sex. The Navajo, for example, have three categories: male, female and *nadle*. Nadles have special status and are consulted for their wisdom (Herdt, 1994).

Gender is a psychological term and refers to ideas which we hold about the behaviour, personality and attitudes of males and females within a given society. It includes terms such as *masculinity*, *femininity* and *androgyny*. Because concepts are ideas and not facts, concepts can change over time and vary both within and between cultures, hence our concept of gender may change over time.

In the past in Western society, anyone in one category having characteristics associated with a person in another category was regarded as deviant. In recent years, however, there has been a move towards explaining gender not in terms of distinct categories but as a continuum of behaviour, from extreme masculinity to extreme femininity.

Practical Activity

The following is a list of characteristics which may be classified as being masculine or feminine. Add a few more of your own to the list.

gentle, sympathetic, dominant, self-reliant, yielding, loyal, affectionate, forceful, independent, ambitious, competitive, aggressive, caring, dependent, nurturing

First, divide the characteristics into two lists which you regard as typically male or female.

Now, draw a five-column grid like the one below. Decide where on the grid you would put each word.

Masculine ←			→ Feminine	
very	quite	neutral	quite	very
forceful				gentle

It is possible that you had difficulty in placing some words. For example, aggressive might be considered a masculine trait, but you may have thought about females being verbally aggressive. Aggression is the external response to internal thoughts and feelings. People may experience the same aggressive feelings but behave in different ways.

Androgyny is a term used to describe people who show characteristics and behaviour regarded as both typically masculine and feminine. Psychologists who study androgyny believe that differences between men and women are socially constructed. They believe that encouraging androgyny may eliminate sex-role stereotyping and increase mental (psychological) health. Sandra Bem (1974) believes that androgyny exists, is measurable and is desirable.

Cherie Booth QC has a traditional female role of wife and mother. At the same time, she is also successful in the traditionally male area of the legal profession, where logical argument and tenacity are called for

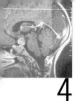
Bem's sex role inventory (BSRI) (1974)

This is a quantitative measure of androgyny. It consists of a list of traits which were originally composed by a panel of judges. They looked at a wide range of personality traits and were asked to state which of the traits was desirable for a man or a woman. The strength of the rating of each trait was recorded, and the final twenty traits of masculine, feminine and neutral were compiled. Some of these can be seen in Figure 4.1.

Masculine items	Feminine items	Neutral items
Self-reliant	Yielding	Helpful
Defends own beliefs	Cheerful	Moody
Independent	Shy	Conscientious
Forceful	Affectionate	Happy
Analytical	Loyal	Unpredictable
Self-sufficient	Sympathetic	Reliable
Aggressive	Soft-spoken	Sincere
Ambitious	Does not use harsh language	Inefficient

Figure 4.1: Twenty-four out of the sixty adjectives in the BSRI

A seven-point **Likert scale** is attached to each item, and respondents indicate how they rate themselves against each item. Respondents can score within the range of 20 to 140 on the masculine and feminine dimension.

The score can then be plotted against two dimensions of masculinity and femininity, as shown in Figure 4.2.

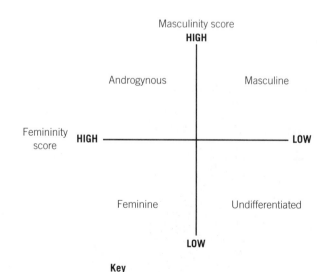

Figure 4.2: Chart illustrating the two dimensions of masculinity and femininity and their classifications

Key
high F score, low M score = feminine
high M score, low F score = masculine
high F score, low M score = androgynous
low F score, low M score = undifferentiated

On its own, this test may tell us little, but it can be used to correlate with other tests, for example mental health and self-esteem. This can allow us to test whether androgyny does correlate with psychological health.

Practical Activity

Conduct a simple study using a Likert scale with a selection of masculine and feminine traits and compare the scores with the type of AS-level subjects your participants have selected.

Do males who select arts subjects and girls who select science subjects show a greater amount of androgyny than those who select the more stereotypical male/female options?

Evaluative Comment

According to Bem (1975), people who score high on androgyny are psychologically healthier than people who suppress their opposite sex traits. Studies by Bem (1975) supported this view; however, studies by Whitely (1985) suggest that the most psychologically healthy individuals are males and females who both rate themselves higher on masculine traits. Does this prove Bem wrong, or could it be that in a male dominated society it is likely to be this way? Even if Bem's scale is a reliable measure of androgyny, it is important to think about how and where the scale was constructed. She used students from Stanford University – a very prestigious academic institution in America. It is always important when looking at psychometric tests to consider if there is any hidden gender or cultural bias.

Sex-role stereotype

A sex-role stereotype is a belief about what is considered appropriate and typical behaviour for people who are classified as male or female. It is an oversimplified, general attitude of how males and females are expected to behave.

Stereotypes *overemphasise* similarities between individuals and *underestimate* the similarities between groups (see Chapter 5). They work on the basis of exclusive categories. Behaviour can only be found in that category and will not be found in another. For example, if women are stereotyped as caring, men cannot also be stereotyped as caring. Any behaviour not consistent with the stereotype is said to be deviant, therefore caring men are acting in a deviant (feminine) manner.

When David Beckham appeared wearing a sarong, it was treated as unconventional, particularly because of the 'macho' nature of his profession. However, his admirers were quick to shave their heads or eyebrows, since that fashion statement did fit with the masculine identity of toughness

Children as young as three years of age show knowledge of sex-role stereotypes (Kuhn, Nash & Brucken, 1978). It is strongest between five and ten years of age (Ullian, 1981); however, people of all ages can be influenced by them. One of the issues for psychologists is to discover how stereotypes arise in the first place. When and where do children start to be influenced by stereotypes? Asking children directly about stereotypes raises serious ethical issues, as you may be exposing children to negative ideas with which they are unfamiliar.

Study

AIM *Williams (1986) conducted a study to discover the impact of television on children's attitudes, including sex-role stereotyping.*

METHOD *Williams studied a community in Canada which was about to receive television for the first time. He assessed the attitudes of children who lived in this town (Notel) before television was introduced and again two years later, after the introduction of television. In order to check that any changes were not due to other variables, he compared his results with children from other towns (Unitel, where there was just one TV station, and Multitel, where there was more than one TV station) who had been exposed to television for several years. This was done at the beginning and end of the study.*

RESULTS *At the start of the study, children from Unitel and Multitel held stronger stereotyped attitudes than those without television. However, two years later, the Notel children showed stronger sex-stereotyped attitudes than earlier, but there was no change in the children from the other two towns.*

CONCLUSIONS *The media exerts a powerful influence on children. Williams further argued that television programme producers should pay particular attention to the way in which the sexes are presented.*

Evaluative Comment

Opportunities for studies such as this are extremely rare, and the results are therefore often taken as being very important indicators of the role of the media in forming and maintaining attitudes. The fact that this event arose naturally also helps to overcome some ethical issues since, although children were exposed to stereotyping, it was not done by the researcher. Although the amount of stereotyping in Notel increased, it was not uniform. Some children would watch more television than others, and the type of programme watched varied. What a child watches (or is permitted to watch) will be influenced by other factors, such as the child's interests and family. The child lives within a strong cultural framework of family and community which also shapes their attitudes and beliefs. (See comments on social-learning theory and its evaluation on page 105.) We must be cautious about assuming that merely because a child is aware of stereotyping, these are attitudes the child holds.

Role and identity

Role refers to a part which a person might expect to play in a given situation, e.g. father, mother. Behaviour which is appropriate to the role will be based on a number of factors, including cultural expectations, norms and stereotypes. A gender role for a man may be that of a father. As a father, he may expect to be the final decision-maker or the financial provider and ensure security for his family.

Identity refers to the sense that someone has of what kind of person they are. In the early days of acquiring a gender identity, children recognise that there are boys and girls and that they are either a boy or a girl (Thomson, 1975). Having established who they are, children then look for behaviour which is characteristic of males and females. This helps to develop their sense of identity, what it means to be male or female. For example, if you identify yourself as a boy, it may be important to you to show independence or mental toughness.

Nature and nurture

Nature refers to a belief that behaviour is controlled by hormonal and genetic factors.

If nature is the dominant force in our development, then 'anatomy is destiny'. This approach assumes that women are programmed to be nurturing and caring, whilst men are programmed to be independent hunter–gatherers and protect their family from physical attack. People who believe that sex and gender are biologically controlled take a *deterministic* view of development. Psychoanalytic theorists such as Freud's believe that gender identity occurs as a result of a universal, unconscious process (see page 112). Psychologists with a biological approach, such as Dabbs (1995), are interested in studying the influence of sex hormones on behaviour (see page 103).

Nurture refers to the idea that gender differences are a result of cultural and social factors and that gender behaviour is the product of the environment. Psychologists who hold this view include learning theorists and cognitive psychologists. Anthropologists such as Mead (1935) have also contributed to this explanation. These researchers often use cross-cultural studies and laboratory investigations to support their view (see page 100).

Cultural diversity

In the early part of the twentieth century, there was a great interest in anthropology, and many researchers spent time studying the roles and belief systems of different cultures and communities. Anthropology is the study of different cultures in the world. Studies such as those by Mead (1935) point to differences between cultures as evidence of environmental factors playing a vital role in the development of gender identity.

Study

AIM *Mead (1935) conducted a cross-cultural study of three societies to investigate whether there were differences in gender roles which would suggest that gender was a product of environment rather than culture.*

METHOD *She visited three tribal communities on the island of New Guinea for a period of six months. The Arapesh lived in the mountain region, the Mundugamor lived by the riverside and the Tchambuli lived on the lakeside. She observed and recorded the behaviour of people within these groups for comparison with traditional Western culture.*

RESULTS *The Arapesh showed personality traits and behaviours similar to those found in Western society, although they were more interested in the community than in pursuing individual goals. The Mundugamor were described as fierce and cannibalistic. Both males and females displayed traits which were described as masculine. The Tchambuli had distinctive gender roles, but the reverse of those in the West; men were more artistic and women held the social and economic power.*

CONCLUSIONS *There is no inevitable relationship between biological sex and gender role. Culture is the major socialising and conditioning agent, particularly in the early years.*

Evaluative Comment

Mead's work is one of the most widely reported pieces of cross-cultural research and has often been used as evidence to support the idea of environment being the main force in gender role. However, the study and its conclusions are not without criticism. Many current anthropologists challenge her methodology as lacking scientific rigour. She was in her early twenties at the time with little life experience. This could certainly have coloured her judgement of what she was observing and influenced the way in

which she was regarded by the islanders, whose culture values age for its wisdom. Prior to her research in New Guinea, she already held a strong belief in the powerful role of the environment in shaping gender behaviour. This could also have clouded her perceptions of what she observed. Errington and Gewertz (1989) have revisited the Tchambuli and re-analysed Mead's original material. They record that the women do not dominate men, nor is the reverse true. The fact that Mead only spent six months in these communities is also a problem. During that period only a limited amount of the yearly cycle would have been observed; any other data would have been secondhand. She herself recognised the problem of being a woman and therefore unable to understand a male perspective, a problem not always recognised by her male counterparts! Regardless of its flaws, the findings of cultural differences in gender behaviour stimulated the argument about the role of nature and nurture in defining gender roles.

Studying gender: methods

Ethical issues

The British Psychological Society and the American Psychological Society provide and update guidelines to be followed before psychological research is carried out. Ethical guidelines are there to protect all participants, whether human or non-human. This means protection from harm, both immediate and long-term, and ensuring that participants are treated with respect. Participants are there to assist the researcher, and the psychologist is dependent upon them, not the reverse.

Some issues which specifically relate to gender are given below. (Chapter 3 (page 80) deals more fully with ethical issues in psychological research.)

Research is not value free, and participants may learn something from the study which is not intended but nevertheless influences their ideas. When conducting experiments, for example, it is important that the material presented does not influence people, particularly children, to think about themselves in a negative manner or behave in an undesirable way towards other people. Young children are particularly vulnerable and may easily acquire negative ideas to which they have not previously been exposed. For example, with Damon's (1977) study of children's attitudes towards gender-appropriate behaviour (see page 111), some children given this story may form the impression that it was wrong for boys to play with dolls. If their parents did not discourage them from playing with dolls, the children might then question their parents' behaviour.

Study

Aim *Lloyd (1989) conducted a study to find out how children developed their gender identity during their first year at school.*

Method *It was an observational study, in a primary-school classroom, which lasted for a year. The psychologists recorded the behaviour and the conversations of both children and teachers.*

Results *Analysis of play behaviour with objects showed that, in free play, boys focused on 'construction play', whereas girls divided their time between construction, creative play and role-play. Girls spread their use of space evenly, whereas boys were more focused in the areas where they played and were 'claiming territory'. When the findings were discussed with the teacher and headteacher, the teachers stated that they were willing to allow boys to occupy certain space because they believed that it was natural for boys to be more active and require more space than girls.*

Conclusions *When children begin school they have already acquired a gender identity, but their identity and behaviour are reinforced by the actions and attitudes of their teachers.*

Evaluative Comment

Before this study was conducted, informed consent would have been obtained from the school. During the course of the investigation, behaviour was observed and this could have had an effect upon the individual development of the children. The ethical issue arises as to whether the researcher should draw attention to these practices and risk having the research suspended or continue with the research and bring the findings to light at the debriefing. Lloyd chose to continue with the research and debrief fully. It is usually only when research is completed that we can provide evidence of what is happening. In this case, the wider use of this research could change classroom practice and benefit many more children. There is no suggestion that Lloyd observed any particular behaviour which was seriously harming a child. If such behaviour were observed, the researcher has a duty of care to report the matter, even though this may risk suspension of the research or cause a change in classroom behaviour making the research unreliable.

Reflective Activity

At the debriefing, issues were raised which surprised the staff but also challenged their beliefs.

- *What might have been the impact of this?*
- *What were the broader issues involved in this study?*
- *What impact might this research have on classroom practice and teacher training?*
- *Should psychologists have a role in changing society or should they merely record what is happening and not make judgements?*

Now imagine that you have conducted a study, and your results suggest that there are genetic differences between men and women which affect their ability to perform certain tasks. Your research could be used by politicians to justify changes in education which you believe could be detrimental to people.

- *Should you have conducted your research?*
- *Is an individual more important than the society in which they live?*
- *Are psychologists somehow different from other scientists because they are researching their own species?*

Science is about understanding and seeking knowledge. In this sense, science is objective, since it only claims to report what already exists. You could argue that the natural world is neutral and that mankind has imposed inequality. Research which exposes inequality would be in the interest of mankind. However, it is important to ensure that your research is conducted in a manner which brings us closer to the truth rather than presenting findings which are unreliable or invalid. There are psychologists who believe that no research is ethical since, by its very nature, it dehumanises human beings. These humanistic psychologists argue that it is the role of psychology to help individuals to reach their potential and that everyone is unique. (See Chapter 1 for more information on the humanistic approach.) By researching gender and categorising males and females as two distinct and homogenous groups, we are ignoring individual differences within men and women and similarities between them.

Early psychologists almost certainly did not recognise that they themselves were part of the scientific study and failed to recognise how they influenced the research. This issue is better understood today, and most psychologists realise that humans studying humans present different problems in terms of designing research and interpretation of results.

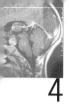

4

Case studies

Case studies give in-depth knowledge about an individual or group of individuals who have a distinctive feature. They may be useful for stimulating other areas of research on broader, normal populations. Unfortunately, their uniqueness can often present problems:

- It is unscientific to generalise from one example.

- The data is largely qualitative (see Chapter 3) or else contains quantitative material which cannot be analysed statistically because it only refers to one person.

- People are aware if they are different from other people, and this may cause them to behave in ways they would not do normally.

- There is a possibility that the researcher may concentrate too much on the individual differences and be less aware of the similarities between the case they are studying and people in general.

Cases often come to the attention of psychologists who already have a strong interest in a particular area of research, and this may then influence their findings and conclusions. Money & Erhardt (1972) have reported a number of studies of children who had ambiguous genitalia. Surgery was performed on these children, and their sex label was reassigned (male to female). Money and Erhardt believe that biological factors have little effect upon gender identity, and there are no side effects if changes occur before three years of age.

Study

AIM *Money & Erhardt (1972) recorded the case of an identical twin boy whose sexual identity was reassigned. They were interested in the development of a child whose sex had been reassigned to see whether he would develop as a biological male or, according to his new identity, as a female.*

METHOD *Due to an accident during surgery, a normal, healthy male child of seven months suffered injuries to his genitals which were so bad that on the advice of their doctors the parents agreed to him being surgically castrated and given plastic surgery to create a female external appearance. During adolescence (s)he was given the female hormone, oestrogen, to promote breast development. The development of the child, known as Joan, was monitored by Money during childhood and into early adolescence.*

RESULTS *Money reported that the development of the child was that of a normal female. She was more feminine in her behaviour than her identical twin brother and assumed a traditional female identity.*

CONCLUSIONS *The case supports the view that gender is socially rather than biologically constructed. It contradicts the view that biological factors are the most important in gender development. In spite of being biologically male (XY chromosomes), the child developed a female gender identity.*

Evaluative Comment

This case provided a rare opportunity to consider the effects of nature and nurture because of the fact that the child had an identical twin brother with whom direct comparisons could be made. In recent years, however, the boy concerned has made his identity public knowledge. His version of his childhood does not agree with Money and Erhardt. He discarded oestrogen tablets at twelve years of age, refused permission for further surgery and subsequently had surgery to reverse all previous plastic surgery. He now lives as a married man. He also states that in spite of the efforts of his parents to feminise him with clothes and toys, he always preferred more masculine toys. School reports also record that he showed masculine traits.

This case also raises ethical issues. The parents of the child believed that they were acting in the child's best interest by putting him through further surgery to give him the best chance of a 'normal' life. Western society can be intolerant of people who do not fit the 'norm'. In changing sexual appearance to conform, the doctors are being complicit in this view. Some would argue that it is the role of doctors and psychologists to help society to understand diversity rather than eliminate it. The boy himself clearly felt that his human rights were violated both by the surgery and the subsequent deception about his sexual identity.

Reflective Activity

Consider the following questions:

- What do the original case notes and the subsequent history suggest to you about biological and environmental influences on development?

- Why do you think that Money and Erhardt gave a different account from the person himself?

Content analysis

Content analysis is a method used to observe communication in the media. This may be visual or verbal, interpersonal as in conversation, or one-way as in books, films, essays or cartoons. The observers select a type of behaviour and systematically look at books, films or cartoons, recording evidence of the type of behaviour and who performed it.

The data is normally collected using a pre-determined coding system. Analysing the content of the message will involve identifying features which correspond to these pre-selected categories and counting the frequency with which they occur. For example, content analysis of sex-role stereotyping would start by firstly classifying different types of behaviour, e.g. caring/cared for, aggressor/victim. Each of these behaviours would then be described, e.g. 'caring' is showing concern, 'cared for' is someone who is receiving help. A tally chart will record every time there is an incident of a category and it can be recorded as follows:

	Male	Female
Carer		
Receiving care		

An advantage of content analysis is that it converts qualitative data to quantitative data and can be used for analysis both in its own right and also for comparing with other data.

Study

Aim Lobban (1974) conducted a content analysis of British reading schemes which were used pre-1960, 1960 and 1970 to investigate the images of males and females shown in children's literature and whether there had been changes over time.

Method She coded the contents of 225 stories, of which 179 had people as their main character. She listed the toys, pets, activities and adult roles shown for each sex.

Results The schemes divided the roles of males and females very rigidly, and males were recorded more frequently. Males were usually shown as active and out of doors. Females were usually shown indoors and only appeared as the heroine in 35 of the 179 stories.

CONCLUSIONS *Lobban felt that the reading schemes which young children were exposed to were suggesting stereotypical but unrealistic roles to young children and that these might adversely influence their understanding of gender identity.*

Evaluative Comment

The researcher found evidence that in these reading schemes sex-role stereotyping did occur; however, her methodology may have influenced the results. Durkin (1985, 1986) believes that the scoring process in content analysis is highly subjective. Although researchers are trained, the training may have a bias. This is not a specific criticism of Lobban, but of content analysis in general. Another problem with the use of pre-determined categories is that the material which is analysed is taken out of its social context. Although stereotyping may have been present in the stories, it has to be understood in the wider context of the story as a whole. In the stories, the majority of images did not portray sex-role stereotypes but were neutral. What is not easy to determine, however, is whether the smaller number of sex-role stereotype images have a greater impact than the majority of neutral images in the story.

Practical Activity

Design a study to analyse either the content of comics aimed at children of three to six years of age, or the pictures and language on a range of children's birthday cards. Select a range of categories relating to clothing, play activities and language. Code the frequency with which these occur for boys and girls.

Having completed the activity, go back and look at all the images which you did not include in your categories. What might happen if you had a neutral category? Think about what determined your choice of categories. How influenced were you by your own stereotyped ideas? Were there more images of females adopting 'masculine' behaviour than males adopting 'feminine' behaviour?

Observation

Observational studies can take place either in a laboratory or in a natural environment. This passage refers *only* to natural observation. The essential feature of a natural observation is that the observer is recording behaviour but not manipulating the situation as would be the case in laboratory or field experiments (see Chapter 3).

Before the observation, the researcher selects the specific behaviour which they wish to study and develops a coding system. For example, if you were studying male and female aggression in a school playground, you would need to decide exactly what you mean by aggressive behaviour – is it physical, verbal or both? If you selected physical aggression, you would need to consider the differences between pushing, shoving, hitting, etc. Girls may show aggression in ways which do not show up on a scale, for example, name-calling. You may need to distinguish between 'play' and 'real' aggression.

In some observational studies, male observers have interpreted the behaviour of females differently to the way female observers might. Parke (1967) studied gender differences in boys and girls who had been told not to touch an attractive toy. The children were left alone in a room with the toy. Girls were less likely to touch the toy than boys. This was interpreted by the male researchers as girls being more conformist than boys. However, it could be interpreted as girls having more respect for other people's property.

Study

Aim *Dweck et al. (1978) conducted an observational study to discover how teachers used negative and positive feedback in a school classroom.*

Method *They observed 79 children in fourth and fifth grade classes twice a week for five weeks. They analysed the type of feedback teachers gave to students. The observers were also students who had not been told the purpose of the study. Each observation was conducted by two observers in order to provide reliable data by cross-referencing.*

The researchers recorded whether the feedback was related to work or behaviour, whether it was positive or negative and whether it was related to what the student produced (intellectual ability) or how they produced it (neatness, etc.).

Results *Positive feedback was more likely to be given to boys about intellectual achievement, but for girls it related to neatness. This was reversed for negative comments.*

Conclusions *Positive and negative feedback differs across gender. Different types of feedback for different types of behaviour contribute to the perception which males and females have about their abilities, and this in turn can influence performance and self-image.*

Evaluative Comment

This study demonstrated that teachers respond in different ways to males and females. However, could the teachers' comments alone account for difference in attitude and belief? The observation only focused on the behaviour of teacher and pupils, but what about the culture of the classroom? The observers were only present for ten sessions, during which time they only recorded selected behaviour. There was no other discussion with students. Both teachers and pupils were aware of the observation, which might have distorted what was observed. Hargreaves (1967), in his observational study of a secondary school, learned from conversations with students in the playground that what he observed in class was not always a true reflection of behaviour.

Practical Activity

Conduct an observational study of male and female behaviour. You could visit a local supermarket to record whether male and female shoppers conform by returning trolleys to the trolley bay after they have unloaded their shopping. You will need to consider whether to record lone shoppers, couples or people with young children.

It is important to remember that ethical guidelines must be applied. What ethical issues are raised in this type of observation and how could they be overcome?

Experiments

Experiments are the most controlled and most scientific of the methods used by psychologists. They normally take place in a laboratory setting, but can also take place in a natural environment, where they are referred to as **field studies** (see Chapter 3).

In the past, many experiments suggested strong gender differences. However, these differences may be the result of the design of the study rather than of actual differences between men and women. For example, in Piaget and Inhelder's 'water-level task' (1958), a bottle is partly filled with water and the participant is asked to predict where the water line will be when the bottle is tipped at an

4

angle. (The water actually remains horizontal regardless of the angle of the bottle – see Figure 4.3.) In tests, 85 per cent of males but only 50–60 per cent of women get this correct. This has lead to claims that women have poorer **spatial ability** than men (Harris, 1978).

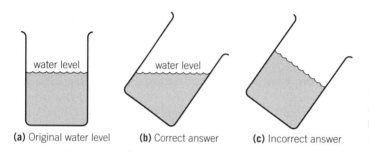

(a) Original water level   (b) Correct answer   (c) Incorrect answer

Figure 4.3: Diagrams showing the water-level task. In (b) and (c), the water line has been drawn onto a blank flask by the participant

Women can solve the problem as well as men, but women prefer to have the actual object in front of them whereas men can solve it on card. Women are better at visualising using 'real-life' objects. The conclusion, therefore, that women have poorer spatial ability is incorrect. It was the materials used in the study which influenced the performance of the men and women.

Practical Activity

Compare the performance of two groups of women using the Piaget and Inhelder bottle task. Give one group a simple outline drawn on card and give the other group a real bottle containing water. Ask each of them to indicate on a piece of card what the water level would look like if tipped at an angle.

Cross-cultural research

This type of research is useful for investigating the nature/nurture debate. If studies are conducted in different cultures and behaviour is found to be similar, regardless of external factors, this leads us to the view that differences are biologically based.

Some cross-cultural research takes the form of anthropological studies (Mead, 1935). It is important when looking at research to consider the types of society investigated. Research within the European community is likely to throw up fewer differences than research in, for instance, America and China.

Study

Aim *Fromboise, Heyle & Ozer (1990) conducted a cross-cultural study to investigate gender roles in Native American cultures and consider whether gender roles were consistent across cultures.*

Method *The researchers undertook a study of the Cheyenne, Blackfeet and Pawnee American Indian tribes of North America. The study involved both observation and interviews.*

Results *Gender roles were clearly defined, but were different from traditional Western roles. Women are known as 'warrior women' and play an active part when conflict occurs between the communities.*

Conclusions *Traditional ideas of men as the natural aggressors are not supported, and physical aggression is not a purely male characteristic.*

Evaluative Comment

Castleden & Kurszewski (2000) draw attention to a specific ethical issue which might influence the findings of cross-cultural research. In the past, research has been a negative experience for indigenous groups because of the idea of Western dominance. Margaret Mead, for example, always called the communities which she observed 'primitive'. Researchers take with them not only different value systems, but also a sense of Western superiority. In the past, anthropologists have frequently misinterpreted gender in Native American Indians. In Western culture, heterosexuality is the norm and homosexuality is often regarded as deviant. This is not the case with the Cherokee, where the culture of the 'berdache', or warrior women, is an important part of tribal life. Castleden and Kurszewski suggest that anyone working with other cultures, for example, Australian Aborigines, should include in the research team at least one member from that culture. This person will be able to educate the researchers about cultural practices and provide a sense of reassurance to the cultural group being studied.

Explaining gender

At the beginning of the twentieth century, there was a strong belief that differences between male and female behaviour was innate and the result of biological factors alone. Rossi (1977) argues that production of the female hormone oxytocin makes women better equipped to care for children both physically and psychologically. Research was focused on observable differences between the two sexes and perpetuated the idea that males and females had different developmental paths. The similarities and overlaps between men and women were ignored. Researchers also largely disregarded environmental factors. Psychoanalytic theorists, such as Freud, reinforced the view that men and women were innately different. He also reinforced the idea of male psychological superiority (Freud, 1905).

During the 1950s and 1960s, psychologists became more focused on mental processes rather than behaviour (see Chapter 1). Cognitive theorists looked at the way in which people define their gender identity and create gender schemas (mental representations). Social learning theorists (Mischel, 1966) combined earlier ideas of learning by conditioning (classical or operant) with cognitive processes. The 1970s saw an increase in research on gender, much of it influenced by feminist psychologists such as Carol Gilligan (1982), who challenged the views of Kohlberg (1966) on moral development in males and females. Feminists also challenged the idea of innate male superiority and focused on the role of the environment in creating different and unequal opportunities for men and women. They also began to draw attention to similarities between males and females (Bem, 1984; see page 90).

Biological theories

Biological theories assume that gender and sex are interrelated. Differences between the sexes are attributed to anatomical differences and the action of hormones.

Study

Aim *Imperato & McGinley (1979) studied a group of people called Machi-embra who live in the Dominican Republic. They wanted to investigate how this group of boys responded to their biological male identity when they had been previously raised as, and believed themselves to be, girls.*

Method *The boys have a rare form of pseudo-hermaphroditism caused by a genetic abnormality in their sex chromosome. This means that whilst they are genetic males (XY), they have the appearance at birth of females. At puberty, normal changes in testosterone levels cause a change in their appearance to*

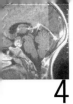

that of normal males. During childhood, they are referred to as girls and socialised into a female role. Thirty-eight boys from 23 extended families spanning four generations have been born with this condition. The researchers interviewed one group of boys and their family about their attitudes towards gender and their new male role.

RESULTS *Although they had been raised as girls, the boys immediately adapted to their new identity with no apparent problems. They assumed the traditional male role within the community and most went on to marry local girls and raise a family as a traditional male.*

CONCLUSIONS *This case study illustrates the importance of biological sex in gender identity, since the boys shed their female role with no harmful psychological effects. They are able to assume a masculine identity more easily because they were biological males and the brain received testosterone in the normal way during foetal development.*

Evaluative Comment

This study illustrates very strongly the influence of biology rather than environment, since the children were raised in a traditional female role but shed this identity with ease because of their biological changes. We must, however, take into consideration the powerful effect of culture on the way in which these children developed and changed their gender identity. The Dominican Republic is both patriarchal (the male is head of the family and descent is traced through the male line) and highly religious. Male children are more important to their family, and the community accepts the transformation from girl to boy as God-given destiny.

Chromosomes

The normal human body contains 23 pairs of chromosomes. A chromosome is a structure containing thousands of genes, which are biochemical units of heredity and govern the development of every human being. Each pair of chromosomes controls different aspects of development, and biological sex is determined by the 23rd chromosome pair. Chromosomes physically resemble the letters X and Y. Twenty-two pairs of chromosomes are X-shaped, however chromosome 23 is different. If the pairing for chromosome 23 is XX, the individual is female, and if it is XY, the individual is male.

Atypical sex chromosomes

There are a number of conditions caused by abnormalities in chromosome pair 23. These include Turner's syndrome and Klinefelter's syndrome. The term **syndrome** refers to a collection of characteristics which are shared by a group with a common problem.

Turner's syndrome (XO) occurs when females develop with only one X chromosome on chromosome 23. It is the only survivable condition where there is a single rather than a pair of chromosomes, and it affects one in 2,500 females.

The absence of the second X chromosome results in a child with a female external appearance but whose ovaries have failed to develop. The physical characteristics of individuals with Turner's syndrome include lack of maturation at puberty and webbing of the neck. In addition to physical differences, there are differences in cognitive skills and behaviour. The affected individuals have higher than average verbal ability but lower than average spatial ability, visual memory and mathematical skills. They also have difficulty in social adjustment at school and generally have poor relationships with their peers.

Klinefelter's syndrome affects males. It is thought that between one in 500 and one in 1,000 males may have the condition. In addition to having a Y chromosome, these men also have an additional

X on the 23rd pair, leading to the arrangement XXY. Physically they appear male, though the effect of the additional X chromosome causes less body hair and under-developed genitals. The syndrome becomes noticeable in childhood, as the boy has poor language skills. At three years of age, the child may still not talk. At school, their poor language skills affect reading ability. When they are babies, their temperament is described as passive and co-operative. This calmness and shyness remains with them throughout their lives.

Reflective Activity

Turner's syndrome and Klinefelter's syndrome might be used by biological theorists to support the idea of a genetic basis for differences in behaviour. Based upon what you have read, to what extent do these characteristics support a biological explanation, and to what extent might they still support an environmental explanation?

Sex hormones and their effect upon behaviour

Hormones are chemical substances secreted by glands throughout the body. The same sex hormones occur in both men and women, but differ in amount and in the effect that they have upon different parts of the body.

Testosterone, which is more present in males than females, affects development and behaviour both before and after birth. The first observable action of this sex hormone occurs in the fifth month of foetal development. Male gonads release testosterone which causes a male foetus to develop external sex organs. At the same time, this hormone acts on the developing brain. The brain is divided into two hemispheres, left and right, with linkage via the corpus callosum (see Chapter 2). In all humans, the left side of the brain is more specialised for language skills and the right for non-verbal and spatial skills. It appears that male hemispheres work more independently than females, and testosterone influences this lateralisation (Lansdell, 1962).

Study

Aim *Waber (1976) investigated the idea of brain lateralisation and the effect that sex hormones might have on the performance of verbal and spatial tasks.*

Method *She tested 80 children in two groups using standard tests for verbal reasoning and spatial ability. Group 1 was classified as early maturers (having reached puberty early (ten-year-old girls and thirteen-year-old boys). Group 2 was classified as late maturers (thirteen-year-old girls and sixteen-year-old boys).*

Results *There was a significant difference in the scores of the two groups. For verbal ability, late maturing girls were better than early maturing girls. The difference was more pronounced in boys, where late maturing boys significantly outperformed the early developers, both male and female. For spatial ability, the difference was less obvious, although late maturing boys and girls had better scores than early maturing boys and girls, boys having the best score of all.*

Conclusions *The difference between males and females in verbal and spatial ability is more likely to be caused by the effect of sex hormones in foetal development and at puberty than by social factors. Gender differences occur not specifically because someone is biologically male or female, but due to the action of hormones on the brain of males and females.*

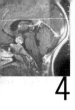

4

Evaluative Comment

*Although Waber's study points to the effect of **lateralisation** as causing differences in performance, it would be wrong to ignore the effect of the social environment. Early developing boys and girls may develop interests which take them away from activities such as reading or sport which help to develop verbal and spatial ability. Studies suggesting male superiority over females in spatial skills have been challenged on the grounds that there is a sex bias in the way in which tests are carried out. Women usually act with greater caution when doing tests involving spatial skills and, as a result, do not complete tests which have a time limit. The scoring system distorts the results when comparing females with males. If the results only relate to questions attempted rather than scoring non-attempts as wrong, no difference between the performance of males and females is found. However Delgado & Prieto (1996), using a much larger sample with this technique, found that males still out-performed females on spatial skills tasks.*

Androgens are associated with normal male development. During foetal development, the effects of androgen can alter development. CAH (Congenital Adrenal Hyperplasia) is a rare condition occurring in both males and females, which causes the adrenal glands to produce androgens regardless of whether testes are present or not. A genetic female (XX) will over-produce male androgens and under-produce cortisol. This can result in malformed exterior genitals and, as a result, the child may be wrongly assigned by sex at birth. If the problem is detected early, the external appearance can be corrected by surgery. However, as the brain has been subject to masculinising hormones during foetal development, girls with this condition are sometimes described as 'tomboyish', and they show greater levels of aggression than other girls, along with a preference for male toys. Their gender orientation and identity is, however, female (Berenbaum, 1998), and their cognitive abilities in spatial tasks are superior to 'normal' females. When the condition occurs in boys, they are more inclined to physical activity but are no more aggressive than their peers.

Study

AIM *Dabbs, Carr, Frady et al. (1995) investigated the link between prisoners' behaviour, the type of crime they had committed and their testosterone levels.*

METHOD *They took saliva samples from 692 male prisoners to test the presence and amount of testosterone. They then looked at the prison records of these men and coded their behaviour in terms of the type of crime committed and whether they had broken prison rules.*

RESULTS *Men with high testosterone levels were more likely to have committed crimes involving sex and violence than men with lower testosterone levels. The lower group were more likely to have committed crimes such as burglary and drug offences. Men with high testosterone levels were also more likely to have broken prison rules.*

CONCLUSIONS *The presence and action of testosterone causes heightened arousal and aggressive behaviour. Since men produce larger amounts of testosterone than females, men are naturally more easily aroused and behave more aggressively.*

Evaluative Comment

There is no doubt that the action of testosterone increases arousal and can cause feelings of aggression. However, we must be careful not to assume that human behaviour is mechanical, or that violent anti-social aggression is programmed into men. The presence of testosterone may be the result of the men feeling aggressive or aroused by a situation rather than the body producing testosterone which leads to arousal, in the same way that the body produces adrenalin to help respond to a threatening situation. Environmental factors such as family background and social opportunity would also play an important role in development and how people respond to frustrating situations. Even if these men do produce high levels of testosterone, the human mind can control behaviour and learn to direct physical energy into mental energy.

Oestrogen is the female hormone responsible for controlling the onset of menstruation and foetal development when pregnant. It is important in females after puberty through its influence on the menstrual cycle. In addition to physical changes which occur in the body due to oestrogen, there are also some behavioural effects.

In some women, these effects can give rise to pre-menstrual syndrome (PMS) or pre-menstrual tension (PMT). The word *tension* is an indicator of the psychological effect. In some women, tension may lead to intense feelings of aggression or cause them to become anti-social in other ways, such as committing criminal acts like shoplifting. Whether this can be directly attributed to hormones is a matter of debate. There have been court cases where PMT has been offered as a mitigating factor in cases of murder and shoplifting, and this defence has been accepted (Easteal, 1991).

Evaluative Comment

*There are clear differences between males and females; however, the total difference between them is slight. At birth, the brain is not fully developed and there are few localised areas. This could mean that the activity of parents, e.g. reading to children, playing football with them, produces differences in the development of male and female brains. The hemispheres are lateralised from birth, the left and right hemispheres having different functions; however, environmental stimulation could reinforce or eliminate these distinctions. Erhardt (1985) rejects the idea of **biological determinism** in favour of what she calls a 'dynamic interactional model'. This means that she stresses the importance of environmental factors. She states that whatever pre-disposing influences biology may have on behaviour, people give meaning to the actions of children in a social context (e.g. girls crying means they are unhappy, boys crying means that they are bored) and therefore gender is socially not biologically constructed.*

Social learning theory (SLT)

Social learning theory (Bandura, 1986) assumes that behaviour is a product of environmental influences and learned as a result of observation and modelling. Whether behaviour is acquired depends upon a person's perception of reinforcement and rewards. Social learning occurs in four stages, as shown in Figure 4.4.

Social learning theory emphasises the importance of the individual actively seeking out behaviour and attitudes. This differs from traditional learning theory, which states that a child is conditioned by stimulus–response and reinforcement and has little choice about the behaviour which they acquire (see Chapter 1).

Social learning theory states that children's behaviour is channelled by the actions of important people within their environment. It is opposed to the view that there are 'natural' categories of behaviour and argues that behaviour is shaped by the social context.

Modelling means either to provide an example – as in the actions of role models – or to imitate the behaviour of a person who has acted as a model.

- A person may be reinforced by the model they are observing. If a boy wants to be accepted by members of a peer group who enjoy playing football, he will begin to play football. This increases the chances of him being accepted by his peers, and their acceptance is his reinforcement.

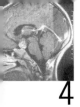

4

- A person may be reinforced by a third person. If a girl observes another girl who dresses in a particular manner which she likes and dresses in a similar way, she may be complimented by her friends on her appearance.

- A person may find reinforcement themselves in modelling behaviour. A woman may notice that a female friend who goes to the gym three times a week is always happy and healthy. She starts to go to the gym herself and finds that she is feeling happier and healthier.

- A person observing a model notices that the model's behaviour is positively reinforced. This is learning through vicarious reinforcement, since the person themselves obtains nothing.

Whether a person chooses to imitate behaviour is determined by a combination of factors concerning the model and the needs of the individual. Factors which are likely to increase the chance of modelling include:

- *Appropriateness* of the model's behaviour in relation to their role. The more appropriate the behaviour is assumed to be, the more likely they are to be imitated. Bandura (1961) found that males would imitate aggressiveness shown by males, but would not imitate the same aggressiveness if the model was female.

- *Relevance*. A model who appears to have similar characteristics to yourself is more likely to be modelled. In young children, the relevance may be seen on lines of gender.

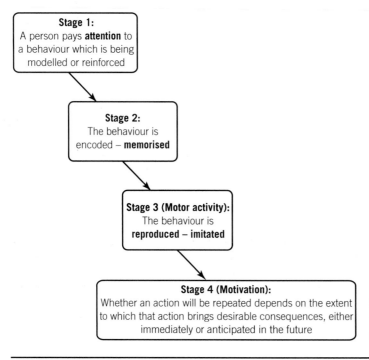

Figure 4.4: The stages involved in the process of social learning

Study

AIM *Janis & Janis (1976) conducted an observational study of the way in which males and females carried their books to see if there was any difference in style.*

METHOD *They first identified five distinct carrying styles, which they classified into two categories: Type I and Type II (see Figure 4.5). They observed a total of 2,626 individuals from kindergarten to college age and also adults as they entered and left a public library. They recorded the carrying behaviour of males and females according to the two types.*

RESULTS *There was a clear division in the types of carrying behaviour between the sexes, with males showing a greater preference for Type II behaviour than females.*

CONCLUSION *The researchers concluded that the differences and the change in behaviour, particularly of the boys, were largely explained by social modelling.*

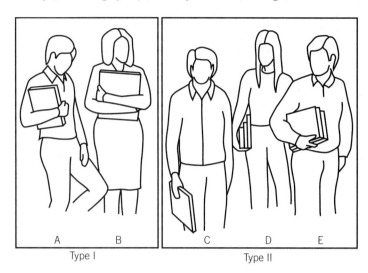

Figure 4.5: Illustration of the types of carrying behaviour identified and classified by Janis and Janis. Any carrying behaviour different from that illustrated was not counted in the observation (Adapted from Jenni, 1976)

Evaluative Comment

This is a good example of an observational study, and the results may be judged as reliable since the sample size was very large and the individuals were observed on several occasions and in a number of different cities. It seems likely that the behaviour of carrying books in this way is social, but to what extent would an individual make a conscious decision to carry their book in a particular way because it reinforces gender identity? It is possible that the explanation also has a biological basis in terms of men having larger hands, enabling them to grasp more easily. Women may find holding the book in Type I ways easier and more comfortable, and thus reinforcing.

Reinforcement

Reinforcement can be external or internal and can be positive or negative. If a child wants approval from parents or peers, this approval is an external reinforcement, but feeling happy about being approved of is an internal reinforcement. A child will behave in a way which it believes will earn approval because it desires approval. Positive (or negative) reinforcement will have little impact if the reinforcement offered externally does not match with an individual's needs. Reinforcement can be positive or negative, but the important factor is that it will usually lead to a change in a person's behaviour.

Mischel (1966) argued that children learn their sex roles by being reinforced directly for behaving in sex-appropriate ways and for imitating same-sex models, especially the same-sex parent. Parents tend to pay more attention to their children when they do this.

Study

AIM *Fagot (1985) studied teachers and two-year-old children (boys and girls) to discover whether there were differences in the way teachers reinforced behaviour in boys and girls, and the effects of peer group reinforcement.*

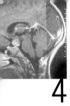

METHOD *She observed two-year-old children in playgroups. She noted how teachers and peers reacted to and reinforced the behaviour of children. Reinforcement was defined as praise or criticism as opposed to ignoring good or bad behaviour.*

RESULTS *She noticed that teachers tended to respond positively more often if the activity was described as 'female preferred'. There was also a difference in the way in which the children responded to who gave the reinforcement. The girls were influenced by both teachers and peers. The boys appeared not to be influenced by teachers and were only influenced by their peers in 'masculine activity', e.g. rough-and-tumble play.*

CONCLUSION *From a very early age, children are reinforced for gender-appropriate behaviour, but whether the child responds to reinforcement will differ between males and females.*

Evaluative Comment

The difference in the behaviour of the boys and girls may be due to earlier conditioning by parents or the fact that the teacher was the same sex as the girls and therefore seen by the girls as a more appropriate role model (see also page 106).

Imitation

This is copying behaviour and is the fastest type of learning in both humans and animals. Behaviour may be imitated because it is seen as rewarding, but if positive reinforcement does not follow or provide the expectation of positive future outcomes, imitation will cease. For example, boys and girls may witness aggressive behaviour which is seen to achieve desired results. If children imitate aggressive actions and the girls are told off but the boys are not, girls are less likely to develop aggressive behaviour.

Study

AIM *Bandura (1965) conducted a study to explore the effect that the consequences of actions have on learning (imitation).*

METHOD *Using the experimental method, he arranged for boys and girls (three to six years of age) to witness a short television programme in which children of a similar age behaved aggressively towards a toy called a 'Bobo doll'. There were three films, each with a different outcome. At the end of Film A, an adult in the film made a positive comment. At the end of Film B, an adult made a critical comment. At the end of Film C, an adult left the room and made no comment.*

After watching the film, each group of children went into a room where there was a similar doll. The children's behaviour both towards the doll and each other was observed.

RESULTS *The graph in Figure 4.6 clearly shows that, whilst the children were exposed to the same behaviour, boys showed high levels of imitation. The girls showed less evidence of imitation and were particularly influenced by negative comments.*

CONCLUSION *Children learn by observation and imitation, but the learning is also mediated by other factors.*

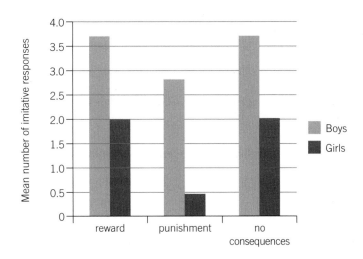

Figure 4.6: Bar chart showing the mean number of imitative responses by boys and girls as a result of the observed consequences

---

Evaluative Comment

The studies by Bandura are often used as powerful evidence to support the idea of learning through imitation. However, these studies were all conducted in experimental conditions, and there was no follow-up to see whether the behaviour observed in the laboratory became incorporated into the behavioural schema of the children. There were also no studies conducted before the laboratory study to determine the natural behaviour of these children. The fact that girls appear to be more influenced by negative comments might also be explained by the demand characteristics of the laboratory situations. Earlier studies have suggested that girls tend to act with greater caution in new situations or possibly that they have more respect for other people's property.

Identification

This relates to attachment to specific models who possess qualities seen as rewarding. Children will have a number of models with whom they identify. These may be people in their immediate world, such as parents or elder siblings, or could be fantasy characters or people in the media. The motivation to identify with a particular model is that they have a quality which the individual would like to possess. By identifying with their role model, the person adds this quality to themselves or believes this will occur in the future.

Reflective Activity

Two six-year-old boys are playing football. They are both wearing football shirts with the name of their favourite player on the back. A six-year-old girl joins them. She is standing with a football and also wearing a team shirt. At first, she plays with the ball by herself and shows skill in controlling and heading the ball. She asks the boys if she can join them. The boys refuse, saying that girls can't play football.

Using your knowledge of social learning theory, explain the boys' and girl's understanding of appropriate gender identity. In your explanation, you should have considered the game of football. Where have the boys picked up their idea? What does the wearing of the shirt suggest? The girl has been exposed to the same external forces as the boys, but apparently has not been affected in the same way. Why might that be?

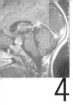

4

Evaluative Comment

Social learning theory places emphasis on the cognitive component in learning and acts as a bridge between traditional learning and cognitive theory. It also explains how and why a person may change their gender behaviour with age and experience, e.g. tomboy to fashion-conscious girl. Sayers (1982) argues that it fails to explain how children build up schemas or ideas of what is appropriate in the first instance. For example, why are children more willing to model themselves on some people rather than others of the same sex? How does the model of appropriate sex-type behaviour emerge within society? Many politicians and teachers are concerned today about the culture of 'lads' and 'laddettes'. Where did this type of behaviour emerge from for it to be modelled?

*In spite of its flexibility, the theory does not account for differences which exist between children of the same sex who may be in the same household. In a review of research on the role of parents in determining a child's personality, Harris (1998) argues that children raised in the same way and the same environment do not show similarity in their development. Even identical twins only show a 0.50 concordance in their characteristics and behaviour. This raises the point that even if a child is biologically similar and raised in the same way, the child must have its own uniqueness which influences its choice of models. This uniqueness is not discussed by social learning theorists. They present a **generic theory** suggesting that boys and girls as groups are influenced by the processes of reinforcement, and that their experience as individuals is less important than their experience as either boys or girls.*

Cognitive theories

Cognitive theories partly answer the criticisms made of other theories of gender. Social learning theory focuses on external factors which channel a child's development. Biological theories emphasise internal factors, but regard the individual as playing a passive role in gender development. Cognitive theorists focus on the internal, mental world of the child and how the child actively constructs and understands gender. According to Spence (1985), a child first acquires knowledge of its identity – 'I am a boy' or 'I am a girl' – then actively looks around to confirm and define their sense of who they are, and how they fit into their world.

Psychologists often refer to gender **schema**, by which they mean a mental representation containing ideas about appropriate behaviour for males and females. When observing the world, we use our gender schema to determine whether or not particular behaviours are appropriate; those that are appropriate are likely to be incorporated into our schema and used to guide our future behaviour.

Reflective Activity

Refer to the activity on page 109. How might cognitive schemas explain the behaviour?

Kohlberg's cognitive development theory

Kohlberg's theory of gender is based on the ideas of the famous developmental psychologist, Piaget. Piaget's theory of cognitive development stated that a child's understanding of the physical world changes with age, and that thinking develops in age-related stages. Kohlberg adopted a similar view, suggesting that understanding of the social world develops in a series of stages in which the child's thinking processes and understanding are quite different. Kohlberg proposed three stages of gender understanding in which he explained how a child's view of gender becomes gradually more sophisticated with age:

* **Gender identity:** At around two years old, a child is able to label his or her own sex correctly, knowing that they are male or female, and is also able to recognise other people as either male or female.

Given the limited language ability of a child at this age, researchers have to use more subtle methods than direct questioning. For example, gender identity can be tested by showing a young child photographs of a 'typical boy' and a 'typical girl', then asking the child, 'Which of these is like you?' Children who have acquired gender identity can usually point correctly to either the boy or the girl photo. It's interesting to note that even before they can correctly label their own sex in this way, children have already started to choose same-sex playmates, as if they are already unconsciously aware of the difference.

● **Gender stability:** Between three-and-a-half and four-and-a-half years old, a child's understanding of gender becomes much more complex, with the realisation that not only are they either male or female now, but that they will always be the same sex. Whether or not a child has developed gender stability can be tested by asking the child what they will be when they grow up. A little boy who has *not yet* developed gender stability might understand quite well that he is a boy now, but think that when he grows up he will 'be a mummy'. Gender is related to specific observable characteristics and behaviours.

● **Gender constancy:** An even more complex understanding of gender is acquired between the ages of four-and-a-half and seven years when the child realises that gender remains the same across time, even where the outside appearance of a person might change. For example, a child who has developed gender constancy would understand that even though a man might wear a kilt (or even a sarong!) and maybe even wear make-up, he is still a man and hasn't changed into a woman.

Kohlberg explains the *process* by which the child creates its gender schema as follows:

● The child *labels* itself as male or female.

● The child *perceives* itself to be masculine or feminine.

● The child *directs and organises its thoughts* along the lines of what it means to be male or female. 'I am a girl therefore I must behave like a girl. What do girls do?'

● The child is *motivated to adopt* gender-appropriate behaviour because it becomes reinforcing to its self-image.

Study

Aim *Damon (1977) investigated the development of the understanding of gender in children of four to nine years of age to see whether the concept changed over time.*

Method *Damon told the children a story about a boy called George who enjoyed playing with dolls. George's parents wanted to discourage him and said that only girls played with dolls. The children were asked questions about whether people were right to interfere with the type of toys children play with and whether it was alright for George to play with dolls if he wanted.*

Result *The children's answers varied according to age. Whilst the four-year-olds thought it was alright for George to play with dolls, the six-year-olds thought it was quite wrong and shouldn't be allowed. The nine-year-olds thought that, whilst it was unusual, it was not a bad thing to do and George should be allowed to play with dolls if he really wanted to.*

Conclusion *Children's understanding of gender-appropriate behaviour changes with age and is a reflection of their cognitive development.*

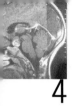

4 Reflective Activity

Four children are playing together. Boy A picks up a doll and starts to dress it. Boy B says, 'That makes you a girl!' Girl C says, 'No, it doesn't. He can play if he wants.' Girl D says, 'No, he can't. Only mummies look after babies.'

From your knowledge of cognitive theories of gender development, approximately what age do you think these children are and why?

Evaluative Comment

Although influential, Kohlberg's theory tends to be descriptive rather than explanatory. In stating that children acquire an understanding of gender identity – male/female – at two years of age, it does not explain why children select the categories they do and the information they incorporate into their schemas. Social learning theory probably provides a better explanation of why the schemas develop through reinforcement and modelling.

Kohlberg's theory does not recognise the different views children hold about what it is to be male or female. Some girls may adopt a very traditional feminine outlook, whereas others prefer a more assertive approach. Kohlberg's 'broad brush' approach does not explain the reason for individual differences in the way males and females see masculinity and femininity. There is a range of schemas which a child may hold about what it means to be male or female, and schemas can change quite radically over time. A few decades ago in Britain, it was considered 'unmanly' for men to be actively involved in child-care or express their emotions in public. Men who may have adopted that identity in the past may today have a very different mental schema of appropriate male behaviour, whereas the understanding of other men may not have changed. Kohlberg does not explain why some individuals may change and others do not. This is better explained by social learning theory.

Psychoanalytic theories

Psychoanalytic theories assume that the development of gender identity is linked to interpersonal relationships between the child and the parent. The parental relationship forms a prototype which remains with a person throughout life. These theories also assume the presence of an unconscious mind (see Chapter 1).

Freud's theory of acquisition of gender identity

This theory is bound up with his ideas surrounding **infantile sexuality** and the development of the self in the first five years of life. During this period, a child passes through three distinct psychosexual stages of development: **oral**, **anal** and **phallic**. It is clear from the naming of the stages that these are linked to biological aspects of an individual.

Freud believed that for the first three years of life a child was bisexual. Sexuality is defined in terms of masculine–activity, feminine–passivity. Males and females show both elements, though the masculine is dominant in both. During the first three years, the child's main, most intense relationship is with the mother. Prior to the phallic stage, the child does not have a strong sense of gender identity and is **bisexual**.

During the phallic stage (three to five years of age), gender division occurs. This occurs as a result of a process which in males is called the **Oedipal complex** and females the **Electra complex** (Freud, 1933).

- **The Oedipal complex:** Sexual energy (**libido**) is directed into the phallus (penis), and a boy's affection for his mother becomes intensely sexual; he desires his mother for himself (id impulses). The boy recognises his father as a powerful rival whom he fears might castrate him if he discovered the boy's feelings for his mother. Torn between love for his mother and fear of castration, the boy resolves his conflict by identification with his father and gives up his desires for his mother. From now on, he assumes an entirely masculine identity, and looks to his father as his role model (ego resolution). The absence of a strong male role model will result in the boy becoming homosexual in his gender identity.

- **The Electra complex:** This involves the girl becoming aware of the male phallus, which is seen as a symbol of power. She realises that she does not have one, but desires it (**penis envy**). She also realises that not only is she 'castrated' and powerless, but so is her mother. She loathes her mother for making her incomplete, but converts her 'penis envy' into the 'penis-baby' project (the desire to have a baby). Having resolved her conflict, she returns to her pre-Electra relationship with her mother and identifies herself as a woman using her mother as her role model.

The fact that the natural male state is one of activity and the female state one of passivity results in the development of gender roles along these lines. The boy abandons the passivity of his bisexual phase and is entirely active and dominant, whereas the girl adopts the passivity of the bisexual stage and relinquishes her active role.

Evaluative Comment

The Oedipal and Electra complexes probably represent the most difficult account of gender acquisition for people to accept. It is made even more difficult by the fact that there is little or no empirical support for their existence. Freud himself was unhappy with the Electra complex, claiming that women were a great mystery to him. The Oedipal complex arose from his own self-analysis, and it appears in the letters he wrote to Fleiss (Masson, 1985). Freud's case study of Little Hans (see below) is often offered as evidence, but this is incorrect. Freud uses the theory as an explanation for Hans's phobia. The fact that Hans's phobia disappeared after his father explained the problem in terms of the Oedipal complex might be taken as very limited evidence for the existence of the phenomena. Freud had already decided that the Oedipal complex existed, and he explained Hans' behaviour in terms of an already-existing theory.

The case of Little Hans

'Hans' was the son of a friend of Freud. Freud had asked the father to write and tell him about his son's development in order that he could understand child development in relation to his own theory of infant sexuality.

The letters from the father suggested that Hans was an unexceptional child until he was four and three quarters when he developed a phobia associated with horses. He was particularly afraid of large white horses with black blinkers and black around the mouth. He was terrified to leave the house and believed that the horses might either bite him or fall down.

At the time that the phobia began Hans' mother was heavily pregnant and Hans had also witnessed an incident when a large horse had fallen down, was lying on its back with feet in the air.

Freud interpreted this anxiety immediately as the conscious expression of the unconscious anxiety which Hans held towards his father and mother. His mother whom he loved was carrying his father's child. The white horse represented his father with dark eyes and a full dark beard. His fear of horses falling down was his unconscious wish to see his father dead.

Figure 4.7: The case of Little Hans

Other psychoanalytic theories - Nancy Chodorow

Freud's theory is based around the relationship between the child and the parents in the phallic stage. Chodorow (1978), however, believes that the early mother–child relationship forms the basis of gender identity.

4

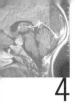

Mothers tend to seek greater proximity to their daughters with activities such as reading, whereas boys play more independently

Because mothers are the same sex as their daughters, the relationship which develops between them from birth is closer. Mothers see daughters as like themselves, but sons are seen as different. The similarity of mothers and daughters leads to a fusion between them, and the mother shows greater closeness and a desire for them to be together. Boys, on the other hand, are seen as distant and different, and therefore mothers are more willing to allow the male child independence because she cannot identify with him to the same extent. The mother's behaviour allows boys to become independent at a much earlier age.

The differences between Freud and Chodorow are shown in Figure 4.8.

Freud's approach to gender identity	Chodorow's approach to gender identity
The development of male and female gender identity is controlled by unconscious and innate forces within the child	The behaviour of the mother influences the different paths of boys and girls
The specific gender identity which emerges is a response to the father	The specific gender identity which emerges is a response by the mother
The process of gender identity occurs at about 4 to 5 years of age	The process of moulding gender identity begins at birth

Figure 4.8: A comparison of Freud and Chodorow's approach to the acquisition of gender identity

Study

Aim *Goldberg & Lewis (1969) observed mother-and-child interactions to discover whether this could account for differences in the behaviour of boys and girls.*

Method *In a laboratory situation, they observed the behaviour of 64 mothers playing with their children. They had previously interviewed each mother when their child was six months old to discover if there were any differences in the way they treated the boys and the girls. At thirteen months of age, the children were brought to a laboratory by their mothers. Each mother-and-child pair was left alone in a room containing a chair and nine toys. Some toys made a noise (drums), others were for quieter play (dolls).*

RESULT *Mother/daughter pairs showed greater physical closeness and played together with the dolls. Mother/son pairs showed less proximity. The boys wandered away from their mothers, played with noisier toys and were generally more independent.*

CONCLUSION *Mothers treat their children differently depending upon the sex of the child, and this difference in treatment accounts for gender differences in behaviour.*

Evaluative Comment

This study was conducted using mothers and their own children. We do not know whether the same mothers would behave differently with their child if they had a child of the opposite sex. However, we do know from other studies that the perceived sex of the child does influence a mother to behave in different ways towards the child. These other studies asked a mother to interact with a baby who is not their own and whose sex has not been revealed to the mother; however, the baby is dressed like a boy (in blue) or a girl (in pink). Mothers showed greater nurturance to girls and held them closer (Davenport, 1994). This suggests that Chodorow's explanation of gender differences is along the right lines. This means that gender differences are not the result of modelling, imitation and reinforcement as suggested by SLT, but the result of more subtle interactions between mother and child. Sayers (1987) considered whether the same relationship that exists between mother and child might occur between teachers and children in schools. Do female teachers nurture girls more than boys because they see girls as similar to themselves and boys as different? In recent years, the number of male teachers has declined and so has male student school performance, whilst female student school achievement has increased. Could there be a causal link? Sayers finally rejects this idea, as it assumes that education merely socialises children into pre-existing roles, rather than education itself socialising children.

Although the theories we have looked at have many distinctive features, they also have similarities and use similar terminology. Figure 4.9 refers to studies which are described in this chapter. It cross-references the methods used to study gender with the factors which are said to influence the development of gender identity.

Method	Influence			
	Biological factors	Parental behaviour	Teachers and peers	Wider society
Case study (including ross-cultural studies)	Imperato & McGinley (1979) (page 101)	Money & Erhardt (1972) (page 96)		Mead (1935) (page 93); Fromboise *et al.* (1990) (page 100)
Observational studies (including content analysis)			Lloyd (1989) (page 94); Fagot (1985) (page 107)	Lobban (1974) (page 97); Dweck (1978) (page 99); Janis & Janis (1976) (page 106)
Experimental method	Waber (1976) (page 103)	Goldberg & Lewis (1969) (page 114)		Bandura (1965) (page 108); Williams (1986) (page 92)
Surveys				Damon (1977) (page 111)
Correlation	Dabbs *et al.* (1995) (page 104)			

Figure 4.9: A cross-reference of methods of studying gender with influences on gender development

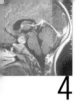

4

	Biological theory	Social learning theory	Cognitive theory	Psychoanalytic theories
Gender is a product of nature	Behaviour is either pre-determined by foetal development or the action of sex hormones	Sex and gender are distinct. Gender is determined solely by environmental influences	Gender is a result of learned responses in the form of schema which develop as a result of the environment	Not strictly speaking biological in terms of genes and hormones but Freud believes that the Oedipal and Electra complex are inherited within the unconscious and hence the process is biologically driven
Role of parents	Parents pass on certain genetic characteristics but after birth they have no specific role in gender development	Parents are important role models for young children in their early gender development but as the child develops their importance can diminish as peers and wider society become important	Not specifically part of the process though their behaviour may be part of what is incorporated into the schema	Same-sex parents form an important part in the acquisition of gender. For Freud, identification with same-sex parent during the phallic stage is crucial in establishing gender identity
Role of society	Gender is universal and innate. Social fators play no role in development	Any feature within society plays an important role in the acquisition of gender identity. These may be significant others such as parents and peers or less direct influences such as the media	Any aspect of society can be an important feature in providing information to be incorporated into the gender schema	Plays no particular role beyond the behaviour of parents
Identification	Not a feature of gender acquisition	Vital component in development of gender identity. Occurs throughout life as the individual's role in society changes	Can form part of the development of schema	For Freud it is crucial during the phallic stage. Identification is based on the child relating to same-sex parents. After the phallic stage identification is complete and the role does not change. Chodorow places the focus of identification with the mother which influences her relationship to the child and moulds behaviour
Timing of gender identity	Gender is fixed prior to birth and occurs during foetal development	Very important in the early years as children acquire their gender identity but it is not fixed and therefore develops and changes throughout life	Occurs over a number of years in childhood. The way in which children think about the concept of gender develops during the first 7/8 years but the actual schema develops and changes throughout life	According to Freud it is fixed during the phallic stage which is a precise biological time between 3 and 5 years of age. Identification occurs at this time and gender identity becomes fixed. Other psychologists such as Chodorow time gender development from birth but is completed in childhood

Figure 4.10: A comparison of key features of each of the four theoretical approaches to gender acquisition

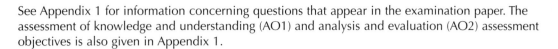

See Appendix 1 for information concerning questions that appear in the examination paper. The assessment of knowledge and understanding (AO1) and analysis and evaluation (AO2) assessment objectives is also given in Appendix 1.

Sample questions

Sample question 4

(a) Describe one effect that oestrogen can have on female behaviour.

   (AO1 = 2)   *(2 marks)*

(b) Explain Freud's concept of the Oedipal complex.

   (AO1 = 1, AO2 = 2)   *(3 marks)*

(c) Name and describe one stage in Kohlberg's theory of the development of gender concept. Give an example of how you would recognise this stage from what a child might say.

   (AO1 = 3, AO2 = 2)   *(5 marks)*

(d) Describe and discuss the social learning theory explanation of the acquisition of gender concept. Refer to at least one study of gender in your answer.

   (AO1 = 5, AO2 = 5)   *(10 marks)*

Total AO1 marks = 11   Total AO2 marks = 9   Total = 20 marks

Questions, answers and comments

Question 2

(a) What is an androgen?

   (AO1 = 2)   *(2 marks)*

(b) Give an example of an atypical sex chromosome arrangement and describe how it might affect either a person's social behaviour or cognitive ability.

   (AO1 = 2, AO2 = 1)   *(3 marks)*

(c) 'I am going to have my hair cut short,' says Mel, aged six years. 'That will make you a boy,' says Beverley, aged three years. 'No, it won't. You don't change just because you have your hair cut,' replies Mel.

   With reference to Kohlberg's cognitive developmental theory of gender, explain what the girls' conversation suggests about their understanding of gender.

   (AO1 = 3, AO2 = 2)   *(5 marks)*

(d) Discuss one similarity and one difference between social learning theory and Freud's psychoanalytic theory of gender.

   (AO1 = 4, AO2 = 6)   *(10 marks)*

Total AO1 marks = 11   Total AO2 marks = 9   Total = 20 marks

Answer to 2 (a)

An androgen is a sex hormone which is found in men and women.

Comment

This answer receives both marks. They have specified that it is a hormone and have also indicated its more specific purpose. Had they only said hormone, they would have received one mark.

Sample questions, answers and comments

4

Answer to 2 (b)

Some girls are born with only one X chromosome on chromosome 23 instead of two, XX. This is called Turner's syndrome. When these girls grow up, their cognitive abilities are different from normal girls. They have much better verbal skills than the average girl, but they are worse than average at arithmetic and visual memory. They can also find it difficult to get on at school and with their peers.

Comment

This answer receives three marks. They have correctly identified an atypical sex chromosome pattern. If the candidate had stated Turner's syndrome without explaining it, this would also have attracted a mark. They have correctly identified an area of difference – cognitive skills. They obtain two marks because they have compared the performance of girls with this syndrome with other girls. The reference to social skills is also appropriate, but not necessary since the question says 'either/or'.

Answer to 2 (c)

Mel has acquired gender stability. This means that she knows that she is a girl and that how long your hair is or whether you wear trousers doesn't make you into someone else. This is shown when she says that she won't change into a boy when she gets her hair cut. Beverley has acquired her gender identity because she knows about boys and girls and she knows that Mel is a girl. She has not yet got gender stability because she thinks that being a boy or a girl depends upon appearance and that when appearance changes, so do you. This is why she says that Mel will change into a boy.

Comment

This answer attracts all five marks. The candidate has correctly identified the terms gender stability and gender identity. They have explained what these terms mean and then related them accurately to the stimulus material. Often candidates can lose the application marks by not expanding enough on the stimulus material. In order to receive full application marks, detail is required. The question specified Kohlberg's theory, and therefore it is important that his terminology is used.

Answer to 2 (d)

One similarity between social learning theory and psychoanalytic theory is that they both talk about identification. Social learning theorists believe that children develop their gender identity by identifying with role models. These role models can be anybody, but for young children these are usually their parents. Psychoanalytic theory also believes in identification and that this happens at around five years of age in the Oedipal complex for boys and Electra complex for girls. During the Oedipal complex, boys are in love with their mothers, but are jealous of their father. They also think that their father will castrate them. In order to protect himself from castration, the boy will identify with his father and become like him.

One difference is that gender identity can be acquired from anyone if you believe in social learning theory. If you believe in the psychoanalytic theory, you can only acquire it from your same-sex parent. Social learning theory believes that people will identify and imitate any behaviour which they think is appropriate for them and is rewarding. This means that gender can be learned from watching television. Williams did a study in Canada where a town was getting television for the first time. He compared the attitudes of children in this town with the attitudes of children in towns which already had television. Two years later, he tested their attitudes again and found that the children who now had television had more sex-stereotyped views than before. This shows that people learn from other places than their parents. Psychoanalytic theory believes that it is only parents who influence gender identity, in fact only your same-sex parents. This means that if a boy is brought up without his father he will not develop a masculine identity because he does not have a father to identify with. Freud believed that if a boy grew up without a father, he would become a homosexual. There is no evidence for this.

Comment

This is a fair attempt at the question. The candidate clearly identifies a similarity and a difference. Although they have given identification as a similarity, they have not explained what this term means. There is some good expansion in relation to the psychoanalytic theory, though it is equated solely with Freud rather than as an approach which others also adopt. More is needed in relation to social learning theory. They have only stated that SLT believes in identification, but not explained how the process works. Although they have described the similarity, there is no real evidence of discussion. They could have discussed the appropriateness of models for SLT, whereas for psychoanalytic theory the only criterion is the same-sex parent.

The response to the difference is better because they have correctly identified a difference and expanded on it. There was no requirement to introduce research, but they have tied the Williams study appropriately into the explanation. There is also an attempt at discussion, but it has not been developed sufficiently.

Of the ten marks available, the candidate would receive seven marks. One mark was lost from lack of explanation of the term identification, and two of the available discussion marks were not awarded.

Total marks for this question: AO1 = 10 marks, AO2 = 7 marks.

4 Further reading

Introductory texts

Banyard, P. & Grayson, A. (1996), *Introducing Psychological Research*, Basingstoke and London, Macmillan

Bernstein, D., Clarke-Stewart, A., Penner, L., Roy, E. & Wickens, C. (2000), *Psychology*, 5th edition, Boston, Houghton Mifflin Company

Gross, R.D. (1990) *Key Studies in Psychology*, 2nd edition, London, Hodder & Stoughton

Gross, R.D. (1996) *Psychology: The Science of Mind and Behaviour*, 3rd edition, London, Hodder & Stoughton

Gross, R., McIlveen, R., Coolican, H., Clamp, A. & Russell, J. (2000), *Psychology: A New Introduction for A Level*, London, Hodder & Stoughton

Taylor, I. (ed.) (1999) *Active Psychology*, Harlow, Pearson Educational Limited

Specialist sources

Archer, J. & Lloyd, B. (1985), *Sex and Gender*, New York, Cambridge University Press

Bee, H. (1997), *The Developing Child*, 8th edition, New York, HarperCollins

Bem, S.L. (1993), *The Lenses of Gender*, London, Yale University Press

Burr, V. (1998), *Gender and Social Psychology*, London, Routledge

Frosh, S. (1989), *Psychoanalysis and Psychology* (Chapter 4), Basingstoke and London, Macmillan

Maccoby, E.E. & Jacklin, C.N. (1974), *Psychology of Sex Difference*, Stanford, California, Stanford University Press

McIlveen, R. & Gross, R. (1997), *Developmental Psychology*, London, Hodder & Stoughton

Turner, P. (1995), *Sex, Gender and Identity*, Leicester, BPS Books

Vasta, R., Haith, M. & Miller, S. (1995) *Child Psychology: The Modern Science*, 2nd edition, Chichester, John Wiley & Sons

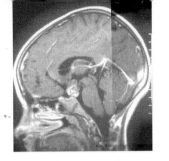

5

Attitudes

Introduction

An **attitude** cannot be directly seen or measured; this is in comparison to many phenomena in the sciences of biology or chemistry. As a consequence, social psychologists have developed many definitions and different approaches to understanding and a range of measurements of attitudes. The term *attitude* is used to represent quite complex mental processes. Attitudes are important in social psychology, since in virtually all aspects of our social lives we continually seek to discover other people's attitudes, tell others of our views, and try to change another person's opinions. Attitudes are also regarded as an important influence on our behaviour. Petty & Cacioppo (1986) define attitudes as:

'general evaluations people make about themselves, others, objects or issues'

and go on to say:

'attitudes have a past, present and future; they were developed from past experience, they guide our current behaviour, and can direct our development in the future.'

Reflective Activity

Think about one person and one issue that you feel strongly in favour of or positive about. Then think of one person and one issue that you feel strongly against or negative about.

Write down:

- *How you think each of your attitudes came about.*

- *How many other people or issues are affected by each of these positive and negative attitudes.*

- *What specific effects each attitude has on your behaviour.*

- *What would cause you to change your attitude to its opposite (that is, change the positive to negative and vice versa).*

From doing this activity you might have referred to past experience, and how your behaviour may be affected by seeking out those things you like and avoiding those you dislike. From this, we learn that attitudes formed from past experiences serve a function and guide our behaviour.

Function and measurement of attitudes

Structure and function of attitudes

The **structural approach** regards attitudes as an evaluation (positive or negative) of an attitude object (person or issue). An attitude may be broken down into three components: *cognitive*, *affective* and *conative*:

- The cognitive component is what the person knows, believes or perceives about the attitude object (person or issue).

- The affective component is how the person evaluates the attitude object: good/bad, like/dislike, etc.

- The conative component is about how we intend to behave towards the person or issue.

This is represented in Figure 5.1 below.

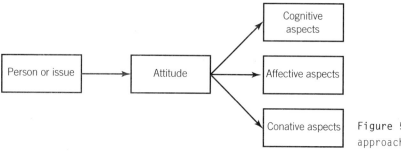

Figure 5.1: The structural approach to attitudes

Practical Activity

Refer back to the activity on page 121 and take the issue you feel strongly in favour of. Write down the cognitive, affective and conative aspects in the form shown in Figure 5.1. Repeat the exercise for the activity that you feel strongly against or negative about.

With the **functional approach to attitudes**, Katz (1960) suggests that the well-being of an individual is promoted through attitudes serving four functions. These functions are as follows:

- *Adaptive* (or utilitarian): to enable a person to achieve a desired goal or avoid undesirable things.

- *Knowledge:* to help structure and organise our social world, thus making the world more familiar and predictable.

- *Ego-expressive* (or self-expressive): to let other people know our opinions and views. As social beings, we need to communicate with others.

- *Ego-defensive:* to protect a person from themselves or other people. This function clearly relates to the psychoanalytic perspective of Freud (see Chapter 1).

The basic idea behind the functional approach is that attitudes help a person to mediate between their own inner needs (self-expression, defence) and the outside world (social and information).

Study

Aim *Martin (1987) conducted an experiment with the aim of investigating how children remembered gender behaviour.*

Method *Children were shown videos of people who behaved in either a gender stereotypical way or in a non-stereotypical way. The children were asked to recall behaviours of both types.*

Results *It was found that children tended to distort their memories to fit in with the stereotypic attitudes of the male or female gender role.*

Conclusions *These results were used to argue that gender stereotypes help the child understand masculine and feminine in a simple way, thus demonstrating the* knowledge *function of attitudes.*

Evaluative Comment

The structural and functional approaches to understanding attitudes are like two sides of the same coin. Neither approach on its own provides a full picture. Which approach you focus on depends upon what interest you have in attitudes. For example, much of the measurement of attitudes (see page 124) has focused on the affective component of the structural approach. This is because it is simple to measure, gives a good summary of an attitude and is often a good predictor of behaviour. By contrast, the functional approach may be important if you are interested in trying to change attitudes. To change a person's attitude, the approach should match the function; for example, an attitude serving a knowledge function is most likely to be changed by showing the person new information (i.e. changing their knowledge).

Reflective Activity

Look back at the notes you made for the activity on page 121. Take the issue or person that you felt strongly in favour of and think about your attitude in relation to each of the four functions described earlier. Try to identify the adaptive, knowledge, ego-expressive and ego-defensive aspects of this attitude. You may not find evidence of each of the four functions, but you may discover two or three. If so, this means that one attitude may serve a number of functions for you.

Cross-cultural research on attitudes has shown that quite general differences between cultures may have specific consequences for changing people's attitudes. For example, Hofstede (1980) studied over 40 countries around the world and tried to locate each one on an 'individualism–collectivism' dimension. A country showing 'individualism' reflects individuals who prize personal choice and achievement. By contrast, a country showing 'collectivism' reflects individuals who value group harmony and collective achievement. Hofstede found Americans (living in the USA) to show individualism and people in Asian countries to show collectivism.

Study

Aim *Han & Shavitt (1993) conducted a study aimed at determining whether advertisements in different countries appealed to individualism or collectivism.*

Method *A range of different advertisements shown in America and Korea were analysed for content and what the people were portrayed doing.*

Results *From analysis of American advertisements, they found that personal success and individualism were promoted; by contrast, Korean advertisements had strong themes of collective or group harmony.*

Conclusions *The research showed that Americans were more likely to be influenced by an advertisement promoting personal achievement rather than an advertisement promoting group harmony.*

Evaluative Comment

Consider the findings by Hofstede (1980) that Western cultures are more individualistic and Eastern cultures more collective minded. The problem here is that this very much accords with the stereotypes that we, as Westerners, hold about Americans and Koreans. It is very difficult in cross-cultural research to separate stereotypes of peoples and/or countries from what the actual attitudes of individuals in any one country are. When devising questionnaires to give to people of different cultures, it is important that the psychologist does not inadvertently make people who answer it focus on the ego-defensive function of attitudes. People then might not tell you their real attitudes because they need to protect themselves.

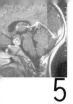

5

Measuring attitudes

Attitudes are subjective; they are not directly observable and have to be inferred from what people do or say. Sometimes psychologists can make **direct measures of attitudes** from physiological recordings. For example, Petty & Cacioppo (1986) claim that attitudes can be measured by recording the activity of facial muscles. They measured the electrical activity of muscles of the mouth and eyes showing that happiness or sadness was associated with muscle activity which could not be detected by the naked eye. Such claims have not gone without criticism and to take such measures requires highly controlled conditions, expertise at measurement and willing participants!

Your facial reaction to another person or attitude object may reveal your own attitude without you knowing it

Practical Activity

Facial expression is often a guide to one person's attitude towards another. Conduct an observational study by sitting in a public area, such as a park or café, and observe how people's facial expressions change when they greet each other. Do people always smile, thus indicating a positive attitude to the other person? Can you detect any facial behaviour which might lead you to infer that one person may not like another? If so, note down the expressions that lead you to make this inference.

Social psychologists can use both **indirect** and **direct measures of attitudes**. Indirect measures fall into two basic groupings: *projective techniques* and *physiological measures*. Direct measures include *self-reports* (asking people their views) and *direct observations* of actual behaviour.

Indirect measures

Projective techniques include the **Rorschach Inkblot Test** and Thematic Apperception Test (TAT) (Murray, 1938). Both stem from a Freudian psychoanalytic approach and ask people to offer interpretations of ambiguous figures. Figure 5.2 shows the type of item that would be included in the TAT. Here, a person would be shown the picture and then asked to write a short story about what they think might be going on in the picture. You may wish to try this yourself and compare your story with your colleagues.

The assumption with this measure of attitudes is that the person will 'project' his or her views, opinions or attitudes into the ambiguous situation, thus revealing the attitudes the person holds.

Figure 5.2: The kind of picture used in the Thematic Apperception Test (TAT). You are asked to make up a short story about what you think may be going on in the picture (Adapted from Murray, 1938)

Practical Activity

Create your own ink blots by folding a piece of paper in two, opening it up and spotting some ink along the fold. Then fold the paper together again. You may use black ink only or black and red ink. Ask a number of different people what they 'see' in the ink blot. Can you infer any attitudes the person might hold from the interpretations of the ink blot they give?

Evaluative Comment

The use of these types of projective technique requires a lot of training as well as skill at interpreting the responses. The main problem with this type of indirect approach to measuring attitudes is that inter-pretation bias may be present and render the technique unreliable. Interpretation bias is where the interpretation given by the psychologist reflects his or her own attitudes or beliefs and is, as a consequence, not objective. Also, different psychologists may give different interpretations, and there is no objective way of saying which is right and which is wrong.

An indirect method known as the *bogus pipeline* has been used when attempting to measure people's attitudes towards sensitive issues such as racial **prejudice**. Here, participants are led to believe that their physiological reactions (such as heart-rate) are being measured (Quigly-Fernandez & Tedeschi, 1978). The idea is that participants fear that dishonest attitudes will be detected through the physiological measures and as a result are more likely to reveal what their actual views are.

A polygraph measures many types of physiological response, such as **galvanic skin response** (GSR), muscle activity (EMG), brain activity (EEG) and is regularly used in the USA as a 'lie detector'. The GSR is a measure of arousal of the autonomic nervous system (the autonomic nervous system is that part of the nervous system that controls blood vessels, body temperature and glands). The underlying assumption is that a GSR will occur when a person is lying or deliberately trying to conceal their real attitude. This measure has many critics who claim, for example, that the response may be caused as much by surprise as fear of telling an untruth.

5

Direct measures

Direct measures of attitudes are self-report approaches and include Likert scales, the **semantic differential** technique of Osgood *et al.* (1957) and Thurstone's (1931) equal interval scale. Attitude scales measure both the direction of an attitude (agree–disagree) and the strength with which the attitude is held (strongly disagree, disagree, etc.). The Likert scale is the most commonly and widely used; here, a series of attitude statements is given to people and they are asked to indicate the extent to which they agree or disagree with each statement. For example, a **Likert scale** to measure attitudes towards asking students to pay for their university education might be as shown in Figure 5.3.

Item					
All students should make a financial contribution to their education	Strongly agree	Agree	Undecided	Disagree	Strongly disagree
Students should spend less on alcohol and more on books	Strongly agree	Agree	Undecided	Disagree	Strongly disagree
Students whose parents are well-off should pay more for their education than those with less well-off parents	Strongly agree	Agree	Undecided	Disagree	Strongly disagree

Figure 5.3: An example of a Likert scale

In constructing a Likert scale, it is important to balance positively and negatively worded statements to avoid *response bias*. This is where a person responds in the same way (for example, 'agree') to all questions. Ensuring that there is a mix of statements means that the respondent has to think about each answer he or she gives to each one.

Practical Activity

Create your own Likert scale by doing the following:

- *Decide upon the attitude topic.*

- *Create five positively worded statements and five negatively worded statements related to this topic.*

- *Use a five-point scale from 'strongly agree' to 'strongly disagree' as shown in Figure 5.3.*

- *Give the questionnaire to 10 people to complete. Convert responses to each statement into a numerical value as follows:*
  Positive statements: strongly agree = 5, agree = 4, undecided = 3, disagree = 2, strongly disagree = 1
  Negative statements: score the other way round.
- *Add up a person's score to the ten statements.*

- *A high score indicates a favourable attitude, a low score an unfavourable attitude to your topic.*

The semantic differential technique of Osgood *et al.* (1957) asks a person to rate an issue or topic on a standard set of bipolar dimensions, each represented by a seven-point scale. For example, people might be asked to consider what they think about cars as a means of transport and asked to indicate their opinion in relation to the following bipolar adjectives:

Good	+3	+2	+1	0	−1	−2	−3	Bad
Valuable	+3	+2	+1	0	−1	−2	−3	Worthless
Clean	+3	+2	+1	0	−1	−2	−3	Dirty
Friendly	+3	+2	+1	0	−1	−2	−3	Unfriendly

The semantic differential technique reveals three basic dimensions of attitudes: *evaluation*, *potency* and *activity*.

- Evaluation is concerned with whether a person thinks positively or negatively about the attitude topic.

- Potency is concerned with how powerful the topic is for the person.

- Activity is concerned with whether the topic is seen as active or passive.

The evaluation dimension has been most used by social psychologists as a measure of a person's attitude, because this dimension reflects the affective, or judgemental, aspect of an attitude.

Evaluative Comment

The advantage of indirect measures of attitudes is that it is often not obvious to the person responding what is being measured. They are therefore less likely to try to misrepresent their views. The disadvantage is that different researchers may offer different interpretations, since there is no objective method to determine who is right and who is wrong. By contrast, the advantage of the direct approach is that a person's view or attitude is being explicitly and clearly asked about. However, the disadvantage is that, since the person knows this, they may not present a true picture of their attitude because, for example, they may want to appear in a socially desirable light. This is a form of what psychologists call **response bias in attitude measurement**.

Attitudes and behaviour

The attitude you hold may not always predict how you will actually behave

Gordon Allport (1935), a famous psychologist, stated that 'attitudes determine for each individual what he (or she) will do'. Nearly 70 years later, social psychologists are still very interested in the relationship between attitudes and behaviour. If psychologists could discover the conditions under which attitudes determine behaviour, then our social world would become a more predictable place.

Attitudes as predictors of behaviour

A famous study by La Piere (1934) provided evidence that attitudes do not always act as a good predictor of behaviour.

Study

Aim *La Piere (1934) devised a study aimed at investigating differences between what people say they will do and what they actually do in a given situation.*

Method *La Piere travelled around America with a Chinese couple and recorded how they were treated at hotels and restaurants. On only one occasion were they treated inhospitably. Six months later, La Piere sent a letter to all the places he had visited, asking them if they would accept Chinese clientele.*

Results *Over 90 per cent of replies were negative: 92 per cent of restaurants and 90 per cent of hotels said that they would refuse Chinese clientele.*

Conclusions *The study demonstrated an enormous difference between what people say they would do and what they actually do.*

Why should there be such inconsistency between attitudes and behaviour in the La Piere study? In this study, *general* attitudes towards Chinese people are being compared to attitudes towards a *specific* Chinese couple. Hence, like is not being compared with like. To do so, La Piere should have made both measures specific to one Chinese couple by, for example, sending a picture of the couple with the letter to the hotels and restaurants.

Principal of consistency

One of the underlying assumptions about the link between attitudes and behaviour is that of *consistency*. This means that we often or usually expect the behaviour of a person to be consistent with the attitudes that they hold. For example, supposing the Government held a referendum on whether Britain should adopt the Euro as common currency. You find out that your friend voted for the Euro; from this, you might assume that your friend has a positive attitude to a common European currency and wants greater integration for Britain in Europe. But there are other reasons why your friend might vote in this way that are not related to their attitude; for example, your friend might want to vote the same way as his/her parents, or might support the present Government no matter what. As you can see, it is not easy or obvious to establish a *behaviour consistency link* between an attitude and a person's behaviour.

The **principle of consistency** reflects the idea that people are rational and attempt to behave rationally at all times. Whilst this principle may be a sound one, it is clear that people do not always follow it, sometimes behaving in seemingly quite illogical ways; for example, smoking cigarettes and knowing that smoking causes lung cancer and heart disease.

Two questions arise with respect to the attitude–behaviour link: *when* and *how* do attitudes influence behaviour? Three factors have been investigated concerning when attitudes determine behaviour; these are:

- the social situation
- attitude strength
- personality factors.

De Bono & Snyder (1995) demonstrated that people tend to prefer social situations where they can behave in ways consistent with their attitudes. It has also been found that in situations where there are time pressures, people have to act fast, and attitudes serve as a quick guide to how to behave. Most social situations in which you find yourself have social norms (unwritten rules of behaviour). Where a person's attitude differs from the social norm, the person is less likely to engage in attitude-consistent behaviour.

Reflective Activity

Think of a number of different social situations that you regularly find yourself in, for example, the coffee bar at college, with a group of friends at your house, in a group discussion in your psychology class, with a group of people you do not know very well. Think about your own attitudes towards fox hunting or wearing clothes made from animals (for example, fur coats). In each of the social situations, would you feel able to speak your mind? Would you agree to go on a march to support or demonstrate against (depending on your attitude) fox hunting? From this analysis, identify where differences and inconsistencies between your attitude and behaviour exist.

The *strength* with which an attitude is held is often a good predictor of behaviour. The strength of an attitude has been taken to mean four things:

*   intensity
*   importance
*   knowledge
*   accessibility.

Importance refers to how significant the attitude is for the person and relates to self-interest, social identification and value (Boninger *et al.*, 1995). If an attitude has high self-interest for a person (i.e. it is held by a group the person is a member of or would like to be a member of, and is related to a person's values), it is going to be extremely important. As a consequence, the attitude will have a very strong influence upon a person's behaviour. By contrast, an attitude will not be important to a person if it does not relate in some way to their life.

The *knowledge* aspect of attitude strength covers how much a person knows about the attitude object; people are generally more knowledgeable about topics that interest them and are likely to hold strong attitudes (positive or negative) as a consequence. Attitudes based on direct experience are more strongly held and influence behaviour more than attitudes formed indirectly (for example, through hear-say, reading or watching television).

Attitude *accessibility* refers to how easily the attitude you hold comes to mind. If the attitude comes to mind quickly and you do not have to think very much about your view, then it is more likely that the attitude will determine behaviour. Generally, the stronger the attitude held, the more easily it comes to mind.

Practical Activity

Interview a friend and find something about which they hold a strong attitude and something about which they hold a weak attitude.

For each of these, establish:

*   *how knowledgeable your friend is about each attitude topic*
*   *the degree of self-interest, social identification and value*

● *the attitude-consistent or -inconsistent behaviours that your friend engages in with respect to each attitude. Do this by creating a list of behaviours under each heading (consistent or inconsistent). Look at your findings and see if your friend behaves more consistently with the strongly held attitude and more inconsistently with the weakly held attitude.*

Attitudes: behaviour and personality

A personality factor found to be related to attitudes and behaviour is called the **self-monitor** (Snyder, 1979). The high self-monitor is a person who is very aware of the demands of the social situation they may be in. In contrast, the low self-monitor is a person who is not so influenced by the social situation. This means that the low self-monitor is more likely to exhibit attitude–behaviour consistency, whilst the high self-monitor will show a poor relationship between attitudes held and actual behaviour. This is because the high self-monitor will conform more to the norms or demands of the situation and less to the attitudes held. Of course, at times, the demands of the social situation and attitudes held will be the same.

How attitudes affect behaviour

We have looked at some aspects of attitude–behaviour consistency, and now turn to the question of *how* attitudes affect behaviour. This has been shown to depend on whether we have time to think and reason about what we should do, or whether we have to act quickly and immediately. When we have little time to think, attitudes influence behaviour automatically. When we think carefully about our attitudes and consider what to do, the theory of Ajzen & Fishbein (1980) best explains how attitudes determine behaviour. This is known as the **theory of reasoned action**.

This theory says that our intentions to behave result from a consideration of three factors:

● *attitudes*: the person's attitudes towards the actual behaviour under consideration

● *subjective norms*: how the person believes others will evaluate the behaviour

● *behavioural control*: the extent to which the person believes he or she is able to behave in that way – is it easy or hard?

When a person holds strong attitudes, believes that others will evaluate the behaviour positively and thinks that it is within their control to behave in that way, they will exhibit very strong intentions to behave in a certain way, enabling a good prediction of behaviour to be made. This is summarised in Figure 5.4.

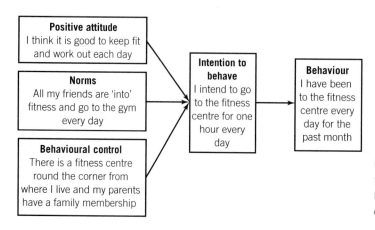

Figure 5.4: The theory of reasoned action by Ajzen and Fishbein (1980) using the example of keeping fit

Study

Aim *Madden et al. (1992) conducted a study aimed at determining how a person's perception of control over different behaviours related to intentions and actual action.*

Method *Participants were asked to rate how much they could control behaviours such as taking vitamin pills (easy to control) and getting a good night's sleep (hard to control).*

Results *Behaviours seen to be easy to control strongly predicted intentions and actual actions, whilst behaviours perceived as hard to control did not predict intentions and actual behaviour very well.*

Conclusions *The study demonstrated the importance of perceived behavioural control as one factor in predicting behaviour.*

Evaluative Comment

Social psychologists have assumed that attitudes determine behaviour. However, early research by La Piere (1934) demonstrated that this may not be so. Theory and research have attempted to understand both when and how attitudes determine behaviour and when they do not. People do seem to show consistency between attitudes and behaviour when attitudes are strongly held, are acquired through direct experience, are important for the individual and readily come to mind. However, some people, because of their personality, will continually show inconsistency between attitudes and behaviours. Such people are called high self-monitors and behave in a way consistent with the social norms of a social situation or behave in a manner that they think will be viewed favourably by the other people in the social group. Such people may be seen as 'social chameleons', changing their behaviour from one social situation to another. From this, it can clearly be seen that the link between attitudes and behaviour is not a simple one, as early social psychologists such as Allport thought.

Attitude change

In our everyday lives, we are exposed to countless attempts to change or strengthen our existing attitudes and form new attitudes. Politicians, teachers, friends and family, to name but a few, often try to persuade us round to their point of view. It is assumed that if our attitudes can be changed, then there will be an effect on our behaviour. Underlying this assumption is the *principle of cognitive consistency*.

Many people try to influence your attitude to make you buy their product

People try to maintain consistency between:

- attitudes, intentions and behaviour
- beliefs, values and attitudes
- a range of related, but different attitudes.

Many philosophers and psychologists regard consistency as an essential element of what it is to be a rational human being.

Reflective Activity

Think about your general attitudes towards leading a healthy lifestyle. Identify two or three specific attitudes, for example, towards eating meat, smoking, drinking alcohol, exercise. For each of these, identify your own attitude – positive or negative – and the strength with which you hold the attitude. Now identify specific behaviours in relation to each of these attitudes. For each specific attitude, identify, using two lists, your behaviours which are consistent *and* inconsistent *with the attitude you hold. You should find that your more strongly held attitudes result in less inconsistent and more consistent behaviours.*

Cognitive consistency and attitude change

Traditional approaches (based on theory and research by social psychologists in the 1950s and 1960s) emphasised the role of *cognition* and developed a number of theories known as *cognitive consistency theories*. These theories addressed both how attitudes are organised and how they may change. These theories are those of **balance** (Heider, 1946), **congruity** (Osgood & Tannenbaum, 1955) and **cognitive dissonance** (Festinger, 1957). By far the most influential has been that of cognitive dissonance.

Balance theory

This considers the relationship between three components: a person (P), another person (O) and an attitude object (X). The relationship – positive or negative, likes or dislikes – between P and O, P and X, and O and X is assessed. This results in eight different combinations, four of which are balanced, or consistent, and four of which are unbalanced, or inconsistent. As a general rule, a combination is balanced if there is an odd number of positive relationships, as the examples in Figure 5.5 show.

Balanced combinations

Peter likes poetry
Olivia likes poetry
Peter likes Olivia

Peter likes pop music
Olivia dislikes pop music
Peter dislikes Olivia

Unbalanced combinations

Peter dislikes foxhunting
Olivia likes foxhunting
Peter likes Olivia

Peter dislikes eating meat
Olivia dislikes eating meat
Peter dislikes Olivia

Figure 5.5: Examples of balanced and unbalanced combinations of attitudes

The theory of balance assumes that people we associate with prefer to agree with each other, and that other people will like what we like. This approach predicts that attitude change will occur when there is an unbalanced combination and there will be a change towards a balanced combination. For example, in the foxhunting example in Figure 5.5, balance can be achieved by Peter changing his attitude towards either foxhunting (from negative to positive) or Olivia changing hers (from positive to negative). A third option is for Peter to attempt to change Olivia's attitude to foxhunting. Any one of these changes will result in a balanced situation.

Practical Activity

Another balanced combination is:

and two unbalanced combinations are:

Create an example of each. Make the examples different to those given in Figure 5.5.

For the two unbalanced combinations, identify how attitude change may take place to achieve balance.

Try to relate these examples to yourself, with you as P and O as a friend of yours. Which attitude would be the easiest to change and why?

Congruity

According to Osgood & Tannenbaum (1955), congruity extends the idea of balance and is related to the direction of attitude change. The principle of congruity states that a person will change their attitude in a way which will reduce inconsistency.

Look, for example, at 'John' and his attitude to the prime minister and government support for the needy (see Figure 5.6). A state of congruity exists when the prime minister is positive about state support for the needy. However, if the prime minister were to disagree with the idea that the state should support those in need, incongruity or inconsistency would exist. To achieve congruity here, John would have to change his attitude to the prime minister or take the same view as the prime minister to state support for the needy. Congruity goes on to give a rating of between one and three for each of the three attitudes involved and predicts that the weakest-held attitude (represented by a one) is most likely to change. This is shown in Figure 5.7. In this state of incongruity, John is most likely to change his attitude to the prime minister, since John is very strongly of the view that the state should support the needy.

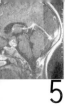
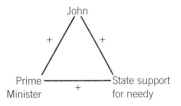

Figure 5.6: An example of consistency in the congruity model of Osgood & Tannenbaum (1955)

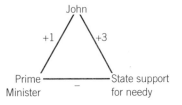

Figure 5.7: State of incongruity showing strength of attitudes. Note that the weakest-held attitude (John's attitude to the prime minister) is most likely to change

Cognitive dissonance and attitude change

By far the most widely researched theory of cognitive consistency is Festinger's (1957) theory of cognitive dissonance. Dissonance is defined by Festinger as:

'a negative drive state which occurs when an individual holds two cognitions (ideas, beliefs, attitudes) which are psychologically inconsistent.'

Basically, cognitive dissonance is experienced as an uncomfortable state of tension or anxiety which a person wishes to change towards a more comfortable, less tense feeling. Cognitive dissonance motivates people to change in some way, with the most likely change being that of the attitudes held.

Study

AIM *Festinger & Carlsmith's (1959) classic study of cognitive dissonance aimed to examine how attitudes may change when a person behaves in a way they cannot justify to themselves. This is called a 'forced-compliance' type of experiment.*

METHOD *In this study, participants were required to perform a boring and meaningless task: placing pegs in holes on a pegboard. Participants were paid either $1 or $20 to tell a new participant that the task was interesting and enjoyable. Festinger assumed that a dissonant situation had been set up in the $1 situation; insufficient reward or justification existed for the participant who had done the boring task to tell somebody else that it was interesting. Festinger predicted that where there is insufficient justification for the behaviour, the discrepant attitude would change.*

RESULTS *The results are shown in Figure 5.8. The control group (who were asked not to mislead the next person) and participants paid $20 to do the task both rating it as boring. By contrast, the participants paid $1 thought the task was more interesting.*

CONCLUSIONS *The study demonstrates that people will change their attitude if they behave in ways opposite to the attitude.*

Cooper & Fazio (1984) reviewed twenty years of research on dissonance and, from this review, proposed that four conditions were necessary for dissonance to occur:

● The person must be aware that the inconsistency between attitude and behaviour has negative consequences.

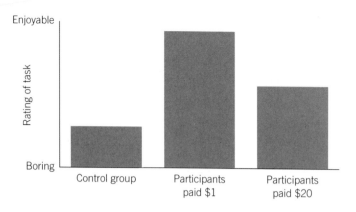

Figure 5.8: Results of the forced-compliance experiment of Festinger & Carlsmith (1959). Participants paid the least rated the boring task as interesting, thus demonstrating attitude change as a result of cognitive dissonance. (Adapted from Festinger & Carlsmith, 1959)

- The person must take personal responsibility for the behaviour.

- Physiological arousal (tension, anxiety, etc.) must be experienced by the person.

- The person must think that the dissonance or discomfort is down to the inconsistency between attitude and behaviour.

Figure 5.9 uses the example of smoking cigarettes to demonstrate when dissonance will and will not arise on the basis of the four conditions proposed by Cooper & Fazio (1984).

Condition	Dissonance present	Dissonance absent
(a) Attitude – behaviour inconsistency has negative consequences	Smoking causes lung cancer	Research has not proved definitely that smoking causes lung cancer
(b) Person takes responsibility for the behaviour	It is my decision to smoke	I am addicted to smoking, I can't do anything about it
(c) Physiological arousal	I feel uncomfortable and anxious about my health because I smoke	Denial – avoiding thinking about the consequences of smoking
(d) Discomfort attributed to attitude–behaviour inconsistency	I am concerned about the fact that I smoke	I feel discomfort because other people are always hassling me about smoking

Figure 5.9: Conditions for dissonance to occur and not to occur using the example of smoking cigarettes

Evaluative Comment

Early research on cognitive dissonance did not take account of specific conditions under which dissonance does and does not occur. The researchers assumed that any attitude–behaviour inconsistency was likely to create cognitive dissonance for the person. This early research also assumed that the way to reduce dissonance was to change attitudes. Festinger recognised this and subsequent research has demonstrated that people employ a range of ways to deal with dissonance. For example, Steele et al. (1981) showed that people may reduce dissonance through the use of alcohol. A more constructive approach is for people to assure themselves of their self-identity (Tesser & Cornell, 1991). Hence, when people experience dissonance, the attitude may not always change to come in line with the behaviour; the person may decide not to behave in that way in the future.

5

Self-perception theory (Bem, 1967) offers an alternative explanation to Festinger's theory of cognitive dissonance. Self-perception theory states that a person *forms* their attitudes on the basis of observing their own behaviour. Bem's famous example to highlight this is 'since I eat brown bread, I must like brown bread'. This approach seems quite good when looking at *attitude formation* and how attitudes are formed when we encounter new situations or experiences; it is less useful when applied to attitude change and more established attitudes that people hold.

Persuasive communication

Persuasive communication is an approach to attitude change based on the question 'who says what to whom with what effect?' That is, an understanding of the source of the communication ('who says'), the content and the nature of the message (what) and the target person or group of people receiving the message (to whom) is required. Early research focused heavily on these three aspects and yielded findings that remain relevant today (Hovland *et al.*, 1953). This approach, with some of the key factors or variables identified as important, is given in Figure 5.10.

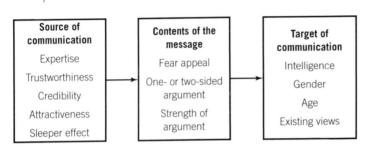

Figure 5.10: The persuasive communication approach to attitude change with key factors, or variables, important for change

With respect to the source of the communication, it has been found that experts, people regarded as trustworthy, people seen as credible and attractive people are more likely to persuade another to change their attitude. The *sleeper effect* is where the target person will believe good arguments from a non-credible or non-expert or unattractive source after a delay (sleeping on it) rather than immediately. The content of the message is more likely to cause attitude change when it arouses fear in us (but not too much!) and tells us what to do. A one-sided argument is more likely to be effective when the person already leans towards a position. A two-sided argument is more effective with an intelligent audience (Hovland *et al.*, 1953). The target of the communication is also an important factor; for example, older people are more difficult to persuade to change their attitudes than younger (18- to 25-year-old) people. Strongly held views or attitudes of the target person are more difficult to change than weakly held views.

Study

AIM *Hovland & Weiss (1952) investigated, in a classic study, the sleeper effect.*

METHOD *Students were asked to read a communication containing strong arguments for the position being put forward. Half the students were told the communication was from a highly credible source (professor), and the other half that the communication was from a low-credibility source (general member of the public). The researchers measured attitude change before the communication was given to the students, immediately after giving the communication and four weeks later.*

RESULTS *As shown in Figure 5.11, a high-credibility source had a strong, immediate effect on attitude change. A low-credibility source only had a small effect immediately. Four weeks later, attitude to change by both groups of students was the same.*

With the low-credibility source, students seemed to dismiss the source itself, but be influenced by the arguments after four weeks. The high-credibility source students were overly influenced immediately and reduced attitude change after four weeks to be in line with the other students.

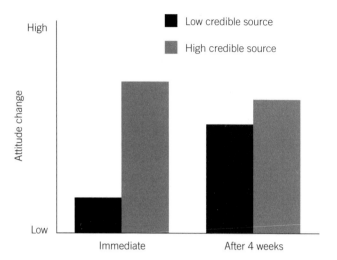

Figure 5.11: Results from the 'sleeper effect' study of Hovland & Weiss (1952). Notice that the low-credibility source does not have immediate effect on attitude change, whilst the high-credibility source does. Adapted from Hovland & Weiss (1952)

CONCLUSIONS *This demonstrates a 'sleeper' effect in that the arguments are paid more attention to than the source after a period of time.*

Dual-process models of persuasion

The early studies identified a wide range of factors and variables related to the source, message and target that may cause attitude change. However, little attention was paid to the underlying cognitive process that may be involved. More recent research has looked at how the target person processes the message and characteristics of the source. Petty *et al.* (1994) claim that people may adopt one of two strategies when presented with persuasive information, such as an advertising campaign. One way is where little attention and cognitive effort are given to the message; this is called *superficial*, or *peripheral processing*. The second way is where attention and cognitive effort are involved; this is called *systematic*, or *central processing*. These two ways of dealing with persuasive communications or messages are called the **dual-process model of persuasion**. When information is processed superficially, attitude change will depend on factors such as attractiveness of the person, status, etc. This means that little cognitive effort is made; by contrast, the systematic processing of information is characterised as a *central route* to attitude change where the person expends considerable time and effort in processing the information. This is summarised in Figure 5.12.

The **elaboration-likelihood model** is the best example of a recent approach to persuasion and attitude change that focuses on the cognitive processes that may be involved in attitude change.

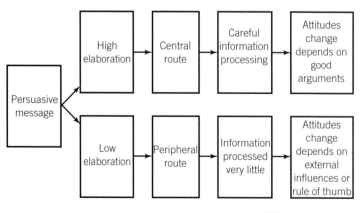

Figure 5.12: The elaboration-likelihood model of Petty *et al.* (1994) showing the two routes of processing information

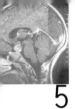

5 Study

AIM *Petty et al. (1981) conducted a study aimed at demonstrating the effects of central and peripheral routes on attitude change.*

METHOD *In this study, students were given a message about an additional examination that final year students would have to take in future. Half the students were told this change would take place next year and hence affect them (high-involvement condition). The other half were told this would not take place for a number of years and hence not affect them (low-involvement). In each of these conditions, half the students were presented with strong, convincing arguments for the change, and the other half were given weak, unconvincing arguments. The experiment thus has four experimental conditions as shown in Figure 5.13.*

High involvement, Strong arguments	**Low involvement, Strong arguments**
High involvement, Weak arguments	**Low involvement, Weak arguments**

Figure 5.13: The four experimental conditions in Petty *et al.*'s study

Students' attitudes about an extra examination were measured after the message had been given to each student.

RESULTS *The results showed that students in the high-involvement condition were more positive and accepting of the additional examination when presented with a strong rather than a weak argument. By contrast, students in the low-involvement condition did not differ much in their view to the additional examination regardless of whether they were presented with a weak or strong argument.*

CONCLUSIONS *The high-involvement condition can be regarded as using a central route to attitude change, with the consequence that students carefully considered the argument presented to them – whether weak or strong. The strong argument was influential in causing attitude change. By contrast, students in the low-involvement condition seemed to take the superficial route and did not systematically or carefully consider either argument because it did not affect them in any way.*

Practical Activity

Look through a glossy magazine or colour supplement of a newspaper and select two advertisements: one which relates to a product important in your life and one that is not important.

For each advertisement, think about how influential it might be in getting you to buy the product.

Try to reflect on whether you have thought more deeply about the product that is related to your life than the one that is not.

Do you think the one related to your life receives high elaboration and more careful processing than the one that does not?

Resisting attitude change

Social psychologists have recently attempted to define and understand the conditions under which we might resist attitude change. Three main ways have been identified:

- reactance (attitude changes in the direction opposite to that intended)

- forewarning (allows us to develop counter arguments)

- selective avoidance (avoiding information that is opposite to the attitudes we hold).

This research asserts the importance of control and choice that people exert in their lives. Not all, or even many, advertising campaigns result in people changing attitudes and/or behaviour. People still drink and drive when there are laws and powerful advertising campaigns to prevent this behaviour and change attitudes. The strategies of reactance, forewarning and selective avoidance may help us understand why this is the case. For example, anti-drink/driving campaigns greatly increase around the Christmas period. People know this and are hence forewarned, with the consequence that attempts to change attitudes might be less effective than if such campaigns were made when people are not expecting them.

Prejudice and discrimination

The terms **prejudice** and **discrimination** are often used interchangeably in everyday life; however, social psychologists make a clear distinction as follows:

- Prejudice is an unjustified or incorrect negative attitude toward an individual based solely on the individual's membership of a group.

- Discrimination is the behaviour or actions, usually negative, towards the individual or a group of people.

This definition of prejudice implies that attitudes towards an individual are always negative; however, this may not always be the case since one can also be prejudiced in favour of an individual or group. Nevertheless, most theory and research has looked at negative attitudes and behaviours, since these are often a source of conflict in society. By distinguishing between prejudice (attitudes) and discrimination (behaviour), it is assumed that a direct link exists between the two. Reread pages 128 to 130 when considering why people hold prejudicial attitudes and the link between attitudes and behaviour.

An extreme example of
prejudice and discrimination

Reflective Activity

Consider three or four social groups, for example, students, cultures different to your own, single parents, unemployed people. Try to identify your own negative and positive attitudes to each social grouping. Next, think of times when you have interacted with an individual from each group. Write down the specific occasion and try to remember your actual behaviour – what was said, your non-verbal actions (such as eye contact, body orientation, etc.).

From these reflections, write down any prejudiced attitudes that you might have. Then identify any discriminative behaviour that you might have shown to the individual for the social group you are considering.

From these reflections, identify to what extent you think you are prejudiced to each social group.

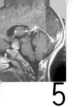

5

Categories of prejudice

We have seen that prejudice refers to negative (although it could be positive) evaluations of individuals perceived to be a member of a group. This is based on the perception that a group has certain characteristics which are then believed to be possessed by every individual in the group. In effect, a **stereotype** of the group is used on the individual. Stereotypes are usually highly simplified, gross overgeneralizations of a set of characteristics used on a person. Stereotypes are unfair and misleading because they fail to take account of individual differences between people, and fail to focus on the unique traits and characteristics of an individual, regardless of his or her membership of a group.

Prejudice, discrimination and stereotypes are usually aimed at minority groups or shown by dominant groups over subordinate groups. A minority group should not always be seen as a group in numerical minority. For example, in the southern states of the USA (Mississippi, Missouri), black African Americans outnumber white Americans. However, it is the black Americans that experience the prejudice and discrimination. In light of this, we may define a minority group as:

> 'a group whose members have significantly less power, control and influence over their lives than do members of the dominant group'. (Schaefer & Lamm, 1992)

Categories of groups that experience prejudice and discrimination range from groups that actually are in a numerical minority (such as homosexuals, Jews, Muslims in Great Britain) to groups that may be in the majority in an area or country (for example, sexism towards females, black African Americans in southern USA states). Figure 5.14 gives a number of categories of prejudice together with a brief explanation, and an example of each.

Perhaps the most prevalent and historically common form of prejudice is **racism**. In the 1800s and early part of the 1900s, native Africans and Aborigines in Australia were blatantly discriminated against – used as slaves or massacred. In the late 1900s and early this millennium, psychologists have talked about 'modern racism' (Surinetal, 1995). This type of racism is covert and subtle, and is revealed in three ways:

- denial by members of the dominant group that a minority group is discriminated against
- impatience and irritation at the continued demands made by the minority group
- resentment that minority groups may be treated favourably or with positive action.

Category of prejudice	Explanation	Examples
Racism	Negative treatment and stereotyping of races other than the dominant one in the society in question	Jews in Nazi Germany in the 1930/40s; Bullying of an Asian by white students
Sexism	Negative treatment of females by males in a particular society; Negative stereotype of men as aggressive, 'spraying testosterone everywhere'	Male view that a woman's place is in the home; 'Glass ceiling' for women trying to reach to top positions in business; Viewing all football supporters as 'mindless hooligans'
Ageism	View that older people are less able, less competent and suffer memory loss	Not employing people in their 50s and early 60s for jobs they could do
Tokenism	Is where positive action is taken towards a person belonging to a group discriminated against	The token 'female' on an all male panel; The token 'ethnic minority person' in a group
Homophobism	Prejudice shown towards homosexuals by heterosexual people	Refusing to serve a homosexual (or lesbian couple) in a public house

Figure 5.14: Categories of prejudice, with an example of each

Evaluative Comment

Categories of prejudice are socially defined rather then defined by numbers of people in the group. The use of the term 'minority group' is a little misleading because of this. Perhaps the term 'socially negatively evaluated group' would be better, although it is awkward. With prejudice and discrimination, it is important to take account of the particular social context – culture, country, etc. – that this takes place in. It is also important to remember that discriminatory behaviour may not always result from a person's prejudiced attitudes. For example, a male businessman may not employ a highly qualified woman for a job because he thinks his clients would go elsewhere if they had to deal with a woman. This is wrong on the part of the businessman, since he should, perhaps, have faith in the abilities of the person rather than the sex of the person.

Most, if not all, people hold prejudiced attitudes and act in discriminating ways at times to other people. Britain has laws to try to stop this, for example, the Race Relations Act and the Sex Discrimination Act. Pettigrew & Meerlens (1995) introduce the ideas of *subtle* and *blatant* racism since many people deny that they are directly or openly racist (blatant) but do exhibit covert or subtle racism. For example, Pettigrew and Meerlens explain subtle forms of racism as follows:

- defence of traditional values with the belief that minority groups receive undeserved rewards and attention;

- exaggeration of cultural differences between a majority and minority group (e.g. different religious groups);

- denying positive emotional responses to groups with which we do not identify and withholding of positive comments and attitudes towards minority groups.

Gaertner & Davidio (1986) regard overt or blatant prejudice to be less in evidence these days; however, they claim that racism often shows itself in situations where the social norms are not clear or publicly known. Evidence for this has come from 'bogus wrong number' telephone calls to garages with a request for help with a broken-down car. Gaertner and Davidio found people who identified themselves as a black caller received a less helpful response from the garage than if the caller identified themselves as white.

Prejudice may be *situationally specific*, which means that in one situation an individual may show prejudice and discrimination and in another situation this may not be shown. The classic study demonstrating this was Minard's (1952) research into the behaviour of miners in a mining community in the USA. Segregation and discrimination of blacks by whites existed in the town; however, below ground in the mine, this disappeared, with black and white workers showing mutual support, interdependence and collaboration.

Study

Aim *Davey (1983) conducted an experiment aimed at establishing the extent of ethnic prejudice that existed in school children.*

Method *In this experiment, children were asked to share out sweets between members of different ethnic groups shown in photographs. Five hundred children participated, and about half distributed sweets in an ethnocentric way, as shown in Figure 5.15. 'Ethnocentric' was defined as when children gave greater numbers of sweets to their own ethnic group.*

Results *As can be seen from Figure 5.15, 60 per cent of white children gave more sweets to their own white group. Such discrimination was less in evidence with West Indian or Asian children.*

| | Ethnic origin of children | | | |
Sweet allocation	White	West Indian	Asian	All
Most to own group	60%	41%	40%	50%
Same to all groups	25%	36%	26%	28%

Figure 5.15: Demonstration of ethnic prejudice amongst children. Notice that all groups allocated most sweets to themselves (Adapted from Davey, 1983)

CONCLUSIONS *All ethnic groups demonstrated in-group favouritism to some extent, thus showing prejudice in children.*

Social psychologists have been interested in understanding and explaining how prejudice and discrimination develop in the first place. It is acknowledged that prejudice only exists where individuals can be placed into social categories or social groupings. Children as young as three years of age are aware of gender and ethnicity as important social categories. Children learn very early about their gender roles, and at the ages of five or six, tend to prefer peers of the same sex as themselves.

Study

AIM *Hayden-Thompson (1987) devised an experiment aimed to investigate gender preference in young children.*

METHOD *Children were asked to 'post' photographs of their classmates into one of three boxes according to how much they liked the classmate. One box had a happy face, one a sad face and one a neutral face. Children were told to put the photograph of a classmate they liked into the 'happy-face' box, those they did not like into the 'sad-face' box and those that did not feel one way or the other about into the 'neutral-face' box.*

'Happy face'

'Sad face'

'Neutral face'

Figure 5.16: Example of faces used on the boxes in the study by Hayden-Thompson (1987)

RESULTS *It was found that children consistently posted more of their same-sex classmates through the happy-face box.*

CONCLUSIONS *Girls tended to show this bias at an earlier age than boys; however, both boys and girls shared gender preference at an early age.*

Explaining prejudiced attitudes

Four main explanations have been put forward by psychologists for how attitudes form and develop:

- The authoritarian personality
- Social influences
- Cognitive factors – stereotyping
- Social identity.

The authoritarian personality

This is based on the idea that hatred by people belonging to one group of people seen as belonging to a different group is regarded as normal. Much of the motivation for this work was based on the persecution of Jews by the Nazis in the 1930s and 1940s, and published by Adorno *et al.* (1950). Adorno argued that the authoritarian personality was prone to prejudice. This type of personality is concerned with upholding convention, conforming and obeying those in authority.

It is claimed that an authoritarian personality results from an over-strict upbringing of a child by parents. Adorno developed the F-scale to measure authoritarianism (F stands for Fascism). Some items of the F-scale are given below:

- Obedience and respect for authority are the most important virtues that children should learn.

- What the youth needs most is strict discipline, rugged determination and the will to work and fight for family and country.

- A person who has bad manners, habits and breeding can hardly expect to get along with decent people.

Evaluative Comment

The items on the F-scale look out of date now, but even at the time there were methodological flaws with the scale. For example, all the items were worded in such a way that agreement implied an authoritarian personality, thus encouraging acquiescence or response bias on the part of the person responding to the statements. On a theoretical level, accounting for prejudice using a personality type does not help explain how whole social groups are prejudiced. Prejudice within a social group is often quite consistent among the individuals. However, each individual has a different personality. Cultural or social norms would seem to offer a better explanation of prejudice and conflict than personality variables.

Social influences

Influences that cause individuals to be racist or sexist, for example, may come from peers, parents and group membership (this latter influence is dealt with later). Children may acquire negative attitudes because they observe role models expressing such views. These role models may reward the child through love, affection or approval for expressing the same views.

Stereotyping

This is where a cognitive representation or set of beliefs exists within an individual to the effect that all members of a social group have the same traits or characteristics. Stereotypes allow us to simplify our social world and may be aids to help us process large amounts of information. But the simplification of our social world is at a cost: the individual is lost to a set of generalisations which allow us to make quick judgements or decisions. Stereotypes are often misleading and may become self-perpetuating, since we may select only that information about a person that confirms the stereotype.

Practical Activity

Using the following social groupings – male homosexuals, Catholics, engineers and people who are obese (greatly overweight) – ask a number of your friends to give the first five descriptions (adjectives) that come to mind when you present them with each grouping.

5

Record each of your friend's responses to each of the social groupings given above.

Once you have done this, identify similarities amongst your friends for each social category of people. These similarities should form the basis of the stereotype that is held for each of these groupings.

Now consider whether the responses given by your friends are simply the repeating of the commonly held stereotype or actually the views that they really hold!

Jussim *et al.* (1995) propose that stereotypes involve both cognitive and affective (emotional or feeling) components which together result in a social judgement being made. This may operate as shown in Figure 5.17.

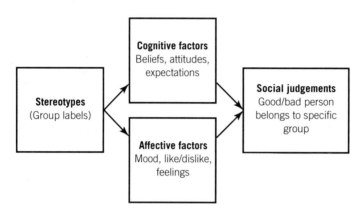

Figure 5.17: Cognitive and affective components of stereotypes and their influences on judgement made about people (Adapted from Jussim *et al.*, 1995)

Social identity

This theory emphasises the role of both cognitive and motivational processes in prejudice and is widely known as **social identity theory** (Tajfel & Turner, 1986). It assumes that we divide the world into 'us' and 'them' through a process of *social categorisation*. More technically, this is known as *ingroup* (us) and *outgroup* (them). Social identity theory proposes that an ingroup will discriminate against an outgroup. By doing this, the members of the ingroup enhance their self-esteem and hence provide rewards for themselves. The central hypothesis of social identity theory is that group members will seek to promote positive aspects for the ingroup. The converse of this is that members of an ingroup will seek to find negative aspects of an outgroup.

Prejudice between cultures may result in racism; in its extreme forms, racism may result in genocide, such as occurred in Germany with Jews, in Rwanda between the Hutus and Tutsis and, more recently, in the former Yugoslavia between Bosnians and Serbs.

Stereotypes have been shown to influence the way we attribute causes or explanations for other people's and our own behaviour (see Chapter 7 for more detail). What is known as the **fundamental attribution error** is where people explain their own behaviour with reference to external causes (the environment) and other people's behaviour with referent to internal causes (the person). Drawing on the ingroup and outgroup distinction made when we looked at social identity theory, it is claimed that negative behaviour (for example, aggression) by an outgroup will be given an internal cause (the individual who is a member of the outgroup is naturally aggressive, for example), whereas, the same negative behaviour will be attributed to an external cause (the person was provoked) by the ingroup.

Study

AIM *Taylor & Jaggi (1974) conducted a study to investigate how Hindu and Muslim office workers explained good and bad behaviour.*

METHOD *Samples of each type of ethnic/religious office workers were presented with scenarios describing desirable and undesirable behaviour.*

RESULTS *It was found that when Hindus were described as engaging in desirable behaviours, Hindus themselves made an internal attribution, that is, the behaviour was caused by the person. By contrast, the same desirable behaviour by Muslims was given an external explanation by the Hindus; that is, some situational or external factor caused the behaviour.*

CONCLUSIONS *The study showed that prejudiced attitudes existed between different religious and cultural groups living in the same city.*

Cultures and prejudice

We all talk about cultures and sub-cultures quite freely, but do we have clear understandings and ways of distinguishing between different cultures? Social psychologists have struggled to provide a definition of 'culture' that will stand up to the test of reality. One definition which has been used extensively is that offered by Rohner (1984):

> 'an organised system of meanings which members of that culture attribute to the persons and objects which make up the culture.'

Notice that this definition restricts the meaning of a culture to the shared understandings that exist between the members of the culture.

Evaluative Comment

This definition does not take account of what role physical objects play in defining a culture. For example, a home in Great Britain is usually thought of as a house or flat of some sort. For a nomadic tribe, it would be a tent or a caravan. Some cultures regard certain animals as sacred and will not eat them, even if they are starving. However, different cultures do seem to have different values and different types of religions, rituals and ceremonies.

Practical Activity

Identify three groupings of people that you think represent three different cultures.

For each culture, write down what you think its key values are, the rituals used for marriage, the type of religion (if appropriate) and the way in which they worship.

What do you think are the two most distinguishing features of each culture? You may wish to ask a friend of a different culture from yourself to do this – you can then compare yours and your friend's view on each others' cultures and identify differences and similarities.

The most influential and highly regarded approach to distinguishing between cultures resulted from Hofstede's (1980) research conducted across 40 countries and from responses from over 117,000 people from these countries. Hofstede assessed this number using people working for large multinational organisations. These employees were asked about work-related values, and Hofstede

5

produced four dimensions by which to classify different countries and hence identify cultural differences. These four dimensions were:

- Power distance: degree of respect shown by subordinates to their superiors.

- Uncertainty avoidance: importance of planning and the creation of stability to deal with life's uncertainties.

- Individualism–collectivism: the importance of personal achievement in relation to the good of the group as a whole.

- Masculinity–femininity: emphasis on achievement and winning or interpersonal harmony respectively.

Hofstede gave each country a score/rating on each of these dimensions, as shown in Figure 5.18. They show that employees in Great Britain are not highly respectful of their superiors (power distance), do plan and create stability for the future (uncertainty avoidance), place great importance on individual achievement (individualism) and like to achieve and win (masculinity).

Country	Power distance	Uncertainty avoidance	Individualism	Masculinity
Great Britain	Low	High	High	High
Greece	Medium	Low	Medium	High
Hong Kong	High	High	Medium	Low
Malaysia	High	Low	Medium	Medium
USA	Medium	High	High	High
Venezuela	High	Medium	Low	High

Figure 5.18: Rating of six countries on each of the four dimensions used to classify different countries/cultures suggested by Hofstede (1980)

The most important of these four to endure and be regarded as central to understanding differences between cultures is that of individualism–collectivism.

Evaluative Comment

Hofstede's (1980) classic study has been criticised on a number of grounds. For example, all respondents were employees of one company, which may have created a culture of its own, and his sample was predominately male. Also, Russia, China and countries from Africa were largely absent from the sample of 40 taken. However, the coverage was unparalleled at the time the research was conducted. In a different way, the four dimensions have not all stood the test of time, and it has been found that the individualism–collectivism dimension correlates negatively with the masculinity–femininity dimension, thus making the latter redundant. Overall, subsequent research, on a large scale, has supported the two dimensions of individualism–collectivism and power distance of ways of separating different cultures.

See Appendix 1 for information concerning questions that appear in the examination paper. The assessment of knowledge and understanding (AO1) and analysis and evaluation (AO2) assessment objectives is also given in Appendix 1.

Sample questions

Sample question 1

(a) Explain what is meant by the *ego-expressive function of attitudes*.
   (AO1 = 1, AO2 = 2) *(3 marks)*

(b) Outline one projective technique used by social psychologists to measure attitudes.
   (AO1 = 3) *(3 marks)*

(c) A psychologist researching attitudes towards a particular political party has decided to use a semantic differential technique. Describe this technique.
   (AO1 = 4) *(4 marks)*

(d) Having identified that a person has a positive attitude towards a political party, how likely is it that the person will vote for the party? Support your answer with empirical evidence.
   (AO1 = 3, AO2 = 7) *(10 marks)*

Total AO1 marks = 11   Total AO2 marks = 9   Total = 20 marks

Questions, answers and comments

(a) Using an example, explain the term *stereotype*.
   (AO1 = 1, AO2 = 2) *(3 marks)*

(b) Research has found that the behaviour of a person is not always consistent with the attitudes held by the person. Using an example, outline one explanation why this may be the case.
   (AO1 = 3) *(3 marks)*

(c) Explain how an attitude may be measured by one direct and one indirect method.
   (AO1 = 2, AO2 = 2) *(4 marks)*

(d) Different people may hold the same attitude but for different reasons. Discuss this statement with reference to a functional approach to understanding attitudes.
   (AO1 = 5, AO2 = 5) *(10 marks)*

Total AO1 marks = 11   Total AO2 marks = 9   Total = 20 marks

Answer to (a)

Stereotypes are grossly exaggerated and often inaccurate categorisations of a group of people who have one or more distinct characteristics such as colour, sex or age. The stereotype may contain some truth. An example would be of a 'hell's angel' biker dressed in leather.

Comment

This answer received the full three marks. One mark was awarded for the idea of categorisation, the second for stating the stereotype may contain some truth and the third for the example. Additional information is also given about age, sex or colour.

5

Sample questions, answers and comments

Answer to (b)

An example of this is La Piere's study where a Chinese couple turned up at hotels and were rarely refused a room. But when the same hotels were sent a letter asking for a reservation for a Chinese couple, most refused. Thus there is consistency when not face to face.

Comment

This answer would score two out of three marks. More on the difference between the two situations in the La Piere study is needed. What is said is correct, but needs expansion.

Answer to (c)

If an attitude on a given topic, for example, school uniform, were to be studied, it would be possible to measure these attitudes, by direct and indirect measures of attitudes. The experimenter gives a situation to which the subject would have to write a response. For example, the situation could be some school pupils being picked on for wearing school uniform, and the subject would have to write what the school pupils would say back. If the subject disliked school uniform, he could write some thing like 'yeah, I hate this school uniform too'. But if the subject liked the school uniform, he could write something like 'go away you big bullies, I actually like my school uniform'.

A direct method is the Likert scale. The experimenter writes a series of statements which are positive and negative to the topic, and the subject has to put the statements on a scale going from 'strongly agree' to 'strongly disagree'. The experimenter then marks the ratings +5 for 'strongly agree' when the statement is positive and 'strongly disagree' when the statement is negative. The higher the score, the stronger the attitude is. The advantage of this method is that there is numerical data, but the disadvantage is that it is hard to put across socially incorrect attitudes.

Comment

The candidate scored five out of six marks for this answer: two marks were awarded for the first part to do with projective tests and marks for the Likert scale. It is clear from this answer that the candidate has an excellent understanding of the construction of a Likert scale and how it is scored. The candidate understands the principles behind projective tests, but is not able to provide an example of an established test, such as the Rorschach Ink Blot test or the Thematic Apperception Test (TAT). The made-up answer to do with the subject and school uniform is not relevant. Incidentally, the term 'participant' should be used instead of 'subject' as required by the British Psychological Society.

Answer to (d)

Many people could hold the same attitudes but for very different reasons. For example, a person might dislike ethnic minorities because of a negative experience from someone from an ethnic minority, or a person might dislike ethnic minorities due to conforming to majority views. The functional approach has three main functions:

1   Adaptive function: our attitudes help us to fulfil our goals
2   Knowledge function: our attitudes help us to make the world simpler and try to make it more predictable
3   Ego-expressive function: our attitudes help us to know what we feel like and help us communicate with others

The main function which gives different people different reasons for having the same attitude is the knowledge function. People may have slightly different stereotypes for particular groups which make their attitudes slightly different. An example is that a person may think all black people are thieves and would not trust any of them at all. But another person may just be conscious of ethnic minorities.

Comment

This answer receives five marks out of ten, for the candidate clearly understands the three functions of attitudes and is able to describe each. This is worth four marks. The candidate is also able to produce a useful
example which scores one mark for application (AO2). But the candidate does not enter into any discussion
– evaluation of the usefulness of the three functions and how easily they may be separated. Questions which
are worth ten marks and ask the candidate to 'Discuss …' have three marks for knowledge and understanding (AO1) and seven marks for evaluation and analysis (AO2).

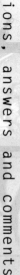

Sample questions, answers and comments

5 Further reading

Introductory texts

Baron, R.A. & Byrne, D. (2000), *Social Psychology*, 9th edition, London, Allyn & Bacon

Hogg, M.A. & Vaughan, G. (2002), *Social Psychology: an introduction*, Third Edition London, Prentice Hall/Harrester

Pennington, D.C., Gillen, K. & Hill, P. (1999), *Social Psychology* (Chapters 3 and 10), London, Arnold

Pennington, D.C. (2000), *Social Cognition* (Chapter 5), London, Routledge

Specialist sources

Brown, R. (1995), *Prejudice: Its Social Psychology*, Oxford, Blackwell Publishers

Eagles, A.H. & Chaiken, S. (1993), *The Psychology of Attitudes*, San Diego, CA, Harcourt, Brace, Jovanovich

Hewstone, M., Stroebe, W. & Stephenson, G. (2001), *Introduction to Social Psychology: A European Perspective*, Third Edition Oxford, Blackwell Publishers

Smith, P.B. & Bond, M.H. (1998), *Social Psychology Across Cultures*, 2nd edition, London, Prentice Hall

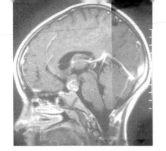

6
Social Influence

Introduction

Social influences are all around us, all the time. Most of the time you are probably completely unaware of them. But read the following three scenarios.

Imagine that you and your best friend go into a clothes shop because you want to buy a new outfit for a party in a couple of weeks' time. Both of you spend a considerable time looking at clothes: you select blue trousers and a white top, but your friend thinks you will look better in an all-black outfit. You go to the checkout and pay for the black outfit. What has happened in between to change your choice of clothes to those selected by your friend?

What influences you when you are buying clothes – your taste in clothes or the views of other people?

Imagine another situation where you go out to eat at an Italian restaurant with a group of friends. The menu is arranged such that if you all have pizzas or all have pasta it is cheaper than if you mix pizza and pasta dishes. Two of the group of six prefer pasta, and the other four prefer pizza. Everyone ends up eating pasta. Here, the minority of two has influenced and persuaded the other four friends to change their preference from pizza to pasta.

Finally, imagine you are going to the cinema and see two queues to buy tickets; one queue is longer than the other. A man in uniform with the name of the cinema on his breast pocket comes up to you and asks you to join the longer queue. You obey and join this queue, even though you have to wait longer to buy the ticket to see the film. Why might you have obeyed?

6

When asked to do something by a person dressed in uniform who looks like an authority figure, do you readily obey?

Reflective Activity

Think about each of the three scenarios described above. For each one, write down:

- *the factors that might have influenced you to buy the black clothes;*
- *the factors that might have persuaded or influenced the majority in the group to agree with the minority and eat pasta;*
- *what might have caused you to obey the uniformed man and join the longer queue for cinema tickets.*

Each of the above scenarios represents a different type of social influence. The first is called **compliance**, the second **minority influence** and the third scenario is **obedience**. Because social influence is such a common feature of our daily lives, it is a topic of central importance in social psychology. Social influence may be defined as:

'Efforts by one or more individuals to change the attitudes, beliefs, perceptions or behaviours of one or more others.' (Baron & Byrne, 2000)

Notice from this definition that at times you may be the target of social influence, whilst at other times be the person, or part of a group, attempting to change another person's attitudes or behaviour. This definition is also useful because it characterises social influence as affecting both cognitions (attitudes, beliefs, perceptions) and actual behaviour. In this chapter, we will consider social influence in relation to compliance, **conformity**, minority influence and obedience to authority.

Practical Activity

In class or whilst having a coffee break, get together with a group of four or five friends. Ask each to think of a situation in which one or more other people influenced what each thought or actually did. Get each of your friends to write down three reasons to explain why they were influenced. Gather all the information together. Look at the reasons given and see if there are any common themes. What are they?

Compliance

Compliance is basically about getting other people to say 'yes' or agree to a request made by yourself. Baron & Byrne (2000) define compliance as follows:

'a form of social influence involving direct requests from one person to another'.

What distinguishes compliance from other forms of social influence is that direct or explicit requests are made, for example, by a salesperson at your door trying to sell you cleaning products or a charity worker coming up to you in the high street asking you to donate money. Advertisements on television are not really examples of compliance, since the use of the medium of television is indirect rather than direct.

Reflective Activity

List between seven and ten examples of compliance where one person or a group of people have asked you to do something. For each example, state whether or not you complied with the request and why (or why not).

Cialdini (1994) researched compliance by looking at jobs in a range of companies where the main task was to get people to agree with their requests. This included salespeople, charities, fund raisers and advertisers. In effect, Cialdini became a participant observer (see Chapter 3) in these companies, but without their knowledge. From his observations, Cialdini (1994) proposed that six principles underlie compliance. These are shown in Figure 6.1. Numerous different techniques are used to gain compliance: we will look at a number of these and link the techniques to the relevant principles.

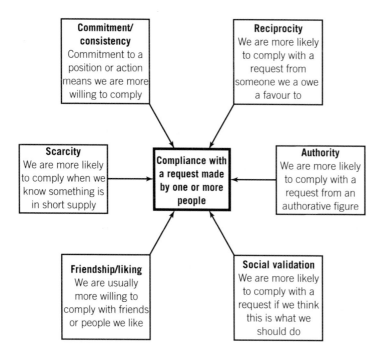

Figure 6.1: Six principles of compliance suggested by Cialdini (1994)

6

Foot-in-the-door technique

The **foot-in-the-door technique** to gain compliance is where you start off by asking for a little or a small request and follow this with a large request. For example, imagine that one of your friends missed the last psychology class and asked to borrow your notes. This is a small request that seems reasonable, so you lend the notes to your friend. A week later, the same friend asks to borrow *all* your psychology class notes. This is a large request – would you agree or not agree?

Study

Aim *Freedman & Fraser (1966) conducted a field study aimed at investigating the foot-in-the-door technique.*

Method *Home owners on a housing estate were asked if they would display a very large sign in their front garden which read 'DRIVE CAREFULLY'. There was an experimental condition and a control group. The control group were simply asked to display the large sign. The experimental group were first asked to display a small sign reading 'DRIVE CAREFULLY'. Those that complied to this small request were asked to display the large sign some time later.*

Results *In the control group, only 17 per cent complied with the request to display the very large sign. In comparison, 75 per cent of the experimental group complied with the larger request.*

Conclusions *The results demonstrate how the foot-in-the-door technique can be successful. The explanation here may be that people like to be helpful and will usually agree to small requests, especially where they agree with the message to drive carefully.*

How willing would you be to put this sign in your front garden, and what reasons might persuade you to do so?

The foot-in-the-door technique works on the principle of consistency (see Figure 6.1). This means that as long as the large request is consistent with or similar in nature to the small request, the technique will work. Freedman & Fraser (1966) included a second experimental group in their study. Individuals in this group were made a small request different or inconsistent with the large request (to sign a petition about a conservation issue). When presented with the large request to display the very large 'DRIVE CAREFULLY' sign, compliance was under 50 per cent, thus demonstrating the importance of consistency between the small and large requests.

Evaluative Comment

Notice that in the Freedman and Fraser experiment, some compliance was found in the control group and quite a high level in the second experimental group. This may be because the large request was something that was in the interests of the home owners on the housing estate. That is, a safer neighbourhood for them and their children might result from displaying the large sign. Therefore, where there is self-interest, the foot-in-the-door technique may be particularly successful in gaining compliance (Reno et al., 1993; Gorassini & Olson, 1995).

Door-in-the-face technique

The **door-in-the-face technique** (Cialdini *et al.*, 1975) is the opposite to the foot-in-the-door technique described above. Here, a large, unreasonable request is made first, which is then followed by a reasonable request. The reasonable request is the one that you really want the person to comply with. In this case, the reasonable request only seems reasonable in the context of the very large, unreasonable request first made. For example, when in negotiation over a pay rise, the workforce representatives of a company may ask for a 20 per cent pay rise. The representatives know this will be unacceptable, and management will 'slam the door in their faces' and refuse. The representatives then go back with a request for a 10 per cent pay rise, which is what they were after all along. The request for a 10 per cent pay rise seems much more reasonable than a 20 per cent pay rise. Given this, it may be that they will stand a better chance of getting 10 per cent than if this had been the request made to management in the first place.

Study

Aim *Cialdini* et al. *(1975) conducted a study to investigate the door-in-the-face technique of gaining compliance.*

Method *College students were approached on campus and asked a large, unreasonable request – to counsel young offenders for two hours a week for the next two years without being paid. A more reasonable request was then made – to take the young offenders on a two-hour trip to the local zoo. A control group were only presented with the reasonable request.*

Results *None of the students complied with the large, unreasonable request. But when the same students were subsequently presented with the reasonable request, about 50 per cent complied. In the control group, just 17 per cent complied with the reasonable request.*

Conclusions *The door-in-the-face technique produces high levels of compliance when the same individuals are presented with a reasonable request similar in nature to the unreasonable request.*

It has also been found that the door-in-the-face technique produces high levels of compliance only when the same person makes the same requests, and the requests are similar in nature (Cann *et al.*, 1978). The door-in-the-face technique works largely due to the principle of reciprocity (see Figure 6.1). Reciprocity is working here because saying 'no' to the large, unreasonable request may make the person feel he or she owes the person who made the request a favour. Generally, we do not like to say 'no' and may feel obliged to be helpful after doing so.

The low-ball technique

The **low-ball technique** (Cialdini *et al.*, 1978; Joule, 1987) is where a person has agreed to a request or agreed to buy an item; subsequently, the person who made the request or agreed to sell the item at a certain price comes back and says a mistake has been made. This results in the request being larger or the price of the item being raised. The most often quoted example is to do with buying a car. The car salesman agrees a price with you, but says he has to check with his manager if this is acceptable. While waiting, you think that you have secured a good deal. The salesman comes back and says his manager would not agree the deal and therefore the price has to be raised. In such situations, most people agree to the higher price.

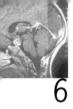

6 Practical Activity

Get together as a group of three or four and devise a study to investigate the low-ball technique of compliance.

Make sure that both requests are ones that can be made of other people and conform to ethical principles of research (see Chapter 3).

Make sure you have a control group and experimental group, and that you have a clear measure of compliance so that results between the two groups can be compared.

Given what you already know about the low-ball technique, devise an alternative hypothesis to test.

The success of the low-ball technique is because of the principle of commitment (see Figure 6.1). Because a person has said 'yes' or agreed to an initial request, commitment has been given. When the request changes and becomes larger or unreasonable, the person will (to a degree) find it difficult to say 'no' because of having originally committed themselves. As with the other change-of-request techniques we have looked at above, greater compliance with the second request is found when it is similar in nature or to do with the same matter as the first request.

Evaluate Comment

The deliberate use of the low-ball technique to achieve compliance with a request does raise some ethical issues. For example, it is of value to society and important in our relationships with other people that we feel we can trust them. Salespeople using the low-ball technique are exploiting this wish to trust others by deliberately getting commitment to one request, knowing they are going to make a larger request less beneficial to you. Also, in many situations, salespeople try to develop a relationship with the customer and foster liking and trust. This is deliberately done to exploit and mislead the customer. The low-ball technique is effective, but may create mistrust of people as a consequence.

Other compliance techniques

Social psychologists have suggested numerous other techniques of compliance (Cialdini, 1994); here, we will consider three others: the 'that's-not-all' technique and tactics based on scarcity and mood.

The 'that's-not-all' technique

The **'that's-not-all' technique** (Burger, 1986) is where an initial request or deal is added to with an incentive before the person has said 'yes' or 'no' to the initial request. For example, imagine that you go into an electrical shop to buy a stereo system. You look at one, and the salesperson says it is normally £299, but if you buy it now, you will also get a personal stereo thrown in with the stereo system. The technique is successful because it is based on the principle of reciprocity (see Figure 6.1). In our example, the adding in of the personal stereo makes you feel that a concession has been granted. Being made a concession usually makes people feel obliged, and hence want to reciprocate. Here, the reciprocation is to agree to the deal.

Scarcity

Seeking compliance through the tactic of scarcity can be quite effective. Perhaps the most common example of this is 'playing hard to get'. If someone initially makes it hard to get to know them, what often results is that the wish to get to know the person becomes stronger. Generally, playing hard to get or giving the impression that something is scarce increases compliance.

Reflective Activity

Imagine you wanted to ask somebody to go out on a date with you. You approach the person, whom you do not know very well, and ask if he or she would like to go to the cinema one night. The person refuses and says they are busy that night. Next day, you ask the person out on another night and get a similar response. At what point do you give up making a request to the person? When does playing hard to get put people off?

Mood

Common sense would indicate that people in a good mood are more likely to comply with a request than people in a bad mood. For example, salespeople may try to put you in a good mood by flattering you and being nice to you (ingratiation). This works up to a point, but if the flattery is too obvious and over the top, or the being nice to you too blatant, it may have the opposite effect (Gordon, 1996).

Study

AIM *Rind & Bordia (1996) conducted a study to see if a sign of friendliness would put customers in a good mood and cause them to leave larger tips.*

METHOD *Waiters, both male and female, in a restaurant were asked either to draw a smiley face on the back of the bill they gave to customers or leave the back of the bill blank.*

RESULTS *The tips of waitresses increased by over 18 per cent when they put a smiley face on the back of the bill. However, no effect was found for waiters (males) for this sign of friendliness.*

CONCLUSIONS *The researchers explained these different findings by arguing that putting smiling faces on the bill by females (waitresses) is gender appropriate, but that it was not gender appropriate for males to do so.*

Evaluative Comment

We have considered a number of different techniques social psychologists have suggested to explain why people comply with requests. These are summarised in Figure 6.2. Most of the research conducted by psychologists has used the experiment. Whilst experiments are generally thought to lack ecological validity (see Chapter 3), one strength of this research is that many of the experiments have been carried out in real-life situations. This means that ecological validity is much greater. Also, Cialdini (1994) acted as a participant observer in companies and was hence able to see what actually caused people to comply.

Personality and compliance

A widely studied personality characteristic that has been investigated in the context of compliance is **need for cognition** (Cacioppo & Petty, 1981). This is to do with the extent that a person likes to think about things. People high in need for cognition like to analyse matters fully, evaluate information and generally spend a lot of effort at thinking. People low in need for cognition do not enjoy thinking deeply and do not show a strong need to understand the world.

Shestowsky *et al.* (1998) showed that people who are high on the personality trait of need for cognition show greater success in getting people to comply with a request than those low on need for cognition. Shestowsky *et al.* suggest that this may be because thinking more deeply and fully about something may result in the person producing stronger arguments and presenting more persuasive information. Showing you have thought about something may also make the person have greater confidence in what you are saying, resulting in the person agreeing to comply with the request.

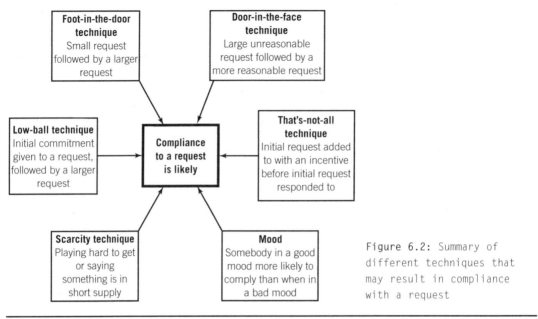

Figure 6.2: Summary of different techniques that may result in compliance with a request

---

Practical Activity

Devise four or five statements to measure need for cognition. Make each statement appropriate to a five-point scale where one end of the scale is 'strongly agree' and the other end is 'strongly disagree'. One such statement might be:

'If I am given a word puzzle to solve, I will not put it down until it is completed.'

If you strongly agreed with this statement, it would indicate high need for cognition.

Give your statements to some of your classmates. At the same time, ask them how they might go about persuading somebody to give up some of their time to do charity work. Try to identify what kind of compliance technique they would use and then see if this relates to high or low need for cognition.

Avoiding compliance - saying 'no'

Cialdini (1993) has suggested a number of techniques that you can use in an attempt to avoid agreeing to requests or being an easy target for salespeople. One technique is simply to say 'no' – people often forget that this is an option open to them. As we have seen from looking at different techniques devised to get our compliance, a degree of distrust of others when they are making requests of us may be a healthy approach to adopt.

Another technique is to avoid being mindless when someone is making a request. As we have seen with the personality variable of need for cognition, thinking about a request more deeply may allow you to resist the request. This may be so because numerous arguments against it may result from thinking more deeply. This would not happen if you were mindless or less thoughtful about the request being made.

The final technique to be mentioned here is to avoid thinking that you have to be consistent in all you do and think. The foot-in-the-door, door-in-the-face and low-ball techniques all play on an assumption that people make about the need to be consistent (see Chapter 4). If someone is trying to get you to comply with a request, it is not logical or rational to be consistent with what you have done or committed yourself to earlier if the request disadvantages you in some way. Being consistent does not necessarily mean that a person is also being rational.

Evaluative Comment

Sometimes we may decide to comply with a request because it seems rational to do so, for example, if it is in our interests, agrees with beliefs or attitudes we hold, or seems a logical result of weighing up the advantages and disadvantages of the request. At other times, we may comply because we give no thought to the request or the justification for it. Langer (1978) showed that people are likely to comply with a small request even if the reason given was not a good justification of the request. In fact, Langer (1978) found low levels of compliance when no reason was given. This shows that any reason results in a higher level of compliance than giving no reason at all.

Conformity

Reflective Activity

Imagine that a small group of you and your friends are standing in a public place, such as a park or shopping area. You have all agreed in advance to look up at the sky for at least five minutes and show interest in what you are looking at. In fact, there is nothing to see, but you are interested in how many passing strangers will stop and look up also. How many people do you think would stop and look? What explanations can you offer for those that do?

What is described in the above activity is an old trick that you may have played on others yourself – it is a good example of *conformity* to what others are doing. Conformity may be defined as follows:

> 'A type of social influence in which individuals change their attitudes, beliefs or behaviour in order to adhere to existing social norms.' (Baron & Byrne, 2000)

Evaluative Comment

This definition emphasises the importance of social norms as a key social cause of people conforming. Social norms are just one example (albeit an important one) of a majority view. As such, conformity can be said to occur in any situation where a person or small group of people are exposed to a majority and conform. Conformity, then, can be seen as majority influence.

In what follows, we shall consider two important and influential studies on conformity, then look at different factors affecting conformity and explanations for conformity. Finally, we shall consider how pressures to conform can be resisted.

The autokinetic effect

Study

Aim *Sherif (1936) conducted an experiment with the aim of demonstrating that people conform to group or social norms when they are put in an ambiguous or novel situation.*

Method *Sherif made use of what is called the **autokinetic effect**. If you are put in a completely dark room and then a small spot of light is projected onto a screen, the spot of light will appear to move, even though it is really stationary. It has been found that individuals in the room on their own make different judgements about how much the light moves – estimates from 20 to 30 centimetres and 60 to 80 cen-*

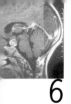

6

timetres are common. The influence of group norms or majority influence was investigated by Sherif by putting three people in the room together. Sherif manipulated the composition of the group by putting together two people whose estimate of the light movement when alone was very similar, and one person whose estimate was very different. Each of the three people in the darkened room had to say aloud how much they thought the light moved. They did this a number of times.

RESULTS Sherif found that over numerous estimates of the movement of the light, the group converged. In effect, as Figure 6.3 below shows, the person whose estimate of movement was greatly different to the other two in the group conformed to the view of the other two.

CONCLUSIONS The results showed that the 'deviant' in the group conformed to the majority view. This took place over a small number of trials at the autokinetic task.

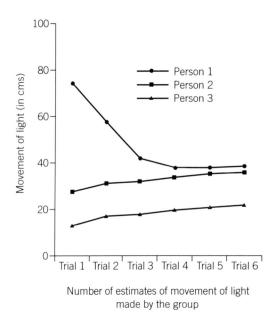

Figure 6.3: Graph showing how the convergence of estimate of movement of light occurred in a three-person group

Sherif (1936) conducted numerous other experiments using the autokinetic effect. Where participants had no previous experience of the autokinetic effect, he found that conformity to a majority view happened very quickly. In general, Sherif found that in ambiguous situations, such as those presented by the autokinetic effect, the less previous experience a person has of the situation, the more powerful will be the influence of a majority with pre-existing, established norms.

Evaluative Comment

The autokinetic effect is not something we come across in everyday life; however, majority influence resulting in conformity occurs in ambiguous social situations where we do not know the correct or accepted way to behave. For example, if you go to an expensive restaurant for a seven-course meal, you will find a large number of knives, forks and spoons laid out at each place. You sit down, look at all this cutlery and do not know which knife, fork or spoon to use with which course. What do you do? You could ask, but this may make you feel you are showing your ignorance. Most likely you will wait until other people start to eat and copy them. You follow the behaviour of the majority. The difference between the autokinetic effect and ambiguous social situations, such as the restaurant scenario given above, is that in most social situations there are social norms or rules about how to behave. With the autokinetic effect, there is no right or wrong answer, since the movement of the light is an illusion anyway.

Asch's study of conformity

Asch (1955) thought that, whilst the studies of Sherif (1936) showed some aspects of conformity, they did not show how social or group pressure would affect tasks where there was an obviously right or wrong answer. Asch wanted to know whether or not people would conform to a majority view when the view was obviously wrong. He investigated conformity using a simple perceptual task in which participants were asked to state which of three comparison lines was the same length as the target line. An example of the task is given in Figure 6.4.

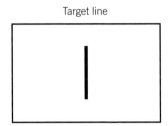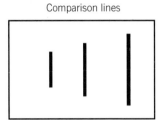

Figure 6.4: An example of the target line and comparison lines used by Asch (1951) in his conformity experiments

Asch conducted a pilot study to ensure that the line-judgement task was easy and unambiguous. In the pilot study Asch (1951), asked 36 people on an individual basis to match the target line with one of the comparison lines. Each person did this twenty times with slightly different versions of the task shown in Figure 6.4. In all, 720 judgements were made with 717 correct responses given, thus showing the task to be clear and unambiguous.

Study

AIM *Asch (1951) conducted an experiment aimed to investigate the influence of a majority view which was wrong on an individual exposed to this view.*

METHOD *Using the line judgement task shown in Figure 6.4, Asch put a participant in the same room as seven other people. These seven people had agreed in advance the responses they were going to give when presented with the line task. The real participant did not know this and was led to believe the other seven people were participants like him or herself. Each person in the room had to state aloud to the others which comparison line was most like the target line in length. The naïve participant sat at the end of the row and gave his or her view last. In some trials, the seven confederates of the experimenter all gave the same and wrong comparison line as answer (for example, Line (c) in Figure 6.4). Typically, the confederates gave the correct response on the first two of eighteen trials. For the remaining sixteen trials, they gave the same wrong answer on twelve occasions and the right answer on just four occasions. Asch was interested in whether or not the naïve or real participant would conform to the unanimous but wrong majority view.*

RESULTS *Asch measured the number of times each participant gave a correct answer or conformed to the incorrect majority view. The results are shown in Figure 6.5. As you can see, just over 22 per cent of participants gave the correct answer on all twelve occasions. This means that 78 per cent of participants gave at least one incorrect response the same as the majority view. About five per cent of participants gave the same answer as the incorrect majority on all twelve occasions.*

CONCLUSIONS *Asch demonstrated that people will conform to a majority view even when it is obvious that the majority is incorrect. Think back to Asch's pilot study, where only three incorrect judgements were made out of 720 answers. Asch concluded that groups exert pressure in some way on an individual to conform to a majority view.*

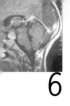

6

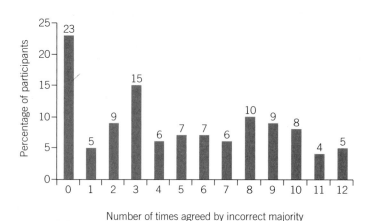

Figure 6.5: Percentage of participants who conformed to an incorrect majority view. (Note: percentages have been rounded to the nearest whole number.) (Adapted from Asch, 1956)

Asch interviewed each participant after they had taken part in the study. The participants who had agreed with the majority gave various reasons for their behaviour. For example, that they did not want to spoil the experimenter's results; that they did not want to be different to the others; that they had actually made the correct judgements; and that they might have been suffering from eye strain. We will look in more detail at explanations psychologists have given for conformity below.

Evaluative Comment

Friend et al. *(1990) drew attention to the fact that psychologists have focused on the participants that conformed to the incorrect majority view. Figure 6.5 shows that over 22 per cent never conformed and around 50 per cent conformed on four of the twelve occasions or more. What explanations are there for resisting majority influence, and how do some individuals manage to do this? We will consider this on page 164. The Asch study also raises ethical issues, in that the naïve participant did not know the other seven in the room were confederates of the experimenter. As such, they were deceived. Pictures of the naïve participant do show shock, surprise and stress when presented with an incorrect majority view.*

Practical Activity

Get a group of two or three together and discuss the following statement: 'Asch was justified in deceiving people in his experiments because we need to know the conditions under which people conform to a majority'. Write down the different arguments produced for and against the statement.

Factors affecting conformity

Many experiments have been carried out since Asch conducted his first studies; some have been shown to increase conformity and others to decrease conformity.

Decreasing conformity

Asch (1955) conducted a series of experiments using the same line task and seven confederates. However, this time one of the confederates always gave the right answer. Asch found that the naïve participants' conformity level dropped to around ten per cent. In another variation which Asch (1955) called the 'extreme dissenter', six of the confederates gave the same wrong answer, whilst the seventh confederate gave a different wrong answer. Conformity levels dropped among participants to around ten per cent also. Asch (1955) also looked at the effect of group size on conformity. Generally, he found that as group size increases, a larger incorrect majority results in higher levels of conformity. With small groups of two or three, where there are one only or two confederates giving the wrong answer, conformity drops to below ten per cent amongst naïve participants.

Study

AIM *Crutchfield (1955) conducted a study to investigate conformity, but where participants sat alone in separate booths. The aim of the study was to determine levels of conformity with other people not present.*

METHOD *Participants sat in separate booths, side by side. In each booth was a set of switches and lights. Each participant was told that they would be given a simple task (some of which were Asch's line task) to make a decision about. They were also told that five other people would be doing the same task and the participant would see their answers (shown as lights) before being asked their own view or decision. Participant had to indicate their view by flipping one of the switches representing their choice.*

RESULTS *Conformity with incorrect majority views by participants dropped to below 50 per cent (in the Asch study, 77 per cent conformed at least once to the majority view). With statements of opinion, conformity was below 35 per cent.*

CONCLUSIONS *When people are placed in situations where they are exposed to an incorrect majority view, but not to the other people, conformity levels are low. Hence, the actual presence of people increases the likelihood of a person conforming to a majority view. This indicates that social pressure has a strong effect on behaviour.*

How does it feel to be the odd one out?

Increasing conformity

Stang (1973) found that the attractiveness of belonging to the group for the individual affects conformity. Generally, the more attractive a group to the participant, the greater will be conformity to the majority view. The cohesiveness of a group has also been found to affect conformity. Cohesiveness concerns the extent to which the individuals in a group like each other and prize being a member of the group. Highly cohesive groups, where each member likes the other and values being part of the group, show higher levels of conformity, whilst low cohesive groups show low levels of conformity (Grandall, 1988; Latane & L'Herrou, 1996).

Culture

Smith & Harris Bond (1993) conducted a review of conformity studies conducted in different cultures around the world between 1957 and 1985. Smith and Harris Bond make a distinction between **individualistic** and *collectivistic* **cultures**. Individualistic cultures are ones such as the USA and Great Britain, where personal choice and individual achievement are valued. Collectivist cultures are ones such as China and Asian countries, where the good of the group is valued over individual achievement. Studies conducted in different cultures showed that conformity is higher in collectivist rather than individualistic cultures. The main explanation for this is that collectivist cultures strive to achieve group harmony more than individualistic cultures.

Explaining conformity

One obvious explanation of conformity is that people follow **social norms**. Social norms are rules, which may be written or unwritten, guiding how people are expected to behave in many social situations. For example, if you go to a classical music concert, speaking while the orchestra is playing would break the social norm of silence.

Reflective Activity

Think of five different social situations – to get you started, one could be sitting around a table in a coffee bar having a drink. List the five situations and write down the social norms that you think apply to each. Also, for each social situation, write down two behaviours which would not be acceptable as a social norm. Why do you think people follow social norms in the situations you have identified? What would be the consequence of not adhering to the social norms?

Many social norms are a product of our upbringing and socialisation. However, other explanations are needed to better account for the majority influence found in the Asch conformity studies. Deutsch & Gerard (1955) put forward a distinction between **normative social influence** and **informational social influence** to account for conformity.

Normative social influence

This is where people conform to maintain the harmony of the group, avoid rejection by the group or gain approval from others. The result of normative social influence is that people publicly comply with the majority view or social norms of the group. However, privately they disagree or hold different views to the majority. Think back to what the participants said when interviewed by Asch after taking part in the study. Some said they wanted to please the experimenter or maintain group harmony, but did not see the target line and comparison line as the same length. This is normative social influence.

Informational social influence

This is where conformity to the majority is as a result of information (things you did not know, persuasive arguments, etc.) presented to you by others in the group. This form of influence results in private acceptance of the majority view. That is, the group is believed to be correct in what it is saying. Private acceptance or internationalisation of views (Kelman, 1958) results in a person stating that view to others. This does not happen with public compliance in normative influence.

Informational social influence is more likely to cause conformity in more ambiguous situations, such as the autokinetic effect. In situations where there is less or little uncertainty, normative social influence is more likely to produce conformity.

Resisting pressures to conform

In the Asch study, over twenty per cent of participants gave the right answer every time and did not conform even once to the incorrect majority view. We have already looked at some factors that reduce conformity. A lone dissenter was found to reduce conformity. More generally, where someone has an ally or good social support, conformity normative social influence pressures are resisted. Allen & Levine (1971) looked at the effect of having either a credible or non-credible form of social support. For example, in one study using the Asch line task, the 'ally', or source of social support, came either from a person who wore thick-lens glasses and said he had a sight problem or someone who did not wear glasses and said he had good sight. Conformity was found to be lowest when the ally was not credible.

Evaluative Comment

Most of the studies that have been conducted on conformity have taken place in a laboratory setting. This raises issues of ecological validity (see Chapter 3). Simply put, how well do these findings generalise to behaviour in everyday life? Look back to the activity on page 159. You may have done this to others or been a victim yourself. Here, both informational influence (what is going on) and normative influence (others are doing this) come into play. For a society such as ours to work well, adherence to both written (laws, etc.) and unwritten (social norms) rules or norms is required. Without conformity to social norms, many of the social interactions that take place between two or more people would become awkward or break down.

Minority influence

The views of a minority of one prevailed, and the other jury members came round to agree with the minority view

Whilst majority social influence and adherence to social norms are common and widespread in society, there are times when a lone voice or minority group can be highly influential. For example, Darwin's theory of evolution, when first proposed back in the 1850s, was widely condemned and rejected by the State, church and many members of the public. Yet 150 years later, the vast majority of people accept the theory of evolution as correct. The film 'Twelve Angry Men', starring Henry Fonda, depicts a jury of twelve men who retire to consider a verdict. At the start, eleven vote for guilty and only one not guilty. Over the course of the film, the lone juror persuades the other eleven jurors to a 'not guilty' verdict.

Moscovici & Faucheux (1972) criticised the traditional experiments on conformity based largely round the Asch approach. They said that the minority (the naïve participant) was always the target for social influence, but not considered as an influential force. Similarly, the majority always exerted influence on the minority, but were not the target of social influence. Since in most of the conformity experiments each member of the group does not talk to each other or discuss the task, the minority is not given the opportunity to persuade the majority to its point of view. Moscovici (1985) stated that an individual in a group who is in a minority can respond in one of three ways:

- conform to the majority view;

- discuss with other group members to achieve a compromise position;

- create conflict in the group and attempt to persuade the majority round to the minority view.

Two main factors have been identified as important for a minority to have an influence over a majority. These are **behavioural style** and *style of thinking*.

Behavioural style

Moscovici and his colleagues (1969) stated that the most important aspect of behavioural style is the consistency with which people hold their position. Being consistent and unchanging in a view is more likely to influence a majority than if a minority is inconsistent and chops and changes its mind. Moscovici *et al.* (1969) conducted a series of studies, called the **blue-green studies**, to investigate the effect of different behavioural styles (consistent/inconsistent) on minority influence.

Practical Activity

Identify three or four minority groups – for example, the environmental group Greenpeace. Look through past newspapers held in your library and see if you can find some articles about these minority groups. Look for evidence of the consistency with which each minority group has given its view. Talk to others about one of these minority groups, and see if the attitudes, views, etc. of the minority group have changed over a period of a few years. What effect might such changes of position have on a majority (yourself, if not a member or supporter of the minority group)?

Study

AIM *Moscovici* et al. *(1969) conducted a study (known as 'the blue-green study') to investigate the effects of a consistent minority on a majority. They hypothesised that a consistent minority will have greater influence on a majority than an inconsistent minority.*

METHOD *The experiment was conducted in two stages. In Stage 1, female participants were put into groups of six; two members of each group of six were confederates of the experimenter and had agreed beforehand what they would say. Each group was shown coloured slides, all of which were blue. In one condition, the two confederates said the slides were green on every trial. In another condition, the two confederates each gave a different answer. A control group consisted of participants only, with no confederates in the group. In Stage 2 of the experiment, participants were put in separate cubicles and shown a further set of coloured slides. In this set of slides, three were obviously blue, three obviously green and ten were blue-green.*

RESULTS *In Stage 1, it was found that the consistent minority had some influence on the majority compared to an inconsistent minority. This is shown in Figure 6.6. Note also that, with the control group, 'green' as a response to seeing the slide was extremely uncommon. In Stage 2, participants who had been exposed to a consistent minority in Stage 1 were much more likely to see the blue-green slides as green than those exposed to an inconsistent minority.*

CONCLUSIONS *A consistent behavioural style by a minority does exert some influence over a majority. In contrast, an inconsistent behavioural style has very little influence over the majority.*

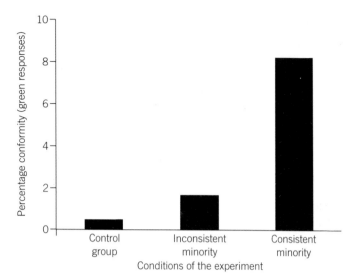

Figure 6.6: The effect of an inconsistent and consistent minority behavioural style on the influence of a minority. Adapted from Moscovici *et al.* (1969)

Evaluative Comment

The conformity rate of a majority to a consistent minority view is much less than the conformity of a minority to a consistent majority view. Compare the findings of the Moscovici et al. (1969) study with that from Asch's (1951) line-judgement task. Further research by Moscovici & Mugny (1983) has shown that a consistent minority is more influential if they are seen to have made sacrifices for their cause. Also, minorities are seen to be more influential if seen to be acting out of principle rather than for motives of gain. Therefore behavioural style of an influential minority entails consistency, making sacrifices and acting on principle.

Style of thinking

Reflective Activity

List three or four minority groups that are reported in the newspapers or on television, for example, the 'flat earth society'. Reflect on how you think about and respond to each of these minority groups and the views they put forward. Do you dismiss their views out of hand and with very little thought, or do you think about what they have to say and discuss their views with other people?

In the above activity, if you dismiss the views of other people without giving them much thought, you would have engaged in *superficial thought*. By contrast, if you had thought deeply about the views being put forward, you would have engaged in *systematic thinking* (Petty *et al.*, 1994). With superficial thought or processing, it is likely that you reject the minority view almost instantly. However, research has shown that if a minority can get the majority to think about an issue and think about arguments for and against, then the minority stands a good chance of influencing the majority (Smith *et al.*, 1996). Furthermore, if the minority can get the majority to discuss and debate the arguments that the minority are putting forward, influence is likely to be stronger (Nemeth, 1995).

6 Study

AIM *Zdaniuk & Levine (1996) predicted that participants in a minority in a group would generate more ideas and arguments for an unpopular view than participants in a majority in a group.*

METHOD *Participants were told they would discuss in a group whether or not examinations should be abolished. Participants were put in groups of six and told how many of the other five in the group agreed with their view. This ranged from one other (minority) to four or five others (majority). Participants were then asked to write down arguments for and against the examination.*

RESULTS *It was found that participants who believed themselves to be in a minority in a group generated more ideas and arguments for the examination issue than those who thought they were in a majority.*

CONCLUSIONS *This finding provides evidence that minorities engage in systematic or deep processing of a position. This results in developing more arguments which can then be used to influence a majority who have thought less (superficial processing) about the issue.*

The use of reason and argument by a minority in an attempt to influence a majority may not have an instant effect. The majority may take time to think about the information and arguments being put forward and change towards the minority view over a period of time. Combining a consistent behavioural style with a systematic style of thinking is likely to put the minority in the best position to influence the majority.

Obedience to authority

Obedience to authority has both a positive and negative side. On the positive side, people obey laws of society, authority figures (such as the cinema attendant mentioned in the scenario at the start of this chapter) and other orders or instructions which seem sensible and reasonable. Obedience in this context is essential to the smooth running of society, and if people did not obey, chaos and disorder would quickly develop. On the negative side, obedience can be destructive and result in terrible crimes. There are plenty such examples from history where one group of people kill another group, for example, the Nazis ordering German soldiers to torture and kill millions of Jews during the Second World War. The Bosnians and Serbs in Eastern Europe, and the Tutsis and Hutus in Rwanda are also examples of mass slaughter resulting from obedience to orders given by high-ranking army officers or government officials.

Ethnic hatred can result in many people obeying the orders of a few - with appalling destructive consequences

Practical Activity

Get together with a group of three or four friends or classmates. Make two lists. In one list, write down ten examples of obedience that are beneficial to society. In the other list, write down ten examples of obedience that harm society – here, try to think of less extreme examples than people killing other people. An example, to get you started, could be the leader of a gang ordering members to shout racist comments at a minority group. Do you think there are any differences in why people obey in each of your lists?

Milgram's study of obedience

Milgram conducted a series of highly controversial studies in the 1960s (Milgram, 1963; 1965; 1974) investigating obedience to authority. The studies investigated the effect of a range of factors on levels of obedience. Milgram recruited participants by placing advertisements in local newspapers asking for volunteers to take part in a experiment on learning. Volunteers were told that the experiment required one person to act as a 'teacher' and another person as a 'learner'. Milgram tossed a coin in front of two participants to assign one to the role of teacher and one to the role of learner. In reality, this was fixed so that the true volunteer or participant was always assigned to the role of teacher and the other person, who was a confederate of Milgram's, to the role of learner. Milgram then explained to the teacher that they had to read a series of word pairs (such as 'blue–girl', 'fat–neck') to the learner. Subsequently, the teacher had to read the first word of the pair, and the learner had to choose the correct second word of the pair from a list of a few words. The teacher was told that if the learner gave the wrong word, the teacher had to give the learner an electric shock. This continued over many sets of word pairs, and each time that the learner gave a wrong answer, the teacher was told they had to give an electric shock of increasing intensity. A sophisticated piece of equipment with a long line of switches and lights was placed in front of the teacher, allowing them to see what the next level of electric shock should be – this is shown in Figure 6.7. On the front panel of the equipment was a voltage scale running from 15 to 450 volts with an indication of the severity of shock, as shown below:

15–60 volts	slight shock
75–120 volts	moderate shock
135–180 volts	strong shock
195–240 volts	very strong shock
255–300 volts	intense shock
315–360 volts	extremely intense shock
375–420 volts	danger, severe shock
425–450 volts	xxx

Prior to beginning the experiment, the teacher was given a sample shock of 45 volts (which is quite painful). The learner (a confederate of Milgram's) did not actually receive any shocks, but the teacher did not know this.

The teacher would see the learner 'wired up', as shown in Figure 6.7, and be told that he had complained of a weak heart. A typical set of responses the learner had rehearsed in advance to say at different levels of shock is shown in Figure 6.8. As the learner kept getting the second word in the word pair wrong, Milgram would order the teacher to carry on and give electric shocks. This would consist of saying 'please go on' or 'the experiment requires that you continue' or 'you have no other choice, you must go on'.

Before conducting his series of experiments, Milgram asked psychiatrists, students and middle-class adults the shock level at which they thought teachers would refuse to go on. All said they would refuse beyond the 'very strong shock' level (195–240 volts), and over 80 per cent said they would refuse to go on beyond the 'strong shock' level (135–180 volts).

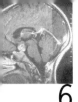

6

Figure 6.7: Stanley Milgram with the sophisticated electric-shock apparatus (left) and the learner having electrodes attached to his wrist (right) (From Milgram, 1974)

Figure 6.8: Responses made by the learner after receiving different levels of electric shock (From Milgram, 1974)

The first experiment was conducted in the Psychology Department at Yale University (a highly prestigious university). Here, the teacher and learner were put in different rooms so that the teacher could hear the learner but not actually see him. Figure 6.9 depicts the results that Milgram obtained. As can be seen, 63 per cent continued to deliver electric shocks up to the very maximum. In dramatic contrast to predictions by psychiatrists, students and adults, all continued to 240 volts, whereas between 90 and 100 per cent were predicted to discontinue at this level. We will look at factors influencing levels of obedience in the next section, and explanations for obedience in the subsequent section.

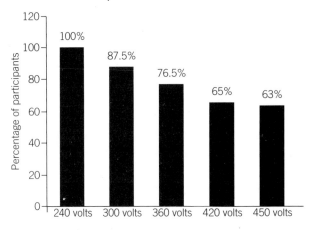

Figure 6.9: Percentage of participant 'teachers' in Milgram's study who continued to give shocks to the learner (Adapted from Milgram, 1974)

Evaluative Comment

Milgram's study raises a number of controversial issues.

Ethical issues: *Two main issues arise: first, participants placed in the teacher role were deceived into thinking that they were actually giving electric shocks to the learner and were not aware that the learner* was in fact a confederate of Milgram's. Second, participants were exposed to an extremely stressful situation that may have had the potential to cause harm. Milgram did debrief each participant fully after taking part in the experiment and followed each up over a period of time to ensure that they came to no harm. Nevertheless, Milgram's experiment does breach the code of ethics published by the British Psychological Society and would not be considered ethical these days.

Validity of findings: We may also ask whether the findings can be regarded as valid. Did the teachers actually believe they were giving electric shocks and causing the learner to suffer pain? If not, then the findings are of little value. Milgram interviewed each of the participants after taking part in the experiment and claimed that they did believe they were giving electric shocks. However, some did say that they thought the experimenters would not allow anyone to be hurt or come to harm in the experiment.

Conditions affecting obedience

Milgram (1974) investigated various situational and social factors affecting obedience in the teacher–learner experiment described above. These include legitimacy of authority, proximity of the learner, proximity of the experimenter, conflicting orders and sex differences.

The legitimacy of authority was varied by conducting the experiment in a run-down office in a less respectable part of town. This 'low legitimacy' experiment resulted in lower levels of obedience – just 48 per cent of participants delivered the maximum shock. The legitimacy of the authority figure – the experimenter – was varied by allowing another participant to give orders to the teacher to carry on, rather than the experiment dressed in a white laboratory coat. Here, obedience dropped to just 20 per cent giving maximum shock. The proximity of the learner was varied by placing the teacher and learner in the same room. Here, obedience dropped to 40 per cent. When the teacher had to put the hand of the learner on a metal plate to deliver the electric shock, obedience dropped to 30 per cent. In another experiment, the experimenter left the room after giving the teacher instructions on what to do. Here, obedience dropped to 20 per cent. Where two experimenters were present with the teacher and one instructed the participant to continue and the other to stop, obedience dropped dramatically, with no one giving the maximum shock. Finally, when females were used as teachers (in the original studies Milgram had used all males) in the original set-up described in the previous section, about the same percentage (65%) delivered the maximum shock.

Numerous replications of the basic Milgram set-up have been conducted in different countries in the 1970s and 1980s. Figure 6.10 summarises some of the findings. However, some caution is needed in interpretation, since slightly different methods to Milgram's were used in different studies. Nevertheless, all show a worryingly high level of obedience to authority.

Study	Country	Participants	Percentage
Milgram (1963)	USA	Male general public	63%
Mantell (1971)	Germany	Male general public	85%
Burley & McGuiness (1977)	UK	Male students	50%
Shanab & Yahga (1978)	Jordan	Students	62%
Miranda et al. (1981)	Spain	Students	90%
Scharz (1985)	Australia	General public	80%

Figure 6.10: Levels of obedience in different countries using the basic Milgram procedure (Adapted from Smith & Harris Bond, 1999)

Explanations for obedience

Kelman & Hamilton (1989) suggest three main factors to explain obedience, and destructive obedience in particular. These are: legitimacy of the system, legitimacy of authority within the system and legitimacy of demands or orders given. The legitimacy of the system concerns the extent to which

6

the government, army, religious group or even family is a legitimate source of authority. The legitimacy of authority is the power individuals hold to give orders because of their position in the system. For example, the prime minister in government or a general in the army would have a high degree of legitimacy. The legitimacy of demands or orders refers to the extent with which the order is perceived to be a legitimate area for the authority figure. For example, if the prime minister tried to order people not to eat meat because he was a vegetarian, you would be unlikely to regard the order as legitimate.

Reflective Activity

Return to the two lists that you constructed in the activity on page 169. Select three examples of obedience from each of the beneficial and harmful lists. For each example, identify the legitimacy of the system, legitimacy of authority, and legitimacy of order. Decide whether each is legitimate or not. Where all three are legitimate, this should be where the highest obedience exists.

Defiance of authority

We have looked at some of the factors which create obedience; now let's consider what factors reduce our likelihood of obeying authority. When individuals are reminded that they are responsible for the consequences of what they do and any harm caused, research has shown large reductions in obedience (Hamilton, 1978). Another factor reducing obedience is to question the reasons the authority figure gives to justify obeying an order. Research has also shown that if participants in a study of obedience watch another person acting disobediently, then levels of obedience will be low (Rochat & Modigliani, 1995).

Study

Aim *Feldman & Scheibe (1972) conducted a study to discover what factors cause people to rebel against an authority figure.*

Method *College students were asked to complete a very personal and embarrassing questionnaire in the presence of other students. The other students were confederates of the experimenter. In one condition, the confederates appeared to willingly complete the questionnaire. In another condition, they refused to complete the questionnaire and asked to leave the experiment.*

Results *The real participants in the first condition were much more likely to complete the questionnaire than those in the condition where the others refused.*

Conclusion *People are likely to refuse authority requests which are unpleasant or harmful when social support from others is available. In this experiment, social support was taken from others refusing to fill in the questionnaire.*

Evaluative Comment

Most of the research dating back to the original and highly influential studies of Milgram has investigated destructive obedience. However, as we saw on page 168, obedience to authority is often beneficial and necessary for a society or system, such as the army, to function. Imagine what it would be like if the soldiers in the army refused to obey the orders of their commanding officer or obeyed only those that they wanted to. People often make conscious decisions to obey orders in everyday life. Whether they do or not may depend quite heavily on the three types of legitimacy that we considered in our explanation of obedience (page 172). It is important to find ways of reducing or avoiding destructive obedience, and the controversial work of Milgram has given psychologists great insight and knowledge into how this can be achieved.

See Appendix 1 for information concerning questions that appear in the examination paper. The assessment of knowledge and understanding (AO1) and analysis and evaluation (AO2) assessment objectives is also given in Appendix 1.

Sample questions

Sample question 1

(a) Outline one ethical issue related to Asch's studies of obedience.

   (AO1 = 2)   *(2 marks)*

(b) Identify two variables shown by Asch to affect conformity.

   (AO1 = 2)   *(2 marks)*

(c) Explain two ways in which a minority of people in a group might change the views of the majority within the same group.

   (AO1 = 2, AO2 = 4)   *(6 marks)*

(d) Describe and discuss two factors that might affect whether or not a person will obey. Refer to empirical evidence in your answer.

   (AO1 = 5, AO2 = 5)   *(10 marks)*

Total AO1 marks = 11   Total AO2 marks = 9   Total = 20 marks

Questions, answers and comments

(a) Identify two ways in which a person may achieve compliance with a request.

   (AO1 = 2)   *(2 marks)*

(b) Using an everyday example, explain what is meant by the term *group pressure*.

   (AO1 = 1, AO2 = 2)   *(3 marks)*

(c) Describe one study which investigated minority influence. Indicate in your answer why the study was conducted, the method used, the results obtained and conclusions drawn.

   (AO1 = 5)   *(5 marks)*

(d) Discuss at least two ways in which a minority may change the views of a majority. Refer to evidence in your answers.

   (AO1 = 3, AO2 = 7)   *(10 marks)*

Total AO1 marks = 11   Total AO2 marks = 9   Total = 20 marks

Answer to (a)

Two ways in which compliance with a request made by somebody may be achieved are the foot-in-the-door method and the low-ball approach.

Comment

This answer would score the full two marks. Both marks are for knowledge (AO1 skills). The terms given are not exactly correct, but good enough.

Answer to (b)

An example of group pressure could be where your friends all want to go to the cinema and you don't. The group exerts pressure and tries to persuade you to go along with the rest of them.

Comment

This answer would score two out of the three marks available. One mark awarded for giving an example of group pressure (AO2 mark, since it relates to application) and one mark for a rather vague explanation of group pressure. More specific detail would be needed – for example, to maintain group harmony – to score the full three marks.

Answer to (c)

The blue–green study by Moscovici was conducted to investigate minority influence and consistency. Participants were shown blue and green colours. Groups of six people were formed. Two were in league with the experimenter and always gave the wrong answer – green instead of blue. The other four in the group were real people. Moscovici found that about ten per cent of the participants were influenced by the minority. He concluded that only if the minority said the same thing each time would they have an influence.

Comment

This answer would score the full five marks. The candidate says why the study was conducted (one mark). The method is full enough to score two marks. The results give some specific detail – ten per cent – and the conclusion is correct. Language a bit awkward at times, but good answer.

Answer to (d)

Psychologists have found many ways in which minorities can influence; two are behavioural style and autonomy. Behavioural style was investigated in the blue-green study by Moscovici. This showed participants blue and green colours where it was obvious what the colour was. When a minority was consistent, the majority was influenced. But this was only to a degree, since only ten per cent were influenced, leaving 90 per cent not influenced by a minority. If the task were less clear about the right answer, then the minority might have influenced more. When the colours were blue-green, then the minority had more sway. These are laboratory experiments and may not generalise to everybody because students are used as participants.

Nemeth (1973) looked at autonomy and showed that the minority has to be seen to be in an influential position when seated at the table. A person at the head of a table is more autonomous than elsewhere. Minorities can influence a majority, but not all the time and only when they behave in certain ways.

Comment

This answer would gain seven out of ten marks (three AO1 marks and four AO2 marks). Two ways are clearly identified, and good description and evaluation is given of the blue-green study. The second way, of autonomy, is less well-developed and a little confused. No discussion is given, so no AO2 marks here. Overall, a good answer.

Further reading

Introductory texts

Baron, R.A. & Byrne, D. (2000), *Social Psychology: An Introduction* (Chapter 9), London, Allyn & Bacon

Hewstone, M. & Stroebe, W. (eds) (2001), *Introduction to Social Psychology*. 3rd edition (Chapter 13), Oxford, Blackwell

Hogg, M.A. & Vaughan, G.M. (2002), *Social Psychology*, 3rd edition (Chapter 6), London, Prentice Hall

Pennington. D.C., Gillen, K. & Hill, P. (1999), *Social Psychology* (Chapter 8), London, Arnold

Specialist sources

Cialdini, R. & Trost, M. (1998), Social Influence: Social Norms, Conformity and Compliance. In D.T. Gilbert, S.T. Fiske & G. Lindzey (Eds), *The Handbook of Social Psychology*, 4th edition, New York, McGraw-Hill

Milgram, S. (1974), *Obedience to Authority*, New York, Harper Row

Miller, A.G., Collins, B.E. & Brief, D.E. (Eds) (1995), 'Perspectives on obedience to authorities: the legacy of the Milgram experiments', *Journal of Social Issues*, 51, 1–212

Shavitt, S. & Brock, T.C. (1994), *Persuasion: Psychological Insights and Perspectives*, Boston, Allyn & Bacon

Smith, P. & Harris Bond, M. (1998), *Social Psychology Across Cultures*, 2nd edition (Chapter 6), London, Prentice Hall

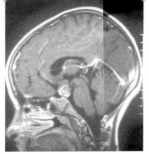

7

Social Cognition

Introduction

The social world is important to us. We need to make judgements about the character and intentions of people around us, and about our own character and personality.

The process of making these judgements is called **impression-formation**, or **social perception**. It is particularly important when we meet people for the first time, for example at a job interview or on a blind date.

We sometimes feel the need to explain the actions of other people, particularly when their behaviour affects us directly. This is called *attribution of causes*. For example, when someone is rude or angry to us, we need to understand why.

These topics together make up what psychologists call **social cognition**, which can be defined as the thought processes, knowledge and beliefs which people use in order to understand the character and behaviour of other people.

Schemas

In order to understand the things which happen around us, each person builds up a set of mental representations of the world. This mental model is mainly constructed during childhood, but details can be added to it at any time as a result of experience. This model might include generalisations such as 'Exercise is good for you', 'Most animals are dirty and dangerous', or 'It is best not to be very happy because if you are, something bad will probably happen'.

A set of linked mental representations of this sort is called a **schema**. (The plural of schema is *schemata*, although *schemas* is also acceptable.)

The schemas a person has about the world enables them to understand and manage their everyday life. Although this is an approximate and often inaccurate description of the real world, for the person it **is** the real world. How they perceive it is how they believe it to be.

Some of our schemas are about people. These are called *social schemas*. They include knowledge, beliefs and expectations about people in general, particular groups of people, particular individuals, social situations and ourselves. For example, having a social schema about football supporters gives you an idea of how they are likely to think and behave.

Impression formation: perception of others

Social perception

When we meet another person for the first time, we observe features of their appearance and behaviour and quickly make judgements about them. The impression we form may not be very detailed or comprehensive.

"He's quite good-looking, looks intelligent too. Wonder if he fancies me? He seems really nice. Maybe he's gay ..."

When we meet another person for the first time, we quickly make judgements about them

Our perception of strangers is usually a rapid, two-stage process. The first stage is to use our sense organs (eyes, ears, etc.) to *observe* the other person. We take in visual information, for example about their sex, clothing, facial features and expression. We also attend to information from other senses – hearing, touch and smell. The second stage is to make *inferences* or judgements about the person. Those judgements are to do with what we really want to know about the person, such as their present emotions, their intentions toward us, their status and abilities.

For example, if you see a girl sitting in a slumped posture, sobbing and wiping tears from her eyes (as shown in Figure 7.1) you are likely to infer that she feels sadness. Your inference might be inaccurate, however. It could be that just before you arrived, someone had told a very funny joke. If you had known that, you might have inferred that her posture and tears were the result of extreme amusement.

Figure 7.1: Social perception is a two-stage process

Observation Melissa is sitting in a slumped position, sobbing and wiping tears from her eyes	→	**Inference** Melissa feels very sad

The process is fast because we need to be able to respond immediately to what the other person is doing. We need to understand and predict their behaviour. In order for our response to be appropriate, we have to make accurate inferences about the other person. This happens even if we can't actually see the person – when we answer the telephone to a stranger, for example. The inferences we make are likely to be influenced by the social schemas we have.

Evaluative Comment

The fact that social perception involves making inferences, or judgements, means that we are quite likely to make mistakes. We observe some, but not all, of the available information about another person, then make a guess about their character, feelings or intentions. Not surprisingly, our inferences risk being biased.

Practical Activity

*The process of forming an impression of another person is complicated by the fact that people often try to influence the impression which others get of them. In the words of the poet T. S. Eliot, you '... prepare a face to meet the faces that you meet'. This is called **impression management**.*

7

Imagine that you are going out with a new boyfriend or girlfriend for the first time. List some of the ways in which you might try to influence the impression the other person forms of you.

Your list might take account of the fact that person perception is influenced not only by a person's appearance, but also by how they sound, smell and feel.

Impression formation

The fact that we often need to form impressions quickly can lead to several kinds of systematic bias. These include the **primacy effect**, the **recency effect** and **stereotyping**.

The primacy effect

Primacy means 'first'. The primacy effect refers to the idea that information presented at the beginning of an encounter has more influence than later information. The *first impression* may shape how the person is perceived much more than what happens afterwards. For example, if you meet a person on a blind date and within the first few minutes they spill a drink in your shoes, the impression you form of them as a clumsy person may never be fully erased by later information. Your first impression might even be enough to prevent a second date from taking place. If the accident happened after you had got to know them, it would have less effect.

The primacy effect is a bias towards attending most to the earliest information we receive about a person. One explanation of this is that we quickly construct a schema about the person, which then affects how we attend to later information. Information which might lead us to change our schema tends to be discounted (ignored).

Study

AIM *Asch (1946) conducted a study to find out whether the order of presentation of information about a person influenced the judgements other people made about this person.*

METHOD *Asch gave participants a description of a person, in the form of a simple list of adjectives. Some participants received a list of adjectives with the most positive qualities first, as follows:*
intelligent, industrious, impulsive, critical, stubborn, envious

Other participants received the same list, but in the reverse order, with the most negative qualities first:
envious, stubborn, critical, impulsive, industrious, intelligent

All the participants were then asked to rate the person described on a series of personality measures, including how honest, sociable, humorous, reliable and happy they thought the person was.

RESULTS *Asch found that participants who had received the reference with positive qualities first, rated the person more positively than the other participants did. The person was judged to be happier and more sociable, for example.*

CONCLUSION *The order of presentation influenced judgements. Information presented first had more effect. This study is evidence that the primacy effect does occur.*

Evaluative Comment

One methodological criticism of the Asch study is that it lacked ecological validity. In other words, it was not true to life. In real-life situations, we usually meet face to face with the people we form impressions of, and we form impressions which are important or relevant to us. In the Asch study, participants did not meet a real person, they just read a description. They were not asked for their impressions of this person, but instead were asked to fill in rating scales. This is a validity problem, because people might behave very differently in a real person-perception situation.

Participants taking part in a version of this study today tend to object that they don't have enough information to make a judgement. It seems so artificial as to be worthless.

A positive feature of the study was that there was good control of variables. For example, the participants in both conditions were given exactly the same words describing the person – only the order was varied.

In many psychology studies, there is a trade-off between good control of variables and artificiality. To put this another way, the more true to life a study is, the less well controlled the variables are likely to be.

The pioneering work by Asch led to further studies with improved ecological validity and similar findings.

Study

AIM *Luchins (1957) conducted a study to find out whether the order of presentation of information about a person influenced the impression formed.*

METHOD *Luchins asked students to read descriptions of a fictional character called 'Jim'. There were two descriptions of Jim – one made him sound like an extrovert, the other like an introvert.*

Group 1 participants were given the extrovert description only.

Group 2 participants were given the introvert description only.

Group 3 participants were given a paragraph containing the introvert description, followed by the extrovert description.

Group 4 participants were given a paragraph containing the extrovert description, followed by the introvert description.

The participants were then asked to rate Jim on a scale of introversion–extroversion. Groups 1 and 2 were really control groups – there to check that participants could correctly recognise a person as extrovert or introvert.

RESULTS *The percentage of participants in each group who rated Jim as extrovert was: Group 1 – 79%; Group 2 – 16%; Group 3 – 34%; Group 4 – 52%. A comparison of the results for Groups 3 and 4 (who received similar descriptions in a different order) shows that the first part of the description had more influence on the impression formed.*

CONCLUSION *This supports the primacy effect. Luchins argued that the primacy effect works because people jump to conclusions early and then ignore or discount any information which conflicts with their first impression.*

Evaluative Comment

This study is an improvement on the Asch (1946) study. The person to be perceived was described and given a name, and the judgement participants were asked to make was typical of the sort of judgements we usually make about others. In other words, the study was a little more ecologically valid. However, participants did not actually see or meet 'Jim', who was a fictional character. A study of impression-formation in which participants do not actually encounter a real person still lacks ecological validity.

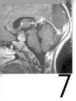

The recency effect

The recency effect is the idea that information presented at the end of an encounter or description has more influence than earlier information. This is the opposite of the primacy effect. In some situations, it seems plausible that we should be most influenced by the latest information we get. For example, two lovers separated for a while might remember each other as they were just before parting. Luchins (1957) found some evidence for this effect when participants were first warned against jumping to conclusions when making their judgements. In the 'Jim' study described above, when Luchins left an interval between presenting the two paragraphs, there was also a recency effect.

Evaluative Comment

The evidence suggests that the recency effect occurs less frequently than the primacy effect. This may be because we form impressions quite quickly. Later information which conflicts with our first impression is more likely to be ignored or discounted.

Study

Aim *Jones* et al. *(1968) conducted a study to find out whether the recency effect occurred when watching someone answer oral test questions.*

Method *Participants watched while a student was asked 30 questions, and was seen getting some of them right and some wrong. Half the participants – Group 1 – watched the student get fifteen answers right, mostly near the beginning of the test. Group 2 watched the same student on a different occasion get fifteen answers right, mostly at the end of the test. The student was a confederate of the experimenters, and was under instructions which questions to answer correctly. Afterwards, each participant was asked to guess how many right answers the student got.*

The researchers expected that Group 2 would make higher guesses than Group 1. They thought that those who had seen the student get the later answers right, but not the earlier answers, would judge him to be more capable because he got better as he went along. In contrast, those who saw the student get the earlier answers right, but not the later ones, might think the student was lucky at first, but was eventually 'found out' by later questions.

Results *On average, Group 1 judged the student to have got 20.6 answers right. On average, Group 2 judged the student to have got 12.5 answers right. This is the opposite to what the researchers expected.*

Conclusion *This does not support the recency effect – in fact, it is good evidence for the primacy effect. Even though the student got the same number of questions right in each case, the participants' perceptions of his performance seems to have been influenced by how they started off rather than on the test as a whole.*

Reflective Activity

This is an opportunity to do some evaluation yourself. Comment on the ecological validity of the Jones et al. *study. In what ways is it an improvement on the studies by Asch and Luchins, and in what ways does it still lack ecological validity?*

Stereotyping

Another bias which is likely to affect impression-formation is stereotyping.

Baron & Byrne (1997) define stereotypes as 'beliefs to the effect that all members of specific social groups share certain traits or characteristics'.

Stereotypes can be formed on the basis of almost any kind of social division, including gender, race, age, ability, class, appearance and occupation. A well-known occupational stereotype, which is widely shared, is that all politicians are liars. Like other stereotypes, this is an unfair and misleading overgeneralisation which is applied to all members of the social group concerned. Its effect on social perception is that a person who had this belief, on meeting a politician for the first time, would assume that he or she was a liar.

Stereotypes are an important ingredient in our social schemas.

Study

AIM *Razran (1950) conducted a study to find out how ethnic stereotypes influence personality judgements.*

METHOD *Razran showed participants a set of photographs of young women and asked them to rate the women for factors such as likeability, beauty, intelligence and ambition. The ratings were recorded. Two months later, the same participants were asked to rate the same photographs, but this time, names were printed on them. These names gave clues about the ethnicity of the women – five were Italian, five Irish, five Jewish and fifteen Anglo-Saxon. For example, one photograph was labelled 'O'Shaughnessy', while others were labelled 'Rabinowitz', 'Fichetti' or 'Adams'. Participants were once again asked to rate the women for likeability, intelligence, ambition and beauty.*

RESULTS *In comparison with the original ratings, the women believed to be Jewish were rated as more ambitious and intelligent, but less likeable or beautiful than they had before. Most of those believed to be Italian or Irish were rated as less likeable and a little less beautiful and intelligent than they had been before.*

CONCLUSION *Ethnic categorisation activated stereotypes which changed or distorted participants' perceptions of the women. Participants who thought that a woman was Jewish made judgements of her which were influenced by their beliefs about Jewish people as a whole. Distortions also resulted from the belief that women were Irish or Italian.*

Reflective Activity

Razran's study also illustrates the trade-off between good control of variables and artificiality. Evaluate Razran's (1950) study by writing down one advantage and one disadvantage of using photographs in the social perception task.

Reflective Activity

Bias in impression formation can have important consequences in some real-life situations. One of the best examples is the job interview, which can be seen as a procedure for enabling impressions to be formed of another person (the applicant).

1 *During job interviews, some interviewees start off rather quietly, look at the floor and give one-word answers. After a while they relax and become more confident, making eye contact and giving longer answers to questions. Decide whether this approach to a job interview is likely to be successful. Refer to one of the three types of bias in person perception which are described above.*

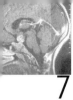
2 *Managers interview six applicants for a job on the same afternoon, before deciding which one to appoint. If you were one of the applicants, and you really wanted the job, would you prefer to be interviewed first, last or in the middle? Refer to types of bias in person perception.*

3 *During an interview, a job applicant refers to some groups she is a member of, but not others. The groups she refers to include an athletics team and a local children's charity. The groups she belongs to but does not mention include Greenpeace and the Anti-Nazi league. Which type of bias is this applicant trying to use in her favour?*

The job interview – a procedure for impression-formation

Note that many job interviews today are conducted by people who have been properly trained to avoid bias and to think carefully about the judgements they make. The selection process rarely relies on the interview alone.

Social schemas

At the start of this chapter, a social schema was described as a set of linked mental representations about people. Fiske & Linville (1980) suggest that schemas allow us to simplify the social world. Because schemas are an oversimplified representation of reality, they enable us to make rapid decisions and predictions about people. They give us expectations of how people will behave and why. Fiske & Taylor (1991) described four different types of social schemas (see Figure 7.2):

* **Self-schemas** are set of cognitions a person has about him or herself. They include the self-image, described on p.185.

* **Person schemas** are sets of cognitions which may be about particular individuals we know or about types of people. These cognitions are likely to include stereotypes.

* **Role schemas** are about the characteristics and behaviour of particular social roles. Social roles include family roles such as 'mother', 'brother', occupational roles such as 'doctor' and 'politician', as well as gender roles. Role schemas are also likely to include stereotypes.

* **Event schemas** refer to our knowledge of the sequence of events which happen in familiar situations, such as when shopping for clothes or buying a meal at a restaurant. Schank & Abelson (1977) called these script schemas. For example, a script schema for a telephone conversation includes the following sequence of steps:

  – identifying yourself;
  – exchanging news and small talk;
  – communicating the main purpose of the call;
  – bringing the conversation to an end.

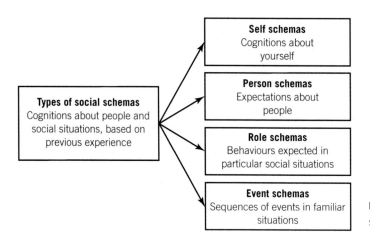

Figure 7.2: Four types of social schema

Practical Activity

Write a list of things which have occurred in your life which you think are typical of you. This could include successes and failures, notable incidents, and habitual activities.

Now get someone else who knows you well to think of events in your life which are typical of you. You could ask a parent or other relative, or an old friend.

Compare the two lists. Your own list is likely to include things which are important in your self-schema. The other person's list reveals something about the person schema they have of you.

If the lists differ, this may be because the other person has a rather inaccurate schema about you. But it could also be because your self-schema is a little inaccurate.

Now think of another everyday social event, and write the script, i.e. list the sequence of steps a person taking part would follow.

Evaluative Comment

Social schemas are useful because they enable us to respond rapidly and appropriately to the actions of others. They enable us to know what to expect of other people in social situations, and so help us to pay attention to relevant information, while ignoring other information.

However, these expectations can lead to bias in impression formation. For example, we tend to ignore or discount information which does not fit our expectations.

Cultural differences

People growing up in different cultural traditions may acquire different social schemas. This leads to cultural differences in the way information is processed, including differences in social perception. Such cultural differences may be found between people living in different parts of the world, but also between people belonging to different sub-cultures within a culture.

For example, children from working-class and middle-class backgrounds may have different perceptions of an individual who studies hard at school. A traditional working-class view of work may include the idea that work is something you have to do for other people (such as 'bosses', who wield coercive and economic power). Your work benefits them more than you, so you should not

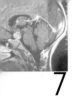

'Well-organised achiever' or 'teacher's pet'? How you perceive this student may depend on your own culture

work any harder than you have to. A traditional middle-class view of work is that it is activity which often brings benefit to the worker, through self-advancement. Work is a route to financial security and social success, so you should work as hard as you can. A school student who works hard may be seen by working-class children as rather weak, because they are allowing themselves to be influenced too much by the demands of teachers. They may be labelled as a 'swot' or 'teacher's pet'. The same student may be seen by middle-class children as ambitious, capable and determined.

Kunda (1999) describes several differences in social perception and self-perception between 'Westerners' (described as North Americans and Europeans) and 'Easterners' (including people from Japan and India). She points out that Westerners see people as unique, independent individuals, concerned with their own personal qualities, ambitious for personal achievement, and seeking opportunities to 'look good' compared with their peers.

In contrast, Easterners see people as part of a web of social relationships, concerned with the welfare of the group (e.g. the family) and seeking opportunities for self-criticism.

Different cultures have rather different ways of thinking about people and social roles – in other words, different social schemas.

Study

AIM *Hoffman et al. (1986) conducted a study to find out whether English and Chinese people had different person schemas.*

METHOD *Short stories were prepared, describing different individuals. One described a person who had what Europeans think of as an 'artistic personality', although this label was not used in the story. Another story described a person who had the personality type described by Chinese people as 'shi-gu'. This type of personality is 'worldly, devoted to the family, socially skilled and reserved'. The stories were printed in English and in Chinese, then English-speaking and Chinese-speaking participants were asked to read each story and to write down their impressions of the character described.*

RESULTS *As shown in Figure 7.3, English speakers wrote down more character traits for the artistic personality than the shi-gu personality. For example, they often suggested that the artistic person would probably be unreliable. This suggests that this was a personality type they recognised and already had a social schema for.*

In contrast, the Chinese speakers wrote down more character traits for the shi-gu personality.

CONCLUSION *English and Chinese people show cultural differences in the schemas they use to think about personality.*

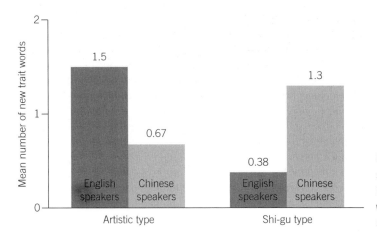

Figure 7.3: Bar chart showing familiarity of English and Chinese speakers with two different person schemas

---

Evaluative Comment

One explanation of such cultural differences is that children learn social schemas from the people around them. In other words, social schemas can be culturally transmitted from parents to children and from peer to peer. This does not mean that everyone within one particular culture will have identical social schemas, but that there will be more similarity in social schemas within that culture than between cultures. To say that 'all Westerners are more concerned with personal achievement than the good of the groups of which they are members' would be an overgeneralisation amounting to stereotyping.

Impression formation: self perception

In addition to perceiving other people, we also perceive ourselves. Just as we use social schemas to make sense of the behaviour of others, we use self-schemas to form our perception of ourselves.

These self-schemas make up what is sometimes called the **self-image**. The self-image is important because it is likely to influence a person's behaviour and experience. For example, a person with a very positive view of themselves is likely to take on challenges and feel good about themselves.

Self-image may have more influence over some people than others. Some people may give little attention to perceiving themselves, while for others this may be a major preoccupation. Apart from these individual differences in the importance of self-concept, there may also be group differences (e.g. along the lines of age or sex).

Cooley's 'looking-glass self'

How do we form an image of ourselves? We know what we think and feel, but we cannot be detached and impartial observers of our own behaviour.

One factor contributing to our self-image is the reactions of other people. This factor was described by Cooley (1902), who referred to it as the **looking-glass self**. Our self is reflected back to us by the way other people treat us. For example, a person who keeps getting invited to parties and who is always the centre of attention is likely to perceive themselves as likeable, interesting and attractive. In contrast, a person who is often the victim of bullying and name-calling may perceive themselves as weak, inadequate and unattractive. Despite the name 'looking-glass self', this is nothing to do with looking in a mirror. Instead of looking at a reflection of ourselves, we watch other people and then infer what sort of a person it is that produces such reactions in them.

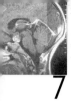

7

Social comparison

Another factor which is likely to influence an individual's self image is the comparisons they make between themselves and others (known as **social comparisons**). It is easy to compare our physical appearance, academic performance, wealth and abilities with those of others. A person who is often in the company of others who are mostly superior to them in these respects is more likely to have a negative self-image. That same person in the company of 'inferiors' would be likely to have a more positive self-image.

Group membership

According to Social Identity Theory (Tajfel 1981), a person's membership of a social group, community or national group (their 'social identity') also contributes to their self-image. For example, the fact that a person is a doctor, Scottish and female, may be important aspects of that person's self-concept.

Practical Activity

Each of the examples below illustrates one of the factors influencing self-image. Decide whether each example illustrates the looking-glass self, social comparison or group membership.

1. *Bruce is an Australian living in London. He feels good about himself because of his country's success at sports. He thinks Englishmen are wimps.*

2. *Mandy thinks of herself as tough and aggressive, and she quite enjoys having this image. Younger children are frightened of her, and her parents describe her as 'bad'.*

3. *Joanne is very unhappy with the way she looks. She often reads magazines illustrated with pictures of fashion models.*

Self-esteem

Self-image includes **self-esteem**, which can be seen as the evaluative aspect of self-image.

A person with high self-esteem has a feeling of self-worth and capability. A person with low self-esteem approves less of themselves and their abilities.

Individuals may also have an image of the sort of person they would like to be. This is called the **ideal self**. If the difference between a person's self-image and ideal self is quite large, they are likely to have low self-esteem.

Rosenberg (1965) measured the self-esteem of a large number of adolescents and found that high self-esteem correlated with higher social class, better school performance and more experience of leadership. This evidence may support the idea of the influence of social comparison, but as it is correlational, a different interpretation could be given.

Study

Aim *Coopersmith (1967) conducted a study to investigate factors which contributed to self-esteem.*

Method *He measured the self-esteem of several hundred middle-class white boys aged between nine and ten years, using three sources of data:*

1. *Scores on a self-esteem inventory (a questionnaire which the boys filled in themselves)*

2. *Teachers' evaluations of the boys' self-esteem*

3. *Scores on a projective test of self-esteem (the Thematic Apperception Test).*

Coopersmith then selected the seventeen boys who scored highest on self-esteem and the seventeen who scored lowest. In this way, he hoped to find factors which systematically differed between the two groups.

RESULTS *Compared with low scorers, the high scorers had more accurate perceptions of themselves, were more popular and performed better at school. The low scorers were more likely to underrate their own abilities, to underachieve at school and to be preoccupied with their own problems.*

There was no significant difference between these two groups in intelligence or physical attractiveness. However, Coopersmith did find a difference in the rearing experiences of the two groups. Parents of the high-esteem boys were more likely to use a democratic rearing style. This style of rearing includes showing approval and providing clear guidelines for behaviour. In contrast, parents of the low-esteem boys tended to be inconsistent, fluctuating between being over-punitive and over-permissive. They were often neglecting and disrespectful towards their children.

CONCLUSION *The reactions of others, particularly parents, have more influence on self-esteem than other factors, such as social comparison. In other words, the study supports the 'looking-glass self' explanation.*

Evaluative Comment

One criticism of Coopersmith's study is that the sample was restricted to one cultural group. The participants were all the same sex, age, social class and ethnicity. The findings cannot therefore be generalised to other groups. For example, it is quite possible that a similar study using female participants might produce different results.

The study can also be criticised on ethical grounds, because it drew the participants' attention to their own self-esteem. For those participants with low self-esteem, this may have been an uncomfortable and embarrassing experience, and may have further decreased their self-esteem.

Theories of attribution

Attribution refers to the tendency we have to make inferences about the causes of people's behaviour. It includes the judgements we make about the reasons for our own behaviour (self-attributions).

Imagine you are watching a well-known personality on a television chat show. You observe that his speech is slurred and that he has a silly, lopsided grin on his face. You might infer a cause for this set of behaviours, for example, you might think he was drunk. An alternative inference might have been that he had suffered a slight stroke, but was carrying on bravely. These inferences about the cause of his behaviour are called *attributions*.

Psychologists often make a distinction between **dispositional** and **situational attributions**. If you make a dispositional attribution, you are saying that the cause of a person's action was their own character or personality. In effect, you claim that they were responsible for this action. If you make a situational attribution, you are saying that the cause of a person's action was the circumstances they were in, and not freely chosen by them. You claim that the situation was responsible for producing this action.

This may strike you as crude – surely the causes of people's actions are both dispositional *and* situational, not one or the other? This is true to a certain extent, but Jones & Nisbett (1971) suggest that ordinary people really do have a simplistic view of human behaviour and really do attribute behaviour to either one sort of cause or the other.

Another way of putting the distinction between dispositional and situational attributions is to call them *internal* and *external* attributions. Internal attributions are dispositional: the cause is inside the person. External attributions are situational: the cause is outside the person.

7

Most examples of attribution refer to situations where an observer makes attributions about the behaviour of another person – the actor. However, we may also make attributions about our own behaviour, particularly if somebody asks us to explain our actions. The attributions we make are likely to be influenced by our social schemas.

Practical Activity

Think back to the example of the TV personality. The belief that he was drunk was a dispositional (internal) attribution. His drunken state was caused by himself. The alternative attribution, that he had had a stroke, is a situational (external) attribution.

Even though the supposed stroke would have happened inside his brain, he could not be held responsible for it and, like most illnesses, it could be seen as situational. (See Figure 7.4.)

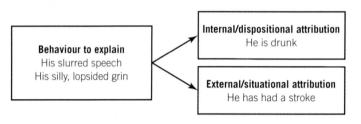

Figure 7.4: Internal and external attributions to explain the TV personality's behaviour

*Decide whether the following **causal attributions** are mainly dispositional or mainly situational:*

1 *I didn't get the work done because basically I'm lazy.*

2 *She didn't get custody of the child because her ex-husband had left her with debts.*

3 *I won the race, mainly because none of the top athletes had entered it.*

4 *Peter really meant to hurt Tom's feelings.*

5 *The reason why few women get top jobs isn't because of lack of opportunity. They simply don't have the necessary determination.*

Notice that items 1 and 3 are self-attributions. The actor is inferring the cause of their own behaviour.

It might be useful to consider in what sorts of situation a person might want to make such attributions. A good example is a situation where someone has suffered some hurt or embarrassment. In this case, they may want to know who or what was to blame. Deciding on blame is an example of attributing cause.

Evaluative Comment

When misunderstandings occur between people, it may be because they do not agree on how to attribute the causes of behaviour. For example, a motorist swerves to avoid a child and collides with a van coming the other way. The van driver may attribute the car driver's behaviour dispositionally – he was driving too fast. However, the car driver attributes his behaviour situationally – the child stepping into the road caused him to swerve.

Attribution theories

These are theories which try to explain and predict what leads us to make situational or dispositional attributions in any particular case.

The correspondent inference model (Jones & Davis, 1965)

Jones & Davis (1965) thought dispositional attributions were more important to us than situational ones, because they provide us with information from which we can make predictions about a person's future behaviour. For example, a student whose car has broken down asks a friend who is passing to help push it. The friend refuses. If the student makes a dispositional attribution (e.g. infers that the friend is not a helpful kind of person), they can predict that the friend will not help in other situations. If the student makes a situational attribution (e.g. maybe he's in a hurry), this does not lead to predictions of future behaviour.

Jones and Davis thought that we pay particular attention to *intentional behaviour* (as opposed to accidental or unthinking behaviour). Their correspondent inference theory describes the conditions under which we make dispositional attributions to behaviours we perceive as intentional. Jones and Davis used the term **correspondent inference** to refer to an occasion when an observer infers that a person's behaviour matches or corresponds with their personality. It is an alternative term to *dispositional attribution*. For example, imagine that Melissa, a school student, has observed that her Biology teacher is often angry with pupils and their parents. When he is angry with Melissa, she is likely to infer that his behaviour corresponds with his personality. She is likely to attribute his behaviour dispositionally, to the extent that Melissa may not feel guilty about what she did to anger him. Melissa has also observed that her History teacher is hardly ever angry with anyone. But today, he is very angry with Melissa. She is likely to attribute his behaviour situationally – and will probably assume that the annoying situation is her behaviour. In the first case, the teacher's behaviour is seen to correspond with his personality. In the second case, the teacher's behaviour does not correspond, so an external cause seems more likely.

The factors which Jones and Davis believe we pay particular attention to include:

- choice
- non-common effects
- social desirability
- hedonic relevance
- personal direction.

Choice

If we perceive that a person's behaviour is freely chosen – not coerced or involuntary – we are more likely to make a correspondent inference. The choices a person makes reveals their personality.

Non-common effects

If a person's behaviour involved a choice between alternatives, and the alternatives are all very similar, we tend to focus our attention on what is different (or 'non-common') between the two alternatives. It is these **non-common effects** which lead to a correspondent inference.

For example, John wants to buy a pair of trainers. He has to choose between two brands – Mikey and Adios. Figure 7.5 shows which effects are common to both brands of trainer and which effects are unique to one brand only.

The two brands have much in common, so the small number of non-common effects give us a clue about John's character. If he chooses the Mikey trainers, we might assume that John is a conformist. If he chooses the Adios trainers, we might assume that he thinks for himself and is concerned about the welfare of child workers.

When there are few non-common effects (as in this example), it is easier to make an internal attribution.

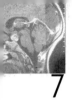

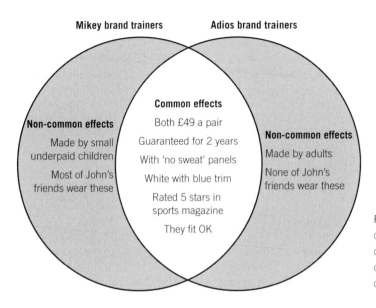

Mikey brand trainers   **Adios brand trainers**

Common effects
Both £49 a pair
Guaranteed for 2 years
With 'no sweat' panels
White with blue trim
Rated 5 stars in
sports magazine
They fit OK

Non-common effects
Made by small
underpaid children
Most of John's
friends wear these

Non-common effects
Made by adults
None of John's
friends wear these

Figure 7.5: The two brands
of trainers have a lot in
common. There are few non-
common effects of John's
choice

Now consider a second example. Jane wants to buy a pair of rock climbing boots. She has two brands to choose between: Sosolo and Scampa (see Figure 7.6). If Jane chooses the Scampa brand, there are so many non-common effects that we get little information about Jane's personality. Perhaps she prefers to climb on granite, or is too lazy to tie laces, or likes to buy British, or wants her climbing boots to match her hair. If there are many non-common effects, your choice reveals little about your disposition.

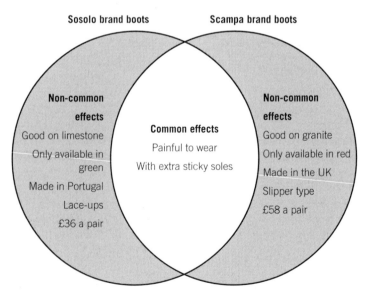

Sosolo brand boots   **Scampa brand boots**

Non-common effects
Good on limestone
Only available in green
Made in Portugal
Lace-ups
£36 a pair

Common effects
Painful to wear
With extra sticky soles

Non-common effects
Good on granite
Only available in red
Made in the UK
Slipper type
£58 a pair

Figure 7.6: The two brands
of rock climbing boots have
little in common. There are
many non-common effects of
Jane's choice

Social desirability

Social desirability means 'conforming to social norms'. Behaviour is low in social desirability if it does not conform to social norms. In this case, you are likely to make a correspondent inference. For example, you observe a person getting on a bus and sitting on the floor instead of one of the seats. Sitting on the floor of a bus is low in social desirability (most people do not do it). In this case, you are likely to infer that this behaviour corresponds with some personality trait of the person.

Hedonic relevance

Another person's behaviour has **hedonic relevance** to us if the behaviour affects us (either pleasantly or unpleasantly). For example, a fellow train passenger doing a crossword is likely to have no hedonic relevance for you, but if they have long conversations on their mobile phone, you might find this annoying and unpleasant. Behaviour with hedonic relevance is more likely to be perceived as dispositional.

Personal direction

Behaviour which seems intentional and deliberately targeted at the observer is more likely to lead to a correspondent inference than behaviour which affects other people or is not directed at anyone. For example, a person who is reading a book and chuckling quietly does not seem to be directing their behaviour at anyone. If they are laughing at a comedian, the behaviour is directed, but not at the observer. If the person is watching the observer and laughing, it seems to be personally directed. In this situation, the observer is most likely to infer something about the person's character.

All of these factors are summed up in Figure 7.7.

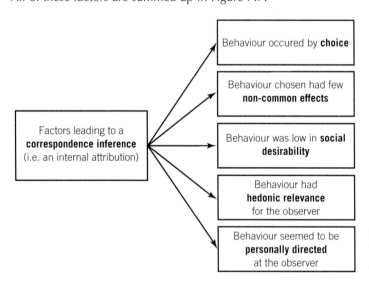

Figure 7.7: Five factors likely to lead to a correspondent inference

---

Practical Activity

Alison said, 'We decided to go out for a meal to celebrate our exam results. Choosing where to go was not easy, because all the places are pretty similar. About half of us, including me, voted to go to the Indian restaurant, and about half wanted to go to the vegetarian restaurant. When it was Pete's turn to vote, he chose the vegetarian restaurant. I don't think Pete knew this, but I can't bear the thought of eating vegetables.'

Use the table below to decide how Pete's voting behaviour is likely to be attributed by Alison.

First decide which of the factors applied in Pete's case, then decide whether this would lead to a correspondent inference or not.

If most or all of the attributions are dispositional, the friend would be likely to make a correspondent inference.

Factor	In Pete's case	Correspondent inference?
Was the behaviour freely chosen?	Yes/No	Yes/No
Were there few non-common effects?	Yes/No	Yes/No
Was the behaviour low in social desirability?	Yes/No	Yes/No
Did it have hedonic relevance for Alison?	Yes/No	Yes/No
Was it personally directed at her?	Yes/No	Yes/No

Study

AIM *Jones* et al. *(1961) conducted a study to investigate the influence of the social desirability factor on attribution.*

METHOD *Participants listened to tape recordings of people who were applying to be an astronaut or a submariner. Before hearing the tape, participants were told of the required qualities for these jobs, including the idea that submariners needed to be extrovert and sociable, whereas astronauts needed to be introverted and self-sufficient. The taped applicants either behaved in a way which was consistent with the required qualities or the opposite way. If a person applying to be a submariner came across as extroverted, this would show high social desirability – that's how you would have to act if you wanted the job. In contrast, if the person wanting to be a submariner seemed introverted, this would show low social desirability.*

Participants were asked to rate personality traits of each applicant, and also to indicate how confident they were in judging the personality of each applicant.

RESULTS *Participants were more confident in rating those applicants who had acted in the opposite to the required characteristics. In other words, those applicants whose behaviour had been low in social desirability were seen as revealing more about themselves.*

CONCLUSION *This suggests that behaviour with low social desirability is likely to be attributed dispositionally, i.e. to tell us something about the person's personality. This supports the correspondent inference theory.*

Evaluative Comment

One strength of the correspondent inference theory is that it recognises that attribution is likely to be influenced by observer bias. Observer bias is the tendency for a person's schemas to lead to inaccuracies in their judgements of the behaviour of other people. The theory also emphasises that we make dispositional attributions when we perceive that a person's behaviour is intentional.

However, Eiser (1983) pointed out that behaviour does not have to be seen to be intentional for us to attribute it dispositionally. For example, if a person keeps forgetting to pay their bills, we are likely to make a dispositional attribution – to describe their personality as 'forgetful' – even though forgetting things is not intentional. Unintentional, accidental behaviour can still be attributable to a person's character.

The theory, in effect, says that we make dispositional attributions when we don't have good evidence of situational factors, but emphasises the social desirability (conformity) factor above others. It may be that other situational factors are just as important in practice.

The co-variation model (Kelley, 1967)

Kelley (1967) argued that our tendency to make dispositional attributions is influenced by our knowledge of how people usually behave in a variety of situations. Kelley believed that when attributing cause to a person's behaviour, we take into account:

* how other people behave

* how that person usually behaves.

The *principle of co-variation* states that:

> 'an effect is attributed to one of its possible causes with which, over time, it co-varies'.

For example, if John is cheerful at all times, we tend to attribute this to John's temperament, rather than the situations he is in.

Kelley believed that there were three types of causal information which influenced our judgements (see Figures 7.8 and 7.9):

* **Consensus:** the extent to which other people behave in the same way in a similar situation. For example, Alison smokes a cigarette when she goes out for a birthday meal with her friends. If all her friends smoke, her behaviour is high in consensus. If she is the only one of the group who smokes, consensus is low.

* **Distinctiveness:** the extent to which the person behaves in the same way in similar situations. If Alison only smokes when she is out with friends, her behaviour is high in distinctiveness, i.e. rather unusual for her. If she smokes at almost any time and place, distinctiveness is low.

* **Consistency:** the extent to which the person behaves like this every time the situation occurs. If Alison always smokes when she is out with friends, consistency is high. If she only smokes on this one special occasion, consistency is low.

Consensus	Distinctiveness	Consistency	Likely attribution
High – all Alison's friends smoke	High – Alison only smokes when out with friends	High – Alison always smokes when out with friends	Situational
Low – none of Alison's friends smoke	Low – Alison smokes in all kinds of situations	High – Alison always smokes when out with friends	Dispositional

Figure 7.8: Patterns of behaviour leading to situational and dispositional attributions (according to Kelley)

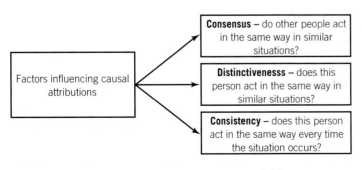

Figure 7.9: Factors influencing causal attributions (according to Kelley)

7

Practical Activity

Apply Kelley's theory to the following example:

Sally often sleeps during her psychology class, as do quite a few other students. She never sleeps during her other subject classes.

Use a grid to label Sally's behaviour in terms of Kelley's three factors and decide how a person is likely to attribute Sally's behaviour in the psychology class.

Study

AIM *McArthur (1972) carried out a study to test the effect of varying consensus, distinctiveness and consistency on attribution; in other words, to test Kelley's theory.*

METHOD *Participants were given one-sentence descriptions of behaviour, followed by information about consensus, distinctiveness and consistency.*

For example, the description 'John laughed at the comedian' might be followed with the consensus information 'Other people also laugh at this comedian' and information about distinctiveness, such as 'John also laughs a lot at other comedians', as well as consistency information such as 'John has almost always laughed at this comedian'.

The information about consensus, distinctiveness and consistency was varied in different conditions of the experiment.

Participants were asked to attribute the John's behaviour to a) the person, b) the situation, or c) a combination of the two.

RESULTS *Participants made more dispositional attributions when consensus and distinctiveness were low, but consistency was high. This means that dispositional attributions were made to statements like:*

> *'John laughs at the comedian, but other people do not.'*
> *'John laughs at the comedian, and he also laughs at other comedians.'*
> *'John has almost always laughed at this comedian.'*

CONCLUSION *These results confirmed Kelley's predictions. Information about the consensus, distinctiveness and consistency of behaviour did affect the attributions made, as in the pattern illustrated by Figure 7.8.*

Evaluative Comment

Just because the factors have the effect Kelley predicted does not mean that we actually use them in our everyday judgements of behaviour. The McArthur study was artificial, it lacked ecological validity.

Major (1980) gave participants the opportunity to request information about consensus, distinctiveness and consistency when engaged in an attribution task. Results showed that participants only requested some of the information available: they were most likely to ask about consistency and least likely to ask about consensus. This study implies that we do not take this kind of information into account to the extent that Kelley claimed.

Nisbett & Borgida (1975) also found that consensus information had little effect. They asked participants to make attributions about a person who had agreed to have an electric shock as part of an experiment. Giving some participants information about consensus (that 16 out of 34 people had agreed to the shock) made no difference to the attributions made.

Another criticism of this theory is that we rarely have access to information about these three variables, so that the theory only describes a 'special case' of attribution.

Another problem is that the theory suggests that we perform what is quite a complicated operation of taking into account the three variables. This is not very plausible, because of the cognitive effort involved.

Finally, the theory implies that the attribution process is logical and rational – a balanced and scientific assessment of probabilities. In practice, people are likely to be biased in their attributions, as in other aspects of social cognition. Sources of attribution bias are described on pages 197–199.

The Causal schemata model (Kelley, 1973)

Kelley produced an alternative and simpler theory of attribution, to explain how we make attributions when we do not have information about consensus, distinctiveness and consistency. Kelley argued that, in the case where we do not know a person and have no information about their previous behaviour, we rely on learned ideas about how causes interact to produce effects. These ideas are schemas about causes, called **causal schemata**.

According to Kelley, our life experience helps us to build up a library of such schemas, enabling us to make snap judgements about the causes of behaviour even for unfamiliar people and situations. These schemas include script schemas which cover a range of standard situations, such as family disputes, being a customer in a shop, being bullied and having encounters with authority figures. Familiarity with such schemas is what enables people to be entertained by sitcoms and soap operas.

Kelley described two contrasting types of causal schemata: **multiple sufficient causes** and **multiple necessary causes**, as shown in Figure 7.10.

Multiple sufficient causes

In a case where we can easily think of several situational causes of a person's behaviour, any one of which would be likely to produce the behaviour shown, we are likely to make a situational attribution. For example, a student decides to attend an open-air concert for which they have been given a free ticket, which is to be held in a park within walking distance of their home, and on a day when the weather is good. Each of the factors mentioned provides sufficient reason to explain the person attending the concert. In this type of situation, the behaviour is likely to be situationally attributed. On the other hand, if the student decided not to go to the concert, a dispositional attribution would be more likely.

Kelley argued that in many cases where there are multiple sufficient causes, we simplify matters by favouring one of them and discounting the others. This is called the **discounting** principle. In the example above, an observer might assume that the student went to the concert because they had a free ticket.

Multiple necessary causes

In a case where several causes must all be present for behaviour to take place, then the absence of one of these is likely to lead to the behaviour being situationally attributed.

For example, in order to play at the concert, a guitarist has to be able to get there, their guitar must also be present and the public address system has to work. If the power fails, we attribute the guitarist's failure to play as due to the situation. Only if all the necessary causes were fulfilled would we attribute the guitarist's failure to play to disposition ('She's a very temperamental person,' etc.).

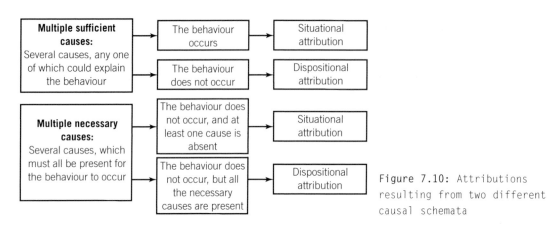

Figure 7.10: Attributions resulting from two different causal schemata

---

Evaluative Comment

This theory is plausible in that it does not claim that people put a great deal of thought and calculation into their attributions of cause. It also recognises that we can attribute causes without having access to much information. In other words, the theory is consistent with the observation that people often make 'snap judgements' about the characteristics and intentions of others.

However, this means that the theory is much less specific than the theories previously described, so it has less predictive power.

One general criticism of attribution theories is that they are of limited use in relation to the effort needed to grasp them. A student who has difficulty in understanding attribution theories might be justified in attributing this externally (to the difficulty of the theory) rather than internally (to their own lack of ability or effort).

A further criticism is that attribution theories are based on the doubtful assumption that we attribute causes to behaviour either internally or externally. In reality, we may be well aware that a particular behaviour is the result of a combination of causes. Whether they are internal or external may not be important to us.

The distinction between internal and external causes is not always clear cut. For example, a person does well in a test, and we judge that this performance is due to their ability and hard work. This looks like a good example of an internal cause. But we might also think that their ability is to some extent due to the encouragement they received during childhood and the motivation provided by an inspirational teacher. These look like external causes.

Another example where the distinction between internal and external causes becomes blurred is in the case where illness influences a person's behaviour. Although this is often given as an example of a situation where an external attribution is appropriate, an illness is, in one sense, obviously internal to the person. In the case of a personality disorder, the distinction breaks down altogether. A personality disorder is clearly an aspect of a person's personality, and therefore behaviour resulting from it will be attributed dispositionally. On the other hand, it is a disorder, an affliction, so that the sufferer cannot be held responsible for its effects, in which case resulting behaviour will be attributed situationally.

The fact that people make causal attributions in research studies does not mean that they frequently do so in more real-life situations. Attribution experiments often require participants to make attributions, using a forced-choice method. Participants have to choose between dispositional, situational or mixed attributions.

Attributional biases

Like impression-formation, attributing causes to people's behaviour is prone to bias.

Reflective Activity

Write down whether you would be more likely to make dispositional or situational attributions in each of the following circumstances.

1 *You see a person reverse their car and collide with a vehicle parked behind.*

2 *You reverse your car into a vehicle parked behind you.*

3 *You come first in a sheep-shearing competition.*

4 *A person you dislike does badly in an exam.*

Now think about the excuses people make for their own behaviour:

   'I'm late because the bus didn't come.'

   'I didn't really forget your birthday, it's just that pressure of work prevented me from buying a present.'

Explain the connection between making excuses and the attribution process.

It should be clear from the examples above that our attributions are susceptible to bias, and that sometimes people behave in a such a way as to modify the attributions we make of their behaviour.

Psychologists have identified several different kinds of **attributional bias**. These include:

* the fundamental attribution error;
* the actor–observer effect;
* the self-serving bias.

The fundamental attribution error

This is the tendency we have to attribute behaviour to dispositional causes rather than situational causes. In other words, we overestimate the role of dispositions and underestimate the role of situations.

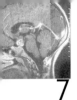

7 Study

AIM *Ross* et al. *(1977) conducted a study to find out whether participants took account of situational factors when judging the performance of people taking part in a quiz.*

METHOD *Students were randomly assigned to be either questioners or contestants in a quiz. The questioners were given fifteen minutes to think up general knowledge questions. Then the contestants were tested on these. This gave an advantage to the questioner, who chose questions on topics they knew well. Later, the questioners, contestants and some other students who observed were asked to rate the general knowledge of the questioners and contestants.*

RESULTS *All the participants rated the questioners' knowledge as superior to the contestants'.*

CONCLUSION *The questioner appears more knowledgeable because he or she knows the answers to all the questions, whereas the contestant gets some answers wrong. However, the questioner has had the advantage of choosing the questions. This is a situational factor. You might expect that an observer who knew that the questioner had this advantage would make an allowance for this when judging the level of knowledge of questioner and contestant. The results suggest that the participants did not make allowances for this situational factor, so the fundamental attribution error has occurred.*

According to Jones & Nisbett (1971), we tend to favour simple explanations over complex ones. It is easier to attribute behaviour to the person who produces it than to the many external influences there may have been. Storms (1973) points out that an observer rarely has information about another person's circumstances. We see the person acting in a certain way and assume it is because of the type of person they are.

Another explanation is that we focus our attention on the person rather than the context they are in. Burger (1991) asked participants to listen while a stranger expressed an opinion. The participants were told that the speaker had been told to express that particular opinion and had no choice in the matter. Even so, participants tended to attribute the views expressed dispositionally. However, participants questioned a week after hearing the speaker made more situational attributions. This supports the view that the presence of the person focuses our attention on themselves rather than the context they are in.

Evaluative Comment

There is convincing evidence to suggest that the fundamental attribution error occurs. However, an opposite bias can occur in some situations.

Quattrone (1982) found that participants who were told about situational factors which played some part in influencing an actor's behaviour tended to overestimate their influence and make situational attributions. This supports Jones and Nisbett's view that we oversimplify when attributing causes to behaviour.

There is also evidence that the fundamental attribution error may not occur in all cultures. Miller (1984) asked American participants and Hindus from India to attribute causes to various good or bad actions. She found that the Hindu participants made about twice as many situational attributions as the Americans, and correspondingly fewer dispositional attributions. This suggests that the fundamental attribution error may occur in some cultures and not others. In most Asian countries, as well as in Africa and South America, people see themselves more as part of a social group and less as distinct individuals. In contrast, the importance of being a distinct individual is emphasised in North American and European cultures.

The actor-observer effect

This bias refers to a kind of double-standard we have. When observing another person's behaviour, you are likely to attribute this behaviour dispositionally. However, when attributing your own behaviour, you are more likely to make a situational attribution. For example, David is playing football and misses an easy shot at goal. Sven, who is an *observer*, attributes David's miss dispositionally. He missed the goal because he is not a very good player. David, who is the *actor*, attributes the miss situationally: he slipped on the waterlogged pitch just as he kicked the ball.

One explanation for the effect is that the actor is much more aware of the situational variables affecting his behaviour than an observer is. Another explanation, suggested by Storms (1973), is that the actor and observer have different points of view. The actor is looking at the situation, but the observer is looking at the actor.

Study

AIM *Storms (1973) conducted a study to find out whether a person who has an observer's point of view is likely to make more dispositional attributions than a person who has the actor's point of view.*

METHOD *Participants were told that they were taking part in a study to find out what happens when two strangers meet and get acquainted. The participants were studied in groups of four. Two of these were the 'actors' and were asked to have a five-minute 'get to know you' conversation. The other two partici-pants were asked to observe the actors. During the conversation, both actors were videotaped. To measure attribution, participants (both actors and observers) were then asked to fill in a questionnaire including items on how much the actor's behaviour was caused by their personality, character, atti-tudes, mood, etc., and on how much it was caused by the situation, such as the topic of conversation which came up and the fact of being in an experiment.*

RESULTS *Observers made more dispositional attributions than actors did.*

Interestingly, when the actors were asked to watch the videotape of themselves, they also tended to make more dispositional attributions.

CONCLUSIONS *Several conclusions follow from this study:*

- *The existence of actor–observer effect was supported.*
- *A person's point of view is a key factor in the effect.*
- *The results also showed that both groups made more dispositional than situational attributions. This supports the fundamental attribution error.*

Evaluative Comment

The existence of the actor–observer effect is supported by Storms' (1973) study. However, the effect does not always occur. Fiske & Taylor (1991) report that when the behaviour involved is helping another person, the effect is reversed. The actor attributes his or her own helpful behaviour dispositionally, but attributes the behaviour of another person who is being helpful situationally.

The self-serving bias

This is the tendency we have to make attributions which are favourable to us and which help to protect our self-esteem. For example, if you have some success, you are likely to attribute it to your own efforts, i.e. dispositionally. If you experience some failure, you are likely to attribute this to circumstances beyond your control, i.e. situationally.

7

Practical Activity

Ask a friend who failed their driving test or did badly in a test or examination what the main reason was for their failure. Answers such as 'I didn't revise' or 'I'm just not very good at it' indicate that the friend has made an internal attribution. Answers such as 'It was a really hard test' or 'I had too much work on at the time' indicate an external attribution which is self-serving.

Try this with a few friends, and vary it by sometimes asking about their successes.

Ask a teacher how many of their students got Grade As last summer (or how many failed).

Then ask why the students did so well (or badly). Again, what you need to find out is whether the teacher attributes the students' success (or failure) internally or externally. If the teacher attributes their students' success to the teacher's efforts, or the students' failures to the students' lack of effort or ability, this is an example of the self-serving bias.

Arkin *et al.* (1980) found that students believed that examinations in which they had performed well were fair, while examinations in which they had performed badly were poor indicators of ability. They also found that teachers are more likely to accept responsibility for their students' performance in examinations if the students did well.

Study

AIM *Kingdon (1967) conducted an interview study to investigate how politicians attributed their own success or failure in elections.*

METHOD *Politicians in the USA were interviewed a few months after an election. Some of them had won their elections, others had lost. They were asked to summarise the reasons why they had won or lost.*

RESULTS *The election winners claimed that their success had been due to hard work, personal service to their electors and their good reputation locally. The losers claimed that their failure was due to a lack of money for publicity, the fact that their opponent was very well known and that the district had a tradition of electing members of another political party.*

CONCLUSION *The reasons given by the winners were mainly dispositional. They claimed that their success was due to their own qualities and effort, and not due to outside circumstances. The reasons given by the losers were mainly situational. They claimed that factors beyond their control had produced the result, and not their own inadequacy or lack of effort. Win or lose, the participants explained the result in a way which was favourable, or not unfavourable, to themselves. This suggests that the participants demonstrated a self-serving bias.*

Evaluative Comment

The self-serving bias does not always occur. Abramson et al. (1978) found that people who were depressed showed the opposite bias. They tended to attribute their successes to circumstances and to blame their failures on themselves. A possible explanation is that depression involves negative cognitions about the self, and a reverse self-serving bias is consistent with these cognitions. Davison and Neale (1994) found that women show a greater tendency towards this reverse bias than men.

Notice that attribution biases sometimes conflict. For example, while the fundamental attribution error and the actor–observer effect both lead to a bias towards dispositional attributions of the behaviour of others, in the case of a teacher attributing the success of his or her students, the self-serving bias leads to a situational attribution. The students' success is attributed to an external factor – the effectiveness of the teacher.

Similarly, the tendency of an actor to attribute their behaviour situationally – as in the actor–observer effect – conflicts with the self-serving bias when the behaviour was successful or praiseworthy.

Reflective Activity

Mr Green is late for his appointment at the dentist. He had set out in time, but then had to go back home to pick up his wallet which he had forgotten. In his hurry, he damaged his car while parking. The dentist, noticing that Mr Green is sweating and agitated, attributes this to an anxiety about dental treatment.

Write down three reasons why Mr Green is more likely to attribute his own behaviour externally than the dentist is.

7

See Appendix 1 for information concerning questions that appear in the examination paper. The assessment of knowledge and understanding (AO1) and analysis and evaluation (AO2) assessment objectives is also given in Appendix 1.

Sample questions

Sample question 1

(a) Mrs Jones says, 'I'm really pleased with my A level results this year. Mind you, I really worked them hard.' Mr Taylor replies, 'My results were disappointing. The students were a dim lot. There wasn't much I could do about that.'
Identify and explain the attribution error which both teachers may be making.
(AO2 = 3) (3 marks)

(b) Identify two factors which are likely to lead someone to develop a high level of self-esteem.
(AO1 = 2) (2 marks)

(c) Describe one study in which self-esteem has been investigated. Indicate in your answer why the study was conducted, the method used, the results obtained and the conclusions drawn.
(AO1 = 5) (5 marks)

(d) Describe and discuss the causal schemata model of attribution.
(AO1 = 4, AO2 = 6) (10 marks)

Total AO1 marks = 11   Total AO2 marks = 9   Total = 20 marks

Questions, answers and comments

(a) What is meant by the term *dispositional attribution*?
(AO1 = 2) (2 marks)

(b) Identify one factor which is likely to influence an observer to make a situational attribution. Illustrate your answer with an example.
(AO1 = 1, AO2 = 1) (2 marks)

(c) Using an example, explain what is meant by each of the following:
(i) the actor–observer effect
(ii) the self-serving bias.
(AO1 = 2, AO2 = 4) (6 marks)

(d) It is Simon's first day at his local college, where he plans to study A levels. The psychology teacher arrives late and tells the class, 'Of course, you can't expect me to teach you anything today with the place in chaos. I'll give you the syllabus to read later if I can get the photocopier to work.' The second meeting of the class is much better organised. With reference to psychological theory and evidence, discuss the likely effect of the events described on the impression Simon forms of the teacher
(AO1= 5, AO2 = 5) (10 marks)

Total AO1 marks = 10   Total AO2 marks = 10   Total = 20 marks

Answer to (a)

A dispositional attribution is made when someone judges that the cause of another person's behaviour is dispositional.

Comment

This answer received one mark, which was awarded for the information that *attribution* means inferring or judging what the cause of a person's behaviour is. However the word *dispositional* has not been explained. To get the second mark, it would be necessary to say that *dispositional* means 'due to the person's personality' or 'internal'. A definition which uses the term to be defined and does not explain it is unlikely to score full marks.

Answer to (b)

If the person had no choice about their behaviour, the observer is likely to make a situational attribution. For example, a person who stays off work for a week because the doctor has told them to.

Comment

This answer would score the full two marks. One mark is awarded for the factor. In this case, the candidate has used one of the factors from the correspondent inference theory. The second mark is gained by a valid example.

Answer to (c)

(i) The actor–observer effect is the tendency to overestimate the importance of dispositional factors in attributing other people's actions. For example, if a car driver sees another driver ahead hesitating at a road junction, he is likely to assume that the other driver is a 'ditherer' or a bad driver, instead of assuming that his car might have a fault.

(ii) The self-serving bias is when we attribute our successes internally, and our failures externally. For example. if I pass my psychology exam, I might think it was because I am intelligent and worked hard; but if I fail my exam, I might say it was because the exam was unfair or my teacher did not teach me properly.

Comment

The candidate scored four out of six marks for this answer. In each part, two marks were available for describing each type of attribution bias, and one mark for each example. Two marks were lost in Part (i) because the candidate has actually described the fundamental attribution error instead of the actor–observer effect. The two are easy to confuse. The candidate should have also referred to a tendency to attribute our own actions more situationally. What the candidate has said is partly relevant, so they get one mark. The example in this part does not score a mark. Part (ii) receives the full three marks.

Answer to (d)

Simon is likely to form a negative impression of the teacher because of the primacy effect. This is the first time Simon has met the teacher, and he is likely to form his impression of him/her right at the start. We usually form impressions quickly because of the need to respond immediately.

The primacy effect means that information received at the start of a relationship is likely to have more influence on impression formation than information received at any later stage. However good the teacher is in later meetings, Simon will see him/her as inefficient because he will ignore or discount information which conflicts with his existing impression. He will already have formed a person schema for him/her, and that schema will influence his judgement of later behaviour.

However, it may be that Simon knows that you should not jump to conclusions about people. If he has kept an open mind, it could be that later information will influence him more. This is called the recency effect. However, it hardly ever occurs in practice.

It may also be that whatever the teacher does, Simon might form a negative impression of him/her, because he might already have quite a negative stereotype of teachers. In that case, his bias against teachers will lead him to think they are all the same and all inefficient. This bias will distort the information he receives about his teacher at the start or later.

Comment

The candidate has described relevant theory, for which three out of the five (AO1) marks were available. They have also applied the theory well to the example of the teacher, and they have done some evaluation of the theory by pointing out alternative or competing explanations. This is worth four out of the five (AO2) marks available.

However, the candidate has not followed the requirement of the question to refer to empirical evidence. They will therefore only score six marks (the maximum allowed if they have not followed the instruction to refer to empirical evidence).

If the candidate had included a brief description and evaluation of studies such as Luchins or Jones *et al.*, full marks could have been obtained.

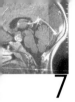

7 Further reading

Introductory texts

Aronson, E., Wilson, T.D. & Akert, R.M. (1999), *Social Psychology*, Addison-Wesley

Baron, R.A. & Byrne, D. (1997), *Social Psychology*, 8th edition, Boston MA, Allyn & Bacon

Deaux, K., Dane, F.C. & Wrightsman, L.S. (1993), *Social Psychology in the '90s*, 6th edition, Brooks/Cole

Hewstone, M. & Stroebe, W. (Eds) (2001), *Introduction to Social Psychology*, 3rd edition, Blackwell Publishers Ltd

Hogg, M.A. & Vaughan, G.M. (1998), *Social Psychology*, 2nd edition, Prentice Hall Europe

Pennington, D.C. (2000) *Social Cognition*, London, Routledge

Lippa, R.A. (1994), *Introduction to Social Psychology*, 2nd edition, Brooks/Cole

Myers, D.G. (1999), *Social Psychology*, 6th edition, McGraw-Hill

Pennington, D.C., Gillen, K. & Hill, P. (1999), *Social Psychology*, Arnold

Specialist sources

Fiske, S.T. & Taylor, S.E. (1991), *Social Cognition*, 2nd edition, McGraw-Hill

Kunda, Z. (1999), *Social Cognition: Making Sense of People*, MIT Press

Smith, P.B. & Bond, M.H. (1998), *Social Psychology Across Cultures*, Prentice Hall Europe

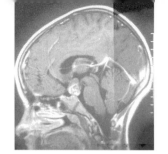

8

Social Psychology of Sport

Introduction

Many sports are played by teams competing with each other

Some sports are played by individuals competing with one another, rather than teams playing each other

Think about a sport that you play, such as hockey, rugby or football, or a game, such as pool or darts. With team sports such as hockey or football, it is common to have other people watching the game. With other games which are more individual, such as pool or darts, they are often played without an **audience** watching. Think about the games you often play and occasions when, where appropriate, people have been watching you and when there has not been an audience. Can you recall whether or not your performance at the game was affected by having an audience present? It is likely that in a one-to-one game you would be much more aware of the people watching you than in a team game. In the first part of this chapter, we shall explore these questions under the topic of **social facilitation**.

Now think about a team game you have played (this may be the same game as above). Playing in a **team** means that all the team members must work together to perform well. It is common sense that if the individuals in a team do not like each other and do not get on very well, then their performance as a team is likely to be poor. In the second part of this chapter, we shall explore these matters under the general topic of **social cohesion**.

8

Social psychology enjoys application to many areas of everyday life. These include application to eyewitness testimony in a legal context, business organisations in relation to leadership and work motivation, understanding human relationships, and sport. In what follows, we will look at social facilitation and team cohesion in relation to sport. In sport psychology, there are many more areas of application, such as attribution theory, self-confidence and self-esteem, which are dealt with generally in Chapter 7 and more specifically in books on sport psychology (e.g. Morris & Summers, 1995; Carron & Hausenblas, 1998).

Social facilitation

It is a commonly made observation that world records are often broken at important events such as the Olympic Games or international championships. In all sports, athletes often improve on their personal best performance in important situations such as finals, when they are performing in front of an audience. Athletes do not usually perform at their best when in training. Hence, the presence of an audience appears to improve the performance of athletes.

Research on social facilitation

Social facilitation is the term used to refer to enhancement of task performance caused by the mere presence of other people (Baron & Byrne, 2000). The use of the phrase 'mere presence of other people' indicates that other people are what may be called **co-actors** or an audience. Co-actors are where two or more people perform the same task or sport as each other and in the presence of each other, for example, cycle racing or a track event such as the 100 or 10,000 metres races. With sports where athletes co-act, there is no concept of team work; each individual is out to do the best for him or herself. By contrast, audiences are a group of people observing individuals or teams playing a sport or performing a task.

Over 100 years ago, Triplett (1898) published one of the first experiments in social psychology. This study was based on the observation that competing cyclists produced faster times when racing with another cyclist than simply competing on their own against the clock. In the first part of the study, Triplett (1898) used archive data from the Racing Board of the league of Wheelmen. He compared times taken by cyclists to cover certain distances in three different conditions: alone (unpaced), with another cyclist as a pace maker and in a racing group. Figure 8.1 depicts Triplett's findings, and shows that cyclists were slowest when racing alone and fastest when racing with a pacemaker or in a racing group.

Figure 8.1: Average time, in seconds per mile, for cyclists racing alone, paced and in a group. Notice that the time for paced and group are similar, but both are faster than when the cyclist races alone (Adapted from Triplett, 1898)

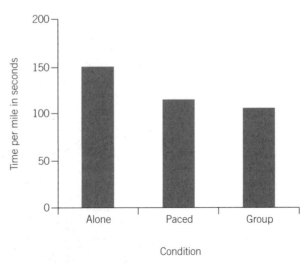

Study

AIM *Triplett (1898) devised a laboratory task to investigate whether or not performance would be enhanced in the presence of other people (co-actors) performing the same task.*

METHOD *Participants were instructed to wind in line on a fishing reel as quickly as they could. Following a practice period, participants performed the task both alone and in pairs, alternating between the two conditions. In each trial, participants were timed at how long about 150 winds of the reel took.*

RESULTS *As can be seen from Figure 8.2, performance was faster in the presence of another person than when the task was performed alone. Participants were about one per cent faster when working in pairs than working alone.*

CONCLUSIONS *Participants' performance at the task was enhanced or facilitated by the presence of another person performing the same task. In other words, a co-acting group produces social facilitation.*

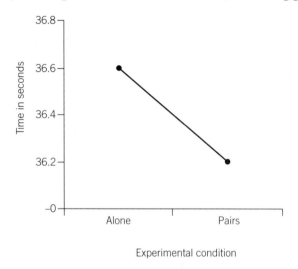

Figure 8.2: Average time to complete the reel-winding task by people working alone and in pairs (Adapted from Triplett, 1898)

Research by Travis (1925) looked at the effect of being observed by other people on performance on a pursuit-rotor task. Participants were first trained to use a pursuit-rotor, which involves holding a pen or stylus and following a moving target. Travis found that participants made fewer errors (that is, kept on target more) when observed by an audience than performing the task alone.

Does performing in front of an audience facilitate or inhibit your performance?

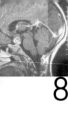
8 Practical Activity

Devise a simple study to investigate either co-action effects or audience effects. You will need to decide upon the type of task, how performance will be measured on the task and how you will determine whether or not an effect has been caused by the presence (co-action or audience) of other people.

Study

AIM *Pessin (1933) investigated the effect of an audience on how well people were able to perform a task.*

METHOD *Participants were asked to learn lists of nonsense syllables (such as KAX), either alone or in the presence of an audience.*

RESULTS *As can be seen from Figure 8.3, performance declined in the presence of an audience. Participants in the audience condition required more trials to learn the list of nonsense syllables. Furthermore, the number of errors made (wrongly recalled nonsense syllables) was higher in the audience condition.*

CONCLUSIONS *The results of Pessin's study directly contradict those obtained by both Triplett and Travis.*

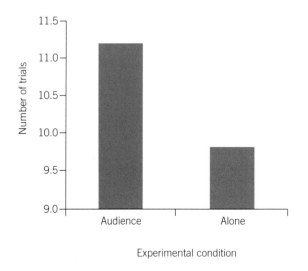

Figure 8.3: Average number of trials required to learn a list of seven nonsense syllables (Adapted from Pessin, 1933)

Pessin (1933) extended the above study and contacted participants several days later and again tested their recall of the nonsense syllables. This time, Pessin found that recall in front of an audience was better than recall alone. Early findings with respect to performance in the presence of other people seem to be contradictory; sometimes performance is enhanced, and at other times it is inhibited.

Evaluative Comment

Numerous studies have been conducted investigating social facilitation with results that seem to be contradictory, as we have seen above. Allport (1924) conducted a series of experiments where participants worked alone in cubicles or sitting round a table together. Allport found that with simple tasks, such as crossing out certain letters in words, performance was better in front of other people. However, with more complex tasks, such as solving complex problems, performance was better when participants worked alone. Dashiell (1930) found that the number of multiplications performed by participants increased in the presence of others, but so did the number of errors made. Schmitt et al. (1986) found that participants typed their name faster in front of an audience, but when asked to type their name backwards, performance was better when they worked alone. Studies with animals have shown that simple mazes are learned faster in the presence of other like animals, whilst complex mazes are learned faster when the animal is on its own (Zajonc et al., 1969).

Reflective Activity

Create a table with two headings; in the first column put 'alone' and in the second column put 'with others'. Read back through the studies mentioned so far. Under the 'alone' column, put those tasks which are performed better when the person is alone. Under the 'with others' column, put those tasks that are performed better in the presence of others. Compare the tasks in the two columns. Can you think of a rule to explain when the presence of others will enhance performance and when the presence of others will inhibit performance?

Facilitation of dominant responses

Zajonc (1965) put forward a theory to explain these apparently contradictory findings. The rule that Zajonc observed was that performance of well-learned or well-practised tasks is enhanced by the presence of other people. In contrast, performance of new or complex tasks is inhibited by the presence of other people. In other words, to quote Zajonc (1965):

'performance is facilitated and learning is impaired by the presence of spectators'.

This is demonstrated in Pessin's (1933) study. Here, we saw that when participants were trying to learn the nonsense syllables, performance was inhibited by the presence of an audience. However, a few days later after the nonsense syllables had been learned, performance was enhanced by an audience and inhibited when alone.

Zajonc (1965) used the term **dominant response** to refer to behaviour we are most likely to perform in a given situation. Zajonc claimed that dominant responses are facilitated by the presence of other people. When a person has learned a behaviour or is highly skilled at a sport, then this is their dominant response. For example, a world-class basketball player who is skilled at throwing the ball through the hoop can be regarded as having this as a dominant response. The basketball player would have practised this behaviour again and again. Hence, in a match, the presence (of both other players and the audience) enhances or facilitates this dominant response. That is, the player will get more balls through the hoop in front an audience than when training alone. In contrast, when somebody is learning a new skill, error or poor performance is the dominant response, so an audience will cause the person to make more errors or perform even more poorly. For example, somebody who has rarely, if ever, played basketball before will get fewer balls through the hoop in front of an audience than when practising alone. Another good example to apply the idea of dominant response to is ice skating.

Highly skilled and experienced ice skaters have their performance facilitated or enhanced by performing in front of an audience

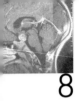

8 Reflective Activity

Identify tasks, games and sports that you think you are skilled at and ones you have rarely, if ever, engaged in. Think about times, if there have been any, when you have had to perform alone and in front of an audience on the same task. Does your experience reflect the idea of dominant responses? A good example is giving a presentation – you practise at home in your room, and then have to deliver it to an audience. How might the two performances differ?

Study

AIM *Michaels et al. (1982) conducted a study to test the prediction that the presence of an audience would facilitate well-learned behaviours and inhibit poorly-learned behaviours.*

METHOD *In the first part of the study, student pool players were observed in a Students' Union building. Following observation, twelve players were selected: six were identified as above average, and six as below average at playing pool. In the second part of the study, four observers stood round a pool table and observed the players over a number of games.*

RESULTS *As can be seen from Figure 8.4, the above average players achieved 80 per cent shot accuracy (balls potted) when observed. In contrast, below average players achieved only 25 per cent shot accuracy when observed and 36 per cent accuracy when not observed.*

CONCLUSIONS *The presence of an audience resulted in performance being affected as predicted by Zajonc's theory of dominant responses. The dominant response of skilled pool players is to pot balls, and the dominant response of unskilled players is to miss shots and not pot balls. An audience facilitates, enhances or exaggerates each of these different dominant responses.*

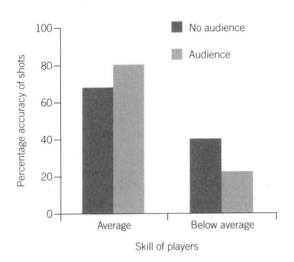

Figure 8.4: Percentage accuracy of shots (percentage of shots resulting in the ball being potted) by above average and below average players with no audience and in front of an audience (Adapted from Michaels *et al.*, 1982)

Similar findings have been reported in numerous studies. For example, MacCracken and Studulis (1985), using eight-year-old children as participants, reported that children skilled at balancing tasks showed higher skills in front of an audience. In contrast, children poor at balancing tasks showed poorer performance in front of an audience. Similar findings supporting the idea of facilitation of dominant response by the presence of others have been reported by Zajonc & Sales (1966) and Geen (1989).

Practical Activity

Working in groups of three or four, design a study to investigate social facilitation of dominant responses. Consider the following:

- *What sport or activity to use, and how you will determine what a dominant response is for each participant (well-learned or inexperienced at).*

- *Who you will use as participants in your study and where these participants will be selected from.*

- *What measures of performance you will take.*

- *What kind of audience you will use, how many people there will be in the audience and what the setting will be.*

Having designed your study, make a prediction or number of predictions based on what you know about the social facilitation of dominant responses.

Facilitation and arousal

Zajonc (1965) put forward the **drive theory of social facilitation**. This states that the presence of other people (co-actors or an audience) increases a person's general level of arousal; this in turn increases the tendency to perform dominant responses. Generally, when arousal is low, such as when we are sleepy, performance at tasks tends to be poor. Similarly, when we are very highly aroused, we show signs of panic and disorganisation, which also results in poor performance. Performance tends to be optimum when arousal is moderate. Zajonc's drive theory of social facilitation suggests that the presence of others when performing dominant responses increases arousal to an optimum level for performance. This is shown in Figure 8.5, where the level of arousal when working alone is not at the optimal level. The presence of others increases arousal level to cause better performance of a dominant response.

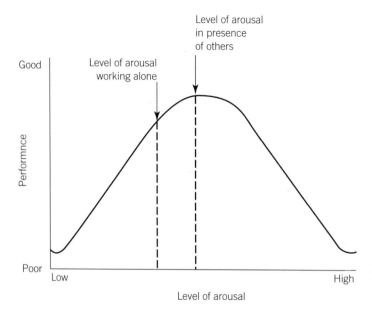

Figure 8.5: Relationship between level of arousal and performance at a task when working alone or in the presence of others

8

Evaluative Comment

The optimal level of arousal also varies according to the type of task to be performed, and whether or not the person has learned the task well. If the task is new or difficult, then a lower level of arousal is the optimal level for the performance of a task, compared to a well-learned or simple task. This is because trying to do well or be successful at a new task will require high levels of concentration, which, in itself, will raise the person's level of arousal.

We have seen how the optimal level of arousal is different for new and well-learned tasks. This can be applied to the context of sport. For example, using a golf club to hit a golf ball a long distance down the fairway is a highly skilled task. If you have never or rarely played golf, you will almost certainly perform better alone than with other people watching you, even if those other people are ones you are playing a round of golf with. Using a golf club requires concentration on many things (the ball, fairway and swing), and therefore results in quite a high level of arousal in the first place. The effect of people watching may push the arousal level too high and over the peak shown in Figure 8.5. The result is that performance will be poorer than if you played a golf shot on your own. This is equally likely to apply to other sports, such as tennis, ice skating and field events such as the javelin and high jump. With team sports, things may be a little different, but generally a team that has played together on many occasions is likely to perform better in front of an audience than a team that is newly formed. Judging how well a team plays is quite difficult and subjective if you do not consider the actual result of the match.

Practical Activity

Select a team sport that you enjoy watching on television. Try to find matches where two types of team are playing: one type of team where the players have played together for some time, and another type of team that has had many new players that have not played together before. The best time to do this is, perhaps, at the start of a sporting season. Try to video the matches of the two teams. Look at the behaviours and skills of each of the players in the two types of team. Try to identify displays of good skills and poor skills. You should find that the poorer skills are displayed more often by the team that has many new members that have not played together before.

Evaluation apprehension

Why should the mere presence of others, either in a co-acting group or an audience, cause arousal? One explanation put forward by Cottrell (1972) and Cottrell *et al.* (1968) revolves around the idea that when in the presence of others, we are concerned that they are evaluating our performance. In the presence of others when performing a task or a sport, Cottrell claims that people experience **evaluation apprehension**. Evaluation apprehension on a simple or well-learned task produces arousal, which results in the performance being enhanced. For a new or complex task, evaluation apprehension increases arousal to too high a level, with the consequence that performance is inhibited.

Study

Aim *Baris et al. (1988) conducted a study to investigate whether or not evaluation apprehension would lead to improvement in performance on a simple task and inhibition of performance on a complex task.*

Method *Participants were all presented with the same basic task involving thinking of different uses of a knife. One group was asked simply to list all the different uses of a knife that they could think of.*

Another group was asked to think only of creative uses of a knife. Some participants in each condition were told that their performance would be identified (the evaluation apprehension condition). Other participants in each condition were told that their ideas would be collected together as a group, but no individual would be identified.

RESULTS *When performing the simple task, participants in the evaluation apprehension condition produced more uses for a knife than participants in the other condition. By contrast, when performing the complex task, those in the evaluation apprehension condition produced fewer uses for a knife.*

CONCLUSIONS *Evaluation apprehension increases performance on simple tasks, but decreases performance on complex tasks.*

In a sporting context, Worringham & Messick (1983) found that male joggers ran faster when observed by a female audience than when a female was present, but had her back to the joggers. Other research has shown that the nature of the audience may also be an important factor in creating evaluation apprehension. Henchy & Glass (1968) found that typing performance declined in the presence of an expert typist, but not in the presence of someone who did not type. MacCracken & Stadulis (1985) found that the presence of an audience had little effect on children under the age of eight years. This suggests that evaluation apprehension may be something we develop as we get older.

Evaluative Comment

Some research, for example Schmitt et al. (1986), has shown that an audience who are all wearing blindfolds and an audience without blindfolds both have the same effect on the person in front of the audience. This contradicts what the evaluation apprehension explanation of social facilitation would predict. Equally, when we know that we will be video-taped performing some task, then arousal increases. If evaluation apprehension is playing a role here, it is because we expect other people to watch the video at some future time. However, even if we are told that no one else will see the video, then arousal increases, but is this as a result of evaluation apprehension?

Distraction-conflict theory

Saunders (1983) proposed an explanation of social facilitation based on the idea that the presence of other people creates a distraction to the person attempting to perform the task. This in turn interferes with the amount of attention the person can give to the task. The person then experiences a conflict between whether to attend to the task or to the audience. This conflict produces an increase in arousal, thus facilitating performance on simple or dominant tasks and inhibiting performance on complex or non-dominant tasks.

Study

AIM *Saunders et al. (1978) conducted a study to test the effect of distraction–conflict on performance of a task.*

METHOD *Participants were presented with either a simple or difficult task to perform in the presence of others performing either the same or a different task. It was hypothesised that a co-actor performing the same task as the participant would produce more distraction since they would be a source of comparison for the participants' performance.*

RESULTS *Participants in the high-distraction condition (same task with co-actors) performed at a higher level on the simple task, but produced more errors on the complex task.*

CONCLUSIONS *The results of this study produced evidence in support of the distraction–conflict theory of social facilitation.*

The **distraction–conflict theory** of social facilitation may also help to explain the results from studies using non-human animals. Social facilitation has been shown to occur in ants and cockroaches, but this is hardly likely to be due to evaluation apprehension! The presence of other animals of the same species may be distracting and draw attention away from the task itself.

Figure 8.6 summarises the different theories used to explain social facilitation.

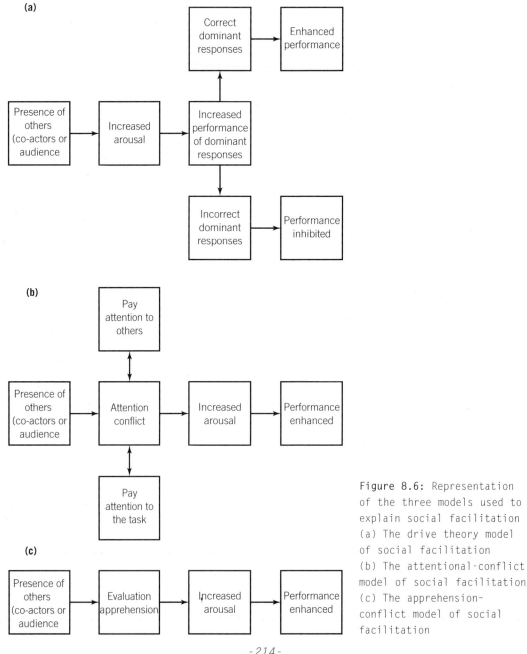

Figure 8.6: Representation of the three models used to explain social facilitation (a) The drive theory model of social facilitation (b) The attentional-conflict model of social facilitation (c) The apprehension-conflict model of social facilitation

Evaluative Comment

Empirical research into social facilitation may be criticised from a number of perspectives. First, audiences in experiments have tended to be passive in that they simply observe the behaviour of participants. In the context of sport, audiences are active, often noisy and respond both positively and negatively to the performance of the players or the team as a whole. Second, research has largely ignored individual differences between people. Triplett (1898) reported that 25 per cent of his participants actually showed social inhibition in the co-action condition of his experiment. There are many examples where leading athletes fail to produce their best performance in conditions where peak performance might be expected. Research on team performance (Ringlemann, 1913; Latane et al., 1979) has often found that individuals in a team show poorer performance in the presence of others. This has been called **social loafing**. *Finally, many of the tasks given to participants are not like real-life situations and are very artificial. Hence, the ecological validity (see Chapter 3) of these studies can be called into question, especially in relation to the application of the findings to sport. Specific research using a wide range of different sports is needed for social facilitation to be seen as a sporting phenomenon.*

Home-ground advantage

At the 1992 Winter Olympic Games, competitors from Japan won more medals than that nation's athletes had won at all previous Winter Olympics combined. One factor which may have contributed to this success is home advantage – the competition was held in Japan. In the sixteen times that the football World Cup has been held, the host nation has won on six occasions. On just one occasion has the competition been won by a nation from a different continent to that in which the competition was being held (in 1958, when Brazil won in Sweden). These two examples illustrate the idea of **home-ground advantage**.

What is home-ground advantage?

Courneya & Carron (1992) define home-ground advantage as:

> 'The consistent finding that home teams in sports competitions win over 50 per cent of games played under a balanced home-and-away schedule.'

Belief in the existence of home-ground advantage is long established. Triplett (1898) made reference to the positive effects of playing at home on the performance of American footballers. Edwards & Archambault (1989) reported that the media made more references to home advantage than any other factor. The effect has been shown to be consistent over time; Pollard (1986) found evidence for home-ground advantage from 1888 to 1984.

Reflective Activity

Select a sport that you are familiar with and enjoy watching. How would you investigate whether or not teams enjoy a home-ground advantage in this sport? What would you need to consider to ensure that your investigation reflected a true state of affairs rather than short-term or temporary fluctuations in form due to injury, for example?

Home-ground advantage and different sports

Evidence for the existence of home-ground advantage has generally relied on archive and historical data. For example, Schwartz & Barsky (1977) and Edwards (1979) both report findings that involved

8

statistical analysis of matches across a variety of different sports. This research demonstrates that home advantage exists, but the magnitude varies from sport to sport, as shown in Figure 8.7. As can be seen from Figure 8.7, football (soccer) enjoys the greatest home advantage at nearly 70 per cent, whilst baseball is only just over the 50 per cent level that would be expected by chance. This high level of home advantage for soccer has remained around 70 per cent for over 100 years (Pollard, 1986).

Sport	Number of studies	Total number of games	Winning percentage
Baseball	6	23,034	53.5%
Football (American)	5	2,592	57.3%
Ice hockey	4	4,322	61.1%
Basketball	8	13,596	64.4%
Soccer	2	37,202	69.0%

Figure 8.7: Home-ground advantage for different sports (Adapted from Cournenya & Carron, 1982)

Research has shown that home advantage is present in both amateur and professional sports, and that the advantage applies equally to team and individual sports (Bray & Carron, 1993). Home advantage is present in sports played by both males and females (Courneya & Carron, 1992).

Practical Activity

Get together as a group of four or five and each identify a different sport watched and enjoyed, and one preferably played.

Conduct an unstructured interview (see Chapter 3) with two or three players of the sport. In the interview, ask them about what it is like to play at home and play away from home. Ask what factors they enjoy about playing at home and away, and whether they think they play better at home.

After conducting the interviews, collect the information together from each of the group members. Look to see if there are any differences and similarities in what the players say about playing at home and away. Do you find one sport where players really do not like playing away and one where they prefer to play away?

Explanations for home-ground advantage

Courneya & Carron (1992) identified five main factors which may each play a role in explaining and creating home advantage. These are shown in Figure 8.8. Pace & Carron (1992) found that if the visiting team had to travel across time zones and little rest took place between games, then they (the visiting team) were disadvantaged. Travelling to a country with a very different climate and altitude may also disadvantage the visiting team if time to adapt to conditions is not provided. Familiarity with the pitch is also said to advantage the home team. Dowrie (1982) compared the advantage of teams with the smallest and largest pitches with other teams in the football league. A one per cent advantage was found for teams that played on a larger- or smaller-sized pitch.

Research on whether or not officials make more decisions that favour the home side does not produce consistent results. Carron & Hausenblas (1998) report no evidence of home-side bias by officials. However, Nevill et al. (1999) found from conducting a study on football referees in England and Scotland that decisions favour the home side. The effect was shown to increase as the size of the audience increased, perhaps reflecting the sheer number of home-side supporters compared to the number of supporters for the visiting team.

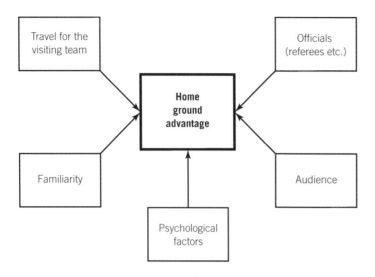

Figure 8.8: The five main factors used to explain home-ground advantage

Are referees and linesmen more likely to make decisions which favour the home team at their home ground?

The audience has a number of effects on both the home and visiting team or player. Generally, there are more people in the audience supporting the home team, and home-team fans may show hostility to the visiting team. Crowd density is also a factor, in that the greater the size of the crowd, the more home-team fans are present and hence the greater volume of noise shown in support. A small number of visiting fans compared to a large home-team audience will make the visiting team feel relatively poorly supported.

Evaluative Comment

Home advantage is much less in evidence, if at all, when teams play at home, but in the absence of an audience. This indicates that home-team advantage may be strongly influenced by the presence of supporting fans and the number of such fans.

The research we have considered so far demonstrates that the performance of athletes often improves on home ground and in front of a home audience. However, other research (Baumeister & Steinhilber, 1984) has shown that performing in front of home supporters on home ground can sometimes have the opposite effect. Generally, this research shows that the more important the game, the less likely the home team are to win on their home ground.

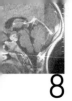

8

Home-ground disadvantage

In the baseball World Series, the championship is decided by a series of seven games between the top two teams. In the first two games, the pressure to win (or not to lose) is therefore less than in the final two games (providing, of course, one team has not lost four or five of the games played already). Baumeister *et al.* (1984) used archive records and studied the results of games in the World Series. They found that in the first two games of the seven, the home side won 60.2 per cent of them. However, in the final two games of the seven-game series, the home team only won 40 per cent of their games. This has been called the **championship choke**, implying that, as a game becomes more important, the home team are somehow 'choked' and perform less well (Baumeister, 1995). The findings of Baumeister & Steinhilber (1984) suggest that for important games, the home audience, instead of being seen as supportive by the home team, has the opposite effect. The performance of the home team is negatively affected by their home audience.

Study

Aim *Butler & Baumeister (1998) investigated the effects of different types of audiences on performance to discover under which conditions the championship choke may and may not occur.*

Method *Participants were asked to complete a difficult mathematical problem (subtracting from 999 in 13s). Half the participants were told that they would be observed through a one-way mirror by a stranger. The other half of the participants were told that they would be observed through a one-way mirror by a friend. The number of correct subtractions in each of these two conditions was recorded.*

Results *Participants who thought they were being observed by a stranger completed more subtractions correctly than participants who thought they were being observed by a friend.*

Conclusions *Even though the audience, stranger or friend, could not be seen by the participant, a friendly and presumably supportive audience negatively affected performance at a complex task.*

Butler & Baumeister (1998) conducted two further experiments similar to that described above. Their overall findings showed two things: first, a supportive audience may facilitate performance on an easy or well-learned task where the players expect to succeed. Second, performance on a difficult task decreases in the presence of a supportive audience, especially when the player is expected to succeed or perform well. This experimental, laboratory-based research does provide general support for the championship choke effect on home players in front of their supporters.

Evaluative Comment

The experiments conducted by Butler & Baumeister (1998) provide some understanding of how individual performance may be affected by different types of audiences. However, the research does not generalise very well to the team-sports setting. This is because the research focused on individual performance at mental-arithmetic tasks, and not team performance at a sport. Further research is needed to look at the effects of home audiences on home-team performance.

Schlenker et al. (1995) updated the original data of Baumeister & Steinhilber (1984) for the subsequent ten years for both the sports of basketball and baseball. This revised data did not provide evidence for a championship choke effect. This highlights the importance of taking archive data over a long period to ensure that a consistent effect is seen over time. What is needed is more experimental research into the idea of the championship choke to get away from undue reliance on the analysis of historical or archive data.

Team cohesion

People who play a sport do so either as individuals or as part of a team. However, this is not really an either/or category, but best seen as a continuum. At one end are individual sportsmen and sportswomen, for example boxers, golfers and singles tennis players. At the other end of this continuum are sports teams, which may vary in size from two or three players up to fifteen or twenty players. In some sports, small groups of people may play together, but are competing with each other and other players at the same time, for example in golf championships. However, much of the theory and research that is considered here looks at teams that play together against other teams.

Reflective Activity

List ten different sports and identify whether each is an individual activity, team activity or both.

For those that are team activities, think about differences that may exist between small teams (two or three) and larger teams (fifteen to twenty). Do all these teams have leaders or captains? If so, why, and if not, why not? What are the three most important things, in your view, that affect how well a team works and plays together?

Group and teams

The study of groups by social psychologists has a long history. It is important to distinguish between a **group** and a **team**. Cartwright & Zander (1968) define a group as follows:

> 'a collection of individuals who have relations to one another that make them interdependent to some significant degree'.

The key point about this definition is that the individuals in the group interact with each other and develop interpersonal relationships. In addition, the success of the group and its ability to achieve and to stay together are reflected by the interdependence of the members. This means that each individual relies on each other for how the group performs. The definition given above also shows a group to be much more than a collection of individuals. A crowd is a collection of people who may come together for a common purpose, but the individuals are not interdependent on each other.

How does a team differ from a group? Basically a team is a special kind of group, and may be defined as follows:

> 'a team is a group of players who have a well-developed collective identity and who work together to achieve a specific goal or set of goals.' (Morris & Summer, 1995)

The distinguishing or defining feature of a team is that it has a clear goal or purpose, for example, to win at the sport that it plays. Groups, such as work groups, may have goals and objectives, but often these are not about competing but about achieving. Leisure and family groups may not have such clearly defined goals or objectives. However, sports teams are not only about achievement at the sport, but about being together, being part of a culture or set of social norms that define the sport.

Reflective Activity

Select five of the sports you have identified in the activity above. Think about other social psychological aspects of the sport, such as culture and norms.

Identify the general culture of the sport and list two or three of the norms you think exist. You may be better to do this activity with a couple of others in your class.

8

The media sometimes speculates about a 'dream team' when there is a national, international or world competition. Here, you are asked to imagine picking the best players who have ever played the sport to produce the 'dream team'. Underlying this bit of speculative fun is the assumption that the best team, i.e. the team that can beat all other teams at the sport, is made up of the best or most able individuals. However, this is not always the case, since teams are people who relate to each other and are interdependent, as stated in our definition above. Team processes or group processes are also important determinants of the success or failure of a team. A team that cannot work together is unlikely to perform well. Hence, achievement at a sport by a team depends on both the ability of the individual members at the sport and how well the individuals come together and relate to each other as a team. Therefore one of the most important factors for success is **team cohesion** (Widmeyer *et al.*, 1993).

Team cohesion and task cohesion

Ask friends and acquaintances you know who play a team sport (or if you are a team player yourself, ask other team mates) 'What makes a team work?' Having good players of course. But you are likely to get other responses, such as 'team spirit' or 'playing as one' or 'high morale'. There are no doubt many more everyday terms for what social psychologists call *team cohesion*, which may be defined as follows:

> 'a dynamic process which is reflected in the tendency for a group to stick together and remain united in the pursuit of its goals'. (Carron, 1982)

Evaluative Comment

This definition has three main points that are important for understanding team cohesion. First, that it is a dynamic process: this means that it changes and evolves over time. At one time, cohesion may be high and at another time low. Second, the group or team sticks together: this means that there is commitment from the members of a group to remain as a team, regardless of lack of success or difficulties in interpersonal relationships. Third, the team remains united: this is an extension of sticking together, but is to do with remaining united in pursuit of goals. The goals or objectives of the team are to beat another team, but also to work well as a team. The concept of team cohesion is quite a complex one which involves a number of psychological factors.

Team cohesion is a special case of the general concept of group cohesiveness, which has been the subject of much theory and research in social psychology (Pennington, 2002). Group cohesiveness may range from very low to very high if it is conceived as a single dimension. The definition given above reflects more what we expect of a team or group which shows a high degree of cohesion or cohesiveness.

Practical Activity

Turn to the sports section of a Sunday newspaper and select an article about a team that has recently lost a game or match.

Identify instances in the article which refer to how well the team played as a team and any problems that the team seemed to be having in working together.

On a scale of one to ten, where one is low and ten is high, how would you rate the team cohesion? Now do this again, but for a group that has recently won a match or a game. On the basis of this, do you think that success goes hand in hand with high team cohesion or not?

Team cohesion is often referred to as the 'glue' or 'cement' binding together the individuals in a group (Schachter, 1955). However, psychologists like to see greater precision and have defined this 'glue' or 'cement' as the extent to which members of the team identify with the goals and aspirations (i.e. winning or being good at the particular sport) and like each other (Hogg, 1992). This reflects two key aspects of cohesion – **task cohesion** and **social cohesion**. Task cohesion refers to the extent to which members of the team work together to achieve the task (in the case of sport, winning or being good at the sport). Social cohesion refers to the extent to which members of the team are attracted to each other. Task and social cohesion are regarded as two different dimensions (Cota *et al.*, 1995), each of which may vary from high to low. If we look at this simplistically, four different categories can be seen to describe a group, as shown in Figure 8.9.

	Task cohesion	
Social cohesion	1 High task cohesion High social cohesion	2 Low task cohesion High social cohesion
	3 High task cohesion Low social cohesion	4 Low task cohesion Low social cohesion

Figure 8.9: Four categories of high and low task and social cohesion

A team in Box 1 represents a group that both works very hard and wins at its sport, where members of the team like each other and enjoy being in the team. By contrast, a team in Box 4 will be in a poor state, where members or players neither work hard at the sport nor like each other very much. Teams in Box 4 may not stay together very long unless changes occur.

Reflective Activity

Think about a team in Box 4 of Figure 8.9.

What might you recommend should be done in order to get the team into Box 2?

What might you recommend should be done to get the team into Box 3?

Why might a long-established team find themselves in Box 4?

Consider both task and social cohesion to answer this question.

Determinants of team cohesion

In this section, we will consider a range of variables psychologists have identified as contributing to the development of cohesion within a team. These factors may be crudely categorised as those external to the team, such as geographical and social environments, and those internal to the team, such as individual characteristics of the team and leadership qualities.

External factors

The environment in which a team operates and competes is an important contextual factor (Carron *et al.*, 1988; Widmeyer *et al.*, 1993). Geographical factors relate to the availability of a particular sporting facility in the area and the opportunity a team has to play their sport against other teams. To take an extreme example, if a group of people in Wigan were interested in developing an American baseball team, they would have to overcome a number of problems. These might include a baseball ground properly marked out on which to play the sport, obtaining appropriate equipment, finding other baseball teams to play against, finding an experienced coach to train the team, etc. If you think about this example, you will realise that sports are culturally determined.

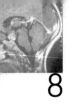
8 Reflective Activity

List ten sports that were played at the Sydney 2000 Olympic Games. For each sport, consider how commonly it is played in countries such as USA, Greece, South Africa, China and Britain. Which highly popular sports were not represented at the Olympic Games?

In contrast, list two or three sports that you think are local to the area that you live in.

The social environment is also important and includes peer pressure, family expectations and, more generally, how children are socialised, through upbringing and school, to regard some sports as acceptable and normal to play and others as unusual; for example, young women at school wanting to play rugby and young men wanting to play netball. Gender enters into determining which sports men and women normally play. You may think that a woman wanting to play a traditional male sport, such as rugby, may be more committed to a female rugby team than when in a team playing a traditional female sport. This relates to the initiation rites of joining a team and its effects on commitment to the team and team cohesion (Aronson & Mills, 1959) – this is considered later in this section.

A very important external factor is competition with another team and **intergroup conflict**. The classic field study of Sherif *et al.* (1961) dramatically demonstrated how competition between two teams for the same resources led to hostility and aggression between teams, and served to strengthen and foster co-operation and cohesion between individuals within the team.

Study

AIM AND METHOD *Sherif et al. (1961) conducted a field study in Robbers' Cave State Park in the USA. The aim of the study was to see how two groups of boys on an American Summer Camp holiday behaved towards each other when (a) they had to compete for the same resource, and (b) when the two groups had to co-operate and work together to achieve a task.*

RESULTS *When competing with each other, with the winning team getting prizes at competitions, hostility broke out and escalated between the two groups.*

CONCLUSIONS *When co-operating to achieve a task, intergroup hostility reduced. However, team cohesion was highest within each team when the two teams were in competition, and reduced for each team when they were required to co-operate.*

The relevance of this research in the context of sports teams is two-fold. First, co-operation and working together in a team leads to cohesiveness, especially when competition and winning is the main goal for the team. Second, coaches should set tasks (which may not necessarily be to do with the sport itself) that require members of the team to co-operate and work together in order to be successful.

Internal factors

Personal factors, such as social background, gender, attitudes, ability at the sport, commitment and personality, all contribute to cohesiveness in the group. Team homogeneity (Cox, 1990) has been suggested as being important to team cohesion. Team homogeneity is the idea that individuals in a team are similar on one or more personal factors. For example, socio-economic status, commitment to the sport and the team. Cox (1990) suggests heterogeneous teams – where individuals differ on one or more personal factors – show lower levels of team cohesion.

Evaluative Comment

Widmeyer & Williams (1991) and Williams & Widmeyer (1991) conducted empirical research investigating teams categorised as homogenous or heterogeneous on a number of different personal factors. This research did not report any strong relationship between levels of team cohesion and team homogeneity. More research is needed in this area. You may be able to produce anecdotal evidence both for and against this idea, for example contrast Olympic teams with local teams.

The stability of a team has been shown to be related to team cohesion (Forsyth, 1990). Teams that have been together longer, both in terms of the existence of the team and the length of time each player has been with the team, are generally higher in cohesiveness. By contrast, teams either newly formed or experiencing a high turnover of players tend to be less cohesive.

Practical Activity

Work with a friend or classmate and pick a sport (football is a good one). Look in the back copies of summer newspapers to identify teams that have bought a lot of new players over the summer and those that have not. You may wish to visit the websites of some football teams to help you with this.

Categorise some teams with extreme cases of high turnover/change of players and low levels of change of players. How have these teams done in the first four or five matches of the season? Does any pattern emerge?

One factor that does need to be taken into account, and may offset high turnover of players, is the ability of the new players joining the team. It may be that, in the early days of a team with many new players, the high-ability level of the new players may offset the decrease in cohesiveness of the team. However, if an extremely able player cannot integrate into the team, cohesiveness may not develop to a sufficiently high level, and other team players may be adversely affected. The consequence is likely to be that the performance of the team will be poor.

Leadership is vital to developing cohesiveness within a team (Westre & Weiss, 1991). Leaders (captains and coaches) should be consistent and give clear directions in respect of both team goals and interpersonal relationships. Westre and Weiss also state that leaders who involve team members in team decisions (tactics, targets, etc.) develop more cohesive teams, since all the players have 'ownership' and agree with the decisions reached. A democratic style of leadership fosters team cohesion, except when the situation is highly unfavourable (for example, the team is facing relegation from a league). Here, a more directive and autocratic style of leadership may be successful (Fiedler, 1965).

Team size has been shown to affect cohesion (Schultz & Schultz, 1994). Generally, research has shown that as group size increases, group cohesion decreases. It may be that large teams (for example, England's football squad of 20 to 25 players) should be put into subgroups at times to develop and foster cohesiveness. However, care is needed not to create competition between subgroups and hence affect overall team cohesion.

The initiation of a new player or member to a team has an important influence on the commitment of that player to the team, and consequently the cohesiveness of the team. Generally, the more severe the initiation rites to join a team, then the greater the subsequent group cohesion. Severe initiation in the sports world can be equated with the effort a player has had to make to join a team. This effort may have taken place over a number of years as a player has progressed from playing a sport at local level, then county level onto national and international levels. People or players who become a member of a group with little or no effort show less commitment to the group, with the consequence that the group is less cohesive (Aronson & Mills, 1959).

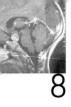

8   Study

Aim Aronson & Mills (1959) conducted a study with the aim of determining the effect of different levels of effort to join a group on commitment to the group.

Method Female students volunteered to take part in a group discussion about sexual matters. However, before they could join the group, they were told that they each had to go through a test which measured the extent to which they were able to speak openly. The female volunteers were assigned to one of two conditions: a severe condition, in which they had to read aloud explicit sexual passages, and a mild condition, in which they had to read aloud words or text that were not sexually explicit.

Results The researchers found that those in the severe-initiation condition showed much greater liking and enjoyment of the group discussion than the mild-initiation participants. Participants in the severe condition rated the group discussion as more interesting and the other participants of the group as more interesting than those in the mild condition.

Conclusions The greater the commitment or effort a person makes to join a group or team, the greater the person will like the group and the people in it.

Evaluative Comment

A range of factors related to external and internal aspects of a team have been shown to affect the development of team cohesion. Much of the research conducted has focused on the effects of just one or two factors on cohesiveness. Such an approach has the strength that we find out a lot about the effects of a single factor or variable. However, this does not provide information about the relative importance of all factors in determining team cohesion. It is probably reasonable to say that all factors need consideration – some you can't do much about, for example, team size. Others are more controllable, such as leadership, individual effort and team homogeneity. However, there is no clear set of guidelines that can be justifiably drawn up to provide a coach or team captain with a recipe to follow to achieve high levels of team cohesion.

Measuring team cohesion

A highly regarded and widely used measure of team cohesion is the **Group Environment Questionnaire** (GEQ) developed by Carron et al. (1985). This questionnaire has been developed from a conceptual model of team cohesion based on two dimensions.

Team perception

One dimension is the individual players' perception of the team, which is subdivided into two components:

● *group integration*, which concerns the individual's perception of the group as a whole – how well or poorly the group work together;

● *individual attraction*, which involves the team players' personal attraction to the group – that is, how much each player likes being in the group or team.

Group orientation

The second dimension is the player's group orientation, which is also subdivided into two components:

● *social cohesion*, which is to do with how well each of the players are attached or bonded to the team as a unit to satisfy social needs;

● *task cohesion*, which concerns how well the players are in agreement and committed or bonded to the team as a unit to satisfy task completion needs.

These four aspects of team cohesion are shown in Figure 8.10. From this, you can see that four separate measures of team cohesion are obtained. The questionnaire developed by Carron *et al.* (1985) – the GEQ – contains eighteen Likert-scale items representing each of the four measures.

		Player's perception of the team	
		Group integration	**Individual attraction**
Group Orientation	**Social**	Bonding or attachment to the team overall in order to satisfy social needs (G1–S)	Attraction to the team and others in the team in order to satisfy social needs (ATG–S)
	Task	Bonding or attachment to the team overall in order to satisfy task completion needs (G1–T)	Attraction to the team and others in the team in order to satisfy task completion needs (ATG–T)

Figure 8.10: The conceptual model of team cohesion proposed by Widmeyer *et al.* (1985)

An example of a G1–T question is as follows:

Our team is united in trying to reach its goal for performance.

1 _____ 2 _____ 3 _____ 4 _____ 5 _____ 6 _____ 7 _____ 8 _____ 9

Strongly agree   Strongly disagree

Obtaining four measures of team cohesion in this way allows the sport psychologist to identify specific areas where team cohesion is high and low. This then permits time and attention to be focused on the areas that need to be improved and cohesion raised. For example, suppose a hockey team were found to score high in three measures but low in ATG-S (attraction to the team to satisfy social needs). This may mean that what individuals are looking for in the team with respect to fulfilling social needs is not forthcoming. Action may require changing perceptions or changing what the team can offer in this respect.

Evaluative Comment

A Likert-scale questionnaire approach is commonly used when social or sport psychologists wish to make quantitative measures. However, there are shortcomings with such an approach. For one thing, what people report when circling a number on a scale may not reflect what they actually think or feel. For example, consider the sample question from the GEQ given earlier. If you felt that your team was not really united over the goals or targets it should attempt to reach, how honestly do you feel you would report this? There may be a social desirability bias working whereby you are wanting to put the team in a better, more positive light than it actually is. Another problem is that each member of the team may interpret the same question slightly differently.

Nevertheless, despite these general shortcomings of Likert scales, the GEQ has been shown to meet quite high standards with respect to its reliability and validity (Carron et al., 1988). It is of vital importance that a psychometric test of any sort can demonstrate reliability and validity (see Chapter 3).

More recently a questionnaire has been developed by Partington & Shangi (1992) to measure 'team chemistry'. This is a much larger questionnaire than the GEQ and is called the *Team Psychology*

Questionnaire (TPQ). It consists of 53 Likert-scale items measuring the following seven dimensions:

- player talent and attitude

- task cohesion

- coach – technical

- team identity

- coach – interpersonal

- style of play

- task integration.

As you can see, some of these dimensions go beyond what might be traditionally seen as team cohesion. However, this does reflect the wider social context in which the development of team cohesion takes place.

Team cohesion and team satisfaction

Common sense would seem to indicate that high levels of team cohesion should result in high levels of **team satisfaction**. Martens & Peterson (1971) confirmed this common sense view and proposed a circular model linking team cohesion to individual satisfaction and performance. This is shown in Figure 8.11.

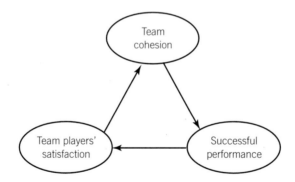

Figure 8.11: Circular model linking team cohesion to satisfaction and performance (After Martens & Peterson, 1971)

Martens & Peterson (1971) state the following in relation to this model:

- high levels of team cohesion lead to high levels of team performance;

- successful team performance leads to high levels of team player satisfaction;

- high levels of team player satisfaction lead to enhanced team cohesiveness.

Evaluative Comment

You may wonder why the direction of arrows in relation to these three factors is shown in Figure 8.11. There seems to be little compelling evidence for such a directional effect, and it may be better to have the arrows pointing both ways. This high team cohesion may be both a cause and effect of both successful performance and satisfaction. We will return to this issue of cause and effect in the next section when we come to look specifically at the relationship between team cohesion and performance.

A different model was put forward by Williams & Hacker (1982), based on the importance of successful or high levels of performance on both team cohesion and satisfaction of the team members. In this model, it is the successful or unsuccessful performance of the team that affects both cohesion and satisfaction. Research has clearly shown that team players or members gain satisfaction and enjoyment from being part of a cohesive team (Carron *et al.*, 1997). Also, where the individuals in the team see their team as highly cohesive, they want to continue to be a member of that team (Spink, 1995).

Study

Aim *Myers (1962) conducted a study aimed at investigating differences in team morale (cohesion) when a team competed with another team or against a standard.*

Method *Army rifle teams took part in either a competitive league with other rifle teams, or a non-competitive league. The non-competitive league was against a standard of rifle-shooting accuracy, not other teams.*

Results *These showed that competency against another team had a stronger effect on morale (cohesion), but was dependent on performance. If a team did well against another team, morale increased; however, if it did badly, morale decreased. When competing against a standard, morale was affected as you would expect, but not in such an extreme way.*

Conclusions *It can be concluded that competition between teams and the outcomes have a strong effect on morale and team cohesion.*

Practical Activity

Identify two or three people you know who play in different sports teams. Find out what their run of wins and losses has been over the past five matches or games. Interview each individual and ask:

- *what level of cohesion the team had five matches ago;*
- *what level of cohesion the team has now;*
- *what effect this has had on their own individual satisfaction as a member of the team;*
- *whether they are happy to remain in the team.*

Team cohesion and team performance

As with team satisfaction, common sense would lead you to think that high levels of team cohesion should correlate positively with high levels of team performance and success. Many empirical studies have reported this positive relationship and at different levels of competition (for example, Slater & Sewell, 1994; Williams & Widmeyer, 1991). Widmeyer *et al.* (1993) conducted a review of the research conducted on cohesion–performance limits. It was found that about 80 per cent of the research reported the expected positive relationship. However, 17 per cent of empirical studies actually reported a negative relationship, i.e. high team cohesion may be associated with poor performance or, the other way round, low team cohesion may be associated with good, successful performance. Finally, three per cent of studies reported no significant relationship between cohesion and performance. Given the outcome of the review conducted by Widmeyer *et al.* (1993), it would seem that the relationship is more complex. We need to look at factors such as different types of sports, different types of teams or other situational factors to explain and understand such a mixed set of findings.

8

Cox (1990) suggests that we categorise sports into one of two types: those where the team players have a high level of interaction amongst each other (for example, football, hockey, basketball) and those where interaction is low amongst team players (such as bowling, archery). Having done this, Cox investigated and measured team cohesion and performance relationships for each category. It was found that high cohesion in sports with high interaction tended to be associated with good performance. By contrast, sports with little or no interaction showed a negative relationship between cohesion and performance. This means that high cohesion in low-interaction sports may lead to poorer performance than low cohesion in such types of sport! This is shown in Figure 8.12.

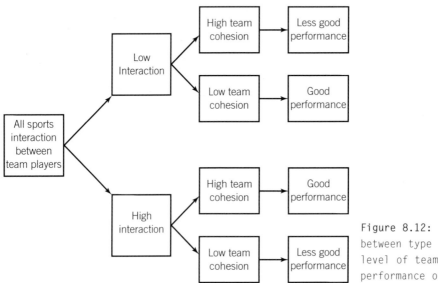

Figure 8.12: Relationship between type of interaction, level of team cohesion and performance of a team

Practical Activity

List twenty sports different from those just mentioned. Think about the level of interaction between the team players (interaction between team players refers to talking to each other whilst playing the sport, or communicating in other ways, such as hand gestures). Include in the idea of interaction all players in the team together when playing a match.

Now try to categorise each sport into high- or low-interaction categories.

Which sports are easy to categorise and which are difficult?

For the sports that are difficult to categorise, write down the difficulties and see what may be in common between them.

For the difficult categories, speculate about what you may think the relationship between team cohesion and performance may be. Offer some justification of this.

Various aspects of what is commonly called **group structure** (Pennington, 2002) in social psychology are related to both team cohesion and team performance. Group structure refers to status and rules for the individuals in the group, and also includes the norms of a group. We will only consider the latter here in the context of sport.

Group norms refer to the values, standards and rules which the individual members are expected to adhere to (Pennington, 2002). Newly formed groups are unlikely to have established a set of norms; however, long-standing groups or sports teams usually have a well-established set of norms. When a new player joins an established team, they will be expected to confirm or adhere to the prevailing team norms. Norms function to hold a group together and hence are a key factor in the level of team cohesion that exists. The relationship between norms and team cohesion is circular; one reinforces the other. Basically, high cohesiveness leads to high conformity to group norms and vice versa.

Stogdill (1972) reviewed a number of studies and found that the group norm for productivity is the main factor that affects the relationship between team cohesion and productivity. Evidence of a team with a norm of a high level of productivity will be all players working as hard as possible, no 'slackers' and a commitment to give 100 per cent all the time.

A group with a norm for a low level of productivity will be the opposite of this. The effect of different levels of this norm for productivity and levels of team cohesion is shown in Figure 8.13. It can be seen that high team cohesion and a high productivity norm lead to good performance. By contrast, a low productivity norm and low team cohesion are linked to poor performance. Notice in Figure 8.13 the two conditions of average performance.

| | | Team cohesion | |
		High	Low
Productivity norm	**High**	Good performance	Average performance
	Low	Poor performance	Average performance

Figure 8.13: Effects of high and low levels of productivity norm and team cohesion on team performance (Adapted from Stogdill, 1972)

Study

AIM *The aim of a study conducted by Slater & Sewell (1994) was to determine the causal relationship between team cohesion and team performance.*

METHOD *Male and female hockey teams were used, and players were given the Group Environment Questionnaire (GEQ) to measure team cohesion. One GEQ was given out at the start of the season and one towards the end of the season. Measures of performance, wins and losses, goals score, etc. were taken throughout the measure.*

RESULTS *Slater and Sewell found that team cohesion early in the season was a better predictor of performance towards the end of the season than team cohesion late in the season.*

CONCLUSIONS *The conclusion to be drawn from this study is that team cohesion is more likely to determine or cause performance than the other way round. You might also conclude that a team with many new players should try to develop high team cohesion before the season starts, rather than let it develop as the team plays together in matches.*

Evaluative Comment

The above study attempts to sort out the direction of causality between team cohesion and team performance. As we have seen, a positive correlation exists between team cohesion and team performance. The issue is what causes what, or whether it is a circular relationship without a direct cause and effect. This is not an easy matter to sort out, and the answer is unlikely to be simply that one causes the other. What sport psychologists and team coaches want to know, however, is how important team cohesion is. As we have seen in the Sewell & Slater (1994) study, high team cohesion does seem to be a strong causal factor in good team performance.

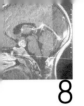

Generally, we have seen that high levels of cohesion lead to good performance, and that winning or success by a team will enhance or at least maintain a high level of team cohesion. But consider teams that have a very poor season at their sport, lose nearly every match, but remain average to high on team cohesion measures.

Study

Aim *Taylor et al. (1983) conducted a longitudinal study to investigate how poor performance may affect team cohesion.*

Method *An ice-hockey team had a poor year in which they won only three out of the 25 games they played, and had experienced some humiliating losses. Team cohesion ratings were obtained from each player after every game.*

Results *It was found that team cohesion remained at a relatively high level throughout the season.*

Conclusions *The likely explanation for the maintenance of high levels of team cohesion throughout the season is to do with the high level of identification each player had to their team. High identification and commitment to the team seems to offset the negative effects of poor performance on team cohesion. Whether this could last over three or four seasons is another matter though!*

If it is generally accepted that high levels of team cohesion play an important role in determining a high level of team performance, we need to know how to *build* a team. Team-building is a process normally carried out by coaches and managers to enhance both social and task cohesion (Carron & Dennis, 1998). The following ten principles are suggested for **team building** (Cox, 1998).

1 Acquaint each player with the responsibilities of the other players in the team.

2 The coach or manager should take time to learn personal matters about each team player.

3 Develop a sense of pride within the team and subgroups of large teams.

4 Develop a sense of 'we' amongst the players.

5 Set goals for the team and get the players to be proud of successes.

6 Ensure that each player understands the importance of their role in the team and that it is enacted.

7 Expect tensions within the team at times and address them as soon as they arise.

8 Avoid the formation of cliques within the team.

9 Establish routines and practice games/matches to encourage co-operation.

10 Emphasise good performance even when a team may lose a game or match.

Practical Activity

Consider a sports team of which you are a member. (If you do not belong to a sports team, find one that your friends are in so that you can talk to the players.)

Conduct interviews with the players in the team to get a sense of the level of the team cohesion and where problems may exist in the team working as a unit.

Relate these problems to one or more of the ten principles given above.

Determine an action plan for each relevant principle to help address the problem. Try to implement it in the team.

See Appendix 1 for information concerning questions that appear in the examination paper. The assessment of knowledge and understanding (AO1) and analysis and evaluation (AO2) assessment objectives is also given in Appendix 1.

Sample questions

Sample question 1

(a) Explain what is meant by the term *evaluation apprehension*.
(AO1 = 1, AO2 = 2)   *(3 marks)*

(b) Describe what is meant by the term *social facilitation*.
(AO1 = 3)   *(3 marks)*

(c) Explain the importance of dominant responses in social facilitation theory.
(AO1 = 2, AO2 = 2)   *(4 marks)*

(d) Discuss one strength and one weakness of social facilitation theory.
(AO1 = 4, AO2 = 6)   *(10 marks)*

Total AO1 marks = 10   Total AO2 marks = 10   Total marks = 20

Questions, answers and comments

(a) Describe what is meant by the term *social cohesion*.
(AO1 = 3)   *(3 marks)*

(b) The following is a list of factors which may increase or decrease team cohesion. For each factor, state whether it would increase or decrease team cohesion.
(i)   team homogeneity
(ii)   competition with another team
(iii) change of team membership.

(AO2 = 3)   *(3 marks)*

(c) Discuss how team cohesion is affected by one of the factors identified above.
(AO1 = 2, AO2 = 2)   *(4 marks)*

(d) Describe and discuss how team cohesion may affect the performance of a team. Refer to empirical evidence in your answer.
(AO1 = 5, AO2 = 5)   *(10 marks)*

Total AO1 marks = 10   Total AO2 marks = 10   Total = 20 marks

Answer to (a)

Social cohesion is to do with the social 'glue' that holds a team together. It is to do with how much each person in the team likes the other members of the team.

Comment

This is a good description worth two marks. The answer identifies the key factor of how much members of the group like each other. To score full marks, this needs to be extended to the idea that social cohesion can range from high to low.

Sample questions, answers and comments

8

Answer to (b)

(i)   will increase team cohesion
(ii) will increase team cohesion
(iii) will decrease team cohesion.

Comment

This is a straightforward question to mark. Here, each of the answers is correct, so the full three marks are awarded.

Answer to (c)

Team homogeneity refers to how similar team members are on factors such as race, social class, etc. By contrast, heterogeneous teams in sport are where there is a mix of different people. For example, in football a team may be made up of both white and black people. Research has shown that there may not be any effect of a homogenous team on cohesion.

Comment

This answer would be awarded three out of the four marks available. Two of the marks are awarded for providing a clear understanding of homogeneity in a team, and the opposite, of a heterogeneous team. The example helps provide further clarification, but is not really needed. One mark is given for the evaluative comment that homogeneity may not affect team cohesion. However, since in a four-mark 'discuss'-type question two marks would be for AO2 (application and analysis), the analysis here is not full enough for the full two marks. Good answer, though.

Answer to (d)

Team cohesion is to do with how well a team works and plays together at a sport. For example, in football, everyone knows what their position on the pitch is and they all try to stick to this. The performance of a team concerns how well the team plays together and how often they win at the matches they play. Sports psychologists have claimed that teams that have cohesion perform better that teams that do not have cohesion. But this is probably too simplistic.

Widmeyer, some time in the 1990s, conducted a review of loads of studies that had looked at this. Generally, he found that teams having cohesion performed better. But this was not always the case. A small percentage of teams were found to perform better if cohesion was not there. This was explained by Cox as due to whether teams talked to each other or not. If teams talked to each other loads, then cohesion was important. If they did not talk much, cohesion did not matter.

One problem with trying to find out if team cohesion affects performance in sport is the circular problem. What causes what? Does cohesion result in good performance or good performance make a team cohesive? It all seems as if sports psychologists do not really know and it is difficult to find out.

Comment

A 'describe and discuss' question such as this can achieve a maximum of five marks for knowledge and understanding. This answer would be awarded four marks because a good understanding is shown of team cohesion and team performance. The answer also correctly states the general position that high levels of team cohesion are associated with good levels of performance. This is backed up to some extent by reference to the literature review of Widmeyer *et al.* (1993); however, the answer does not refer specifically to any empirical studies, so this is a minus feature. The answer does go on to mention that the above association may not always be there; however, confusion is present at this stage, since the answer should refer to the interaction patterns of teams representing different sports, not just how much players in a team talk to each other. Nevertheless, it is along the right road. Finally, the answer does refer to the cause–effect problem. So for AO2 (application and analysis), this answer would be awarded four marks. Overall, the answer is quite good and would achieve eight out of the total ten marks available. A very good answer!

Further reading

Introductory texts

Cox, R.H. (1998), *Sport Psychology: Concepts and Applications*, 4th edition, Boston, McGraw-Hill

Morris, T. & Summers, J. (1995), *Sport Psychology: Theory, Application and Issues*, Brisbane, John Wiley & Sons

Pennington, D.C., Gillen, K. & Hill, P. (1999), *Social Psychology* (Chapter 11), London, Arnold

Wann, D.L. (1997) *Sport Psychology*, Upper Saddle River, NJ, Prentice Hall

Specialist sources

Pennington, D.C. (2002), *The Social Psychology of Behaviour in Small Groups*, London, Psychology Press Ltd

Williams, J.M. (Ed.) (1998), *Applied Sport Psychology: Personal Growth to Peak Performance*, London, Mayfield Publishing Company

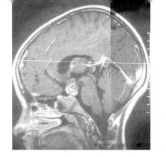

9
Perception and Attention

Introduction

When we look at something like an apple, how do we process it? How do we experience and understand what we are seeing? If someone gives us an apple, how do we know whether to eat it, wear it, chase it or smile at it? Psychologists interested in perception and attention try to explain our processing and interpretation of all sorts of sensory information. As **perception** and **attention** occur early on in the processing system, they are often the focus for the debate about whether human information processing is **bottom-up** or **top-down**. By bottom-up, we mean that processing relies mostly on the sense information from the things we experience, like the shine and fruity smell of an apple, or the sparkle of light reflected on the surface of a lake. In contrast, top-down means that processing depends not just on the information coming to us from our senses, but also on our store of existing knowledge which comes from past experience. For example, our complete interpretation of an apple might depend not just on the sensory cues we get from it at the time, but also on our previous 'apple' experiences and our knowledge of the world in general. Although the apple in front of us may look shiny and smell fruity (bottom-up information), our previous knowledge might tell us that this type of apple is more suitable for baking (top-down information), and therefore we would perceive it as not a very good one to bite into. The bottom-up versus top-down debate will be explored in depth on pages 235–239, but it is useful to think about it in relation to everything that is covered in this chapter.

Perception

Perception has been referred to as the process of 'assembling of sensations into a useable mental representation of the world' (Coon, 1983). Gregory (1966), meanwhile, refers to perception as a 'dynamic searching for the best interpretation of the available data'. Look at Figure 9.1 and try to 'assemble the sensations' into something sensible you might later be able to think about or 'use'. As you look, can you feel yourself 'searching' for the best interpretation? See the bottom of the page to see whether you have identified the figure correctly.

Figure 9.1: At first glance, this may seem like a random collection of splodges, but if you look carefully, especially through half-closed eyes, a picture may emerge (see page 258 for solution)

Processing sensory information

Sensory information from the environment is received in many forms. Light, sound, touch, tastes and smells are received by receptor cells in our sensory organs and converted by the body into electro-chemical information that is transmitted through our nervous system to be processed in the brain. Here, our processing systems translate the information from these external stimuli into our experience and understanding of the external world. Whilst the focus of most research and most texts, including this one, has been on visual perception, we should not forget that perception of the world takes place through all our senses. The task for psychologists studying and researching perception is to explain how we make sense of the external sensory information. Note that 'external sensory information' would also include sensory information coming from our own physical body, like an itch or a pain, for example.

Reflective Activity

Concentrate on your experiences of the environment at this moment. What is the exact nature of the visual stimulus you are receiving? What sounds are you hearing? What can you feel, smell, taste?

Imagine the activity of the neurons in your nervous system as they transmit this information to your brain, and the electro-chemical activity within the brain as these external sensations are processed to give you an understanding of your current environment.

Would someone else experience the same sensations in exactly the same way as you?

Bottom-up theory of information processing

J.J. Gibson's (1966) theory of perception is an example of a bottom-up theory of information processing and is sometimes known as a theory of *direct* perception or a theory of *ecological* perception. The term *ecological* is used to emphasise the importance of cues from the environment in Gibson's theory. The theory can be summarised as follows:

- Stimulus cues drive perception.

- The visual array contains visual cues, for example, light reflected from objects and graded textures.

- As we move around our world, these cues change.

- The changes in visual cues allow us to perceive depth and objects.

- Properties afforded by objects are instantly perceived; for example, when we see a table, we instantly and automatically perceive its hardness, stability, etc. from the visual cues. We can understand that objects may be placed on the table without having had any previous experience of tables. Gibson would say that the visual cues from the table indicate that the table 'affords' these properties. This is known as the theory of **affordances**.

- The human eye has evolved to be an acutely sensitive organ, able to detect very fine stimulus cues like changes in light and texture. This extreme sensitivity enables bottom-up or data-driven perception.

Reflective Activity

Explore the concept of 'affordances'. Look at an everyday object in your bedroom, kitchen or classroom.

Now imagine you have never seen the object before and have no knowledge that would enable you to understand what it was for. Look at it from different angles, but don't touch it.

9

Does the visual information enable you to tell whether it is hard or soft, smooth or rough, warm or cold, stable or wobbly? If it were a completely unfamiliar object made of unfamiliar materials, would you be able to tell what properties it 'affords'?

Gibson studied the visual experience of World War Two pilots landing aircraft, referring to their entire view as the **optic array**. He said that factors like the optic-flow pattern and the changes in gradient of textures as the pilot moved forward enabled the pilots to make correct judgement of distances. To understand what he meant by optic flow, imagine what it is like to travel fast in a car, and how, if you focus ahead of you, the rest of the visual information from the outer edges of your visual field appears at first to get larger and then flows past you out of your field of vision. To understand what Gibson meant by gradient of textures, look closely at a carpet and observe how you can identify each tiny, individual tuft of material. Now look at the carpet further away, and notice how the texture is much finer, and individual tufts are no longer clear. Gibson thought the pilot would similarly experience changes in the texture of grass and trees as the plane travelled along the runway. This flow of visual information and outward, or radial, expansion of textures from the point to which the pilot approached he called **optic-flow patterns**.

As the pilot approaches the runway, the visual information at first expands and then flows out of sight – optic flow

Although the concept of affordances has been criticised, there are several points to make in favour of Gibson's theory. First, the theory is all about the way in which changes in visual cues occur with movement, and how our perception depends on these changes. As such, it is a really sensible theory, since people do move around as they perceive their world and don't see things from a static point. Remember that the theory stems from applied research with pilots and therefore shows how real-life perception occurs. Second, it is quite unlikely that simple creatures, such as insects and fish, use past experience, for example, to perceive depth, so their perception is probably entirely stimulus-driven. If we believe that all creatures are related, as in the theory of evolution, then perhaps human perception uses the same mechanisms as other, less complex creatures. Third, some infant research (see the Study on page 238) suggests that certain perceptual abilities may be innate and therefore cannot depend on the use of stored information. Finally, whatever critics may say about bottom-up theory, it cannot be disputed that stimulus information is a necessity for perception.

Evaluative Comment

Critics of Gibson's theory argue that it cannot be used to explain illusions and instances of mistaken perception, yet clearly we do make perceptual errors, as several examples of illusions on pages 248 and 249 illustrate. According to Gibson, all we need to perceive accurately is the stimulus information; but in illusions, we often perceive the stimulus inaccurately, sometimes even to the extent that we think *something is there when it isn't, as with fiction illusions (see Figure 9.8). The concept of affordances is difficult for many to accept, and of course it is hard to believe that we do not need or use past knowledge (or top-down information) to establish the properties of objects and what they might be used for. Finally, the theory implies there is no distinction between sensation and perception, and yet from experience we know there is a distinction. This was demonstrated by looking at Figure 9.1, where we **saw** an array of black blobs on the white background, but we **perceived** a horse and rider.*

In conclusion, Eysenck & Keane (1995) suggest that perception is perhaps mostly bottom-up in good, clear viewing conditions when the visual cues are obvious and easy to determine, but probably more dependent on top-down information when viewing conditions are not so clear and we need to fill in the missing bits.

Top-down theory of information processing

Richard Gregory (1966) proposed a top-down theory of perception, stating that our perceptions of the world are hypotheses based on past experience and stored information. According to Gregory, our sensory receptors receive information from the environment, which is then combined with previously stored information about the world that we have built up as a result of experience. Together, these two sets of information enable us to produce a hypothesis about what we are currently seeing. For example, if we are driving along a road through the woods and we catch a glimpse of a small reddish-brown creature running across the road, we would probably form the hypothesis that it is a fox. This hypothesis is formed not just on the available data, but also through the use of *inference* about what animals we might expect to see in the forest at night. The hypothesis is then tested and reformulated as we receive more information; for example, if we look through the trees as we pass, we might see a furry tail, enabling us to confirm our original hypothesis about the fox. Thus the theory suggests that perception is active, constructive and requires some degree of inference. This means that we must go beyond the information given and add to stimulus information in order to make sense of it. Because Gregory's theory emphasises the role of stored information in perception, it is sometimes referred to as **concept-driven processing**.

The top-down theory of perception emphasises the role of inference in interpreting our experience, and indeed we often use inference to help us perceive. Just consider how, for example, when we look at two-dimensional or flat images in books and on TV screens, we are inferring depth and distance in our mind. It is reasonable, then, to expect that we use inference all the time as part of our normal perception.

Many studies support the proposal that we use stored information in perception. Most of the studies involve the perception of visual information, but some research has been carried out on auditory (sound) perception.

Study

AIM *Lieberman (1963) set out to show that the surrounding context and past experience influence the perception of single spoken words.*

METHOD *Participants listened to recordings of phrases such as 'A stitch in time saves nine' and had no difficulty perceiving the phrases when presented as a whole. In the experimental condition, however, participants heard single words spliced out of the phrases and presented on their own, for example, the word 'time' without anything before or after it.*

RESULTS *Words presented in isolation were much more difficult to perceive; for example, the word 'nine' was recognised only 50 per cent of the time in the isolation condition, but was never misperceived in the control condition.*

9

CONCLUSION *Lieberman concluded that participants were making use of previous stored information about the context to recognise single words within a phrase. Use of context to enable perception has similarly been found in other work on auditory perception by Warren & Warren (1970), who discovered that participants 'heard' letters and even parts of words, even though they had been deleted from the tape recordings. The Lieberman study is an example of how perception can be affected by our perceptual set, a phenomenon which is fully described on page 240.*

Whilst top-down theory is able to explain many of our perceptual activities, including the way we misperceive when we look at illusions (see pages 248–249) and perceptual set, it is often argued that empirical demonstrations, like experiments which use **ambiguous figures**, involve artificial stimuli which are deliberately misleading and not like our real, everyday perceptual experiences. In support of top-down theory, it seems only logical that past experience influences our perception; after all, our store of personal experiences is what makes us who we are, so we cannot disregard its influence on our present experiences.

Evaluative Comment

One argument against top-down theory suggests that in emphasising the use of already stored information, the richness of stimulus information is neglected. Furthermore, if perception relied on top-down information, then how would a newborn baby who has no stored information ever be able to interpret any sensory experience and begin to build a mental model of the world? Studies with infants indicate that some perceptual abilities are present at birth, and therefore probably do not require top-down processing.

Study

AIM *Bower, Broughton & Moore (1970) set out to show that very young babies were capable of perceiving distance.*

METHOD *Infants aged between 6 and 21 days were positioned facing an object suspended in front of them at a distance. As the object was released from the start position and 'loomed' towards the infants' faces, the researchers observed their response.*

RESULTS *As the object loomed closer, babies made a typical 'collision' response, pulling their heads upwards and away from the approaching object in an attempt to avoid collision. The babies' visual experience of a rapid expansion of the retinal image as the object moved closer enabled them to interpret this as a change in distance.*

CONCLUSION *Infants can perceive depth at just a few days old, as indicated by their avoidance response to the looming object. It is questionable whether six-day-old babies could have had sufficient visual experience to enable them to have learned about depth perception, so the study appear to contradict the top-down hypothesis. It seems, therefore, that nature endows us with certain abilities, such as depth perception.*

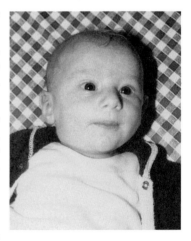

Bower *et al.* (1970) showed how young babies could perceive an object looming towards them

Work with illusions seems at first sight to be good evidence for top-down processing, but some illusions still persist, even when we know we are making a perceptual error. For example, even when we are told that the horizontal lines in Figure 9.2 are straight and parallel, we continue to experience them as slightly curved or convex. According to top-down theory, once we know the lines are straight, then we should no longer experience the illusion. How is it that mistaken hypotheses still persist even when we know they are wrong?

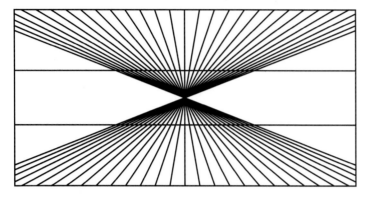

Figure 9.2: The two horizontal lines are parallel, although they don't look it

Neisser (1976) proposed a dynamic theory of perception which takes account of both bottom-up and top-down information. The **analysis-by-synthesis** model proposes that past experience in the form of schema leads us to look for particular features in the environment. A schema is an organised unit of knowledge about the world. The sensory data from the features we explore then lead to revision of our schema and adjustment of what we expect, and therefore what sense data we notice and analyse. For example, a 'plant' schema might consist of information about the colour of flowers and leaves, so when you visit a garden, you seek out plants of a certain colour. As you inspect your chosen plants, you notice the aromatic smell of the lavender, which now becomes part of your plant schema. From now on, you will focus not only on colour and leaf texture, but also on the scent of the plants.

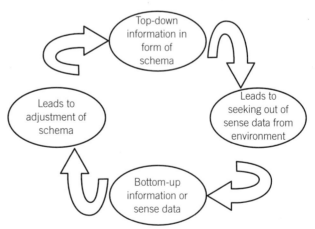

Figure 9.3: Neisser's model combines the bottom-up view of Gibson with the top-down view of Gregory

Factors influencing perception

We have all developed our own way of perceiving the world. Sometimes this is referred to as a **perceptual set** which can be defined as a predisposition to attend to and perceive certain aspects of a stimulus and disregard others. *Set* is related to the concept of *schema*, which is our own personal way of organising past events into units of knowledge that are meaningful to us. Many factors affect

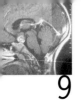

our perceptual set, including expectation, motivation, emotion and culture. All of these can be understood as top-down influences on our perception and therefore relevant to the broader theoretical debate about the top-down or bottom-up basis of perception.

Expectation and perceptual set

Expectations arise for many reasons and influence perceptual set very powerfully. Most experiments conducted by psychologists involve creating an expectation by manipulating the context in which a stimulus is shown. This is usually achieved by showing a set of pictures, and then exposing the participant to a stimulus that can be perceived in more than one way. Such a stimulus is known as an **ambiguous figure**. One very well-known example of an ambiguous figure used in 'set' experiments is the rat/man figure shown in Figure 9.4 (Bugelski & Alampay, 1962). The rat/man figure is shown at the end of a sequence of pictures, either of faces or of animals. It is usually found that participants

Figure 9.4: 'It's a rat!' 'No, it's a man!' The Rat-Man figure illustrates how we can have two possible hypotheses for the same stimulus

who see the face sequence perceive the figure as that of a man's face, whereas those participants who see the animal picture sequence perceive the ambiguous figure to be that of a rat or a mouse.

Study

AIM *Bruner & Minturn (1955) set out to demonstrate how the immediate physical context could influence perception of an ambiguous figure.*

METHOD *In an independent design, participants were shown either a series of numbers or a series of letters. In each case, the centre stimulus was exactly the same – I3. Participants were asked to look at the letters or numbers and state what they saw.*

RESULTS *The perceptions of the two groups were quite different. The group who saw the ambiguous figure alongside letters reported seeing the figure as a 'B', whilst the number-context group reported seeing the figure as a '13'.*

CONCLUSION *Bruner and Minturn concluded that perception of sensory information varies according to the context in which a stimulus is presented and that by altering immediate context, it is possible to predispose participants to interpret visual information differently. The study therefore supports the existence of context-induced perceptual set.*

Practical Activity

You could try your own version of the Bruner and Minturn study using your own hand-written stimulus.

Experiment with writing words that could be seen in two different ways. Then set your ambiguous word into two different context groups. For example, if your ambiguous word was 'dog/clog', you could produce two lists like those in Figure 9.5.

pony, rabbit, hamster, cat, clog

trainer, boot, sandal, shoe, clog

Figure 9.5: 'Ambiguous word' lists

Put the handwritten lists on separate sheets of paper and check that each list has an identical version of the ambiguous word. You can photocopy it to make sure they are the same. Then present your stimulus lists to people and ask them to read the words. If most people tend to read the ambiguous word in line with the surrounding context words, then your results are similar to those of Bruner and Minturn.

Evaluative Comment

It is often remarked that the stimuli used in studies of perception are artificial because the images are specially produced to 'trick' people into making perceptual errors. However, if you look carefully, there are also many real-life examples of how perception can be affected by the context. How many times have you been reading a book, or for that matter a notice or a menu, and found that there are errors in typing or 'typos'? These ought to have been identified by the proof-reader, whose job involves going carefully through the text to make sure it is correct. However, some some errors are inevitably missed because perception of written words is influenced by context in just the same way as perception of ambiguous pictures. Look at the notice in Figure 9.6 and read the words out loud. Next time you go to a park, check to see whether the park keeper is playing a joke on you.

Figure 9.6: Did you spot the error?

Motivation and perceptual set

The idea that wanting something increases its attractiveness is a familiar one and is illustrated in old sayings like 'the grass is always greener on the other side of the fence'. This phenomenon of increased awareness and/or attractiveness is known as **perceptual accentuation**. This means that our perception of something we need or want becomes accentuated or heightened simply because of our motivation or desire for it.

Practical Activity

Make a list of real-life occasions where something appeared brighter, nicer and generally more attractive just because you wanted it. For example, you might have set your heart on a new jacket or pair of shoes that you couldn't afford.

Perhaps if you had had the money to go and buy it there and then, it wouldn't have seemed so desirable. Very often we find that when we do eventually get whatever it is we want, it turns out to be a bit of a disappointment.

Study

AIM *Gilchrist & Nesberg (1952) set out to test the effect of motivation induced by hunger and thirst on perception of pictures.*

METHOD *Participants viewed food-related and non-food-related pictures, which they were then asked to rate on a scale for colour and brightness. Some participants had been deprived of food and liquid for several hours, others had not.*

RESULTS *The 'deprived' participants rated the food-related pictures as brighter and more colourful than non-food-related pictures.*

CONCLUSION *Gilchrist and Nesberg suggested that hunger and thirst were motives which led to perceptual accentuation, producing perceptions which were stronger and brighter than normal. The study is an example of how motivation can induce a perceptual set.*

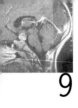

9 Practical Activity

Try your own version of the Gilchrist and Nesberg study using a type of inkblot picture. On a plain sheet of paper, daub some colourful paint splodges to give an abstract pattern that could be interpreted in lots of different ways. A traditional inkblot effect can be achieved by folding the paper in half when the paint is still wet and then opening it up to dry, a bit like a 'butterfly painting' children often make at nursery school. Try showing your picture to people and asking them what they can 'see' in it. You could ask some people just before lunchtime when they're hungry and ask other people after lunch. Record how many times people mention food- or drink-related items in the two conditions.

Evaluative Comment

In the Gilchrist and Nesberg study, participants went without food for just a few hours, so they were hardly being starved, although this is sometimes presented as a criticism because it sounds a bit unethical. If they had been deprived of food long enough to make them uncomfortable, or even ill, then of course it would have been unethical, but this wasn't the case, so the criticism is not justified. However, consider the implications of the study, and how the findings could be applied to the behaviour of people who are on a strict diet and have reduced their food consumption dramatically. How would this affect their perception of food images, for example, in magazines, on TV and in real life? Not surprisingly, diet magazines recommend that dieters should go to the supermarket when they have just eaten, so that they don't end up buying a trolley full of things that look good simply because they are hungry at the time.

Emotion and perceptual set

Both positive and negative emotions have been found to affect perception. An example of a positive emotion that could affect how we interpret what we see or hear is excitement, which might lead us to perceive a forthcoming event more positively because of eager anticipation. An example of a negative emotion that might affect perception would be fear, which would lead us to perceive something bad as worse than it really is because we would rather avoid it.

Several studies show that it takes us longer to perceive stimuli we find unpleasant. In a way, this is a form of perceptual set, since we are affected by a predisposition, although in this case, we are less rather than more likely to perceive certain aspects of a stimulus. This phenomenon of delayed perception is referred to as **perceptual defence** and has been illustrated by McGinnies (1949), who looked at the time it took for participants to recognise words presented using a tachistoscope. The words were very rapidly projected at first with gradually increasing display times. The task was to say aloud each word as soon as it was recognised. The results showed that it took participants a lot longer to recognise taboo words like 'crotch' than it did for them to recognise neutral, inoffensive words like 'plate'. The perceptual defence interpretation of these findings rests on the Freudian concept of defence mechanisms like repression and denial (see Chapter 1). According to Sigmund Freud (1901, 1976), these unconscious defence mechanisms act to protect us from consciously experiencing unpleasant events and thoughts.

Evaluative Comment

Can you think of any criticisms of the taboo-word research? Did people really take longer because their unconscious perceptual defence mechanism was operating to protect them, or was there another reason? People might have been too embarrassed to say the rude words aloud in front of the experimenter. Even if they were not embarrassed, they presumably wanted to be quite sure that the word was really what they thought it was, probably thinking that it was unlikely to be such a rude word in an experiment.

For this reason, perhaps they would have waited fractionally longer before saying the word out loud. The study could also be criticised from an ethical point of view, since participants were likely to have been at least a little uncomfortable, if not completely embarrassed and affronted.

Study

Aim *The question of whether or not unconscious perception can occur was explored in a famous study by Lazarus & McCleary (1951).*

Method *They presented participants with ten nonsense syllables on a screen; for five of these syllables, presentation was accompanied by a mild electric shock. After the initial training period, they were shown the syllables again without the shocks but at a presentation rate that was too fast for them to consciously perceive the words. Participants were wired to a galvanic skin response (GSR) meter which records minute changes in the surface moisture of the skin which occur when a person becomes aroused, as would happen when a person is afraid or shocked in some way.*

Results *Even though the participants were not aware they had seen anything during the second lot of presentations, when the syllables which had previously been paired with electric shocks were shown again, they experienced anxiety evidenced by their GSR.*

Conclusion *Lazarus and McCleary concluded that an effect known as subliminal or unconscious perception was taking place, as the participants had experienced perception without any conscious awareness. Perhaps, then, it is possible that our perceptual systems can screen out some undesirable material before we become consciously aware of it.*

Culture and perceptual set

If perceptual set and expectation can be induced by immediate context, then it is likely that the enduring context of the culture in which we are raised and currently live will also influence our perception. Many studies from the 1960s suggest that people from different cultural backgrounds, with different visual experiences, perceive the world differently. For example, Turnbull (1961) studied people who lived in dense forest, taking them to the open plain to watch herds of buffalo. The forest dwellers thought the buffalo were ants and suspected witchcraft. Turnbull concluded they had not developed size constancy because of their restricted visual environment.

Many cross-cultural studies with illusions have suggested that Westerners are generally much more susceptible to visual illusions. Segall *et al.* (1963) proposed the **carpentered-world hypothesis**, which suggested that Westerners are tricked by line illusions because of the tendency to read three dimensions into a two-dimensional stimulus. In the case of the famous distortion illusion, known as the Müller-Lyer illusion (see Figure 9.7), the line with the in-going fins (line (b)) is unconsciously perceived as the outer corner of a building projecting towards us, and the line with the out-going fins (line (a)) as the inner corner of a room stretching far away from us. In this case, then, it is no wonder that we are tricked by the illusion into seeing the out-going fin line (line (a)) as longer. If we believe it is further away and yet it still makes the same sized retinal image as the other line, then we are

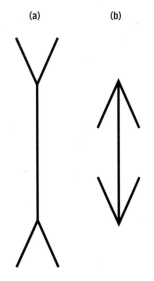

(a)   (b)

Figure 9.7: The Müller-Lyer illusion. The fins act as linear perspective, giving the illusion of 3D so that the vertical line on the left appears longer than the one on the right

forced to conclude that it must be longer. Constancy scaling is 'misapplied' so that the line with the out-going fins is mentally scaled up to compensate for its apparent perceived distance.

Here, the linear perspective cues have been added to the outer edge of a building and the inner corner of a room. According to the carpentered world hypothesis, this is how people from structured, or 'carpentered', cultures unconsciously perceive the Müller-Lyer illusion

Evaluative Comment

Not all psychologists agree with the carpentered world interpretation of the Müller-Lyer illusion; for example, Eysenck (1984) notes that the illusion still persists when spheres are used in place of the fins. Without the fins, there are no depth cues, making it impossible to perceive the lines as the corner of a room or the edge of a building, yet people still experience the illusion. It seems that exposure to Western culture, especially pictures, may have been a confounding variable in many studies of cultural differences in perception. Interpretation of pictures involves inference, yet studies by Deregowski (1972) and Hudson (1960) appear to show that people who have no experience with two-dimensional images of three-dimensional scenes do not understand the need to make a three-dimensional interpretation. Whilst it is generally assumed that cross-cultural studies imply that ecology, or surrounding environment, is linked to susceptibility to illusions and perception of depth, we must remember that there are methodological criticisms.

Visual perception

The nature of constancy

Although retinal images made by objects may vary according to how near or far they are, or the angle from which they are viewed, our perceptual systems keep our mental representation of the object constant. For example, even though a person may walk away from us, or twirl around, and the image they make on our retina changes dramatically as a result, we usually perceive them as remaining the same size and shape. This is made possible by the automatic mental application of our perceptual constancies.

Size constancy

Size constancy enables us to keep the perceived size of objects constant despite changes in the size of the retinal image. We use depth cues from the visual field to determine the distance of objects, and once we determine they are distant, we mentally enlarge them to make them appear normal sized. Such a process is known as **constancy scaling** and is an integral feature in the working of many illusions.

Even though objects or people in the distance make a much smaller retinal image, we perceive them as normal sized

Shape constancy

When we view objects or people from different angles, the image they make on our retina changes considerably, yet **shape constancy** means that we perceive the shape of the object or person as constant.

Different retinal image, but we perceive the same object

Colour constancy

Colour constancy means that we perceive colours of objects as constant, although the wavelengths of light reflected from them may change considerably as lighting conditions vary.

Practical Activity

Do this on a dull day when you have the lights on inside the house or classroom. Look around the room and focus on a brightly coloured object. It might be someone's jumper or a cushion.

Look carefully at the colour of the object and think about your experience of it. Concentrate also on the texture and surface – is it shiny, patterned, rough, etc.? Now turn off the light and view the object again in the semi-light. How do you experience its colour and brightness now? Do you still perceive the colour as you did previously? Your colour constancy should enable you to perceive the colour of the object as just the same as in light conditions.

The problem of illusion

In order to understand how illusions work, we need to know about the process of depth perception, or three-dimensional perception.

9

Depth perception

There are a number of visual cues that we use to perceive depth. Some are **monocular** (possible with just one eye) and some **binocular** (requiring the use of both eyes). Remember that Gibson's bottom-up theory of perception says that certain visual cues are especially important for perception.

One-eye (monocular) cues

- Decreasing size: we learn that the size of an image made by an object is not constant. It appears smaller as it moves away.

- Height in visual field: things further away are higher up in two dimensions.

- Gradient of texture: the finer the texture, the further the distance.

- Clarity/light: near objects are clearer/brighter, we can see details.

- Superimposition: close objects obscure those further away.

- Linear perspective: parallel lines appear to converge as they go into the distance.

- Motion parallax: distant objects move more slowly across our visual field as we move than near objects.

How many monocular depth cues can you see in this photograph?

Practical Activity

Find a picture of a scenic painting in a magazine or book, either a country scene with lots of hills and trees and animals, or a lively town scene.

Look carefully at the picture and see what depth cues the artist has used to convey the illusion of three dimensions in the painting.

Make a list of all the cues; for example, if some things are higher up in the painting, that could be an indication that they are meant to appear to be further away.

Now compare your list from the painting with the list of one-eye depth cues above to see how many you have found. Note that motion parallax is dependent on movement, so will not occur when looking at a picture.

Two-eye (binocular) cues

- Retinal disparity: each eye receives a slightly different view because each sees the world from a slightly different angle. The nearer the object is to you, the greater the difference in the view each eye receives. The brain analyses the difference in the two images and computes the distance (see the activity below).

- Convergence: a cue from the eye muscles as they feed back information to the brain about the angle of vision. The harder the muscles work to turn the eyes, the greater the amount of feedback. This would indicate the closeness of the object being viewed.

Practical Activity

To understand the extent of the difference in the view from each eye, try the following exercise: close your right eye and hold your forefinger vertically in front of you at arm's length, lining your finger up with a vertical surface in the room, like the edge of the door.

As you continue to look at the finger, switch eyes, closing the right and opening the left, but keep the finger quite still. Notice how the finger is no longer lined up with the door edge but appears to have jumped slightly to the left.

Now do the same again, this time with your hand quite close to your face. This time you will see the finger 'jump' dramatically to the left. This shows how retinal disparity (the difference in view from each eye) is much greater when things are close than when they are far away.

The problem of illusion

So far, we have seen how perception may be a combination of both bottom-up and top-down processing using both current data and stored information. We have also seen how basic perceptual abilities like depth perception and the organisation of visual information are influenced by depth cues and constancies. This exploration of the normal processes involved in perception provides us with several possible explanations for our susceptibility to visual illusions.

General explanations of illusions

We have a natural tendency to convert a two-dimensional visual stimulus into a three-dimensional perception. This tendency is triggered by intentional use of depth cues in illusions, for example linear perspective in the fins of the Müller-Lyer illusion. The presence of depth cues causes us to engage in constancy scaling, whereby our perceptual processes lead us to unconsciously mentally enlarge any stimulus we believe to be further away. Many distortion illusions work because we misapply constancy scaling, falsely believing some parts of the stimulus to be further away than others.

Past experience or immediate context creates expectations about what is likely to be perceived. This top-down information in turn leads to the development of a *perceptual set* which predisposes us first to see certain aspects of a stimulus and second to interpret the stimulus in a particular way.

Some illusions exist because there are two possible hypotheses in a stimulus, neither of which can be disconfirmed by the data. These illusions are known as *ambiguous figures* and include the rat-man (see Figure 9.4).

Our desire for symmetry and order in our world, and the constant striving to extract shapes from the background, leads us to identify figures which do not really exist. This explanation for illusions rests on the **Gestalt** theory of perception, which suggests that we perceive our world according to certain principles or laws. These Gestalt Laws include:

9

- the law of symmetry, where we seek out and prefer to experience symmetrical objects;
- the law of closure, where we mentally complete incomplete figures;
- the law of figure-ground, where we continually seek to distinguish objects from the background.

Practical Activity

Look at each of the illusions shown in Figures 9.8 to 9.11 and make a note of which explanations relate to each of the different illusions. Sometimes more than one explanation can be used for a single illusion. For example, in Figure 9.8, we perceive a three-dimensional object which isn't there, so we are inferring depth inappropriately. We are also using our past experience of objects in the world to recognise the non-existent object as a pyramid. The Gestalt explanation also applies, as we are seeking to organise the available data into a symmetrical object, distinct from the background.

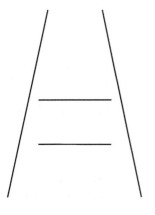

Figure 9.8: Richardson's pyramid is an example of a non-existent figure or fiction, where we perceive a figure that does not exist

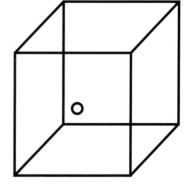

Figure 9.9: The Necker cube is an example of an ambiguous figure, where there is more than one perceptual hypothesis. If you find it difficult to perceive the cube at a different orientation, try blinking your eyes

Figure 9.10: The Ponzo illusion is an example of a distortion illusion. Viewers normally perceive the top horizontal line as longer than the bottom one

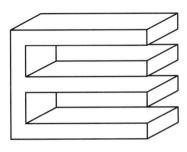

Figure 9.11: The Huffman figure is an example of an impossible figure. It can exist only as a drawing in 2D and not as a 3D object

Evaluative Comment

Critics of illusion research point to the artificial nature of the stimuli and say that illusion research contributes little to our understanding of real-life perception. According to Gibson (1966), whose approach to perception was ecological and concerned with real-life perception in a dynamic and changing environment, studies involving illusions are of minimal importance and tell us very little at all about normal perceptual processes. However, the illusions in the above activity do serve to illustrate how the normal perceptual processes of depth-cue analysis, conversion of two dimensions into three dimensions, hypothesis testing, constancy scaling and object recognition are mistakenly applied in the processing of illusions, showing us quite a lot about normal perception.

Attention

When something comes to our attention, what happens first? Do we sense it, then select it and then consciously focus on it and work out what it means? If we are studying quietly in the library with the general hum of whispering students and computers around us, how is it that we pick out and attend to a sound, which is at first hardly noticeable, but becomes increasingly obvious, like the tapping of a pen by an absent-minded student sitting opposite. Most cognitive psychologists suggest that the processing of information happens in a stage-by-stage sequence, and adopt what is known as the *information-processing* approach to the study of mental processes. Let's see how this stage-by-stage sequence might be applied to the library example:

- Stage 1 Attention: We would be drawn by the sound to the unusual noise in the library and start to consciously focus on it.

- Stage 2 Perception: We would interpret the sound, perceiving it as the noise of a pen tapping on a desk.

- Stage 3 Memory: To make a full interpretation, we would need to use our memory of what a pen is, and how they are made of hard material and would make a noise if banged on a desk.

- Stage 4 Thinking: We might go on to think about how annoying the noise is, and how the student must be daydreaming instead of getting on with his work.

Using this example, we can see how information from the senses might be processed in series of systems or stages involving attention, perception, memory and thinking in a sequence. Cognitive research is directed at specifying the processes and structures involved at each of these stages, and investigating how information is altered in some way at each stage in the system. The information processing approach also sees parallels between human information processing and the processing that occurs in computers.

Attention is sometimes considered to be the gateway to the rest of the cognitive system and the point at which the mass of sensory information in the environment must be reduced to an amount with which our cognitive systems can cope. For this reason, attention theories are often thought of

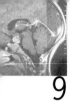

as the best examples of information-processing models, and are represented in typical information-processing terms as models with boxes, each box representing a stage in the process, with arrows showing the flow of information through the system.

Definitions of attention

The following definitions of attention are taken from Gross (2001):

> Definition 1: 'mechanisms by which certain information is registered and other information is rejected'

> Definition 2: 'some upper limit to the amount of processing that can be performed on incoming information at any one time'.

Notice how the first definition implies selection of certain stimuli in preference to others, whilst the second definition implies some upper capacity to our ability to attend to the mass of incoming stimuli. The differing emphasis in these definitions is reflected in theories of attention and the experimental techniques employed.

Studies by researchers who understand attention in terms of the first definition usually involve participants hearing two simultaneous messages, then **shadowing**, or repeating, one of the messages. The shadowed message is known as the *attended* message, and participants are then tested to see whether they know anything about the unattended message. Theories of attention centre round the search for the point at which the narrowing down of the messages or filtering occurs.

Researchers who understand attention in terms of the second definition conduct experiments that involve **dual-task** performance, seeing how much and what type of tasks can be performed simultaneously. Theories are focused on explaining how we allocate a limited pool of attentional resources to two or more concurrent tasks.

Selective and divided attention

Selective attention is the ability to attend to and process a single stimulus and disregard all other stimuli or inputs. An example of selective attention might be the ability to attend exclusively to the voice of a person on the telephone even when there is a lot of noise and other people speaking in the room around you.

Divided attention is the ability to attend to and process more than one stimulus or input at the same time. An example of divided attention might be the ability to attend to this task whilst at the same time carrying on a conversation with a colleague or friend at the next desk.

Reflective Activity

Think of your own examples of how and when you might use selective attention and divided attention in everyday life.

Consider what inputs you are disregarding when you selectively attend to your chosen input and whether other information that you don't pay attention to might sometimes creep into your conscious awareness.

Think about the example of divided attention, and how many different inputs you can attend to at any one time. Is there an upper limit? Does it depend on the types of stimuli or task you are performing?

Models of attention

Broadbent's model of attention

Donald Broadbent (1958) proposed that all information comes through a single channel and that there is a filter early in the system that screens out all unwanted information. The information to be attended to is selected on the basis of gross physical characteristics, for example, whether a voice is male or female, or whether a message consists of words or a tone. Figure 9.12 shows Broadbent's model of attention.

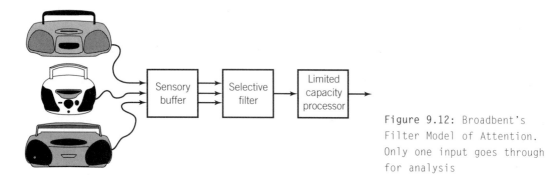

Figure 9.12: Broadbent's Filter Model of Attention. Only one input goes through for analysis

Broadbent is best known for his experimental technique known as **dichotic listening**, where participants are simultaneously presented with two different messages, one in each ear, through stereophonic headphones.

Study

Aim *Broadbent (1958) set out to show that incoming stimuli were selected on the basis of 'gross physical characteristics' and that only one channel of information could be processed at any one time.*

Method *Participants took part in a procedure known as a split-span task. Using stereophonic headphones, two sets of three digits were presented simultaneously, one set to the right ear and one to the left ear. The digits were presented at one-second intervals. Participants were required to report back what they had heard after all the digits had been presented.*

Results *Broadbent found that ear-by-ear reporting was much easier for participants than pair-by-pair recall. This means that participants were much better at saying the three digits from one ear first, followed by the three from the other ear, than they were at reporting the first digit from both ears, then the second digit from both ears, and finally the third digit from both ears. He presumed that this was because pair-by-pair recall would require constant switching from ear to ear and would therefore reduce efficiency.*

Conclusion *Broadbent concluded that attention occurred very early in the system and that the decision about which input to attend to is made on the basis of physical characteristics (in this case which ear) and not on the basis of meaning. He also concluded that people could only attend to two different inputs by rapidly switching between input channels.*

In summary, Broadbent's theory states that attention is preconscious, in that any decision about which stimulus to attend to is made before the content is known. This suggests that attention is a bottom-up process, meaning selection is based on sensory properties of stimulus rather than what the stimulus means. Attention involves serial processing, which means that, just like a computer, we can only deal with one message or input at a time. Broadbent reasoned that if both messages were recalled, it was because the listener had been switching input channels (or ears) rapidly.

Evaluative Comment

*Broadbent's theory and his research formed the basis for much attention research that was to follow. Many critics argue that his dichotic listening experiment was a very artificial task and therefore that his findings had very little ecological validity. Undoubtedly the task was extremely difficult, but there are everyday parallels, for example, when we are trying to carry on a telephone conversation and also listen to someone speaking in the room. Teachers understand very well the problem of having multiple inputs at once, which is why they often have to ask for 'one question at a time please!' The main criticism of Broadbent's theory was the observation that occasionally information from the apparently unattended channel could be analysed for meaning, which the filter model would not have predicted. To explain this, we must look at Anne Treisman's **attenuation** model of attention.*

Treisman's model of attention (1964)

Treisman was a student of Broadbent's who refined his original theory about a selective all-or-none filter using a technique invented by Cherry (1953). Cherry asked participants to shadow (repeat) one of the messages in a dichotic experiment, thus ensuring that they were carefully attending to the shadowed message. According to the filter model, no information from the unattended ear would be processed. However, it was found that participants would often be able to hear their own name in the message to the unattended ear, an effect which became known as the **cocktail-party phenomenon**. Gray & Wedderburn (1960) gave participants items like 'mice five cheese' in one ear and 'four eat six' in the other, and found they reported what made sense, such as 'mice eat cheese' and 'four, five, six', demonstrating some semantic analysis of the unattended message. Such findings were incompatible with Broadbent's notion of an early pre-perceptual filter, and Treisman herself went on to show that semantic information from the unattended ear would influence interpretation of a shadowed message.

Study

Aim *Treisman attempted to show how information from the supposedly unattended channel in a shadowing experiment could be processed in preference to the attended message if it made more sense.*

Method *Participants were asked to shadow a message in one ear whilst another message was played in the unattended ear. At a certain point, the sentence from the attended ear was switched to the unattended ear whilst a non-consecutive message continued in the ear that was supposed to be being shadowed. For example, participants would hear the following message in the shadowed ear: 'While walking through the forest/a bank can lend you money' and another message in the unshadowed ear: 'If you want to buy a car/a tree fell across his path'.*

Result *Shadowing confirmed that participants would switch attention from the shadowed to the unshadowed ear if it made more sense to do so; for example, they would report, 'While walking through the forest, a tree fell across his path'. Despite having been told to attend to the message from just one ear, participants could not help switching in order to preserve the sense of the material.*

Conclusion *There must be some semantic analysis of the unattended channel, otherwise participants would not have switched ears. This evidence seems to suggest that Broadbent's view of an all-or-none filter based on gross physical characteristics is incorrect.*

To accommodate these findings, Treisman (1964) adapted Broadbent's filter model, proposing that after initial selection, information that is screened out is not eliminated altogether but is *attenuated* or toned down. She proposed stages of selection based on:

- gross physical characteristics (for example whether the voice is male or female);
- keywords and syllables (for example, our own name) and word meanings (for example, reference to an issue that concerns us like our favourite football team's name or home ground).

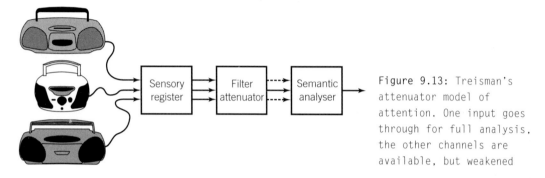

Figure 9.13: Treisman's attenuator model of attention. One input goes through for full analysis, the other channels are available, but weakened

Treisman's model (see Figure 9.13) is an example of a single-channel model that is sequential, but unlike in Broadbent's theory, selection for Treisman is not all or nothing. Rather than being entirely bottom-up, Treisman's model is a combination of both bottom-up and top-down processing, with the decision about what to attend to being made not only on the basis of stimulus characteristics, but also on the basis of previously stored information and meaning.

Practical Activity

Make a list of keywords, syllables and meanings that you think would grab your attention if you heard them in the 'unattended' channel in a shadowing experiment. Obviously your own name would be one, but what about other stimuli? What sorts of things are you especially tuned to notice?

Evaluative Comment

Treisman's model is much more flexible than the original filter model and offers an adequate explanation for the findings of experiments that Broadbent's model could not explain. However, Treisman offers little explanation of what was doing the attenuating and how the process of attenuation works. Given that attenuation depends on semantic content of competing messages, there must be some fairly high-level analysis involved, which cannot simply be explained away as 'turning down the volume' of unwanted messages. There is also the problem that participants could be switching channels rapidly. Massaro (1989) suggests that the attenuator might be better considered as a 'probabilistic filter', since the probability of a word being recognised in the attended channel is much higher than the likelihood of it being recognised in the unattended channel.

Deutsch and Deutsch's model of attention

Deutsch & Deutsch (1963) and Norman (1976) proposed a model of attention involving late selection, according to which the bottleneck in the system is much nearer to the response end of the attentional process than to the input end (see Figure 9.14). They proposed that all sensory information is unconsciously recognised at the start and goes to a short-term store, where selection

9

then occurs on the basis of relevance or pertinence. Many critics say that if all information is analysed anyway, then there is no economy (Solso, 1979), as you might expect from a theory of selective attention; but according to late-selection theory, the recognition is unconscious and therefore requires no cognitive effort. Research shows that there is some evidence for analysis of information from the unattended channel without conscious awareness.

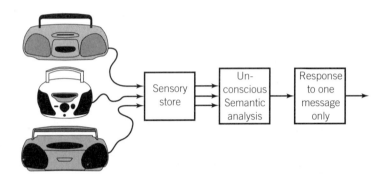

Figure 9.14: Deutsch & Deutsch's Late-Selection Model of Attention. All inputs go through for semantic analysis, but only one is responded to

---

Study

AIM *MacKay (1973) set out to demonstrate that there could be unconscious analysis of information in the unattended ear.*

METHOD *Participants heard a different message in each ear, one of which they had to 'shadow' or repeat after the speaker. In the shadowed ear, they heard ambiguous sentences like 'They threw stones towards the bank yesterday'. At the same time, in the unshadowed ear, they were presented with single words like 'money' or 'river'.*

RESULTS *When asked later about the meaning of the shadowed sentences, participants reported interpretations that tallied with the context of the word in the unattended ear, even though they could not consciously recall anything of the unattended message. For example, if they had heard 'river' in the unattended ear they reported hearing a sentence about children throwing stones into the water, whereas if the word in the unattended ear had been 'money', they recalled hearing about a riot outside a bank.*

CONCLUSION *Interpretations of the ambiguous sentences were unconsciously affected by the meaning of words from the unattended ear, suggesting that attention can be pre-conscious and that any narrowing down to one channel is at the response end of the process rather than early on. Note that these findings could equally be used to support the Treisman model of attention.*

Evaluative Comment

Similar studies involve presenting information to the unattended ear which, in prior training sessions, has been accompanied by mild electric shocks. Participants showed a galvanic skin response (GSR) to this information although they could not consciously report having heard anything. A galvanic skin response is a measurement of the momentary changes in moisture on the surface of the skin that occur when an individual is stressed or aroused. However, Corteen & Wood (1972) note that this effect is unreliable. In summary, the late-selection model of attention is more top-down than other selection theories and involves parallel processing up to the response stage. Critics suggest that is it not economical and no real improvement on Treisman's theory, since she can also explain intrusions from the unattended ear.

Kahneman's model of attention

Kahneman's resource-allocation theory of attention (1973) states that a limited amount of processing capacity is allocated flexibly, according to task demands. Research shows that well-practised tasks require less attentional capacity; thus several easy, well-practised tasks can be performed simultaneously, whereas one unfamiliar task may require all our processing resources, leaving no unused capacity to allocate to another task at the same time. With enough practice, it seems that even difficult tasks can be performed simultaneously because they are so well-learned that they each require very little conscious attention. In general, dual-task performance has found to be affected by task difficulty, task similarity and practice.

Study

AIM *Spelke* et al. *(1976) investigated the effects of practice on dual-task performance.*

METHOD *Two student participants were given approximately 90 hours training at dual tasks. The students were required to read short stories for comprehension, whilst at the same time taking down words at dictation.*

RESULTS *At the start of training, reading speed was slow and handwriting during dictation was of poor quality. After 30 hours of practice, however, their reading speed and comprehension had improved to normal single task level, and their handwriting had improved markedly.*

CONCLUSION *With practice, participants can demonstrate remarkable ability in dual-task studies, even where the two tasks are similar and therefore require the same processing mechanisms.*

According to Kahneman (1973), attentional ability depends on overall processing capacity which is variously affected by the demands of the task, both in terms of its difficulty and salience, and the arousal, motivation, momentary intention and skill of the actor. Rather than the one-way flow of information proposed by the selective-attention models, Kahneman's model has a greater emphasis on top-down processing, involving constant evaluation and adjustment in the light of feedback about task performance (see Figure 9.15).

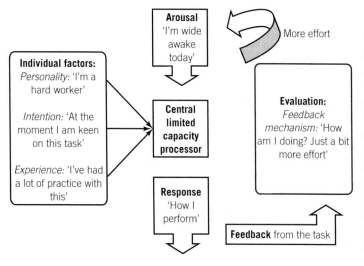

Figure 9.15: Kahneman's resource-allocation model of attention. The model illustrates how task and personality factors can influence the amount of available attention. Here, the task is an easy one with which the actor can easily cope. What would the verbal responses be like if it was a difficult task and the actor was generally less keen?

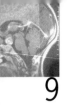

9

Evaluative Comment

Whilst the Kahneman model is more flexible than traditional filter theories and can explain findings from many attention studies, there is no clear statement about the amount of capacity and precisely how it is allocated. Despite a general acceptance that the ability to perform dual tasks is affected by how similar the tasks are, the model makes no attempt to differentiate between attention for different types of task and assumes we have a single pool of attention that can be allocated to any type of activity. Later resource-allocation theories have taken a modular approach, proposing several specialised processing modules (Navon & Gopher, 1979; Wickens 1980), each with a limited capacity, responsible for different types of task.

Kahneman's model of attention and findings of dual-task studies indicate the likelihood that some of our information processing is automatic. Eysenck & Keane (1995) state that automatic processing is fast, unconscious, makes no demands on attention (leaving lots of capacity free to attend to other tasks) and is unavoidable, meaning that it always happens in response to a certain situation.

Practical Activity

Think of some of the behaviours you perform regularly. Some of them will be so well practised that you really don't have to think very hard about them at all. People sometimes say things like 'I could do it with my eyes closed' or 'I could do it without thinking'.

Make a list of your behaviours which you think involve automatic processing and then consider them in relation to Eysenck and Keane's criteria above. Is the behaviour fast, unavoidable, etc.? Are some of the things you mention so automatic that you do them almost entirely without thinking?

Stroop (1935) devised an experimental procedure to illustrate a phenomenon known as the **Stroop effect**. There are many variations on the original study, which involves naming the colour of ink in which words are written. Sometimes the words are non-colour words and sometimes they are colour words, but written in ink of a conflicting colour. Participants normally take significantly longer to name the colour of ink in which conflicting colour words are written than the colour of ink for the non-colour words. The difference in naming times has been taken to illustrate the unavoidable, automatic processing of written words. Since reading is such an automatic skill for an accomplished reader, when presented with a word it is impossible to avoid reading it. The Stroop experiment is sometimes also taken as evidence that Broadbent's theory of an all-or-none filter that works at the level of gross physical characteristics is incorrect, since participants are apparently unable to screen out the meaning of the stimulus words and attend solely to the colour of ink.

Evaluative Comment

*A general distinction is sometimes made between automatic processing, or automaticity, and controlled processing. **Automaticity** is passive and unconscious, whereas controlled processing is active and conscious. Norman & Shallice (1980) question the distinction between controlled and automatic processing, arguing instead that there are at least three levels of functioning:*

1 Fully automatic processing, which requires little conscious awareness and is governed by existing schema (organised units of knowledge/plans of action).

2 Partially automatic processing, which involves some conscious awareness, but no deliberate direction or control.

3 *Deliberate control, which involves conscious and focused control to allow decision-making and coping in novel situations.*

Cheng (1985) argues there is no such thing as automatic processing, suggesting that with practice people use different and more efficient ways of doing things, but this does not mean they are carried out automatically.

Interaction between perception and attention

Although the two processes of perception and attention have been considered separately in this chapter, it is apparent that there is interaction between them. Several theories of attention and the concept of automatic processing seem to suggest a top-down influence on attention, whilst at the same time, certain theories of attention, like Broadbent's, imply a stimulus-driven or bottom-up process. In conclusion, we can note how the two processes have been simultaneously investigated and linked in an applied study by Cooper & Fairburn (1992).

Study

AIM *Cooper & Fairburn (1992) investigated information-processing in people suffering from eating disorders, looking to demonstrate how it might differ from the processing of non-sufferers.*

METHOD *Three groups of women performed in a repeated measures design. In a variation on the Stroop scenario, women suffering from eating disorders, normal female dieters and a female control group of normal eaters were asked to name the colour of ink in which both neutral and diet-linked or shape-linked words (e.g. fat, cake, thighs) were written. Naming times for each group in the two conditions were recorded.*

RESULTS *The eating disorder group took significantly longer to name the colour of diet-related and shape-related words than they took to name colours for the neutral words, whilst the other two groups showed no difference in time taken in the two conditions.*

CONCLUSION *Cooper and Fairburn concluded that the eating disorder group took longer to name the colour because they were less able to filter out the meaning of the words, since these words were so salient to them. Cooper and Fairburn suggested this might contribute to the maintenance of eating disorders, since these people perhaps notice food-related stimuli more than other people do.*

Practical Activity

Consider the results of the Cooper and Fairburn study described above and note down how they relate to the contents of this chapter. Think about the results in relation to:

- *Broadbent's filter theory of attention*
- *Treisman's attenuation theory of attention*
- *The phenomenon of perceptual set*
- *The role of motivation in perception*
- *Top-down and bottom-up processing.*

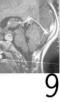

9 Evaluative Comment

As is often the case in cognitive psychology, many of the studies reported in this chapter have been carried out in artificial environments and using artificial stimuli. Undoubtedly, the lack of ecological validity in perception and attention research is a problem if we want to generalise the results of laboratory studies to real-life human experiences. It is refreshing to look at an investigation like the eating disorders study on page 257, where the research is linked to theoretical issues but has a real-life application, and could perhaps be used to explain and treat a potentially life-threatening condition. However, although it might have greater ecological validity, applied research often suffers from other problems. For example, in conducting their study on page 257, Cooper and Fairburn would have had several ethical issues to consider, not least the possibility of negative psychological and behavioural effects on the participants.

Solution to Figure 9.1, page 234

The image is a horse and rider, facing the left-hand side of the page.

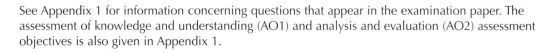

See Appendix 1 for information concerning questions that appear in the examination paper. The assessment of knowledge and understanding (AO1) and analysis and evaluation (AO2) assessment objectives is also given in Appendix 1.

Sample questions

Sample question 1

(a) Psychologists often refer to *models of attention*. Explain what is meant by the term *model* in this context.
   (AO1 = 2, AO2 = 1)   *(3 marks)*

(b) Identify three features of Deutsch and Deutsch's model of attention.
   (AO1 = 3)   *(3 marks)*

(c) Luke is able to talk face-to-face with his friend and send a text message on his mobile phone to another friend all at the same time. Sam is quite unaware of what people around him are saying when he concentrates on playing his guitar. With reference to Luke and Sam's behaviours, outline what is meant by selective and divided attention.
   (AO1 = 2, AO2 = 2)   *(4 marks)*

(d) Describe and discuss Broadbent's model of attention.
   (AO1 = 5, AO2 = 5)   *(10 marks)*

Total AO1 marks = 12   Total AO2 marks = 8   Total = 20 marks

Questions, answers and comments

(a) According to Kahneman, there are several factors which affect a person's ability to perform tasks simultaneously. Identify three of the factors proposed by Kahneman.
   (AO1 = 3)   *(3 marks)*

(b) Identify and explain one difference between Broadbent's and Treisman's theories of attention.
   (AO1 = 2, AO2 = 1)   *(3 marks)*

(c) Describe one psychological explanation for a named illusion.
   (AO1 = 4)   *(4 marks)*

(d) Discuss the influence of both emotion and expectation on perception.
   (AO1 = 3, AO2 = 7)   *(10 marks)*

Total AO1 marks = 12   Total AO2 marks = 8   Total = 20 marks

Answer to (a)

Kahneman's theory is a limited capacity theory and it says that our attention depends on how awake or aroused we are at the time we perform the task. It also depends on how much we really want to carry out the task we have to do and it is also affected by the difficulty of the task. For example, two difficult tasks would be harder to carry out than two simple ones.

Comment

The full three (AO1) marks are awarded here for reference to three valid factors: arousal, motivation and task difficulty. Notice that the candidate has not referred to motivation by name, but there is nevertheless an acceptable description of the factor in the candidate's own words.

Answer to (b)

One difference between Broadbent's and Treisman's is that they disagree about what happens to information the person is not properly attending to. Broadbent says that all this information is lost forever, whereas Treisman says that it is not lost and is weaker.

Comment

The feeling is that the candidate understands full well the difference about the fate of the unattended message, but unfortunately the language used to express their knowledge is fairly non-psychological. An examiner would be loath to give full marks here simply because of the seemingly anecdotal content. One mark (AO1) is given for identification of a difference and one (AO1) for elaboration. However, the analysis mark is not awarded, as there is no real evidence of analysis or application as there might have been had they gone on to explain the point about the message being 'weaker'.

Answer to (c)

I am going to talk about the Ponzo illusion which looks like railway lines going into the distance. This works because of how we always look at things in 3D even when they are only meant to be 2D. The cues in the Ponzo illusion, like the diagonal lines on each side, act to make us believe the lines are going into the distance. So we (mis)apply constancy scaling, even though we shouldn't, and this makes the top line appear bigger than it really is because we are compensating for the 'distance'. Constancy scaling is triggered here by false depth cues.

Comment

Full four (AO1) marks here for a very thorough answer. An illusion is clearly identified (the candidate could also have produced a quick sketch to make it even clearer) and the misapplied constancy scaling explanation is appropriate and complete.

Answer to (d)

The area of perception we are talking about here is all to do with perceptual set. Set is a pre-disposition to attend to certain stimuli or aspects of certain stimuli and disregard others. Set also acts as a factor influencing not just what we perceive, but also how we perceive it. Perceptual set can be initiated either by factors within the perceiver or by external factors like the context in which we see something.

Perceptual set research has often focused on the role of emotion in perceiving the world. In everyday terms, we know that if we are excited, we see things more positively than if we are depressed.

Studies of emotion research focus on perceptual defence which happens if we are afraid or dislike something, and so we deliberately unconsciously do not let ourselves perceive it. In the taboo-words study, people took longer to perceive rude words than ordinary words, presumably because their emotions had set up a perceptual defence to protect them from seeing the words consciously. All of this explanation relies on the Freud theory about repression and cannot really be demonstrated. Freud's work is notorious for its lack of evidence. There could also be another explanation for the taboo-word effect. Perhaps people were simply embarrassed to say the words out loud and couldn't believe their eyes so hesitated before speaking.

Expectation can easily be shown to affect perception in studies like Bruner and Minturn's B/13 study and the Rat Man study. In these experiments, context is used to set up an expectation that certain things will follow, and sure enough that is what people tend to perceive. These are examples of ambiguous figures used to show expectation. Critics would say that these studies are artificial and that real-life perception doesn't usually involve ambiguous figures. In general, work on expectation is more convincing than work on emotion, but undoubtedly they do both have an effect on how we perceive the world.

Comment

The candidate has produced a competent answer to the question, although unfortunately the piece is somewhat brief and perhaps a bit vague. There is a clear definition of terms at the start and the answer is well organised, with no irrelevant material. For AO2, there is some evidence of analysis in respect of the emotion factor, although this is less evident for expectation. The candidate could have done much better on AO2 by linking the answer to the broad theoretical debate about top-down and bottom-up. This answer is awarded three marks for AO1 and three marks for AO2, making a total of six marks for section (d).

Overall, this is a good answer, showing all-round competence and a good grasp of the subject matter. Occasionally, the candidate seems to be struggling to use the appropriate terminology, but answers are to the point and address the questions clearly. The answer as a whole has been awarded a total of fifteen marks out of twenty (AO1 = 12, AO2 = 3).

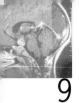

9 Further reading

Introductory texts

Eysenck, M.W. (2001), *Principles of Cognitive Psychology*, 2nd edition, Hove, Psychology Press

Eysenck, M.W. & Flanagan, C. (2001), *Psychology for AS Level*, Hove, Psychology Press

Eysenck, M.W. & Keane, M.T. (2000), *Cognitive Psychology: A Student's Handbook*, 4th edition, Hove, Psychology Press

Gross, R.D. (2001) *Psychology: The Science of Mind and Behaviour*, 4th edition, London, Hodder & Stoughton

Hill, G. (1998), *Advanced Psychology Through Diagrams*, Oxford, Oxford University Press

Specialist sources

Block, J.R. & Yuker, H.E. (1991), *Can You Believe Your Eyes?*, London, Robson Books

Gordon, I.E. (1997), *Theories of Visual Perception*, 2nd edition, London, John Wiley & Sons Ltd.

Gregory, R. (1997) *Eye and Brain*, 5th edition, Oxford, Oxford University Press

Ninio, J. (2000), *The Science of Illusions*, Ithaca, NY, Cornell University Press

Rookes, P. & Willson, J. (2000), *Perception*, London, Routledge

Roth, I.A. & Bruce, V. (1995), *Perception and Representation*, 2nd edition, Milton Keynes, Open University Press

Smyth, M.M., Collins, A.F., Morris, P.E. & Levy, P. (1994), *Cognition in Action*, Hove, Psychology Press

Wade, N.J. & Swanston, M. (1991), *Visual Perception: An Introduction*, London, Routledge

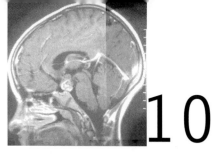

10

Remembering and Forgetting

Introduction: the nature of memory

The role that memory plays in our everyday lives cannot be underestimated. Remembering where we live and how to get home, recognising our friends and family, remembering how to ride a bicycle are all activities which rely on our ability to store and retrieve information. We can remember an enormous amount of information about events that we have personally experienced, as well as the knowledge we have acquired about the world. However, we don't remember everything that happens to us; our memories represent a selection of events that we have experienced. Many of our memories aren't permanent – we forget things. We forget where we left our keys, we forget telephone numbers and unfortunately we also forget information we have learned for examinations.

Reflective Activity

What did you do yesterday? Make a list of ten things.

Now consider how your memory was involved in the activities you listed. For example, consider the different types of information you used when you were carrying out the activity.

This activity should help you recognise the role that memory plays in everyday life. It should also indicate the range of different types of information we store in our memory.

In order to answer the question posed in the above activity, 'What did you do yesterday?', you must have a stored representation of the events that can be retrieved from memory. It also means that in some way you must have encoded information about the events as they were happening. The three stages of **encoding**, **storage** and **retrieval** form the basis of learning and memory. When theorising about memory, psychologists make a distinction between *structure* and *process*. Structure concerns the way in which the memory system is organised, whereas process is concerned with the activities

Stages of learning and memory	Encoding Storage Retrieval
Structure of memory: key questions	(a) How many different memory stores do we need to cope with encoding storing and retrieving information? (b) What are the characteristics of the different memory stores?
Memory processes: key questions	(a) How is information encoded? (b) How do we forget? (c) How is information retrieved?

Figure 10.1: The nature of memory

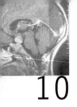

10

occurring within the system. If we are interested in structure, then we would be concerned with questions such as, 'How many different memory stores are needed to account for all the different types of information we can store and remember?' On the other hand, if we are interested in process, then we might ask questions such as, 'How is information retrieved?' and 'Why do we remember some things more clearly than others?' Structure and process are both important in memory – we can't have one without the other. Figure 10.1 provides an overview of the nature of memory.

Models of memory

The multi-store model

Atkinson & Shiffrin (1968) developed one of the most influential models of memory, the **multi-store model**. It was developed at a time when the information-processing approach (see Chapter 2) was becoming increasingly influential in psychology. This approach assumes that mental processes can be understood by comparing them with the operations of a computer, and also that mental processes can be interpreted as information progressing through a system in a series of stages, one step at a time (Eysenck, 1993). Atkinson and Shiffrin's model of memory is probably the most important example of the information-processing approach (Matlin, 2002). Atkinson and Shiffrin included both process and structure in their model. They proposed a basic structure consisting of three memory stores: a sensory store, a short-term store and a long-term store. They also suggested that the processes of *attention* and *rehearsal* were responsible for controlling the flow of information between the stores. This is shown in Figure 10.2.

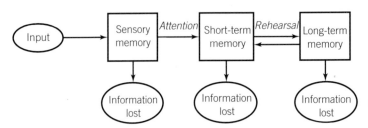

Figure 10.2: Atkinson and Shiffrin's (1968) model of memory (Based on Atkinson & Shiffrin, 1968)

The **sensory memory** stores are considered to be large-capacity storage systems that hold information for very brief periods of time, no more than two seconds. According to the model, all of our senses – seeing, touch, hearing, taste and smell – have a separate sensory memory store. However, research has focused largely on visual sensory memory (usually referred to as **iconic memory**) and to a lesser extent on the auditory sensory memory (usually called **echoic memory**). Atkinson and Shiffrin's model proposes that a vast amount of information is held in sensory memory for a couple of seconds, or less, and then most of it is lost. The information that isn't lost is then transferred to our short-term memory. They propose that the processes of 'attention' are responsible for transferring information from sensory memory to short-term memory. In other words, some information is selected (i.e. 'attended to') for further processing, and it is this information which will be transferred into short-term memory. The two key characteristics of short-term memory are:

* it has a very limited capacity (about seven items);

* any distraction usually causes forgetting (Eysenck & Keane, 2000).

According to the model, the process of rehearsal enables information to be transferred from **short-term memory** into the **long-term memory**. Long-term memory has a very large capacity and can retain information for many years. Atkinson and Shiffrin argued that once information has been stored in long-term memory, it is relatively permanent.

People retain large amounts of information in sensory memory stores. Some of this information finds its way into our short-term memory, but most of it fades away just like the after-image of a sparkler

Much of the evidence supporting the existence of sensory memory stores comes from research investigating iconic memory. The classic studies in this area were conducted by Sperling (1960). In one experiment, Sperling presented three rows of four letters to participants using a tachistoscope (a piece of equipment capable of displaying stimuli for very short periods of time). The letters were displayed for 50 milliseconds (1/20 of a second – faster than you can blink your eyes), followed by a blank white screen. Participants were then asked to recall the letters in the display. Under these conditions, participants were only able to recall four or five of the twelve letters. There are two possible explanations for this finding. It could be that, because of the brief period of time the letters were displayed, the participants were only able to see a limited number of letters. On the other hand, participants might have seen all the letters but forgot some of them in the time it took to report four or five of the letters. Sperling carried out a further experiment to investigate which of these possible explanations was correct.

Study

AIM *Sperling (1960) set out to investigate the capacity of visual sensory memory (iconic memory).*

METHOD *A three-by-four array of letters was displayed for 50 milliseconds. This was followed by a cue which indicated which row participants had to recall. The cue consisted of a sound: a high-pitched tone indicated that participants should recall the top line, a medium tone for the middle row and a low tone for the bottom row.*

RESULTS *In many cases, the participants were able to correctly recall all the letters in the row that had been cued. On average, participants correctly recalled three out of the four letters in the cued row.*

CONCLUSIONS *As the participants didn't know in advance which row was going to be cued and yet still managed to get most of them correct, we can assume that for a brief period of time information about the letters in all three rows was available for recall. These results indicate that large amounts of information can be held in sensory memory for very brief periods of time.*

Sperling's work provided the basis for the commonly accepted view that our sensory memory stores are rapidly decaying, large-capacity memory stores. It has been estimated that our sensory stores can hold information for between 250 milliseconds and 500 milliseconds before it decays.

One of the key components of Atkinson and Shiffrin's model is the existence of separate short-term and long-term memory stores. Evidence for this distinction comes from a number of sources, including the storage capacity and duration of the two stores, and the code used to store information. In terms of storage capacity, research suggests that short-term memory can

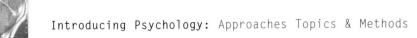
accommodate approximately seven 'chunks' of information (Miller, 1956), whereas long-term memory can hold vast quantities of information. Without rehearsal, information is rapidly lost from short-term memory, whereas long-term memory is capable of retaining information for many years.

The view that short-term memory and long-term memory use different codes to store information is based on the idea that the code for words can be based on three different types of information:

- the visual pattern of letters which go to make up the word (orthographic code);
- the sound of the word (phonological code);
- the meaning of the word (semantic code).

Evidence that short-term memory could be based on a phonological code and not on orthographic came from a study by Conrad (1964). He found that when you present participants with a list of letters and immediately ask them to recall the list, they tend to make mistakes based on the sound of the letter (phonological mistakes). In other words, participants often confused letters such as 'C' and 'V', which sound similar but are not similar in appearance (orthography). On the other hand, he also found that participants tended not to confuse letters which had a similar shape, such as 'V' and 'X' (see Figure 10.3). This suggests that short-term memory is based on a phonological code rather than an orthographic code. But Conrad's study does not rule out the possibility that the coding in short-term memory is based on meaning.

Stimuli material	Frequency of errors in immediate recall task
Letters that have a similar sound (e.g. C, V)	High
Letters that have a similar shape (e.g. P, R)	Low

Figure 10.3: Summary of findings of Conrad's (1964) study

Study

Aim *Baddeley (1966a) carried out this study to investigate the coding of words in short-term memory.*

Method *He presented participants with a list of words and immediately asked them to recall the list. The list contained some words that sounded the same, such as 'cap', 'can', 'cat', and words that had a similar meaning, such as 'small', 'tiny', 'little'.*

Results *Participants made errors with similar-sounding words, but did not make mistakes when the words had a similar meaning.*

Conclusions *These findings were taken to indicate that coding in short-term memory was based on the sound of the word.*

The experiments of Conrad and Baddeley, together with numerous other studies, provided strong support for the view that information in short-term memory is based on a phonological code. But what about long-term memory?

Study

AIM *Baddeley (1966b) carried out this study to investigate the coding of words in long-term memory.*

METHOD *Participants were presented with a list of words. There was then a delay before participants were asked to recall the list. This ensured that it was long-term memory that was being tested. As in the previous experiment, the list contained some words that sounded the same and words that had a similar meaning.*

RESULTS *Errors were based on the meaning of the word (semantic) and not the sound (phonology).*

CONCLUSIONS *These findings were interpreted as supporting the view that information in long-term memory is based on a semantic code.*

These two experiments by Baddeley (1966a, 1966b) provide strong support for the view that long-term memory uses a semantic code to store information, whereas short-term memory uses a phonological code.

Evaluative Comment

Atkinson & Shiffrin (1968) present a systematic model of memory that includes both structure and process. There is no doubt that the model was extremely successful in terms of stimulating a considerable amount of research and theorising into memory. However, the model's main emphasis was on structure and it tends to neglect the process elements of memory. The model is oversimplified, in particular when it suggests that both short-term and long-term memory each operate in a single, uniform fashion. It has now become apparent that both short-term memory and long-term memory are much more complex than was originally thought. Case studies of patients with brain damage have provided a rich source of data. For example, the patient KF suffered brain damage following a motorcycle accident. His short-term memory for verbal materials was very poor, but more or less normal for visual material (Shallice & Warrington, 1970). Findings such as this suggest that short-term memory is not a single store. In the case of long-term memory, it is unlikely that different kinds of knowledge, such as remembering how to play a video game, the rules for subtraction and remembering what we did yesterday are all stored within a single, long-term memory store. Finally, the role of rehearsal as a means of transferring information from short-term memory to long-term memory is much less important than Atkinson & Shiffrin (1968) claimed in their model. As Eysenck and Keane (2000) point out, in everyday life we very rarely rehearse information, and yet we have little problem in acquiring huge amounts of it.

Episodic, semantic and procedural memory

The multi-store model of memory proposed by Atkinson and Shiffrin and subsequent developments, such as Baddeley & Hitch's (1974) working-memory model, make a distinction between a relatively short-term memory (working memory) and long-term memory. Our long-term memories consist of a range of different types of knowledge. For example, we can remember what we did yesterday, but we also know that London is the capital of England, and most of us know how to ride a bicycle. This had led psychologists to propose that there are different long-term memory systems, each of which is specialised to deal with particular types of information (Eysenck & Keane, 2000).

One of the earliest and most influential distinctions of this kind was proposed by Tulving (1972). He proposed a distinction between **episodic memory** and **semantic memory**. Episodic memory refers to our memories for events that we have experienced (they describe episodes in our lives (Matlin, 2002). Most of us can remember our first day at secondary school, and we can probably also remember a conversation we had yesterday. These are both examples of episodic memories.

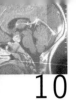

Semantic memory focuses on our general knowledge about the world. This includes our knowledge about the meanings of words, as well as general knowledge, such as knowing that New York is on the east coast of North America and a robin is a small bird. The distinction between episodic memory and semantic memory is a reasonable one that makes a great deal of common sense. However, finding experimental evidence to support the view that they are separate and distinct memory stores has proved difficult. Some evidence has come from studies monitoring blood flow in the brain while participants complete different tasks.

Study

Aim *Tulving (1989) carried out this study to investigate the extent to which episodic and semantic memory were independent memory systems located in different parts of the brain.*

Method *Tulving used himself as a participant. Small quantities of radioactive gold were injected into his bloodstream. He then thought about semantic memories (e.g. historical facts, such as the work of famous astronomers) or he thought about episodic memories (e.g. what he did during summer vacation as a child). The blood flow within his brain was monitored by radioactivity detectors positioned around his head.*

Results *The two tasks gave different patterns of blood flow in the brain. Episodic memories were associated with increased blood flow in the front of the brain, whereas, semantic memories were associated with an increase in blood flow in areas towards the back of the brain.*

Conclusions *These results were taken to support the view that episodic and semantic memory may be based in different parts of the brain. However, Tulving (1989) himself pointed out that, as this was a preliminary study, the findings should be interpreted with caution.*

Most laboratory tests of memory rely on episodic memory. A typical experiment involves presenting a participant with a list of words and then, after a period of time, another list will be presented and participants are asked to decide which words were on the original list. In other words, participants are being asked about a previous episode they had experienced, namely learning the list. A test of semantic memory would involve asking the participant to make judgements about the meaning of words, such as answering the question, 'Is a dog an animal?'.

Practical Activity

Try using words to describe the following in enough detail that someone else would be able to repeat the activity:

* *How you go around a sharp corner on a bicycle.*

* *The route from your home to school/college.*

* *What you had for breakfast.*

This activity demonstrates that some knowledge is much easier to put into words than other forms of knowledge. In particular, knowledge about how to carry out skilled activities, such as riding a bicycle, is very difficult to express verbally.

The knowledge that we hold in semantic and episodic memories focuses on 'knowing that' something is the case. For example, we might have a semantic memory knowing that Paris is the capital of France, and we might have an episodic memory knowing that we caught the bus to school yesterday. This kind of 'knowing that' knowledge is referred to as **declarative knowledge**.

During our daily lives, we take part in lots of activities which rely on our memory for skills. Remembering how to ride a bicycle, skate, play the piano all rely on procedural memory, which is where this type of knowledge is stored

Cohen & Squire (1980) drew a distinction between declarative knowledge and **procedural knowledge**. Procedural knowledge involves 'knowing how' to do things. It includes skills, such as playing the piano, riding a bicycle and other motor skills. One of the differences between procedural and declarative knowledge lies in the extent to which the knowledge can be expressed in words. Declarative knowledge, episodic and semantic memories, can be expressed verbally. You can tell people what you did yesterday or how much geography you know. On the other hand, procedural knowledge is very difficult to express verbally.

Evidence for the distinction between declarative and procedural memory has come from research on patients with **amnesia**. Typically, amnesic patients have great difficulty in retaining episodic and semantic information following the onset of amnesia. Their memory for events and knowledge acquired before onset of the condition tends to remain intact. In other words, it appears that their ability to retain declarative information is impaired. However, amnesic patients do appear to be able to acquire new motor skills, which suggests that their ability to acquire procedural knowledge remains intact (Cohen, 1984).

Study

Aim *Corkin (1968) aimed to investigate the ability to acquire new motor skills in a person with amnesia.*

Method *Corkin used a case-study methodology with an amnesic patient (HM). HM's memory problems were so severe that he appeared to be unable to remember new information. HM spent some time learning and practising a task which involved tracking a curvy line on a rotating disc. Several days later, he performed the same task again.*

Results *Initially, HM's performance was poor, but he improved considerably with practice. When he performed the task again after several days, he had no recollection of the first session. Nevertheless, his performance was as good as it had been at the end of the first session.*

Conclusions *These results show that although HM is unable to acquire declarative knowledge, he is capable of learning and retaining new motor skills. This supports the view that procedural knowledge and declarative knowledge are dependent on separate memory systems.*

Evidence for the opposite pattern of deficits – intact declarative system and impaired procedural system – has been reported in patients with the degenerative condition **Huntington's disease**. These patients find it very difficult to acquire new motor skills, but appeared to have the ability to acquire declarative knowledge (Heindel, Butters & Salmon, 1988). Taken together with the findings of Corkin (1968), this pattern suggests that there are different systems underlying procedural and declarative knowledge.

10 Evaluative Comment

Although it is possible to make a clear distinction between episodic and semantic memories in terms of their content, the extent to which they rely on different brain structures and processes is unclear. Some researchers (e.g. Medin et al., 2001) suggest that episodic memory and semantic memory are both part of the same system. There is empirical support for the view that declarative and procedural memory rely on different encoding systems and brain structures. The distinction made by Tulving (1972) between episodic and semantic memory focused on the type of information held by the two different systems. More recently Wheeler et al. (1997) have provided an alternative definition of episodic memory which focuses on the thoughts and feelings that accompany the retrieval of episodic and semantic memories. They argue that when we remember an event that has happened to us, it is associated with an aware-ness of ourselves actually experiencing the event, whereas the retrieval of semantic memories involves thinking objectively about something that we know and is not associated with the conscious recollection of past events.

Levels of processing

Craik & Lockhart (1972) present an alternative to the structural models of memory discussed above. They argued that it might be fruitful to focus on the processes that contribute to memory, rather than structure. Two important assumptions concerning the **levels of processing** approach were made by Craik and Lockhart:

- that the way in which information is processed can affect the likelihood of it being retrieved at some point in the future;

- that there are a range of different levels at which information can be processed, starting at a shallow and superficial level and proceeding through to deeper and richer levels.

Craik and Lockhart argued that deeper levels of processing give rise to more durable and more retrievable memories, whereas shallow levels of processing result in memories that are less likely to be retrieved.

Practical Activity

Read each of the following questions and answer 'yes' or 'no' with respect to the word in the right-hand column.

1 *Is the word in capital letters?* chair

2 *Does the word rhyme with GREEN?* BEAN

3 *Does the word fit this sentence:*

'The soldier picked up his _____ '? rifle

4 *Is the word in lower-case letters?* FLOWER

5 *Does the word fit this sentence:*

'The woman _____ on the train'? slept

6 *Does the word rhyme with MEND?* pool

7 *Is the word in capital letters?* MEANING

8 *Does the word fit this sentence:*

'Yesterday we saw a _____ '? fence

9 *Does the word rhyme with HOUSE?*   *MOUSE*

10 *Does the word fit this sentence:*

    'There are _____ growing in my garden'?   *DOORS*

11 *Is the word in lower-case letters?*   *spend*

12 *Does the word rhyme with TABLE?*   *GENERAL*

13 *Is the word in capital letters?*   *article*

14 *Does the word fit this sentence:*

    'The _____ should not exceed 1,000 words'?   *castle*

15 *Does the word rhyme with STOOL?*   *POND*

Now turn the book over and see how many of the of the words that were in the right-hand column you can remember.

This activity is based on an experiment carried out by Craik & Tulving (1975). There were three kinds of task in the activity

- making judgements about physical appearance (capitals or lower-case letters)
- deciding whether or not a word rhymed with another
- making a decision about the meaning of a word (does it fit into a sentence).

There were five examples of each task. How many words did you remember from each task? Did you remember more from the 'meaning' task?

The levels-of-processing approach predicts that when we process a word for meaning, we are more likely to remember it than if we simply process its physical appearance. Did the words you remembered provide any support for this prediction?

The above activity provides an example of different levels of processing. Making judgements about whether letters are upper or lower case is an example of shallow processing, in that only superficial information about the words is processed, whereas making judgements about whether or not a word fits into a sentence requires processing at a much deeper level. It is necessary to understand the meaning of the word and the sentence. This is sometimes referred to as *semantic processing*. The task of making judgements about the sound of words, deciding whether or not one word rhymes with another word, lies somewhere in between the previous two levels of processing. Craik and Lockhart's theory would predict that words where we are processing for meaning (deep processing) will be remembered better than words processed for sound, which in turn will be better recalled than words which are processed for shape and size (shallow processing).

Study

AIM *Craik & Tulving (1975) conducted an experiment with the aim of investigating the effects of different types of processing on the recall of words*

METHOD *They presented participants with a list of 60 words, about which they had to answer one of three questions. The questions required participants to make decisions about the case of the word, the sound of the word or the meaning of the word. The questions were presented auditorily and were followed by a brief visual presentation of the word. Participants then answered the question. When the 60 questions had been competed, participants were given a recognition test. They were presented with a list of 180 words and had to tick the words about which they had been asked questions.*

RESULTS *The findings confirmed Craik & Lockhart's (1972) ideas about depth of processing. Approximately seventeen per cent of words in the physical-appearance condition were correctly recognised, 37 per cent in the rhyming condition and 65 per cent in the meaning condition.*

CONCLUSIONS *These results were used to support the view that the type of processing which takes place when information is encoded has an effect on subsequent recall.*

The technique used by Craik and Tulving to test participants' performance is referred to as an **incidental-learning procedure**. This means that the participants were not aware at the start of the experiment that they would be required to remember the words in a subsequent test.

Although they emphasise process rather than structure, Craik and Lockhart do assume the existence of separate short-term and long-term memory systems. However, they see the function of short-term memory in terms of the processes it carries out (Baddeley, 1997).

In Craik and Lockhart's theory, two of the most important processes carried out in short-term memory are **maintenance rehearsal** and **elaborative rehearsal**. Maintenance rehearsal, as the name suggests, involves holding information without transforming it. For example, repeating a list of words to yourself over and over again. This means that the information is retained while it is being rehearsed, but it doesn't lead to long-term learning. On the other hand, elaborative rehearsal involves a deeper and more meaningful analysis of the material. For example, suppose you see the word 'cat' in a list of items you have been asked to remember; elaborative rehearsal could involve generating an image of a cat or thinking about the last time you stroked a cat. Elaborative rehearsal can add all kinds of extra images, associations and memories to enrich the material which has to be learned, resulting in better recall (Matlin, 2002).

Evaluative Comment

Craik & Lockhart's (1972) theory provided an interesting and credible alternative to the dominant approach to memory, which focused on structural issues. They focused attention on the fact that processes occurring during learning have a major impact on the extent to which material can be retrieved from long-term memory (Medin, Ross & Markham, 2001). However, one of the main criticisms levelled at the theory concerned the way in which depth of processing was measured. There was no independent measure of whether processing was deep or shallow. Determining whether or not processing was deep or shallow relied on a circular definition which argued that if recall was good, then deep processing must have taken place, and if recall was poor, then the processing must have been shallow. More recently, Lockhart & Craik (1990) have updated their model in response to criticisms and research findings. Although the basic ideas behind the model remain the same, they accept that their original model was rather oversimplified and agreed that they had not considered retrieval processes in sufficient detail. In addition, Lockhart & Craik (1990) accepted that in some cases, shallow processing does not lead to rapid forgetting.

Working memory

Atkinson & Shiffrin's (1968) model was extremely successful in terms of the amount of research activity it generated. However, as a result of some of this research, it became clear that there were a number of problems with their ideas concerning the characteristics of short-term memory. Building on this research, Baddeley & Hitch (1974) developed an alternative model of short-term memory which they called *working memory*.

The model of working memory proposed by Baddeley and Hitch consists of a **central executive** which controls and co-ordinates the operation of two subsystems: the **phonological loop** and the

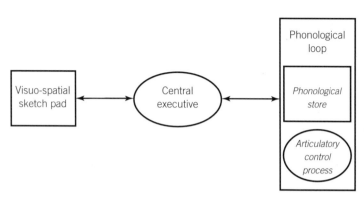

Figure 10.4: A simplified representation of Baddeley and Hitch's (1974) working-memory model

visuo-spatial sketchpad. The labels given to the components of working memory reflect their function and the type of information they process and manipulate. The phonological loop is assumed to be responsible for the manipulation of speech-based information, whereas the visuo-spatial sketchpad is assumed to be responsible for manipulating visual images (Baddeley, 1997). The model proposes that every component of working memory has a limited capacity, and also that the components are relatively independent of each other.

Like many everyday activities, playing chess involves processing information, manipulating images and solving problems. This processing relies on our working-memory system to store, process and manipulate information in an active manner

Baddeley & Hitch (1974) proposed that the phonological loop consists of two components: a store (phonological store) and a process for refreshing and rehearsing the information in the store (articulatory control process). It is necessary to have means of refreshing the information held in the phonological store, since it assumed that the information is only retained for about two seconds before it decays. Evidence that the phonological loop comprises two subsystems comes from techniques which monitor the blood flow in participants' brains when they are carrying out specific tasks. These studies are based on the idea that increased blood flow indicates those parts of the brain which are active.

Study

AIM *Paulesu et al. (1993) carried out this study to investigate the nature of the phonological loop in working memory.*

METHOD *Participants were required to either store a series of letters or mentally rehearse the sounds of the letters. While they were carrying out these tasks, the blood flow in their brains was monitored using a technique called **positron emission tomography**.*

RESULTS *The two tasks gave quite different patterns of blood flow in the brain. The rehearsal of letter sounds was associated with increased blood flow in Broca's area of the brain, whereas the letter-memory task was associated with a different area of the brain.*

CONCLUSIONS *These results were taken to support the view that the phonological loop comprises two components, one which stores sounds and one which is capable of the mental rehearsal of items (Logie, 1999).*

Baddeley (1997) suggests that the phonological loop plays an important role in the acquisition of a range of language skills. Learning to read is one language skill that could involve the phonological loop. Children with normal levels of intelligence who have difficulties learning to read tend to perform badly on tasks which rely on the phonological loop, such as deciding whether or not two words rhyme. Although there are many factors which can influence the ease with which children learn to read, it seems likely that for some children at least, deficits in the phonological loop system are related to difficulties in learning to read (Baddeley *et al.*, 1998). A similar pattern is also found in research investigating the acquisition of a vocabulary in children (Gathercole & Baddeley, 1989). It would also seem to be the case that the phonological loop plays a significant role in the comprehension of language (Baddeley, 1997).

Reflective Activity

Think of your bedroom. Which side of the door is the door handle on? How many panels are there in the door? When you are answering questions like this, most people generate a mental image of their door and use that to answer the question. Our visuo-spatial sketchpad enables us generate and manipulate visual and spatial images

As its name suggests, the visuo-spatial sketchpad stores and manipulates visual and spatial information and has a limited capacity (Baddeley, 1997). The sketchpad also stores visual information that has been encoded from verbal stimuli, such as words. For example, if someone says the word 'cat', you might find yourself visualising an image of a cat. The limited capacity of the visuo-spatial sketchpad means that if we try and perform two tasks simultaneously, both of which involve a visual and spatial component, our performance will suffer. It is likely that the visuo-spatial sketchpad plays an important role in helping us keep track of where we are in relation to other objects as we move through our environment (Baddeley, 1997). As we move around, our position in relation to objects is constantly changing and it is important that we can update this information. For example, being aware of where we are in relation to desks, chairs and tables when we are walking around a classroom means that we don't bump into things too often! We also need to update constantly on how the locations of moving objects are changing (Medin *et al.*, 2001).

The central executive is the most versatile and important component of the working-memory system (Eysenck & Keane, 2000). However, despite its importance in the working-memory model, we know considerably less about this component than the two subsystems it controls (Baddeley, 1997). Baddeley suggests that the central executive acts more like a system which controls attentional processes rather than as a memory store. This is unlike the phonological loop and the visuo-spatial sketchpad, which are specialized storage systems. The central executive enables the working-memory system to selectively attend to some stimuli and ignore others. It also plays a role in retrieving information from long-term memory. In our everyday activities, the central executive helps us to decide what to do, and also what not to do (Matlin, 2002). Baddeley (1986, 1999) uses the metaphor of a company boss to describe the way in which the central executive operates. The company boss makes decisions about which issues deserve attention and which should be ignored. They also select strategies for dealing with problems, but like any person in the company, the boss can only do a limited number of things at the same time. The boss of a company will collect information from a number of different sources. If we continue applying this metaphor, then we can see the central executive in working memory integrating information from two assistants (the phonological loop and the visuo-spatial sketchpad) and also drawing on information held in a large database (long-term memory) (Matlin, 2000).

Evaluative Comment

Working memory is a very flexible system which controls and co-ordinates a range of cognitive activities. This is considerably different from the relatively rigid fixed-capacity, short-term store proposed by Atkinson & Shiffrin (1968). Eysenck & Keane (2000) identify a number of advantages that the working-memory model has over Atkinson & Shiffrin's (1968) model. First, the working-memory model places more emphasis on the active processing of information rather than the storage of information. This ensures that working memory can be seen to be playing a significant role in complex cognitive tasks such as understanding and producing language. Second, the pattern of deficits observed in patients with brain damage can be explained using the working-memory model. For example, if only the visuo-spatial sketchpad is damaged, then performance on tasks which rely on the phonological loop will remain unimpaired. Research into the operation of the phonological loop has suggested that it plays an important role in learning to speak and read as well as understanding spoken language. However, Baddeley (1997) points out that we still do not have a detailed understanding of the way in which working memory actually works!

Reasons for forgetting

Rather surprisingly, research into forgetting has been rather limited in recent years. Perhaps this has something to do with the dominance of the computer metaphor in cognitive psychology and the fact that computers tend not to forget (Baddeley, 1997). On the other hand, people have a tendency to forget lots of things. We forget appointments, have difficulty remembering someone's name, lose our keys and can't remember the precise details of books we read last week. Numerous different explanations have been proposed to try and explain why we forget. The five most common of these are **decay**, **interference**, **retrieval failure** and lack of consolidation.

One of the earliest explanations of forgetting was proposed by Ebbinghaus (1885), who argued that memory traces spontaneously decay over time. In other words, our memories gradually fade away over a period time. Ebbinghaus used himself as a participant, and his basic experiment consisted of learning a list of nonsense syllables made up of consonant-vowel-consonant sequences (e.g. BEJ, ZUX) and then testing himself after different intervals of time. He found that forgetting followed a particular pattern (Figure 10.5) which became known as the 'forgetting curve'.

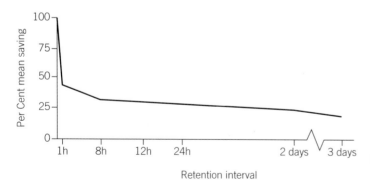

Retention interval

Figure 10.5: Ebbinghaus' (1885) forgetting curve

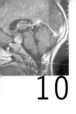

10

Reflective Activity

Make a list of thirteen syllables. Now learn the list so that you can recall it perfectly, with all the items in the correct order.

After a period of time, for example 24 hours, test yourself to see how much of the original list you can recall.

Imagine constructing thousands of these lists! This activity will have given you some idea of the kind of research carried out by Ebbinghaus.

No one disputes the fact that memory tends to get worse the longer the delay between learning and recall, but there is disagreement about the explanation for this effect. In the decay theory of forgetting, the events between learning and recall have no effect whatsoever on recall. It is the length of time the information has to be retained that is important. The longer the time, the more the memory trace decays and as a consequence more information is forgotten. There are a number of methodological problems confronting researchers trying to investigate the decay theory. One of the major problems is controlling for the events that occur between learning and recall. Clearly, in any real-life situation, the time between learning something and recalling it will be filled with all kinds of different events. This makes it very difficult to be sure that any forgetting which takes place is the result of decay rather than a consequence of the intervening events.

Support for the idea that forgetting from short-term memory might be the result of decay over time came from research carried out by Brown (1958) in the United Kingdom, and Peterson and Peterson (1959) in the United States. The technique they developed has become known as the **Brown–Peterson task**.

Practical Activity

Try this activity with a friend. You will need a watch with a second hand and four pieces of card. Write the following on each the cards:

Card 1   Front: incubate, literate, flicker; Back: 764
Card 2   Front: soothe, hostile, viable; Back: 357
Card 3   Front: attend, phrase, sober; Back: 563
Card 4   Front: ascend, sparse, hatching; Back: 967

The task involves counting backwards in threes, so give your friend a few minutes to practise. Ask them to count backwards in threes from 578, and keep going until they have got used to it. Show your friend the words on the first card for about two seconds and then immediately turn the card over and ask them to count backwards in threes, as fast as possible, from the number on the card. After twenty seconds, see if they can remember the three words on the card. Repeat this process with the other three cards. This activity is a modified version of the Brown–Peterson technique; in their original studies, sequences of three consonants (e.g. L Z M), referred to as trigrams, were commonly used. Counting backwards in threes prevents people from rehearsing the information in short-term memory. It should demonstrate that if we are unable to rehearse information in our short-term memory, it is very quickly forgotten. One point to bear in mind is that studies using this technique usually find that people do quite well on the first trial, but the more trials they carry out, the worse their performance becomes.

Studies using the Brown–Peterson technique show that when people are prevented from rehearsing information, it is very quickly lost from short-term memory. Performance drops by more than 50 per cent in less than six seconds (Figure 10.6).

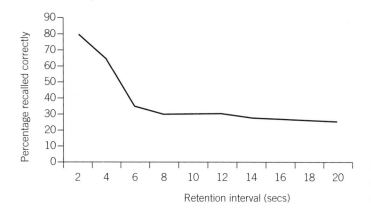

Figure 10.6: Typical pattern of results using the Brown-Peterson technique

The findings of studies using the Brown–Peterson technique were used as support for the view that information is lost from short-term memory through a process of decay. If they were correct, then the duration of time between presentation and recall should be the only factor influencing recall. However, research by Waugh & Norman (1965) showed that this is not the case.

Study

AIM *Waugh & Norman (1965) aimed to investigate the process of forgetting from short-term memory.*

METHOD *Participants were presented with a list of sixteen digits which were read at a rate of either one per second or four per second. This meant that one list took sixteen seconds to read out whereas the other took four seconds. After the list had been presented, participants were given a cue which indicated which of the sequence of sixteen digits they had to recall. If decay alone is responsible for forgetting, then the more time that has passed, the more information will be forgotten. This means that there should be more forgetting from the list that took sixteen seconds to read out.*

RESULTS *There was no significant difference between the two conditions in terms of recall.*

CONCLUSIONS *The absence of any significant difference between the two conditions suggests that decay alone cannot account for forgetting from short-term memory.*

Evaluative Comment

*There is very little direct support for decay theory as an explanation for the loss of information from short-term and long-term memory. One of the problems with decay theory is that it is more or less impossible to test it. In practice, it is not possible to create a situation in which there is a blank period of time between presentation of material and recall. Having presented information participants will rehearse it. If you prevent rehearsal by introducing a **distracter task**, it results in interference. Decay theory has difficulty explaining the observation that many people can remember events that happened several years previously with great clarity, even though they haven't thought about them during the intervening period. If our memories gradually decayed over time, then people should not have clear memories of distant events which have lain dormant for several years. However, the work of Sperling (1960), discussed earlier, suggests that information is lost from sensory memory through the process of decay.*

10

Interference

The basic assumption of interference as a reason for forgetting is that our memory traces are disrupted or obscured by other information, in other words forgetting occurs because of interference from other memories (Baddeley, 1999). There are two ways in which interference can cause forgetting:

- When what we already know interferes with what we are currently learning. This type of interference is referred to as **proactive interference** (pro = forward).

- When what we have learned is interfered with by subsequent learning. In other words, later learning interferes with earlier learning. This form of interference is referred to as **retroactive interference** (retro = backward).

Numerous studies have reliably demonstrated proactive and retroactive interference (for example, Warr, 1964; Underwood & Ekstrand, 1967). The basic methods for testing proactive and retroactive interference are shown in Figure 10.7.

| | Retroactive interference | | Proactive interference | |
	Experimental group	Control group	Experimental group	Control group
Phase 1	Learn A	Learn A	Learn A	Rest or unrelated task
Phase 2	Learn B	Rest or unrelated task	Learn B	Learn B
Phase 3	Recall A	Recall A	Recall B	Recall B

Figure 10.7: Typical procedure for studying retroactive and proactive interference

A number of studies have attempted to directly compare decay theory and interference theory as explanations of forgetting from long-term memory. One of the earliest was an experiment carried out by Jenkins & Dallenbach (1924).

Study

AIM *Jenkins & Dallenbach (1924) set out to test the decay theory of forgetting.*

METHOD *Two participants learned a list of nonsense syllables, either in the morning or in the evening just before going to sleep. Their recall was tested at intervals between one and eight hours. The participants were either awake or asleep during the period between learning the list and recalling it.*

RESULTS *There was much less forgetting when the participants were asleep between learning and recall.*

CONCLUSIONS *Trace decay theory would predict that the time elapsed between learning and recall should be the only factor that influenced forgetting; it should make no difference whether participants are awake or asleep during the retention interval. Jenkins and Dallenbach interpreted their findings as providing support for interference theory on the grounds that there is much more interference with memory when people are awake than when they are asleep.*

One of the problems with the study carried out by Jenkins and Dallenbach is that it did not control for the time at which learning took place. When participants slept during the time between learning and recall they always learned the list in the evening. On the other hand, when they were awake during the retention interval, learning always took place in the morning. This flaw in the design of the study means that we cannot tell whether forgetting depends on time of learning or what happens during the period between learning and recall.

More recently, studies have used naturally occurring events to compare interference theory and decay theory. An interesting example is the study reported by Baddeley & Hitch (1977).

Study

AIM *Baddeley & Hitch (1977) compared the effects of interference and the amount of time that has elapsed since an event on forgetting.*

METHOD *They asked rugby players to recall the names of the teams they had played earlier in the season. Because some players had missed games through injury or some other reason, Baddeley and Hitch were able to assess the effect of the number of intervening games (interference) and time since the game was played (decay) on recall.*

RESULTS *A larger number of intervening games was associated with poorer recall. Time elapsed alone had very little influence on levels of forgetting.*

CONCLUSIONS *They interpreted their findings as providing support for the view that forgetting was due to interference rather than decay.*

Evidence for retroactive interference in a naturalistic context also comes from Schmidt *et al.* (2000). In their study, participants who had grown up in the same area completed a questionnaire which contained a map of their childhood neighbourhood. They were asked to name the streets on the map as well as provide other information, such as how long they had lived in the area, how often they had moved to other areas and where they usually played. The level of retroactive interference was defined as the number of times participants had moved to other neighbourhoods or cities. This was based on the notion that moving home will result in similar learning experiences in terms of becoming familiar with a different set of street names, which will then interfere with the recall of the names of streets in their childhood neighbourhood. Schmidt *et al.* found that the more frequently participants had moved house, the fewer street names they were able to recall from their childhood neighbourhood (see Figure 10.8). These findings suggest that participants' recall of street names from their childhood neighbourhood is influenced by retroactive interference.

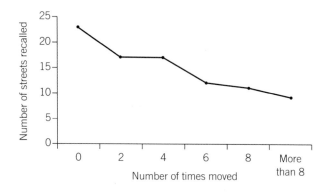

Figure 10.8: Number of street names recalled as a function of the number of times participants had moved house (From Schmidt, Peeck, Paas & van Breukelen, 2000)

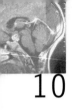

10 Evaluative Comment

Although proactive and retroactive interference are reliable and robust effects, there are a number of problems with interference theory as an explanation of forgetting. First, interference theory tells us little about the cognitive processes involved in forgetting. Secondly, the majority of research into the role of interference in forgetting has been carried out in a laboratory using lists of words, a situation which is likely to occur fairly infrequently in everyday life (Eysenck & Keane, 2000). Nevertheless, recent research has attempted to address this by investigating 'real-life' events and has provided support for interference theory. However, there is no doubt that interference plays a role in forgetting, but how much forgetting can be attributed to interference remains unclear (Anderson, 2000).

Retrieval failure

The basic premise underlying retrieval failure as an explanation for forgetting from long-term memory is that information is stored in memory, but cannot be retrieved because the **retrieval cues** are inadequate. Such material is said to be available, because it is still stored in memory, but inaccessible; in other words, it cannot be retrieved.

Study

Aim *Tulving & Pearlstone (1966) aimed to investigate retrieval failure in memory.*

Method *Participants studied 48 words, comprising four words from each of twelve different categories, such as animals, fruits and sports. The words were preceded by the name of the category, for example, 'sport – cricket, football, tennis, rugby', but the participants were told that they did not need to remember the category titles, they only needed to remember the items in each of the categories. In the recall phase of the study, there were two different conditions. In one, participants were simply asked to recall as many of the words as possible (**free recall**); in the other condition, participants were given the category names as retrieval cues (**cued recall**).*

Results *The difference between the two conditions was considerable. In the free-recall condition, participants remembered approximately 40 per cent of the words, whereas in the cued-recall condition, participants recalled over 60 per cent of the target words.*

Conclusions *This study provided clear evidence that the free-recall group knew more than they could recall. We can draw this conclusion because both groups had experienced exactly the same conditions during the learning phase and yet the cued-recall group was able to recall far more words. So it is reasonable to assume that if the free-recall group had been provided with the categories as cues, they would have been able to recall more words from the original list. In other words, their poor performance was due to retrieval failure.*

Tulving & Thompson (1973) proposed that the retrieval of information from memory depends on the availability of retrieval cues which match up with some aspect of the stored memory trace. The idea that recall is better if the retrieval context is similar to the encoding context has been termed the encoding-specificity principle (Tulving & Thompson, 1973). One of the key features of the encoding-specificity principle is that it assumes a relationship between encoding and retrieval. However, Baddeley (1997) points out that the **encoding-specificity principle** is impossible to test experimentally. This is because it argues that if a stimulus leads to the retrieval of a memory, then it must have been encoded with the memory. On the other hand, if the stimulus does not lead to retrieval of a memory, then the encoding-specificity principle argues that it cannot have been encoded. Since there is no independent way of determining whether or not information has been encoded, it is not possible to design an experiment which will test the encoding-specificity principle. This is a similar problem to some of the criticisms aimed at the concept of 'depth' in the levels of processing approach. It is a circular argument, which means it is not possible to test the encoding-specificity principle empirically. However, it must also be pointed out that there is no doubt about the importance of cues in retrieving information from our memory, and Tulving's research into retrieval cues forms an important and impressive body of work (Baddeley, 1997).

Reflective Activity

*One example of temporary retrieval failure is referred to as a **tip-of-the-tongue** (TOT) **state** (Brown & McNeill, 1966). TOT state is when a person feels that they know the word but are temporarily unable to retrieve it. The questions below were used in a study by Burke et al. (1991) to elicit a TOT state. Do any of the questions produce a TOT state in you? The answers are at the bottom of the page.*

1 *What is the navigation instrument used at sea to plot position by the stars?*

2 *What do you call a stone building (often found in a cemetery) with places for entombment of the dead above ground?*

3 *What do you call an instrument for performing calculations by sliding beads along rods?*

4 *What is the name of the art of Japanese paper folding?*

5 *What do you call a sentence which reads the same backward or forward, such as 'Madam, I'm Adam'?*

1 Sextant   2 Mausoleum   3 Abacus   4 Origami   5 Palindrome

The context within which we learn something is important when we come to recall that information. Recall is better if it takes place in the same context as the learning. So if you learn something when you are underwater, you will recall it better underwater than on dry land!

The role of context in aiding retrieval of memories is shown very clearly in an interesting study carried out by Godden & Baddeley (1975). Their participants were divers who learned a list of words either underwater ('wet' condition) or on dry land ('dry' condition). Their recall scores are shown in Figure 10.9. What is clear from these results is that recall performance is best when the context for learning and recall are the same. In other words, if the words were learned underwater, then recall performance was better underwater than on dry land and vice versa. In Godden and Baddeley's study, participants recalled approximately 40 per cent more if the recall took place in the same environment as the learning. However, other studies in which the change in context was less drastic than the Godden and Baddeley study have tended to find smaller effects on recall performance (Baddeley, 1997).

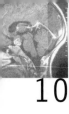

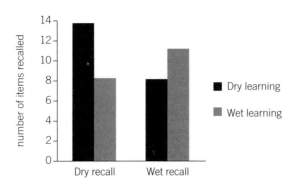

Figure 10.9: The recall of words by divers under 'dry' and 'wet' conditions during learning and recall (Source: Godden & Baddeley, 1975)

Interestingly, it would appear that it is not always necessary to be physically in the same environment to benefit from the effects of context-dependency. Jerabek & Standing (1992) demonstrated that the beneficial effect of contextual information can also occur when people simply imagine the context in which the learning took place. This confirms the findings of an earlier study (Smith, 1979), who found that imagining the room in which material was learned resulted in performance which was not significantly different from participants who had actually been in the same room.

Evaluative Comment

The relationship between the cues available at learning and recall have a considerable influence on a person's ability to retrieve information. The encoding-specificity principle can be used to provide an explanation of the 'levels of processing' effects on memory in the following way. We can assume that 'deep processing' produces numerous links and associations with other information stored in our memories, which increases the likelihood of one or more of these associations matching up with a retrieval cue (Groome, 1999). The examples of retrieval failure considered so far have all involved the use of external cues, such as category names. However, internal cues, such as a person's mood, have also been associated with failure to retrieve information. For example, if a person is depressed when they learn something, they are more likely to recall the information when they are in a depressed than when they are in a happy mood. This effect is strongest in situations when the encoding context involves positive moods and personal events rather than lists of word which lack any personal relevance (Eysenck & Keane, 2000).

Displacement

The short-term memory store in Atkinson & Shiffrin's (1968) model of memory was assumed to have certain characteristics, including a limited capacity, and if information was not rehearsed, it would be forgotten. In the late 1960s and early 1970s, when Atkinson and Shiffrin's model was at its most popular, it was thought that the loss of information could be explained through the concept of displacement (Groeger, 1997).

It was assumed that the limited capacity of the short-term store resulted in new information 'pushing out', or displacing, information already in the store. It was also assumed that the information that had been in the short-term store for the longest was the first to be displaced by new information, similar to the way in which boxes might fall off the end of a conveyor belt – as new boxes are put on one end, the boxes which have been on the conveyor belt the longest drop off the end. Support for the view that displacement was responsible for the loss of information from short-term memory came from studies using the 'free-recall' method. A typical study would use the following procedure: participants listen to a list of words read out at a steady rate, usually two seconds per word; they are then asked to recall as many of the words as possible. They are free to recall the words in any order, hence the term 'free recall'.

Practical Activity

Before you start, make sure you have a pen or pencil and a piece of blank paper to write on. Read the list of words below, spending no longer than one second on each word. After you have read the last word on the list, immediately turn over the book and see how many words you can write down. You can write them down in any order,

Floor	*House*	*Accurate*
Youth	*Soothe*	*Careless*
Night	*Hostile*	*Double*
Comedy	*Goblet*	*Chamber*

Now compare the words you remembered with their position on the list. You should find that you tended to remember words from the beginning of the list and the end of the list, but not many from the middle of the list.

The findings from studies using free recall are fairly reliable and they produce similar results on each occasion. If you take each item in the list and calculate the probability of participants recalling it (by averaging recall of the word over all participants) and plot this against the item's position in the list, it results in the **serial position curve** (Figure 10.10).

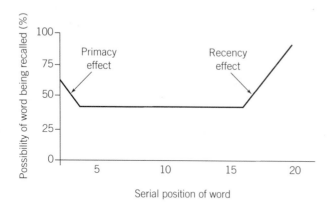

Figure 10.10: Simplified representation of serial position curve for immediate recall (Adapted from Rundus, 1971)

The two key features of the serial position curve are:

- items presented early in the list are more likely to be recalled than those in the middle of the list;
- items presented at the end of the list are also more likely to be recalled than items in the middle of the list.

Good recall of items at the beginning of the list is referred to as the **primacy effect**, and good recall of items at the end of the list is referred to as the **recency effect**. The displacement theory of forgetting from short-term memory can explain the recency effect quite easily. The last few words that were presented in the list have not yet been displaced from short-term memory and so are available for recall. The primacy effect can be explained using Atkinson & Shiffrin's (1968) model which proposes that information is transferred into long-term memory by means of rehearsal. The first words in the list are rehearsed more frequently because at the time they are presented they do not have to compete with other words for the limited capacity of the short-term store. This means that words early in the list are more likely to be transferred to long-term memory. So the primacy effect reflects items that are available for recall from long-term memory. Displacement theory predicts that it should be possible to disrupt the recency effect by giving participants another task, such as a simple arithmetical task, after the end of the list of words but before the free recall. According to displacement theory, the new information associated with the additional task would replace the words held in the short-term store and thereby abolish the recency effect. Postman & Phillips (1965) found that when they asked their participants to count backwards in threes from 100 for fifteen seconds between the list being read out and free recall, they observed no recency effect. Glanzer & Cunitz (1966) provided support for the view that displacement was a major cause of forgetting, but also recognised that other factors, including decay, played a role in forgetting from short-term memory.

Evaluative Comment

Displacement theory provided a good account of how forgetting might take place in Atkinson & Shiffrin's (1968) model of short term memory. However, it became clear that the short-term memory store is much more complex than proposed in Atkinson and Shiffrin's model. As a result, displacement theory fell out of favour as a means of explaining forgetting from short-term memory. More recently, research has focused on the role of interference in forgetting from short-term memory.

Lack of consolidation

The previous accounts of forgetting have focused primarily on psychological evidence, but memory also relies on biological processes. For example, we can define a memory trace as:

> 'some permanent alteration of the brain substrate in order to represent some aspect of a past experience'.
> (Parkin, 1993)

The brain consists of a vast number of cells called neurons, connected to each other by synapses. Synapses enable chemicals to be passed from one neuron to another. These chemicals, called neurotransmitters, can either inhibit or stimulate the performance of neurons. So if you can imagine a network of neurons all connected via synapses, there will be a pattern of stimulation and inhibition. It has been suggested that this pattern of inhibition and stimulation can be used as a basis for storing information. This process of modifying neurons in order form new permanent memories is referred to as **consolidation** (Parkin, 1993).

One of the earliest and most influential models of the relationship between brain physiology and memory was developed by Hebb (1949). He proposed that groups of neurons, which Hebb (1949) referred to as **cell assemblies**, were activated in response to information being transferred from our senses (vision, auditory, etc.). The role of the cell assemblies is to maintain a representation of the information long enough for a permanent memory to be formed. Hebb (1949) proposed that the process of consolidation and formation of a permanent memory took about 30 minutes. However, it is likely that the process occurs much more rapidly than this (Parkin, 1993). If consolidation is a chemical process relying on neurotransmitters, it should be possible to disrupt it by the administration of drugs. One neurotransmitter in particular (acetylcholine) has been identified as playing a significant role in the consolidation of memories.

Study

Aim *Drachman & Sahakian (1979) aimed to investigate how the process of consolidation can be disrupted.*

Method *A drug which blocked the action of the neurotransmitter acetylcholine was administered to the experimental group. Participants were required to learn a list of words and then recall them after a delay of 60 seconds. During the delay, participants performed a distracter task which was designed to stop participants simply rehearsing the information in working memory. This ensured that the task would involve the process of consolidation. Performance was compared with a control group who received no drug treatment.*

Results *The control group recalled approximately twice as many words as the treatment group.*

Conclusions *The findings show that consolidation requires the action of specific neurotransmitters and also that this process can be disrupted.*

One of the questions that has concerned researchers investigating the processes involved in the consolidation of memories is, 'How long does it take for the process of consolidation to be completed?'. Parkin (1993) suggests that the process of consolidation continues over a relatively long time period. He argues that consolidation involves different phases: the first occurs very rapidly and results in an 'initial fixation' of the memory. This is followed by a much longer process, in which the memory trace becomes more fully integrated with our other memories. Some support for the extended duration of consolidation comes from the study of an amnesic patient, HM. In 1953, HM had brain surgery to treat his epilepsy which had become extremely severe. The surgery removed parts of his brain, and although it relieved his epilepsy, it left him with a range of memory problems. Not surprisingly, the surgery undergone by HM has not been performed again on any other patients. HM has been one of the most extensively studied individuals in the history of psychology, and Pinel (1993) suggests that he has contributed more than any other to our understanding of memory. The main problem experienced by HM is his inability to remember and learn new things. This inability to form new memories is referred to as **anterograde amnesia**. However, of interest in our understanding of the duration of the process of consolidation is HM's memory for events before his surgery. In general, his memory for events before the surgery remains intact, but he does have some memory loss for events which occurred in the two years leading up to surgery. Pinel (1993) suggests that this challenges Hebb's (1949) idea that the process of consolidation takes approximately 30 minutes. The fact that HM's memory is disrupted for the two-year period leading up to the surgery indicates that the process of consolidation continues for a number of years.

Evaluative Comment

The research into the processes involved in consolidation reminds us that memory relies on biological processes, although the exact manner by which neurons are altered during the formation of new memories has not yet been fully explained. Hebb's pioneering work has opened up the way for research that draws together biological and psychological models of memory and forgetting. There is no doubt that investigating the role of neurons and neurotransmitters will provide new and important insights into memory and forgetting.

10

See Appendix 1 for information concerning questions that appear in the examination paper. The assessment of knowledge and understanding (AO1) and analysis and evaluation (AO2) assessment objectives is also given in Appendix 1.

Sample questions

Sample question 1

(a) Explain how 'lack of consolidation' might account for forgetting.

   (AO1 = 1, AO2 = 2)   *(3 marks)*

(b) Identify and describe one strength and one weakness of the 'levels of processing' approach to memory.

   (AO1 = 4)   *(4 marks)*

(c) Describe the difference between *displacement* and *decay* as explanations of forgetting.

   (AO1 = 3)   *(3 marks)*

(d) Discuss how Atkinson & Shiffrin's (1968) model of memory has contributed to our understanding of human memory.

   (AO1 = 4, AO2 = 6)   *(10 marks)*

Total AO1 marks = 12   Total AO2 marks = 8   Total = 20 marks

Sample question 2

(a) Using your knowledge of models of memory, explain how we can remember a telephone number in the period between looking it up in the telephone directory and dialling the number.

   (AO1 = 1, AO2 = 2)   *(3 marks)*

(b) Describe a study which illustrates how retrieval failure can account for forgetting. In your answer, indicate why the study was conducted, the method used, results obtained and conclusions drawn.

   (AO1 = 5)   *(5 marks)*

(c) Using your knowledge of explanations of forgetting, describe what is meant by *interference*.

   (AO1 = 2)   *(2 marks)*

(d) With reference to at least one study, discuss how lack of consolidation can account for failure to recall information.

   (AO1 = 3, AO2 = 7)   *(10 marks)*

Total AO1 marks = 11 Total AO2 marks = 9 Total = 20 marks

Sample question 3

(a) Describe the difference between episodic and semantic memory.

   (AO1 = 3)   *(3 marks)*

(b) Explain how knowledge of the levels of processing approach could help someone preparing for an exam.

   (AO1 = 1, AO2 = 2)   *(3 marks)*

(c) Describe Atkinson & Shiffrin's (1968) multi-store model of memory.

   (AO1 = 4)   *(4 marks)*

(d) Discuss Baddeley & Hitch's (1974) model of working memory.

   (AO1 = 4, AO2 = 6)   *(10 marks)*

Total AO1 marks = 12 Total AO2 marks = 8 Total = 20 marks

Questions, answers and comments

(a) Discuss one way in which knowledge about 'retrieval failure' as an explanation of forgetting might help a student prepare for an examination.

(AO1 = 1, AO2 = 2) *(3 marks)*

(b) Atkinson & Shiffrin's (1968) model of memory proposes that there are three separate parts that go to make up our memory system: sensory memory, short-term memory and long-term memory. Describe one study which has investigated the differences between long-term memory and short-term memory. In your answer, indicate why the study was conducted, the method used, results obtained and conclusions drawn.

(AO1 = 5) *(5 marks)*

(c) Identify two differences between episodic memory and procedural memory.

(AO1 = 2) *(2 marks)*

(d) Discuss the working memory model. Refer to empirical evidence in your answer.

(AO1 = 3, AO2 = 7) *(10 marks)*

Total AO1 marks = 11   Total AO2 marks = 9   Total = 20 marks

Answer to (a)

Retrieval failure means that someone has a memory for something but cannot recall it when they want to. One of the reasons for this is that the cues they have available are not effective when it comes to accessing the memory. This means that the person has a memory for something but can't retrieve it.

Comment

This answer would score two out of the three marks. One mark for identifying and describing retrieval failure, the second mark for expanding this to include the role of cues in retrieval. However, they have not related this to preparation for examinations which would be necessary for the full three marks.

Answer to (b)

Baddeley (1966) carried out an experiment to look at the way in which information is coded in long-term and short-term memories.

Method: He presented his participants with a list of words. Some of the words sounded the same, like 'car' and 'bar'. Some of the words had a similar meaning, like 'bench' and 'chair'. After the words had been presented, there was a delay. This was to make sure that the words were in long-term memory.

Results: Baddeley found that when his participants made mistakes, they were based on the meaning of the word and not the sound of the word.

Conclusions: These findings were interpreted as supporting the view that information in long-term memory is based on meaning and not sound. This evidence can be used to support Atkinson & Shiffrin's (1968) model, which has separate long-term and short-term memory stores.

Baddeley also carried out a similar experiment which looked at the coding in short-term memory. It was basically the same as the experiment above, but didn't have a delay between presenting the list and recall. In this situation, people were making mistakes based on the sound of the word and not the meaning. Both these studies supported the idea of separate memory stores.

Comment

This answer would receive the full five marks. The candidate has described an appropriate study in which the aim, method, results and conclusion are clearly stated; four marks would be awarded for this. The additional mark is awarded for the expansion where the candidate provides additional contextual information relating the study to other research.

Sample questions, answers and comments

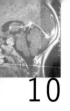

Answer to (c)

One difference is that episodic memory is memory about things that have happened to us, events that we were involved in, like remembering our birthday party. Procedural memory is our memory for how to do things like playing the piano or riding a bike. Another difference is that we can describe our episodic memories in words, but it is very difficult to put procedural memories into words.

Comment

This answer would be awarded the full two marks. The candidate has correctly identified two differences between episodic and procedural memory and has also provided examples to support the points made. It is clear that the candidate understands the difference between the two types of memory.

Answer to (d)

The working-memory model was developed by Baddeley & Hitch (1974). It was developed because the short-term memory store in Atkinson and Shiffrin's multi-store model didn't cope very well with some of the research evidence. For example, Warrington & Shallice (1970) conducted a case study with a patient (KM) who had suffered brain damage. KM had a good short-term memory for visual information, but had a very poor short-term memory for words. This indicates that short-term memory isn't a single unit, as suggested by Atkinson and Shiffrin, but is made up of different components. Another problem with the Atkinson and Shiffrin model concerned the role of rehearsal in transferring information into long-term memory. Our experience in everyday life shows that lots of information can be transferred into our long-term memory without any rehearsal. In response to these criticisms, Baddeley and Hitch developed an alternative model of short-term memory. They used the term 'working memory' rather than short-term memory to indicate that it wasn't just a passive store holding information, but was much more active in processing information. The working-memory model has three basic components. These are called the visuo-spatial sketchpad, the phonological loop and the central executive. The central executive controls the other two systems, just like the boss in a big company. The visuo-spatial sketchpad deals with visual and spatial information and helps us keep a track of where we are in our environment. The phonological loop deals with sounds and language. It has two parts, one which stores information for short periods of time and the other part rehearses information so that it isn't lost. Evidence for the fact that there are two components to the phonological loop comes from a study carried out by Paulesu *et al.* (1993), which used a PET scan to monitor blood flow in participants' brains while they carried out two different tasks. One task involved rehearsing letters by repeating the sounds of the letters over and over again to themselves. The other task consisted of simply remembering the letters without rehearsing the sounds. The two tasks gave different patterns of blood flow in the brain. The findings were taken to support the view that the phonological loop consists of two different components. The phonological loop plays a role in learning to read and other language skills. Evidence based on case studies with patients suffering from brain damage has provided evidence that some patients can have damage to the visuo-spatial sketchpad, but their phonological loop operates normally. There are also patients with the opposite pattern of damage – intact visuo-spatial sketchpad and damaged phonological loop. This suggests that the phonological loop and visuo-spatial sketchpad are separate systems. The working-memory model has been very successful in terms of the amount of research it has generated, and it is a significant improvement on the model of short-term memory proposed by Atkinson and Shiffrin. But there are still some criticisms that have been made of the working-memory model. In particular, it has been pointed out that the details about how working memory actually works have not been fully specified.

Comment

This answer would score full marks. It presents a good and accurate description of the components of the working memory. It also identifies the role that the phonological loop plays in the acquisition and use of language. The three AO1 marks would be awarded for the description and three AO2 marks for the expansions relating to the development of the model and the role of the phonological loop in language acquisition. The remaining four AO2 marks would be awarded for the empirical evidence referred to by the candidate and also the discussion/evaluation.

Further reading

Introductory texts

Eysenck, M.W. (1993), *Principles of Cognitive Psychology* (Chapter 4), Hove, LEA

Scott, P. & Spencer, C. (1998), *Psychology: A Contemporary Introduction* (Chapter 7), Oxford, Blackwell

Sternberg, R.J. (1995), *In Search of the Human Mind* (Chapter 8), Fort Worth, Harcourt Brace College Publishers

Westen, D. (1996), *Psychology: Mind, Brain and Culture* (Chapter 6), New York, John Wiley & Sons

Specialist sources

Anderson, J.R. (2000), *Learning and Memory*, New York, John Wiley & Sons

Baddeley, A.D. (1997), *Human Memory: Theory and Practice*, Hove, Psychology Press

Baddeley, A.D. (1999), *Essentials of Human Memory*, Hove, Psychology Press

Eysenck, M.W. & Keane, M.T. (2000), *Cognitive Psychology: A Student's Handbook*, Hove, Psychology Press

Groeger, J.A. (1997), *Memory and Remembering: Everyday Memory in Context*, New York, Addison Wesley Longman

Matlin, M.W. (2002), *Cognition*, Orlando, Harcourt College Publishers

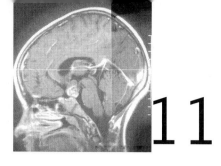

11

Language and Thinking

Introduction: the nature of language

Language is essential to many of our activities in everyday life. We use language to communicate with other people and also as a means of representing our own thoughts. In many situations, we simply take language for granted, but it is difficult to imagine what life would be like without it. It has been suggested that language is probably one of the most complex behaviours humans engage in (Gleitman & Liberman, 1995). Despite the complexity of language, humans acquire a huge vocabulary; for example, a typical college student will have a vocabulary of approximately 90,000 words (Wingfield, 1993). In addition, one of the important characteristics of language is the way in which it is possible to create new and unique utterances. It has been estimated that if we were able to list all the possible twenty-word sentences it would take ten billion years to read them out (Pinker, 1993).

Definitions of language

Psycholinguistics is the term used to describe the study of the psychological processes involved in language. However, defining language is not an easy task. In fact, there have been several books devoted solely to answering the question 'What is language?'

Greene (1990) identifies four different ways in which language has been investigated.

- as a universal human ability, something that we all acquire and use throughout our lives;
- in terms of how it is understood by communities who share a common language;
- in terms of the knowledge individuals have of the language they use;
- how it is used to communicate in social contexts.

Kellogg (1995), proposes that language is:

'a system of symbols that allow communication of ideas among two or more individuals'.

This definition makes a distinction between communication and language, in that language provides a vehicle for communication to take place. Communication is much more easy to define than language – it is the transmission of a signal that conveys information (Harley, 1995). There are an infinite number of ways in which we can communicate with other people; for example, ordering a meal at a restaurant, asking a question in class and writing an essay are all acts of communication.

Hockett (1960) has provided an alternative approach, and rather than focusing on producing a definition, he attempted to identify the essential characteristics of language. He produced several lists which reflected his developing ideas, the longest of which was sixteen characteristics. Some of the more important ones are presented in Figure 11.1.

Characteristic	Description of term
Semanticity	Words have a meaning: they relate in some way to features of the world.
Arbitrariness	Symbols and words are abstract, they do not look like the objects they stand for.
Displacement	Language can be used to refer to things not physically present.
Openness	Language can be used to create new and unique messages.
Tradition	Language can be taught and learned.
Duality of Patterning	Unless they are put together in appropriate ways combinations of sounds, words and sentences are meaningless.
Prevarication	Language provides us with the ability to lie and deceive.
Reflectiveness	We can communicate about the communication system itself, just as this book is doing.
Learnability	The speaker of one language can learn another.

Figure 11.1: Characteristics of language (From Hockett, 1960)

One of the common features of the characteristics of language presented by Hockett (1960) is their emphasis on the fact that language is about meaning and also provides us with the opportunity to communicate about almost anything. Hockett (1960) uses the term *semanticity* to refer to the fact that language is used to convey meaning. The sounds we use in spoken language and the words we use in written language refer to objects, emotions, events, beliefs and intentions. If someone says to you, 'I had a really good time last night,' then it tells you something about their state of mind and also about the events of the previous evening. The sounds and words are capable of conveying a clear meaning. On the other hand, if you hear someone whistling a tune while they are walking down the road it does not tell us anything specific about their mood or how they are feeling. It could be that they always whistle when they are happy; on the other hand, they could be whistling because they are sad, angry, depressed or full of energy. So, unlike language, whistling is not specialised to convey a clear meaning (Kellogg, 1995).

Although words carry a specific meaning – for example, we all know that 'cat' refers to a small, furry mammal – there is no obvious connection between the word and the meaning it carries. Hockett (1960) uses the term *arbitrariness* to refer to this property of language. 'Chat', 'kat', 'Katze' and 'cat' are all words referring to the same thing in different languages (French, Dutch, German and English), and there is no obvious connection between the sounds of the words and the object. In other words, there is an arbitrary relationship between the word and the object. Knowing that 'cat' refers to a small, furry animal is a relationship that is learned as we acquire language, it is not something that comes from the word itself. However, there are some words that do sound like the things they describe, for example, 'buzz', 'ding-dong', 'bang' and 'pop'. The term used to describe words like this is *onomatopoeic*, but there are relatively few of these kinds of word in any language.

Evaluative Comment

The characteristics of language identified by Hockett (1960) have proved to be very useful, for example, in deciding whether or not a system of communication is a language. This approach to defining language avoids many of the problems associated with other definitions. However, Hockett's (1960) list is by no means exhaustive, and a number of other characteristics of language have been proposed more recently. For example, Marshall (1970) points out that language is intentional*: it is under our voluntary control and we use it to communicate particular messages. Anderson (2000) suggests that another feature of language is that we can use it to create extremely long sentences by combining phrases using words such as 'and' or by embedding parts of sentences in other sentences.*

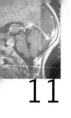

11 Comparison of human language and communication in other species

There are two basic views on the relationship between human language and communication in other species. They are referred to as **continuity theory** and **discontinuity theory**. Both of these viewpoints recognise the long evolutionary history of humans and accept that animals are capable of communicating with each other. However, continuity theory sees human language as having gradually evolved from a more primitive form of communication used by our non-human ancestors. In other words, human language can be seen as a more advanced, complex and sophisticated version of the language used by chimpanzees. On the other hand, discontinuity theory sees human language as being something completely different from the forms of communication used by animals. According to discontinuity theory, human language exists alongside the other forms of communicating which reflect our evolutionary history. So the systems of calls used by monkeys may be closely related to the cries of pain and delight expressed by adults and the different types of crying observed in children (Aitchison, 1989), whereas, according to discontinuity theory, the language used in everyday conversation is not directly related to the calls and sounds used by monkeys. At present, it is not clear whether continuity or discontinuity theorists are correct. One of the key questions in this area concerns the extent to which animals have a language which is comparable to human language.

Study

AIM *The aim of Seyfarth et al.'s (1980) study was to investigate the alarm calls of vervet monkeys to see if they represent a communication system.*

METHOD *Vervet monkeys have a range of different alarm calls they use in the presence of different predators. A 'chirp' is used for lions and leopards, a 'rraup' warns of an eagle and 'chutter' announces the presence of a snake. A concealed loudspeaker played recordings of these alarm calls and the behaviour of the monkeys was observed.*

RESULTS *The behaviour of the monkeys was related to the type of alarm call being played. When a 'chirp' was played, they rapidly climbed a tree, and at the sound of a 'rraup' they ran into the vegetation as if to hide from an eagle.*

CONCLUSIONS *The vervet monkeys have a system of alarm calls that signify specific predators.*

The study carried out by Seyfarth *et al.* (1980) clearly demonstrates that animals can communicate, but it does not tell us whether or not animal communication is the same as human language. One way to address this question is to use the characteristics of language identified by Hockett (1960) to animal communication. Hockett's (1960) notion of *openness* appears to be of crucial importance when comparing human and animal communication. The ability to generate and understand an almost infinite number of utterances seems to be unique to humans. Most animals have a limited number of signals which are only used in specific circumstances. For example, the North American grasshopper has only four signals, two of which relate to courtship displays, whilst the vervet monkey has just 36 distinct vocal sounds (Aitchison, 1989). However, insects such as bees have more complex and sophisticated communications systems; for example, bees perform a 'dance' which communicates information about the location of food sources. But is there any evidence that their communication systems meet Hockett's (1960) criteria of openness?

Study

AIM *The aim of von Frisch's (1954) study was to investigate the communication of vertical distances by bees.*

METHOD *A hive of bees was placed at the foot of a radio tower and a supply of sugar was placed at the top of the tower. A small number of bees were taken to the sugar. If the bees are capable of communicating information about vertical distance then they should be able to communicate this to the other bees in the hive.*

RESULTS *The other bees were unable to find the sugar.*

CONCLUSIONS *Bees are capable of communicating information about horizontal distance, but not vertical distance.*

It would appear from the work of von Frisch (1954) that bees are not capable of creating new and unique messages. In other words, they do not have a language according to Hockett's (1960) criteria.

More recently, there have been several research programmes investigating the extent to which it is possible to teach human language to chimpanzees. Washoe and Sarah were two chimps who were the focus of a considerable amount of research in the 1970s. Washoe was taught to use a modified version of American Sign Language (ASL). In sign language, a combination of movements and hand shapes are used to stand for words. For example, Washoe's sign for 'funny' was to press the tip of her finger on to her nose and utter a snort. Washoe was not taught language through the use of training schedules, rather she was surrounded by humans who communicated with her and each other by signs (Gardner & Gardner, 1969). Washoe very quickly acquired a vocabulary of 34 single words after a period of about two years, which gradually increased to well over 100. In the early stages, her language acquisition was similar to that of a human child. There was clear evidence that Washoe understood that certain signs stood for specific objects. For example, she made the sign for flower when she was shown the picture of a flower and also when she was walking towards the garden. Perhaps the most impressive aspect of Washoe's language use was her ability to put together combinations of signs in novel and new ways, such as 'gimme tickle' and 'hurry gimme toothbrush' (Aitchison, 1989). However, unlike children, Washoe did not appear to put her signs in a consistent order. When children first start to string together sequences of words, they put the action word after the subject word, for example, 'Daddy gone' and 'Amy eat', whereas Washoe was just as likely to say 'tickle gimme' as she was to say 'gimme tickle'. This would appear to indicate that although Washoe understood the meaning of words, she did not understand the way in which language is patterned and structured (Aitchison, 1989).

There have been several research studies aimed at teaching chimpanzees to use language. Some chimps have acquired a vocabulary of over 100 words, but there is a considerable debate about whether or not they use language in the same way as humans

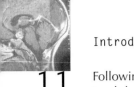

Following on from the Washoe project, there were a number of other studies which attempted to teach language to primates. Perhaps one of the most interesting of these was the one which used Koko, a female gorilla. After a period of approximately five years of training, Koko had acquired a vocabulary of approximately 400 words (Patterson, 1978).

Evaluative Comment

Aitchison (1989) argues that the findings from the attempts to teach language to Washoe and Sarah are not clear cut. There is no doubt that the systems of communication learned by Washoe is less complicated than human language. For example, Premack & Premack (1974) point out that children with severe learning difficulties who are unable to acquire normal language can learn to use the system taught to Sarah. But it is also the case that Washoe did show some grasp of language previously thought to be restricted to humans (Aitchison, 1989). The debate concerning whether or not primates can acquire language continues, and Aitchison (1989) suggests that we should not consider language as an 'all or none' matter. The studies with apes have demonstrated that they can acquire some aspects of language that had previously been thought to be exclusively human. However, there is no conclusive evidence that apes can understand the structural aspects of human language.

The relationship between language and thought

One of the issues debated by philosophers, linguists and psychologists is the relationship between language and thought. Throughout our daily lives, we are constantly thinking and using language; we communicate with other people and solve problems on a regular basis. A number of different views on the relationship between language and thinking have been proposed, and the ideas of Whorf (1956), Piaget (1968) and Vygotsky (1934/1962) will be discussed later in this section.

The relationship between language and thought

The traditional view on the relationship between language and thought is that thought determines the language we use. This idea can be traced back to the Ancient Greek philosopher Aristotle, who believed that languages have developed in order to enable people to express their thoughts (Garnham & Oakhill, 1994). However, in the twentieth century, alternative views on the relationship between language and thought were developed.

Practical Activity

You will need a couple of friends to carry out this activity, the aim of which is to demonstrate the effect that language can have on perception and memory.

The activity involves showing the same picture, but with different labels, to different people and asking them to draw the picture from memory. In order to do this, you will need copies of the six cards in Figure 11.2.

Next, you will need two people who are willing to help you. Show Cards 1, 3 and 5 to one person and Cards 2, 4 and 6 to the other person. Display each of the cards for about two seconds (long enough for them to read the label). After a suitable delay, for example, fifteen minutes, ask your participants to draw the pictures they saw on the cards. It is important that each person only sees one set of cards.

Compare the drawings. Is there any evidence that their recall of the cards has been influenced by the label?

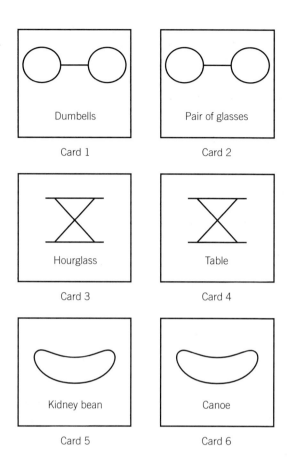

Figure 11.2: Use copies of these cards for the activity

The above activity demonstrates the effect that verbal labels have on the way in which people perceive and recall simple line drawings. It can also be taken to suggest that there is a relationship between thought and language. Hartland (1991) states that three possible relationships between language and thought have been explored in some detail. They are:

- Thinking depends on language (Whorf, 1956).

- Language depends on thought (Piaget, 1968).

- Language and thought develop independently in children until they are approximately two years old. At this point, they become interdependent and develop together (Vygotsky, 1934, 1962).

Each of these views will be considered in more detail in the following sections.

Whorf's views on the relationship between language and thought

Whorf (1956) proposed that the form of our language determines the structure of our thought processes. The work of Whorf is closely associated with that of his teacher, Edward Sapir, and as a result, the view that language determines thought is usually referred to as the **Sapir–Whorf hypothesis**. Whorf worked for a time as an insurance claims engineer and noted that accidents sometimes occurred when people were misled by words. An example that is often used to illustrate this point is the case of a fire that was started when a worker threw a cigarette into an 'empty' drum

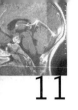

of petrol. Although the drum was empty of liquid petrol, it was full of petrol vapour which exploded in contact with the cigarette (Harley, 1995). In other words, the word 'empty' was misleading and may have contributed to the accident.

Whorf's ideas concerning the relationship between language and thought were developed through studies of Native American languages, such as Apache and Hopi. He focused on the ways in which different languages were used to describe aspects of the world. Whorf (1956) claimed that different languages impose different ways of viewing the world on their speakers. For example, Whorf (1956) argued that because the Hopi have no words that refer to time, they must have a very different conception of time to ourselves. The idea that language determines thought is referred to as **linguistic determinism**. Unfortunately, some of Whorf's writings are rather vague and inconsistent (Garnham & Oakhill, 1994), and as a result, there are at least two versions of his views on the extent to which language determines thought. These different versions are frequently referred to as 'strong' and 'weak' versions of the Sapir–Whorf hypothesis. 'Strong' versions of the hypothesis argue that that our language determines the way we think, remember and perceive our environment. 'Weak' versions of the hypothesis stop short of arguing that language determines thought and propose that there is a relationship between language and thought. For example, our language may influence the way we perceive different objects or aspects of our environment (Harley, 1995).

The way in which people perceive and remember colours has formed the basis for a considerable amount of research into the relationship between language and thought. One of the reasons for this is that colours can be categorised independently of the language used to describe them. For example, colours can be described in terms of their position in the spectrum and their wavelength. One of the first experiments using colour to test the Sapir–Whorf hypothesis was carried out by Brown & Lennenberg (1954).

Study

AIM *The aim of Brown & Lennenberg's (1954) study was to test the Sapir–Whorf hypothesis that language influences thought.*

METHOD *Brown and Lennenberg identified eight colours (red, orange, yellow, green, blue, purple, pink and brown) that people described using a single word and sixteen colours that people described using additional words, such as light green, pale blue and dark red. Participants were shown examples of each of the colours for a short period of time and then were asked to pick out the colour from a chart with 120 colours on it.*

RESULTS *There was a moderately high correlation between how easily the colours were to name and recognition. In other words, the colours identified by a single name were also easier to recall.*

CONCLUSIONS *These findings were taken to support the Sapir–Whorf hypothesis, since the names for colours apparently influenced the cognitive task of recalling the colour.*

If Brown & Lennenberg (1954) are correct in their view that the names we give colours influence their recall, then it should be possible to identify differences between cultures who label colours in different ways in terms of their ability to remember colours. A cross-cultural study was carried out by Heider (1972) with the Dani people in Indonesian New Guinea. The Dani have only two basic colour words: 'mili' for dark or cold colours and 'mola' for bright and warm colours. When the Dani are talking about other colours, they use longer phrases which tend to describe the colour. If the Sapir–Whorf hypothesis is correct, then there should be significant differences between the Dani's ability to recall colours which are easily named in their language and those that are more difficult to name. In fact, Heider (1972) found that the colours which were easy to recall in the Brown & Lennenberg (1954) study were also better recalled by the Dani, even though they did not have specific words for some of the colours. This finding would appear to cast doubt on the idea that thought is dependent on language in the manner proposed by the Sapir–Whorf hypothesis.

Evaluative Comment

Recently, the Sapir–Whorf hypothesis has enjoyed a revival, as it has become clear that some of the data which were used to challenge it have been called into question. Hunt & Agnoli (1991) have proposed a version of the Sapir–Whorf hypothesis based on cognitive psychology. They argue that in any language it is easy to think in certain ways and more difficult to think in other ways, and this is why thinking is influenced by language (Eysenck & Keane, 2000). Although there is a reasonable amount of evidence which is consistent with Hunt & Agnoli's (1991) position, Eysenck & Keane (2000) argue that there is still the need for a systematic programme of research to test out their specific predictions concerning the relationship between language and thought.

Piaget's views on the relationship between language and thought

Piaget's views on the relationship between language and thought are more or less the opposite of those taken by Whorf. Piaget was opposed to the idea that language is responsible for thought (Greene, 1990). One of the main arguments presented by Piaget (1968) in support of the view that thought precedes language comes from observations of the way in which language use develops in children. His view is that it is impossible for children to understand what is meant by particular words or phrases until they understand the underlying concept. For example, anyone who has tried playing a board game with very young children will know that they do not understand the concept of 'turn-taking'. So using the phrase 'It's not your turn' will not be very helpful if the child does not understand the concept of taking turns in a game. According to Piaget's theory, a child's way of thinking changes first; this is followed by a change in the language used by the child in order to express new ideas and a new way of thinking (Garnham & Oakhill, 1994).

Piaget (1968) argued that young children use speech to express their thoughts rather than communicate with other people. He used the term **egocentric speech** to describe this use of language. Piaget (1968) observed that young children use language in the presence of other people, such as parents, but their speech is not directed towards them. The child's speech is merely a reflection of their own thoughts and intentions. As the child grows older, they become able to consider the thoughts and feelings of other people, and egocentric speech disappears.

Harley (1995) argues that one way of testing the view that thought precedes language would be to examine the language skills of children with some form of cognitive impairment. The rationale here is that if thinking is necessary for language, then children whose cognitive development is impaired should also have poor language skills. Although in general this tends to be the case, there are some instances of children whose language skills are considerably greater than their other cognitive abilities.

Study

Aim *Yamada (1990) aimed to investigate the relationship between language and other cognitive abilities.*

Method *A case study was carried out with a participant called 'Laura', who completed a number of tests of cognitive and linguistic ability.*

Results *Laura's general cognitive ability was very poor; for example, her IQ was estimated to be 41. However, her linguistic abilities were considerably greater, and she was capable of producing complex sentences.*

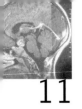
CONCLUSIONS *The findings led Yamada (1990) to conclude that cognitive abilities and language develop independently.*

Evaluative Comment

There is very little empirical support for Piaget's view that thought precedes language. It would appear to be the case that Piaget underestimated the extent to which children use language to ask questions and learn about the world from other people (Hartland, 1991). In other words, he underestimated the social function of language. There is currently little active research on the Piagetian approach to language (Harley, 1995).

Vygotsky's views on the relationship between language and thought

Vygotsky was a Russian psychologist whose ideas became increasingly influential in the latter part of the twentieth century. Although his work was published in Russia in the 1930s, it was not translated into English until 1962. Vygotsky's (1934/1962) basic position concerning the relationship between language and thought is that language and thought develop independently in young children (up to about two years of age), but as the child grows older, language and thought become interdependent. Vygotsky (1934/1986) uses the term *pre-intellectual language* to refer to the crying and babbling used by children up to the age of two. In this stage, the words children use to name objects are properties of the objects. For example, children might refer to dogs as 'bow wows' because of the sounds that dogs make. Vygotsky (1934/1962) argued that thought during this stage of development was 'non-verbal' and relied on perceptions and images. However, at some point language and thought become connected and this enables the child to use verbal thought.

Practical Activity

In order to carry out this activity, you will need to be able to observe a young child who is approximately two years old and one who is six or seven years old. Pay attention to the following:

* *How frequently does the child say aloud what they are going to do? For example, do they say 'I'm going to draw' or 'The car's going to crash'?*

* *Do they wait for an answer or do they carry on playing?*

* *How often do they use the word 'I' or 'Me' at the beginning of a sentence?*

* *What are the differences between the older child and the younger child in the way they talk while they are playing?*

This activity illustrates the changes that occur in language use as children develop.

As children get older, they start to use language to describe their actions, almost giving a running commentary on what they have just done. For example, if a ball which the child is playing with disappears from view, the child is likely to say 'Ball gone'. As this stage progresses, verbal descriptions will begin to be expressed before the child completes an action rather than following it. For example, rather than the child saying 'Hit ball' after they have hit the ball, it will occur before the action takes place. Vygotsky (1934/1962) interpreted this as an indication that language and thought are becoming more interdependent. According to Vygotsky, language now has two different functions for the child. The first involves using language internally as means of thinking and problem-solving. The second is an external function which involves engaging in social interaction and communicating with other people (see Figure 11.3).

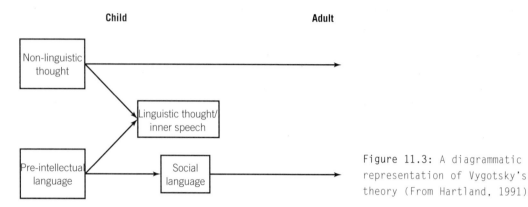

Figure 11.3: A diagrammatic representation of Vygotsky's theory (From Hartland, 1991)

Anyone who has observed young children playing will have noticed that they constantly talk to themselves. Piaget referred to this as *egocentric speech*, as there is no attempt being made to communicate with another person; the speech is associated with the activities being carried out by the child. Vygotsky and Piaget had completely different views on the function of egocentric speech (Garnham & Oakhill, 1994). Piaget's view was that egocentric speech was related to a particular developmental stage when children do not understand that other people have a different perspective or point of view than they do. According to Piaget, as the child matures and realises that other people see things differently to themselves, egocentric speech simply disappears. On the other hand, Vygotsky believed that egocentric speech becomes transformed into the 'inner speech' that is associated with much of our complex thinking. Inner speech is somewhat different from the speech that is used in conversations. For example, words used in inner speech contain much more than the dictionary definition of the word. The word 'dog' used in inner speech would be associated with all your personal memories of dogs, how it feels to stroke a dog, your emotional feelings towards dogs and so on. In some ways, inner speech can be seen as providing a bridge between thought itself and the expression of those thoughts in language (Hayes, 1994). Figure 11.4 provides a comparison of Piaget and Vygotsky's views.

Piaget	Vygotsky
Cognitive development determines the language used by individuals	Language develops as a result of the social interactions between people, but thinking develops as a result of an individual's actions on the environment
Egocentric speech is relatively shortlived, disappears and is replaced by social speech	Egocentric speech develops into verbal thinking which forms the basis of much adult thought. Social speech is developed as a means of communicating with other people

Figure 11.4: Summary of the main differences between Piaget and Vygotsky's views on the relationship between language and thought (Based on Hartland, 1991)

Evaluative Comment

As a theory of the developing relationship between language and thought, Vygotsky's theory appears more plausible than Piaget's (Garnham & Oakhill, 1994). Although Vygotsky (1934/1962) conducted a

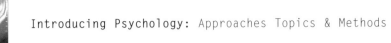
number of experiments, they are difficult to evaluate, because his reports omitted many details of the procedure he used. In a number of these, he attempted to compare his theory with Piaget's. Surprisingly, they have not been repeated under more stringent conditions (Harley, 1995).

Ways of thinking

Burton & Radford (1991) propose that the task of understanding thinking is one of the most important challenges for psychology. Defining thinking is difficult because it is involved in nearly all human activities, for example, making decisions, planning what to do, imagining what might happen in certain circumstances. One quite straightforward definition is that thinking is 'going beyond the information given' (Galotti, 1989). This definition highlights the point that thinking involves more than simply reproducing our existing knowledge.

Insight

Practical Activity

To complete this activity, you will need six small sticks of the same length. You could use matchsticks.

The task is to make four equilateral triangles (i.e. triangles with sides of equal length and where all the internal angles are 60 degrees).

Need a clue? You have to stop thinking in two dimensions and think in three dimensions.

If you still can't find the solution, the answer is at the bottom of the page.

Solving problems is often associated with a 'flash of insight' which enables us to see the solution immediately

The above activity presents a problem that requires a solution. There are a number of different psychological models which have been proposed to explain the processes involved in problem-solving. **Gestalt psychology** would argue that trying to solve the problem in the above activity involves a process of reorganisation. You were trying to reorganise the parts of the problem (the

---

In order to create four equilateral triangles with six sticks, you need to create a three-dimensional shape. The base is made up of three sticks forming a triangle. The remaining three sticks are placed at each corner of the triangle and rest against each other to form an apex. The base forms one triangle and the three sides of the structure provide another three triangles, making four in total.

sticks) so that they fit together in a new and different way. Quite often, people get 'stuck' when they are attempting to solve problems – maybe you experienced that when trying to solve the 'stick problem'. In many situations, people continue to try similar ways of solving the problem, even though it is clearly not working. Sometimes giving people a hint or a clue can help them think about the problem in a different way, and suddenly the answer to the problem becomes clear. This experience of suddenly discovering the solution to a problem is referred to as **insight**. It is frequently called the **'aha' phenomenon**, as it is often accompanied by the exclamation 'aha'!

Study

Aim *Kohler (1927) aimed to investigate problem-solving behaviour in a chimpanzee called Sultan.*

Method *The chimpanzee was in a cage, and bananas were placed outside the cage, out of his reach. In order to reach the bananas, Sultan had to join together two sticks which had been placed inside the cage.*

Results *After a period of trial and error with one of the sticks, Sultan sat quietly for a short time. Then he took the two sticks and joined them together to reach the bananas.*

Conclusion *Kohler (1927) argued that Sultan's behaviour was more than trial and error, and the problem solution was arrived at through the process of insight.*

Gestalt psychologists such Kohler (1927) argued that the process of insight was different from normal, everyday thinking. Wertheimer (1945) made a distinction between **reproductive thinking** and **productive thinking**. Reproductive thinking involves the production of responses and behaviours that have been used before; in other words, it is based on applying old solutions to new problems, whereas productive thinking involves going beyond what the person already knows and producing new and different solutions to problems. Gestalt psychologists proposed that the process of insight involves productive thinking.

An alternative view concerning the nature of insight has been presented by Weisberg (1986). He argues that insight is merely an extension of normal, everyday thought processes such as perceiving and recognising. This view is often referred to as the 'nothing-special view' (Sternberg, 1999).

Study

Aim *Weisberg & Alba (1981) aimed to investigate the role of insight in solving the nine-dot problem.*

Method *Four groups of participants were presented with different versions of the nine-dot problem. Three of the groups were presented with additional information to make the problem easier to solve. Group 1 (the control group) were given no additional information. Group 2 was told that you have go outside the square formed by the dots. Group 3 was given the same instruction as Group 2, and the first line was already drawn. Group 4 was given the verbal instruction and the first two lines. Weisberg & Alba's (1981) rationale was that insight would be indicated by a sudden increase in performance associated with the additional information given to participants.*

Results *The additional information given to participants resulted in gradual increase in performance. There was no evidence of a sudden increase in performance indicative of insight (see Figure 11.5 on page 302).*

Conclusion *Weisberg and Alba used these findings to support the view that insight was not a special form of thinking and did not account for the way in which people solve the nine-dot problem.*

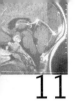

11

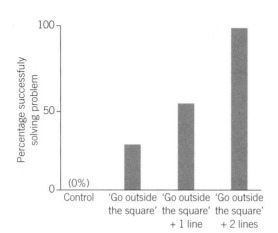

Figure 11.5: Percentage of participants solving the nine-dot problem (Based on Weisberg & Alba, 1981)

Weisberg & Alba's (1981) study cast considerable doubt over the usefulness of insight as a concept in problem-solving. However, subsequent research suggests that Weisberg & Alba's (1981) lack of support for the notion of insight reflected the method that they used in their research. Metcalfe (1986), using a different approach, reported findings which indicate that insight does occur when solving some problems.

Evaluative Comment

Kohler's (1927) findings with Sultan have proved to be very difficult to replicate. For example, Birch (1945) found little evidence of insight in chimpanzees who had been reared in captivity. Nevertheless, Kohler's (1927) work did provide the basis for subsequent research into the role of insight in human problem-solving (Eysenck & Keane, 2000). Like many Gestalt concepts, insight is one which is easily understood and which reflects the phenomena people experience in solving problems on a day-to-day basis. Nevertheless, as a theoretical concept, 'insight' has been criticised because it lacks detail and specificity. The conditions under which insight will occur were not made clear within Gestalt psychology. Ohlson (1992) has attempted to develop a theory which interprets insight within an information-processing framework. He argues that insight occurs in situations when the original representation of the problem does not act as an appropriate cue to retrieve information necessary to solve the problem. According to Ohlson (1992), insight occurs when the representation of the problem is changed in a way that allows the information required to solve the problem to be retrieved from our memory.

Cognitive styles (convergent and divergent thinking)

The majority of research conducted within cognitive psychology aims to establish models and theories that apply to everyone. This is based on the assumption that there are aspects of cognitive functioning which we all have in common. For example, Baddeley & Hitch's (1974) model of working memory is intended to be applicable to the whole population (see Chapter 10). However, this approach ignores what psychologists call individual differences, i.e. differences in cognitive performance across individuals. The individual-differences approach reflects the view that different people can approach the same task in different ways. Psychologists who study personality and intelligence are largely concerned with individual differences between people. Within cognitive psychology, interest in individual differences has focused on **cognitive style**, i.e. the way in which people perform cognitive tasks. This implies that when people are carrying out a cognitive task, such as solving a problem, they have a preferred way of approaching it. During his research into the nature of intelligence, Guilford (1967) identified two different cognitive styles that reflected different ways in which people attempted to solve a variety of problems. He labelled these two different styles of thinking **convergent thinking** and **divergent thinking**.

Practical Activity

Try to answer the following questions:

* *Write down as many different uses that you can think of for a brick.*

* *Multiply 36 by 27.*

Discuss the following points with a friend who has also answered the questions.

* *How are the two questions different?*

* *Is there a correct answer to Question 1? Is there a correct answer to Question 2?*

* *How can you judge the quality of the answers to Question 1?*

* *How can you judge the quality of the answers to Question 2?*

This activity illustrates the difference between divergent thinking and convergent thinking. Question 1 requires divergent thinking, whereas Question 2 is an example of convergent thinking.

People who have a convergent thinking style tend to try and find a single best solution to a problem. As a result, convergent thinkers tend to perform well on problems that have a single, unique solution. On the other hand, people with a divergent thinking style tend to focus on producing a variety of different solutions to problems they are faced with. Divergent thinkers perform better on problems that are open ended and do not have a single solution (Colman, 1990).

Convergent thinking is the type of thinking responsible for performance on traditional intelligence tests. In these tests, there is a single correct answer to each question, and a person's score is normally calculated on the basis of the number of questions they answered correctly. An example of a question from a widely used intelligence test (The British Ability Scales) is presented in Figure 11.6.

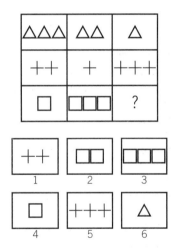

Figure 11.6: An example of a question used in the British Ability Scales

Tests of divergent thinking (e.g. Torrance, 1968) usually measure three aspects of an individual's performance, namely fluency, flexibility and originality. Fluency refers to the extent to which the person is able to generate a number of alternative solutions to a problem. Flexibility is the ability to change approaches when solving a problem, and originality refers to the ability to generate novel or unusual solutions (Ellis & Hunt, 1993).

Practical Activity

Suppose that all humans were born with six fingers on each hand instead of five. Give yourself three minutes to list all the consequences or implications that you can think of. Now ask a friend to try this task and compare your answers.

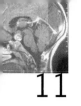

This question is taken from Torrance's (1966) test of creative thinking. The problems on this test are intended to measure divergent thinking.

Several studies have investigated differences between convergent and divergent thinkers. For example, Hudson (1966, 1968), in a study of English schoolboys, found that participants who performed well on convergent-thinking tasks tended to specialise in the sciences and hold conventional attitudes. On the other hand, divergent thinkers tended to specialise in the arts or biology and hold unconventional attitudes and opinions. Interestingly, Hudson (1966, 1968) also reported that convergent thinkers tended to be emotionally inhibited, whereas divergent thinkers tended to be emotionally uninhibited.

Evaluative Comment

Convergent thinking underpins performance on most tests of intelligence. There is some evidence that convergent and divergent thinking reflect different styles of thinking. Recent evidence indicates that convergent and divergent thinking rely on different areas of the brain. Razoumnikova (2000) suggests that convergent thinking relies primarily on the right side of the brain, whereas divergent thinking appears to rely heavily on both sides of the brain. Guilford's (1956, 1967) ideas on divergent thinking have been responsible for the development of a number of tests aimed at measuring creativity. However, as Garnham & Oakhill (1994) point out, whether or not these tests actually measure creativity is unclear. Focusing on creativity in terms of an individual's ability, such as their capacity for divergent thinking, tends to neglect the fact that creative acts take place within a social context. Creative acts also depend on other factors, such as social and economic circumstances and the availability of appropriate role models (Simonton, 1997).

Reasoning (inductive, deductive and probabilistic)

The psychology of reasoning is concerned with investigating the extent to which people can arrive at correct conclusions from information they have been provided with. At a more basic level, research into reasoning is concerned with the question 'Are human beings rational?' (Eysenck & Keane, 2000). It is possible to identify several different forms of reasoning, including inductive, deductive and probabilistic. Each of these will be examined in turn.

Inductive reasoning

Inductive reasoning is the type of thinking which takes place when you arrive at a conclusion on the basis of some evidence (Manktelow, (1999). Detective work is based on inductive reasoning since it relies on the collection of evidence which is then put together to decide who is most likely to have committed the crime and to rule out people who are unlikely to have committed the crime. However, there is a potential problem with inductive reasoning, namely the conclusion cannot be guaranteed to be true. This is because the conclusion may be based on irrelevant evidence, new evidence may emerge after the decision has been arrived at, or the evidence could be biased in some way. Inductive reasoning involves a process of generating a general rule from a set of specific observations (Kahney, 1993).

Reflective Activity

Try to imagine you are a visitor from another planet and you decide to observe what happens to traffic at a junction with traffic lights. What rules might you arrive at concerning the relationship between the traffic lights and the movement of the traffic? This is an exercise in induction, since you are going from specific observations (for example, cars moving across the junction when the lights are green) to a general rule (for example, 'If the light is green, cars cross the junction').

Induction is a risky kind of reasoning because it is not always possible to observe every possible event, so you can never be completely certain that a rule will apply to every situation. For example, in the situation you considered in the above activity, it is possible that you came up with the rule 'If the light is red, cars stop'. However, as we all know, if you observe behaviour at traffic lights for a sufficiently long period of time, a car will break this rule and go through a set of red lights. But if you only observe for a short period of time, there could be no instances of cars going through red traffic lights. One of the main advantages of induction as a cognitive process is that it enables us to generate rules from our everyday experiences (Kahney, 1993).

Inductive reasoning has been investigated using **analogical reasoning** tasks. An **analogy** is when we identify a similarity between two quite different things, objects or events. Kahney (1993) uses the example of friend's child who said, 'Mowing the lawn is like giving the grass a haircut' to illustrate the way in which young children can reason using analogy.

Study

AIM *Gentner and Gentner (1983) aimed to investigate the effect of using different analogies in an inductive reasoning task.*

METHOD *The experiment used two groups of participants. Participants had to solve a physics problem based on electricity and resistors. Each of the groups was given a different analogy to represent the way in which electricity and resistors operate. The first group was told that the flow of electricity was like the movement of crowds of people and that a resistor was like a turnstile which only allowed one person to pass through at a time. The second group was told that the flow of electricity was like water flowing through a pipe and that a resistor could be thought of as a narrow section of pipe which produced a decrease in the flow of water.*

RESULTS *Participants who used the 'crowd' analogy performed better in solving the problems involving electricity and resistors.*

CONCLUSION *The analogy people use when they reason inductively can have a significant effect on their performance.*

Deductive reasoning

Deductive reasoning involves drawing logical conclusions from information that is given. It has been argued that deductive reasoning is necessary in order to develop plans, pursue arguments and negotiations, assess evidence and solve problems (Johnson-Laird & Byrne, 1991). One of the most common forms of deductive reasoning is called *conditional* (or *propositional*) *reasoning*.

Reflective Activity

Read the following information:

If it is raining, there are puddles on the pavement.
There are no puddles on the pavement.

Which of the following conclusions is valid?

1   *Therefore it is not raining.*

2   *Therefore it is raining.*

The above activity is an example of conditional reasoning. The information we are presented with tells us something about the relationship between different conditions. In this example, the conditions relate to rain and the presence of puddles on the pavement. In other words, **if** there are puddles on the pavement, **then** it is raining. This type of relationship between conditions is referred to as an 'if–then' relationship. Research investigating deductive reasoning in the form of 'if–then' relationships typically relies on the task you have just completed in this activity, i.e. presenting participants with information and asking them to determine whether or not the conclusion is valid. The answer to the activity is 1: there are no puddles, therefore it is not raining.

Deductive reasoning involves arriving at a conclusion from a set of assumptions. It starts with general principles or rules and applies them to specific instances. This is different from inductive reasoning, which draws conclusions based on specific observations

One of the most widely used problems in research investigating deductive reasoning is **Wason's** (1966) **selection task**. The standard Wason selection task is presented in Figure 11.7.

You are given this statement about the four cards. "If a card has a vowel on one side it has an even number on the other side." You are told that each of the four cards has a single number on one side and a single letter on the other. Your task is to decide which of the cards you need to turn over to test whether the rule is true or false.

Figure 11.7: The standard abstract Wason selection task

In the standard Wason's selection task, participants are presented with a conditional sentence of the form 'If-then'. But what is the answer? The only way to determine whether or not the statement is true or false is to look for cases that would falsify the statement. In other words, you need to look for a card with a vowel on one side and an odd number on the other side. (Note that a card with a consonant on one side and an even number on the other would not falsify the statement. This is because the rule refers to cards with a vowel on one side.) The important point here is that it is not possible to prove the rule by finding 'true' cases, it is only possible to disprove it by finding 'false' cases. Going through each card in turn, we need to check the 'E' card because if there is an odd number on the back, it would falsify the statement. We do not need to check the 'K' card, because whatever is on the other side, it will not disprove the rule. The same is true for the '4' card. If there is a vowel on the other side it confirms the rule, but does not disprove it, and if there is a consonant it does not disprove the rule either. The '7' card needs to be checked. If there is a vowel on the other side, it will disprove the statement. Therefore the two cards that need to be turned over to test whether or not the statement is true or false are the 'E' card and the '7' card (see Figure 11.8).

Card	Possible letter/number on reverse of card	Status of information
E	Even number	Confirms the rule
E	Odd number	Falsifies the rule
K	Even number	Irrelevant to the rule
K	Odd number	Irrelevant to the rule
4	Vowel	Confirms the rule
4	Consonant	Irrelevant to the rule
7	Vowel	Falsifies the rule
7	Consonant	Irrelevant to the rule

Figure 11.8: The status of the possible information on the reverse of cards in the Wason selection task

People have great difficulty selecting the correct cards in Wason's selection task. In fact, in many studies using the original form of Wason's selection task, none of the participants select the correct cards. Wason's (1966) original explanation was that people were making errors because they were attempting to find evidence which confirmed the rule rather than evidence which disproves it. A number of variations of Wason's selection task have been used, for example, a number of studies have investigated the effect of using different types of information on the cards.

Probabilistic reasoning

Probabilistic reasoning focuses on the way in which people make judgements about the probability, or likelihood, of particular events occurring. Try the following activity before you continue reading the rest of the section.

Reflective Activity

Imagine you have a coin with a head (H) on one side and a tail (T) on the other side. You toss it in the air six times. Which of the following outcomes is most likely?

1 *THHTHT*

2 *TTTHHH*

3 *HHHHTT*

Did you choose 1? Most people guess that Answer 1 is the most likely outcome because it looks random. We all know that tossing a coin should produce heads and tails randomly, so we choose the pattern which looks random. In fact, all three outcomes have exactly the same chance of occurring.

The above activity demonstrates one of the ways in which people make errors when they are reasoning about the probability of events occurring. Tversky & Kahneman (1974) proposed that when people are making judgements about probability, they rely on heuristics (rules of thumb or short-cuts for solving problems) to help themselves arrive at a solution. One of the advantages of heuristics is that they enable people to make quick and often efficient judgements. The drawback is that heuristics often result in people making judgements that are incorrect. Tversky and Kahneman identified a number of heuristics which people appear to use when making decisions about probability. The two most common are the **representativeness heuristic** and the **availability heuristic**.

- The representativeness heuristic is responsible for the choices people make when they are answering questions similar to the one in the above activity. According to the representativeness heuristic,

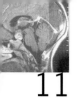

people ignore information about the probability of an event occurring. Instead, they make a judgement based on the extent to which the outcome represents what we consider to be a 'typical' outcome. In the example used in the activity, people incorrectly believe that outcomes that look 'random' are more likely to occur than outcomes that appear orderly.

● The availability heuristic refers to the way in which people make judgements about the frequency of an event occurring on the basis of how easy it is to recall. In other words, people assume that events they can easily recall are more common than events or occurrences that they find it more difficult to recall.

Evaluative Comment

Inductive reasoning enables us to reach conclusions that are probable, but not logically certain. When we use inductive reason, we are going beyond the evidence that we have available. Research into inductive reasoning has traditionally focused on category-learning tasks. As a result, there is an impressive body of research concerning the way in which people use inductive reasoning in the formation and use of categories. However, Mayer (1992) points out that the extent to which we can generalise from laboratory studies to the way in which people develop and use categories in everyday life is not clear. As a result, attention has shifted to investigating the way in which people use inductive reasoning in more natural situations. Deductive reasoning is a task that people find extremely difficult, especially when abstract materials are used. When attempting to use deductive reasoning to solve Wason's selection task, people often try to confirm the rule or hypothesis rather than trying to disprove it. However, their accuracy is improved when the task describes a concrete situation. Since the content of deductive reasoning tasks appears to have an effect on the extent to which people are able to solve it, some researchers have argued that induction and deduction are more closely related than has been thought (Rips, 1990). Unlike deductive and inductive reasoning, which rely on logic to explain the way in which people reason, probabilistic reasoning uses probability theory rather than logic. There is some evidence that the availability heuristic can occur in situations when parents are making decisions about whether or not to have their child vaccinated (Ritov & Baron, 1990). News stories about children who have an adverse reaction to reaction to a vaccine appear to be far more memorable than stories of children who suffer as a result of not being vaccinated. This could result in parents making the decision not to have their child vaccinated without considering the probabilities of different outcomes.

Representation of knowledge

Schemata and scripts

We have a lot of knowledge about our day-to-day lifestyles that we take for granted. For example, we know what is expected when it is someone's birthday and how to pay for a meal in a restaurant. We continually use this kind of everyday knowledge in our lives to help make decisions about what to do and to make sense of what is happening around us.

It has often been assumed that this generalised knowledge about situations and events is stored in the form of memory packages collectively referred to as **schemata** (*schemata* is the plural form; the singular is *schema*). For example, we may have a 'birthday schema' which represents the actions and activities associated with birthdays. We also have schemata that contain information about what we are likely to find in different types of shop. For example, in a baker's shop we would expect to find different kinds of bread, cakes, sandwiches, but we would not expect to find psychology textbooks, garden tools or clothes for sale. This schema-based knowledge ensures that we know what to expect when we go into a baker's shop to buy a loaf of bread. A schema is generalised knowledge about a situation or an event that has been acquired from past experience (Cohen, 1996).

It has been suggested that our everyday knowledge about the world is represented in the form of schemata. Schemata influence the way in which we encode information and also influence the way we remember events

Schemata influence the way in which we encode, interpret and store new information (Cohen, 1996). An important implication of this view is that it suggests that new experiences are not just copied directly into our memory. Our representation of events and experiences is actively constructed as a result of the interaction between our existing schemata-based knowledge and the new information we are currently encountering. If this is the case, then we would expect that information which is consistent with our pre-existing schemata will be remembered better than information that is irrelevant or unexpected.

Study

AIM *Brewer & Treyens (1981) set out to test the hypothesis that schemata-consistent information will be recalled better than schemata-inconsistent information.*

METHOD *Participants were asked to wait in a room for 35 seconds. They were then called into another room and given the unexpected task of recalling everything they had seen in the first room. The first room contained 61 objects and had been arranged to look like a student's study room. Some of the objects were schemata consistent; in other words, they were objects you would expect to find in such a room, such as a calendar, posters, a desk and chair. Other objects were schemata inconsistent, such as a skull and a piece of bark.*

RESULTS *Participants demonstrated good recall of schemata-consistent items. They also reported items, such as a telephone, which were not present in the room, but were consistent with the schemata. Unusual objects, such as the skull and piece of bark, were also recalled quite frequently.*

CONCLUSIONS *The results of this study show that people remember objects that are consistent with the currently active schemata. However, the study also shows that schemata-inconsistent items which are unusual or bizarre are also well remembered.*

A **script** is:

> 'a simple, well-structured sequence of events associated with a familiar activity'.
> (Matlin, 2002)

People have scripts for a variety of everyday activities, such as eating a meal in a restaurant, going to see the doctor, buying sweets in a shop and so on. The concept of scripts was developed by Schank & Abelson (1977) as a way of trying to understand how we make sense of language used in everyday situations. A script provides us with a set of expectations about what will happen next in a familiar situation. Schank & Abelson (1995) argue that scripts are useful for a variety of reasons. They make it easier to cope with complex situations; for example, we don't have to start from scratch to work out what to do every time we enter restaurant. All we need to know is the restaurant script (see Figure 11.9) and what part we play in it. Scripts also help us understand the behaviour of other people. If we know what script they are following, we can make sense of their actions with very little effort.

Like schemata, scripts change over time. When something new and different happens to us, this knowledge is incorporated into the appropriate script and schema. This means that although there will be similarities between your restaurant script and mine, there will also be differences which reflect our different experiences in restaurants. Schank & Abelson (1995) suggest that, in most situations, thinking means finding the correct script to use, rather than generating new ideas and solutions.

Evaluative Comment

Schema theories are very useful in situations where psychologists are trying to explain how people cope with complex situations and events (Markman, 1999). However, in many situations, schema often fail to operate as we would expect. For example, we often remember information that is inconsistent with our schemata, and we frequently recall the exact words of a passage of text (Matlin, 2002). One criticism of the research into schemata is that it has relied on information provided by the experimenter. Wynn and Logie (1998) argue that when people are recalling information from their actual experiences, they are more accurate than when the information is supplied by researchers. In Schank and Abelson's (1977) original model of scripts, it was assumed that every situation we experience in everyday life is represented in the form of a script which contains a fixed series of actions. There are two problems with this assumption. First, the number of scripts required to cope with the range of events and situations we experience would be enormous and a very uneconomical way of representing knowledge. For example, we would need a different script for every different type of restaurant and café. Second, the rigid structure of the scripts would make it very difficult to deal with novel and new situations, something that most of us deal with on a regular basis.

Script:	Restaurant
Roles:	Customer, waitress, chef, cashier
Goal:	To obtain food to eat
Subscript 1:	Entering
	move into restaurant
	look for empty tables
	decide where to sit
	move to table
	sit down
Subscript 2:	Ordering
	receive menu
	read menu
	decide what to eat
	give order to waitress
Subscript 3:	Eating
	receive food
	eat food
Subscript 4:	Leaving
	ask for bill
	receive bill
	give tip to waitress
	move to cashier
	pay bill
	leave restaurant

Figure 11.9: An example of a restaurant script (Based on Schank & Abelson, 1977)

Imagery

In psychology, an 'image' is a mental representation of something that is not physically present. Although it is possible to use imagery in all of our senses, the majority of research has focused on the characteristics and properties of visual images. Research into mental imagery is difficult to carry out because mental images are not directly observable and because they fade so quickly (Richardson, 1999). Shepard & Metzler (1971) developed a pioneering technique for investigating mental images. The basic task requires participants to mentally rotate a figure to determine whether or not it is the same as another figure that is presented at the same time.

Study

AIM *Cooper & Shepard (1973) aimed to investigate the way people use imagery in a mental-rotation task.*

METHOD *Participants were presented with a letter which had been rotated from the vertical position (Figure 11.10).*

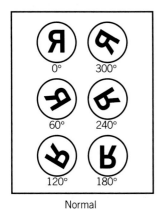
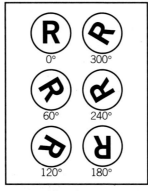

Normal   Mirror image

Figure 11.10: The different degrees of rotation performed on the letters in Cooper & Shepard (1973)

The letters were either in their normal form or a mirror-image. Participants had to decide whether the presented letter was either normal or a mirror-image. The dependent variable was reaction time.

RESULTS *The further the letter was rotated from the upright position, the longer participants took to make their decision (Figure 11.11).*

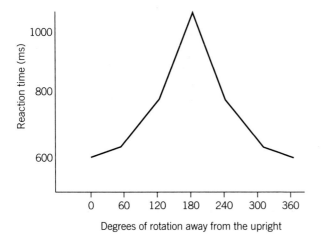

Figure 11.11: The mean time to decide whether the letter was in the normal or mirror-image orientation (From Cooper & Shepard, 1973)

CONCLUSION *Participants were using visual imagery to rotate the letters back to the upright position in order to make their judgement. Cooper & Shepard (1973) argued that these findings support the view that we use mental images in the same way as we would manipulate physical objects in the real world.*

The findings of Cooper & Shepard (1973) appear to suggest that people manipulate images in the same way as they manipulate physical objects. Finke (1989) uses the term *structural equivalence* to refer to this property of images. Structural equivalence is the idea that the structure of mental images corresponds to that of physical objects in the real world (Finke, 1989).

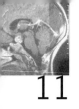

11 Evaluative Comment

Over the years, since the pioneering work of Shepard & Metzler (1971), there has been considerable debate over the nature of images. Pylyshyn (1973, 1984) has argued consistently that images are a superficial phenomena derived from a more basic representation of knowledge. Pylyshyn (1973) argued that knowledge is stored in the form of abstract concepts that represent the relationship between items. He used the term propositions *to refer to this form of knowledge and argued that it would be impossible to store information in the form of images because of the huge storage capacity required to store all the images people have (Matlin, 2002). Perhaps the most comprehensive model of the processes involved in generating and using mental imagery has been developed by Kosslyn (1980, 1994). Kosslyn (1980) argued that an image consists of two components. The first is a 'surface' representation which is responsible for our experience of having a picture-like mental image. This representation is held in an active memory store. The second component is a 'deep' representation, held in long-term memory, which is used to generate the surface representation. Kosslyn (1980) specified in detail the processes necessary to generate and transform images.*

Hierarchical model of concept organisation

The world we live in is an extremely complex environment. Every day, we encounter countless objects and events; if we did not have some way of organising this knowledge, everyday life would be impossible to deal with.

Reflective Activity

Think about what you have done in the last two hours. Imagine what it would be like if you remembered every single detail of every object and event you encountered during that time. Consider how much information you would have accumulated just in that short period of time.

One way to reduce the storage demands on our cognitive system is to try and avoid storing the same information more than once. For example, most of us will have encountered several different types of tree, such as oak, sycamore, elm, ash and so on. Although these trees are all different in some ways, for example, the shape of their leaves, they all have certain things in common, such as branches and an outer layer that we refer to as 'bark'. So rather than storing the information 'has bark' and 'has branches' with every single type of tree we know about, it is more economic to store this information only once at a higher level with the general concept of 'tree'. This is referred to as the principle of *cognitive economy* and it is achieved by dividing our environment into groups of things in order to reduce the amount of information we have to deal with (Collins & Quillian, 1969).

Collins & Quillian (1969) developed a model which incorporated the idea of cognitive economy. Their model was based on the notion that concepts and knowledge are organised in a hierarchical manner and is illustrated in Figure 11.12.

The dots in Figure 11.12 represent concepts such as 'bird' and 'canary'. The more inclusive a concept is, the higher it is located in the hierarchy, so 'animal' is located above 'bird' because the category 'bird' is a subset of 'animal'. Each concept has attributes associated with it, for example, the concept 'fish' has the attributes 'Has fins', 'Can swim' and 'Has gills'. One of the characteristics of Collins & Quillian's (1969) model is that it views our knowledge as highly organised and interrelated.

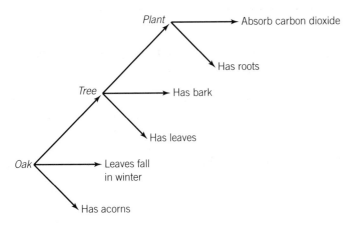

Figure 11.12: Hypothetical hierarchical model of concept organisation (Adapted from Collins & Quillian, 1969)

Study

AIM The aim of Collins & Quillian's (1969) study was to test their hierarchical model of concept organisation.

METHOD Participants were presented with true statements such as (1) 'Canaries can sing', (2) 'Canaries have feathers' and (3) 'Canaries have skin', and also false statements such as 'Apples have feathers'. The task for participants was to decide as quickly as possible whether or not the statement was true. The rationale was that participants would respond more quickly to statements where the information was stored closely together (see Figure 11.12). For example, the attribute 'can sing' is stored directly with the concept 'canary', whereas the attribute 'has feathers' is stored at the next level in the hierarchy and is therefore further away from the concept 'canary'. The attribute 'has skin' is common to all animals and is therefore stored at the highest level in the hierarchy, even further away from the concept 'canary'.

RESULTS The time taken to make judgements about statements similar to (1) was significantly faster than the time taken to make judgements about statements similar to (2), which in turn was significantly faster than the time taken to make judgements about statements similar to (3).

CONCLUSION The findings were taken to support Collins & Quillian's (1969) hierarchical model of concept organisation.

Collins & Quillian's (1969) model was extremely successful in that it stimulated a considerable amount of research. Some of this research began to produce some findings which were problematic for the model. For example, the model predicts that it should take longer to verify the statement 'A bear is an animal' than 'A bear is a mammal' because the concept 'animal' is further away from 'bear' than the concept 'mammal'. Rips *et al.* (1973) found exactly the opposite: it takes longer to verify 'A bear is a mammal'. It also became clear that it was easier to make judgements about some examples of a category more quickly than others, even though they were at the same level in the hierarchy. For example, responses to statements such as 'A robin is a bird' were faster than responses to 'A turkey is a bird' (Smith *et al.*, 1974). This is often referred to as the *typicality effect*. This is a problem for Collins & Quillian's (1969) model, which does not predict typicality effects.

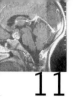

11 Evaluative Comment

Early models of concept organisation, such as Collins & Quillian (1969), assumed that once represen-
tations of concepts have been developed, they remain fairly static and unchanging. However, Barsalou
(1993) suggests that our representation of concepts develops and changes over time. This view is sup-
ported by the research of Johnson & Mervis (1997) on the changing nature of concepts as people
become experts. Barsalou (1993) points out that the way in which a concept is represented is influ-
enced by the context within which it appears. For example, under normal circumstances, Americans
regard a robin to be a more typical bird than a swan. However, if they are instructed to take the view-
point of someone who lives in China, Americans believe that a swan is a more typical bird than a robin
(Matlin, 2002).

See Appendix 1 for information concerning questions that appear in the examination paper. The assessment of knowledge and understanding (AO1) and analysis and evaluation (AO2) assessment objectives is also given in Appendix 1.

Sample questions

Sample question 1

(a) Describe what psychologists mean by *insight*. Use an example to illustrate your answer.

   (AO1 = 3)   *(3 marks)*

(b) Describe Vygotsky's ideas about the relationship between language and thought. Use an example to illustrate your answer.

   (AO1 = 2, AO2 = 1)   *(3 marks)*

(c) Describe what psychologists mean when they use the term *probabilistic reasoning*. Explain at least one type of error that people make when they are making decisions using probabilistic reasoning.

   (AO1 = 1, AO2 = 3)   *(4 marks)*

(d) Describe and discuss how script theory can account for everyday behaviour.

   (AO1 = 5, AO2 = 5)   *(10 marks)*

Total AO1 marks = 11 Total AO2 marks = 9 Total = 20 marks

Sample question 2

(a) Describe two features of Piaget's ideas about the relationship between language and thought.

   (AO1 = 2)   *(2 marks)*

(b) Using an example, describe what is meant by *cognitive styles*.

   (AO1 = 1, AO2 = 2)   *(3 marks)*

(c) Describe one study in which human reasoning was investigated. Indicate in your answer why the study was conducted, the method used, results obtained and the conclusions drawn.

   (AO1 = 5)   *(5 marks)*

(d) A psychologist carried out a study in which she was attempting to teach a chimpanzee to communicate with humans. She taught the chimpanzee to use sign language. The chimpanzee was able to make the sign for 'flower' when he was shown the picture of a flower.

   Using your knowledge of the characteristics of human language, discuss the extent to which the chimpanzee was using language to communicate.

   (AO1 = 4, AO2 = 6)   *(10 marks)*

Total AO1 marks = 12   Total AO2 marks = 8   Total = 20 marks

Sample question 3

(a) Describe one method that has been used to investigate mental imagery.

   (AO1 = 2)   *(2 marks)*

(b) Describe and explain one feature of the hierarchical model of concept organisation.

   (AO1 = 1, AO2 = 2)   *(3 marks)*

(c) Describe a communication system used in one non-human species.

   (AO1 = 5)   *(5 marks)*

(d) Discuss one advantage and one disadvantage of using inductive reasoning in everyday life.

(AO1 = 4, AO2 = 6) *(10 marks)*

Total AO1 marks = 12   Total AO2 marks = 8   Total = 20 marks

Questions, answers and comments

(a) Describe probabilistic reasoning and explain one type of error people can make when using it.

(AO1 = 1, AO2 = 2) *(3 marks)*

(b) Psychologists have argued that our knowledge about events and situations is stored in the form of *schemata*. Describe one study which has investigated schemata. In your answer, indicate why the study was conducted, the method used, results obtained and conclusions drawn.

(AO1 = 5) *(5 marks)*

(c) Identify two differences between convergent and divergent thinking styles.

(AO1 = 2) *(2 marks)*

(d) Discuss Whorf's theory of the relationship between language and thought.

(AO1 = 4, AO2 = 6) *(10 marks)*

Total AO1 marks = 12   Total AO2 marks = 8   Total = 20 marks

Answer to (a)

Probabilistic reasoning is when people are making judgements about the likelihood of something happening. People are not very good at probabilistic reasoning and they tend to make a lot of mistakes.

Comment

This answer would score one (AO1) out of the three marks. The mark would be awarded for correctly describing probabilistic reasoning. No AO2 marks would be awarded to this answer. The candidate has not presented any information about the types of errors people make when using probabilistic reasoning. Appropriate information here would include an explanation of one of the heuristics identified by Kahneman & Tversky (1974), such as 'availability' or 'representativeness'.

Answer to (b)

One of the predictions made by schemata theory is that information that is consistent with our schema will be remembered better. Brewer & Treyens (1981) carried out an experiment to test this hypothesis.

Method: *They asked participants to wait in room for a short time. They were then called into another room and given the unexpected task of recalling everything they had seen in the first room. In the first room, there were objects that had been placed there to make it look like a student's room. Some of the objects were consistent with a student's-room schema, other objects were inconsistent – like a skull.*

Results: *Participants remembered the schemata-consistent items very well. But they also recalled items, such as a telephone, that were not present in the room, but were consistent with the schemata. Unusual objects, such as the skull, were also recalled quite frequently.*

Conclusions: *The results of this study showed that people remember objects that are consistent with their schemata. But the study also shows that schemata-inconsistent items which are unusual or bizarre are also well remembered. This finding is a problem for schemata theory.*

Comment

This answer would score full marks. The answer has presented an appropriate study which is accurately described using the correct headings. When asked to describe a study, it is helpful to use the headings 'Aim', 'Method', 'Results' and 'Conclusions' as a way of presenting the information.

Answer to (c)

Divergent thinking is when you produce a lot of answers to a question like 'How many uses can you think of for a brick.' It is used in tests of creativity. Divergent thinkers try to produce lots of answers to a problem.

Comment

This answer would score one out of the two marks. It correctly identifies and describes divergent thinking, but does not present any information on convergent thinking. A better answer would have clearly identified the differences between convergent and divergent thinking. For example, divergent thinking involves producing lots of answers to problems, whereas convergent thinking focuses on producing the single, correct answer. Tests of intelligence tend to test convergent-thinking skills, whereas tests of creativity tend to test divergent-thinking skills.

Answer to (d)

Whorf's view was that our language determines the way we think. His ideas came from his work as an insurance claims engineer when he noticed that sometimes people seem to be misled by words that are used. For example, one fire was started when a worker threw a cigarette into an 'empty' drum of petrol. The drum didn't have any liquid petrol in, but was full of fumes which exploded when the cigarette was thrown in. Whorf said this happened because the worker was mislead by the word 'empty'. One study carried out to test Whorf's ideas presented participants with ambiguous drawings. One group saw the drawings with one set of labels and another group saw the same drawings with different labels.

After a delay, they were asked to recall the drawings. The drawings they produced were affected by the labels. So the group with the glasses label drew a picture that looked more like a pair of glasses than the original drawing, and the group with the dumbbells label drew something that looked more like a set of dumbbells. This study seemed to show that the language we use influences the way that we think and was used to support Whorf's ideas. Research using colours has also been used to test Whorf's ideas. Brown and Lennenberg used colours that were described using a single word (such as red, blue) and colours that were described using more than one word (light green, pale blue). They presented participants with the different colours and tested their recall. They found that the colours with one name were remembered better than the colours with more than one name. This was used to support the view that language influences thought because the names were affecting participants' ability to remember the colour. But more recently, research carried out by Heider found that some colours were easier to recall regardless of their name. Heider carried out research with people from New Guinea who have quite long names for some colours. Heider found that the name of the colour had no effect on how easy it was to remember the colour. This finding cast some doubt on Whorf's ideas.

The ideas of Whorf are the opposite to those put forward by Piaget on the relationship between language and thought. Piaget argued that thought comes before language. Piaget used his observations of the way in which language develops in children to support his ideas. He argued that young children use language to express their thoughts, and this develops through to adulthood. But there is very little research to support Piaget's ideas.

Comment

This is a good answer that would be awarded full marks. The answer provides an accurate description of Whorf's ideas and discusses some of the research that has been carried out to test his ideas. The answer also compares Whorf's ideas with those of another psychologist, Piaget. When questions ask you to 'discuss' a particular theory, it is usually a good idea to present an alternative theory. This enables you to compare and contrast different viewpoints. The answer also includes a drawing that makes it much easier to understand the study which is being discussed.

Sample questions, answers and comments

11 Further reading

Introductory texts

Roth, I. (ed.) (1990), *Introduction to Psychology* (Vols 1 & 2, Chapters 7 & 13), Hove, Psychology Press

Scott, P. & Spencer, C. (1998), *Psychology: A Contemporary Introduction* (Chapters 9 & 10), Oxford, Blackwell

Westen, D. (2002), *Psychology: Mind, Brain & Culture* (Chapters 6 & 7), New York, John Wiley & Sons

Specialist sources

Cohen, G. (1996), *Memory in the Real World*, Hove, Psychology Press

Eysenck, M.W. & Keane, M.T. (2000) *Cognitive Psychology: A Student's Handbook*, Hove, Psychology Press

Garnham, A. & Oakhill, J. (1994), *Thinking and Reasoning*, Oxford, Blackwell

Harley, T.A. (1995), *The Psychology of Language: From Data to Theory*, Hove, Psychology Press

Manketlow, K. (1999), *Reasoning and Thinking*, Hove, Psychology Press

Matlin, M.W. (2002), *Cognition*, Orlando, Harcourt College Publishers

Richardson, J.T.E. (1999), *Imagery*, Hove, Psychology Press

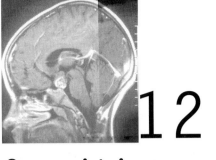

12

Cognition and Law

Introduction

Many of us have been embarrassed when we have bumped into someone we used to know long ago and can't recall where we know them from or what they are called. We've all had the peculiar experience of meeting someone in a place where we wouldn't normally see them, like meeting a teacher on holiday, and not recognising them instantly as we would normally do if we saw them at school or college. Just occasionally, when someone disagrees with you about who said what to whom, you might begin to doubt yourself and wonder whether what you think happened really did happen. Most of these everyday memory problems are quite common and happen to all of us at some time, but some people experience special difficulties if they suffer from serious memory problems like **amnesia**. Cognition and Law is an area of applied psychology and is all about how aspects of cognitive psychology relate to real life. The topic area is divided into two sub-sections: *Face Recognition and Eyewitness Testimony* and *Amnesia and Recovered False Memories*.

Face recognition

Processes involved in face recognition

Remembering and recognising faces is an essential skill we use every day. Although most of the studies in this chapter involve recognition of 'faces', rarely in real life do we identify someone from just their face. Information about people's clothes, voice, mannerisms and where we usually meet them all help the identification process. Sometimes we struggle to recognise someone because the person is not wearing their usual type of clothes or because they are in an unexpected context.

Cohen (1989) distinguishes between:

● Face identification: looking at a person's face and knowing who it is;

● Face recognition: recognising the face as one we have seen before;

● Face recall: when, from memory, we try to verbally describe a face, draw a face or form a 'mental image' of the face.

Practical Activity

Find some photographs of famous people. Pick some who are very famous and some who are less so. Show them to people and:

● *ask them to identify the faces;*

● *if they can't identify them, ask if they have seen the person in the photograph before, and if they know anything about them;*

- *put the photographs away and ask them to write a description of one of the faces;*
- *compare these descriptions to see if they are similar and how well they describe the face.*

The above activity shows the difference between identification, recognition and recall. Sometimes we recognise the face and know something about the person, but cannot name them. This tells us something about the processes involved in face recognition. Putting the stored mental image of a face into words for the description shows how difficult it is to convert the stored 'whole' into a list of 'features'.

Study

Aim *Bahrick (1984) set out to show that face recognition tends to be better if the materials used are more realistic.*

Method *Participants looked at twenty target faces for five seconds each and were later tested on their ability to pick out the target faces from distracters. In a more realistic version of the same study, they studied another twenty target faces, but this time the faces were those of their classmates. The distracter faces were non-classmates, but students from the same university.*

Results *The original test showed 29 per cent correct recognitions and the classmates condition showed 38 per cent.*

Conclusion *The results indicated significant improvement in recognition in ecologically valid conditions. This brings into question results from many other studies in which researchers used photographs of strangers in an attempt to control the experiment.*

Evaluative Comment

This study illustrates a problem with face-recognition research and cognitive research in general. For control purposes, researchers like to use materials that have no personal meaning to participants, but this means that the findings may not tell us how the behaviour happens in real life. Face recognition research is often laboratory based, using time-controlled exposure and a front view of a motionless face. In real life, faces are moving and at different angles. In addition, real-life encounters involve a range of social, emotional and motivational factors.

Two fairly general findings from studies of face recognition are that people are better at recognition than identification, and that the ability to recognise faces deteriorates over time. Bahrick (1984) used a sample of teachers to investigate differences in recognition and identification at various time intervals. Teachers were asked to recognise/identify faces of present and former students when they were shown sets of five faces, four of which were distracters. Their tasks were to a) identify the known student from the set (recognition task), and b) name the student (identification task). As shown in Figure 12.1 below, recognition was better than identification, but in general, memory for faces deteriorated over time.

	Time period between exposure and identification		
Type of task	11 days	1 year	8 years
Recognition task	69	47.5	26
Identification task	35.5	6	0

Figure 12.1: Table showing percentage of correct responses

Explanations for face recognition

Feature-analysis theory

Feature-analysis theory is an example of a bottom-up theory in which it is suggested that analysing individual features is the most important factor in face recognition. According to bottom-up theory, the visual cues from the face we are currently viewing are the most important information for recognition, and so we would need to focus on the detail of the face, analysing the separate features closely. Visual cues would include the way the light and shade appear on the face and the texture of the hair and skin. All these visual cues combine to enable us to perceive the broader features of the face like the shape of the nose and mouth.

Look back at the descriptions you obtained in the activity on page 319 and you will see they are mostly lists of features. There may be other information, too, for example 'it's a friendly face', but much of the description will consist of features. Shepherd, Davies & Ellis (1981) investigated how features are used in free-recall descriptions by showing participants some faces of people they had never seen before for a brief period of time. Participants were then asked to describe from memory the faces they had been shown. In describing these unfamiliar faces, the features most often referred to were: hair, eyes, nose, mouth, eyebrows, chin and forehead (in that order). This research suggests that faces of unfamiliar people tend to be recalled using the main features of the face.

Ellis *et al.* (1979) discovered that descriptions of unfamiliar faces focus more on external facial features such as hair, face shape, etc., whereas we tend to use internal features when recalling faces of familiar people. Obviously external features are more noticeable, particularly from a distance. However, they are also more likely to change, as when people dye or cut their hair, so internal features are probably more reliable for long-term recognition.

External features are more likely to change

Practical Activity

● *Using the written descriptions of faces from the activity on page 319, count the number of times different features have been used to see whether the results are similar to those of Shepherd, Davies and Ellis. Which features appear most frequently and which are rarely mentioned?*

● *Investigate the importance of internal and external features for recognition using photographs of famous people. Get two copies of the same photographs and on one, obscure the external features like hair and jaw line. For the other, obscure internal facial features like nose, eyes and mouth. Now see if people can identify the faces. Use different participants for each set of pictures.*

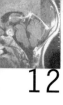

12 Evaluative Comment

Think about the above activity and consider the problem with this and other studies using photographs of famous people. It is hard to find photographs of people who are equally familiar to everyone. Sample variables can be important; for example, younger participants would more easily recognise people from certain TV programmes, and sporty people would be better at recognising sports personalities.

Holistic-form theory

Holistic-form theory is an alternative to the feature-analysis approach. Although visual cues and facial features are important in describing faces and must have a role in face recognition, relying just on bottom-up processing for such a complex activity is unlikely. Bruce & Young (1986) proposed a top-down approach, suggesting that recognising a face requires stored semantic and emotional information, and is more complex than simply adding together a set of features. For example, when we see someone in the street, we would need to refer back to previously stored information about where we know the person from in order to say that we have recognised them fully.

According to the holistic approach, a face is recognised as a whole, analysing the relationship between features, feelings aroused by the face and semantic information about the person. Ellis (1975) suggests we have a stored template or pattern for the face of each person we know, and when presented with a face, we try to match this stimulus to our mental pattern. Young & Hay (1986) demonstrated the importance of layout or configuration in the processing of faces. Pictures of famous faces were cut in half horizontally, and participants' recognition of the people in the two separate halves was tested. These halves were then combined together in non-matching pairs and participants were asked to name the person in each half. It was found that recognition time from the halves was much longer when two were put together. Apparently, recognition was difficult because the two halves combined seemed to produce an entirely new holistic face, making it harder to recognise the separate halves. This demonstrates that visual cues and features are not the only important information for recognition, as the overall layout of the face is equally, if not more important.

It is more difficult to recognise the people in the two halves of face (c) in Figure 12.2 than it is to recognise the two halves shown independently ((a) and (b)).

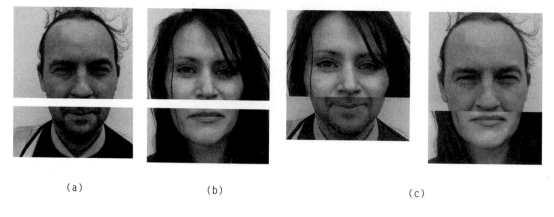

(a)　　　　　　(b)　　　　　　(c)

Figure 12.2: Young & Hay (1986) demonstrated the importance of configuration by making up a composite face from two original faces.

Similar research involves changing the layout of faces in other ways, either by scrambling the facial features or by inverting the face as shown in Figure 12.3.

Haig (1984) showed how recognition times increased for faces of famous people where the spacing between features was altered, and Yin (1969) found that upside-down or inverted faces are much harder to recognise. Cohen (1989) suggests this shows that faces:

'are normally recognised holistically, and inversion destroys the global pattern relationships between features.'

Such findings seem to support the holistic approach to face recognition.

Figure 12.3: It takes longer to identify faces that are shown upside down because the pattern of the features is changed

Practical Activity

Try your own versions of the scrambled-face and inverted-face studies using photographs or computer images.

* **Scrambled faces:** *Get two identical photographs/images then alter one for the experimental condition and keep the other for the control condition. Cut the photo into three bands across the face: eyes, nose and mouth areas. These can then be swapped around and pasted onto card. Time how long it takes participants to identify the normal and scrambled faces.*

* **Inverted faces:** *Paste the photographs/images onto a card and present either the correct way up or upside down. For a set of eight or ten faces you could measure the overall identification time. You might need to set an upper time limit, just in case participants really can't recognise one of the faces at all. Alternatively, you could just record the number of correct identifications in a given time.*

Further support for a holistic model of face recognition comes from studies comparing recognition and recall. People are usually better at recognising faces seen before than they are at recalling them.

Study

Aim *Ellis et al. (1975) aimed to show the difficulties involved in verbally recalling faces.*

Method *Participants were shown six photographs of male faces for ten seconds and were asked immediately to recall the face so that it could be reconstructed using photofit materials. Judges then attempted to pick out the target face from the photofit reconstructions.*

Results *Only 12.5 per cent of identifications were correct, indicating that the reconstructed faces were not much like the original stimulus.*

Conclusion *To describe a face, we must convert our stored mental image of it into words, which is a difficult and not very effective process, as this study shows, suggesting we probably store faces as wholes rather than as sets of features.*

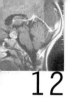

12   Evaluative Comment

*Consider how eyewitnesses help police to identify suspects. One method is to produce a list of features from a verbal description, and then make up a **photofit** (or e-fit). Davis et al. (1978) found most participants had difficulty producing a photofit likeness even when the real face was in front of them! When new participants were asked to match photofit efforts to the originals, their performance was only slightly better than would have happened by chance. Woodhead et al. (1979) evaluated the use of component features in face recognition by looking at the effectiveness of a feature-based face recognition training course. Participants spent three days learning to recognise features like 'full mouth', 'thin mouth', etc. and then took part in recognition tests of full faces. In one task where participants had to identify a 'wanted criminal' from 240 other faces, the feature training resulted in inferior performance. If faces are stored as features, then training in feature analysis and recognition should help recognition of whole faces. This research seems to indicate faces are stored as wholes and not as sets of features.*

Recognition disorders

Clinical studies provide intriguing insights into the processes involved in face recognition (Ellis & Shepherd, 1992). **Prosopagnosia** is a rare disorder where patients lose the ability to recognise familiar human faces. In extreme cases, they cannot even recognise their own reflection. Sufferers describe how they get the emotional feeling of recognition, but have no conscious awareness of knowing the person.

In **Capgras syndrome**, patients experience the delusion that 'doubles' have replaced people they know. Capgras syndrome is almost the opposite of prosopagnosia, as Capgras patients experience cognitive recognition, but have no sense of emotional recognition. In a case reported by Hirstein & Ramachandran (1997), a Capgras patient (DS) was shown pictures of strangers and of his mother whilst he was attached to GSR machine (a device which records minute changes in surface moisture of the skin). Normally, when we see someone we recognise, the surface moisture of our skin increases; but although the patient stated that the picture of his mother was a person who looked exactly like his mother, he was quite certain that it was not her and did not show the usual sweat response that comes with emotional recognition. In fact, his response to the photograph of his mother was just the same as his response to the pictures of strangers.

Clinical evidence suggests face recognition is an extremely complex activity involving both cognitive and emotional processes. Cases show how face recognition cannot rely just on features, as prosopagnosics and Capgras sufferers can name and describe individual features of familiar faces. This and other evidence points to a more holistic model of face recognition.

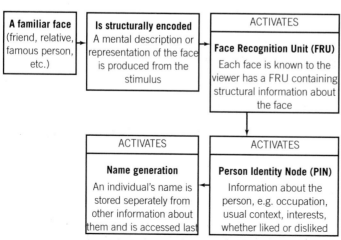

Figure 12.4: A holistic model of face recognition (Adapted from Bruce & Young, 1986)

According to Bruce & Young (1986), a face is firstly encoded structurally, meaning we take in the visual information, processing the look of the face. If this matches an existing **Face Recognition Unit** (FRU), then this will be activated. The FRU contains physical information and semantic knowledge. Activation of the FRU triggers activation of the **Person Identity Node** (PIN), giving personal information such as occupation, interests, where we normally meet the person and whether we like them or not. The final stage in the process is name generation. According to Bruce and Young, names are stored separately to the FRUs and PINs, but can only be accessed via the PIN. This would explain the embarrassing experience of knowing lots about a person we meet, but not being able to think of their name.

Study

Aim *Young, Hay & Ellis (1985) set out to test the holistic model.*

Method *Participants kept a daily diary of problems in face recognition. These were then analysed for content.*

Results *Out of 1,008 incidents, there were no reports of naming someone without knowing other information about them. In 190 cases, the opposite occurred; for example, occupation was known, but not the person's name. In 233 cases, participants reported experiencing familiarity, but nothing else.*

Conclusion *The findings support the sequence proposed by the holistic model whereby names can only be accessed if semantic information has been accessed first. The 233 cases where familiarity was experienced without full recognition would be times where a FRU has been triggered, but the PIN has failed to activate, again supporting the sequence proposed by Bruce and Young.*

Practical Activity

Keep a diary about face- or person-recognition events. Consider your recognition experiences when you encounter people you have not seen for some time, like someone from your old school. Do you recognise them instantly, or do you have to work at it? Do you feel you know the person, but don't know anything about them? Do you remember their name?

Evaluative Comment

Evidence from diary studies, laboratory research and clinical case histories supports the Bruce and Young model, suggesting that:

* *information about familiar faces is accessed in a sequence;*
* *the sequence of events is in the order indicated by the model;*
* *faces are analysed as wholes rather than as separate features.*
* *Face recognition is complex and involves emotion as well as cognition.*

However, the model has been criticised, particularly over the lack of information about recognition of unfamiliar faces.

Eyewitness testimony

How accurately can people recall events they have witnessed? As early as 1895, J.M. Cattell reported a study indicating poor recall for frequently observed events. In one study, Cattell asked

12

his students about the previous week's weather. Although it had snowed, only seven of the 56 responses mentioned snow.

Studies involving memory for everyday objects also show very poor recall. Nickerson & Adams (1979) asked participants to draw a US penny piece from memory and found that, on average, only three of the eight critical features of the coin were recalled correctly, and these were often incorrectly located.

French & Richards (1984) asked participants to draw a clock face from memory and found that the Roman numeral IIII was incorrectly shown as IV in most drawings (see Figure 12.5).* These studies illustrate how existing schemas can influence our memory for everyday items.

Figure 12.5: Participants usually draw the four as IV, instead of IIII, as it usually appears on clocks

In a famous study, Bartlett (1932) showed that human memory is not just a factual recording of what has occurred, but that we make 'effort after meaning'. By this, Bartlett meant that we try to fit what we remember with what we already know and understand about the world. As a result, we quite often change our memories so they become more sensible to us. Bartlett was especially interested in how memories could be distorted by existing knowledge about the world. His participants heard a story and had to tell the story to another person and so on, like a game of 'Chinese Whispers'. The story was a North American folk tale entitled 'The War of the Ghosts'. When asked to recount the detail of the story, each person seemed to recall it in their own individual way, although there were consistent tendencies. With repeated telling, the passages became shorter, puzzling ideas were rationalised or omitted altogether and details were changed to become more familiar and conventional. For example, the information about the ghosts was often omitted as it was difficult to explain, whilst participants frequently recalled the idea of 'not going because he hadn't told his parents where he was going' because that situation was a familiar one. From this research, Bartlett concluded that memory is not exact and is distorted by our existing schema, or what we already know about the world.

Practical Activity

Wait for a big news story to appear and make detailed notes as you hear it at the time. Then ask people about the story the next day, some days later and then in two weeks' time.

Write down their versions of the story each time and compare them, both with the original and with each other. Are people making 'effort after meaning' as Bartlett suggested?

These findings suggest memory for events and objects is active and reconstructive, meaning that we reconstruct the details based on existing knowledge. For example, if we hear the sentence 'The bottle was broken during the pub fight', we might assume that the bottle was a beer bottle because we would expect to find a beer bottle in a pub rather than a milk bottle. This process of adjusting memories to fit with expectations, beliefs and stereotypes is known as confabulation.

* Although the Roman numeral for four is usually represented as IV, clock faces are the exception, as the four is always represented as IIII, apparently as a symmetrical balance for the VIII (eight) on the opposite side.

Evaluative Comment

*Cases of miscarriages of justice on the basis of **eyewitness testimonies** which later turn out to be incorrect have been reported. Loftus (1979) describes the case of the Sawyer brothers who were arrested for a store robbery in 1975. Both men denied the offence, but at the trial the store manager identified them and they were convicted. The real culprit later confessed, and the Sawyers were released. The jury relied on the eyewitness testimony despite a lot of contradictory evidence.*

In 1976, the Devlin Committee investigated all the identification parades held in England and Wales in 1973. They found that:

- 45 per cent of ID parades led to a suspect being identified;
- 82 per cent of those identified were later convicted.

In many cases, eyewitness identification was the only evidence, but even then 74 per cent were convicted.

The Devlin Committee recommended that juries do not convict on the strength of a single eyewitness testimony alone, so miscarriages of justice, as in the case of the Sawyer brothers above, would be much less likely to occur today. Since the Devlin Report (1976), less weight is given to single eyewitness identifications, and other sources of evidence are expected to be used to support the eyewitness report.

Factors affecting the reliability of eyewitness accounts

Psychologists have identified a number of factors about witnesses themselves, or about the situation, which can affect the **reliability** of eyewitness recall. Five factors will be considered here, although several other factors are also supported by research and may be reported in various other textbooks.

Context

In most cases, the surroundings at the time of testimony are different to the surroundings in which the initial event was witnessed. Much laboratory research on memory indicates that recall is better if participants are in the same context as when the information was encoded, and specific eyewitness research seems to show the same effect.

Study

AIM *Malpass & Devine (1981) set out to investigate the role of context in recall of events.*

METHOD *Participants were shown an act of vandalism and interviewed about the event five months later. Participants in one group were given cues in the form of information about what day it was, details about the room and the immediate reactions of people as they witnessed the event. Participants in the control group were given no contextual information.*

RESULTS *The group given information about the context had significantly better recall than the control group.*

CONCLUSION *Giving information about the context aids recall of events. This finding could be linked to the retrieval failure explanation for forgetting, according to which information is stored but not always accessible without the relevant cues (see Chapter 10).*

Use of questions

In a famous series of studies in the 1970s, Loftus *et al.* (1974) found that a witness's memory for events could be significantly distorted at interview in a number of ways:

- **Leading questions** can influence recall, showing that suggestion by the power of language can extensively alter what we remember of an event.

- Non-existent items can be inserted into memory so that if a person is asked 'Did you see *the* knife?' rather than 'Did you see *a* knife?', they are more likely to believe there was a knife just because of the use of the word 'the' in the sentence.

- Memories can be transformed by deleting and replacing information, so that events that did happen are forgotten and events that didn't happen are 'recalled'.

Study

AIM *To explore the influence of question-wording on memory for events.*

METHOD *Loftus (1975) showed two groups of participants a film of a car accident and then asked the following questions:*

Control group: 'How fast was the white sports car going when it passed the stop sign?'

Experimental Group: 'How fast was the white sports car going when it passed the barn while travelling along the country road?'

In the film, the car did pass a stop sign, but there was no barn.

RESULTS *Seventeen per cent of the participants who had been exposed to the false information in the 'misled group' reported seeing a barn, whereas less than three per cent in the control group made this mistake.*

CONCLUSION *A non-existent item – the barn – had been inserted into the witnesses' memories for the film, suggesting that participants had indeed been influenced by the wording of the question. If this is possible in an experiment, where people probably know beforehand that they are likely to be asked to recall the information, then the effect of leading questions is even more likely to apply in real-life situations. Real witnesses' recall for people, items and events could be affected by the way they are questioned by the police and members of the legal profession, just as Loftus's participants were.*

Practical Activity

Imagine you have seen a car crash. Would it make any difference to your memory for the event if you were asked 'How fast were the cars going when they smashed into each other?' rather than 'How fast were the cars going when they hit each other?'? In a study by Loftus & Palmer (1974), the average speed estimates for 'smashed' were 40.8 mph and for 'hit' 34 mph. Make a list of other words you could use instead of 'smashed' and 'hit' and see if you can decide what the estimates of speed might be when your words are used in the questions.

Evaluative Comment

Several factors have been found to limit the influence of leading questions on our memory for events. For example, where misleading information is quite clearly and obviously incorrect, it tends to have no effect on a witness's memory. The importance of the detail also seems to matter, such that less crucial details are more easily distorted than critical facts. Thus, in a report of a robbery, it would be easier to distort the detail about the item that was stolen than to distort the information about the look of the robber.

Emotion/stress

Clifford & Scott (1978) found that people who saw a film of a violent attack remembered fewer of the 40 items of information about the event than a control group who saw a less violent, less stressful version. As witnessing a real crime is probably much more stressful than taking part in an experiment, memory accuracy may well be even more affected in real life. Loftus (1979) refers to an effect, now known as **weapon focus**, where a witness's attention is drawn to the weapon in a crime scene, so they recall few other details.

However, a study by Yuille & Cutshall (1986) showed that witnesses of a real-life incident had remarkably accurate memories of a stressful event involving weapons. A thief stole guns and money, but was shot six times and died. The police interviewed witnesses, and thirteen of them were re-interviewed five months later. Recall was found to be accurate, even after a long time, and the two misleading questions inserted by the research team had no effect.

Evaluative Comment

The Yuille and Cutshall study illustrates three important points.

- *First, there are cases of real-life recall where memory for an emotional event is accurate, even some months later.*

- *Second, misleading questions need not have the same effect as has been found in laboratory studies.*

- *Third, contrary to some research, 'weapon focus' does not always affect recall.*

Age

It is generally believed that children make less reliable eyewitnesses than adults, and there has been much research in this area.

Study

AIM *Marin et al. (1979) set out to test age differences in children's and young adults' memory for events.*

METHOD *Children of primary-school age, junior-school age, senior-school age and college students viewed a fifteen-second scene where an adult male in a distressed state entered the room. Participants were tested on their memory for the person and the event immediately afterwards and again two weeks later.*

RESULTS *Recall of both correct and incorrect material increased with age, but, crucially, there was no significant difference in accuracy of identification, ability to answer specific questions and influence of leading questions.*

CONCLUSION *Although younger children seem to recall less general information about an event, recall of key information is no worse in younger children. Findings from this type of study might be used to inform court proceedings where children are called to give evidence, and may be relevant to the discussion about false memories on pages 338–343.*

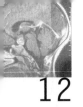

How well do you recall
events from your childhood?

Evaluative Comment

Reviewing data from studies of pre-school children, Fivush & Shukat (1995) conclude that 'very young children are able to give accurate, detailed accounts of their personal experiences, even after extended periods of time'. However, they caution against generalising these results to the courtroom for three reasons.

- *Laboratory studies involve recall of emotionally positive events, like holidays and birthdays, rather than the kind of event an eye witness must recall.*

- *In research studies, the children are not overly encouraged to recall, unlike child witnesses who may be put under much greater pressure.*

- *Researchers are careful not to use leading questions, whereas leading questioning would probably be a factor in real-life testimony.*

Practical Activity

Students with younger brothers, sisters or cousins might like to ask what they remember of a specific event. Choose something pleasant they will enjoy talking about, such as a birthday party or a day out. Look at the following:

- *Content: what information do they remember best? Is it people, objects, actions?*

- *Consistency: do they recall the same information each time you ask them?*

- *Coherence: do they put memories into context, for example, do they explain about who was present at certain events and who those people are?*

At the other end of the age spectrum, we might expect older people to give less accurate eyewitness accounts. Indeed, many laboratory studies show a decline in memory ability from the age of about 60 years. However, some studies actually show that older people have better memories than younger participants. See page 336 on age-related amnesia.

Stereotyping

Studies show that eyewitness accounts often reflect commonly held stereotypes. Baddeley (1982) found that errors are more likely to occur when the suspect is of a different race to the witness, perhaps due to racial stereotypes, or perhaps because we do not attend to distinctive features of people from other races. The influence of racial stereotyping on memory for events was demonstrated by Howitt (1991), who presented participants with a story as follows:

> 'The time was 5.30 p.m., the underground train was overcrowded as usual ... Two men of different ethnic origins were standing up facing each other; one of them had an open, double-edged knife and a newspaper in his hand ... In the struggle to get in and out of the train, a passenger stepped on the foot of one of the men. A fight ensued ...'

Howitt found that participants' recollections revealed distortions based on stereotypical racist assumptions. For example, one report stated 'there were two black men there. One was carrying a rolled-up newspaper with a knife partly hidden ...' In this case, it seems that memory was distorted by racial stereotypes. Gender stereotyping also affects memory, as demonstrated by Gruneberg (1992), who found witnesses to a bag-snatch incident frequently reported that the thief was male, even though it had been a female who had snatched the bag.

How might recall of events be improved?

Findings concerning the reliability of eyewitness accounts have led researchers to attempt to devise methods for improving retrieval. One of these is the **cognitive interview**, proposed by Fisher & Geiselman (1992). This involves four procedures which have been found to enhance eyewitness accounts of events:

- The interviewer mentally reinstates the context of the crime for the witness, perhaps by asking them about their general activities and feelings on the day.

- Witnesses are encouraged to report every detail of the event, however unimportant the information might seem. In this way, apparently unimportant detail might act as a trigger for key information about the event.

- Witnesses are asked to recount the incident in a different order. For example, the person might be asked 'What happened just *before* the robber shouted at the bank cashier?'

- Witnesses are asked to report from different perspectives, describing what they think other witnesses might have seen.

Study

AIM *Geiselman et al. (1985) set out to investigate the effectiveness of the cognitive interview.*

METHOD *Participants viewed a film of a violent crime and, after 48 hours, were interviewed by a policeman using one of three methods: the cognitive interview; a standard interview used by the Los Angeles police; or an interview using hypnosis. The number of facts accurately recalled and the number of errors were recorded.*

RESULTS *The mean number of correctly recalled facts for the cognitive interview was 41.2; for the hypnosis condition was 38.0 and in the standard interview was 29.4. In addition, no significant difference in the number of incorrect responses was found.*

CONCLUSION *The cognitive interview leads to better memory for events, with witnesses able to recall more relevant information than when the interviews are conducted in the traditional way. Of course, it is very important that any interview technique does not increase the tendency for people to recall more incorrect information, and the usefulness of the cognitive interview was further demonstrated in a follow-up study which showed that people were less likely to be misled by false information when the cognitive interview was being used.*

12 Amnesia - types of memory deficit

Amnesia refers to some form of memory failure and can have a variety of causes. Memory loss is usually fairly specific, rather than a general forgetfulness. Most patients with selective amnesia show normal intelligence and short-term memory span, but have impaired recall and recognition for facts and events experienced either before or after the critical brain damage (Mayes 1992).

Retrograde amnesia refers to loss of memory for events before an incident.

Anterograde amnesia refers to loss of memory for events after an incident – often such cases are examples of what are known as *pure amnesiacs*.

Pure amnesia is a term usually used to refer to cases of anterograde amnesia where patients suffer severe, dense memory loss but without general intellectual impairment.

Retrograde amnesia

Retrograde amnesia refers to memory loss extending back in time, usually from a brief period of unconsciousness, for example where a person cannot recall events immediately before a car accident or where a child cannot remember events leading up to a fall from a tree. On recovering consciousness, the patient may have retrospective memory loss for events extending back several months or years, but most memories are gradually restored as time goes by after the accident. Quite often, however, people suffer permanent loss of memory for the few minutes and seconds just before the incident. So, for example, an accident victim might make a full recovery, but never be able to recall the moments just before the accident.

Common-sense explanations for retrograde amnesia suggest that the person deliberately forgets because it would be too upsetting to know the details, or that the person does not attend to the information just immediately before the injury. Baddeley (1982) does not accept these explanations. First, they don't explain why only cases involving concussion lead to such memory loss. Second, there is evidence to show that the memory loss is not due to failure to take in the information leading up to the event.

Study

Aim *To investigate the effects of concussion on memory loss.*

Method *Yarnell & Lynch (1970) carried out a field study of American footballers who had been con-cussed during a game. As soon as they came round, they were asked about the details of play at the time of the incident and asked again between three and twenty minutes later.*

Results *When asked immediately, they gave accurate information; however, when asked between three and twenty minutes after regaining consciousness, they could give no information about the play just before the accident.*

Conclusion *The blows to the head received by the players led to a disruption of the consolidation process needed to make a memory trace permanent. Failure to recall events from before concussion cannot be due to a failure to take in the information in the first place, as it was available for recall immediately after regaining consciousness.*

Anterograde amnesia

Patients with anterograde amnesia often show normal memory for events before the incident responsible for the memory deficit, but have trouble recalling information about events occurring after the incident. Whereas with retrograde amnesia there is almost always a gradual restoration of most of the lost information, with anterograde amnesia there is quite often no such recovery. The case which led to the discovery of anterograde amnesia is that of HM (Milner *et al.*, 1968).

A case of anterograde amnesia

HM had brain surgery in 1953 when he was 27 years old to reduce symptoms of epilepsy. As a side effect, he suffered serious memory loss. His short-term memory was normal, but he was completely unable to transfer new information into his long-term memory. He showed almost no knowledge of current affairs, because he forgot news items as soon as he had read them; he knew nothing of recent family events, including moving house and the death of his father. He could remember people from long ago, but could not store information about new people he met. Generally, HM seemed cognitively 'normal', as he was able to use perceptual and motor skills.

This case and others (Gross, 1996; Baddeley, 1994) illustrate the selective nature of the problems of anterograde amnesia following brain damage. Some abilities, such as learning new information, are severely impaired, whilst others, including language and memory span, are quite normal.

Reflective Activity

Think what it must be like to be HM. How would it affect your life? What would it be like to come to school or college, and how would you cope at home? Would you still be able to travel on the bus or train? Would you be able to prepare a meal or speak to your friends on the telephone? How would you pass the time? Thinking about these things enables us to at least partly understand what it must be like to live with such a disability.

Pure amnesia

Pure amnesia is the term given to a condition of dense memory impairment in which there is no general intellectual difficulty. Patients often suffer from anterograde amnesia following surgery, like HM, and in all such cases described, the patient has apparently suffered damage to both sides of the temporal lobes in the brain and possibly to other brain structures.

Pure amnesiacs appear entirely normal in their speech and social behaviours. They can have a conversation about their early life quite easily and often use strategies to hide their problem. They might have a store of useful conversational phrases so they can hide the fact that they have no real knowledge of the content of the conversation. For example, when asked about a news item, the person might say 'Well of course, it's all bad news these days, isn't it?'. However, if asked a direct question like 'What did you have for breakfast this morning?' or 'When did we last meet?', they would not be able to answer.

Evaluative Comment

Pure amnesiacs seem completely unable to learn anything following the brain-damage incident. However, sometimes they can learn but not be consciously aware of their learning. Clarapede, a Swiss psychiatrist, related the tale of how he hid a pin in his hand when he shook hands with an amnesiac patient on his hospital rounds. The following day, when he went to shake hands with the patient again, the man refused to take his hand, but could not explain why he was so reluctant.

Most cases of pure amnesia are not due to surgery and are more likely to be caused by brain infections from either Herpes simplex encephalitis, where the cold-sore virus attacks the brain, or from meningitis (Gruneberg & Morris, 1992). The most common cause of pure amnesia, however, is

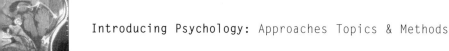

Korsakoff's syndrome, which occurs in alcoholic patients whose excessive and prolonged drinking has resulted in a vitamin deficiency (see pages 335–336).

Explanations for amnesiac syndromes

There are several reasons why people might suffer from serious memory loss more acute than that we would call ordinary forgetting. In general, amnesia occurs as a result of some physical experience, although the type of experience can vary widely. The reasons described here all have one factor in common in that they all involve either temporary or permanent physical damage to the brain. Non-physical amnesia, sometimes known as **fugue amnesia**, occurring as a result of repression, is referred to on page 338.

Traumatic amnesia

Every year in Britain, there are thousands of serious head-injury cases. Most of the victims survive, but many are permanently affected, either physically or mentally, by their experience. A severe blow to the head (physical trauma) quite often leads to a period of unconsciousness lasting for just a few seconds or for several months. In extreme cases, the patient might never regain consciousness. Following an unconscious episode, the patient may be confused and suffer from what is known as **post-traumatic amnesia**. Patients can usually hold a conversation, but may have difficulty understanding where they are and will keep on asking the same questions. There may also be difficulty recognising people and objects. Although this confusion usually passes, the patient may have no memory for the accident or events prior to the accident, suffering from retrograde amnesia.

Practical Activity

Watch out for a film or book dealing with the subject of accident-induced amnesia. Observe the pattern of behaviour demonstrated by the amnesiac character in the film. Does their behaviour conform to the pattern described above? Can they function normally in the present, indicating no problem with short-term memory? Can they recall any information from before the accident?

ECT-induced amnesia

Electro-convulsive therapy (ECT) patients often show a similar pattern of memory impairment to that of trauma-affected patients. ECT is sometimes used as a treatment for acute depression and involves passing a small electric current through the brain. The patient experiences a seizure and brief loss of consciousness which somehow appears to cure their depression. On regaining consciousness, the patient usually has a headache, appears confused and cannot recall events immediately before treatment, although memory for much earlier events is unaffected. Apparently, the memory loss occurs because there is disruption to the consolidation of the memory traces. Squire & Cohen (1982) investigated memory problems in ECT patients, giving a long-term memory questionnaire before and after ECT treatment. In the questionnaire, patients were asked to identify the title of TV programmes screened between 1957 and 1972. Analysis of percentages of programme titles correctly remembered showed that there was no difference in pre- and post-ECT performance for the programmes dated between 1957 and 1970, but that there was a marked decrease on post-ECT performance for the most recent programme titles. These findings suggest that ECT disrupts most recent memories only and leaves much of long-term memory unaffected.

Evaluative Comment

Many people are unhappy about the use of ECT, perhaps because it appears barbaric and also because there is no satisfactory explanation as to how it helps depression. In addition to the retrograde memory deficit seen in Cohen and Squire's research above, patients also appear to experience some difficulties with learning new information and occasional absent-mindedness. It has been found that the side effects of ECT can be reduced if the shock is administered to one side of the brain only, although Butcher & Carson (1992) report that many psychiatrists still prefer to use the two-sided version.

Surgery-induced amnesia

In the case of HM, tissue was removed from both sides of the brain, resulting in the severe deficit. Surgeons are now careful to limit tissue removal to one side of the brain if possible. Before HM, there had been other cases of patients receiving similar treatments for mental disorders. Following the discovery of HM's memory disability, eight psychotic patients who had previously has similar surgery were tested by Scoville & Milner (1957). These patients, too, had anterograde amnesia.

Evaluative Comment

In the 1950s, brain operations were often routinely carried out to treat depression, and were even used to change behaviour in cases where people behaved in ways that were thought to be socially unaccept-able. Surgically induced amnesia is quite rare nowadays because surgical procedures are not often carried out for mental/behavioural disorders, and also because new scanning techniques mean that surgery can be precisely and accurately targeted without incidental damage to surrounding brain tissue.

Alcohol-induced amnesia

In 1889, Sergei Korsakoff described a severe memory disorder due to brain damage. The most obvious symptom is severe anterograde amnesia, where patients appear unable to form any new memories but can still remember some old ones. Korsakoff's syndrome usually results from a thiamine (vitamin B1) deficiency after years of alcohol abuse. Alcoholics often have a poor diet because they get most of their calories from their alcohol intake. In addition, alcohol interferes with the absorption of thiamine in the intestines. Very occasionally, Korsakoff's syndrome can result from doses of glucose given to people suffering from severe malnutrition.

Many patients go through an acute phase, known as **Wernicke's encephalopathy**, during which they suffer from cognitive, emotional and motor problems. In the chronic phase that follows, the main symptom is amnesia, mostly anterograde but also retrograde.

Study

Aim *To test cognitive deficits in Korsakoff's patients.*

Method *Bloom & Lazerson (1988) report how patients are shown geometric shapes and have to point to the 'correct' shape. The patient is then told either 'Yes, correct' or 'No, incorrect'. The next part of the task involves changing the solution from, say, a circle to a square to see whether the patient realises that the solution has changed. After picking a circle and being told it is the wrong answer, normal people would try different shapes until they eventually pick a square.*

Results *In the second part of the experiment, Korsakoff's patients keep on choosing the circle, even though they are told it is the wrong answer.*

CONCLUSION *Korsakoff's patients seem unable to solve simple cognitive problems, apparently unable to learn from their earlier mistakes.*

The brain damage in Korsakoff's syndrome appears to be widespread, with loss of nerve cells in several regions of the brain, including the frontal lobe. Interestingly, patients who have suffered frontal-lobe damage due to injury often have similar problem-solving difficulties to those in the above study (Carlson, 1994).

Age-related amnesia

Fortunately, most people are unaffected by amnesia due to trauma, ECT, surgery and alcohol, but many people experience some form of memory deficit with increasing age. Here, we should distinguish between gradual decrease in memory function affecting most elderly people eventually, and the more severe memory loss found in people with **age-related dementia**.

Working memory	Particularly when performing some simultaneous tasks or when playing a game like chess. Rabbitt (1989) found older players were more likely to reconsider a move they had thought about and previously rejected.
Visuo-spatial memory	For example, the ability to create and use mental images of a street or town.
Long-term memory	Both visual and verbal recognition and visual and verbal recall.
Prospective memory	Where people are required to remember to do something at a particular time in the future. For example, when told to 'place a cross at the end of the next paragraph' participants aged over 60 perform worse than younger people.

Figure 12.6: Normal age-related difficulties in memory function (Baddeley, 1994)

Figure 12.6 illustrates the types of memory difficulties that most of us will experience as we grow older.

Study

AIM *To investigate differences in visual and verbal memory with age.*

METHOD *Baddeley et al. (1994) tested people aged sixteen to 80+ using the 'Doors and names' test. For the visual task, participants were presented with pictures of house doors of different styles, one of which they had seen in a priming stage of the experiment. The task was to identify from the set the door that had been seen previously. In the verbal version, participants performed the same task, but this time using people's names.*

RESULTS *The sixteen to 31 age group averaged over 75 per cent correct identifications, and the 80+ group just over 50 per cent. There was no notable difference due to the use of visual or verbal material.*

CONCLUSION *There was a gradual decline in memory performance with age.*

Evaluative Comment

Part of the problem for older people seems to be that they don't put as much effort into encoding. Younger people will spontaneously use elaborative coding if they think they will have to remember something later. For example, they might make the material they want to remember more distinctive somehow, perhaps by use of a rhyme or by incorporating images. Older participants, however, don't tend to elaborate material unless they are told they should. Similar effects have been found in other areas of cognitive research with older people. Quite often, they can function as well as younger participants if given strategies and encouraged. In some areas of cognitive functioning, particularly language and vocabulary, knowledge improves with age, so it's not all bad news!

Practical Activity

Harris & Sutherland (1981) found that retired older people between 69 and 80 years experienced fewer everyday memory lapses than people aged between twenty and 36. In a later study comparing the young people with people aged 50 to 60 who all worked, they found an even greater difference in ability in favour of the older group. Keep a diary for yourself for the next week. Every time you forget something, note it down. Then check to see how many memory lapses you've recorded and what sort of things you forgot. Ask an older relative, a grandparent perhaps, to do the same, so you can compare performances. Tell them about Harris and Sutherland's findings and they'll probably be quite keen!

Severe loss of memory with age may be due to brain degeneration leading to age-related (senile) dementia or Alzheimer's disease. Although Alzheimer's disease mainly affects elderly people, occasional cases of early onset have been reported. Certain brain changes take place in Alzheimer's patients; the brain's cavities or ventricles are enlarged; the neurons become tangled; small holes appear in the neuronal tissue and senile plaques (small patches of waste substance from nerve cells) appear. There are many symptoms of Alzheimer's, but the most predominant early symptom is confusion and memory impairment.

Long term memory for events	Patients have difficulty recalling events throughout the lifespan, but recent experiences, even before the onset of the disease, are especially poorly recalled.
Semantic memory problems	For example, a patient asked to name as many vegetables as possible in 1 minute will perform very poorly compared to normally functioning people.
Short-term memory problems	For example, on the digit span test.

Figure 12.7: Memory deficits in Alzheimer's patients (Baddeley, 1994)

Figure 12.7 shows the kinds of memory difficulties experienced by patients with Alzheimer's disease. The short-term memory difficulties create serious problems for everyday living, because severely affected patients become quite unable to perform simple tasks, as they constantly forget what they are doing. As the link between short- and long-term memory deteriorates, it becomes almost impossible for patients to store any new information permanently, so in many ways they become like the case of HM (see page 333).

Unlike normal older people who experience mild memory impairment, Alzheimer's patients tend not to benefit from memory aids and new memory strategies. There are several hypotheses about the causes of Alzheimer's disease, including low levels of the brain chemical acetylcholine and genetic factors, but, whatever the cause, there is not yet any effective treatment, and the outlook for Alzheimer's patients is not good.

12 Recovered and false memories

The term *recovered memory* refers to the emergence of an apparent recollection of a childhood event of which the person had no previous knowledge. Most controversially, this would be a memory of childhood sexual abuse.

A **false memory** is a memory of an event which did not take place, but which is believed by the individual to have happened. *False memory syndrome* (FMS) is described by Kihlstrom (1998) as:

> 'a condition in which a person's identity and interpersonal relationships are centred around a memory of a traumatic experience which is objectively false, but in which the person strongly believes. The memory often rules the individual's entire personality and lifestyle and disrupts all sorts of other adaptive behaviours. The memory tends to take on a life of its own, encapsulated and resistant to correction. The individual avoids confrontation with any evidence that might challenge the memory and may be effectively distracted from coping with the real problems of living.'

The key questions in relation to the debate are whether real memories can be repressed so that we are completely unaware of them, then later be recovered, and whether false memories of events that never took place can be either deliberately or accidentally implanted so that people think that they really happened.

Can real memories be repressed and then recovered?

Is it really possible for people to have experienced events, have no conscious memory of them for many years and then later recall them quite clearly? The theoretical basis for recovered memories rests on the Freudian defence mechanism of **repression**. According to Freud, memories can be repressed so we are not consciously aware of them. This happens because to have conscious recollection of the events, particularly unpleasant events from early childhood, would be too upsetting. These memories might remain forever repressed, although they could affect behaviour in later life. According to Freud, many of his women patients who came for psychoanalysis were suffering anxieties due to repression of childhood memories of sexual encounters with parents or other adults. In extraordinarily severe cases, repression is said to result in **fugue amnesia**, where the patient shuts out all memories of their life, possibly taking on a new identity.

Certainly, most people remember little from their first few years particularly before the age of about five. This **infantile amnesia** appears strongest before the age of three. However, contrary to Freud's predictions, the lost memories of childhood are for all types of experience and not just unpleasant events.

Reflective Activity

Think about your earliest childhood memories. How old were you when the events you recall took place? You may have to ask your parents or family about this. Do you remember many details? Are the memories visual, or is it more of a vague idea about the event? How many times have you talked to people about the event in the past? Have you got any old photographs taken at the time? Have you really remembered, or are you just 'remembering' what other people have told you about what happened?

Some experimental studies, such as the study below, have provided support for the concept of repression, although many studies do not.

Study

AIM *Levinger & Clark (1961) attempted to test the Freudian repression hypothesis experimentally.*

METHOD *Participants were given a set of emotionally negative words like 'argument' and 'unhappiness' and a set of neutral words. They were then asked to provide an associated word for each stimulus word. For example, if given the word 'star', the participant might say 'moon'. Later on, participants had to say the word that went with the cue word.*

RESULTS *Fewer associated words for the emotionally negative set were recalled than for the neutral set; thus, for example, participants could not recall associated words like 'cry' or 'hurt'.*

CONCLUSION *The difficulty recalling the negative word associations was taken as an indication of repression, although there may have been other explanations for the failure to recall the emotionally negative words. From carrying out memory studies with lists of words, we know that many variables affect recall, such as word length, frequency and importance to the individual.*

There are examples where traumatic experiences occurring over a prolonged period have been held back from consciousness, although such studies have been severely criticised (see below).

Study

AIM *Williams (1994) set out to see whether women recalled incidents of childhood abuse.*

METHOD *Participants were 129 women, shown by hospital documentation to have been abused between the ages of ten months and twelve years. When interviewed seventeen years later, they were aged between eighteen and 31.*

RESULTS *In extended interviews about their sexual histories, 38 per cent of the women failed to report the abusive episode documented by the hospital authorities. They did, however, quite often report their general experience of having been abused.*

CONCLUSION *Some participants failed to recall specific incidents of abuse because they had been repressed.*

Evaluative Comment

Other studies suggest that repression may not be the only explanation for the women's failure to report the incidents. In follow-up interviews, former victims of abuse give various reasons for choosing not to talk about events they can clearly recall. For example, they might wish to forget the past and get on with the future; they might be embarrassed; they may wish to protect their parents; or they may just prefer not to disclose to the interviewer (Femina et al., 1990).

Can false memories be implanted?

The theoretical basis of False Memory Syndrome relies on the reconstructive nature of memory. An interesting case study of reconstructed memory comes from the famous child psychologist Jean Piaget, whose earliest memory was of an attempt to kidnap him from his pram when he was out with his nurse in Paris. Piaget clearly recalled the event and believed the memory to be true until, when he was fifteen, his former nurse wrote to his parents confessing she had made up the whole story. The role of reconstruction has been studied extensively by Elizabeth Loftus who, in a recent article (Loftus, 2001), refers to several studies that show how asking people to imagine events that never happened leads them to confidently believe that these non-existent events had actually taken place. According to Loftus, guided imagination used by therapists may be a prime factor in false memories.

Study

AIM *Loftus & Ketcham (1994) studied whether a false memory of an unpleasant event could be implanted into a person's memory.*

METHOD *The study involved a sample of five people – three children and two adults – to whom the idea that they had once been lost in a shopping mall was casually introduced into conversation. With the assistance of parents or other family members, Loftus subsequently reintroduced the topic into conversation several times and asked questions about the event.*

RESULTS *The participants' memories of the event were at first uncertain, but each time the incident was mentioned, they seemed more and more sure, and finally were able to provide details, which they had not been told, about an event that never occurred.*

CONCLUSION *It is possible to make people believe something happened using suggestion (and remember, two of Loftus and Ketcham's participants were adults, so it is not just children who experience false memories).*

Evaluative Comment

*The 'Lost in the Shopping Mall' study has been referred to by Loftus as **existence proof** that it is possible to implant false memories into people's minds. By existence proof, Loftus means simply evidence that something exists. If such an effect is possible, then it is also possible that children who accuse their parents or relatives of child abuse in cases of recovered memory following therapy are making the mistake of believing a false memory. Critics of the 'Shopping Mall' study focus on the small sample, whether it was ethical to 'trick' children into believing an unpleasant event had occurred to them, and the validity of generalising from this to real-life cases of abuse.*

Ethical and theoretical implications of the false memory debate

---

Ethical implications

What if someone is wrongly accused?

What if a person is more unhappy after a memory is recovered than they were before?

Do therapists let their own beliefs influence the way they interpret what the patient says?

Theoretical implications

If lost memories can be recovered, perhaps Freud's repression theory is correct.

If memories can be false, then this could support the theory of reconstructive memory.

Figure 12.8: Distinguishing between ethical and theoretical implications

The growth in the USA of therapy for recovered memories has caused widespread public and professional concern. In the 1980s, many women and children who had recently undergone therapy spoke out about their memories of early childhood abuse. In many cases, there were direct accusations against elderly parents, causing widespread family disruption. Some accusations led to legal proceedings, with parents accused of offences against their own children, sometimes dating back decades. Since the early 1980s, many people have retracted their accusations against the parent, instead accusing their therapist of implanting false memories. Accused families have formed themselves into self-help and pressure groups to expose the therapists they accuse of ruining their lives.

The two largest societies for the families of accusers are the False Memory Syndrome Foundation (FMSF), formed in Philadelphia in 1992, and the British False Memory Society (BFMS), set up in 1993. Analysis of membership and background of the BFMS shows that:

- most accusers were female (87%);
- most accusations were made against the biological father;
- most accusations arose after a period of therapy;
- many people who had recently been in therapy had been suffering from either depression or eating disorders;
- many patients reported having relationship problems before making accusations.

Consequences of accusations were:

- broken contact with family (59%);
- legal proceedings (14%);
- seeking further treatment for stress (29%).

(Gudjonsson, 1997)

Brandon *et al.* (1998) reviewed the literature for the Royal College of Psychiatrists to consider the issues surrounding recovered memories of childhood sexual abuse and the circumstances in which such memories arise. Although many cases involve therapy, some instances appear to have been triggered by popular therapy books that suggest child sexual abuse is the root of many adult problems. Where therapy is involved, the Brandon report outlines some of the techniques used by therapists to enhance memory recovery:

- Checklists of symptoms (a bit like those to be found in magazine quizzes) where a given number of ticks indicates the existence of certain events in the past.

- Drugs given to relax the patient and reduce inhibition.

- Hypnosis (although hypnosis increases the amount of information recalled, it also leads to decrease in memory accuracy).

- Age regression, where the patient is encouraged to go back in time.

- Dream interpretation.

- Imagistic work, where the patient is guided to create and 'work on' images and feelings.

Following the Brandon review, draft guidelines were proposed for psychologists. First, they state that there is no doubt that child sexual abuse does exist and that some cases of recovered memory are recollections of events that really occurred. At the same time, they note concern that some therapeutic practices can lead to false memories.

Guidelines for Psychologists

Whilst practitioners should be open to the idea that memories of real events may be recovered, they should be alert to the possibility that such memories may be 'literally/historically true or false, or may be partly true, thematically true, or metaphorically true, or may derive from fantasy or dream material.' Psychologists should guard against actively seeking for memories of abuse and should avoid suggestion. (Frankland and Cohen 1999)

Figure 12.9: Guidelines for psychologists (Frankland & Cohen, 1999)

Summary of the false/recovered memory debate

The argument about recovered/false memories and the existence of False Memory Syndrome continues. There is theoretical support and evidence for a number of possibilities: that it is possible for memories to be withheld from consciousness; that under certain circumstances, such memories may be recalled; and that people can reconstruct memories such that they believe they have experienced events that never happened. Andrews *et al.* (1995) report the results of a British Psychological Society (BPS) survey of 1,083 practitioner members, in which the majority of respondents believed that false memories are possible, but also believed that recovered memories could sometimes be accurate.

Reflective Activity

Analyse the role of the expert by imagining the following:

- *What it would be like to be an expert involved in a case of recovered/false memory?*

- *What are the ethical problems?*

- *What are the likely outcomes for the patient and the patient's family?*

- *What will happen if the accuser decides to take legal action?*

- *Which other experts might be called to give evidence in court?*

Evaluative Comment

Thinking about the above activity helps us to understand the problems for any professional working in a context in which false memories might arise. Perhaps more interestingly from a student's point of view, this chapter as a whole shows just how much psychology is involved in real life. Very often in psychology we concentrate on laboratory research and theoretical points, sometimes forgetting how the theory and research can be applied to people's real experiences. Applications of psychology show just how relevant psychology is to many important aspects of our lives.

12

See Appendix 1 for information concerning questions that appear in the examination paper. The assessment of knowledge and understanding (AO1) and analysis and evaluation (AO2) assessment objectives is also given in Appendix 1.

Sample questions

Sample question 1

(a)   Name two features of the holistic form approach to face recognition.

(AO1 = 2)   *(2 marks)*

(b)   Explain what is meant by the *feature-analysis approach to face recognition*.

(AO1 = 1, AO2 = 2)   *(3 marks)*

(c)   Describe one study in which the process of face recognition was investigated. In your answer, you should refer to why the study was conducted, the method used, the results obtained and the conclusions drawn.

(AO1 = 5)   *(5 marks)*

(d)   Discuss at least two factors affecting the reliability of eyewitness identification.

(AO1 = 4, AO2 = 6)   *(10 marks)*

Total AO1 marks = 12   Total AO2 marks = 8   Total = 20 marks

Questions, answers and comments

(a)   Identify two psychological factors which might affect the reliability of eyewitness testimony.

(AO1 = 2)   *(2 marks)*

(b)   Suggest one way in which reliability of an eyewitness account might be improved.

(AO1 = 1, AO2 = 2)   *(3 marks)*

(c)   Describe one study in which the reliability of eyewitness testimony was investigated. In your answer, you should refer to why the study was conducted, the method used, the results obtained and the conclusions drawn.

(AO1 = 5)   *(5 marks)*

(d)   Discuss one theoretical explanation for face recognition.

(AO1 = 4, AO2 = 6)   *(10 marks)*

Total AO1 marks = 12   Total AO2 marks = 8   Total = 20 marks

Answer to (a)

One factor is a person's racial background. If you are a different race to someone, then it is harder to tell the person's features. The second factor is emotion. People who are afraid are less likely to be able to tell who the culprit is.

Comment

Two marks for correct identification of race and emotion. Explanations are not required and cannot gain extra credit.

Answer to (b)

One way to improve memory for a robbery is to take them back to the scene of the crime and ask them what happened. They could be told to imagine what else was going on and how they felt. This would bring the memory flooding back.

Comment

This is quite a good answer. Although it seems mostly common sense, there is a valid strategy. Context is not named, but the description is appropriate. Two marks were awarded for application. Reference to 'context' would have scored the AO1 mark.

Answer to (c)

A study was carried out to see if weapons affect ability to recall events. People watched a film about a person who was carrying a knife, and it was found that these people remembered the knife and could not remember the face of the person carrying the knife. This study concluded people remember only the weapon and not the person.

Comment

The candidate refers vaguely to aim, method, results and conclusion, but there is insufficient detail here. The method and results are extremely vague, and the conclusion is a repetition of the results. Overall, a rather generous three marks were awarded: one each for the aim and method, plus one for the results/conclusion.

Answer to (d)

There are two main theories of face recognition. One says features are important, and the other says we need to recognise the whole face at once. The holistic model will be discussed here with evidence and criticism.

Bruce and Young said that to recognise a face, we had to process the whole, that is the features and their configuration. Other factors like context and background information about a person were also important too. The holistic theory is an example of a top-down theory, because it stresses the importance of previously stored information when it comes to process new information. Bruce and Young said that for everyone we know, we have a face recognition unit (FRU) stored, and when we see someone, we try to match their face to one of our FRUs. If matching occurs, that triggers lots of other information about the person.

Critics of the theory say that features too are important, and many studies show this. The most important features for people we know are internal ones like eyes, mouth, etc. However, lots of studies show that it's not just the features that are important, but the whole arrangement. Yin found it took longer to identify faces presented upside down, because even though the features were the same, the layout was different. Baddeley also describes how people trained to recognise separate features are no better at recognising faces, so it's not just feature based. Also, when we look at the sequence of events, we usually remember names of people last, like Bruce and Young predicted.

Finally, we probably do need to look at features more in people we don't know very well, but with familiar people it is more about the whole face and person and everything about them.

Comment

There is considerable description of the model here. It could perhaps be better expressed, but shows knowledge about the meaning of holistic and the basics of Bruce and Young's model. The discussion has just enough evidence for and against. Sadly, the candidate mentions naming and the recognition sequence, but doesn't really explain this point. This answer gained six marks (three AO1 marks and three AO2 marks); a fairly good answer, but with the emphasis on description; not detailed or evaluative enough for the top band.

Overall Mark: 13/20 (AO1 = 8, AO2 = 5)

General advice to this candidate would be to spend a little less time on the earlier questions, particularly if the instruction is simply to 'name', 'identify' or 'give'. This would leave more time available to concentrate on detail for part (c) and more thorough evaluation for part (d).

12 Further reading

Introductory texts

Baddeley, A. (1994), *Your Memory: A User's Guide*, Harmondsworth, Penguin Books

Gross, R. (1996) *Psychology, the Science of Mind and Behaviour*, 3rd edition, London, Hodder & Stoughton

Gross, R. (2001) *Psychology, the Science of Mind and Behaviour*, 4th edition, London, Hodder & Stoughton

Gross, R., McIlveen, R. & Coolican, H. (2000), *Psychology: A New Introduction for AS Level*, London, Hodder & Stoughton

Hayes, N. (1999), *Foundations of Psychology: An Introductory Text*, 3rd edition, Surrey, Nelson

Moxon, D. (2000), *Memory*, London, Heinemann

Specialist Sources

Ainsworth, P.B. (1998), *Psychology, Law and Eye-witness Testimony*, London, Wiley

Bruce, V. (1988), *Recognising Faces*, Hove, Lawrence Erlbaum Associates

Bruce, V. & Young, A. (1998), *In the Eye of the Beholder: The Science of Face Perception*, Oxford, Oxford University Press

Cohen, G. (1989), *Memory in the Real World*, Hove, Lawrence Erlbaum Associates

Gruneberg, M. & Morris, P. (eds) (1992), *Aspects of Memory* (Volume 1: Practical Aspects), 2nd edition, London, Routledge

Kellogg, R.T. (1995), *Cognitive Psychology*, London, Sage Publications

Loftus, E.F. (1979), *Eye-witness Testimony*, Cambridge, MA, Harvard University Press

Loftus, E. & Ketcham, K. (1994), *The Myth of Repressed Memory*, New York, St Martin's Press

Smyth, M.M., Collins, A.F., Morris, P.E. & Levy, P. (1994), *Cognition in Action*, 2nd edition, Hove, Lawrence Erlbaum Associates

Zaragoza, M.S., Graham, J.R., Hall, G.C.N., Hirschman, R. & Ben-Yorath, Y.S. (1995), *Memory and Testimony in the Child Witness*, London, Sage Publications

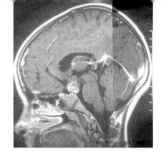

Appendix 1

Questions and Assessment Objectives in the AS Examinations

Question selection and question structure

The questions that appear in the AS-level examination papers for Unit 1 (Introducing Psychology) and Unit 2 (Social and Cognitive Psychology) adhere to certain principles and are all structured in a standard way. An explanation of the principles and structure of question setting is given below.

Question selection

Unit 1 (Introducing Psychology) contains four topic areas:

- key approaches and the study of psychology;
- methods of research;
- the biological approach;
- the psychology of gender.

There are five questions in the examination paper, divided into three sections as follows:

- Section A: one question on key approaches and the study of psychology and one question on the biological approach.
- Section B: one question on research methods.
- Section C: two questions on the psychology of gender.

You are required to answer one question from Section (a), the compulsory research-methods paper in Section (b), and one question from Section (c). To answer a question in Section (a), you must have studied and revised all the content given in the specification for **either** key approaches **or** the biological approach. This content is provided in Chapters 1 and 2 of this book respectively. The compulsory Section (b) question on research methods is covered in Chapter 3. In the specification, the psychology of gender is divided into two areas: studying gender and explaining gender. The two gender questions in the examination are based on each area. However, for study and revision purposes, you must cover both areas to be in the best position to answer one of the questions.

Unit 2 (Social and Cognitive Psychology) contains four topic areas in social psychology and four topic areas in cognitive psychology:

Social Psychology	Cognitive Psychology
• Attitudes	• Perception and attention
• Social influence	• Remembering and forgetting
• Social cognition	• Language and thought
• Social psychology of sport	• Cognition and law

You are required to answer three questions in total: one from social psychology, one from cognitive psychology and the third question from either area. The examination paper has eight questions, one from each of the eight topic areas listed above. To be properly prepared to answer a question in one of the topic areas, you must study and revise all the content for that topic area given in the specification. Eight chapters in this text book (Chapters 5 to 12) closely and carefully follow the content specified.

Question structure

All of the questions in the examination papers for Unit 1 (Introducing Psychology) and Unit 2 (Social and Cognitive Psychology) carry twenty marks and have 30 minutes allocated to answering each. All questions, except the compulsory research-methods question in Unit 1, conform to the following structure:

• Four subsections per question: (a), (b), (c) and (d)

• Subsections (a) and (b) can only be worth between two and three marks each

• Subsection (c) can only be worth between four and six marks

• Subsection (d) will always be worth ten marks

The research-methods question will contain numerous subsections, as shown in Chapter 3, where each may be worth between one and a maximum of four marks.

Further details and guidance are given in Appendix 2 under the heading 'Dealing with questions'.

Assessment objectives

The term *assessment objectives* sounds complicated, but it's not; however, it is very important that you understand the three assessment objectives of the AQA Specification B AS Psychology. This is because the questions, mark schemes and actual marking of the answers that you write in the examination all directly relate to them. There are three assessment objectives, as shown in Figure A1.1.

Assessment Objective 3 (AO3) relates solely to Unit 3 (Psychological Investigations). For more on this, see Appendix 3, where the assessment of skills related to the practical report write-up that you have to do are dealt with fully.

AO1 Knowledge and understanding

This assessment objective concerns how well you know about and understand theories, concepts, methods and studies in psychology. It is to do with how well you are able to offer written description of these different aspects of psychology. Terms used in questions on the examination papers which attempt to assess AO1 knowledge and understanding include the following:

Give	Outline
Identify	State
List or name	Describe

Assessment objective	Explanation
AO1 – Knowledge and understanding	Involves knowledge and understanding of psychological theories, terminology, concepts and methods in psychology. Also involved is the clear and effective communication of knowledge and understanding.
AO2 – Analysis and evaluation	Involves the analysis and evaluation of psychological theories, concepts, studies and methods in psychology. Also involved is the clear and effective communication of this.
AO3 – Psychological investigations	Design, conduct and report psychological investigations choosing from a range of methods, and taking into account issues of reliability, validity and ethics, and collect and draw conclusions from data.

Figure A1.1: Explanation of the three assessment objectives used for AS-level psychology

How effectively you can communicate, in written form, your knowledge and understanding of psychology will directly relate to the marks you are awarded when answering questions with the above terms in them. Hence, in your studies and revision of topic areas in Unit 1 and Unit 2, you must know and understand all the content specified in the areas that you chose to study.

AO2 Analysis and evaluation

This assessment objective is concerned with how well you are able to use your knowledge and understanding of psychology to provide critical evaluation of a topic and demonstrate its application to everyday life. Analysis and evaluation requires you to be able to discuss strengths and weaknesses, advantages and disadvantages, shortcomings and application of theory, concepts and research findings in psychology. The skills of analysis and evaluation are higher-level cognitive or intellectual skills which you would have to demonstrate in written form to gain a Grade A or B at AS-level psychology. Terms used in questions which assess AO2 analysis and evaluation include the following:

Discuss   Distinguish

Evaluate   Explain

Apply   Compare

In each of the twelve chapters of this book, there are numerous sections headed 'Evaluative comment'. These are designed to help develop your skills of analysis and evaluation. It is very important that you not only understand the point being made in an evaluative comment, but that you are able to discuss and expand upon it further. One way to do this is to get together with a group of three or four of your classmates. Another way is to hold a discussion based on an evaluative comment in class. You may also be able to develop the point further by taking up some of the suggestions for further reading given at the end of each chapter.

Assessment objectives and examination questions

In each of the specimen questions given at the end of each chapter, an indication of marks for AO1 (knowledge and understanding) and AO2 (analysis and evaluation) is provided. Consider a sample question from 'Key Approaches and the Study of Psychology' (Chapter 1), as follows:

(a) Outline one way in which psychology scientifically studies human behaviour.
(AO1 = 2)   (2 marks)

(b) Explain the difference between scientific and common-sense explanations of human behaviour.
(AO1 = 1, AO2 = 2)   (3 marks)

(c) Identify and discuss one key influence of Darwin on the development of psychology.
(AO1 = 2, AO2 = 3)   (5 marks)

(d) Describe and discuss two assumptions of the cognitive approach in psychology.
(AO1 = 5, AO2 = 5)   (10 marks)

Total AO1 marks = 10   Total AO2 marks = 10   Total = 20 marks

From this, you can see that the balance of AO1 (knowledge and understanding) and AO2 (analysis and evaluation) marks for the whole twenty-mark question is ten for each assessment objective. This means that to score high marks for your answer, you must show evidence of both a good knowledge of psychology and critical analysis and application, as appropriate.

If you look at each subsection of the question, you will see that (d) has the most AO2 marks attached to it (five marks in this example). As we have seen earlier, key terms like 'discuss', 'explain', 'distinguish', 'evaluate', etc. indicate a requirement for AO2 (analysis and evaluation). With subsection (b) in the specimen question, you are asked to 'Explain the difference …': here, one mark is given for AO1 (knowledge and understanding) and two marks for AO2 (analysis and evaluation).

To understand better what examiners award marks for when marking what you write in examinations, you are referred to past examination papers and associated schemes of marking. The schemes of marking are detailed and are what the examiners use to determine the marks to award for what you write in an examination. These are available from the AQA or visit their website at www.aqa.org.uk.

When studying, revising and preparing for the AS-level examinations associated with Unit 1 and Unit 2, you must ensure that you provide analysis and evaluation (critical discussion) when the terms given above are present in the wording of the question. One of the most common problem with answers to questions, especially to subsection (d), is that too much is written that is descriptive (knowledge and understanding) and not enough that represents critical discussion (analysis and evaluation). It is tempting to write down all that you know about the topic under examination. However, lots of description will not score any of the marks for AO2 in the question.

For the ten-mark sub-section (d) questions in both Unit 1 and Unit 2, the following guidelines generally apply;

• 'Describe and discuss' indicates that there are five marks for AO1 (knowledge and understanding) and five marks for AO2 (analysis and evaluation).

• 'Discuss' indicates slightly fewer marks for AO1 (three or four marks) and more marks for AO2 (six or seven marks).

Recommendations

The above explanation of how questions are set, structured and assessed in Unit 1 and Unit 2 at AS level is important to understand. Read this appendix carefully and ask your teacher if there are bits that you do not understand clearly enough. Remember that success at examinations is about studying hard, good examination preparation and being well organised.

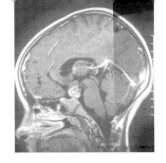

Appendix 2
Study and Examination Skills

Sarah and Daniel have a psychology examination in a few weeks' time. They chat about how to revise.

Sarah: Did you know that if someone reads out a lot of facts to you while you're asleep, you can remember them when you wake up?

Daniel: I tried it in last week's psychology class – it didn't work for me.

Sarah: Maybe we could use one of those memory techniques, like that guy – you know, the Russian guy did a study about him. How did he do it?

Daniel: I can't remember.

Sarah: If only someone would teach *us* how to revise.

Sarah and Daniel need to learn effective study techniques

Sarah and Daniel are right in thinking that there are effective techniques for revision, and that these techniques can be learned quite easily. Most students will be able to improve their performance if they adopt some of the suggestions described in this appendix. Much of the good practice described below can also be applied to other subjects you are studying.

What to study

Most examinations allow candidates some choice of questions; however, it is not always necessary or practical to study all the material in the syllabus specifications. For example, in the AQA Specification B AS-level Unit 1 (Introducing Psychology) examination paper, there are five questions, but each candidate is required to answer only three. You can choose between Question 1 (key approaches) and Question 2 (the biological approach). In revising for the examination, you might choose to revise only one of these topics. This means you will have less to revise in terms of breadth, so that you can spend more time revising your chosen topics in depth.

In the Unit 2 (Social and Cognitive Psychology) examination paper, the candidate has to answer three questions out of eight.

A possible approach is to revise for only four topics (say two from social and two from cognitive psychology) and answer the best three questions which come up. If you adopt this approach, it is very important to revise all the content mentioned in the relevant syllabus sections.

The examinations mentioned above require you to be able to:

● define terms, explain concepts and give examples;

● describe methods and techniques used in research;

● describe and evaluate research studies which have been carried out;

● describe and evaluate theories and methods of research;

● briefly outline or cite (quote) studies to support or challenge theories.

How to study

The start of a psychology course can be an exciting, but also a puzzling time. You may be studying psychology for the first time, perhaps with a new teacher or in a new college. At first, the subject may seem confusing and difficult. However, you should soon master it if you use some of the techniques described here from the start of the course.

Studying during your course

Building up revision notes

Revising directly from textbooks is rarely effective. It is better to extract information to form short notes which make sense to you, and which you can use for revision purposes. It may be that your teacher provides you with notes or handouts which are in a suitable form for revision; however, there are strong advantages in producing your own revision notes.

Making summary notes requires you to think carefully about the topic, and this is an effective way of learning. You should not try to include a lot of detail in summary notes. The notes should act as a kind of key to unlock your memory for details. Figure A2.1 gives an example of what these notes might look like.

Using the language

A psychology examination tests your ability to express psychological ideas and evidence, so it is very important that you practise this skill. Students studying psychology for the first time often find the new terminology unfamiliar. To gain confidence in expressing psychological ideas, it helps if you try to use them in everyday conversation with friends, partners or parents. For example, a parent who wants to know what you learned at school (or college) today is providing a helpful opportunity for you to express yourself clearly to someone else. Explaining Social Learning Theory or cognitive dissonance to them will help you get a clearer understanding of these ideas. However, you may have to choose your topic of conversation carefully. For example, if you have just learned about some of Freud's ideas and wish to apply them, it may not be a good idea to tell a friend that they have an anal personality.

Practice in writing answers to examination questions is also important. Some students show a tendency to avoid doing homework. This is a poor strategy. Homework gives you the opportunity of practising the skill of writing about psychology and getting feedback. In addition, you may be lucky enough to come across a question in the examination which is similar to one you already answered for homework.

Methods of studying genetic basis of behaviour – intelligence

1. <u>Selective breeding</u> – mate most intelligent male+ female – keep selecting for several generations.

If intelligence increases – genetics must play a part.

(Study) Tryon (1940) bred rats for speed of maze learning – it increased
      Ads: – good control of variables – experiment – conclusive
      Disads: – not with humans – ethics
               – maze running not same as intelligence
               – does not measure effect of environment.

2. <u>Adoption studies</u> – find correlations between IQs of grown-up adopted child
   and –
      1. adoptive parent (environment) 0.26 (Study)
      2. biological parent (genetics)   0.57 Kamin (1974)

Biol. effect seems bigger – HOWEVER Skodak + Skeels (1945) found adopted children usually higher IQs than biol. parent – so environment important too.
Ads: humans studied, measured IQ
Disads: no control over adoption + rearing environment
          correlational study – not as conclusive as expt.

3. <u>Twin studies</u> – correlate IQs of 3 sets of twins –

Figure A2.1: An example of revision notes

Asking questions

A teacher might mention *empirical research* or *cognitive processes* without realising that you may not understand these terms. And you might assume that everyone else knows what the teacher means, and think that if you ask for explanation, other people will think you are stupid. It is much better to ask for explanation than to put up with confusion in silence. Asking a question is likely to benefit everyone in the classroom. Asking questions is a sign of competence, not stupidity.

Processing the information

Cognitive psychologists claim that recall of information is improved if that information has been processed deeply according to its meaning (see Chapter 10). When this idea is applied to revision, it means that actively processing information is much more effective than just reading through notes.

Information can be actively processed in several ways. One way is to change the form of the information. For example, you can extract information from text and put it in the form of a table. The process of doing this aids learning and also produces a summary which is useful for further revision. An example is shown in Figure A2.2.

Some students find that so-called *spider diagrams* are also useful. A spider diagram provides a visual image which stores key information and also the relationship between different pieces of information. Students who are good at recalling visual images benefit most from this method. An example is shown in Figure A2.3.

Revising

Using cued recall

Cued recall means recalling information by linking it with other information which acts as a key to unlock the memory store. One way of doing this is to use a *mnemonic* – this is a trick or routine for memorising information. A common example is the use of a mnemonic based on the first letters of

Method	Key features	Advantages	Disadvantages
Experiment	An IV is manipulated and the DV is measured to see its effect. All other variables controlled.	Good control of variables. Most conclusive method for testing cause–effect hypotheses.	Artificial. May lack ecological validity. Ethical problems likely e.g. deception.
Observation	Behaviour is systematically observed and recorded, using categories and coding.	High ecological validity – records actual behaviour.	Little control of variables. Not conclusive test of cause–effect hypotheses. Presence of observer may affect participant behaviour.
Study using correlational analysis	Two variables are measured to see if there is a link.	Easy – few ethical problems.	Not conclusive test of cause–effect hypotheses – correlation does not imply causation. Little control of variables.
Interview	Researcher asks a schedule of questions and records replies	Can judge respondent's sincerity/ involvement. One way of studying attitudes.	Self-report is subjective. Risk of respondent bias. Inconclusive. Time-consuming.
Questionnaire	Participant given schedule of questions and records own replies.	Data can be quickly collected from a large sample. Less risk of researcher bias.	Self-report is subjective. Risk of respondent bias. Low rate of return may lead to unrepresentative sample.
Case study	In-depth study of an unusual individual.	Used where a group of similar participants is not available.	Small sample – cannot be generalised, often retrospective, no control of variables, risk of researcher subjectivity.

Figure A2.2: Table showing advantages and disadvantages of different research methods

a list. Most people can recall the colours of the visible spectrum by using the phrase *Richard Of York Gave Battle In Vain* (ROYGBIV). Remember this phrase, and you can then recall the sequence Red, Orange, Yellow, Green, Blue, Indigo, Violet. For example, a student studying for the Module 2 section on memory might want to remember a list of explanations for forgetting. This list includes:

- Decay
- Lack of consolidation
- Displacement
- Retrieval failure
- Interference
- Repression

The student might use the mnemonic *Dead Lemmings Don't Run In Races*. Alternatively, they may reorder the list and think of a mnemonic with more personal relevance to themselves, such as *I Really Do Despise Rugby League* or possibly even *I Don't Remember Lighting Rachel's Dress*.

Cued recall can also be used to recall large numbers of research studies.

Make a list of the studies you want to remember, by the name(s) of those who reported each study. Next to the name, write a few words which indicate some key feature of the study (see Figure A2.4).

Learn this list, using the self-testing method described below. When you need to cite a study in an exam question, you only need to think of a key feature of the study, and this will cue your recall of the relevant name. This technique is very efficient, because you are learning even as you draw up the list. The same applies to a list of technical terms and their definitions.

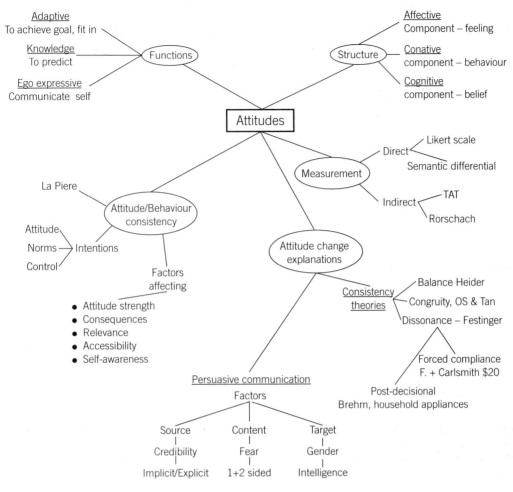

Figure A2.3: Example of a spider diagram

Who carried out the study	Key feature
Asch	Line conformity
Sherif	Autokinetic conformity
Moscovici & Lage	Blue–green minority influence
Milgram	Shockingly obedient volunteers
Hofling	Overdosing nurses

Figure A2.4: Method of cued recall for learning studies

Self-testing

This is the single most important technique for successful revision, yet many students do not use it. Self-testing can be used with any of the revision approaches already suggested above. For example, with the list of researchers and studies, you can cover up the description of the study, look at the name and guess the key features – then check whether you were right or not. You can soon work through a long list in this way. Next, cover up the names column, look at the key features and try to recall the name of the researcher.

As you get better, you might get someone to read items from the list in a random order, asking you to recall at one time the name and at another time the key feature.

Self-testing can also be done with a page of revision notes or a spider diagram (see Figure A2.3). Read the spider diagram carefully for a few minutes, then cover it up and try to reproduce it from memory. Then check your reproduction with the original and notice any gaps. As your recall improves, you should try to reproduce the page the day after you last looked at it.

One useful effect of self-testing is that it provides you with feedback about how well you know the material. Self-testing can be quite demanding, so once you have learned some material fairly well, you can get someone else to help by testing you. Ideally, you should do this with another student studying for the same examination, so that both of you benefit.

Provided that you have summarised the material to be learned, revision in the last few days before the examination is a simple matter of re-testing yourself on your knowledge of perhaps fifteen to twenty revision sheets.

Using time efficiently

Some people assume that spending a lot of time in revision will bring success. This is not necessarily the case. Reading and rereading a textbook for hours is a very ineffective way to revise. It is much better to spend shorter periods of time revising, then you can concentrate fully. After half an hour of self-testing, you will need a break, but you may well achieve more than in one hour of less efficient revision.

Having a revision timetable which indicates when you are going to revise each topic may help you to manage the task without putting too much pressure on yourself. Figure A2.5 gives an example.

Monday 8th	1830–1930	Revise psychoanalytic theory of gender
	2015–2030	Self-test on experimental design
Tuesday 9th	0915–1000	Revise cognitive theory of gender
Wednesday 10th	1400–1430	Revise social learning theory/gender
	1830–1845	Self-test on psychoanalytic theory
Thursday 11th	1830–1930	Revise biological theory of gender Self-test on sampling and cognitive theory of gender
Friday 12th	1130–1215	Draw chart of methods of studying gender – self-test
Saturday 13th	Day off	

Figure A2.5: Example of a revision timetable for part of Unit 1 (Introducing Psychology)

Effective revision should leave you with time to relax and time to get the sleep you need. If a parent or other caring individual asks you whether you should spend more time revising, you could reply by inviting them to test you.

Examination technique

An effective approach to examination technique enables you to enter the examination room with a mental plan – a clear idea of the skills you wish to demonstrate, with a realistic expectation of what the questions will be like, and with the intention of using the questions to demonstrate as much knowledge as possible. This active approach to examination technique enables you to be in control of the situation.

However, some students approach examinations with a fatalistic attitude, rather like helpless victims facing torment. They respond passively to the questions and then hope for the best. The first approach is more likely to succeed.

A mental plan

You could plan to jot down some of your mnemonics or spider diagrams before you start answering any questions. In that way, you can refer back to your plan when writing your answer, without fear of forgetting what you were going to write next.

Showing off knowledge

It can be quite frustrating to do a lot of revision and then find that you are not asked questions that reflect what you have learned. However, it sometimes happens that examination questions give you the opportunity to show off knowledge. For example, if you have learned a lot about the psychoanalytic and humanistic approaches for Unit 1 (Introducing Psychology), but a ten-mark question asks you to evaluate the biological approach, you can still use your knowledge of the other approaches by using it to criticise or contrast with the biological approach.

Answer plans

For longer answers, it is very useful to jot down a skeleton plan of the answer before you start. That way, you can 'empty' your head of detail in one go, so you don't have to think of things as you go along. The plan should be in very brief note form and should list the main points you want to include in your answer. This will also help you to order the points logically and spot any gaps.

Coping with examination pressure

You may have learned during your psychology course that arousal can improve performance (see Chapter 8). In examinations, people tend to be fairly highly aroused, and this often has positive effects. They think more clearly and quickly, and write more fluently. If you feel a little anxious before an examination, don't worry about it. Remember, it may improve your performance. However, a few people become so anxious about examinations that their high arousal level leads to a worsening of performance. It is quite important for such people to find ways of coping with their anxiety.

One way is to try to control the way you think about exams. If you find yourself thinking or saying things which reflect negative thoughts, you should try to stop yourself. It is no use saying to yourself (or to others) 'I'm no good at exams'. That can easily become a self-fulfilling prophecy. If you really believe you are no good at exams, you may not bother to revise properly, because you assume it will not lead to success. Because of this, you may perform poorly.

Someone who is over-anxious about examinations should try to think of some positive thoughts, such as 'I have done enough revision for my exam' and 'Exams never hurt anyone'. Of course, it is essential that you really have done enough revision and prepared well for the examination. A useful plan is to think through or visualise what will happen during the examination, so as to gain control over the situation.

The plan or script might run like this:

> I shall arrive at least half an hour before the start of the exam, but sit in a quiet place away from other anxious students. I shall read a magazine while waiting.

> In the exam room, there will probably be a mix-up over where to sit, or what centre number to write on the paper.

> When I open the paper and look at the questions, my mind will go blank, but that will pass. While I am waiting to calm down, I'll write down my mnemonic or spider diagram for research methods. Then I'll read the questions again and answers will begin to occur to me. I will take my time, even though the person next to me is already scribbling furiously …

The value of this sort of visualisation is that you are prepared for your moment of anxiety, and have a way of dealing with it. In effect, you are taking control of the examination situation rather than feeling that it controls you.

It is also important to avoid self-punishing behaviour. An example of this is to set impossibly high targets for yourself, so that you end up staying awake late into the night to do all the revision you have set yourself. Examinations should be challenging, but preparing for them should not be an ordeal.

The mock examination

A mock examination is very useful, provided that it takes place within about two weeks of the real examination. At that time, it is a realistic test, because you will already have done most of your revision. Provided that the mock is marked and returned to you before the real examination, it is also useful in detecting mistakes or confusions in your knowledge of psychology. The most useful mock examination will make use of a previous paper you have not seen before.

The mock examination gives you an opportunity to check whether your use of time is about right, and whether you need to write more or less for each question. You can also use it to practise using any techniques which are new to you, such as using spider diagrams as answer plans. Finally, the mock examination is a great opportunity to get any silly mistakes out of your system, such as answering all the questions on the paper, instead of the three you are instructed to answer.

If you do not have an opportunity to sit a mock examination, you should certainly practise writing answers to the specimen questions included in this book as well as previous examination questions, available from your teacher or direct from AQA.

Dealing with questions

Typically, a question includes four sections. A common error is to write more than necessary for the subsections with few marks attached, and less than necessary for sections (c) and especially (d), which carries half the marks for the entire question.

Sections (a) and (b) usually have two or three marks attached to them. Each should be answered briefly. A useful rule of thumb is to make two points for a two-mark section, but to say more in a three-mark section. For example, if a two-mark section asks you to 'Identify two functions that holding an attitude might serve for an individual', all you need to do is to name two functions. The answer 'The knowledge function and the adaptive function' will get you two marks. There is no point in writing an explanation or even in giving an example in this case.

If a subsection asks you explain what is meant by something, and three marks are available, you need to define the term, but then say a little more – either add some detail or give an example.

For example, the three-mark question 'Explain what is meant by the term sex-role *stereotype*', could be answered as follows:

> 'A sex-role stereotype is a widely held belief that all men share the same characteristic, or that all women are the same in some way. This belief is usually inaccurate. Examples include the belief that all men are insensitive, or that all women are indecisive.'

This answer would score all three marks available. Notice that it is still quite brief and that the word *stereotype* is not used as part of the definition. If the candidate had written 'A sex-role stereotype is a stereotype about the characteristics of men or women', they would have failed to say what a stereotype actually is.

Section (c) may be awarded four, five or six marks. Sometimes section (c) asks you to 'describe one study', and requires you to state the aim, method, results and conclusions of this study. You will get one mark each for doing each of these. The fifth mark is gained by giving some extra detail. To score all these marks, it is only necessary to state each point briefly, but to give more detail in one area – often this is done in the description of the method, i.e. the procedure used in the study.

Alternatively, section (c) may require you to apply your knowledge of psychology to a situation, or to explain a psychological technique or theory. For example, the question 'Explain the use of selective breeding as a way of investigating the genetic basis of behaviour' has five marks attached. This requires some detail, including describing the technique, pointing out how it might help to investigate the topic and referring to an actual study. (See Figure A2.6 for an example of an answer plan for this.)

Section (d) always has ten marks attached. Even though this is half the mark allocation for the question, you may need to spend more than half the time in answering it. This section requires an answer which is in the form of a short essay. A brief introduction and a brief conclusion may be appropriate. Before starting to write your answer, it may be useful for you to quickly plan the structure of the essay – and jot down any names or ideas you might forget later (see the section on answer plans above). Sometimes the question may need to be decoded. This means that you have to decide exactly what the question is asking you to do.

Waffling

A candidate who does not stop to think about what answer the question requires is likely to fall into the temptation to waffle. Waffling typically includes making broad, impressionistic generalisations, describing your personal experiences or beliefs, using many words to explain a simple idea and being repetitive.

What you write in an examination should mainly feature actual detail of studies and concepts you have learned about. It is possible that you know the information required to answer the question, but you may have failed to connect this information with the question. If you find yourself making it up as you go along, stop and think.

Writing style

The ideal style for an examination is clear, concise and precise. Good answers often show a certain pattern of explanation, as follows:

1 An idea, factor or definition is clearly expressed.

2 It is elaborated and explained.

3 It is supported with an example or by reference to a study.

4 It is evaluated critically.

5 The criticism is commented on and perhaps modified with a 'However' point (see below).

An answer in *short notes* style is unlikely to score well.

Evaluation and description

In section (d) questions, at least half the marks allocated are for evaluation or related skills such as analysis and application. This means that half the marks or less are allocated for factual description.

A classic mistake many candidates make – both during revision and during the examination – is to concentrate too much on factual detail. It is essential to be able to discuss and evaluate, for example by pointing out advantages and disadvantages.

'However' points

A simple way of ensuring that your answer includes some relevant evaluation is to get into the habit of writing *However...* after expressing an idea. This cues you to make some critical comment or evaluation.

(See Appendix 1 for more detail on different assessment objectives in the examination.)

Summary

Each student is different. You may find some study techniques effective which other people find unhelpful. An important part of learning to study is to try out different techniques, adapt them and so find out what works best for you. The key guidelines can be summarised as follows:

- Build up a set of clear condensed revision notes, right from the start.
- Practise expressing psychological ideas.
- Use memory aids.
- Self-test.
- Plan your revision ahead.
- Know what to expect of the examination.

Remember that the organisational and planning skills you pick up while studying at AS/A level may well be useful to you in higher education and in your working life.

Further reading

Cottrell, S. (1999), *The Study Skills Handbook*, Palgrave

Marshall, P. (1997), *How to Study and Learn – Your Practical Guide to Effective Study Skills*, 2nd edition, How to Books

Northedge, A. (1994), *The Good Study Guide*, Open University

Rowntree, D. (1998), *Learn How to Study*, Time Warner

Saunders, D. (1994), *The Complete Student Handbook*, Oxford, Blackwell

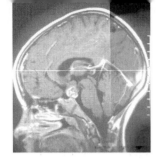

Appendix 3

The Practical Investigation Report

Introduction to the Practical Investigation

Most courses in psychology require students to investigate human behaviour and thought by designing, implementing and reporting their own research. In AQA Specification B, Unit 3 is the Practical Investigation, and marks are awarded for the quality of the report, which is marked externally by the examination board. When you have understood the methods used by psychologists (see Chapter 3), you will need to present a proposal for an investigation to your teacher. Your teacher will decide whether the design you have outlined is appropriate and ethically acceptable. Your teacher has to sign a form which states that the research was your own independent work and that the design had been approved before you conducted the study. Before you start your coursework, there are some important issues to bear in mind.

Originality

The marks awarded will be based on your own independent work. This means that you should produce your own investigation and not work with other people. It is difficult for an external marker to be sure that the report contains evidence of the skills of one person that a group of people were working together. Also, if you copy a design of a study from a textbook or from information given by your teacher, then you cannot claim credit for the work. Students sometimes write in their reports that they are replicating the work of a famous psychologist. However, this is inadvisable, as it means conducting a copy of the research, and copying another person's work means that you could not gain marks for the design of the investigation. It is perfectly acceptable to design an investigation based on famous studies. The key point is that you must produce your own version of the study. If you use a questionnaire or task which has been produced by someone else, it is your responsibility to check that the material is not under copyright.

Ethical considerations

The investigation you carry out and report must be ethical (see Chapter 3). People who take part in your study should not have any of their rights abused, and you will need to be sure that the proposal you present to your teacher is ethical, otherwise your teacher will refuse to allow the investigation to be conducted.

Outside help

Once your proposal has been accepted, you are on your own. Your teacher should explain all the skills the examiner will be looking for, but once you have designed the investigation, you should not expect extra help. You will need to apply your understanding of what each skill means to your investigation. Your teacher will keep a check on your progress and activities and will sign your Candidate Record Form to show that the report is the result of your independent work. Remember, as the examination board considers the practical investigation to be a script, you have to imagine that it is a 'long examination'. Your teacher could not stand in the examination room telling you what the answers to the questions are, and they cannot tell you what to do or write for your coursework.

Skill marks for the write-up of the practical investigation

In total, you can be awarded 30 marks by the external marker for your practical investigation. The criteria for each of the skills are in the specification for the course, but the detail of each skill is covered in the following information.

Skill A: Design

There are fourteen skill marks allocated to design. There is no requirement for any candidate to use a particular methodology; however, it is expected that each candidate will present coursework which was designed so that there was the opportunity to gain full marks. There are some methodologies you will have learned about as part of your course which will make it difficult for you to obtain all the skill marks if you choose them for your practical investigation. We will return to this point once you have seen all the skill-mark criteria. The skills are numbered A1–A14.

A1 **Aim stated** means you must make a clear statement of the purpose of your investigation.

A2 **Background material** requires that the proposed investigated is drawn from psychological theory and/or research presented in the content of the other units (Unit 1 and Unit 2) of the AS course. Sufficient detail of theory or other studies relevant to your proposal must be included so that the marker can understand the aim and hypotheses of the investigation.

A3 **Hypothesis stated** means either the null hypothesis (H_0) or experimental/alternative hypothesis (Ha or H_1) is appropriate and written as a testable statement.

A4 **Variables identified** refers to the key variables presented in the H_0 or H_1. These may or may not be an independent variable and a dependent variable, but they must be operational.

A5 An **extraneous variable** is one which may confound the results, and you must be aware of the possible effects of this in your investigation.

A6 **Control for extraneous variable** should be a practical suggestion about how you will ensure that the extraneous variable you identified does not confound the results.

A7 The **target population** must be identified precisely, including location, so that the following skills can be assessed accurately.

A8 **Sampling method** means you must identify the sampling method used to get people to participate in your study.

A9 **Justification of sampling method** means that you should explain why the sampling method you chose was appropriate.

A10 **Description of task and materials** means that you should explain how these items were designed for the investigation.

A11 **Ethical issue identified** means that you will write about at least one issue which is relevant to your particular study rather than producing a list of all issues in general.

A12 **Ethical issue controlled** means that one of the issues you identified has been addressed successfully in the design.

A13 **Procedure described** will be credited if the marker can follow the description presented.

A14 **Procedure replicable** will be credited if all materials and information are presented so that the marker could conduct a replication of the study described above.

Skill B: Implementing

There are just two marks available for this skill; this reflects the difficulty of assessing a skill which the marker cannot have seen taking place. Credit will be given when there is detail in the written report to support this decision. The skills are numbered B1 and B2.

B1 **Appropriate treatment of participants** means there will be some reference in the report to ethical and/or safe treatment of the participants. There must be more than a simple statement such as 'they were treated ethically'.

B2 **Procedures carried out appropriately** will be judged by the marker using the detail provided by the candidate.

Skill C: Analysis and Interpretation

This section of skills carries ten of the 30 marks available. The skills are numbered C1–C10.

C1 **Data presented in appropriate forms** means you will choose a suitable form for your data, probably a table, chart or graph. You may choose to include more than one, but that is not a requirement. Remember, the data now needs to be summarised as the results of the investigation, and you must avoid tables, charts or graphs which display raw data.

C2 The form chosen, which could be a table, chart or graph, will be **headed properly** with an inform-ative title.

C3 **Raw data** must be converted into summary statistic(s), and evidence of calculations presented. Suitable calculations include measures of central tendency and measures of dispersion.

C4 However the data are summarised statistically, there will also be a **verbal summary** describing the direction/differences found/not found.

C5 The results will be **related to the hypothesis/es** stating which is supported. If only one hypothesis was presented, then the statement will relate to this.

C6 The results will be **compared with the background material**. This means you must discuss how the results of your investigation fit with the theory or research you presented at the start of your report.

C7 An appropriate **conclusion** will be drawn based on the results presented. You must avoid re-stat-ing the results and should discuss what the results tell you about human behaviour.

C8 A possible **limitation** of the investigation will be explored. This might be related to sample size, sampling technique, procedure or ecological validity.

C9 An appropriate **suggestion for improvement** will be discussed, probably based on the limitation presented previously.

C10 A **future research aim** will be presented. There is no need for excessive detail, but it should be a different key variable.

Skill D: Communication

There are four marks allocated to this skill area. The skills are numbered D1–D4.

D1 The **components present** means that you have organised the report under the following headings: Title, Abstract, Introduction, Method, Results, Discussion, References and Appendix. There is more detail on page 365 about what information should be in each of the components.

D2 **Terminology relevant** to the investigation is used appropriately. This means that you have included in your report terms and concepts used in psychology and have used these accurately.

D3   There will be an **abstract** which summarises the investigation. More detail of exactly what should be in the abstract can be found on page 366.

D4   Any relevant **reference(s)** will be presented at the end of the report. There is more information about how to write references on page 369.

Once you have understood what is meant by each of these skill marks, you should be able to see that it is very important that you design an investigation which will enable you to gain all the marks. In the Chapter 3, you learned about many different methods psychologists use to find out about human behaviour and thought. However, you should be able to see that some types of investigation might restrict your ability to gain all the skill marks – it is very difficult to perform a calculation on the verbal responses from an interview. Your teacher will help you to choose between the methods, and as long as you understand each skill, you should have no difficulty making a suitable choice.

Writing up the Report of the Practical Investigation

The following notes will provide you with information about how you could present a write-up of a complete investigation. There are no hard-and-fast rules which say it must be done in a certain way, and if you look at journal articles, you will see that the professionals do not follow a rigid format. However, the suggestions below will provide you with enough information for you to achieve the highest number of marks possible for your own written report. The use of the following standardised subheadings will help you to include relevant information in your report; but remember that you may adopt a slightly different structure to accommodate detail of your investigation if you feel that is necessary. Take care to ensure that you can still achieve skill D1 if you have a novel arrangement of sections in your report.

Title
Abstract
Introduction
Method
  Design
  Participants
  Apparatus and materials
  Procedure
Results
Discussion (including Conclusion)
References
Appendices

Below, you will find more detailed guidance on what to include under each of the subheadings suggested above.

Title

The best approach here is to write a sentence which includes the variables under investigation. So, in an experimental study, you might produce a sentence like 'An investigation into the effect of order of presentation of information on the impression formed of an individual', whereas in a study using correlational analysis, a suitable title might be 'An investigation into the relationship between memory ability and numerical ability'.

You should avoid writing the title as a question, and should avoid bland sentences like 'A Questionnaire' or 'A Memory Experiment'.

Abstract

This is a brief and clear summary of the complete investigation. It should be about 200 words long and include the following:

- the background theory and research on which the investigation is based. (this should be brief);
- the aim(s) and hypothesis/es of this investigation;
- details of the research method used; for example, experiment/observation and the design chosen, as in repeated measures or independent groups;
- the sampling method and sample of participants;
- the results of the investigation, including appropriate descriptive statistics and display of data;
- the conclusion drawn about the relationship between results obtained and hypothesis/es;
- how the findings were interpreted.

The abstract is the first piece of information the reader meets about the study; it is best written after the rest of the report has been finalised and should be left until all other sections have been written.

Introduction

This begins in a general way and presents key concepts involved in the subject area. There is no need to write all you know about the topic, as this is not an essay. It continues with a review of both previous theory and research which are relevant to the investigation which is to be undertaken. This should be written briefly, for example:

> 'In a study of organisation and memory, participants in one condition were presented with words arranged in hierarchical categories while participants in the other condition were given the same words but they were presented in random groups. When recall was tested, those whose words were categorised hierarchically were able to remember all the words, whereas those with randomly arranged words could recall on average only half of the words.' (Bower *et al.*, 1969)

Having presented the ideas and work of other psychologists, you must then state the aim of the investigation and its hypothesis/es. Remember, these must be operational statements, which means they must be testable, and it must be clear from the background information presented why a particular hypothesis has been written. Therefore, the task is to move from general information to specific information which is particularly relevant to the proposed investigation in a logical way, so that the reader is able to follow the reasoning behind the investigation to be undertaken. This section should be about 400 words long.

Method

In this section, the reader is told exactly what was done in the preparation for and conduct of the investigation. The best way of checking that all appropriate detail is included is to ask someone who has not been involved in the investigation to read this section; they should be sure they would be able to repeat/replicate the study from the detail you provide. You are expected to subdivide this section as follows, so that the information is organised in a logical way for the reader. Remember to check off all the Skill A and B marks as you write this section.

Design

In this section, you should state the research method used and justify that choice, for example 'an experiment was conducted because this method ...'. The key variables of the investigation will need to be stated and the extraneous variables identified, and the steps taken to control these should be detailed. Only one needs to be identified to gain credit, but it is good practice to also identify others that might be confounding variables and suggest ways they could be controlled.

Then you might need to explain why a particular type of experimental design, related or unrelated, was chosen, together with an indication of how participants were allocated to conditions. The number of participants in a group/condition and the number of trials undertaken may be relevant. Some students like to give details of the construction of materials/apparatus required in this section. This is because the section is concerned with items which have been created, for example, production of word lists, pictures or cards participants will be asked to use. Also, ethical considerations, the written form of all that will be said to participants to ensure ethical treatment, and record sheets or response sheets need to be included. The reader needs to know what the investigator produced, and a copy of each piece of these materials can be numbered and placed in the appendix so that the main body of the report is not cluttered.

Participants

In this section, you need to identify the target population, the sampling method used and the final number of participants gathered for the sample. If age and gender are relevant to the investigation, then details of these or other variables can be stated.

Apparatus and materials

All apparatus and/or materials must be listed here. If the apparatus is commercially available, then details of the make and model number should be given. Materials specially prepared should be described here if that has not already been done in the Design section. Remember, you don't want to give description of stimulus material such as word lists or pictures twice, or the report will become repetitive.

Procedure

This consists of a step-by-step description of exactly what was said and done from the point at which a prospective participant was approached and asked to take part to the thanking of that participant for their time after taking part in your experiment. It should not be written as a numbered list of steps, and the reader should be able to replicate the procedure from the detail given.

It is essential that whatever is said to participants is written word for word, and a logical way of doing this is to produce three written pieces:

1 Briefing: what is said to a prospective participant. At the end of this, the person agrees or refuses to take part.

2 Standardised instructions: these are given in the chosen location, and there may be more than one set for different conditions of the investigation.

3 Debriefing: this is where all is explained to the participant who is thanked at the end of their contribution.

This approach allows you to demonstrate clearly the ethical treatment of people who may or may not agree to take part in your investigation. Again, the construction of these materials should not be described here if that has been done in the Design or Apparatus sections. These pieces of apparatus can be referred to by number, and the reader can look them up in the appendix. However, marks will not be given for materials which are referred to but are not to be found in any section of the report, hence 'the participants were treated ethically' or 'the participants were debriefed' would not gain credit if the evidence for these statements has not been given in the report.

If participants are dealt with on an individual basis, then the Procedure section can be written as it applies to one participant, and you can state that this procedure was repeated for all other participants in the same condition/trial.

At this point, all of your planning and designing is complete, and it is worth thinking about writing up the report so far. It can sometimes be a mistake to write up a report in numerous short bursts, as the whole project can lose its coherence. However, it can be equally inadvisable to leave the writing until the investigation has been completed. Two major problems can be:

● those notes which seemed so clear when planning the investigation now seem incomprehensible;

● once the investigation has been completed, you know what the results are, and this knowledge can creep into your writing of those sections of the report which come before the Results and Discussion sections.

You must make a decision about how you will proceed; your teacher will be able to advise you.

Results

The results of the investigation must be presented as clearly and simply as possible, since you cannot assume that the reader is familiar with the area you are studying. This is *not* the place for raw data, which should be in the appendix. Summarised data, for example, measures of central tendency, (mean, median and mode) or ranges and standard deviations or percentages as appropriate, presented in tables with explicit headings will allow the reader to see immediately the overall pattern of results. Similarly, graphical displays may be presented, as long as they add to the reader's understanding of the data. However the results are displayed, there should be a verbal summary of the results shown with the table/chart/graph.

Calculations should be shown in the appendix so that they can be checked by the marker.

Discussion

This starts with the results of the statistical analysis and what they mean in relation to the hypothesis or hypotheses presented in the Introduction. Remember to comment on any anomalies which may have occurred and be careful of generalising the results without reference to the sample used.

Then you will need to relate the results to the background theory and research presented in the Introduction. Look for methodological similarities or differences between the studies, especially if your results do not fit with previous evidence.

Limitations of the usefulness of the study and the results should be considered. It may be that certain variables were avoidably or unavoidably left uncontrolled. Possible effects of this should be considered. Then you can move on to suggestions for improving the present investigation.

Depending on the nature of the investigation, you may be able to assess the wider practical or theoretical implications of the results you have found. It is also useful to consider ethical issues.

Finally, you should think about future research which could be conducted in the light of the results of the present investigation. Try to give a brief outline of the plan, rather than just making a general suggestion.

Conclusion

It is not strictly necessary to have a separate section for this, but it will round off the report if you provide a brief verbal summary of the main findings in relation to the aims and hypotheses. The conclusion must not merely be a restatement of the results, but show an appreciation of what the researcher now knows about a specific human behaviour.

References

Any theories, research and ideas or materials which you have used and which are the product of someone else's work or thinking must be referenced. This enables the reader to sort out whether what you are saying is original or from published work, and you should keep an accurate record of references. If you do not provide a reference for information, you are saying it is your idea, and the reader may well spot that it was proposed by another person and will not be impressed by this plagiarism.

References should be given in alphabetical order of author using the following format:

Author, date of publication, title (of book, article etc.), publisher.

Here are examples of some different types of references:

(a)
Bousfield, W.A. (1953), The occurrence of clustering in recall of randomly arranged associates. In R.D. Gross (1996), *Psychology: The Science of Mind and Behaviour*, London, Hodder & Stoughton

(b)
Bower, G.H., Clarke M., Lesgold A. & Winzenz D. (1969), Hierarchical retrieval schemes in recall of categorized word lists. *Journal of Verbal Learning and Verbal Behaviour*, 8, 323–343

(c)
Coolican, H. (1994), *Research Methods and Statistics in Psychology*, London, Hodder & Stoughton

(d)
Gruneberg, M.M., Morris, P.E. & Sykes R.N. (Eds) (1978), *Practical Aspects of Memory*, Academic Press, London, Routledge

Notice how book references (c) and (d) differ slightly from references for articles appearing in books (a) and from articles appearing in journals (b). Look at the reference sections in books and journals for an understanding of how this is done. You will not gain the mark for References if you do not follow the format given above.

Appendix

Copies of materials such as word lists, raw data and calculations, answer sheets and so on should be in the appendix so the marker can check the information in the main report.

Other points to bear in mind

When you do begin to write up the practical report, you should not use 'I' or 'we' in the description you present. This is too informal for a scientific report. Instead of 'I decided to use repeated measures as this would eliminate differences between participants ...' write 'A related design using repeated measures was chosen so that differences between participants were eliminated ...'.

In order to check that you have included the information necessary to gain full marks for all four skill areas, you must refer to the marking criteria given on pages 363–365.

One final point: if you cannot find any information in the form of theory and previous research for your proposed investigation, then you should not proceed with your idea. You cannot omit this material and expect to achieve reasonable marks for the report.

Summary of report writing

● Title: an informative sentence.

● Abstract: a concise and informative summary of the investigation.

● Introduction: background material in which relevant terms, theory and research are presented. Finishes with statement of the aim and hypothesis or hypotheses for present investigation.

● Method: variables under investigation identified appropriately, extraneous variable identified and control suggested; task and materials described; ethical issue identified and control suggested; target population identified, sampling method identified and justified; procedure explicit and replicable.

● Results: appropriate form chosen and headed, statistical and verbal summary, (calculations in appendix).

● Discussion: results related to hypothesis/es and background material; conclusion based on results; appreciation of limitation(s) stated and appropriate suggestion for improvement; suggestion for further research.

● References.

● Appendix.

Proposal form for the Practical Investigation

When you have understood the methodologies available to researchers and the skill marks which will be used to award marks for your report write-up, you will need to submit a proposal to your teacher, who will advise you about the suitability of your intended research. The following is an outline of the information you need to provide for your teacher so that they can judge whether your design decisions are appropriate.

Design for Practical Investigation

You must provide the answers to the following so that your teacher can be sure that the experiment you wish to conduct will provide you with the opportunity to collect as many marks as possible from the marking scheme.

● Identify the aim of your experiment.

● Identify the key variables in the investigation and then use this information to write the H_1 and H_0 for the study.

● Identify any extraneous variables which might affect the dependent variable if they are not controlled and suggest ways of controlling these that are practical.

● Outline any other standardised procedures that you think are necessary to ensure that the study will not suffer from *confounding* – this means that the results have been produced by something other than the key variables under investigation.

● Describe the task you have devised for the participants in your study and remember to give detail of how the materials which make up your apparatus were constructed. The actual materials should be appended to this information/discussed with your teacher.

● Identify the target population for your study and also the sampling method you will use to generate an appropriate group of participants. Justify this choice.

- Say which experimental design you will use. You must justify your choice. This means that you must explain why the related or unrelated design is appropriate.

- Write a set of *verbatim* instructions. This means that everything you say to your participants must be written down as you would say it. There are three sets of written information you must prepare:
(a) the briefing in which you write down what you say to a person you approach in the hope that they will agree to take part;
(b) the standardised instructions, which give the precise information about how to complete the task;
(c) the debriefing in which you explain fully the aim of the study and also how it has been implemented.
In each of these pieces of writing, you must also include the relevant ethical points.

- Give a very brief outline of the background information which you will use in the Introduction section of the report. You need only list the research of others at this stage.

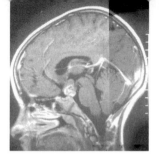

Glossary

Acetylcholine A neurotransmitter that has been identified as playing a significant role in the consolidation of memories.

Actor–observer effect A bias towards making more situational attributions of some behaviour when you are doing it yourself than when you see another person doing it.

Adoption studies Compare characteristics of adopted children to children of biological parents. Normally, adopted children in one family are compared with biological children in another family in efforts to determine the heritability of a characteristic.

Adrenal glands These are located above the kidneys and secrete a number of hormones, the most important being adrenalin. Adrenalin prepares the body for action.

Affordances Aspect of Gibson's theory of perception that states visual information alone is sufficient to enable perception of properties of objects. For example, when we see an object with a shiny surface, we perceive its smoothness and hardness.

Age-related dementia Also known as Alzheimer's disease, dementia of the Alzheimer's type (DAT). Disorder resulting in memory impairment and confusion that occurs in some elderly people.

'Aha' phenomenon The experience of suddenly finding the answer to a problem.

Alternative hypothesis Also know as the experimental or research hypothesis. This states that there is a relationship (association or difference) between the two variables being studied. Often shown as H1.

Alzheimer's disease See *age-related dementia*.

Ambiguous figure Figure with two or more possible interpretations.

Amnesia Partial or complete loss of memory, often as a result of damage to the brain.

Anal stage The second stage of development when the sexual energy is mainly focused in the anal region and the child receives sexual gratification from urination and defecation.

Analogical reasoning A form of problem-solving in which people understand a new situation by making comparisons with a familiar situation.

Analogy A comparison between two different objects or situations that allows you to make a judgement which may or may not be correct.

Analysis by synthesis Neisser's theory of perception in which the top-down and bottom-up approaches are combined.

Androgyny The appearance of both typically masculine and typically feminine traits within one individual's personality.

Anterograde amnesia Loss of memory after the onset of amnesia as a result of which the person cannot learn new material.

Anthropological studies Research which is conducted on societies to understand mankind and social relationships.

Anthropology The study of different cultures that exist across the world, including their historical origins and development.

Articulatory control process A feature of Baddeley and Hitch's working-memory model responsible for maintaining information in the *phonological loop* by means of rehearsal.

Asch's line study Asch used an unambiguous and clear task whereby participants were shown a target line and three comparison lines. The target line had to be matched in length with one of the comparison lines. Also known as *Asch's study of conformity*.

Attention Commonly used to refer to the process by which certain information is selected for further processing. The means by which information is transferred from sensory stores to the short-term store in Atkinson and Shiffrin's model of memory.

Attenuation Process by which the attentional system weakens any input which is not the prime focus of current attention, but still makes it available for lower-level analysis.

Attitude A general evaluation people make about themselves, others, objects or issues which are developed from past experience and guide behaviour.

Attributional bias A source of bias in making inferences about the causes of a person's behaviour.

Audience People observing individuals or teams playing or performing a sport or task. See also *co-actors*.

Authoritarian personality Characterised as upholding convention, conforming and obeying those in authority, but being authoritarian to subordinates. Linked to *prejudice* and *discrimination*.

Autobiographical memory Memory for events that have happened in one's own life.

Autokinetic effect The apparent movement people see with a stationery spot of light in a darkened room. Used to investigate conformity by Sherif.

Automaticity The ability to perform a task or tasks without conscious, controlled or focused attention.

Autonomic nervous system This consists of two subsystems: the sympathetic and parasympathetic nervous systems.

Availability heuristic One of the heuristics used in making judgements about the likelihood of an event occurring (*probabilistic reasoning*). Information that can easily be recalled (available) will influence the judgements people make.

Balance A theory considers the relationship between a person (P), another person (O) and an attitude object. The relationship may be balanced or unbalanced. See also *congruity*.

Basic level An intermediate-level category (identified by Rosch), which usually contains the most information about an object, such as 'chairs' and 'desks'. Usually correspond to the categories normally used.

Behaviour genetics Concerned with how our genetic make-up (*genotype*) influences characteristics such as personality, intelligence and mental disorder (schizophrenia).

Behavioural sciences See *social sciences*.

Behavioural style An important factor in *minority influence*. For a minority to be influential they should show a consistent style.

Behaviourism An approach in psychology which states that only the objective measurement of

behaviour is scientific, and that all learning comes from reinforcement or punishment of responses. See also *classical conditioning* and *operant conditioning*.

Binocular cues Cues to depth or distance perception that require the use of both eyes.

Biological approach An approach which is interested in how physical structures, especially the central nervous system, and our genes influence thought and behaviour.

Biological determinism The view that individuals have no control over the development of their behaviour, but that it is controlled by genetic forces.

Biology Concerned with understanding the structure and function of the physical aspects of the body. Of interest to psychologists is the study of the central and peripheral nervous systems.

Bisexual Possessing the characteristics of both sexes and finding attraction in the qualities of both the same and opposite sex.

Blue–green study A study conducted by Moscovici and his colleagues to investigate minority influence. Blue- and green-coloured slides were shown to participants who had to say which colour they were.

Bottom-up approach An approach that suggests our cognitive processes are mainly influenced by incoming stimuli rather than previously stored information. Sometimes known as a *data-driven* or *sense-data approach*.

Broca's area An area of the frontal cortical lobe responsible for the function of speech. If damaged, it results in Broca's aphasia: speech will be slow, laborious and hesitant.

Brown–Peterson task A method developed to investigate the characteristics of short-term memory. It typically involves the use of lists of three-letter sequences which participants are required to learn and recall.

Capgras syndrome A clinical disorder affecting face recognition where patients believe their world is inhabited by people who look like people they know, but who are strangers.

Carpentered-world hypothesis Suggestion that people from Western cultures, where buildings are structured or carpentered with right angles and level floors, perceive the world differently to people from less structured environments.

Case study An in-depth or detailed study of one individual or a small group of individuals, event or organisation which might take place over a period of time. Case studies are usually conducted using an open-ended interview technique.

Category A grouping based on common properties.

Causal attribution An inference about whether the cause of a person's behaviour was dispositional or situational.

Causal schemata Organised sets of cognitions about the causes of commonly occurring behaviour.

Cell assemblies A feature of Hebb's ideas concerning the relationship between physiology and memory. He suggested that groups of neurons are activated in response to new information and they then form the basis for the formation of permanent memories.

Central executive The part of Baddeley and Hitch's working-memory model responsible for controlling the operation of the *phonological loop* and the *visuo-spatial sketchpad*.

Central nervous system Made up of the brain and the spinal cord. The human brain has three major parts: the brain stem, cerebellum and cerebral cortex.

Championship choke Where the home team performs worse at home due to a game being very important to the home team. This results in home-ground disadvantage.

Classical conditioning The pairing of a neutral stimulus with a stimulus that automatically elicits a response so that the neutral stimulus comes to elicit a response. First developed by Ivan Pavlov and his experiments with dogs.

Cluster sampling Where clusters are identified and selected at random, then a sample is randomly selected from each sample.

Co-actors Where two or more people perform the same task as each other in each other's presence.

Cocktail-party phenomenon Where a person responds to their own name or other piece of information important to them personally from an unattended source whilst listening to an attended source.

Cognitive approach The dominant approach in contemporary psychology which studies thought and mental processes more generally. Areas of study include perception, attention, memory, language and thought. See also *information-processing approach*.

Cognitive dissonance Occurs when the attitude a person holds is inconsistent with the person's behaviour. This creates tension or feelings of discomfort and motivates attitude change towards consistency.

Cognitive interview Interview technique involving four special ways of questioning to help witnesses recall events more clearly.

Cognitive style A distinctive way of thinking which varies across people.

Collectivistic cultures Cultures where the good of the group and achievement of the group is valued over individual achievement. For example, China and Asian countries. See also *individualistic cultures*.

Colour constancy The ability to perceive colours as constant despite changes in the retinal cues with varying light conditions.

Common sense Observations and knowledge about human behaviour based on subjective experience, folk psychology, lay psychology or naïve scientist. What is commonly believed to be true may or may not be supported by psychological science.

Communication The transmission of a signal that conveys information.

Compliance A type of social influence whereby direct requests are made from one person to another.

Concept-driven processing See *top-down processing*.

Concept A mental representation of a group of events, ideas or objects that share common properties.

Conditional reasoning The type of deductive reasoning carried out using 'if-then' statements. Also referred to as *propositional reasoning*.

Confabulation Where memories of events are altered in line with what we think happened, based on our previous knowledge of the world, so that the memory is no longer a true record of events.

Confirmation bias The tendency for people to look for information that confirms their expectations.

Conformity A type of social influence in which a person changes their attitudes, beliefs or behaviours to adhere to social norms. Usually seen as *majority influence*.

Confounding variable Also known as extraneous variable. A variable which the psychologist has not controlled in an experiment, but which may influence how people behave and hence influence in an unwanted way the dependent variable.

Congruity Similar to balance theory, it measures the strength of attitude held and attempts to predict the direction of attitude change. See also *balance*.

Consensus The extent to which other people also engage in a particular behaviour. One of the factors referred to in the covariation model of attribution.

Consistency The extent to which a person always or reliably engages in a particular behaviour in particular circumstances. One of the factors referred to in the covariation model of attribution.

Consolidation The process by which memories become permanent. Lack of consolidation is one explanation that has been used to try and account for forgetting.

Constancy scaling Process by which we mentally enlarge our perception of a distant object to compensate for its distance from us.

Continuity theory The view that human language has evolved from our non-human ancestors.

Convergent thinking A thinking style that is directed towards getting the single 'correct' answer to a problem.

Correlation A statistical technique used to determine whether or not there is a relationship between two variables. A correlation statistic can range from positive through zero to negative.

Correspondent inference The inference that a person's behaviour is a good guide to their character.

Cross-cultural psychology How people behave and think in different cultures. Topic areas of psychology applied to different cultures to look for cross-cultural differences. See also *anthropology*.

Cued recall A technique used in memory research. Participants learn some information, usually a list of words, and are required to recall them after a delay. In the recall phase, participants are given cues, such as parts of words or categories, to aid their recall.

Cultural relativitity The view that behaviour and development are linked to the particular society in which a person lives rather than an innate and universal programming of behaviour.

Data-driven approach See *bottom-up approach.*

Decay The idea that memories are lost because the memory trace fades away as a result of the passage of time.

Declarative knowledge Knowledge stored in long-term memory that includes our episodic and semantic memories. It is knowledge that can be translated into words and described, such as 'knowing' that Paris is the capital of France.

Deductive reasoning A form of reasoning that draws logical conclusions from facts that are known or supposed to be true.

Dependent variable (DV) The measure or measures taken by the psychologist of people's behaviour in an experiment.

Descriptive statistics Used to summarise and present the findings of quantitative data or raw data. Descriptive statistics include *measures of central tendency* and *measures of dispersion.*

Determinism The idea that behaviour (and thought) is determined by either or both genetic inheritance and the environment. The belief that behaviour is programmed for an individual and that the person has no free will to chose their behaviour. See also *free will.*

Dichotic listening Technique used in attention studies where participants hear a different message through left and right earphones.

Digit span test Frequently used to test the capacity of short-term memory. The test involves participants repeating back sequences of auditorily presented digits. The maximum number of digits to be recalled correctly in sequence indicates the short-term memory capacity.

Direct measures of attitudes Self-report approaches whereby a person is asked directly about their attitude. The most commonly used direct measure is the *Likert scale.*

Discontinuity theory The view that human language is completely different from the forms of communication used by animals.

Discounting principle The tendency to focus on one cause and ignore other possible causes when a behaviour is perceived as having *multiple sufficient causes.*

Discounting The tendency to ignore new information which conflicts with existing schemas.

Discrimination Behaviour or actions, usually negative, towards individuals or groups of people.

Dispositional attribution The inference that the cause of some behaviour is the character of the person who produced the behaviour, rather than the circumstances they are in.

Distinctiveness The extent to which a person's behaviour is restricted only to a specific set of circumstances. One of the factors referred to in the covariation model of attribution.

Distraction–conflict theory States that the presence of others when performing a task creates a distraction, which in turn interferes with the attention the person can give to the task. This increases arousal, hence the tendency to perform the *dominant response.*

Distracter task A task given to participants in memory experiments to ensure that they do not simply remember information by silently rehearsing it to themselves.

Divergent thinking A thinking style that involves producing numerous alternative solutions to problems. Often associated with creative thinking.

Dizygotic twins Also known as fraternal twins. They are no more alike than ordinary brothers and sisters, since they come from two different fertilised eggs.

Dominant response What an individual is most likely to perform when asked to do a task. The person may be highly skilled at a task or have little previous experience – either is a dominant response.

Door-in-the-face-technique A method used to gain compliance by first making a large unreasonable request, which is almost certain to be refused, followed by a smaller, more reasonable request.

Drive theory of social facilitation States that the presence of others when performing a task increases the person's general level of arousal. This in turn increases the likelihood that the person will perform their *dominant response*.

Dual-process model of persuasion Proposes two processes of attitude change resulting from automatic or deliberative processing of information. The elaboration-likelihood model is an example is the dual-process model.

Dual task Type of task used to investigate the ability to perform two tasks concurrently, used with a view to specifying some upper limit on attentional capacity.

Echoic memory A sensory memory store specialised for holding sounds for two to three seconds.

Ecological validity The extent to which a study can be generalised to real life. If a study has low ecological validity, then the behaviour has not been measured in circumstances similar to the way in which that behaviour occurs in real life.

Ego One of the aspects of personality identified by Freud, it serves to satisfy the needs of the *id*.

Ego resolution A state when the child is able to come to terms with conflict by working out a way in which internal conflict can be resolved and the self remains intact.

Egocentric Only seeing things from your own point of view.

Egocentric speech A term used by Piaget to describe the type of speech used by children when they use language to express their own thoughts rather than communicate with other people.

Elaboration-likelihood model of attitude change An example of a dual-process model of persuasion. It states that people adopt either a superficial or systematic approach to processing information.

Elaborative rehearsal One of the two types of rehearsal proposed by Craik and Lockhart in their levels-of-processing model. Involves the deep and meaningful analysis of information rather than simply repeating it over and over. See also *maintenance rehearsal*.

Electra complex Freudian theory that girls develop *penis envy*, identify with their father and reject their mother.

Electro-convulsive therapy (ECT) Treatment involving the passing of a brief electric current through the brain. Nowadays used mostly as a therapy for depression.

Encoding-specificity principle Proposes that our ability to recall memories is dependent on the extent to which the information held in a memory trace matches the information available at retrieval.

Encoding The process by which information is extracted from a stimulus to form memory trace.

Endocrine system Made up of a number of glands that secrete chemicals called hormones into the bloodstream.

Episodic memory A memory system proposed by Tulving which stores our memories of personal experiences and events.

Evaluation apprehension Occurs when performing a task in the presence of others. It causes arousal which in turn increases the likelihood of the *dominant response*.

Event schema A cognitive structure which represents the typical sequence of events in a familiar situation.

Evolutionary psychology An area of psychology which uses evolutionary mechanisms and explanations for human thought, behaviour and culture.

Existence proof Proof that something exists, for example, that it is possible to implant in a person's mind a memory of something that never happened.

Experimental Experimental designs in psychology are of three basic sorts: repeated measures, matched pairs and independent groups.

Experimental hypothesis See *alternative hypothesis*.

External attribution See *situational attribution*.

Extraneous variable See *confounding variable*.

Extroversion A group of personality traits including sociability, out-goingness and stimulation-seeking.

Eye-witness testimony Verbal or written account of an event given by a person who witnessed the event.

Face recognition unit (FRU) Feature of the Bruce and Young model of face recognition containing structural information about the face of a person we know.

False memory A memory of an event which has never taken place but is thought by the person remembering it to have really happened.

Feature-analysis theory Theory of face recognition emphasising the importance of individual facial features.

Field study An experiment carried out in a natural setting or real-life situation, but where the psychologist has control over some variables.

Foot-in-the-door technique A method used to gain compliance by first securing agreement to a small request which is then followed by a large request.

Free association A technique where participants are encouraged to respond to a stimulus with the first thing that occurs to them.

Free recall A technique used in memory research. After learning some information, participants are instructed to recall as much of the information as they can in any order.

Free will The idea that people are free to choose and that their behaviour is not pre-determined by either genetics or the environment. See also *determinism*.

Fugue amnesia A type of amnesia associated with the Freudian theory of repression where the sufferer apparently loses all memory of their life, forgetting relationships, job and even their own name, and takes on a whole new identity.

Functional approach to attitudes Suggests that a person's general well-being is promoted through attitudes serving four functions: adaptive, knowledge, ego-expressive and ego-defensive.

Fundamental attribution error A source of bias in *causal attribution* which leads to more *dispositional* than *situational* attributions being made.

Galvanic skin response (GSR) Method for detecting emotion or stress which involves placing electrodes on the surface of the skin to record minute changes in surface moisture.

Gender This refers to the social and cultural interpretation of behaviour expected of men and women

Generic theory Ideas which have no particular class, but include features of several classes.

Genetics The study of the genetic make-up of organisms and how this influences physical and behavioural characteristics.

Genotype The actual genetic make-up of a person as represented in the 23 pairs of human chromosomes. See also *phenotype*.

Gestalt approach An approach to psychology originating in Germany. Gestalt psychologists were interested primarily in perception and problem-solving, proposing that organisation of perceptual information was determined by the least effort needed to interpret the sense data. An approach which emphasises the 'wholeness' of experience and thinking.

Group Environment Questionnaire (GEQ) A widely used questionnaire used to measure *team cohesion*; it is based on group integration and individual attraction.

Group A collection of individuals who interact with each other and are interdependent on each other to an extent.

Group structure The statuses and roles of individuals in a group; also the group norms.

Hedonic relevance The extent to which another person's behaviour affects me. One of the factors referred to in the *correspondent inference* theory of attribution.

Hemispheric specialisation See *lateralisation of function*.

Heredity The traits, tendencies and characteristics inherited from a person's parents and their ancestors.

Heritability coefficient A number between zero and one showing the extent to which a behaviour or psychological characteristic is a result of heredity. A value of one means the characteristic is solely due to heredity, a value of zero that heredity has no influence at all.

Heuristic A strategy for solving problems which is based on 'rules of thumb' and cognitive short-cuts. It is not guaranteed to produce the correct solution but is highly likely to solve the problem.

Hierarchical model of concept organisation A model that represents the way in which concepts are represented in our cognitive system. It proposes that concepts are stored in a hierarchy.

Holistic-form theory Theory of face recognition emphasising the importance of the face as a whole, including the general layout or configuration of the features, and information about the person, such as where we know them from and whether or not we like them.

Home-ground advantage Where home teams in sports competitions win more games at home under a balanced home-and-away schedule. Geography, familiarity with pitch, player confidence at home, and home audience all contribute to this effect.

Humanistic psychology Also known as the 'third force' in psychology. An approach which places value on human experience and sees each person as unique. Also known as a *phenomenological* or *ideographic* approach.

Huntington's disease An inherited disorder which causes damage to the motor areas of the brain. Patients experience increasing problems with their motor skills but retain the ability to acquire declarative knowledge.

Iconic memory A sensory memory store specialised for holding visual information for about half a second.

Id Also known as 'das est' (the it), this refers to the fact that the child at birth only contains instinctive needs which require gratification at any cost.

Ideal self A person's view of how they would like to be. Linked to a person's *self-schema*.

Idiographic approach A general approach in psychology which places emphasis on the importance of an indepth understanding of the individual. See, by contrast, the *nomothetic approach*.

Image A form of mental representation which is based on physical sensations such as sight and sound.

Impression formation The process of making inferences about another person's character, mood, abilities and intentions.

Impression management Attempting to influence the impressions other people form of you.

Incidental-learning procedure A technique used in memory research. Participants are presented with information, but they are not aware that they are going to be asked to recall it. Used in research investigating the levels of processing approach to memory.

Independent variable (IV) The variable which is manipulated and controlled by the psychologist in an experiment.

Indirect measures of attitude Do not measure an attitude directly, but use projective techniques and physiological measures as an indirect indication of the attitude a person holds.

Individualistic cultures Cultures where individual achievement and personal choice are highly valued. For example, the USA and United Kingdom. See also *collectivistic cultures*.

Inductive reasoning A type of reasoning in which people go from specific observations to making generalisations. In this type of reasoning, you cannot be sure that the conclusion is correct.

Infantile amnesia Loss of memory for events that took place in early childhood.

Infantile sexuality A Freudian idea which maintains that infants relate to their parent (mother) as a result of innate sexual desires.

Inference Going beyond, or adding to, the information given in order to make a sensible interpretation of a stimulus or event.

Information-processing approach An approach to cognition popularised in the 1960s and 1970s, which likens the human mind to the operation of a computer where information is coded, stored, retrieved and used to make a response. See also *cognitive approach*.

Informational social influence Where conformity to the majority view results from new information or reasoned arguments presented to a minority by a majority in the group. This form of social influence results in private acceptance of the view.

Insight The sudden restructuring of a problem which usually results in the correct solution.

Intelligence A person's ability to learn and remember, recognise concepts and their relationships and apply information to behaviour in an adaptive way.

Interference Proposes that forgetting is the result of our memories being disrupted or interfered with by other information.

Intergroup conflict Where two groups or teams compete with each other for the same prize or resource; as a result, competition and conflict between the two teams develop.

Internal attribution See *dispositional attribution*.

Interviews Usually take place face-to-face between the researcher and a participant. Interviews can be either structured (formal) or unstructured (informal).

Introspection Technique first used by Wilhelm Wundt to establish psychology as a science. Requires a person to report on conscious experience. Realised that introspection is subjective and not scientific.

Introversion A group of personality traits including shyness, a preference for solitude and avoidance of stimulation.

Korsakoff's syndrome Severe memory loss due to brain damage as a result of prolonged alcohol abuse.

Laboratory experiment A type of experiment that is carried out in a highly controlled environment. This is often, but not always, in a psychology laboratory.

Language A system of symbols and sounds that enables people to communicate ideas.

Lateralisation The division of the brain into two distinct hemispheres, each having specific functions.

Lateralisation of function Also known as *hemispheric specialisation*. This refers to the finding that the left hemisphere in most people is dominant for language and logical thought, whilst the right hemisphere is dominant for artistic creativity, music and intuition.

Law of effect Proposed by Thorndike, this states that the tendency of an individual to produce behaviour depends on the effect the behaviour has on the environment.

Laws of Pragnanz Laws of perceptual organisation proposed by the Gestalt psychologists. The laws govern the way in which we interpret sensory information and lead us to make the simplest interpretation of a given stimulus. For example, the law of similarity states that similar objects would be perceived as a group rather than as a number of individual objects.

Leading question Question in which the answer is suggested, perhaps by the way the question is phrased or by the tone of the interviewer's voice.

Levels of processing An alternative to the multi-store model of memory. Developed by Craik and Lockhart, it proposes that how information is processed determines whether or not it is remembered. 'Deep' processing is more likely to lead to successful recall than 'shallow' processing.

Libido A form of sexual energy which the person is born with and which forms the motivation for behaviour

Likert scale Usually a five-point scale used in testing attitudes to behaviour in which a person indicates their acceptance of the statement from 'strong agreement' to 'strong disagreement'. The scale is measured from one to seven, and by counting the individual responses to each statement, the strength of opinion on a particular topic can be calculated.

Linguistic determinism The term used to describe Whorf's view that language must determine thought.

Localisation of (cortical) function The idea that different parts or areas of the brain are specialised at certain tasks or activities. See also *Broca's area* and *Wernicke's area*.

Long-term memory Our permanent store of knowledge which has a more or less infinite capacity and can retain information for a lifetime.

Looking-glass self The idea that *self-image* results from the reactions and behaviour of other people towards us.

Low-ball technique A method to gain compliance where a person who has already agreed a request or to purchase an item is then asked for more or to pay more. Car salesman are often said to use this technique when selling a car.

Maintenance rehearsal One of the two types of rehearsal proposed by Craik and Lockhart in their levels-of-processing model. It involves retaining information by repeating it over and over again. See also *elaborative rehearsal*.

Majority influence The influence of a majority view on a minority, with the result that the minority conform to the view of the majority.

Mean The sum of all the raw scores divided by the number of raw scores.

Measures of central tendency Commonly used to describe data and include the *mean, median* and *mode*.

Measures of dispersion Describe the spread of scores. The most commonly used measures of dispersion are the *range* and *standard deviation*.

Median The central or middle value of a set of raw scores.

Minority influence Where a minority in a group changes the attitudes, perceptions, beliefs or behaviours of the majority in the group. The minority influence the majority to their point of view.

Mode The most commonly occurring score or value in a set of data.

Monocular cues Cues to depth or distance perception that require the use of only one eye.

Monozygotic twins Also known as identical twins. They share exactly the same genetic make-up, since they both come from the sane fertilised egg. See also *dizygotic twins*.

Multiple necessary causes When every one of a number of conditions has to be fulfilled in order for some behaviour to occur. An aspect of the *causal schemata* model of attribution.

Multiple sufficient causes When any one of a number of conditions can lead to some behaviour occurring. An aspect of the *causal schemata* model of attribution.

Multi-store model A model of memory which proposes three types of memory store, each with different characteristics: a sensory store which holds large amounts of information for very brief periods of time; a short-term store which has a limited capacity; and a long-term store which can hold large amounts of information for very long periods of time.

Natural selection An evolutionary process in which genetically influenced characteristics either benefit a species and help individuals survive better in their environment, or do not aid survival. Important concept in Darwin's theory of evolution. See also *survival of the fittest*.

Need for cognition A personality characteristic to do with the extent to which a person likes to engage in and enjoys thinking. This ranges from high to low as a variable.

Neuron The basic building block of the nervous system. The neuron, or nerve cell, transmits and receives information in the form of electrical impulses in the nervous system.

Neurotransmitters Chemicals found in the synaptic vesicles in the *synapse*. These chemicals may increase or decrease the firing of a neuron. Several different neurotransmitters are found in the brain.

Nomothetic approach A general approach in psychology that looks for laws of human behaviour and, as a consequence, makes scientific comparisons across people. See, in contrast, the *ideographic approach*.

Non-common effect Any difference which results from a choice between alternatives. One of the factors referred to in the *correspondent inference model* of attribution.

Non-participant observation Where the researcher observes the behaviour of other people but does not become a member of the group. See also *participant observation*.

Normative social influence Where people conform to the majority view in order to maintain group harmony, avoid reflection by the group or gain approval from other group members.

Null hypothesis This states that there is no relationship (association or difference) between the two variables being studied. Often shown as Ho.

Obedience to authority A type of social influence in which one or more other people [???]. Investigated in Milgram's famous experiments.

Objective This is what science aspires to be: value free and lacking in subjectivity.

Oedipus complex Freud's theory that, at a certain stage in their development, boys develop a sexual attachment to their mother.

Operant conditioning The shaping of behaviour to achieve a response which is then reinforced. The reinforcement or reward is conditional upon the behaviour being performed. Developed by Skinner.

Opportunity sampling Where a sample is selected according to availability or convenience of people. For example, sampling people from those leaving a library.

Optic array All the visual information currently in our field of vision.

Optic-flow patterns Flow of visual information across the visual field and radial expansion of textures that occurs as we move forward.

Oral stage The first stage in development when the sexual energy of the libido is located around the mouth and the child finds sexual satisfaction from objects placed around the mouth.

Parasympathetic nervous system Maintains normal bodily activity by regulating, for example, breathing and heart rate. Reduces the activity of the *sympathetic nervous system*.

Participant observation Where the researcher observes the behaviour of other people in a group by actually becoming a full member of the group. See also *non-participant observation*.

Penis envy Experienced by girls during the phallic stage when they recognise the power of the penis which they desire and at the same realise that they have not got one.

Perceptual accentuation Heightened or increased awareness, usually in relation to something we want or need.

Perceptual defence Decreased perceptual awareness or reluctance to perceive due to the use of unconscious Freudian defence mechanisms. Perceptual defence supposedly prevents us from perceiving a stimulus we would find unpleasant or upsetting.

Perceptual set Predisposition to perceive and attend to certain aspects of a stimulus rather than others.

Peripheral nervous system Has two sub-systems: the somatic and autonomic nervous systems. The peripheral nervous system transmits and conveys information to and from the *central nervous system*.

Person Identity Node (PIN) A feature of the Bruce and Young model of face recognition containing personal information about a person we know, for example, where they live, their job, etc.

Person schema A cognitive structure which represents a person's knowledge about other individuals or types of individual.

Persuasive communication An approach to attitude change based on the question 'who says what to whom and with what effect?'

Phallic stage The third stage in development when the libido transfers itself to the genitals resulting in sexual desire of the boy child for the mother.

Phenotype The expression of a person's genetic make-up: physical appearance, behavioural characteristics, personality, etc.

Phenylketonuria A disorder (known as PKU) which results from a double recessive gene and which can cause severe learning difficulties for the person. The condition results in the inability to synthesise the amine **phenylanaline**. Special diets without this amine result in the person developing normally.

Phobia An irrational fear or anxiety directed to a specific object which cannot itself cause harm.

Phonological loop The part of Baddeley and Hitch's working-memory model that deals with auditory information. Consists of the phonological store which holds information and the *articulatory control process* which is capable of rehearsing information.

Phonological store A feature of Baddeley and Hitch's working-memory model. A passive store which is capable of holding auditory information for about two seconds. Operates in collaboration with the articulatory control process, which is capable of rehearsing and refreshing the information.

Photofit A technique used by the police to construct an image of a face from a witness's description using five component features. Nowadays done on a computer and known as an *e-fit*.

Pilot study An initial run through of a questionnaire or experiment to check for problems, flaws or difficulties that participants may have. Modifications may be made to the study or questionnaire as a result of this.

Positron emission tomography (PET) A computerised brain-scanning technique that enables researchers to monitor the activity of neurons in different parts of the brain.

Post-traumatic amnesia Memory loss occurring after a severe blow to the head, as might happen in a car accident or a fall.

Prejudice An unjustified or incorrect negative (or positive) attitude towards an individual based solely on the individual's membership of a group.

Primacy effect The tendency for the first few items on a list to be remembered better than the items that appear in the middle of the list. May cause bias in *impression formation*.

Principle of consistency The assumption that attitudes and behaviour link together in a consistent way such that the attitude predicts the behaviour of a person.

Proactive interference Where old memories that have already been stored interfere with the storage and retrieval of new information.

Probabilistic reasoning The type of reasoning used to make judgements about the likelihood, or probability, of an event occurring.

Procedural knowledge Knowledge held in long-term memory of skills and abilities. The type of knowledge that consists of knowing how to do something, such as playing a musical instrument, and is very difficult to express verbally.

Productive thinking A type of thinking in which our existing knowledge has been changed or adapted in some way to make it applicable to a particular problem.

Propositional reasoning See *conditional reasoning*.

Prosopagnosia A disorder of face recognition in which sufferers are unable to recognise the faces of people they know.

Prospective memory Memory for events in the future, for example, when we need to remember to do something at a certain time or on a certain day.

Psychoanalysis Theory and therapy developed by Sigmund Freud emphasising the importance of the unconscious, sexual instinct and psychosexual development in childhood. See also *psychodynamics*.

Psychodynamics An approach in psychology, originating with Freudian theory, which emphasises the importance of unconscious conflicts within the individual and instructual energy. Therapies based on a psychodynamic approach may analyse dreams to uncover and help resolve mental conflicts.

Psycholinguistics The study of language and the structure of language, in particular its interaction with thinking.

Psychology The scientific study of mind and behaviour. Derived from the Greek words *psyche* meaning 'mind' and *logos* meaning 'the study of'.

Pure amnesia A particularly dense form of memory loss, usually resulting in a complete inability to store any new information.

Qualitative data Verbal or written rather than numerical data. The methods commonly used to collect qualitative data are observations, interviews and examination of written or pictorial material.

Quantitative data Numerical data which can then be subjected to various types of statistical analysis.

Questionnaires Can be used to obtain people's views and attitudes about a topic or measure a specific aspect of personality. Questionnaires can use both open-ended and closed questions.

Quota sampling Where a sample is selected on the basis of the groups that make up the population. Samples of each group, or quota, are taken according to their proportion in the population.

Racism Prejudice and discrimination aimed at one group of people by another group of people. Racism these days is more likely to be subtle rather than blatant.

Radical behaviourism See *behaviourism.*

Random sampling Where each person in the target population has an equal chance of being selected for a sample. This can be achieved by putting all names or numbers in a hat and drawing the number of participants needed for the study.

Range The difference between the highest score and lowest score in a set of data.

Rational–emotive therapy Developed by Albert Ellis to treat people with depressive or anxiety disorders. It attempts to change the way people think about themselves and other people in order to remove defeatist thoughts and replace them with positive ones. A therapy representing the cognitive approach in psychology.

Recency effect The tendency for the last few items on a list to be remembered better than those in the middle of the list. This may cause bias in impression formation. See also *primacy effect.*

Reconstructive memory Where recall is achieved through the use of extra information, such as previously stored knowledge in the form of schema or stereotypes.

Recovered memory Apparent memory of an event of which the person had no previous knowledge.

Reliability Consistency between the actual event and an eye-witness's recollection of it. Can also be used to refer to the consistency of accounts between two or more witnesses.

Representativeness heuristic One of the heuristics used in making judgements about the likelihood of an event occurring (*probabilistic reasoning*). Information that is seen as being representative or typical will be assumed to occur most frequently. Often leads to people making inaccurate judgements.

Repression Freudian defence mechanism which suggests that forgetting has an emotional basis. According to Freud's theory of motivated forgetting,

unpleasant memories are held in the unconscious because they are so distressing.

Reproductive thinking A type of thinking in which our existing knowledge is simply re-applied to a new problem. There is no attempt made to modify the knowledge to make it applicable to the new situation.

Retrieval Remembering information by bringing it from long-term memory into short-term or working memory.

Retrieval cues Stimuli or thoughts that can be used as an aid to the retrieval of information from long-term memory.

Retrieval failure Information is stored in the memory but cannot be retrieved because the retrieval cues are inadequate. Such material is said to be available, because it is still stored in memory, but inaccessible, because it cannot be retrieved.

Retroactive interference Where new information interferes with the retrieval of older information already stored in long-term memory.

Retrograde amnesia A form of amnesia or memory loss in which the person is unable to recall memories for events which occurred before the onset of the amnesia.

Role schema A cognitive structure about the character and behaviour to be expected from people in a particular social role.

Rorschach inkblot test An example of a projective test where people are asked to make an interpretation of a pattern of abstract blobs. The interpretation is taken to indicate something about the person being tested, most usually their personality.

Sampling Where a psychologist selects a sample of people to take part in a study or experiment. Sampling techniques include: quota sampling, systematic sampling, stratified sampling, opportunity sampling and cluster sampling.

Sapir–Whorf hypothesis A hypothesis based on the work of Whorf and Sapir that language and thought must be closely connected.

Scattergram A type of graph on which pairs of data are plotted to see whether a relationship (correlation) exists between two variables. See also *correlation.*

Schema (plural schemata) An organised unit of knowledge or collection of beliefs and feelings about some aspect of the world. A schema helps to structure and interpret new information and is stored in long-term memory.

Schizophrenia A serious mental disorder characterised by hallucinations (visual and auditory), delusions and emotional withdrawal. Twin studies and adoption studies point to a strong degree of heritability.

Science The use of theory to generate hypotheses which can then be tested in controlled, laboratory conditions. Empirical evidence is used to provide support or refute a theory/hypothesis.

Script schema See *event schema*.

Scripts A term used by Schank & Abelson (1977) to describe the way in which we store information about the sequence of events in everyday situations.

Selective breeding A method used in an attempt to determine the heritability of a characteristic. It involves artificial selection of males and females to breed, as compared with natural breeding.

Self-esteem How favourably a person evaluates themselves.

Self-image The set of perceptions a person has about themselves. The complete set of a person's *self-schemas*.

Self-monitor A personality dimension related to attitudes and behaviour. The high self-monitor is a person aware of the demands of social situations. The low self-monitor is less influenced by a social situation but more by attitudes held.

Self-perception theory States that a person forms attitudes on the basis of observing their own behaviour. It offers an alternative explanation to cognitive dissonance for attitude change.

Self-schema An integrated set of memories, beliefs and generalisations about oneself.

Self-serving bias A type of attribution bias in which you attribute your successes dispositionally, but your failures situationally.

Semantic differential A direct measurement of attitudes whereby a person is asked to rate an attitude topic on a set of standard bipolar dimensions each on a seven-point scale.

Semantic memory A long-term memory system which contains our general knowledge about the world, including the rules of language and the meaning of words.

Sense-data approach See *bottom-up approach*.

Sensory memory The memory stores that hold sensory information for brief periods of time. Each of our senses (vision, hearing, touch, taste, smell) has a separate store.

Serial position curve The U-shaped curve produced when the results of people remembering a list of words is plotted on a graph. The curve reflects the fact that people are more likely to remember the first few and last few items than those items in the middle of the list.

Sex This refers to the biological distinction between males and females based on chromosomes. See also *gender*.

Shadowing Where participants hear a different message in each ear and are asked to repeat one of them as they hear it to ensure they are attending to it fully.

Shape constancy The ability to perceive objects as having a constant shape despite changes in the retinal image when viewed from different angles.

Short-term memory A component of the multi-store model of memory. A limited capacity storage that is capable of holding information for short periods of time if rehearsal is prevented. Information can be held for longer periods by means of rehearsal.

Situational attribution The inference that the cause of a person's behaviour is the circumstances the person is in, rather than their character.

Size constancy The ability to perceive the size of objects as constant despite changes in the size of the retinal image with distance.

Social cognition The thought processes, knowledge and beliefs which people use in order to understand the character and behaviour of other people.

Social cohesion The extent to which individuals in a team are attracted to each other and to belonging to the team as a whole. See also *task cohesion* and *team cohesion*.

Social comparison The idea that self-image results from assessments we make about our qualities and abilities in relation to those of other people (especially peers).

Social desirability How consistent an action is with group or cultural norms. One of the factors referred to in the *correspondent inference model* of attribution.

Social facilitation The enhancement of task performance caused by the mere presence of other people.

Social identity theory States that we divide the world into groups of people which are 'us' or 'them' through a process called social categorisation.

Social influence Efforts by one or more people to change the attitudes, beliefs, perceptions or behaviours of one or more other people.

Social loafing Where individuals in a team perform less well at a task than when working alone.

Social norms Written or unwritten rules guiding how people are expected to behave in social situations. Social norms often reflect majority views and are a source of social influence.

Social perception Observing other people and making inferences about them.

Social schema A cognitive structure which represents a person's knowledge or beliefs about groups of people or individuals.

Social sciences A family or cluster of related disciplines including psychology, sociology, anthropology and biology. Also called *behavioural sciences*.

Sociology The study of groups and institutions within society, or of different societies. Includes study of the family, ethnic groups, subcultures, religious institutions and the workplace.

Somatic nervous system This transmits information from our senses (ears, eyes, etc.) through receptors to the *central nervous system*.

Spatial ability A cognitive skill where a person is able to mentally visualise a physical object and its movement.

Standard deviation A measure of dispersion which tells you how the scores spread around the mean. If the standard deviation is a high value, the scores are widely spread round the mean and the range will be large. If the standard deviation is small, the scores are all close to the mean and the range will be small.

Stereotype A highly simplified, gross overgeneralisation of a group of people that is then applied to an individual seen to be a member of that group. Often based on a single attribute such as race, gender, disability or social class.

Stereotyping A source of bias in *impression formation* in which shared beliefs about a specific group of people leads to overgeneralised and often inaccurate inferences about a member of that group.

Storage The process of keeping memories for retrieval.

Stratified sampling A combination of *quota* and *random sampling*. The different strata or types of people in the population are identified, and a random sample taken from each of the strata.

Stroop effect Taking longer to name the colour of ink in which words are written when the words are colour words written in a conflicting colour. For example, it would take longer to name the colour if the word 'red' was written in blue ink than if a non-colour word was written in blue ink.

Structural approach An approach to attitudes which consists of three components: cognitive, affective and conative aspects of attitudes.

Subliminal perception Perception without conscious awareness.

Subjective Where the interpretation can vary, depending on the point of view of the observer.

Superego The third aspect of personality identified by Freud, representing a person's conscience and ideal self.

Survival of the fittest Characteristics which help an individual survive better will be passed on to future generations and hence help the species adapt better to their environment.

Sympathetic nervous system This responds to threat by preparing the body for flight or fight. Works in opposition to the *parasympathetic nervous system*.

Synapse A small gap between neurons through which neurons communicate. Neurotransmitters are responsible for transmitting information across the gap. See also *neurotransmitters*.

Systematic sampling Where every nth member of the target population is selected, for example, every fifth person on a register.

Syndrome A collection of symptoms associated with a particular disease or disorder.

Tabula rasa Idea deriving from the philosopher John Locke that people enter the world as 'blank sheets' and the environment (nurture) determines our behaviour. As opposed to nature, when genetic inheritance is important.

Task cohesion The extent to which members of a team work together to achieve a common task or goal. See also *social cohesion* and *team cohesion*.

Team building Usually carried out by coaches and team captains to produce a more cohesive and better performing team.

Team cohesion A dynamic process in which a group stick together and remain united in the pursuit of common goals. See also *task cohesion* and *social cohesion*.

Team A group of players who have a collective identity and who work together to achieve a specific or common set of goals.

Team satisfaction The extent to which individuals in a team are satisfied with the performance of the team as a whole and with being part of the team.

That's-not-all-technique A method used to gain compliance where an initial request or deal when buying is added to with an incentive. The incentive is offered before the person has agreed the request or deal.

Theory of evolution First proposed by Charles Darwin, it states that all creatures, including human beings, have evolved biologically and share common ancestors.

Theory of reasoned action Regards intentions to behave as resulting from attitudes, subjective norms and behavioural control.

Tip-of-the-tongue state When people are attempting to recall information from long-term memory, but failing. They know the information is 'in there', but they are unable to retrieve it.

Top-down approach An approach that suggests our cognitive processes are mainly influenced by previously stored information rather than the incoming data. Sometimes known as *concept-driven processing*.

Traumatic amnesia See *post-traumatic amnesia*.

Verbal ability An understanding of the meaning of language.

Visuo-spatial sketchpad A part of Baddeley and Hitch's working memory model. It is controlled by the central executive and deals with visual and spatial information and helps us keep a track of where we are in our environment.

Wason's selection task A task widely used in the study of human reasoning. The participant is shown one face of each of four cards and has to select the cards that must be turned over to find out if a particular rule is true.

Weapon focus Where a weapon is involved, witnesses pay attention to the weapon and fail to notice other aspects of the situation.

Wernicke's area An area of the left temporal lobe responsible for the language function of comprehension or word recognition. Damage to this area results in Wernicke's aphasia: a person will have difficulty understanding what others say, and speech will be meaningless.

Wernicke's encephalopathy Initial acute stage of Korsakoff's syndrome where the patient suffers a range of symptoms, not just memory loss.

Working memory A development of the model of short-term memory proposed by Atkinson and Shiffrin. It consists of a 'central executive' which controls and co-ordinates the operation of two subsystems – the *phonological loop* and the *visuo-spatial sketchpad*.

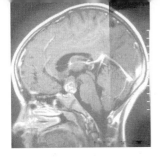

References

ABRAMSON, L.Y., SELIGMAN, M.E.P. & TEASDALE, J.D. (1978), Learned helplessness in humans: Critique and reformulation. *Journal of Abnormal Psychology*, 87, 49–74

ADORNO, T.W., FRENKEL-BRONSWICK, E., LEVINSON, D.J. & SANFORD, R.N. (1950), *The authoritarian personality*, New York, Harper

AITCHISON, J. (1989), *The articulate mammal: an introduction to psycholinguistics*, London, Unwin Hyman

AJZEN, I. & FISHBEIN, M. (1980), *Understanding attitudes and predicting social behaviour*, Englewood Cliffs, Prentice Hall

ALLEN, V.L. & LEVINE, J.M. (1971), Social pressure and personal influence. *Journal of Experimental Social Psychology*, 7, 122–124

ALLPORT, F. H. (1924), *Social psychology*, Cambridge, MA, Houghton Mifflin

ALLPORT, G. (1935), Attitudes. In G. Murchison (Ed.), *Handbook of social psychology*, Worcester, Clark University Press

ANDERSON, J.R. (2000), *Learning and memory*, John Wiley & Sons, New York

ANDERSON, J.R. (2000), *Cognitive psychology and its implications*, 5th edition, New York, Worth

ANDREWS, B., BEKERIAN, D.A., BREWIN, C.R., DAVIES, G.M. & MOLLON, P. (1995), The recovery of memories in clinical practice: Experiences and beliefs of British Psychological Society practitioners. *The Psychologist*, Vol. 8, No. 5. 209–214

ARKIN, R., COOPER, H. & KOLDITZ, T. (1980), A statistical review of the literature concerning the self-serving attribution bias in interpersonal situations. *Journal of Personality*, 48, 435–448

ARONSON, E. & MILLS, J. (1959), The effects of severity of initiation on liking for a group. *Journal of Abnormal and Social Psychology*, 59, 177–181

ASCH, S. (1951), Effects of group pressure on the modification and distortion of judgements. In H. Gretzikow (Ed.), *Groups, leadership and men*, Pittsburgh, Carnegie Press

ASCH, S. (1955), Opinions and social pressure. *Scientific American*, 193, 5, 31–35

ASCH, S.E. (1946), Forming impressions of personality. *Journal of Abnormal and Social Psychology*, 4, 258–290

ATKINSON, R.C., & SHIFFRIN, R.M. (1968), Human memory: A proposed system and its control processes. In K.W. Spence (Ed.), *The psychology of learning and motivation: advances in research and theory*, Vol. 2, New York, Academic Press

BADDELEY, A. (1994), *Your memory: a user's guide*, Harmondsworth, Penguin Books

BADDELEY, A.D. (1966A) Short-term memory for word sequences as a function of acoustic, semantic and formal similarity. *Quarterly Journal of Experimental Psychology*, 18, 362–365

BADDELEY, A.D. (1966B) The influence of acoustic and semantic similarity on long-term memory for word sequences. *Quarterly Journal of Experimental Psychology*, 18, 302–309

BADDELEY, A.D. (1986), *Working memory*, Oxford, OUP

BADDELEY, A.D. (1997), *Human memory: theory and practice*, Hove, Psychology Press

BADDELEY, A.D. (1999), *Essentials of human memory*, Hove, Psychology Press

BADDELEY, A.D. & HITCH, G.J. (1974), Working memory. In G. Bower (Ed.), *Recent advances in learning and memory* (Vol. 8), New York, Academic Press

BADDELEY, A.D. & HITCH, G.J. (1977), Recency re-examined. In S. Dornic (Ed.) *Attention and performance VI*, Hillsdale, NJ, LEA

BADDELEY, A.D., GATHERCOLE, S. & PAPAGNO, C. (1998), The phonological loop as a language learning device. *Psychological Review*, 105, 158–173

BAHRICK H.P. (1984), Memory for people. In J.E. Harris and P.E. Morris (Eds), *Everyday memory, actions and absentmindedness*, London, Academic Press

BANDURA, A. (1965), Influence of model's reinforcement contingencies on the acquisition of imitative responses. *Journal of Personality and Social Psychology*, 1, 589–595

BANDURA, A. (1986), *Social foundations of thought and action: a social-cognitive theory*, Englewood Cliffs, NJ, Prentice Hall

BANDURA, A., ROSS, D. & ROSS, S. (1961), Transmission of aggression through imitation of aggressive models. *Journal of Abnormal and Social Psychology*, 63 (3), 575–582

BARKOW, J.H., COSMIDES, L. & JOOBY, J. (Eds) (1992), *The adapted mind: evolutionary psychology and the generation of culture*, New York, Oxford University Press

BARLEY, P.M. & McGUINESS, I. (1977), Effects of social intelligence on the Milgram paradigm. *Psychological Reports*, 40, 767–770

BARON, R.A. & BYRNE, D. (2000), *Social psychology*, 9th edition, Boston, MA, Allyn & Bacon

BARSALOU, L.W. (1993), Flexibility, structure and linguistic vagary in concepts: Manifestations of a compositional system of perceptual symbols. In A.F. Collins, S.E. Gathercole, M.A. Conway & P.E. Morris (Eds.), *Theories of memory*, Hove, Erlbaum

BARTIS, S., SZYMANSTIC, K. & HARKINS. S.G. (1988), Evaluation and performance: a two-edged knife. *Personality and Social Psychology Bulletin*, 14, 242–251

BARTLETT, F.C. (1932), *Remembering: a study in experimental and social psychology*, Cambridge, Cambridge University Press

BAUMEISTER, R.F. & STEINHILBER, A. (1984), Paradoxical effects of supportive audiences on performance under pressure: The home field disadvantage in sports championships. *Journal of Personality and Social Psychology*, 47, 85–93

BAUMEISTER, R.F. (1995), Disputing the effects of championship pressures and home audiences. *Journal of Personality and Social Psychology*, 68, 644–648

BAUMRIND, D. (1985), Research using intentional deception: ethical issues revisited. *American Psychologist*, 40, 165–174

BEM, D.J. (1967), Self-perception: an alternative interpretation of cognitive dissonance phenomena. *Psychological Review*, 74, 183–200

BEM, S. (1974), The measurement of psychological androgyny. *Journal of Consulting and Clinical Psychology*. 42, 155–162

BERENBAUM, S.A. (1998), How hormones affect behavioural and neural development. *Developmental Neuropsychology*, 14, 175–196

BICKMAN, L. (1974), The social power of a uniform. *Journal of Applied Social Psychology*, 7, 47–61

BIRCH, H.G. (1945), The relationship of previous experience to insightful problem solving. *Journal of Comparative Psychology*, 38, 267–383

BISHOP, J.A. & COOK, L.M. (1975), Moths, melanism and clean air. *Scientific American*, 232, 90–99

BLOOM, F.E. & LAZERSON, A. (1988), *Brain, mind and behaviour*, 2nd edition, New York, W.H. Freedman

BONNINGER, D.S., KROSTRICK, J.A. & BERENT, M.K. (1995), Origins of attitude importance: self-interest, social identification and value relevance. *Journal of Personality and Social Psychology*, 68, 61–80

BOWER, T.G.R., BROUGHTON, J.M. & MOORE, M.K. (1970), The coordination of visual and tactual input in infants. *Perception and Psychophysics*, 8, 51–53. In G. Butterworth & M. Harris, *Principles of developmental psychology*, Hove, Lawrence Erlbaum Associates

BOWLBY, J. (1969), *Attachment and loss*. Vol. 1: Attachment, Harmondsworth, Penguin

BRANDON, S., BOAKES, J., GLASER, D. & GREEN, R. (1998), Recovered memories of childhood sexual abuse. *The British Journal of Psychiatry*, 172, 296–307

BRAY, S. & CARRON, A.V. (1993), The home advantage in alpine skiing. *The Australian Journal of Science and Medicine in sport*, 25, 76–81

BREWER, W.F. & TREYENS, J.C. (1981), Role of schemata in memory for places. *Cognitive Psychology*, 13, 207–230

BRITISH PSYCHOLOGICAL SOCIETY (1995), *Recovered memories; report of the working party of the British Psychological Society*, Leicester, British Psychological Society

BROADBENT, D.E. (1958), *Perception and communication*, Oxford, Pergamon Press

BROWN, J. (1958), Some tests of the decay theory of immediate memory. *Quarterly Journal of Experimental Psychology*, 10, 12–21

BROWN, R. (2000), *Group processes*, 2nd edition, Oxford, Blackwell

BROWN, R. & LENNENBERG, E.H. (1954), A study in language and cognition. *Journal of Abnormal and Social Psychology*, 49, 454–462

BROWN, R. & MCNEILL, D. (1966), The 'tip-of-the-tongue' phenomenon. *Journal of Verbal Learning & Verbal Behaviour*, 5, 325–337

BRUCE, V. & YOUNG, A. (1986), Understanding face recognition. *British Journal of Psychology*, 77, 305–327

BRUNER, J.S. & MINTURN, A.L. (1955), Perceptual identification and perceptual organisation. *Journal of General Psychology*, 53, 21

BUGELSKI, B.R. & ALAMPAY, D.A. (1962), The role of frequency in developing perceptual sets. *Canadian Journal of Psychology*, 15, 205–211

BURGER, J.M. (1986), Increasing compliance by improving the deal: the that's-not-all technique. *Journal of Personality and Social Psychology*, 51, 277–283

BURGER, J.M. (1991), Changes in attributions over time: the ephemeral fundamental attribution error. *Social Cognition*, 9, 182–193

BURKE, D.M., MACKAY, D.G., WORTHLEY, J.S. & WADE, E. (1991), On the tip of the tongue: What causes word-finding failures in young and older adults? *Journal of Memory & Language*, 30, 542–579

BURTON, A. & RADFORD, J. (1991), Thinking. In J. Radford and E. Govier (Eds), *A textbook of psychology*, 2nd edition, London, Routledge

BUSS, D.M. (1995), Evolutionary psychology: a new paradigm for psychological science. *Psychological Inquiry*, 6, 1–49

BUTCHER, R.C. & CARSON, J.N. (1992), *Abnormal psychology and modern life*, 9th edition, New York, Harper Collins

BUTLER, J.L. & BAUMEISTER, R.F. (1998), The trouble with friendly faces: skilled performance with a supportive audience. *Journal of Personality and Social Psychology*, 75, 1213–1230

CACIOPPO, J.T. & PETTY, R.E. (1981), Effects of need for cognition on message evaluation, recall and persuasion. *Journal of Personality and Social Psychology*, 45, 805–818

CANN, A., SHERMAN, S.J. & ELKES, R. (1978), Effects of initial request size and timing of second request on compliance. *Journal of Personality and Social Psychology*, 38, 382–395

CARLSON, N.R. & BUSKITT, W. (1977), *Psychology: the science of behaviour*, 5th edition, Boston, MA, Allyn & Bacon

CARLSON, R. (1994), *Physiology of behaviour*, 5th edition, Boston, MA, Allyn & Bacon

CARMICHAEL, L., HOGAN, H.P. & WALTER, A.A. (1932), An experimental study of the effect of language on the representation of visually perceived form. *Journal of Experimental Psychology*, 15, 73–86

CARRON, A.V. & DENNIS, P.W. (1998), The sport team as an effective group. In J. M. Williams (Ed.), *Applied sport psychology: personal growth and peak performance*, Mountain View, CA, Mayfield Publishing Company

CARRON, A.V., WIDMEYER, W.N. & BRAWLEY, L.R. (1985), The development of an instrument to assess team cohesion in sport teams: The Group Environment Questionnaire. *Journal of Sport Psychology*, 7, 244–266

CARRON, A.V., SPINK, K.S. AND PRAPAVESSIS, H. (1997), Team building and cohesiveness in the sport and exercise setting. *Journal of Applied Sport Psychology*, 9, 61–72

CARRON, A.V. & HAUSENBLAUS, H.A. (1998), *Group dynamics in sport*, 2nd edition, Morgantown, WV, Fitness Information Technology

CARRON, A.V. (1982), *Social psychology of sport*, Ithaca, NY, Movement Publications

CARRON, A.V., WIDMEYER, W.N. & BRAWLEY, L.R. (1988), Group cohesion in individual adherence to group activity. *Journal of Sport and Exercise Psychology*, 10, 127–138

CARTWRIGHT, D. & ZANDER, A. (1968), *Group dynamics: Research and theory*, New York, Harper & Row

CASTLEDEN, H. & KURSZEWSKI, D. (2000), Life narratives on collaborative research in Aboriginal communities. *2000 AERC Proceedings*

CATTELL, J.M. (1895), Measurement of the accuracy of recollection. *Science*, 20, 761–776

CHAMBERS TWENTIETH CENTURY DICTIONARY (1977), Edinburgh, W.&R. Chambers

CHENG, P.W. (1985), Restructuring versus automaticity: alternative accounts of skill acquisition. *Psychological Review*, 92, 414–423

CHERRY, E.C. (1953), Some experiments on the recognition of speech with one and two ears. *Journal of the Acoustical Society of America*, 26, 554–559

CHODOROW, N. (1978), *The reproduction of mothering*, Berkeley, CA, University of California Press

CIALDINI, R.B. (1993), *Influence: science and practice*, 3rd edition, New York, Harper Collins

CIALDINI, R.B. (1994), Interpersonal influence. In S. Shavitt & T. C. Brock (Eds), *Persuasion*, Boston, MA, Allyn & Bacon

CIALDINI, R.B., CACIOPPO, J.T., BASSETT, R. & MILLER, J.A. (1978), Low-ball procedure for producing compliance: commitment then cost. *Journal of Personality and Social Psychology*, 36, 463–476

CIALDINI, R.B., VINCENT, J.E., LEWIS, S.K., CATALAN, J., WHEELER, D. & DARBY, B.L. (1975), Reciprocal concessions procedure for inducing compliance: the door-in-the-face technique. *Journal of Personality and Social Psychology*, 31, 206–215

CLIFFORD, B.R. & SCOTT, J. (1978), Individual and situational factors in eyewitness testimony. *Journal of Applied Psychology*, 63, 342–359

CLONINGER, C.R. (1987), Neurogenetic adaptive mechanisms in alcoholism. *Science*, 236, 410–416

COHEN, G. (1989), *Memory in the real world*, Hove, Lawrence Erlbaum Associates

COHEN, G. (1996), *Memory in the real world*, 2nd edition, Hove, Psychology Press

COHEN, N.J. & SQUIRE, L.R. (1980), Preserved learning and retention of pattern analyzing skill in amnesia: dissociation of knowing how and knowing that. *Science*, 210, 207–210

COHEN, N.J. (1984), Preserved learning capacity in amnesia: Evidence for multiple memory systems. In L.R.

Squire & N. Butters (Eds), *The neuropsychology of memory*, New York, Guilford

COLLINS, A.M. & QUILLIAN, M.R. (1969), Retrieval time from semantic memory. *Journal of Verbal Learning and Verbal Behaviour*, 8, 240–247

COLMAN, A.M. (1990), Aspects of intelligence. In I. Roth (Ed.), *Introduction to psychology*, Vol. 1, Hove, Lawrence Erlbaum

CONRAD, R. (1964), Acoustic confusion in immediate memory. *British Journal of Psychology*, 55, 75–84

COOLEY, C.H. (1902), *Human nature and social order*, New York, Shocken

COOLICAN, H. (1999), *Research methods and statistics in psychology*, 2nd edition, London, Hodder & Stoughton

COON, D. (1983), *Introduction to psychology*, 3rd edition, St Paul, Minnesota, West Publishing Co.

COOPER, J. & FAZIO, R.H. (1984), A new look at dissonance theory. In L. Berkowitz (Ed.), *Advances in experimental social psychology*, Vol. 17, New York, Academic Press

COOPER, L.A. & SHEPARD, R.N. (1973), Chronometric studies of the rotation of mental images. In W.G. Chase (Ed.), *Visual information processing*, New York, Academic Press

COOPER, M.J. & FAIRBURN, C.G. (1992), Selective processing of eating, shape and weight related words in patients with eating disorders and dieters. *British Journal of Clinical Psychology*, 31, 363–365

COOPER, R.M. & ZUBEK, J. P. (1958), Effects of enriched and restricted environments on the learning ability of bright and dull rats. *Canadian Journal of Psychology*, 12, 159–164

COOPERSMITH, S. (1967), *The antecedents of self-esteem*, New York, W.H. Freeman

CORTEEN, R.S. & WOOD, B. (1972), Automatic responses to shock-associated words in an unattended channel. *Journal of Experimental Psychology*, 94, 308–313

COTA, A.A, EVANS, C.R., DION, K.L., KILIK, L. & LONGMAN, R.S. (1995), The structure of group cohesion. *Personality and Social Psychology Bulletin*, 21, 512–580

COTTRELL, N.B. (1972), Social facilitation. In C. McClintock (Ed.), *Experimental social psychology*, pp. 185–236, New York, Holt, Rinehart & Winston

COTTRELL, N.B., WACK, D.L., SEKERAT, G.J. & RITTLE, R.H. (1968), Social facilitation of dominant responses by the presence of others. *Journal of Personality and Social Psychology*, 9, 245–250

COURNEYA, K.S. & CARRON, A.V. (1992), The home advantages of sports competitions: a literature review. *Journal of Sport and Exercise Psychology*, 14, 13–27

COX, R.H. (1998), *Sport psychology: concepts and applications*, 4th edition, Boston, McGraw-Hill

CRAIK, F.I.M. & LOCKHART, R.S. (1972), Levels of processing: a framework for memory research. *Journal of Verbal Learning and Verbal Behaviour*, 11, 671–684

CRAIK, F.I.M. & TULVING, E. (1975), Depth of processing and the retention of words in episodic memory. *Journal of Experimental Psychology: General*, 104, 268–294

CRANDALL, C.S. (1998), Social contagion of binge eating. *Journal of Personality and Social Psychology*, 55, 588–598

CRUTCHFIELD, R.S. (1955), Conformity and character. *American Psychologist*, 10, 191–198

DABBS, J.M., CARR, T.S., FRADY, R.L. *et al.* (1995), Testosterone, Crime and Misbehaviour among 692 Male Inmates. *Personality and Individual Differences*, 18.5, 627–633

DAMON, W. (1977), *The social world of the child*, San Francisco, CA, Jossey-Bass

DARWIN, C. (1859), *The origin of the species by means of natural selection*, London, John Murray

DARWIN, C. (1871), *The descent of man and selection in relation to sex*, London, John Murray

DARWIN, C. (1872), *The expression of emotion in man and animals*, London, John Murray

DASHIELL, J.E. (1930), An experimental analysis of some group effects. *Journal of Abnormal and Social Psychology*, 25, 190–199

DAVEY, A. (1983), *Learning to be prejudiced*, London, Edward Arnold

DAVIS, G., ELLIS, H. & SHEPHERD, J. (1978), Face recognition accuracy as a function of mode of representation. *Journal of Applied Psychology*, 63, 180–187

DAVISON, G. & NEALE, J. (1994), *Abnormal psychology*, 6th edition, New York, Wiley

DEBONO, K.G. & SNYDER, M. (1995), Acting on one's attitudes: the role of a history of choosing actions. *Personality and Social Psychology*, 21, 629–636

DELGADO, A.R. & PRIETO, G. (1996), Sex differences in visuo-spatial ability. Do performance factors play such an important role? *Memory and Cognition*, 24, 504–510

DEREGOWSKI, J. (1972), Pictorial perception and culture. *Scientific American*, 227, 82–88

DEUTSCH, J.A. & DEUTSCH, D. (1963), Attention: Some theoretical considerations. *Psychological Review*, 70, 80–90

DEUTSCH, M. & GERARD, H.B. (1955), A study of normative and informational influence upon individual judgement. *Journal of Abnormal and Social Psychology*, 51, 629–639

DEVLIN, P. (1976), *Report to the Secretary of State for the Home Department Committee on evidence of identification in criminal cases*, HMSO, London

DOWIE, J. (1982), Why Spain should win the World Cup. *New Scientist*, 94, 541–553

DRACHMAN, D.A. & SAHAKIAN, B.J. (1979), Effects of cholinergic agents on human learning and memory. In R. Barbeau *et al.* (Eds) *Nutrition and the brain*, 5, pp. 351–366, New York, Raven Press.

DURKIN, K. (1985), *Television, sex roles and children*, Milton Keynes, Open University

DWECK, C.S., DAVIDSON, W., NELSON, S. & ENNA, B. (1978), Sex differences in learned helplessness: II The contingencies of evaluative feedback in the classroom and III An experimental analysis. *Developmental Psychology*, 14. 268–276

DYER, C. (1995), *Beginning research in psychology*, Oxford, Blackwell

EASTEAL, D. (1991), Women and Crime, pre-menstrual issues. *Australian Institute of Criminology, Trends and Issues in Crime and Criminal Justice*, 31

EBBINGHAUS, H. (1885), *Memory*, New York, Columbia University/Dover 1964

EDWARDS, J. (1979), The home field advantage. In J.H. Goldstein (Ed.), *Sports, games and play: social and psychological viewpoints*, 1st edition, Hillsdale, NJ, Erlbaum

EDWARDS, J. & ARCHAMBAULT, D. (1989), The home field advantage. In J.H. Goldstein (Ed.), *Sports, games* and play: social and psychological viewpoints, Hillsdale, NJ, Erlbaum

EISER, J.R. (1983), From attributions to behaviour. In M. Hewstone (Ed.), Attribution theory: social and functional extensions, Oxford, Basil Blackwell

EKMAN, P. (1992), Facial expression of emotion: new fundings, new questions. Psychological Science, 3, 34–38

ELLIS, A. (1962), Reason and emotion in psychotherapy, New York, Lyle Stuart

ELLIS, A. (1989), Inside rational-emotive therapy: a critical appraisal of the theory and therapy of Albert Ellis, New York, Academic Press

ELLIS, H.D. & SHEPHERD, J.W. (1992), Face Memory – Theory and Practice. In M. Gruneberg & P. Morris (Eds), Aspects of memory, Vol. 1, 2nd edition, London, Routledge

ELLIS, H.D. (1975), Recognising faces. British Journal of Psychology, 66, 409–426

ELLIS, H.D., SHEPHERD, J.W. & DAVIES, G.M. (1979), Identification of familiar and unfamiliar faces from internal and external features: Some implications for theories of face recognition. Perception, 8, 431–439

ERHARDT, A.A. (1985), Gender differences: a Biosocial Perspective. Nebraska Symposium on Motivation. 1984 37–57

ERIKSON, E. (1968), Identity: youth and crisis, New York, Norton

ERRINGTON, F. & GEWERTZ, D. (1989), Cultural alternatives and a feminist anthropology, Cambridge, Cambridge University Press

EYSENCK, M.W. (1984), A handbook of cognitive psychology, London, Lawrence Erlbaum Associates Ltd

EYSENCK, M.W. (1994), Perspectives on psychology, Hove, Lawrence Erlbaum

EYSENCK, M.W. & KEANE, M.T. (2000), Cognitive psychology: a student's handbook, 4th edition, Hove, Psychology Press

EYSENCK, M.W. (1993) Principles of cognitive psychology (Chapter 4), Hove, LEA

FAGOT, B. (1985), Beyond the reinforcement principle: another step toward understanding sex role development. Developmental Psychology, 21, 1097–1104

FANCHO, R.E. (1996), Pioneers of psychology, 3rd edition, New York, Norton

FELDMAN, R.S. & SCHREIBE, K.E. (1972), Determinants of dissent in a psychological experiment. Journal of Personality, 40, 331–348

FEMINA, D.D., YEAGAR, C.A. & LEWIS, D.O. (1990), Child abuse: adolescent records vs adult recall. Child Abuse and Neglect, 14, 227–231

FESTINGER, L. & CARLSMITH, J.M. (1959), Cognitive consequences of forced compliance. Journal of Abnormal and Social Psychology, 58, 203–210

FESTINGER, L. (1957), A theory of cognitive dissonance, Stanford, CA, Stanford University Press

FIEDLER, F.E. (1965), A contingency model of leadership effectiveness. In L. Berkowitz (Ed.), Advances in experimental social psychology, Vol. 1, New York, Academic Press

FIEZ, J.A. (1996), Cerebellar contributions to cognition. Neuron, 16, 13–15

FINKE, R.A. (1989), Principles of mental imagery, Cambridge, MA, MIT Press

FISHER, R.P. & GEISELMAN, R.E. (1992), Memory-enhancing techniques for investigative interviewing: the cognitive interview, Springfield, IL, Charles C. Thomas

FISKE, S.T. & LINVILLE, P.W. (1980), What does the schema concept buy us? Personality and Social Psychology Bulletin, 6, 543–557

FISKE, S.T. & TAYLOR, S.E. (1991), Social cognition, 2nd edition, New York, McGraw-Hill

FIVUSH, R. & SHUKAT, J.R. (1995), Content, Consistency and Coherence of Early Autobiographical Recall. In M.S. Zaragoza, J.R. Granham, G.C.N. Hall, R. Hirschman & Y.S. Ben-Yorath (Eds), Memory and testimony in the child witness, London, Sage Publications

FORSYTH, D.R. (1990), Group dynamics, 2nd edition, Pacific Grove, CA, Brooks/Cole

FRANKLAND, A. & COHEN, L. (1999), Working with recovered memories. The Psychologist, Vol. 12, 2, 82–83

FREEDMAN, J.L. & FRASER, S.C. (1966), Compliance without pressure: the foot in the door technique. Journal of Personality and Social Psychology, 4, 195–202

FRENCH, C.C. & RICHARDS, A. (1993), Clock this! An everyday example of schema-driven error in memory. British Journal of Psychology, 84, 249–253

FREUD, A. (1966), *Normality and pathology in childhood*, London, Hogarth Press

FREUD, S. (1900/1976), *The interpretation of dreams*, Pelican Freud Library, Vol. 4, Harmondsworth, Penguin

FREUD, S. (1905), *Three essays on the theory of sexuality*, Pelican Freud Library, Vol. 7, Harmondsworth, Penguin

FREUD, S. (1909/1977), *Analysis of a phobia in a five-year-old boy*, Pelican Freud Library, Vol. 8, Harmondsworth, Penguin

FREUD, S. (1901/1976), *The psychopathology of everyday life*, Pelican Freud Library, Vol. 5, Harmondsworth, Penguin

FREUD, S. (1933/1973), *New introductory lectures on psychoanalysis*, Pelican Freud Library, Vol. 2, Harmondsworth, Penguin

FRIEND, R., RAFFERTY, Y. & BRAMEL, D. (1990), A puzzling misinterpretation of the Asch conformity study. *European Journal of Social Psychology*, 20, 29–44

GAERTNER, S.L. & DAVIDIO, J.F. (1986), The aversive form of racism. In J.F. Davidio & S.L. Gaertner (Eds), *Prejudice, discrimination and racism*, Academic Press

GALE, A. (1995), Ethical issues in psychological research. In A.M. Coleman (Ed.), *Psychological Research Methods and Statistics*, London, Longman

GALOTTI, K.M. (1989), Approaches to studying formal and everyday reasoning. *Psychological Bulletin*, 105, 331–351

GALTON, F. (1869), *Hereditary genius: an inquiry into its laws and consequences*, Cleveland, OH, World Publishing

GANNON, P.J., HOLLOWAY, R.L., BROADFIELD, D.C. & BRAIN, A.R. (1998), Asymmetry of chimpanzee planum temporale. *Science*, 279, 220–222

GARDNER, R.A. & GARDNER, B.T. (1969), Teaching sign language to a chimpanzee. *Science*, 165, 664–672

GARNHAM, A. & OAKHILL, J. (1994), *Thinking and reasoning*, Oxford, Blackwell

GAZZANIGA, M. (1967), The split brain in man. *Scientific American*, 217, 24–29

GEARY, D.C. (1995), Reflections of evolution and culture in children's cognitions: implications for mathematical development and instruction. *American Psychologist*, 50, 24–37

GEEN, R.G. (1989), Alternative conceptions of social facilitation. In P.B. Paulus (Ed.), *Psychology of group influence*, 2nd edition, New York, Academic Press

GEISELMAN, R.E., FISHER, R.P., MACKINNON, D.P. & HOOLAND, H.L. (1985), Eyewitness memory enhancement in the police interview: Cognitive retrieval mnemonics versus hypnosis. *Journal of Applied Psychology*, 70, 401–410

GENTNER, D. & GENTNER, D.R. (1983), Flowing waters or teeming crowds: mental models of electricity. In D. Gentner & A. Stevens (Eds), *Mental models*, Hillsdale, NJ, Erlbaum

GIBSON, J.J. (1966), *The senses considered as perceptual systems*, Boston, Houghton & Mifflin

GILCHRIST, J.C. & NESBERG, L.S. (1952), Need and perceptual change in need-related objects. *Journal of Experimental Psychology*, 44, 369

GILLIGAN, C. (1982), *In a different voice*, Cambridge, MA, Harvard University Press

GLANZER, M. & CUNITZ, A.R. (1966), Two storage mechanisms in free recall. *Journal of Verbal Learning and Verbal Behavior*, 5 (4), 351–360

GLEITMAN, L. & LIBERMAN, M. (1995), The cognitive science of language: Introduction. In L. Gleitman & M. Liberman (Eds.), *Language: an invitation to cognitive science*, 2nd edition, Cambridge, MA, MIT Press

GODDEN, D. & BADDELEY, A.D. (1975), Context-dependent memory in two natural environments: On land and under water. *British Journal of Psychology*, 66, 325–331

GOLDBERG, S. & LEWIS, M. (1969), Play Behaviour in the year-old infant: Early sex differences. *Child Development*, 40, 21–32

GORASSINI, D.R. & OLSON, J.M. (1995), Does self-perception change explain the foot-in-the-door technique? *Journal of Personality and Social Psychology*, 69, 91–105

GORDON, R.A. (1996), Impact of ingratiation in judgements and evaluations: a meta-analytic investigation. *Journal of Personality and Social Psychology*, 71, 54–70

GOTTESMAN, I.I. & BERTELSEN, A. (1989), Confirming unexpressed genotypes for schizophrenia. *Archives of General Psychiatry*, 46, 867–872

GOTTESMAN, I.I. (1991), *Schizophrenia genesis*, New York, W.H. Freeman

GRAY, J. & WEDDERBURN, A. (1960), Grouping strategies with simultaneous stimuli. *Quarterly Journal of Experimental Psychology*, 12, 180–184

GREENE, J. (1990), Topics in language and communication. In I. Roth (Ed.), *Introduction to psychology*, Vol. 2, Hove, Lawrence Erlbaum

GREGORY, R.L. (1966), *Eye and brain*, London, Weidenfeld & Nicholson

GRIGGS, R.A. & COX, J.R. (1982), The elusive thematic materials effect in Wason's selection task. *British Journal of Psychology*, 73, 407–420

GROEGER, J.A. (1997), *Memory & remembering: everyday memory in context*, New York, Addison Wesley Longman

GROOME, D. (1999), *An introduction to cognitive psychology: processes and disorders*, Hove, Psychology Press

GROSS, R. (1995), *Themes, issues and debates in psychology*, London, Hodder & Stoughton.

GROSS, R.D. (2001), *Psychology, the science of mind and behaviour*, 4th edition, London, Hodder & Stoughton

GRUNEBERG, M. & MORRIS, P. (1992), *Aspects of memory*, Vol. 1, 2nd edition, London, Routledge

GRUNEBERG, M. (1992), In J. McCrone, *My family and other strangers*, The Independent on Sunday, 1.3.92

GUDJONSSON, G.H. (1997), The members of the BFMS, the accusers and their siblings. *The Psychologist*, 10, 111–114

GUILFORD, J.P. (1967), *The nature of human intelligence*, New York, McGraw-Hill

HAIG, N.D. (1984), The effect of feature displacement on face recognition. *Perception*, 13, 505–512

HAN, S. & SHAVITT, S. (1993), *Persuasion and culture: advertising appeals in individualistic and collective societies*. Unpublished Thesis, University of Illinois

HARGREAVES, D.H. (1967), *Social relations in a secondary school*, London, Routledge & Kegan Paul

HARLEY, T.A. (1995), *The psychology of language: from data to theory*, Hove, Erlbaum, (UK) Taylor & Francis

HARRIS, J.E. & SUTHERLAND, A. (1981), Effects of age and instructions on an everyday memory questionnaire. *British Psychological Society, Cognitive Psychology Section Conference*, Plymouth

HARRIS, J.R. (1978), In M. Kingsbourne (Ed.), *Sex differences in spatial ability*

HARRIS, J.R. (1998), Where is the Child's Environment? A group socialization theory of Development. *APA Journals*

HARTLAND, J. (1991), *Language and thought*, Leicester, BPS Books

HAYDEN-THOMSON, L. *et al.* (1987), Sex preferences in sociometric choices. *Developmental Psychology*, 23, 558–562

HAYES, N. (1994), *Foundations of psychology: an introductory text*, London, Routledge

HEBB, D.O. (1949), *Organization of behaviour*, New York, Wiley

HEIDER, E.R. (1972), Universals in color naming and memory. *Journal of Experimental Psychology*, 93 (1), 10–20

HEIDER, F. (1944), Social perception and phenomenal causality. *Psychological Review*, 51, 358–374

HEIDER, F. (1946), Attitudes and cognitive organisation. *Journal of Psychology*, 21, 107–112

HEINDEL, W.C., BUTTERS, N. & SALMON, D.P. (1988), Impaired learning of a motor skill in patients with Huntington's disease. *Behavioural Neuroscience*, 102, 141–147

HEIT, E. (1998), A Bayesian analysis of some forms of inductive reasoning. In M.R. Oaksford & N. Chater (Eds), *Rational models of cognition*, Oxford, Oxford University Press

HENAHAN, D. *Sex differences in cognition*

HENCHY, T.P. & GLASS, D.C. (1968), Evaluation apprehension and social facilitation of dominant and subordinate responses. *Journal of Personality and Social Psychology*, 10, 446–454

HENDERSON, N.D. (1982), Human behaviour genetics. *Annual Review of Psychology*, 33, 403–440

HERDT, G. (1994), *Third sex, third gender*, New York, Zone Books

HIRSTEIN, R. & RAMACHANDRAN, V.S. (1997), Capgras syndrome: a novel probe for understanding the representation of the identity and familiarity of persons. *Proceedings: Biological Sciences*, Vol. 264, No. 1380, 437–444, The Royal Society

HOCKETT, C.F. (1960), The origin of speech. *Scientific American*, 203, 88–96

HOFFMAN, C., LAU, I. & JOHNSON, D.R. (1986), The linguistic relativity of person cognition: an English-Chinese comparison. *Journal of Personality and Social Psychology*, 51, 1097–1105

HOFSTEDE, G. (1980), *Culture's consequences: international differences in work-related values*, Beverly Hills, Sage

HOGG, M.A. (1992), *The social psychology of group cohesiveness: from attraction to social identity*, London, Harvester Wheatsheaf

HOVLAND, C.I. & WEISS (1952), The influence of source credibility on communication effectiveness. *Public Opinion Quarterly*, 15, 635–650

HOVLAND, C.I., JANIS, I.L. & KELLEY, H.H. (1953), *Communication and persuasion: psychological studies of opinion change*. New Haven, CT. Yale University Press

HOWITT, D. (1991), *Concerning psychology: psychology applied to social issues*, Milton Keynes, Open University Press

HUBEL, D.H. & WEISEL, T.N. (1979), Brain mechanisms of vision. *Scientific American*, 241, 150–162

HUDSON, L. (1966), *Contrary imaginations: a psychological study of the English schoolboy*, London, Methuen

HUDSON, L. (1968), *Frames of mind: ability, perception and self-perception in the arts and sciences*, London, Methuen

HUDSON, W. (1960), Pictorial depth perception in sub-cultural groups in Africa. *Journal of Social Psychology*, 52, 183–208

HUNT, E. & AGNOLI, F. (1991), The Whorfian hypothesis: A cognitive psychology perspective. *Psychological Review*, 99, 377–389

IMPERATO-MCGINLEY, J., GUERRO, I., GAUTIER, T. & PETERSON, R.E. (1974), Steroid 5-reductase deficiency in man. An inherited form of pseudo-hermaphroditism. *Science*, 186, 1213–16

INHELDER, B. & PIAGET, J. (1958), *The growth of logical thinking from childhood to adolescence*, New York, Basic Books

JACOB, T., KRAHN, G.L. & LEONARD, K. (1991), Parent-child interactions in families with alcoholic fathers. *Journal of Consulting and Clinical Psychology*, 59, 176–181

JAQUISH, G.A. & RIPPLE, E. (1980), Divergent thinking and self-esteem in preadolescents and adolescents. *Journal of Youth and Adolescence*. Vol. 9 (2), 143–152

JENKINS, J.G. & DALLENBACH, K.M. (1924), Obliviscence during sleeping and waking. *American Journal of Psychology*, 35, 605–612

JERABEK, I. & STANDING, L. (1992), Imagined test situations produce contextual memory enhancement. *Perceptual and Motor Skills*, 75, 400

JOHNSON, K.E. & MERVIS, C.B. (1997), Effects of varying levels of expertise on the basic level of categorization. *Journal of Experimental Psychology: General*, 126, 248–277

JOHNSON-LAIRD, P.N. & BYRNE, R.M.J. (1991), *Deduction*, London, Psychology Press

JONES, E.E. & NISBETT, R.E. (1971), *The actor and the observer: divergent perceptions of the causes of behaviour*, Morristown, NJ, General Learning Press

JONES, E.E. & DAVIS, K.E. (1965), From acts to dispositions: The attribution process in person perception. In L. Berkowitz (Ed.), *Advances in experimental social psychology*, Vol. 2, New York, Academic Press

JONES, E.E., DAVIS, K. & GERGEN, K. (1961), Role-playing variations and their informational value for person perception. *Journal of Abnormal and Social Psychology*, 63, 302–310

JONES, E.E., ROCK, L., SHAVER, K.G., GOETHALS, G.R. & WARD, L.M. (1968), Patterns of performance and ability attribution: An unexpected primacy effect. *Journal of Personality and Social Psychology*, 10, 317–340

JOULE, R.V. (1987), Tobacco deprivation: the foot-in-the-door technique versus the low-ball technique. *Journal of Social Psychology*, 17, 361–365

JUNG, C. (1964), *Man and his symbols*, London, Aldus-Jupiter Books

JUSSIM, L. *et al.* (1995), Prejudice, stereotypes and labelling effects: sources of bias in person perception. *Journal of Personality and Social Psychology*, 68, 228–246

KAGAN, J. (1994), *Galen's prophecy: temperament in human nature*, New York, Basic Books

KAHNEMAN, D. (1973), *Attention and effort*, Englewood Cliffs, NJ, Prentice Hall

KAHNEY, H. (1993), *Problem solving: current issues*, Buckingham, Open University Press

KASSIN, S. & KIECHEL, K. (1996), The social psychology of false confessions: Compliance, internalisation, and confabulation. *Psychological Science*, 7, 125–128

KATZ, D. (1960), The functional approach to the study of attitudes. *Public Opinion Quarterly*, 24, 163–204

KELLEY, H.H. (1967), Attribution theory in social psychology. In D. Levine (Ed.), *Nebraska Symposium on Motivation*, Vol. 15, Lincoln, Nebraska University Press

KELLEY, H.H. (1973), The process of causal attribution. *American Psychologist,* 28, 107–28

KELLOGG, R.T. (1995), *Cognitive psychology*, Thousand Oaks, Sage

KELMAN, H.C. & HAMILTON, V.L. (1989), *Crimes of obedience*, New Haven, CT, Yale University Press

KELMAN, H.C. (1958), Compliance, identification and internalisation; three processes of attitude change. *Journal of Conflict Resolution*, 2, 51–60

KENDLER, K.S. & DIEHL, S.R. (1993), The genetics of schizophrenia: a current genetic-epidemiologic perspective. *Schizophrenia Bulletin*, 19, 261–285

KETY, S.S. (1988), Schizophrenic illness in the families of schizophrenic adoptees: findings from the Danish national sample. *Schizophrenia Bulletin*, 14, 217–222

KIHLSTROM, J. (1998), Exhumed memory. In S.J. Lynn & K.M. McConkey (Eds), *Truth and memory*, New York, Guilford Press

KINGDON, J.W. (1967), Politicians' beliefs about voters. *The American Political Science Review*, 61, 137–145

KOHLBERG, L. (1964), Development of moral character and moral ideology In M.L. Hoffman & L.W. Hoffman (Eds), *Review of Child Development Research*, Vol. 1, New York, Russel Sage Foundation

KOHLBERG, L. (1984), *Essays on moral development: the psychology of moral development*, Vol. 2, New York, Harper & Row

KOHLER, W. (1927), *The mentality of apes*, 2nd edition, New York, Harcourt Brace

KOLB, B. & WHISHAW, I.Q. (2000), *An introduction to brain and behaviour*, New York, Worth Publishers

KOSSLYN, S.M. (1994), *Image and brain: the resolution of the imagery debate*, Cambridge, MA, MIT Press

KOSSLYN, S.M., BALL, T.M. & REISER, B.J. (1978), Visual images preserve metric information: Evidence from studies of image scanning. *Journal of Experimental Psychology: Human Perception and Performance*, 4, 47–60

KRUPA, D.J., THOMPSON, J.K. & THOMPSON, R.F. (1993), Localisation of a memory trace in a mammalian brain. *Science*, 260, 989–991

KUHN, T.S. (1970), *The structure of scientific revolutions*, 2nd edition, Chicago, Chicago University Press

KUHN, D., NASH, S.C. & BRUCKEN, L. (1978), Sex role concepts of two-and three-year-olds. *Child Development*, 49, 445–451

KUNDA, Z. (1999), *Social cognition: making sense of people*, Cambridge, MA, MIT Press

LA FRAMBOISE, T.D., HEYLE, A.M. & OZER, E.J. (1990), Gender and Ethnicity: Perspectives on Dual Status. *Sex Roles*, 22, 455–476

LA PIERE, R.T. (1934), Attitudes and actions. *Social Forces*, 13, 230–237

LANGER, E. J. (1978), Rethinking the role of thought in social interaction. In J. H. Harvey, W. I. Ickes & R. F. Kidd (Eds), *New directions in attribution research*, Vol. 2. Hillsdale, NJ, Erlbaum

LANSDELL, H. (1964), Sex Differences in Hemispheric Asymmetries of the Human Brain. *Nature*, 203 (4944), 550

LASHLEY, K.S. (1950), In search of the engram. In *Symposium for the Society of Experimental Biology*, Vol. 4, New York, Cambridge University Press

LATANÉ, B. & L'HERRON, T. (1996), Spatial clustering in the conformity game: dynamic social impact of electronic groups. *Journal of Personality and Social Psychology*, 70, 1218–1230

LATANÉ, B., WILLIAMS, K.D. & HARKINS, S.G. (1979), Many hands make light work: the causes and consequences of social loafing. *Journal of Personality and Social Psychology*, 37, 822–832

LAZARUS, R.S. (1991), *Emotion and adaptation*, New York, Oxford University Press

LAZARUS, R.S. & MCCLEARY, R.A. (1951), Autonomic discrimination without awareness. *Psychological Review*, 58, 113

LEGGE, D. (1975), *An introduction to psychological science*, London, Methuen

LEVINGER, G. & CLARK, J. (1961), Emotional factors in the forgetting of word association. *Journal of Abnormal and Social Psychology*, 62, 99–105

LIEBERMAN, P. (1963), Some effects of semantic and grammatical context on the production and comprehension of speech. *Language and Speech*, 6, 172–187. In M.M. Smyth, P.E. Morris, P. Levy & A.W. Ellis, 1987 *Cognition in action*, London, Lawrence Erlbaum Associates

LLOYD, B. (1989), Rules of the gender game. *New Scientist*, 1693, 60–64

LOCKHART, R.S. & CRAIK, F.I.M. (1990), Levels of processing: A retrospective commentary on a framework for memory research. *Canadian Journal of Psychology*, 44, 87–112

LOFTUS, E. & KETCHAM, K. (1994), *The myth of repressed memory*, New York, St Martin's Press

LOFTUS, E.F. (1979), *Eyewitness testimony*, Cambridge MA, Harvard University Press

LOFTUS, E.F. (2001), Imagining the past. *The Psychologist*, Vol. 4, No. 11, 584–587

LOFTUS, E.F. & PALMER, J.C. (1974), Reconstruction of automobile destruction: An example of the ineraction between language and memory. *Journal of Verbal Learning and Verbal Behaviour*, 13, 585–589

LOFTUS, E.F. (1975), Leading questions and the eyewitness report. *Cognitive Psychology*, 7, 560–572

LOGIE, R.H. (1999), Working memory. *The Psychologist*, 12, 174–178

LUCHINS, A.S. (1957), Primacy-recency in impression formation. In C. Hovland (Ed.), *The order of presentation in persuasion*, New Haven, CT, Yale University Press

LURIA, A.R. (1973), *The working brain*, Harmondsworth, Penguin

MACCRACKEN, M.J. & STADULIS, R.E. (1985), Social facilitation of young children's dynamic performance balance. *Journal of Sport Psychology*, 7, 150–165

MACKAY, D.G. (1973), Aspects of the theory of comprehension, memory and attention. *Quarterly Journal of Experimental Psychology*, 25, 22–40

MADDEN, T.J., ELLEN, P.S. & AJZEN, I. (1992), A comparison of the theory of planned behaviour and reasoned action. *Personality and Social Psychology Bulletin*, 18, 3–9

MAJOR, B. (1980), Information acquisition and attribution processes. *Journal of Personality and Social Psychology*, 39, 1010–1024

MALPASS, R.S. & DEVINE, P.G. (1981), Guided memory in eyewitness identification. *Journal of Applied Psychology*, 66, 343–350

MANKTELOW, K. (1999), *Reasoning and thinking*, Hove, Psychology Press

MANSTEAD, A.S.R. & MCCULLOCH, C. (1981), Sex-role stereotyping in British Television Advertisements. *British Journal of Social Psychology*, 20, 171–80

MANTELL, D.M. (1971), The potential for violence in Germany. *Journal of Social Issues*, 27, 101–112

MARIN, B.V., HOLMES, D.L., GUTH, M. & KOVAC, P. (1979), The potential of children as eyewitnesses. *Law and Human Behaviour*, 3, 295–305

MARKMAN, E.M. (1999), *Knowledge representations*, Mahwah, NJ, Erlbaum

MARSHALL, J.C. (1970), The biology of communication in man and animals. In J. Lyons (Ed.), *New horizons in linguistics*, Vol. 1, Harmondsworth, Penguin

MARTENS, R. & PETERSON, J.A. (1971), Group cohesiveness as a determinant of success and member satisfaction in team performance. *International Review of Sport Sociology*, 6, 49–61

MARTENS, R. (1969), Sweating and the presence of an audience. *Journal of Experimental Social Psychology*, 5, 371–374

MARTIN, C.L. (1987), A ratio measure of sex stereotyping. *Journal of Personality and Social Psychology*, 52, 489–499

MASLOW, A.H. (1970), *Motivation and personality*, 2nd edition, New York, Harper & Row

MASSARO, D.W. (1989), *Experimental psychology: an information processing approach*, Orlando, FL, Harcourt Brace Jovanovich

MASSON, J.M. (1985), *The complete letters of Sigmund Freud to Wilhelm Fleiss, 1887–1904*, Mass. & London, Cambridge

MATLIN, M. (2002), *Cognition*, 5th edition, Fort Worth, Harcourt College Publishers

MAYER, R.E. (1992), *Thinking, problem solving, cognition,* 2nd edition, New York, W.H. Freeman

MAYES, A. (1992), Brain damage and memory disorders. In M. Gruneberg, & P. Morris, *Aspects of memory*, Vol. 1, 2nd edition, London, Routledge

MCARTHUR, L.A. (1972), The how and why of why: some determinants and consequences of causal attribution. *Journal of Personality and Social Psychology*, 22, 171–93

MCGINNIES, E. (1949), Emotionality and perceptual defence. *Psychological Review*, 56, 244

MEAD, M. (1935), *Sex and temperament in three primitive societies*, New York, Dell

MEDIN, D.L., ROSS, B.H., & MARKHAM, A.B. (2001), *Cognitive psychology*, 3rd edition, New York, Harcourt College Publishers

METCALFE, J. (1986), Premonitions of insight predict impending error. *Journal of Experimental Psychology: Learning, Memory and Cognition*, 12, 623–634

MICHAELS, J.W., BLOMMEL, J.M., BROCATO, R.M., LINKOUS, R.A. & ROWE, J.S. (1982), Social facilitation and inhibition in a natural setting. *Replications in Social Psychology*, 2, 21–24

MILGRAM, S. (1963), Behaviour study of obedience. *Journal of Abnormal and Social Psychology*, 67, 371–378

MILGRAM, S. (1965), Some conditions of obedience and disobedience to authority. *Human Relations*, 18, 57–76

MILGRAM, S. (1974), *Obedience to authority*, New York, Harper

MILLER, G.A. (1956), The magical number seven, plus or minus two: Some limits on our capacity for processing information. *Psychological Review*, 63, 81–97

MILLER, J.G. (1984), Culture and the development of everyday social explanation. *Journal of Personality and Social Psychology*, 46, 961–978

MILNER, B., CORKIN, S. & TEUBER, H.L. (1968), Further analysis of the hippocampal amnesic syndrome: 14-year follow-up study of HM. *Neuropsychologia*, 6, 215–234

MINARD, R.D. (1952), Race relations in the Pocahontas coal field. *Journal of Social Issues*, 8, 29–44

MIRANDA, F., CALLABERO, R.B., GOMEZ, M. & ZAMORANO, M. (1981), Obediencia a la autoridad. *Psiquis*, 2, 212–221

MISCHEL, W. (1966), A social-learning view of sex differences in behaviour. In E.E. Maccoby (Ed.), *The development of sex differences*, Stanford, Stanford University Press

MONEY, J. & ERHARDT, A.A. (1972), *Man and woman, boy and girl*, Baltimore, Johns Hopkins University Press

MORRIS, T. & SUMMERS, J. (1995), *Sport psychology: theory, applications and issues*, Brisbane, John Wiley & Sons

MOSCOVICI, S. & FAUCHEAUX, C. (1972), Social influence, conformity bias and the study of active minorities. In L. Berkowitz (Ed.), *Advances in experimental social psychology*, Vol. 6, London, Academic Press

MOSCOVICI, S. & MUGNY, G. (1983), Studies in social influence. In B. Paulus (Ed.), *Basic group processes*, New York, Springler-Verlag

MOSCOVICI, S. (1985), Social influence and conformity. In G. Lindzey & E. Aronson (Eds), *Handbook of social psychology*, New York, Random House

MOSCOVICI, S., LAGE, E. & NAFFRECHOUX (1969), Influence of a consistent minority on the response of a majority in a colour perception task. *Sociometry*, 32, 365–379

MURRAY, H.A. (1938), *Explorations in personality*, New York, Oxford University Press

MYERS, A. (1962), Team competition, success, and the adjustment of group members. *Journal of Abnormal and Social Psychology*, 65, 325–332

NAESAR, M.A., PALUMBO, C.L., HELM-ESTABROOKS, N., STAISSY-EDER, D. & ALBERT, M.L. (1989), Severe non-fluency in aphasia. *Brain*, 112, 1–38

NAVON, D. & GOPHER, D. (1979), On the economy of the human processing system. *Psychological Review*, 86, 214–255

NEISSER, U. (1976), *Cognition and reality*, San Francisco, W.H. Freeman

NEMETH, C.J. (1995), Dissent as driving cognition, attitudes and judgement. *Social Cognition*, 13, 273–291

NEVILLE, A.M. & HOLDER, R.L. (1999), Home advantage in sport: an overview of studies on the advantage of playing at home. *Sports Medicine*, 28, 221–236

NICKERSON, R.S. & ADAMS, M.J. (1979), Long-term memory for a common object. *Cognitive Psychology*, 11, 287–307

NICKERSON, R.S., PERKLINS, D.N. & SMITH, E.E. (1985), *The teaching of thinking*, Hillsdale, NJ, Erlbaum

NISBETT, R.E. & BORGIDA, E. (1975), Attribution and the psychology of prediction. *Journal of Personality and Social Psychology*, 32, 923–943

NORMAN, D.A. & SHALLICE, T. (1980), *Attention to action: willed and automatic control of behaviour* (CHIP Report 99), University of California

NORMAN, D.A. (1976), *Memory and attention*, 2nd edition, Chichester, Wiley

NYE, R.D. (2000), *Three psychologies: perspectives from Freud, Skinner and Rogers*, 6th edition, Belmont, CA, Wadsworth

OHLSON, S. (1992), Information processing explanations of insight and related phenomena. In M.T. Keane & K.J. Gilhooly (Eds.), *Advances in the psychology of thinking*, London, Harvester Wheatsheaf

OSGOOD, C.E. & TANNENBAUM, P.H. (1955), The principle of congruity in the prediction of attitude change. *Psychological Review*. 62, 42–55

PACE, A. & CARRON, A.V. (1992), Travel and the home advantage. *Canadian Journal of Sport Sciences*, 17, 60–64

PARKE, R.D. (1967), Nurturance, nurturance withdrawl and resistance to deviation. *Child Development*, 38, 1101–1110

PARKIN, A.J. (1993), *Memory: phenomena, experiment and theory*, Oxford, Blackwell

PARTINGTON, J.T. & SHANGI, G.M. (1992), Developing an understanding of team psychology. *International Journal of Sport Psychology*, 23, 28–47

PATTERSON, F.G. (1978), The gestures of a gorilla: language acquisition in another pongid. *Brain and Language*, 5, 72–97

PAULESU, E., FRITH, C.D. & FRACKOWIACK, R.S.J. (1993), The neural correlates of the verbal component of working memory. *Nature*, 362, 342–345

PENNINGTON, D.C. (2002), *Social psychology of behaviour in small groups*, London, Routledge

PENNINGTON, D.C. (2003), *Essential personality*, London, Hodder Arnold

PENNINGTON, D.C., GILLEN, K. & Hill, P. (1999), *Social psychology*, London, Arnold

PESSIN, J. (1933), The comparative effects of social and mechanical stimulation on memorising. *American Journal of Psychology*, 45, 263–270

PETERSEN, S.E., FOX, P.T., POSNER, M.I., MINTIN, M. & RAICHLE, M.E. (1988), Positron emission tomographic studies of the cortical anatomy of single word processing. *Nature*, 331, 585–589

PETERSON, L.R. & PETERSON, M.J. (1959), Short-term retention of individual verbal items. *Journal of Experimental Psychology*, 58, 193–198

PETTIGREW, T.F. & MEERSTENS, R.W. (1995), Subtle and blatant prejudice in Western Europe. *Journal of European Social Psychology*, 25, 57–75

PETTY, R.E., CACIOPPO, J.T., STRATHMAN, A.J. & PREISTER, J.R. (1994), To think or not to think: exploring two routes to persuasion. In S. Shavitt & T. C. Brock (Eds.). *Persuasion*, Boston, Allyn & Bacon

PETTY, R.E. & CAPCIOPPO, J.T. (1986), *Communication and persuasion: central and peripheral routes to attitude change*, New York, Springer-Verlag

PETTY, R.E., CACIOPPO, J.T. & GOLDMAN, R. (1981), Personal involvement as a determinant of argument-based persuasion. *Journal of Personality and Social Psychology*, 41, 847–855

PIAGET, J. (1963), *The origins of intelligence in children*, New York, Norton

PIAGET, J. (1968), *Six psychological studies*, New York, NY, Random House

PINEL, J.P.J. (1993), *Biopsychology*, Boston, Allyn & Bacon

PINKER, S. (1993), The central problem for the psycholinguist. In G. Harman (Ed.), *Conceptions of the human mind*, Hillsdale, NJ, Lawrence Erlbaum

PLOMIN, R. & DEFRIES, J.C. (1998), The genetics of cognitive abilities and disabilities. *Scientific American*, May, 62–69

PLOMIN, R. (1988), The nature and nurture of cognitive abilities. In R. Steinberg (Ed.), *Advances in the psychology of human intelligence*, Hillsdale, NJ, Erlbaum

PLOMIN, R., DE FRIES, J.C., McCLEAN. G.E. & RUTTER, R. (1997), *Behavioural Genetics*, 3rd edition, New York, Freeman

POLLARD, R. (1986), Home advantage in soccer: a retrospective analysis. *Journal of Sport Sciences*, 4, 237–248

POPPER, K. (1963), *Conjectures and refutations: the growth of scientific knowledge*, New York, Basic Books

PREMACK, D. & PREMACK, A.J. (1972), Teaching language to an ape. *Scientific American*, 227, 92–99

PREMACK, D. & PREMACK, A.J. (1974), Teaching visual language to apes and language deficient persons. In R.L. Schiefelbusch, & L.L. Lloyd (Eds), *Language perspectives: acquisition, retardation and intervention*, Baltimore, University Park Press

PYLYSHYN, Z.W. (1973), What the mind's eye tells the mind's brain: A critique of mental imagery. *Psychological Bulletin*, 80, 1–24

PYLYSHYN, Z.W. (1984), *Computation and cognition*, Cambridge, MA, MIT Press

QUATTRONE, G.A. (1982), Overattribution and unit formation: When behaviour engulfs the person. *Journal of Personality and Social Psychology*, 42, 593–607

QUIGLEY-FERNANDEZ, B. & TEDESCHI, J.T. (1978), The bogus pipeline as a lie detector: two validity studies. *Journal of Personality and Social Psychology*, 36, 247–256

RABBITT, P.N.A. (1989), Inner City Decay: Age changes in structure and process in recall of familiar topographical information. In L. Poon, D. Rubin & B.A. Wilson, *Everyday cognition in adult and later life*, Cambridge, Cambridge University Press

RAZOUMNIKOVA, O.M. (2000), Functional organization of different brain areas during convergent and divergent thinking: An EEG investigation. *Cognitive Brain Research*, 10, 11–18

RAZRAN, G. (1950), Ethnic dislikes and stereotypes: A laboratory study. *Journal of Abnormal and Social Psychology*, 45, 7–27

RENO, R.R., CIALDINI, R.B. & KALLGREN, C.A. (1993), The trans-situational influence of social norms. *Journal of Personality and Social Psychology*, 64, 104–112

RICHARDSON, J.T.E. (1999), *Imagery*, Hove, Psychology Press

RIND, B. & BORDIA, P. (1996), Effect on restaurant tipping of male and female servers drawing a happy smiling face on the backs of customers' checks. *Journal of Applied Social Psychology*, 26, 218–225

RINGLEMANN, M. (1913), Recherches sur les moteurs animés: travail de l'homme. *Annales de l'Institut National Agromonique*, 2 (12), 1–40

RIPS, L.J. (1990), Reasoning. *Annual Review of Psychology*, 41, 321–353

RIPS, L.J., SHOBEN, E.J. & SMITH, E.E. (1973), Semantic distance and the verification of semantic relations. *Journal of Verbal Learning and Verbal Behaviour*, 12, 1–20

RITOV, I. & BARON, J. (1990), Reluctance to vaccinate: Omission bias and ambiguity. *Journal of Behavioral Decision Making*, 3 (4), 263–277

ROGERS, C. (1961), *On becoming a person: a therapist's view of psychotherapy*, Boston, Houghton-Mifflin

ROGERS, C. (1980), *A way of being*, Boston, Houghton-Mifflin

ROHNER, R. (1984), Toward a Conception of Culture for Cross-Cultural Psychology. *Journal of Cross-Cultural Psychology*, 15, 111–138

ROSCH, E.H., MERVIS, C.B., GRAY, W.D., JOHNSON, D.M. & BOYES-BRAEM, P. (1976), Basic objects in natural categories. *Cognitive Psychology*, 8, 382–439

ROSENBERG, M. (1965), *Society and the adolescent self-image*, Princeton, NJ, Princeton University Press

ROSS, L., AMABILE, T.M. & STEINMETZ, J.L. (1977), Social roles, social control and biases in social perception processes. *Journal of Personality and Social Psychology*, 35, 485–494

ROSSI, A. (1977), A biosocial perspective on parenting, *Daedalus* 106, 1–32

RUNDUS, D. (1971), Analysis of rehearsal processes in free recall. *Journal of Experimental Psychology*, 89, 63–77

SAPOLSKY, R.M. (1992), *Stress, the aging brain and mechanisms of neuron death*, Cambridge MA, MIT Press

SAUNDERS, G.G. (1983), An attentional process model of social facilitation. In A. Hare, H. Blumberg, V. Kent & M. Davies (Eds), *Small groups*, London, Wiley

SAUNDERS, G.S., BORAN, R.S. & MOORE, D.L. (1978), Distraction and social comparison as mediators of social facilitation effects. *Journal of Experimental Social Psychology*, 14, 291–303

SAYERS, J. (1982), *Biological politics: feminist and anti-feminist perspectives*, London, Tavistock

SCARR, S. & WEINBERG, R.A. (1978), The influence of 'family background' on intellectual attainment. *American Sociological Review*, 43, 674–692

SCHACHTER, S. (1951), Deviation, rejection and communication. *Journal of Abnormal and Social Psychology*, 46, 190–207

SCHAEFER, R.T. & LAMM, R.P. (1992), *Sociology*, 4th edition, New York, McGraw-Hill

SCHANK, R.C. (1982), *Dynamic memory: a theory of reminding and learning in computers and people*, New York, Cambridge University Press

SCHANK, R.C. & ABELSON, R. (1977), *Scripts, plans, goals and understanding*, Hillsdale, NJ, Lawrence Erlbaum

SCHANK, R.C. & ABELSON, R. (1995), Knowledge and memory: The real story. In R.S. Wyer (Ed.), *Advances in Social Cognition*, Vol. VIII, Hillsdale, NJ, Lawrence Erlbaum

SCHLENKER, B.R., PHILLIPS, S.T., BONIECKI, K.A. & SCHLENKER, D.R. (1995), Where is the home choke? *Journal of Personality and Social Psychology*, 68, 649–652

SCHMIDT, H.G., PEECK, V.H., PAAS, F. & VAN BREUKELEN, G.J.P. (2000), Remembering the street names of one's childhood neighbourhood: A study of very long-term retention. *Memory*, 8, 37–49

SCHMITT, B.H., GILOVICH, T., GOORE, N. & JOSEPH, L. (1986), Mere presence and socio-facilitation: one more time. *Journal of Experimental Social Psychology*, 22, 242–248

SCHULTZ, D.P. & SCHULTZ, S.E. (1994), *Psychology and work today: an introduction to industrial and organisational psychology*, 6th edition, New York, Macmillan

SCHURZ, G. (1985), Experimentelle Überprufung des Zusammenhangszwischen Personlichkeitmerkmalen und der Bereitschaft der destruktiven Gehorsam gegenüber Autoritäten. *Zeitschrift für Experimentele und Angewandte Psychologice*, 32, 160–177

SCHWARTZ, B. & BARSKY, S.F. (1977), The home advantage. *Social Sciences,* 55, 641–661

SCOVILLE, W.B. & MILNER, B. (1957), Loss of recent memory after bilateral hippocampal lesions. *Journal of Neurology, Neurosurgery and Psychiatry*, 20, 11–18

SEGALL, M.H., CAMPBELL, D.T. & HERSKOVITS, M.J. (1963), Cultural differences in the perception of geometrical illusions. *Science*, 139, 769–771

SEYFARTH, R.M., CHENEY, D.L. & MARLER, P. (1980), Monkey responses to three different alarm calls: Evidence for predator classification and semantic communication. *Science,* 210, 801–803

SHALLICE, T. & WARRINGTON, E.K. (1970), Independent functioning of of verbal memory stores: A neuropsychological study. *Quarterly Journal of Experimental Psychology*, 22, 261–273

SHANAB, M.E. & YAHGA, K.A. (1978), A cross-cultural study of obedience. *Bulletin of the Psychonomic Society*, 11, 267–269

SHEPARD, R.N. & METZLER, J. (1971), Mental rotation of three-dimensional objects. *Science,* 171, 701–703

SHEPHERD, J.W., DAVIES, G.M. & ELLIS, H.D. (1981), Studies of cue saliency. In G. Gavies, H. Ellis & J. Shepherd (Eds), *Perceiving and Remembering Faces*, London, Academic Press

SHERIF, M. (1936), *The psychology of social norms*, New York, Harper Row

SHERIF, M., HARVEY, O.J., WHITE, B.J., HOOD, W.R. & SHERIF, C.W. (1961), *Intergroup conflict and co-operation: the robber's cave experiment*, Norman, OK, University of Oklahoma

SHESTOWSKY, D., WEGENER, D.T. & FABRIGER, L.R. (1998), Need for cognition and interpersonal influence: individual differences in impact on dyadic decisions. *Journal of Personality and Social Psychology*, 74, 1317–1328

SIMONTON, D.K. (1997), Creative productivity: A predictive and explanatory model of career trajectories and landmarks. *Psychological Review*, 104, 66–89

SKINNER, B.F. (1953), *Science and human behaviour*, New York, Knopf

SKINNER, B.F. (1990), Can psychology be a science of mind? *American Psychologist*, 45, 1206–1210

SLATER, M.R. & SEWELL, D.F. (1994), An examination of the cohesion – performance relationship in current hockey teams. *Journal of Sport Sciences*, 12, 423–431

SMITH, C.M., TINDALE, R.S. & DUGONI, B.L. (1996), Minority and majority influence in freely interacting groups: qualitative versus quantitative differences. *British Journal of Social Psychology*, 35, 137–149

SMITH, E.E., SHOBEN, E.J. & RIPS, L.J. (1974), Structure and process in semantic memory: A feature model for semantic decisions. *Psychological Review*, 81, 214–241

SMITH, P.B. & HARRIS BOND, M. (1998), *Social psychology across cultures: analysis and perspective*, London, Prentice Hall

SMITH, S.M. (1979), Remembering in and out of context. *Journal of Experimental Psychology: Human Learning and Memory*, 5, 460–471

SNYDER, M. (1979), Self-Monitoring Processes. In L. Berkowitz (Ed.) *Advances in Experimental Social Psychology*, Vol. 12, 88–131, New York, Academic Press

SOLSO, R. L. (1979), *Cognitive psychology*, New York, Harcourt Brace Jovanovich

SPELKE, E., HIRST, W. & NEISSER, U. (1976), Skills of divided attention. *Cognition*, 4, 215–230

SPENCE, J. (1985), Gender Identity and its implications for the concepts of Masculinity and Feminity. *Nebraska Symposium on Motivation*, 1984, 59–95

SPERLING, G. (1960), The information available in brief visual presentations. *Psychological Monographs*, 74, 1–29

SPERRY, R. (1984), Consciousness, personal identity and divided brain. *Neuropsychologica*, 22, 661–673

SPINK, K.S. (1995), Cohesion and intention to participate of female sport team athletes. *Journal of Sport and Exercise Psychology*, 17, 416–427

SQUIRE, L.R. & COHEN, N.J. (1982), Remote memory, retrograde amnesia, and the neuropsychology of human memory. In L.S. Cermak (Ed.), *Human memory and amnesia*, Hillsdale, NJ, Erlbaum.

STANG, D. J. (1973), Effects of interaction rate on ratings of leadership and liking. *Journal of Personality and Social Psychology*, 27, 405–408

STEELE, C.M., SOUTHWICK, L.L. & CRITCHLOW, B. (1981), Dissonance and alcohol: drinking your troubles away. *Journal of Personality and Social Psychology*, 41, 831–846

STEINBERG, R.J. (2001), *Psychology: in search of the human mind*, Fort Worth, Harcourt College Publishers

STENBERG, R.J. (1999), *Cognitive psychology*. 2nd edition, Fort Worth, TX, Harcourt Brace

STOGDILL, R.M. (1972), Group productivity, drive and cohesiveness. *Organisational Behaviour and Human Performance*, 8, 26–43

STORMS, M.D. (1973), Videotape and the attribution process: Reversing actors' and observers' points of view. *Journal of Personality and Social Psychology*, 27, 165–75

STROOP, J.R. (1935), Interference in serial verbal reactions. *Journal of Experimental Psychology*, 18, 643–661

SUNRI, K., AIKIN, K.J., HALL, W.S. & HUNTER, B.A. (1995), Sexism and racism: old-fashioned and modern prejudices. *Journal of Personality and Social Psychology*, 68, 199–214

SUTTON, S.K. & DAVIDSON, J.R. (1997), Prefrontal brain asymmetry: a biological substrate of the behavioural approach and inhibition centres. *Psychological Science*, 8, 204–210

SYLVA, K.D., ROY, C. & PAINTER, M. (1980), *Childwatching at playgroup and nursery school*, London, Grant McIntyre

TAJFEL, H. (1981), *Human group and social categories*, Cambridge, Cambridge University Press

TAYLOR, D.M., DORICE, J. & TYLER, J.K. (1983), Group Performance and cohesiveness: an attributional analysis. *Journal of Social Psychology*, 119, 187–198

TAYLOR, D.M. & JAGGI, V.(1974), Ethnocentrism and causal attribution in a South Indian context. *Journal of Cross-Cultural Psychology.* 5, 162–171

TEASDALE, J.D. & BARNARD, P. (1993), *Affect, cognition and change*, Mawah, NJ, Erlbaum

TESSER, A. & CONNELL, D.P. (1991), On the confluence of self-process. *Journal of Experimental Social Psychology*, 27, 501–526

THOMSON, S.K. (1975), Gender labels and early sex-role development. *Child Development*, 46, 339–347

THORNDIKE, E.L. (1911), *Animal intelligence*, New York, Macmillan

THURSTONE, L.L. (1931), The measurement of social attitudes. *Journal of Abnormal and Social Psychology*, 26, 249–269

TORRANCE, E.P. (1966), *Torrance tests of creative thinking*, Princeton, NJ, Personnel Press

TRAVIS, L.E. (1925), The effect of a small audience on eye-hand coordination. *Journal of Abnormal and Social Psychology*, 20, 142–146

TREISMAN, A.M. (1964), Verbal cues, language and meaning in selective attention. *American Journal of Psychology*, 77, 206–219

TRIPLETT, N. (1898), The dynomogenic factors in pacemaking and competition. *American Journal of Psychology*, 9, 507–533

TULVING, E. (1972), Episodic and semantic memory. In E. Tulving & W. Donaldson (Eds), *Organisation of memory*, London, Academic Press

TULVING, E. (1989), Memory: Performance, knowledge and experience. *European Journal of Cognitive Psychology*, 1, 3–26

TULVING, E. & PEARLSTONE, Z. (1966), Availability versus accessibility of information in memory for words. *Journal of Verbal Learning and Verbal Behaviour*, 5, 381–391

TULVING, E. & THOMPSON, D.M. (1973), Encoding specificity and retrieval processes in episodic memory. *Psychological Review*, 80, 352–373

TURNBULL, C.M. (1961), *The forest people*, New York, Simon & Schuster

TVERSKY, A. & KAHNEMAN, D. (1973), Availability: A heuristic for judging frequency and probability. *Cognitive Psychology*, 5, 207–232

TVERSKY, A. & KAHNEMAN, D. (1974), Judgements under uncertainty: Heuristics and biases. *Science*, 185, 1124–1131

TYRON, R. (1940), Genetic differences in maze-learning ability in rats. *Yearbook of the National Society for the Study of Education*, 39, 111–119

ULLIAN, D. Z. (1981), The Child's Construction of Gender Anatomy as Destiny. In E.K. Shapiro & E. Weber (Eds), *Cognitive and affective growth*, Hillsdale, NJ, Erlbaum

UNDERWOOD, B.J. & EKSTRAND, B.R. (1967), Word frequency and accumulative proactive inhibition. *Journal of Experimental Psychology*, 74, 193–198

VON FRISCH, K. (1954), *The dancing bees*, London, Methuen

VYGOTSKY, L.S. (1934/1962), *Thought and language*, Cambridge, MA, MIT Press

WABER, D. (1976), Sex Differences in Cognition: A Function of Maturation Rate? *Science*, 192, 572–573

WANN, D.L. (1997), *Sport psychology*, Upper Saddle River, NJ, Prentice Hall

WARR, P.B. (1964), The relative importance of proactive inhibition and degree of learning in retention of paired associate items. *British Journal of Psychology*, 55, 19–30

WARREN, R.M. & WARREN, R.P. (1970), Auditory illusions and confusions. *Scientific American*, 223, 30–36

WASON, P.C. (1966), Reasoning. In B.M. Foss (Ed.), *New horizons in psychology* I, Harmondsworth, Penguin

WAUGH, N.C. & NORMAN, D.A. (1965), Primary memory. *Psychological Review*, 72, 89–104

WEISBERG, R.W. (1986), *Creativity: genius and other myths*, New York, Freeman

WEISBERG, R.W. & ALBA, J.W. (1981), An examination of the alleged role of 'fixation' in the solution of several insight problems. *Journal of Experimental Psychology: General*, 110, 169–192

WERTHEIMER, M. (1945), *Productive thinking*, New York, Harper & Row

WESTEN, D. (1999), *Psychology: mind, brain and culture*, 2nd edition, New York, John Wiley

WESTRE, K.R. & WEISS, M.R. (1991), The relationship between perceived coaching behaviours and group cohesion in a high school football team. *The Sport Psychologist*, 5, 41–54

WHEELER, M.A., STUSS, D.T. & TULVING, E. (1997), Toward a theory of episodic memory: The frontal lobes and autonoetic consciousness. *Psychological Bulletin*, 121, 331–354

WHITELEY B.E. (1985), Sex role orientation and psychological well-being: two meta-analyses. *Sex Roles*, 12, 207–225

WHORF, B.L. (1956), *Language, thought and reality*, Cambridge, MIT Press

WICKENS, C.D. (1980), The structure of attentional resources. In R.S. Nickerson (Ed.), *Attention and performance*, Vol. VIII, Hillsdale, NJ, Lawrence Erlbaum

WIDMEYER, W.N., BRAWLEY, L.R. & CARRON, A.V. (1985), *The measurement of cohesion in sport teams: the Group Environment Questionnaire*, Eastbourne, Spodym Publishers

WIDMEYER, W.N. & WILLIAMS, J. M. (1991), Predicting cohesion in a coacting sport. *Small Group Research*, 22, 548–570

WIDMEYER, W.N., CARRON, A.W. & BRAWLEY, L.R. (1993), Group cohesion in sport and exercise. In R.N. Singer, M. Murphey & L.K. Tennant (Eds), *Handbook of research on sport psychology*, New York, Macmillan

WILLIAMS, J.M. & HACKER, C.M. (1982), Causal relationships among cohesion, satisfaction and performance in women's intercollegiate field hockey teams. *Journal of Sport Psychology*, 4, 324–337

WILLIAMS, J.M. & WIDMEYER, W.N. (1991), The cohesion–performance outcome relationship in a coacting sport. *Journal of Sport and Exercise Psychology*, 13, 364–371

WILLIAMS, J.M. (Ed.) (1998), *Applied sport psychology: personal growth to peak performance,* London, Mayfield Publishing Company

WILLIAMS, L.M. (1994), Recall of childhood trauma: a prospective study of women's memories of child sexual abuse. *Journal of Consulting and Clinical Psychology*, 62, 1167–1176

WILLIAMS, T.M. (Ed.) (1986), *The impact of television: a national experiment in three communities*, New York, Academic Press

WILSON, E.O. (1976), *Sociobiology – the new synthesis,* Cambridge, MA, Harvard University Press

WINGFIELD, A. (1993), Sentence processing. In J.B. Gleason & N.B. Ratner (Eds), *Psycholinguistics*, Fort Worth, Harcourt Brace

WOLPE, J. (1958), *Psychotherapy by reciprocal inhibition*, Stanford, CA, Stanford University Press

WOODHEAD, M.M., BADDELEY, A.D. & SIMMONDS, D.C.V. (1979), On training people to recognise faces. *Ergonomics*, 22, 333–343

WORRINGHAM, C.J. & MESSICK, D.M. (1983), Social facilitation of running: an unobtrusive study. *The Journal of Social Psychology*, 121, 23–29

WYNN, V.E. & LOGIE, R.H. (1998), The veracity of long-term memories – Did Bartlett get it right? *Applied Cognitive Psychology*, 12, 1–20

YAMADA, J.E. (1990), *Laura: a case for the modularity of language*, Cambridge, MA, MIT Press

YARNELL, P.R. & LYNCH, S. (1970), Retrograde memory immediately after concussion. *Lancet*, 1, 863–865

YIN, R.K. (1969), Looking at upside-down faces. *Journal of Experimental Psychology*, 81, 141–145

YOUNG, A. & HAY, D. (1986), Configural information in face perception. In V. Bruce (1988), *Recognising faces*, London, Lawrence Erlbaum Associates

YOUNG, A., HAY, D. & ELLIS, A.W. (1985), The faces that launched a thousand slips: everyday difficulties and errors in recognising people. *British Journal of Psychology*, 76, 495–423

YUILLE, J.C. & CUTSHALL, J.L. (1986), A case study of eye-witness memory of a crime. *Journal of Applied Psychology*, 71, 291–301

ZAJONC, R.B. (1965), Social facilitation. *Science*, 149, 269–274

ZAJONC, R.B. (1983), Validating the confluence model. *Psychological Bulletin*, 93, 457–480

ZAJONC, R.B., HEINGARTER, A. & HERMAN, E.M. (1966), Social enhancement and impairment of performance of the cockroach. *Journal of Personality and Social Psychology*, 13, 83–92

ZDANUIK, B. & LEVINE, J.M. (1996), Anticipated interaction and thought generation: the role of faction size. *British Journal of Social Psychology*, 35, 201–218

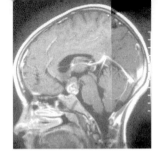

Index

MIDDLESBROUGH COLLEGE
LEARNING RESOURCES CENTRE
WITHDRAWN